WAR AT ANY PRICE

WAR AT ANY PRICE
World War II in Europe, 1939–1945

Second Edition

M. K. Dziewanowski

University of Wisconsin at Milwaukee

PRENTICE HALL, Englewood Cliffs, New Jersey 07632

Library of Congress Cataloging-in-Publication Data

Dziewanowski, M. K.
War at any price : World War II in Europe, 1939-1945 / M.K. Dziewanowski. -- 2nd ed.
p. cm.
Includes index.
Includes bibliographical references.
ISBN 0-13-946658-4
1. World War, 1939-1945. 2. World War, 1939-1945--Europe.
I. Title.
D743.D95 1991
940.53--dc20 90-7544
CIP

Editorial/production supervision and
interior design: KATHLEEN SCHIAPARELLI
Cover design: RAY LUNDGREN GRAPHICS, LTD.
Cover photos: COURTESY OF THE SOVIET EMBASSY, WASHINGTON, D.C.
Manufacturing buyer: DEBBIE KESAR AND MARY ANN GLORIANDE

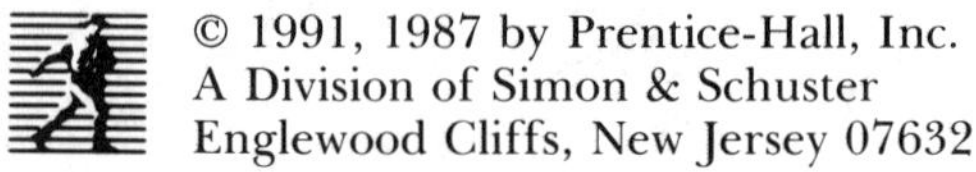

A Division of Simon & Schuster
Englewood Cliffs, New Jersey 07632

Printed in the United States of America

10 9 8 7 6 5 4 3 2 1

ISBN 0-13-946658-4

PRENTICE-HALL INTERNATIONAL (UK) LIMITED, *London*
PRENTICE-HALL OF AUSTRALIA PTY. LIMITED, *Sydney*
PRENTICE-HALL CANADA INC., *Toronto*
PRENTICE-HALL HISPANOAMERICANA, S.A., *Mexico*
PRENTICE-HALL OF INDIA PRIVATE LIMITED, *New Delhi*
PRENTICE-HALL OF JAPAN, INC., *Tokyo*
SIMON & SCHUSTER ASIA PTE. LTD., *Singapore*
EDITORA PRENTICE-HALL DO BRASIL, LTDA., *Rio de Janeiro*

To my first teacher of military history,
Colonel Dr. Władysław Dziewanowski,
and
to my friends and comrades-in-arms
who lost their lives during the war.

Contents

Preface xi

Maps xiv

Chronology xvi

Part One The Origins

1

World War I and Its Aftermath 1

Europe before the War 1
World War I Breaks Out 4
The United States and Soviet Russia 13

2

Fascism, National Socialism, and the Formation of the Axis 19

The Rise of Fascism in Italy 19
The Rise of Nazism in Germany 22
Hitler's Rise to Power 23
The Nazis Gain a Foothold 26
The Nazis Seize Power 27
The Nazi Party in Action 28
A New German Military 30
The West's Response to Hitler 31
The Soviet Response 32
Franco-Soviet Relations 33
Italian Adventurism and the Spanish Civil War 35
The Axis and the Anti-Comintern Pact 37
Hitler's Grand Strategy 38

3

The Prelude 41

Austria: The First Victim 41
From Austria to Czechoslovakia 44

Confrontation 46
The Munich Conference 46
International Reaction to Munich 48
The Polish Crisis 49
The Strengthening of the Rome-Berlin Axis 54

Part Two The Axis on the Offensive

4

World War II: The Overture 61

The Polish Campaign 61
The British and French Response 68
Continued British and French Passivity 70
Soviet Expansionism in Eastern Europe 72
Enigma 74

5

The Scandinavian Gambles 76

The Rival Camps during the "Phony War" 76
The Allied Blockade and the Sea War 77
The Finnish Campaign 78
Allied Interests in Scandinavia 82
Helsinki Negotiates 84
Hitler Moves North 86
The Allies Respond 89
The German Victory in Scandinavia 90
Gambles Won and Lost 92

6

A Decisive Victory in the West? 93

Planning the Western Offensive 93
The Orders of Battle 95
The German Attack 97
The "Impassable" Ardennes 99
The German Advance 100
Churchill Becomes Prime Minister 101
New French Leadership and the British Expeditionary Force 104
The Evacuation of Dunkirk 105
France's Defenses Fail 107
The Fall of France 108
Hitler's Triumph 109
Italian Opportunism 110
Reasons for the German Success 111
Blood, Sweat, and Tears 112

7

Britain's Lonely Stand 114

Hitler's View of Britain 114
Britain Refuses to Yield 115
The Destruction of the French Navy 116
Invasion Plans and the Balance of Forces 121
The Battle of Britain 124
Why Germany Lost the Battle 127
New Armed Forces in the Making 131
The Mobilization of the Home Front 131

8

The Struggle for the Mediterranean 134

The North African and Mediterranean Theater of Operation 134
Consequences of the African and Mediterranean Triumphs 143

9

The Balkans 147

The Italian Campaign against Greece 149
Yugoslavia's Predicament 151
The Political Struggle for and in Yugoslavia 152
The Axis Attacks 155
Britain Aids Greece 157
The Invasion of Greece 158
The Battle of Crete 160
The Significance of the African and Balkan Conflicts 162

10
Toward Cairo and Moscow 163

German Preparations for Entering North Africa 163
Rommel Lands in Africa 165
The Political Situation in the Middle East 167
Increasing Russo-German Tensions 168
Germany Strikes 169
The Battle of Russia 172
The German Drive Falters 175
Stalin's Response to the Crisis 176
The Atlantic Conference 177
Soviet-Polish Relations 179
The Battle of Moscow 180
Reasons for the German Failure 182
The United States Enters the War 183
Timing and Resources 186

Part Three The Axis in Retreat

11
The Turn of the Tide in the West: The Battle of the Atlantic and El Alamein 187

Allied Strategy 187
The Battle of the Atlantic 190
Britain's Desperate Measures 195
The War in Africa 196

12
The North African Landing 205

The Politics of Torch 205
Hitler Responds to the Allied Landing 208
The Casablanca Conference 210
The Battle of Tunisia 212
The Significance of the Allied Victories 215

13
The Turn of the Tide in the East: Stalingrad and Kursk 218

A New German Offensive in Russia 218

14
The Invasion of Italy, the Air Offensive, and the Teheran Conference 233

The "Major Martin" Ruse 234
The Allies Strike 235
Italy Changes Sides 239
The Allied Air Offensive 243
Arrival of the U.S. Air Force 244
The Teheran Conference 246

15
The New Order 251

The Nature and Structure of the New Order 252
The Expansion of the Third Reich 254
Hitler's Vassals 256
Eastern Troops 259
The "Resettlement" of the Jews 261
The Final Solution 263
The Allied Response and Jewish Resistance 265
Attempting to Understand the Holocaust 267
Other Holocausts 267

16
The Resistance 272

East and West 273
Communism and the Resistance Movement 274
The Resistance in Eastern Europe 278
The French Resistance 279
The SOE and the OSS 281
Daring Exploits 283
Allied Intelligence Networks 284
Espionage in the Neutral Countries 286
Opposition and Conspiracy in Germany 287

The Opposition in Italy 291
Other Resistance Activities 292

17

The Reconquest of Europe 294

Preparing for D-Day 294
German Preparations 296
Operation Overlord 297
Hitler Taken Off Guard 299
The Battle of the Beaches 300
The Battle of Normandy 302
A Change of Command 303
Hitler's Secret Weapons 304
An Attempt on Hitler's Life 305
The Latter Phases of the Battle 305
Toward Paris 307
The Soviet Drive Westward 308
The Balkans 310
The End of the Second Battle of France 311
Two Strategies 312
The Battle of Arnhem 314
The German Counteroffensive 317
The Yalta Conference 320
Concessions and Ambivalence 323

18

The Last Battles 325

The Bombing of Dresden 325
The Value of Strategic Bombing 327
The Battle of Germany 328
"Who Will Take Berlin?" 330
The Death of Roosevelt 333
On the Eve of the Fall of Berlin 334
Hitler's Death 335
Hitler in Retrospect 336
The Italian Campaign 337
Germany Surrenders 339
The End of the War in Europe 341

Part Four The Aftermath

19

The Potsdam Conference and the New Status Quo 343

The Potsdam Conference 343
The Trial at Nuremberg 349

20

The War in Retrospect 353

A Beastly Madness 353
Why Germany Lost the War 354
Further Reasons for Germany's Defeat 356
Armies and Strategy 358
New Methods of Warfare 361
The Postwar World 362

Selected Bibliography 367

Index 375

Preface

This is the second, corrected, updated and expanded edition of the original version of my outline of the history of World War II, entitled *War at Any Price*. New research necessitated only a few changes to the text, but the dramatic events in east-central Europe of 1989 called for a thorough rewriting of the last part of the final chapter, which deals with post–World War II Europe. Also, numerous new photographs have been added.

This book has been long in gestation. For nearly fifty years I have been involved in World War II in one way or another. Before the war, from 1937 to mid-1939, I watched Hitler's preparations for aggression as a diplomatic correspondent of the news agency PAT in Berlin. During this period I reported on the invasion of Austria, the Munich Pact, and the German occupation of the Sudetenland. This provided me with an opportunity to observe Hitler, Goering, Goebbels, and many other Nazi leaders at fairly close range.

During the war, I fought as a platoon commander in Poland in September 1939 and watched the campaign in France during the spring of 1940. In 1941/42 I served as an instructor-interpreter at a school for parachutists and saboteurs near London. From 1942 to 1944 I took a dual assignment as both an editor of a secret radio station, which kept in touch with the Polish resistance movement, and a BBC news commentator. In 1944 I served as assistant to the military attaché at the Polish embassy in Washington. All these activities enabled me to participate in the war in four different capacities: field service, training, intelligence, and diplomacy. I met many top Allied leaders, including Prime Minister Winston Churchill and Generals Charles de

Gaulle, Collin Gubbins, and Władysław Sikorski, as well as many other prominent personalities.

After the war, while studying history at Harvard (1947–1951) and preparing my doctoral dissertation as research fellow of the Russian Research Center and of MIT, I utilized several grants to investigate American, German, and Polish archives pertaining to both world wars—research I have continued until the present.

My experience with teaching courses on World War II at the University of Wisconsin has convinced me that there is no adequate one-volume synthesis on the subject, although the 1980s and 1970s witnessed publication of numerous books that threw a great deal of new light on some vital aspects of the war. For instance, two seminal books revealed one of the best-kept secrets of the twentieth century, namely, that the highest form of intelligence obtained from the captured German cipher machine "Enigma" had been available to the Allied leaders throughout the war. The books were written by General Gustave Bertrand (*Enigma,* Plon, Paris, 1973) and by F. W. Winterbotham (*The Ultra Goes to War,* Futura, London, 1973). The fact that many of Hitler's and Mussolini's secret orders were often on the desk of the Allied war leaders before they reached the hands of the German and Italian field commanders invalidated some of the previous assumptions about the conduct of the war and the reasons for the defeat of the Axis powers. Despite this revelation, as of this writing no general history of World War II has adequately taken this fundamental factor into consideration.

The book's title places me squarely in opposition to A. J. P. Taylor's thesis, expressed in his well-known monograph *The Origins of the Second World War,* which asserts that Hitler stumbled into the war by accident. I am more in agreement with the thesis of the Swiss historian Walter Hofer and his work, *War Premeditated.* Like Hofer I stress Hitler's responsibility not only for the launching of the war but also for its character and outcome. Hitler forced it on his mostly reluctant generals and admirals and conducted it in accordance with his whims, which he called "my intuition," while lacking broader strategic vision and operational experience. Germany was losing the global war and Hitler realized that at least by 1942/43. Yet, like a true berserker he dragged the hopeless struggle on even at the price of bleeding his own people white and turning his country into a heap of ruins. Hence the title *War at Any Price.*

The documentation of the war is overwhelming. Over 70,000 books have been written on this theme and the number is growing every day. The National Archives in Washington alone contain 164,000 cubic feet of World War II material, including some 3 million photographs. There are other such large repositories of sources on World War II located in the United States—the Hoover Institution on War, Revolution, and Peace at Stanford, California, to mention only the most important one. Equally massive archives are located in Britain, France, Germany, and the USSR. Most of the Western repositories are now largely, although not completely, open to researchers, and I used these to the limits of my ability. Yet, mastery of so vast a subject as World War II is beyond the reach of any individual scholar.

Another factor that limits one's perspective is lack of access to the repositories of one major participant in the War. The relevant archives of the Soviet Union are still closed to Western students. In 1960, while staying in the Soviet Union as an exchange scholar, I tried to make up for this limitation by at least visiting some of the battlefields of what the Russians call "The Great Patriotic War." Until the Soviet archives are opened, our perception of the history of World War II will be fragmentary, and our picture of the war will largely remain what an ancient Chinese historian called "a glimpse through a crack in the wall at a galloping wild stallion."

Although I tried to peep through many cracks in the walls of the available repositories of sources, by visiting British, German,

French, Polish, and American archives, I cannot claim to have done more than skim the surface of an ocean of material. Consequently, my book is only partly a result of research in the aforementioned archives; it is largely an attempt at a new synthesis of an overwhelming amount of published material, supplemented by numerous personal interviews. It is a work by a participant in the war, now a historian, written both for the college student and the general reader. For the sake of space and at the insistence of the publisher, the footnotes are reduced to an absolute minimum. Primary sources are referred to only in the case of some of the most important controversial problems, for instance, the French view of the Polish campaign or the British attitude toward the Tito-Mihajlović controversy. Monographs in foreign languages are mentioned only when there are no adequate comparable works in English. The bibliography is highly selective and excludes non–Western-language publications.

My debt to other people is huge. It would take a good many pages to name all the historians, soldiers, statesmen, archivists, and librarians, as well as participants in the war, who have helped me over nearly five decades with advice, information, and encouragement. I have to limit myself to a few people who either read my manuscript or gave me some other assistance. The entire manuscript was checked by my most helpful departmental colleagues at the University of Wisconsin–Milwaukee: Professors John F. McGovern, Hans Pawlishch, and Neal H. Pease. The eagle eye they cast over my original text was invaluable. My gratitude is due also to the following people whom I either interviewed or who saw parts of my book: Major Dr. Aleksander Blum, Professor Józef Garliński, Mr. Alex Jordan, Dr. Erich Kordt, Dr. J. M. A. H. Luns, Brigadier General Fitzroy Maclean, Major David M. Marshall, Colonel Leon Śliwiński, Major Melden E. Smith, Jr., David Stefancic, and Colonel Stanisław Żochowski. Of course, I am entirely responsible for all the opinions expressed in this book and for all its shortcomings.

I am also indebted to the aforementioned academic institutions which financed my travel and research over many years. My special thanks go also to the American Philosophical Society of Philadelphia, which recently gave me three research grants that allowed me to visit the British, French, and German archives and thus to finish my work.

I would also like to thank the following reviewers, whose comments and opinions I found very helpful: David Detzer, Western Connecticut State University; Béla K. Kiraly, President, Atlantic Research and Publications, Inc.; Robert J. Maddox, Pennsylvania State University; John A. Maxwell, West Virginia University; William L. O'Neill, Rutgers University; James P. Shenton, Columbia University; Brian R. Sullivan, Yale University; and Donald S. Birn, SUNY at Albany. Most deserving of recognition is my old friend Professor Henryk Batowski, who has read, analyzed, and corrected the first version of the book with extraordinary erudition and professionalism.

May I take this opportunity to express my thanks to the typists, Mary Marshall, Kathy Reck, and Nancy Taylor. I am also grateful to Nancy Jaeger for drawing most of the maps, to Kathleen Schiaparelli of Prentice Hall for her editorial help, Uta Hoffman for providing me with many illustrations, and last but not least, my wife, Ada.

M.K.D.

Maps

Europe, 1914–1918 **5**
Territorial Settlements in Europe **12**
The Occupation of Austria, March 1938 **43**
Europe on the Eve of World War II August 1939 **55**
The German and Soviet Invasion of Poland, September 1939 **67**
The Soviet-Finnish Treaty of Moscow, March 1940 **83**
The German Invasion of Denmark and Norway, April 9, 1940 **87**
The German Invasion of Holland, Belgium, Luxembourg and the Penetration of the French Northern Defense Line, May 10–20, 1940 **98**
The German and Italian Invasions of France, May 10–June 24, 1940 **102**
The Battle of Britain, July–December 1940 **122**
The Mediterranean Theater of Operations, 1940–1943 **136**
The Western Desert Force Offensive against the Italians, December 7 & 8, 1940–February 9, 1941 **140**
The Invasion of Yugoslavia and Greece by the Axis, April 6, 1941 **153**
The Invasion of Crete (Operation Mercury), May 20–31, 1944 **159**
Rommel's First Lightning Offensive, March 24–April 25, 1941 **165**

The German Invasion of Soviet Russia, June 22–December 6, 1941 **171**

United Nations Counter Offensives in the Asian and Pacific Theaters, 1942–1945 **184**

The Battle of the Atlantic, 1940–1943 **192**

The Battle of el-Alamein, October 24–November 4, 1942 **203**

The Allied Pincers in North Africa **208**

The Battle of Tunisia, December 1942–May 1943 **212**

German Sixth Army Trapped and Destroyed at Stalingrad, November 23, 1942–February 1943 **223**

The Battle of Kursk, July 1943, and the Subsequent Soviet Offensive **230**

The Italian Campaign, July 1943 to the End of 1944 **236**

Allied Invasions of Europe, 1944–1945 **303**

Operation "Market Garden," September 17–25, 1944 **313**

The German Offensive in the Ardennes, December 16–31, 1944 (The Battle of the Bulge) **318**

The Last Battles on Three Main Fronts: Eastern, Western, and Southern, from Late January 1944 to May 8, 1945 **332**

Soviet Territorial Gains in Europe, 1939–1945 **363**

Chronology

1914

28 July:	Austro-Hungarian declaration of war on Serbia—beginning of World War I.

1917

25 February:	Liberal Revolution in Russia. Tsar abdicates.
7 November:	Bolshevik Revolution in Russia.

1918

3 March:	Treaty of Brest-Litovsk—peace between imperial Germany and Soviet Russia.
11 November:	Armistice is signed—World War I ends.

1919

2 March:	Foundation of Third International.
28 June:	Treaty of Versailles signed. France, Britain, and United States sign Mutual Assistance Treaty, but it is never approved by U.S. Senate.
10 September:	Treaty of Saint-Germain signed—breakup of Austrian Empire. Establishment of German Republic.

1922

16 April:	Treaty of Rapallo—agreement between Soviet Russia and Germany.

31 October:	Benito Mussolini made Italian prime minister.

1923

8–11 November:	Beer Hall (Munich) Putsch by Adolf Hitler fails.

1929

28 October:	Stock market crash on Wall Street.

1931

11 May:	Failure of Kredit-Anstalt. Beginning of Great Depression in Europe. German reparation payments end.
18 September:	Japan invades Manchuria.

1933

30 January:	Hitler becomes chancellor of Germany.
27 February:	Reichstag fire.
4 March:	Franklin D. Roosevelt becomes president of United States.
19 October:	Germany leaves disarmament conference and League of Nations.

1934

30 June:	"Night of the Long Knives"—purge of Nazi party by Hitler.
25 July:	Nazi coup attempted in Austria. Engelbert Dollfuss assassinated.
2 August:	Death of von Hindenburg. Hitler becomes head of German state.
18 September:	Soviet Russia joins League of Nations.

1935

11 January:	Saar plebiscite.
16 March:	Hitler denounces disarmament clauses of Versailles treaty and begins massive rearmament program in open. Universal compulsory military service begun.
25 July:	Seventh Communist International calls for "Popular Front" with other left-wing parties in opposition to fascism.

1936

7 March:	Denunciation of Locarno Pact by Hitler. German troops march into Rhineland armed with blank ammunition.
28 July:	Spanish civil war begins.
25 October:	Formation of Rome-Berlin Axis.
25 November:	Signing of Anti-Comintern Pact between Germany and Japan.

1936–1938	Joseph Stalin carries out massive purges of party and military leaders.

1937

1 May:	President Roosevelt signs U.S. Neutrality Act.
6 November:	Italy joins Anti-Comintern Pact.

1938

4 February:	Hitler assumes supreme command of German armed forces.
12–13 March:	Austria incorporated into Germany.
29–30 September:	Munich Conference.
1–10 October:	Annexation of Sudetenland by Germany.

1939

14 March:	Slovakia becomes German puppet state.
15 March:	German annexation of Bohemia and Moravia under guise of "protectorate."
16 March:	Hungarian occupation of Ruthenia.
21 March:	German annexation of Memel.
28 March:	Spanish civil war ends with fall of Madrid and Valencia.
31 March:	Neville Chamberlain announces British and French guarantees to Poland.
7 April:	Italy invades and annexes Albania. Spain joins Anti-Comintern Pact.
23 August:	Signing of Russo-German Nonaggression Pact.
1 September:	4:45 A.M., Germany invades Poland—World War II unleashed.
3 September:	Britain, France, Australia, Canada, and New Zealand declare war on Germany.
5 September:	United States declares neutrality in European war.
15 September:	Soviet-Japanese ceasefire in Manchuria.
17 September:	Soviet Russia attacks Poland.
6 October:	Last Polish units capitulate.
30 November:	Soviet Russia attacks Finland.
13–17 December:	Naval battle of Rio de la Plata—*Admiral Graf Spee* scuttled.

1940

12 March:	Finland signs peace treaty with Russia in Moscow.
9 April:	Hitler invades Norway and Denmark.
10 April:	Fall of Neville Chamberlain—Winston Churchill becomes prime minister of Great Britain.
10 May:	German invasion of Holland, Belgium, and France begins.
10 June:	Italy declares war on France.
22 June:	Franco-German armistice.
3 July:	Royal Navy attacks French naval base of Mersel-Kébir and seizes fifty-nine French warships in British harbors.
Mid-August to Mid-September:	Battle of Britain.
28 October:	Italy invades Greece.
11 November:	British attack cripples Italian fleet at Taranto.
12–13 November:	Viacheslav Molotov's visit to Berlin. RAF bombs Berlin.
18 December:	Hitler orders preparations for "Operation Barbarossa."

1941

31 March:	Erwin Rommel begins his offensive in North Africa.
6 April:	German invasion of Yugoslavia and Greece.
25 May:	*Bismarck* sunk.
22 June:	Hitler and his satellites invade Russia.
14 August:	Roosevelt and Churchill meet and draft Atlantic Charter.
16 September:	Kiev falls.
2 October:	German attack on Moscow begins.
7 December:	Pearl Harbor bombed. United States enters war.
8 December:	Battle of Moscow ends in failure.

1942

May–June:	Rommel's second offensive in Egypt—capturing of Tobruk.
May–September:	Renewed German offensive in Russia.
October to November:	Battle of Stalingrad reaches its peak.
23 October to 3 November:	Bernard Montgomery defeats Axis forces at el-Alamein.
8 November:	American and British troops land in Morocco and Algeria.
11 November:	Germans occupy southern France. French fleet scuttled at Toulon.
19–20 November:	Soviet army counterattacks at Stalingrad and encircles German Sixth Army.

1943

3 February:	Germans capitulate at Stalingrad.
19 April:	Jewish Uprising in the Warsaw ghetto.
12 May:	End of all organized Axis resistance in Tunisia.
May:	Dissolution of Comintern by Stalin. Battle of the Atlantic won by Allies.
4–12 July:	Battle of Kursk.
9–10 July:	Allied landing in Sicily.
24 July:	Mussolini overthrown by Italian Grand Council.
6–8 September:	Italian armistice. Disarmament of most of Italian troops by Germans.
1 October:	Allies capture Naples.
28 November–1 December:	Teheran Conference of "Big Three."

1944

14–23 January:	Casablanca Conference
22 January:	Allies land at Anzio, Italy.
April–May:	Battle of Monte Cassino.
4 June:	Allies capture Rome.
6 June:	Cross-channel operation—Allied landing in Normandy (D-Day).
20 July:	Plot to assassinate Hitler fails.
1 August to 3 October:	Warsaw Uprising.
15 August:	Allies land in south of France.
25 August	Liberation of Paris.
18–28 September:	Soviet-Finnish armistice. Hungary tries to secede from Axis. Failure of Allies' airborne forces to cross Rhine at Arnhem, Holland.
16–31 December:	The Battle of the Bulge.

1945

12 January:	Beginning of great Soviet offensive.
17 January:	Warsaw captured by Soviet and Polish troops formed in Russia.
7–12 February:	Second summit conference at Yalta.
13 February:	Bombing of Dresden.
7 March:	Western Allies cross Rhine and invade Germany.
13 April:	Soviet troops capture Vienna.
30 April:	Hitler commits suicide.
2 May:	Fall of Berlin.
7–8 May:	Germany capitulates—end of war in Europe.
17 July to 2 August:	Potsdam Conference.
6 August:	First atom bomb dropped on Hiroshima, Japan.
9 August:	Destruction of Nagasaki by second atom bomb.
12 August:	Soviet Russia enters war against Japan.
2 September:	Capitulation of Japan.

WAR AT ANY PRICE

1

World War I and Its Aftermath

EUROPE BEFORE THE WAR

At the turn of the nineteenth and twentieth centuries the prestige of Europe was at its peak. During the closing phases of the European era, Great Britain, seconded by France and Germany, was setting not only economic but also political standards of civilized conduct. Most Western political institutions were based on the parliamentary rules evolved by the British people.

From the eighteenth to the late nineteenth century, Great Britain, with its empire stretching across the world, was the dominant power of the globe. British business was the chief creator and exporter of both capital and manufactured goods. Not Wall Street but London, or "the City," was the financial hub, the principal marketplace and economic clearinghouse of the world. The Royal Navy was the main protector of international trade routes. The stability of *Pax Britannica* was paralleled by a slow but steady progress toward an international organization aimed at safeguarding the peace of the world, based on a balance of power. International trade was booming; the generally accepted gold standard made trade and travel easy, and among the principal states of the world only Russia and Turkey required visas for foreign visitors.

Yet beneath the glittering facade there was a host of pent-up ethnic tensions, class hatreds, and barely controlled violence. The last two generations before World War I lived through a period of the swiftest social change and economic progress in the history of humankind. The scientific and industrial revolution had transformed the world of horse, cart, and muscle power beyond recognition, making steam and electric power the chief instruments of mass production and swift communication. The early twentieth century had at its disposal a technology more complex than the mental and moral ability to guide its practical application. Most existing political institutions did not keep pace with the fast-changing balance of socioeconomic forces, thus generating acute tensions.

Moreover, unrealized slogans of the French Revolution haunted the restless urban masses. They resented not only the capitalistic ownership of industry and trade but also the phenomenon of managerial bureaucrats increasingly controlling industrial and commercial enterprises on behalf of often distant and anonymous corporate capital. The *Communist Manifesto* was still vividly in the minds of the leaders of the proletariat. The class conflicts generated by the birth of Marxist socialism, organized into a net of Social Democratic parties, covered most of the countries, including those ruled by the colonial powers.

Another source of tension had its roots in the intensification of nationalism, especially in the subjected ethnic groups of east-central Europe and the Balkans. Some Serbs were dreaming about uniting the South Slavs at the expense of the Habsburg Empire; and many Poles, about their country's reunification. The Rumanians passionately coveted Transylvania; and the Italians, Trieste and South Tirol. These nationalistic strivings were intertwined with the changes in the traditional global balance of power.

The Rise of Germany and Realignment

For three centuries or so British statesmen had skillfully manipulated the delicate European balance of power. But at the close of the nineteenth century some symptoms augured ill for the continued preeminence of the "Mistress of the Seven Seas," and for the stability of the Western world in general. After 1871 the balance was upset by the unification of Italy, but especially by the rise of a mighty German Empire. Within one generation or so, the Second Reich, welded together by the "Iron Chancellor," Prince Otto von Bismarck, from a congeries of lesser states after Prussia's victory over France in 1871, became the most powerful nation in Europe.

Germany's progress was regarded with a mixture of admiration and envy by the outside world. Soon the more modern industries of the Ruhr, Westphalia, and Silesia began to outproduce and undersell British wares in foreign markets. By the very end of the century Britain's industrial output per capita had been surpassed not only by the United States but also by Germany. Moreover, under the leadership of a young emperor, William II, Germany embarked upon a crash naval program that was a challenge to the well-established British naval supremacy. German self-confidence and pride knew no bounds. Numerous official and private pronouncements of prominent Germans extolled the martial virtues of the "Teutonic race," while voicing contempt for the rights of other "inferior" peoples and preaching a religion of race superiority and violence. As liberal a thinker as Max Weber defined Germany's historic mission as opposing "Latin rationalism," "Anglo-Saxon materialism," and the "Russian's crude barbarity." The British were the chief obstacle to German ambitions. Great Britain owned the world and Germany wanted it.

The groping for the Second Reich's historic mission was accompanied by a tendency to emphasize the paramount role of the state at the expense of society. This trend was combined with a naive admiration for power and a willingness to leave it in the hands of an essentially irresponsible government, increasingly dominated by the military establishment. Germany's fast-growing power and worldwide imperial ambitions produced a great deal of tension and mutual suspicion in its relations with other powers, especially Britain, France, and Russia.

British statesmen, deeply attached to their imperial mission, embodied in the "white man's burden" concept looked down at the newly formed German empire as a dangerous rival, as well as an arrogant upstart. This attitude produced an intense reaction on the part of the Germans, who looked at "proud Albion" with a mixture of hatred and envy. As the naval, commercial, and colonial race between the British and the Germans intensified and as the fleet of William II loomed ever more menacingly, the concept of "splendid isolation" appeared more and more outdated. Consequently, at the beginning of the century London began to search for allies to counterbalance and curb the growing dynamism of the Second Reich. France, smarting under the consequences of the humiliating defeat of 1871, was an obvious first choice for such a partner. The embittered French patriots passionately desired revenge and a chance to recover Alsace-Lorraine. Since 1871 the statue of Strasbourg in the Place de la Concorde in Paris had been symbolically draped in black. France's leaders were worried about their nation's diplomatic isolation and were also looking for ways of ending it by means of alliances that could help them to restore their country's former position on the continent of Europe. French intellectuals were irritated by the spread of German philosophic and scientific thought and were jealous of the growing ascendancy of the German universities.

Germany's leader, the young Emperor William II, was ambitious and restless. In 1890 he dismissed his venerable premier, Bismarck, and refused to renew the agreement hitherto binding Germany and Russia. This left Russia isolated and suspicious of the increasing German support for the Habsburg's expansive drive in the Balkans, which threatened the traditional Russian position as protector of the Slavic Greek Orthodox peoples of the region. Saint Petersburg became more and more fearful that the Germans and the Austrians harbored plans to make all the Near East and Middle East their sphere of influence and that they desired to open a pathway through the Ottoman Empire to the Persian Gulf, "from Berlin to Baghdad."

At the same time, the Pan-Germanic stirrings among the Baltic Germans of the Tsarist Empire also worried St. Petersburg. A series of Russian discriminatory measures against the Baltic Germans triggered a financial boycott of the Russian market by the Berlin bankers, who had followed the guidance of their government. This crisis was promptly taken advantage of by French financial circles, which offered generous loans to industrialize the Tsarist Empire. A series of economic deals led to political rapprochement. Finally, in 1894 the French and the Russians signed a defense alliance. Its terms provided that, should one of the partners be attacked without provocation by a third party, the other would come to its aid with all necessary forces. The treaty was soon followed by a military convention. Thus, already by the close of the nineteenth century two systems of alliances began to take shape, with Britain in the middle, still uncommitted but suspiciously watching the shifting balance of power.

In the meantime British disputes with both France and Russia were still numerous and substantial. At the turn of the century it was the fear of Russia's ambitions in Asia that eventually pushed London to conclude an alliance with Japan in 1902. But Tokyo's victory in the Russo-Japanese War of 1904/5 weakened the Russian position and largely dispelled those fears. Meanwhile, the growing British-German tensions were pushing London toward improving relations first with France, and finally with Russia. In 1904 Britain gave France a free hand in Morocco, and the French reciprocated by giving London a free hand in Egypt; this was followed by a gradual ironing out of various outstanding differences between the two powers in other parts of the world. This in turn led toward close military and naval cooperation in case of war, which amounted for all practical purposes to an informal alliance, known as the Entente Cordiale, or Franco-British cordial understanding.

The definite formation of a loose defensive grouping of the main nations threatened by Germany came in 1907. That year Russia, weakened and humiliated by her recent defeat at the hands of the Japanese and increasingly threatened by the German-Austro-Hungarian expansion in the Balkans, came to an understanding with Great Britain. Both powers made concessions in areas where they had been rivals, such as Persia, Afghanistan, and Tibet, and promised to cooperate with each other in matters of common concern.

Thus, the turn of the century saw a far-reaching realignment on the European diplomatic scene. By 1907 two distinct rival constellations were already facing each other in mutual mistrust and hostility. On the one hand, there was France, Great Britain, and Russia, or the Entente as they were called; on the other there was Germany, Austria-Hungary, and Italy, or the Triple Alliance. Italy's position was paradoxical; it had joined the dual alliance of Germany and Austria-Hungary in 1882, largely as a protest against the French occupation of Tunisia, coveted by the Italians. Yet Italy's main enemy was obviously the Habsburg monarchy controlling such territories as South Tirol, Trieste, and the Dalmatian coast, formerly a part of the Republic of Venice.

WORLD WAR I BREAKS OUT

Amidst the mounting tension, Archduke Francis Ferdinand of Habsburg, heir to the thrones of Austria and Hungary, was assassinated on June 28, 1914, in the Bosnian town of Sarajevo by a Serbian patriot conspiring to pry the Southern Slavs loose from the Dual monarchy. Although Vienna and Budapest had no indisputable proof of the Serbian government's complicity in the crime, they assumed it. Despite the nearly complete acceptance of a stiff ultimatum by Belgrade, the government of Austria-Hungary, urged on by the German General Staff, decided to use the tragic incident as a pretext for crushing Serbia. The assassination was regarded as a "gift from Mars." It was an opportunity to knock France out of the war before Russia, suffering from the disastrous defeat inflicted by Japan in 1904/5, could rearm. This "window of vulnerability" was not to be missed. Serbia, Russia's main ally in the Balkans, seemed to Berlin and Vienna a shaky obstacle to their joint push toward the Near East and Middle East with their bases, markets, and oil resources. It was a threat not only to Russia but also to Britain and France. Saint Petersburg's determination to support Serbia as Russia's ally and to maintain its status as a great power triggered the mechanism of the Franco-Russian alliance. Great Britain, although united with France by the "cordial understanding," initially remained neutral. Only German violation of Belgian neutrality, regarded as vital to Britain's security, compelled London to declare war on Germany and Austria-Hungary. What might have been another Balkan war now became World War I.[1]

Although the actual outbreak of the war did involve numerous miscalculations on both sides, the stubborn efforts of Berlin and Vienna to exploit the assassination of the archduke, almost at any price, shifted upon them much of the guilt for the general conflagration. As a German historian has demonstrated on the basis of documents, the Germans and Austrians did not stumble into the war; they had plotted and planned it for a long time. Prodded by the military and industrial circles, the German leaders evolved a vast expansionist program for European domination, to be known as *Mitteleuropa.* The scheme envisioned an economic and political hegemony that involved partial annexation of Belgium and northeastern France, the establishment of a rump Poland as a vassal state, and the dismemberment of the Tsarist Empire. Ample annexations in Africa were also part and parcel of the ambitious plan, which would give to Germany control of some 10 percent of the surface of the globe. Such a fundamental reconstruction of the international order

---

[1]The conflict between Serbia, which tried to act as the Piedmont of the Balkans and unite the Southern Slavs, and the Habsburg monarchy defending the status quo is described in Vladimir Dedijer, *The Road to Sarajevo* (New York: Simon & Schuster, 1966).

would leave Germany as the greatest world power, dominant throughout the globe.[2]

The Course of the War

Despite the strategic initiative and initial successes in both Belgium and France, as well as on the Russian front, Germany and Austria-Hungary, the Central Powers, were unable to break the resistance of France, Britain, and Russia, or the Entente. The resulting stalemate was not broken by the adherence of Turkey and Bulgaria to the Central Powers. Italy, which defected from the original Triple Alliance in 1915 and joined the Entente, did not materially alter the balance of the war forces either. Despite the fact that the conflict soon spilled over to the colonial possessions of the Great Powers, and despite the rather nominal participation of Japan on the side of the Entente, the war was largely fought on European soil. Only the entry of the United States in April 1917 turned it into a truly global conflict.

---

[2]Hitherto unknown, Fritz Fischer has demonstrated how Germany's expansionist ambitions were not limited only to Europe and Africa. He also pointed out that these ambitions could only succeed through a war that would smash the Great Power positions of all its principal opponents: Great Britain, France, and Russia; see Fritz Fisher, *Germany's Aims in the First World War* (New York: W. W. Norton, 1967). The German title, *Grif nach der Weltmacht* (Grasp for World Power), reflects much better the general thrust of this seminal work.

As early as the fall of 1914 the struggle became a fruitless, frustrating, and static trench war. The campaign in the Middle East and two great German guerrilla operations in East Africa were the only ones in World War I in which mobile warfare exerted an important influence on its outcome. Human losses on all the fronts, east and west, were appalling. In the west, the French bore the brunt of the struggle. During the four days of the battle of the Marne, at the beginning of August 1914, their casualties amounted to 140,000, or twice the number of the whole British Expeditionary Force at the time. Within four weeks after the mobilization General Ferdinand Foch (future marshal and commander in chief of the Inter-Allied armed forces at the end of the war) lost his only son and son-in-law. Not a single member of St. Cyr's class of 1914 (the French West Point) survived the war. The casualties of the Russian army after the first year of the war amounted to some 4 million men (dead, wounded, missing, or prisoners of war), or more than one-fourth of all soldiers mobilized in 1914.

The war marked the nadir of monumental mismanagement of human and material resources of both belligerent camps. Strategy was largely reduced to mutual slaughter. A typical example of this type of war of attrition was the battle of Verdun, the key fortress of the French defenses. Throughout most of 1916 around Verdun, the French and German armies were walloping each other with all the obstinacy of two half-blind drunks in a dark alley on Saturday night. The German goal was not so much to capture the French system of fortifications as to bleed the enemy to death. The battle of Verdun lasted some ten months and cost both antagonists at least seven hundred thousand casualties along a front of some 15 miles.

The main weapon of war responsible for these casualties was the machine gun, firing an average of some 300–600 rounds per minute. Other technological novelties were the gasoline-powered airplane (used initially mostly for reconnaissance and dogfights), the submarine, poison gas, and the tank. The latter represented the marriage of an armored gun with a tractor and was devised and first used in 1916 by the British. The use of tanks and the entry of the large, fresh U.S. contingents were largely responsible for the breaking of the German defense lines on the western front in the summer of 1918. Economically exhausted and half starved by the Allied blockade, Germany, victorious on the east-

American tanks advance in the Argonne Region, October 15, 1918. National Archives

ern front, had to capitulate in the west and ask for an armistice on November 11, 1918. World War I was over.[3]

World War I lasted four years and three months and was fought by thirty nations that had mobilized the near totality of their resources. Its balance sheet was frightening. Some 8.5 million men were dead; at least 20 million were wounded. Well over 8 million were listed as missing or as having been taken prisoner of war. The war squandered the cream of Europe's manhood. The direct final cost of the cataclysm has been estimated at over 200 billion pre-1914 dollars. Never before had there been a struggle so gigantic, so murderous, and so costly. The traumatic impact of the prolonged carnage and the omnipresence of death on the psyches of the combatants is difficult to imagine. As a result of World War I, the Europeans became not only thoroughly anesthetized to mass butchery but also inclined to accept conditions that had made such appalling carnage possible: the imposition of militarylike discipline, hero worship, and indoctrination through mass media, such as the newly born radio. These were some of the phenomena contributing to the spread of the totalitarian movements that were to follow the war.

Revolt of the Masses

The first of them was born in war-weary Tsarist Russia. Already in March 1917 a revolt of the discouraged man-in-the-street, combined with mutinies among demoralized soldiers, toppled the shaky old regime in Russia and brought to power an improvised provisional government. The Bolshevik coup d'état that smashed this weak but essentially democratic coalition in November was soon followed by Russia signing a separate peace with the Central Powers at Brest-Litovsk in March 1918.

One of the most immediate and dramatic results of the war was the downfall of four great dynastic empires: first the tsarist, then the Ottoman-Turkish, and finally the Habsburg as well as the German. The Ottoman Empire and the Austro-Hungarian, or Dual, Monarchy went to pieces beyond redeeming. Germany, although it lost some of its colonial and peripheral European conquests, preserved intact the heartland of its nation-state and became more solidly united than ever.

Every major war is a great divide, a watershed, since it usually helps to bring to the surface the rising political, social, and cultural undercurrents of the time. So it was with World War I, which was a historic turning point in many respects. One of the chief changes involved the balance of social classes. Before, the historic ruling classes, in alliance with the old bourgeoisie and the new business community, were certain of their social position and secure in their control of power. The war upset the intricate equilibrium that had characterized prewar European society.

The most glaring manifestation of the breakdown was the Bolshevik Revolution of November 1917, which skillfully exploited the war-weariness of the masses, as well as their longing for social reform and national emancipation. Soon, the Communist regime in Russia became a natural pole of attraction for the many discontented elements of the world and thus a phenomenon of global significance. Even the subsequent follies and crimes of the Soviet regime should not conceal the initial magnetic attraction the Bolshevik triumph in Russia held for the underprivileged masses of the globe. To many exploited and oppressed peoples, especially in the colonies, it appeared as a stern yet promising experiment in socioeconomic equality and national self-determination. Under the impact of the Bolshevik victory most Social Democratic movements split one after another, and their radical wings began to form Communist parties in their respective countries.

[3]For an attempt at a brief revisionist summary of the conflict see Marc Ferro, *The Great War, 1914–1918* (London: Routledge & Kegan Paul, 1973). For a standard conventional history of the war see Bernadotte E. Schmitt and Harold C. Vedeler, *The World in the Crucible, 1914–1919* (New York: Harper & Row, 1984).

The Making of a Peace

By 1919 the old pre-1914 order was in full decay and dissolution. The peoples of the old Tsarist Empire were fighting a bloody civil war. Several "White" generals, largely supported by the French, British, and United States governments, waged war on the fringes, contesting the power of the Bolsheviks in the heartland of old Russia, and the outcome of the struggle was not yet quite clear to the peacemakers of Paris, who gathered there in January 1919. Subject nationalities from Finland to Arabia had set up their independent states. The republics of Poland and Czechoslovakia in east-central Europe and the Kingdom of Serbs, Croats, and Slovenes in the Balkans were in the process of formation. The spring of 1919 seemed like another spring of nations.

The unexpectedly swift collapse of the Central Powers found the victors unprepared for an orderly transition to peace. During the war there had been numerous public formulations of war aims, but most of them were vague and contradictory. Among the congeries of statements of war aims, however, President Woodrow Wilson's declaration of January 8, 1918, known as the Fourteen Points and Five Particulars, shined by its compactness, consistency, and breadth of vision. Speaking from a position of strength, President Wilson not only managed to force the Central Powers to surrender but induced the Allies to accept his peace program, which in many instances was not to their liking either. Besides reiterating such general principles as freedom of the seas and stipulating such aims as disarmament, President Wilson's proclamation made a series of concrete proposals for settling the main outstanding territorial questions and stipulated the establishment of an international association of nations to guarantee universal peace. According to Wilson's declaration, "The peoples of Austro-Hungary . . . should be accorded the freest opportunity of autonomous development." France was to regain Alsace-Lorraine; Italy was to have its frontiers adjusted "along clearly recognizable lines of nationality"; Belgium, Serbia, and Rumania were to be restored, and an independent Poland was to be set up "with free and secure access to the sea."

Delegates of the Central Powers were not admitted to the deliberations of the conference; nevertheless, they were allowed to make written "observations." The Germans made full, and often very effective, use of this privilege, for instance, in the matter of the status of Danzig or Upper Silesia. Thus, in contrast to the end of World War II, there was actually no unconditional surrender, and the Treaty of Versailles was not a unilateral dictation, or *Diktat,* as the Germans liked to claim.

The Paris Peace Conference is often referred to as that of Versailles, where the treaty between the thirty-two "Allied and Associated Powers" and Germany was finally signed on June 28. But various deliberations leading to minor treaties were held in a variety of small palaces in the vicinity of Paris, for instance, Trianon or St.-Germain-en-Laye, where treaties with Hungary and Austria were signed.

The Terms of Peace: To the Victors

The French delegation was determined to assure that their almost Pyrrhic victory, which had cost them some one and a half million corpses, would not be in vain and that their country's security would not be jeopardized in the future by a revival of German militarism. The French delegates were headed by their almost octogenarian prime minister, Georges Clemenceau, "the Old Tiger." He came to the conference with the wisdom of an old, disillusioned man who remembered the Franco-Prussian War. He was firmly convinced that it would be a criminal folly not to use the opportunity to extend for as long as possible the advantages of the victory over what he believed was the main hereditary enemy of his country.

Consequently, the French tried to carry out the military disablement of Germany by cutting its armed forces to the bone. They also insisted on vast war indemnities, or reparations, and on the permanent occupation of the Rhineland, and tried to achieve a dismemberment of the Reich into its components as before 1815. The creation of a ring of border states, such as Czechoslovakia, Poland, Rumania, and Yugoslavia—all of them bound by defensive alliances with Paris—was to grant added security to the exhausted French. This program had the firm support of their military establishment, headed by the former generalissimo of the Allied forces, Marshal Ferdinand Foch. He considered that unless the French proposals were adopted without much change, the peace would be nothing but an armistice of some twenty years, to be followed by another outburst of German avenging fury.

The program represented by Foch and Clemenceau was carried out only partially, largely because of British opposition. Yet, under the political clauses of the Treaty of Versailles, Germany was compelled to return Alsace-Lorraine to France, restore northern Schleswig to Denmark, and cede the areas of Eupen and Malmédy to Belgium. The Germans were forbidden to build fortifications and assemble armed forces on the left bank of the Rhine, or within 50 kilometers of the right bank. They had to relinquish to the French the coal resources of the Saar basin for a period of fifteen years, "as a compensation for the destruction of the coal mines in the North of France." During this period the Saar would be administered by the League of Nations, and at the end of the fifteen years a plebiscite of the inhabitants would decide the future status of the territory.

The Treaty of Versailles confirmed Germany's abrogation of the Treaty of Brest-Litovsk of March 1918 and also renounced "all the rights and titles over her overseas possessions," a colonial empire of over a million square miles, now to be submitted to the new mandate system administered by the League of Nations. Germany also accepted the independence of the newly established Republic of Austria and promised not to merge with it. Germany was to hand over to Poland most of the territories Prussia had annexed in the three partitions at the end of the eighteenth century, that is, Polish Pomerania, Posnania, Danzig (now Gdańsk), and segments of East Prussia, as well as Upper Silesia. Using its right to make "observations," the German delegation, supported by the British prime minister, Lloyd George, managed to arrange for plebiscites in Upper Silesia and East Prussia and have Danzig established as a "free city" to be administered by the League of Nations.

The delimitation of the eastern frontiers of Germany was among the thorniest problems of the conference. In view of the fact that the settlement eventually triggered the outbreak of World War II, it merits close attention. On the whole, the advisers of the conference who outlined the Polish-German boundaries followed the German census of 1910. Danzig was one of the few major exceptions to the linguistic criteria applied by them. As the United States East European expert, Professor R. H. Lord of Harvard declared, the failure to provide the Poles with control of the mouth of their main river, the Vistula, would favor the interests of 200,000 German inhabitants of Danzig over those of 20 million Polish inhabitants of its hinterland. This, argued Professor Lord, would be equivalent to leaving control of the Mississippi Delta to Mexico.[4]

The compromise solution adopted gave complete self-government to the Germans of the "Free City of Danzig," under the supervision of the League of Nations, and granted merely a set of special economic and administrative privileges allowing Poland "free access to the sea" in accordance with the thirteenth point of President Wilson's declaration. Another old Hanseatic city, Memel (Klaipėda), at the mouth of the Niemen, was placed at the disposal of the Allies, eventually to serve as Lithuania's access to the sea until 1939.

---

[4]For territorial and boundary problems see the essays by two experts of the U.S. delegation: Charles H. Haskins and Robert H. Lord, *Some Problems of the Peace Conference* (Cambridge: Harvard University Press, 1920).

On the strength of the plebiscites conducted in East Prussia and Upper Silesia in 1920 and 1921, respectively, both areas were split, with Germany gaining larger shares in both cases. Also, in both cases substantial segments of a Polish-speaking population were left within the territory of the Weimar Republic, and a considerable number of Germans remained in Poland, mostly in its western provinces. No absolutely fair settlement was possible, plebiscites or no plebiscites, in view of the hopeless intermingling of the ethnic elements.

Under the military clauses of the Versailles treaty Germany's army was to be reduced to one hundred thousand men recruited by voluntary enlistment. Soldiers were to serve for twelve years; officers' service was to last for twenty-five. The General Staff was to be disbanded. Germany was not to maintain a navy in excess of six battleships of 10,000 tons, six light cruisers, twelve destroyers, and twelve torpedo boats and was neither to manufacture nor to possess submarines, military aircraft, heavy artillery, tanks, or poison gas. The military clauses were to be carried out under the supervision of an Allied control commission.

Under the financial and economic clauses, the Germans agreed to make war reparations in cash and in kind, and to make them a first charge upon their nation's revenues. The French had the largest share in the war indemnities: it amounted to 52 percent of the total. Responsibility for precipitating the war, which Germany was to share with Austria, was written into the treaty. Those responsible for the worst atrocities were to be punished. The planned trial of war criminals never actually took place, however.

The Terms of Peace: To the Losers

The Treaty of Versailles was a harsh, but not a Carthaginian, peace: It did not aim at destroying the German state or exterminating the German people. With the exception of Alsace-Lorraine, Danzig, and Memel, most other losses of the former territories of the old Reich were carried out largely either in accordance with the principles of national self-determination—the freely expressed wishes of the population—or in accordance with the linguistic criteria of the German census of 1910. The losses in the east, such as Danzig, Pomerania, Posnania, and Silesia, were mostly colonial lands acquired by Prussia during the eighteenth century. The abolition of the dynastic states that survived until the downfall of the German Empire in November 1918 enhanced national unity. For the first time in history, Germany became a fully unified and integrated national entity.

Despite the territorial losses and despite the disarmament and the reparations, the defeated Germany remained potentially by far the greatest power on the continent of Europe. Because the war had been fought on foreign soil, Germany was not ruined, and its industrial production was hardly affected by the hostilities. Thus, potentially, Germany remained stronger than France and Britain. Germany's remaining population of some 65 million was far superior to France's mere 39 million. The contrast between a unified Germany and an atomized Europe was striking. As events were to prove, Germany's recovery was not essentially affected either by the peripheral territory losses or by military disarmament, nor even by the war indemnities, which were never fully paid anyway. Free from its old, obsolete equipment, the new German army could start experimenting with new weapons and new methods of mobile warfare, especially tanks.

Paradoxically enough, it was not Germany but such lesser associates as Austria and Hungary that were more harshly treated by the peacemakers of Paris. Under the territorial clauses, Austria ceded Galicia to Poland and Trieste, Istria, and South Tirol to Italy, which included over 250,000 German-speaking Austrians. To the newly established Republic of Czechoslovakia the Austrians had to leave the old historic frontiers of the kingdoms of Bohemia and Moravia, including the Sudetenland, with some 3 million German-speaking people. To Rumania the Austrians ceded Bukovina; and to the Kingdom of Serbs, Croats, and Slovenes, the provinces of Carniola Bosnia, Hercegovina, and Dalmatia. Thus, Austria, shorn of its empire, was reduced to a small remnant of its former self. It was left with only 32,000 square miles (from 115,000) and some 6 million people (from 30 million).

Hungary was punished more harshly by the Treaty of Trianon than any other defeated country. It was shorn of almost three-quarters of its territory and two-thirds of its inhabitants. Slovakia had to be joined to Bohemia and Moravia to form Czechoslovakia, and Austria was given the largely German Burgenland. Yugoslavia took Croatia-Slavonia and part of the Banat, the area just north of Belgrade. The Rumanians received the rest of the Banat and above all the mixed Rumanian-Hungarian province of Transylvania, with some 1.5 million Hungarians. Like Germany and Austria, the new Hungary had to maintain a greatly reduced army, pay reparations, and assume a part of the old Austro-Hungarian debt.

Italy inherited from the Habsburgs the areas of the South Tirol, Trieste, and a large share of the east Adriatic coast up to the city of Fiume (Rijeka), which had once belonged to Hungary and was now split into two segments. President Wilson's refusal to grant to Italy the entire city of Fiume so angered the Italian delegation that it left the conference as a sign of protest. The controversial Dalmation settlement set the stage for a Yugoslav-Italian conflict and greatly embittered Italy's relations with the western powers, especially France, Yugoslavia's sponsor and ally.

The last stipulation of President Wilson's Fourteen Points provided for the creation of a "General Assembly of Nations . . . for the purpose of maintaining peace." And indeed, such an association was established in 1920 in Geneva under the name of the League of Nations. Initially the former Central Powers were excluded from the organization: They were to earn their way back into the community of nations gradually through good behavior. Soviet Russia denounced the league as a "bourgeois and imperialistic body," a "capitalistic conspiracy," and refused to join it.

The Covenant of the League of Nations was based on two crucial articles, 10 and 16; they guaranteed the new status quo and obligated all the league's members to protect jointly each other's independence and integrity. Article 10 specified that "the members of the League undertake to respect and preserve against external aggression the territorial integrity and existing political independence of all members of the League." Article 16 specified that "should any member of the League resort to war . . . it would *ipso facto* be deemed to have committed an act of war against all other members of the League."

To correct the inevitable shortcomings of the territorial settlements, the League tried to shelter the rights of minorities "without distinction of birth, nationality, language, race, or religion." Though imperfectly implemented, minority protection was a step forward in the struggle against oppression. It is noteworthy that by comparison with the pre-1914 status quo, the number of people classified as minorities was reduced from sixty to twenty million. Initially, in its heyday, the League seemed to be a qualified success, and during the 1920s Geneva began to look like the world's capital.

Whatever the shortcomings of the peace of Versailles, it was the first treaty to be based not merely on the sheer physical preponderance of the victors but largely on the principle of national determination. For the first time in history frontiers were drawn in accordance with statistical data and consultation of the people concerned in the form of internationally supervised plebiscites. Peoples and provinces, as President Wilson had promised, were "not bartered about from sovereignty to sovereignty as if they were but chattels or pawns in a game." The Treaty of Versailles liberated from foreign domination more peoples than any other peace settlement.

Territorial Settlements in Europe, 1919-1926

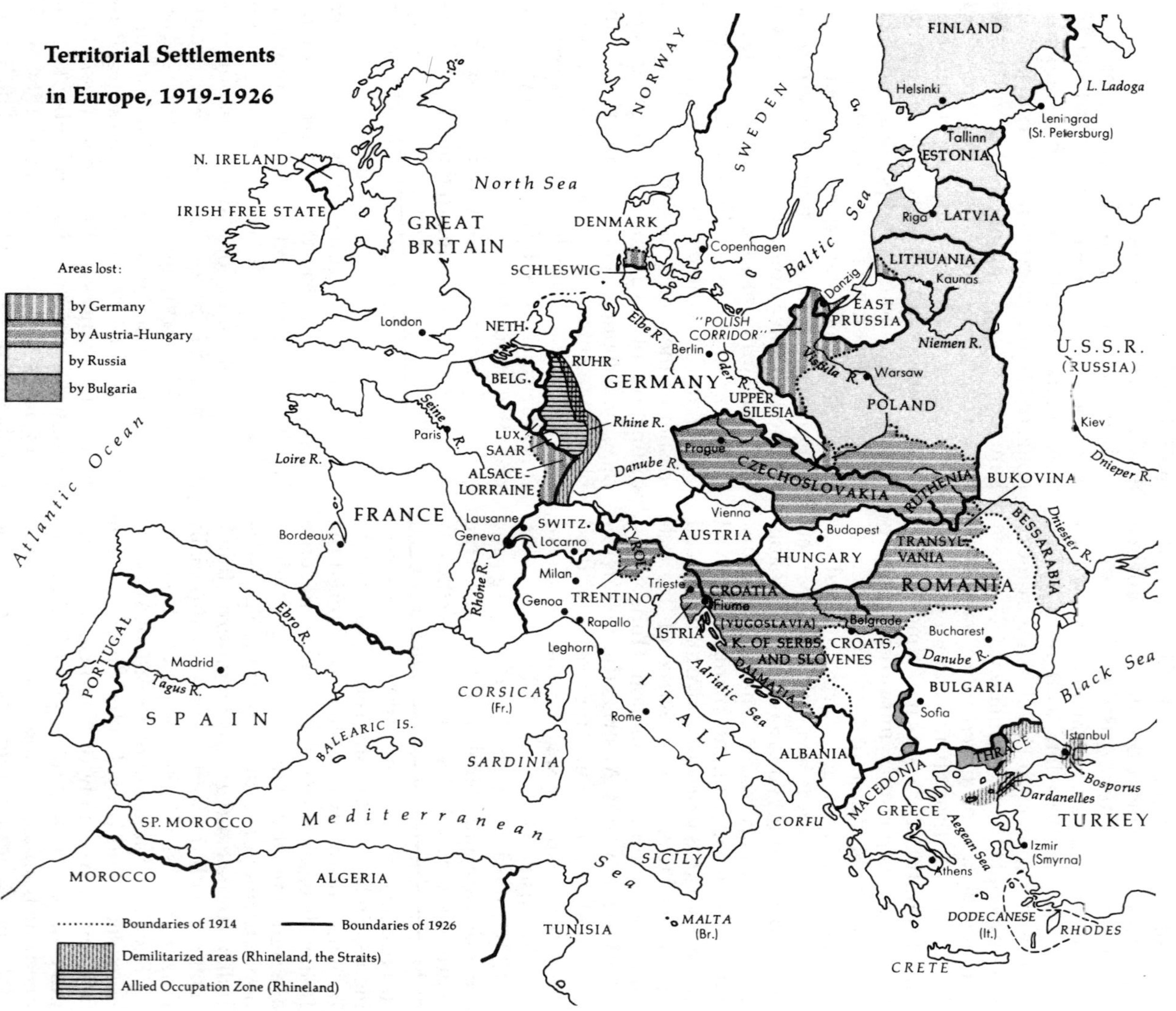

THE UNITED STATES AND SOVIET RUSSIA

Europe emerged from World War I half ruined. The power that, in the long run, benefited most from World War I was neither France nor Britain but the United States. Because of their own needs, the European states had been unable to supply their foreign, especially overseas, markets with their customary exports. The vacated markets, meanwhile, were taken over in part by the neutrals, such as Switzerland and Sweden, but mainly by the United States. As a result of the war, the industrial plant of Europe was run down or partially destroyed, and it took years to rehabilitate it. Although the Central Powers had had to rely on domestic borrowing, the Entente had made full use of the American capital market. The financing of the war was an intolerable burden for the belligerents, and all of them ended the conflict with greatly inflated national debts.

On the other hand, the war bolstered the American economy, thus further widening the gap between the United States and its European competitors. Before the war the United States had been a debtor nation. As a consequence of the Allied wartime borrowing, the United States ended as the great creditor of the world. The increasingly favorable balance of trade, plus the accumulation of most of the then existing reserves of gold, gave to the United States a unique position—that of the globe's dominant capitalist power.

Another consequence of World War I, the full impact of which was to be felt only during the second global conflict and after, was the emergence of Soviet Russia as a state of a new political and socioeconomic type with a new concept of international relations. The Bolsheviks, who seized power in November 1917, with the slogan "dictatorship of the proletariat," entered the international arena by signing a separate peace treaty with the Central Powers at Brest-Litovsk in March 1918. This abandonment of the Western alliance by Russia's new rulers was aggravated by the fact that at the same time Lenin was proclaiming a program radically opposed to everything the liberal democracies stood for. The Bolsheviks not only established a ruthlessly, bloody dictatorial regime but also repudiated all debts to the West, public or private; "nationalized" (that is, confiscated without indemnity) all banks, insurance companies, commercial and industrial enterprises, and all means of communication; established strict thought control; aggressively propagated atheism; and exported revolutionary agitation. Thus, they represented the first and most fundamental challenge to the established order, both domestic and international.

Meanwhile, the newly formed Soviet state was already shaping institutions that were to give it a new importance as a center of a supranational movement transcending national borders and traditional loyalties. In March 1919, while the victors were getting ready to deal with the aftermath of the war, the Bolshevik party laid down the organizational foundations of the world Communist movement in the form of the Third Communist International, or Comintern.

From Moscow the movement soon spread to each and every country of the globe. Thus, from 1919 to 1930 the infant Soviet state managed to construct not only an instrument of struggle against the established socioeconomic and political system but also a unique source of intelligence and a tool of infiltration and subversion to be used in accordance with the Kremlin's wishes.

Sporadic encouragement of internal subversion among rival nation-states was not a new phenomenon in history. What was novel was the open, organized, and worldwide character of the Communist challenge to the established domestic and international order. Consequently, the Bolsheviks vitriolicly condemned the League of Nations as a "capitalistic conspiracy" aimed at the preservation of the "rapacious gains of the predatory war" that had been condemned by Lenin as "imperialistic" on both sides.

Simultaneously with the establishment of

The newly formed Red Army's first official parade in front of the Moscow Kremlin, May 1, 1918.
National Archives

the Comintern, the Soviet leaders were forging another instrument of their policy: "the Red Army of workers and peasants." Like the Soviet state itself, the Red Army was also an institution of a new type. It was to be motivated not by traditional patriotism but by "proletarian internationalism," or the solidarity of the workers in all lands united through their hatred of the capitalistic system and fired by a loyalty to the Communist revolutionary cause.

As long as the Soviet Union was still recovering from the revolutionary convulsion of the civil war, it did not play a significant role in the international forum. But by the end of the 1930s, with the Soviet economy reshaped by Joseph Stalin along collectivist lines and its armed forces modernized, the USSR would soon reenter the concert of Great Powers.

The Victors at Odds

In retrospect, it is clear that the Treaty of Versailles was destroyed almost as much by quarrels among the victors of World War I as by the aggressive steps of Hitler, Mussolini, and Stalin. The United States was the first to abandon the coalition, repudiate the League of Nations, and relapse into easygoing isolationism. Almost to the eve of World War II the French and British worked at cross-purposes, with London acting more as an arbiter between Paris and Berlin than as an ally of the French. The French resolutely opposed any substantial revision of the stipulation arrived at in 1919, which they considered a seamless web, and were determined to fight for every inch of the settlement. The Germans were still potentially dangerous and should be kept disarmed indefinitely and surrounded by a tight net of military alliances capable of curbing their revanchism. For the British, on the other hand, security simply meant freedom from a threat to the British Isles and their trade routes with overseas markets and sources of raw materials. For them imperial Germany had represented a menace as a rising naval power challenging their supremacy and as a commercial competitor as well as a colonial claimant. With their navy destroyed, their economy in shambles, and their colonial possessions divided, the Germans were no longer a dangerous rival.

The 1922 British appeal for an across-the-board cancellation of war debts was immediately condemned by Paris as a selfish move aimed as much at weakening the French economically as at exonerating the Germans from the just retribution of their misdeeds. The entire northeastern segment of France had been devastated by the "Huns," the French argued, and it was only fair that they should pay for the restoration of the region. The Germans, argued the French, were borrowing from the West more than they were paying as war indemnities. How were the French to repay 18.5 billion gold francs to the United States and 15 billion to Britain without collecting their war reparations from Germany?

Another factor that made the British suspicious of the French was the net of eastern European alliances. French policy aroused in London some of its ingrained suspicions dating back to Louis XIV and Napoleon. For Paris, the ties with Poland, Czechoslovakia, Rumania, and Yugoslavia were a collective substitute for the vanished might of tsarist Russia, now ruled by vocal enemies of the whole Versailles system. To face the German potential of some 65 million people with barely 39 million, France needed at least 25 million Poles and 12 million Czechs and Slovaks. For the French, bled white by the war and burdened with a stagnant population, these alliances were necessary to counterbalance the Germans.

The Soviet-German Rapprochement

The quarrels among the victors and the growing weariness of the French prepared the ground for forces determined to destroy the post-Versailles status quo. Its eventual destruction, mainly by Germany and Italy, should not obscure the fact that Soviet Russia was at first as opposed to the settlement as was the Weimar Republic. The Soviet-German collaboration against the Western powers preceded the formation of the Rome-Berlin Axis by some fourteen years and played a crucial role in the destruction of the Versailles status quo in 1939.

Soviet Russia emerged from World War I almost as much a defeated country as Germany. Even the German Social Democrats, who succeeded the imperial regime, opposed Soviet communism because of its subversive propaganda. But even the bloody suppression of the Communist coup d'état in Germany in January 1919 did not stop the Social Democrats from discovering a basic community of political interests between Germany and Russia. Both countries were the main outcasts of the Versailles system—boycotted, ostracized, and isolated from the rest of the world. The French alliances with Poland, Czechoslovakia, Rumania, and Yugoslavia were directed almost as much against communism as against Germany. The *cordon sanitaire* was to help the French to isolate the Soviets as well as to contain the Germans. The hostility of Paris and London toward the two pariahs of the Versailles system automatically tended to push them into each other's arms.

From the Soviet point of view, the Weimar Republic represented a large reservoir of unemployed military personnel and a source of superior technology, so badly needed for Russia's economic rehabilitation and for the modernization and training of the Red Army. The German objective, on the other hand, was to use the distant Russian airfields and training grounds, out of reach of the Allied control commissions, to train their aircraft and tank crews and thus evade the disarmament clauses of the Versailles treaty.

The first step toward a rapprochement between the Weimar Republic and Soviet Russia was taken by them at the International Economic Conference of Genoa, Italy, in April 1922. Both outcasts were invited because it was believed that their eventual collaboration would be indispensable to general European economic recovery. The Germans and the Russians, on the other hand, feared the stiffening of the western position concerning reparations and repayment of the tsarist debts, respectively. This induced Berlin and Moscow to form a common front as debtor powers. On April 16 in the Italian port of Rapallo, the Russians and the Germans signed an agreement innocuously called one of "Friendship and Cooperation." The Treaty of Rapallo stipulated not only resumption of diplomatic relations and trade but also mutual renunciation of all war reparations and debts. The treaty also provided for mutual consultations prior to all important international agreements.[5]

This outwardly benign agreement was soon extended to a series of secret military arrangements that helped Soviet Russia to rebuild its economy, as well as its armed forces, and the Germans to evade the military stipulations of the Treaty of Versailles, to build tanks, planes, and to train crews for these forbidden instruments of war.

Soon after the treaty, German experts began to build poison gas, tank, and aircraft factories on Soviet soil. Such companies as Krupp, IG Farben Industries, Daimler, and Rhine-Metal established their branches in Soviet territory. These industrial ventures were paralleled by a vigorous exchange of military personnel. Three secret German military schools were established in Russia—for tanks, aviation, and chemical warfare. The highly conservative German navy refused to take part in these arrangements and contracted a Dutch company, which secretly assembled parts of the forbidden submarines, manufactured in Germany. As a result of Rapallo, the foundations of Germany's secret rearmament had been laid down long before Hitler.

While the Germans and the Russians were joining their forces to destabilize the settlement of Versailles, the French developed their own hesitations about the security arrangement they had so laboriously erected during the early 1920s. For the first few years after the war, at least until 1925, Paris resolved to stand firm by its smaller allies. But as the mood of pacifism and self-doubt began to spread, some of the French leaders came to the conclusion that they might have been overextending themselves by trying to be the main guardian of the status quo; to induce Berlin to accept of its own will the settlement of 1919 would be a cheaper bargain. Consequently, the French tried to maintain their eastern European alliances on the back burner, just in case France itself would one day need a military diversion against Germany, but tended to manipulate their diplomacy to fit good relations both with Great Britain and with their fast rebounding neighbor across the Rhine. A good example of this new French attitude was the Locarno Pact, concluded in October 1925, in Locarno, Switzerland, which guaranteed France's frontiers with Germany, but not Germany's with Poland and Czechoslovakia.[6]

In the spring of that year the new head of the Quai d'Orsay, Aristide Briand, conceived the idea that to make the hostile Germans voluntarily accept the Versailles settlement, he had only to scale down war reparations and reduce the military occupation of the Rhineland to a minimum. This corresponded to the hopes of the German business establishment, convinced that for full economic recovery it needed cooperation not so much with backward and impoverished Soviet Russia as with the capital-rich Western democracies. The spokesman of the Western-oriented circles was Germany's foreign minister, Gustav Stresemann. He believed that a limited fulfillment of the Treaty of Versailles and gradual reconciliation with the West, if rewarded by adequate political and economic concessions, would be well worthwhile.

To help the German recovery and to encourage Berlin to loosen its collaboration with Moscow, Briand withdrew the French troops from the industrial region of the Ruhr by August 1925. In October at Locarno, on the Swiss side of Lake Maggiore, German, British, Italian, Belgian, and French representatives met to discuss how to make Berlin accept, of its own free will, the frontiers of 1919. Stresemann at once grasped the opportunity of driving a wedge between Paris and its eastern allies. He

[5]For an introduction to Soviet-German dealings during the Weimar Republic see Gerald Freund, *Unholy Alliance: Russo-German Relations from the Treaty of Brest-Litovsk to the Treaty of Berlin* (San Diego: Harcourt Brace Jovanovich, 1957).

[6]For a discussion of the problem see Piotr Wandycz, *France and Her Eastern Allies, 1919–1925* (Minneapolis: University of Minnesota Press 1962).

insisted on the elimination of Allied supervision of the German disarmament and a further speeding up of the evacuation of the Rhineland in exchange for Berlin's confirmation of the status quo in the West.

In the Locarno Pact, the postwar French and Belgian frontiers were freely accepted by Berlin, but the Polish and Czech boundaries were not. The French and Belgian borders with Germany were formally guaranteed by the British and Italians, who pledged to come to France's assistance in case of a German aggression, but the Czech and Polish borders were opened to discussion. Stresemann not only managed to draw a clear distinction between western and eastern German borders, the former recognized and guaranteed and the latter open to a possible revision, but he obtained French withdrawal from the occupation zone around the key city of the Rhineland, Cologne. Consequently, by restricting the French military foothold on German soil, he limited the French capacity for acting on behalf of their allies in eastern Europe, in the event of a German aggression. Before Locarno, the French could have given immediate and effective aid to Poland and Czechoslovakia in any situation considered by them to be a threat to their security. After Locarno, Paris could help the Czechs or the Poles only if they invoked Article 16 of the covenant, which would be a very long and involved procedure. "The spirit of Locarno" created an illusion of security and thus further stimulated the spread of pacifist sentiments in the West.

The French system of alliances could function only if the French were both willing and able to come to the instant and effective military aid of their eastern European allies by starting an offensive action across the Rhine, deep into the main industrial areas of Germany. Before 1925 such a drive could start from the right bank of the Rhine. The gradual evacuation of these vital positions, however, radically limited the possibility of such an action. What still remained was the possibility of an unopposed march of French troops into the demilitarized left bank of the Rhine.

Postwar Military Developments

Another factor hampering the western powers was the trend toward pacifism and disarmament. Soon after the war Britain abandoned conscription and demobilized its army, reducing it to a mere skeleton. After 1920 Britain's armed forces were based mainly on the strength of the Royal Navy supplemented by a small, professional land army and air force designed mainly for imperial garrison service. The more insecure French retained the system of the nation in arms but gradually reduced the terms of conscript service from three years to eighteen months in 1923, and to one year in 1928.

It was the political climate of pacifism and inertia that made the French restructure their defenses by building a chain of powerful fortifications stretching from the Swiss to the Belgian frontiers. The chain was constructed during the years 1929 to 1938. The Maginot Line, as the chain came to be called, was a marvel of modern technique. Besides the most up-to-date military installations, such as batteries of "disappearing" guns, the forts contained very comfortable living quarters for the garrison: kitchens, telephone exchanges, miniature railways, power stations, and hospitals. Elaborate charts indicated fire plans covering every square yard of terrain in front of the line. The Maginot Line was the largest, most intricate, and costly chain of fortifications since the Great Wall of China.

The construction of the Maginot Line was an undertaking that left little for the modernization of the French armed forces. Moreover, feeling blissfully secure behind the line, the French leaders came to believe that they could afford to relax and take only a limited interest in the progress of military technology outside their borders. They also brushed aside the lessons of the last stages of World War I pertaining to the strategic implications of the tank and aircraft.

The French military doctrine insisted that the offensive role of the tank would eventually be counterbalanced by defensive weapons, especially antitank guns, as the cavalry had been by machine guns in the last war. Such views shocked a few more farsighted French experts. In 1936 a veteran French infantry officer, Charles de Gaulle, published his book *Toward a Professional Army,* in which he tried to draw some practical conclusions from the experiences of the closing phases of World War I. In the future, he argued, a conscript army would not be sufficient and should be supplemented by a professional force trained to handle complex mechanized equipment, especially tanks. Armored units should operate, not in small groups merely supporting infantry, but in large masses of divisional strength. Such tank divisions, de Gaulle argued, should not be tied down to slow-moving infantry but act as armored battering rams to penetrate enemy defenses. His book, however, was either completely ignored or sharply criticized by the older members of the French military establishment.

Similar ideas were propagated with limited results by some British military experts, such as General J. F. C. Fuller, Basil Liddell Hart, and Giffort Martell. Only 500 copies of General Fuller's handbook, *Operations Between Mechanized Forces,* were distributed in Britain, while 30,000 copies were sold in Germany. The British experimental mechanized corps was disbanded. Until 1936 Great Britain spent five times as much on horse calvary as on armored and mechanized forces.

While the mood of indolence and inertia was overcoming the military establishments of France and Great Britain, in Germany war veteran Heinz Guderian avidly studied Liddell Hart's and Fuller's books and drew from them far-reaching conclusions. After a number of experimental war games, some of them conducted in Russia, Guderian resolved that armor could achieve deep penetration of the enemy's rear, thus paralyzing his defenses. He also came to believe that aviation should cooperate closely with the mechanized land forces; together they could greatly increase the capacity for threatening faraway targets, especially communication centers and command posts, consequently causing moral paralysis and physical disintegration of the enemy even before the destruction of his main forces on the battlefield. Thus, by the early 1930s the concept of *blitzkrieg,* or "lightning warfare," had already been born.[7]

---

[7]For the attitude of the German military leaders toward mechanization of the Reichswehr see B. H. Liddell Hart, *The German Generals Talk* (New York: Morrow, Quill, 1979), especially Chapter IX, "The Rise of Armor," pp. 90–104.

2

Fascism, National Socialism, and the Formation of the Axis

THE RISE OF FASCISM IN ITALY

In the immediate postwar period Italy was a minor factor, owing to its military weakness and internal instability. During the 1920s and early 1930s Italy, despite sporadic bellicose gestures, remained a loyal member of the Entente. Italy had abandoned the Triple Alliance in 1915 to join the Entente in exchange for promises of territorial advantages that included not only Trieste and South Tirol but also the Dalmatian coast. These promises conflicted, however, with Point IX of President Wilson's Fourteen Points, the principle of self-determination. The compromise reached at the Paris Peace Conference gave Italy Trieste, South Tirol, and Istria, as well as many of the Adriatic islands, but not all of Dalmatia. Most of Dalmatia was allotted to the emerging Kingdom of Serbs, Croats, and Slovenes, or Yugoslavia, on ethnic grounds. Thus Dalmatia became a major bone of contention between Italy and Yugoslavia, an ally and protégé of France.

To this point of friction one should add the grievances against France itself. The fact that in 1859 Piedmont-Sardinia had to pay for the aid of Napoleon III in unifying northern Italy with the then largely Italian provinces of Nice and Savoy was never forgotten by Rome. Neither was the basically Italian ethnic character of Corsica, nor the French preemptive occupation of Tunisia in 1881, carried out to forestall an impending Italian move in that direction.

To keep the Italian soldiers fighting, the pro-Entente politicians were overly lavish with promises of postwar social and economic benefits to be bestowed on the veterans. When these pledges were not kept, the demobilized soldiers felt cheated. By 1919/

20 the dissatisfaction reached menacing proportions. The Bolshevik Revolution gave a powerful push to Italy's leftist groups. Numerous strikes and other demonstrations led to street riots, looting, and bloodshed. At that time the Italian Communists were still a small sect, yet they were increasingly aggressive and vociferous. Together with the Socialists and militant Syndicalists, they took over some factories and committed numerous acts of violence, sabotage, and terror.

By 1919 "the Red Spectre" had frightened the Italian upper and middle classes so much that they responded by organizing various forms of active self-defense. Since the army and security forces often could not be relied upon, the rightist elements began to form their own fighting squads to oppose the encroachment of the increasingly aggressive Left. The most energetic and best-organized detachments were those led by Benito Mussolini, son of a village blacksmith, a former socialist journalist, and a leading proponent of Italy's entry into World War I on the side of the Entente.[1] Short, stumpy, and stagy, he was a skilled demagogic orator. His followers, dressed in black shirts, greeted each other with the Roman salute of the outstretched hand; they used as their symbol the emblem of the old Roman magistrates, a bundle of rods bound together about an ax with a blade projecting. From this symbol of Roman power, or *fasces,* the members of Mussolini's militia came to be known as Fascists.

Benito Mussolini in a Fascist party uniform.
National Archives

In October 1922, taking advantage of the near paralysis of the administrative apparatus, Mussolini staged a concentric march of armed Fascist detachments from various parts of the country, all focusing on Rome, to claim power for their movement. Frightened by this massive and noisy demonstration, King Victor Emmanuel III summoned Mussolini, then cautiously waiting in Milan, the stronghold of Fascism, to form a new government. Only then, on October 30, traveling by sleeping car, Mussolini appeared in the capital to assume the premiership of a new coalition government. At the time of the March on Rome the Fascist party held only 6 percent of the seats in the lower chamber of the parliament.

Mussolini's avowed goal was to remake not only the country's political system but also its psyche. To overcome his countrymen's proclivity for sluggish, happy-go-lucky individualism, often bordering on anarchy, he proclaimed the necessity of imposing martial virtues: military discipline and obedience to the all-powerful Fascist state. Ruthlessly exploiting the temporary special powers granted to him by the fright-

[1]For a recent attempt at presenting him against a broad background, see Denis Mack Smith, *Mussolini* (New York: Knopf, 1982).

ened parliament, he gradually turned them into a permanent dictatorship of his party. Already by the late 1920s Italy had taken the shape of a one-party state with Mussolini as its infallible leader, "Il Duce."

One of the most obsessive features of the Fascist ideology was its glorification of the martial virtues of courage, ruthlessness, and physical force. Fascism, fulminated Mussolini in one of his speeches, "does not believe either in the possibility or the utility of universal peace. It rejects the pacifism which masks surrender and cowardice. War alone brings all human energies to their highest tension and imprints a seal of nobility on the peoples who have the virtue to face it." Modern Italians were heirs to the old Roman Empire, and that is why the Mediterranean should again become Italy's *mare nostrum,* or "our sea."

The philosophic foundations of fascism were rather meager. Selectively and often inconsistently, Mussolini amalgamated various ideas borrowed left and right from Machiavelli, Georges Sorel, Friedrich Nietzsche, Vilfredo Pareto, and Philipo Corradini. To this mixture he added some of his own concepts, such as that of "totalitarianism," or absolute supremacy of an all-powerful state, ruled by a single hierarchically organized party headed by an infallible leader. Mussolini's goal was not so much to create a consistent theory as to provide an instrument for action, a technique for capturing and holding power. His success in this respect encouraged imitation. By the late 1920s and early 1930s fascism had become a favorite fad of a number of conservative politicians. Soon, despite Mussolini's repeated vocal denials, fascism became a major Italian export. Hungary soon would have its Arrow Cross, Rumania its Iron Guard, and Spain its Falange, to mention only a few most striking examples.[2]

An Italian child, member of the Youngest Party Organization, "Bambini," is taught how to make a Fascist salute. National Archives

Mussolini's Expansionist Ambitions

The realization of the ambitious expansionist schemes required a considerable bolstering of Italy's limited military capabilities. To fulfill his dream, Mussolini embarked upon a vast program of modernization of the country's armed forces, especially its navy and air force.

In 1921 the Italian general Giulio Douhet published a book entitled *Air Mastery.* Douhet's main thesis was that a powerful air force could dominate the future war. Once aviation had won control of the skies, command of land and sea would follow as the night follows the day. His concept of victory through air power won wide acclaim and profoundly influenced not only many airmen but also the thinking of some politicians. Similar theories were propagated in Germany by a veteran of Baron von Richthofen's "Flying Circus," General Ernst Udet, and by a United States World War I air ace, General William ("Billy") Mitchell.

Mussolini was fascinated by Douhet's

[2]For an interpretation of Fascist doctrine and practice, see Benzo de Felice, *Interpretations of Fascism* (Cambridge: Harvard University Press, 1977).

book and made Douhet a vice minister of aviation in his first cabinet. During the 1920s the Italian air force was greatly expanded and became the Fascist party's stronghold and pride. Although the Italians were the first to create large motorized units, the economic backwardness of the country prevented them from developing really strong armored forces.

The extensive Italian territorial claims implied a conflict with the main Mediterranean naval power, Britain, which controlled not only Gibraltar and the Suez Canal but also Egypt and the island of Malta; Greece was almost a British protectorate, and Palestine was a British mandate. On the other hand, large stretches of Africa were in the hands of the French, who firmly held Tunisia, Algeria, and Morocco, while exercising a League of Nations mandate over Syria and Lebanon, and guarding the island of Corsica. Thus, the French, who exercised jointly with the British an informal condominium over the Mediterranean, were also a major obstacle to the eventual realization of the objectives of the Italian Fascists.

Yet for over a decade and a half Mussolini, while voicing his disappointment with the Versailles settlement, did enjoy its tangible benefits. After all, Italy's main enemy had been the old Habsburg Empire. Its destruction gave Italy South Tirol, Trieste, and a chunk of the Dalmatian coast and thus enhanced Italy's security in the north and east, in the Danubian basin, and in the Balkans. By the late 1920s rump Austria and Hungary had become Rome's clients politically and economically. Yet in the long run it was this sense of security in the area along the Alpine frontier that encouraged the Italians to stumble into a series of adventurous undertakings in the Mediterranean, in Africa, and eventually in Europe.

THE RISE OF NAZISM IN GERMANY

The movement that eventually proved to be the most dangerous enemy of the peace was born in Germany. The roots of National Socialism were deeply imbedded in the political situation of Germany since November 1918. From the very beginning a great majority of the German people adopted an attitude of implacable hostility toward the Versailles treaty. Even those Germans who had formally accepted the settlement were determined at heart to sabotage it by all available means. The grudging and reluctant acceptance of the treaty by the German people legitimized all forms of secret evasion of the *Diktat*. Consequently, the slogan Destruction of the Treaty of Versailles won nearly unanimous public support.

The groups that best exploited the outraged German nationalism originally called itself the German Workers' party, later becoming known as the National Socialist German Workers' party, or Nazi party for short. Formed in 1919, the party was soon in the forefront of those who insisted that the war had not actually been lost on the battlefield

Hitler is offered roses by a member of the Nazi Youth Organization. National Archives

but on the home front as a result of the domestic treason of the allegedly Jewish-inspired socialist-communist revolt. It was this Marxist-Jewish treachery that had deprived the valiant German soldiers at the front of a well-deserved victory that had been just around the corner. This "stab-in-the-back" legend was a stock in trade of the entire German Right, but the German Workers' party stressed it with an especially vitriolic vehemence, persistence, and skill.

Although the Versailles settlement was the number one target of the German Workers' party, the Weimar Republic was next on the list of its enemies. The party furiously attacked "the self-seeking band of weak and corrupt party bosses" as well as "the greedy money barons of big business," among whom, they argued, the Jewish speculators and "spiderlike money monopolists" were predominant. The Jews, who were a pet target of Nazi demagoguery, were accused of a variety of contradictory machinations. They were responsible, the Nazis fulminated, not only for controlling the world of finance but at the same time for manipulating the leftist movements, the social democrats and communists, as well as the pacifist movement. According to the Nazis, the Jewish-inspired corruption and revolutionary agitation had been largely responsible not only for the German defeat but also for Germany's inability to overcome its effects. By fostering class hatred, cosmopolitanism, and pacifism, the Jews were perpetuating national weakness and degradation and thus diverting the Germans from their main goal, that of national revival and military revenge.

The German Workers' party urged the Germans to overthrow the rule of the allegedly alien, cosmopolitan cliques running the Weimar Republic, and to give power to its best sons, who had risked their lives at the front—the genuine, pure-blooded Germans. They were to restore Germany's dignity, prosperity, and power, which was Germany's birthright. Like the Fascists, the German Workers' party stressed the importance of martial virtues and of the strong leadership of a charismatic, infallible *Führer.*

HITLER'S RISE TO POWER

The German Workers' party vegetated on the fringe of the Weimar Republic's political spectrum until it was taken over by an obscure war veteran, Adolf Hitler. It was he who firmly grasped the leadership of the movement in 1920, never to relinquish it until his suicide in 1945.

Hitler was born on April 20, 1889, at Braunau, in Austria, just across the German border. He was the son of a peasant-craftsman who eventually became a minor Austrian customs official. Adolf was a morose sort of boy, always in sullen rebellion against his father and his schoolmasters. His only strong affection was for his mother. Hitler's early career was erratic and undistinguished. He wanted to be either a painter or an architect but failed in both fields. He spent his twentieth to twenty-seventh years wandering through Linz, Vienna, and Munich, seeking out his living by various means, including house painting and paperhanging. It was at that time that he developed his hatred of the Jews, whom he accused of dominating economic as well as intellectual life in the Habsburg Empire. Soon this hatred became an obsession.[3]

The outbreak of World War I was Hitler's "road to Damascus." According to Hitler, "that hour brought redemption from all the vexations of my youth. I am not ashamed to say that, in a transport of rapture, I sank down to my knees and thanked Heaven . . . for having given me the good fortune of being alive in such times." Although an Austrian subject, he evaded conscription in his native armed forces and volunteered into the German army, as an infantry private. He fought enthusiastically throughout the war, suffered wounds, and earned two Iron Crosses. Nevertheless, he ended the war as only lance corporal because his military supe-

---

[3]Allan Bullock, *Hitler: A Study in Tyranny* (New York: Harper & Row, 1962) is still the best work; see also Joachim C. Fest, *Hitler* (San Diego: Harcourt Brace Jovanovich, 1974) and Norman Stone, *Hitler* (London: Hodder, 1988).

riors considered him incapable of strong leadership and deficient in native intelligence.

Soon after the war Hitler joined the German Workers' party and was put in charge of its propaganda section. Endowed with remarkable oratorical and organizing skills, he soon became the party's dominant personality and eventually its acknowledged leader. It was he who changed the original bland name of German Workers' party into National Socialist German Workers' party, thus ambivalently but astutely drawing together the two dominant strands of German society, nationalism and socialism. Soon Hitler, an ardent admirer of Mussolini, wanted to emulate the March on Rome and launched a bid for power. In November 1923 his attempted coup, or *Putsch,* in Munich was bloodily suppressed by the Bavarian local government backed by the army. For his part in the Munich *Putsch,* Hitler was condemned to five years in the Fortress of Landsberg on the Lech. He served, however, only eight and a half months and used this time for dictating the greater part of his main work, *Mein Kampf* (My Struggle), the canon-to-be of the Nazi movement.[4]

The criminal viciousness of Hitler's policies made his opponents berate him as a theoretician and condemn his outlook as "nihilistic," if not entirely insane. Our natural revulsion toward most of Hitler's objectives and methods should not obfuscate the fact that Hitler harbored definite convictions and fought for a well-integrated vision of the world, as frightening as his *weltanschauung* appears to us. Behind the morose, pallid, common, and cruel face, with its toothbrush mustache and long reddish nose, was hidden a man of uncommon intelligence, prodigious memory, and instant insight into the motives of his opponents, a gift which he called "my intuition." These attributes, combined with hypnotic qualities and remarkable public-speaking talents, made him a formidable political figure. Soon, for many Germans, he became a prophet with a vision of revenge and a better future.

The quintessence of his philosophy was racism. Hitler's ideology was a specific concept of race borrowed from various sources, including Houston S. Chamberlain and Friedrich Nietzsche. In the hierarchy of races the Nordic-Germanic race of tall, blond, blue-eyed individuals occupied the top place. It was supposedly this breed that had always created the highest sociopolitical and cultural values, whereas other races, especially the Jews, always opposed those values and tried to pervert them. Hitler maintained that Christianity was a product of the Judaic ethos and was essentially a Jewish sect. Its morbid morality had a debilitating effect on the Germanic peoples because it preached the creed of charity, meekness, and universal brotherhood, which resulted in a bastardization of the Nordic race and its progressive softness and cowardice. That is why the Christian values had to be rejected as paralyzing the natural Teutonic virility and aggressiveness. The road to national recovery and greatness should lead through repudiation of both Judeo-Marxist and Judeo-Christian values, which had rendered Germany decadent, sluggish, and ideologically confused.

According to Hitler, the struggle of races and not that of classes was the driving force of history. The state was nothing but the race in being, and merely its instrument. The individual was a biological product of his or her race before he or she became a subject of a state, which was a secondary concept. The individual was primarily an integral, organic part of his or her racial community, happiest in a complete merger with its life. Freedom, as understood by liberals, was an effete, outworn, and dangerous concept. The race was weakened by nonconformity of its members. The citizen's highest privilege was to live and work for the nation. Hence, *Gleichschaltung* (integration, subjugation, total merger) was one of the key terms of the Nazi jargon.

---

[4]*Mein Kampf* is a highly stylized autobiography of Hitler, and a history of his movements in three parts. Part I was published in 1924, part 2 in 1926. The third part of the sequence was never completed or published in his lifetime but only edited from his notes, and it saw the light of day in 1961 under the title *Hitler's Secret Book.*

The unification of all German-speaking peoples was declared to be an overriding objective. All scattered segments of the Germanic race in Europe were to be united in one state, under one leader. One Folk, One State, One Leader was another of Hitler's slogans. The race's purity, and hence superior quality, would be enhanced by planned eugenics. The preservation of racial purity was threatened by other, "inferior," races, mainly by the Jews, intermarriage with whom should be forbidden as a cardinal sin against the Germanic nationhood. Numerical growth and territorial expansion were symptoms of health and vitality. In *Mein Kampf* Hitler wrote: "Today we count 80,000,000 Germans in Europe. We can only consider our foreign policy a success if, in less than 100 years, 250,000,000 Germans come to live on the Continent."

In Hitler's mind, the state was not an end in itself but a means to two ends: the preservation of racial purity and territorial expansion. The two objectives were closely interconnected because both served to preserve and enhance the race. German blood and German soil and territory were two supreme values. The race must multiply in numbers and expand its territorial base, or living space (*Lebensraum*). The new living space for the Germanic race could be found in eastern Europe, Poland, and the western fringes of Soviet Russia, mainly in the fertile plains of the Soviet Ukraine.

According to Hitler, Germany's main hereditary enemy was France, not Great Britain as Emperor William II had believed. The British objected only to Germany as a world power; the French hated any united Germany as such. Moreover, the British, as Anglo-Saxons, were blood brothers of the Germans, while the French, as mongrels, were an "inferior race." Thus, Hitler's radical domestic program was closely interconnected with his ambitious foreign policy vision. Germany's aspirations, he argued, could not be carried out by the Germans alone but in alliance with other nations whose interests were not basically in conflict with the essentially eastward drive. These were primarily France's potential rivals, the Italians and the British, neither of whom would oppose Germany's ambitions in eastern Europe, which they regarded as peripheral.

It was the occupation of the Ruhr by French troops in 1923, to compel the recalcitrant Germans to deliver coal and pay other war indemnities, that alerted Hitler to the possibility of a German-British rapprochement against France. The fact that the British radically disassociated themselves from the French occupation made him conceive a future Anglo-German alliance first against France, and eventually also against Communist Russia. He would return to this idea repeatedly in his conversations and his speeches. Hitler's hopes were based on London's traditional policy of balance of power on the Continent. That is why he was very critical of imperial Germany's foreign policy. Faced with a choice between land expansion toward the east or naval and colonial expansion at the expense of Britain, he argued, the Second Reich opted for both, thus risking a war on two fronts. Never again, reiterated Hitler, should such an error be committed.

At that time Hitler also noticed the growing estrangement of Italy from the other victors of the war, especially France. Hence his early conclusion that Germany should draw closer to the sulking Italy and offer help against France. This implied acquiescence in the Italian control of the largely German South Tirol: It was a decision obviously contrary to his principle of gathering all Germanic people in one state, but he was willing to make this relatively small sacrifice to achieve a larger goal, that of forging a broad anti-French coalition. His idea of ties with other powers was not determined by ideological factors but by power-political motives. For instance, his idea of an alliance with Italy predated the triumph of fascism, since it had appeared in Hitler's speeches already in 1920. The triumph of fascism in 1922 merely strengthened Hitler's original inclination to side with Italy against the hated French.

Many historians often err by asserting that Hitler's main objective was revenge for the last war and restitution of the frontiers of 1914. Such an opinion finds no corroboration in his views as expressed in his speeches and writings, as well as in confidential pronouncements. Hitler early rejected the idea of simply reestablishing the boundaries of 1914, considering them purely accidental, illogical, militarily indefensible, and therefore geopolitically irrational. His objective was not restitution but expansion of Germany's *Lebensraum* far beyond the unacceptable frontiers of the Second Reich.

As has already been noted, the initial merely continental European goals of Hitler could be achieved in alliance with two other nations whose objectives did not conflict with those of the Germans: Britain, interested mainly in its imperial overseas possessions, and Italy, whose natural sphere of activity was the Mediterranean basin. Such a triple alliance of Germany, Britain, and Italy would isolate France, thwart her hegemony on the Continent, and thus secure Germany's free hand in the east, mainly toward Soviet Russia, estranged from bourgeois France by communism.

Two of Hitler's fundamental assumptions were also crucial to his calculations. The first was that of an eventual clash of political and economic interests between Britain and the United States, which would prevent collusion of the two Anglo-Saxon powers against Germany; the second was the allegedly insurmountable weakness of the USSR, ruled by incompetent "Jewish Bolsheviks and Slavs," both, in Hitler's opinion, subhuman, uncreative races organically incapable of an effective organization of their vast resources.

THE NAZIS GAIN A FOOTHOLD

The circumstances that brought Hitler to power in 1933 are, in retrospect, of much less significance for a historian of World War II than the consequences of this momentous event. During the years 1926 to 1929, or during the relative stability and prosperity of the Weimar Republic, the Nazi party continued to grow, but it couldn't be said to be flourishing. Its membership was 27,000 in 1925, and 178,000 in 1929. What gave it another chance was the Great Depression, which hit Germany like a mighty tornado. By 1931/32 the country's industrial production had fallen by nearly half. Unemployment had risen from 2 million to 6 million by January 1932. That was the month in which the German government repudiated its "political debts," including reparations. By that time the Nazi movement was swollen partly by the broad masses of unemployed workers and partly by the impoverished, destitute lower middle class, who were among the chief victims of the economic depression.

Since 1930 the whole country had been in turmoil and on the brink of a fierce civil war. Almost every day, in the streets of various cities and towns, strikes, demonstrations, lockouts, and riots were taking place. Not only Nazi but also Communist, Socialist, and other fighting squads were roaming the streets, lynching and murdering their opponents, while remaining largely unpunished. The police were helpless, paralyzed by the scale and intensity of these mass incidents. By January 1932 the Nazi party had more than quadrupled its membership, which passed the 900,000 mark. In the riots, brawls, and clashes with various groups, the Nazis distinguished themselves by their superior organization, efficiency, and ruthlessness. In hand-to-hand fighting with their Marxist opponents, they were more often than not victorious, and their demagogic, unscrupulous propaganda was more persuasive than that of their rivals. This gave them the reputation of being the main obstacle to the allegedly impending Bolshevik coup d'état.

In January 1933, threatened by an almost equally rapidly expanding Communist movement and unable to form a stable coalition government from a plethora of small, shifting political groups, a leader of the Catholic Center party and the vice-chancellor of a bankrupt right-of-center cabinet, Franz von Papen, had an apparently brilliant idea. He persuaded the aging and ailing president of the Republic, Field Marshal von Hindenburg, to entrust the chancellorship of the Reich to Hitler. This would be merely a temporary measure, argued Papen. As the head of the most dynamic non-Marxist political movement, the upstart "Bohemian corporal," as Hitler was called by his rivals, should be able to stem the rising Red tide and exhaust the Nazi movement in the process. Having played himself out, he would be dismissed and replaced by another responsible rightist coalition.

It was Papen who on January 4, 1933, made a secret deal with Hitler at the house of the Cologne banker Kurt von Schroeder, one of the German tycoons who had financed the Nazi movement. The secret pact assured the vice-chancellorship for Papen, and only three of eleven cabinet posts to the Nazis. As a result of this deal, on January 30, 1933, President Hindenburg entrusted Hitler with the task of forming what seemed to be another musical-chair cabinet.[5]

The cabinet's composition was highly deceptive. The foreign ministry and that of defense were to be in the hands of the president's men, the former to Baron Konstantin von Neurath and the latter to General Werner von Blomberg. Together with Papen as vice-chancellor, they were to keep Hitler under control. All that was left for the Nazis, besides the chancellorship, was the Reich's ministry of the interior, which did not control the police, and a ministry without portfolio, which was given to Hermann Goering. This Hitler crony and a former aviation ace was also entrusted with the Prussian ministry of the interior. Unlike the Reich's interior ministry, that of Prussia did control the police force. Since Prussia was a major stronghold of the Social Democratic and Communist parties and since Prussia's territory and population amounted to some two-thirds of the Reich, Goering's double post was actually of crucial importance.

THE NAZIS SEIZE POWER

Pretending that the formation of a working majority had proved impossible, Hitler persuaded Hindenburg to dissolve the *Reichstag,*

[5]For a recent study that downplays the role of German big business see Henry Ashby Turner, Jr., *German Big Business* (New York: Oxford University Press, 1985).

Hitler as chancellor of the Reich appears with the president of the republic, von Hindenburg, at a military parade in Potsdam in the spring of 1933.
National Archives

or parliament, and proclaim a new election. The electoral campaign of 1933 was a textbook case of intimidation and terrorism applied by the Nazi machine to the confused electorate. Hitler put to full use the efforts of Goering, who purged hundreds of Prussian officials and policemen and replaced them mostly with members of the S.A. and S.S., the Nazi party's protection Squads and storm troopers, respectively.

On the night of February 27 the Reichstag building went up in flames. A young Dutchman, van der Lubbe, found there in suspicious circumstances, was accused of having set the fire as the supposed signal for a Communist coup. The incident was used by the Nazis as a pretext for pouncing on the Communist party. The day after the Reichstag fire, Hitler prompted Hindenburg to promulgate a presidential decree "for the protection of the People and the State." The decree suspended the constitutional guarantees of individual liberty and authorized the Reich government, if necessary, to seize full powers in any federal state. Provided with clear dictatorial powers, Hitler could then initiate any action that suited him.

Parallel with the subordination of the political life of the country to the only remaining organized political force, the Nazi party, went the brutal destruction of the independent trade unions upon which the Social Democratic party largely rested. The civil service was soon purged of all Jews and people of Jewish descent, as well as officials with leftist views. The same happened to the bar. The artistic professions and the mass media were in turn brought under the control of Hitler's fanatical henchman, Dr. Joseph Goebbels, and his newly created Ministry of Propaganda and Education. In July, all political parties except the National Socialist party were officially banned. After the adoption of the so-called Nuremberg Laws of September 15, 1935, Jews were systematically excluded from most professions. Thereafter, doctrinal racism ceased to be a mere eccentricity of the Nazi regime and became its integral feature.

The Nazi revolution was accomplished by the use of violence on a massive scale, systematically employed by the government to intimidate or coerce its opponents. The two new instruments of official violence were the state secret police, or *Gestapo,* and a net of concentration camps. The camps at Dachau and Oranienburg were the first to open their gates to a mounting stream of actual and potential enemies of the new regime. Prior to 1939 some 200,000 Germans passed through various concentration camps. Thus, the use of violence was institutionalized and became a quintessential part of the Nazi system.

THE NAZI PARTY IN ACTION

The Nazi seizure of power had been accompanied by a resurgence of Socialist trends within the party: Its left wing insisted that the political revolution should be followed by a radical social upheaval. But Hitler, who never was deeply interested in purely social and economic affairs, gave a free hand to an expert of conservative views, Dr. Hjalmar Schacht, the man responsible for the business recovery during the 1920s. Hitler also entrusted the Ministry of National Economy and Trade to the general manager of the largest insurance company in Germany. The presence of these two representatives of the establishment was to guarantee that there would be no undesirable experiments and that the reconstruction of the country's economy was to be achieved in cooperation with industry and big business, which had largely financed the Nazi movement. Soon the German economy was harnessed to serve the ultimate purposes of the Nazis. All exports and imports were strictly controlled by the government and so carefully balanced that the fast-expanding armament industries would receive everything they needed, including ample stockpiles of strategic raw materials.

Like John Maynard Keynes, Schacht insisted on borrowing by the government and the controlled expenditure of the accumulated funds. By expanding employment and granting purchasing power to workers, the economy could be forced into activity and a prosperous business life reestablished. Thus, Schacht not only created wealth but enforced its rapid recycling to reduce the rampant unemployment.[6]

By 1936—that is, within three years—Dr. Schacht had fully succeeded in ending the depression and in almost totally erasing the country's huge unemployment, while maintaining stability of prices and wages. All this was accomplished by masterfully utilizing Germany's limited natural resources, mainly coal, and the greatest asset of the country, a large reservoir of skilled labor, disciplined and devoted to hard work. There is no doubt that Schacht's resounding success in regenerating the country's shattered economic fabric was something of a miracle, which the outside world refused to recognize because it was horrified by the cruel aspects of Hitler's domestic policies. Hitler skillfully exploited Schacht's triumphs to strengthen his grip on the masses of the German people, most of them grateful to him for their steady jobs and a modicum of prosperity.

The jettisoning of the original quasi-Socialist objectives of the party, however, aroused bitter opposition within the left wing of the movement, headed by Major Ernst Roehm. As the chief of staff of the S.A., which numbered some two to three million men, he was a key figure of the Nazi movement. He and most of his fanatical supporters were not satisfied with this first political phase of the upheaval, which actually ended with the apparent triumph of the old establishment, big business and the army. What the radical left wing of the S.A. hoped for was a "second Revolution." Such a revolution would not only give more power to the workers but also make the S.A. squads, or the "old fighters," the framework of a future expansion and reconstruction of the armed forces. Far from desiring to be incorporated into the cadres of the small regular army, these armed squads insisted on becoming the backbone of a new popular mass army.

Hitler realized that the army's benevolent neutrality not only had been a major factor in his seizure of power but could also serve to guarantee achievement of a crucial further objective, that of making Germany the dominant military power in Europe. Consequently, Hitler was bent on securing a closer cooperation with the leading generals. When Roehm, despite numerous warnings, persisted in his criticism of Hitler's partnership with the establishment, the Führer decided to act. On June 30 his blow fell. In a series of sudden and savage night raids, Heinrich Himmler, at the head of the elite S.S., had several hundred S.A. leaders shot, including Roehm.

As a reward for his services in aborting the Roehm plot, Himmler was reaffirmed in his indisputable leadership of the party's elite storm troopers. The ascendance of the S.S. was largely a result of Himmler's patient spade work at making himself useful to Hitler. It was he who, already in March 1933, had established in Dachau, Bavaria, the first model concentration camp for political dissenters. Then in April 1934, Goering, overburdened with preparing his pet task, the reconstruction of the German air force, handed over to Himmler's control the entire fast-spreading net of concentration camps. By the summer of 1934, in addition to the remnants of the S.A. militia, Himmler commanded some 200,000 well-trained and armed fanatics, a praetorian guard of the Nazi regime. A nucleus of the future military unit, called the *Waffen S.S.,* was soon formed. They were to be trained even more intensively than the regular army and amply supplied with standard army equipment, including armor. By 1936 Himmler controlled most of the domestic affairs by directing the militarized arms of the party as well as the regular police, the secret police or

[6]For a "revisionist" article on Schacht's economic policies, calling them definitely "Keynesian," see J. K. Galbraith, "John Maynard Keynes and Germany," *Harvard Magazine,* May 1977; for a recent overall study of Hitler's achievement see K. Hilderbrand, *The Third Reich* (Winchester, Mass.: Allen & Unwin, 1985).

Gestapo, and the concentration camps; thus, Himmler became the second most important man of the regime.

Meanwhile the army, intoxicated by its apparently decisive victory over what seemed its main rival, was lulled into a false sense of security. The military establishment would for a long time overlook Himmler's expanding semimilitary police and S.S. empire, which was eventually to encroach upon the proud domain of the armed forces and supervise the political loyalty of their personnel.[7]

A NEW GERMAN MILITARY

On August 30, 1934, President Hindenburg died. Hitler, who had anticipated the event, acted swiftly in immediately issuing an announcement that the office of president would henceforward be merged with that of the chancellor. Thus, to his office of chief executive Hitler added that of head of state, which meant also that he became Supreme Commander in Chief of the armed forces of the Reich. Now the soldiers and sailors were called on to swear allegiance, not to the Weimar constitution, which was still formally in force, but to Hitler personally.

Now Hitler could devote more of his time to rearmament and international affairs. In January 1935 the coal-rich region of the Saar, since 1919 administered by the French under the League of Nations mandate, held a plebiscite to determine its fate. Most of the inhabitants were Catholics, many of them Social-Democrats, yet over 90 percent of them voted to return to the Reich. With the recovery of the Saar and with full sovereignty over the entire territory of the Reich, Hitler bolstered his domestic and international prestige. Thus strengthened, Hitler took another step toward his goal. In March 1935 he declared that Germany would ignore the disarmament clauses of the Versailles treaty.

Secret rearmament had been going on since the early 1920s, but it had been hampered by its clandestine character and distant experimentation, mainly on Soviet soil. Hitler defended the existence of various paramilitary organizations, such as the S.A. or S.S., but he had carefully masked the training given to them as little more than cross-country runs, Swedish gymnastics, and target practice with small weapons, which was, he insisted, necessary in view of the latent danger of a violent Communist resurgence.

A start on naval rearmament was made in reviving submarine construction in 1922 when Berlin subsidized Dutch, Swedish, and Finnish shipbuilding firms. The firms built U-boats on contract and this gave German submarine engineers the opportunity to experiment with new designs and technical improvements. A small nucleus for the future air force, the *Luftwaffe,* was formed within Lufthansa, the state controlled airline, shortly after its creation in 1926. By 1931 the secret air force had a total of four fighter, eight observation, and three bomber squadrons. On March 9, 1935, the formation of the Luftwaffe was decreed, and on March 16 the introduction of compulsory military service was ordered. So far nothing was said about the fleet, or *Kriegsmarine,* but it was no secret that the German shipyards were already building at home submarines and battleships far larger than those permitted under the treaty.

Despite the extensive and shrewdly secretive efforts of the Weimar Republic, full-scale open rearmament was a formidable task that taxed most of the resources of the Third Reich. The elite professional army of 100,000 organized in twelve small divisions was to serve now as a training cadre for a conscription army that was to number nearly 600,000 men, or thirty-six divisions, three of them armored. Still thornier were the problems of the navy, which had to expand its program from modest beginnings. The

[7]For military factors see Sir John Wheeler-Bennett, *The Nemesis of Power; The German Army in Politics, 1918–1945* (London: Macmillan, 1954); Gordon A. Craig, *The Politics of the Prussian Army, 1640–1945* (New York: Oxford University Press, 1964); F. I. Carsten, *The Reichswehr and Politics, 1918–1939* (Oxford: Clarendon Press, 1966).

Luftwaffe was in a slightly better position thanks to Goering's persistent efforts. He had ingeniously capitalized on the practices of the Weimar Republic's military leaders, who had developed various aircraft types both in Soviet Russia and in Sweden, and had extensively used the commercial airlines to train men and test new machines.[8]

One of the marvels of military technology created by the Germans was the top-secret coding machine, known as Enigma, or Riddle. Outwardly, the machine looked like an old-fashioned cash register or typewriter. Yet it was the most sophisticated ciphering machine of its kind in the world. It was so constructed that each time a key was pressed, the same combination of letters or numbers could, for all practical purposes, never be duplicated. It was a forerunner of computers, since it was capable of 6 billion, billion, billion different coding arrangements. All services of the German forces were rapidly equipped with this most clever device, and the German High Command was supremely confident that its coding system was absolutely impregnable.[9]

In the field of intelligence another innovation was fostered. In the mid-1930s there were nearly thirty million Germans scattered over the world. The Nazi doctrine proclaimed the superiority of the idea of the nation to that of the state. Consequently, it was to the Reich that the Germans abroad owed their loyalty, and they were to work for its benefit under direct orders of the German authorities. For this purpose a special institute had been established in Stuttgart. Although outwardly it was represented as an essentially cultural organization, it was extensively used for collecting political, economic, and military intelligence for Berlin.

The defensive mentality of the old, small *Reichswehr* was now to be abandoned in favor of a new offensive philosophy. On May 2, 1935, the defense ministry was renamed the war ministry, and its head, Gernal Werner von Blomberg, became commander in chief of the armed forces acting under Hitler as Supreme Commander of the Third Reich armed forces. The name *Reichswehr* (or defense force) was replaced by that of *Wehrmacht* (or fighting force).

From now on, the new Nazi spirit was to energize the old cadres. The largely defensive "strategy of attrition," long envisaged in case of an enemy attack on the Reich's territory, was to be replaced by that of "annihilation": not only destruction of the enemy forces on their own ground but devastation of an invader's entire resources, human and material, to prevent any possibility of a revenge war in the foreseeable future. This "total war" was to be inflicted not solely by force of arms but equally by propaganda, subversion, and economic reprisals. Not the recovery of the old frontiers of 1914, but the securing of a vast new living space, or *Lebensraum,* for the German people was henceforth the Third Reich's main objective.[10]

THE WEST'S RESPONSE TO HITLER

What was the reaction of the main guardians of the Versailles system to these flagrant violations of the treaty? True, all three European victors of the previous war protested against them. But France and Britain limited their indignation to diplomatic notes and appeals to the League of Nations, while Italy alone went as far as to mobilize two classes of conscripts immediately after Hitler's decision to rearm. Indeed, as was mentioned previously, it was Mussolini who summoned a conference of France, Britain, and

---

[8]For the German rearmament see E. M. Robertson, *Hitler's Pre-War Policy and Military Plans 1933–1939* (Secaucus, N.J.: Citadel Press, 1967) and Wilhelm Deist, *The Wehrmacht and German Rearmament,* (Toronto: University of Toronto Press, 1981).

[9]For the origins of Enigma see Józef Garliński, *Intercept: The Enigma War* (London, Melbourne, Don Mills, Ont., Canada: J.M. Dent, 1979), chaps. 1–3.

[10]For the Nazi objectives see Norman Rich, *Hitler's War Aims,* 2 vols. (New York: W. W. Norton, 1974), especially Vol. I; see also Eberhard Jaeckel, *Hitler's World View: A Blueprint for Power* (Cambridge: Harvard University Press, 1981).

Italy to meet on April 11, 1935, in Stresa, to decide upon measures to be taken against this threat to peace. Il Duce hoped to achieve two goals: first, to gain French and British support against Hitler's expected machinations in Austria; second, as compensation for his help in curbing Hitler, Mussolini expected at least the tacit approval of the two main colonial powers for his planned absorption of Ethiopia. At Stresa, however, Franco-British hesitations concerning Italy's African aspirations, as well as Britain's flat refusal to undertake any new commitments in central Europe, dealt a sharp blow to Mussolini's exaggerated hopes.

Here London's attitude was crucial. While paying lip service to the status quo, London was secretly negotiating with Berlin for limitations on Germany's naval rearmament. On June 18, 1935, the signing of the British-German naval agreement was announced. Germany's future fleet was to have not more than 35 percent of the British surface tonnage, and 50 percent of the Royal Navy's submarines. The pact actually provided that in the submarine category Germany could claim parity with Great Britain under certain circumstances. Behind this move was the British Admiralty's firm belief that its antisubmarine detection instrument, the perfected "underwater eye" of 1917 vintage, known as ASDIC, was deadly effective in locating submerged enemy craft. By using sound waves reflected from large metal objects, ASDIC, as an official report concluded, finally removed from the submarine that cloak of invisibility that was its principal weapon.

The 1935 Anglo-German naval agreement was extremely favorable to Germany and actually exceeded the Reich's capacity for shipbuilding in the near future. But by far the most important impact of the deal was psychological. Only a few weeks after an attempt to form a united front with France and Italy at Stresa, London had struck a separate deal with Hitler. This made a mockery not only of the "Stresa front" but of the disarmament clauses of the Versailles treaty and, for that matter, of the treaty as a whole.

THE SOVIET RESPONSE

Four days after Hitler had become chancellor on January 30, 1933, he said to General Blomberg: "Now we shall see whether France has statesmen or not; if so she won't let us have time but attack us." But neither France nor Britain was in a mood to do so. Within a few weeks the Oxford Union Society passed its resolution that "under no circumstances will this house fight for King and Country." Both Britain and France were reducing their military budgets, while Germany was embarking on its rearmament program. In January 1935 General Maxime Weygand, the retiring inspector general of the armed forces, told the Supreme War Council that France would be unable alone to face a rearmed Germany.

This estimate pushed the French government toward taking advantage of the gradual reorientation of Soviet foreign policy. The Soviet government had been hostile to the western democracies and the League of Nations but now inclined toward cooperation with them. The reorientation was cautious and gradual, but the establishment of the puppet state of Manchukuo by Japan in 1931 and Hitler's rise in Germany in 1933 had altered the hitherto relatively secure strategic position of the USSR. When Hitler came to power, Stalin was little disturbed and tried to continue the good relations with Berlin. Even the massacre of the German Communist party by the Nazis did not upset the smooth functioning of the economic and military collaboration between the two governments. The continuing German-Soviet cooperation was, however, difficult to reconcile with the Nazis' proclaimed anticommunism. For Hitler, at this point embarking on an open rearmament, the Soviet training grounds and airfields were no longer indispensable. Consequently, he let lapse the pro-Soviet Rapallo treaty of 1922 after his seizure of power.

Isolated and increasingly menaced in Asia and Europe, Stalin began to probe for new security arrangements. Now needed was a system of alliances to provide the USSR with military assistance from France and possibly Great Britain. This quest for security through ties with Germany's opponents meant that Moscow must quell the fears generated by its explosive revolutionary propaganda in Britain and France and its denunciations of the league as an imperialistic instrument of the "status quo" powers.

The Soviet shift came step by step. Under the guidance of the skillful commissar for foreign affairs, Maksim Litvinov, in the autumn of 1934 the Soviet Union entered the League of Nations as a member with a prominent seat on the council. Litvinov now became one of the most eloquent defenders of the league, praising its system of collective security.

The dramatic reversal of Soviet foreign policy had immediate consequences for the Comintern. Having previously refused to cooperate with the non-Communist Left, the Comintern in 1935 proclaimed a policy of "Popular Fronts." In August 1935 the Comintern Congress ordered its national sections to cooperate with all "democratic and peace-loving" forces to form "broad anti-Fascist coalitions." The first to follow the order were the French Communists, who joined forces with the Social Democrats and Social Radicals in an electoral alliance. Instructions were soon issued to the Communist party of France to support the French rearmament effort.

The domestication of the French Communist party paid immediate dividends. In May 1936 French parliamentary elections resulted in an impressive victory for the coalition of the Communists, Socialists, and Social Radicals. Five million out of 9 million voters cast their ballots for the Popular Front. More than a million votes went for the Communist party, and the number of its deputies increased by 700 percent.

FRANCO-SOVIET RELATIONS

Even before the triumph of the Popular Front, the USSR and France had signed on May 2, 1935, a treaty of alliance that pledged mutual assistance "in case of an unprovoked attack by a European state." A few days later, France's ally, Czechoslovakia, followed the example of its western protector and agreed to a similar treaty. The Soviet-Czechoslovak pact, however, included an additional clause: Any Soviet aid to Czechoslovakia, in case of war, hinged on a previous French entry into the conflict.

The Franco-Soviet alliance of 1935 was actually a modest document, much more restrictive than the diplomatic and military pact of 1894. The new treaty did not envisage automatic action in case of aggression by a third power against one of the contracting parties and spoke only about "mutual consultations" in case of an act of aggression. Moreover, the aggression had to be recognized as such by the League of Nations under Article 16 of the covenant. Effective military cooperation in wartime assumes close peacetime exchanges and detailed planning of future moves. France and the USSR conducted some preliminary General Staff exchanges immediately after the signing of the pact, but they were soon interrupted. The French lacked trust, shocked by the Stalinist purge of top Soviet military personnel, and were hesitant owing to an inveterate suspicion of communism. Consequently, the new French-Soviet alliance was only a pale shadow of its 1894 predecessor. Without a specific, detailed military convention furnishing muscle to the alliance, the pact of 1935 was more a declaration of intent than an effective instrument of defense.

The fact that the new Franco-Soviet pact was signed under different geopolitical conditions also affected the practical usefulness of the alliance. In contrast with the situation prior to World War I, Russia and Germany were not immediate neighbors. They were now separated by a chain of independent states: Rumania, Poland, Lithuania, Latvia, and Estonia. The lack of a common border between the USSR and Germany made it necessary to assure the adherence of the intermediary states to the new security arrangements. For the Red Army to render effective assistance to France in case of an attack by Germany, units would require the right of passage through some of these states to reach German soil. Here the key countries were Poland and Rumania. Obtaining Soviet bases on Polish and Rumanian territory proved to be an insurmountable obstacle to any more effective coordination of Soviet and French preparations. Although allied with the French since 1921 and committed to a nonaggression pact with the USSR since 1932, the Poles, although willing to discuss military cooperation in case of German attack, rejected any idea of allowing the Red Army to be stationed on their territory in time of peace. The Rumanians were equally adamant. Both were firmly convinced that the Red Army, once established on their soil, would never leave it.

Even the lame and halfhearted alliance with the USSR caused a great deal of hesitation and soul-searching among French moderate and rightist politicians. Finally, at the end of February 1936, after a long series of bitter debates, the French parliament ratified the treaty. Hitler at once seized this pretext to decry the alliance as an attempt at "encircling" Germany. He immediately denounced the Locarno Pact as "dead" and on March 7, 1936, sent three regiments onto the left bank of the Rhine. Immediately after this step, he ordered a chain of fortifications to be built as a crash program along Germany's western frontier. The remilitarization of the Rhineland was a gamble. It was taken against the advice of most of Hitler's military and diplomatic advisers, anxious not to precipitate a war crisis before Germany was ready to fight. Hitler brushed aside the objections as cowardice. Yet he played it safe: The commanders of the three regiments were ordered to withdraw at the first sign of any possible active resistance. The rearmament of the Third Reich, started only one year before, had not progressed to the point where German forces could hope to resist successfully a military intervention by France, even if acting alone without support from its allies, Britain, Belgium, Czechoslovakia, and Poland. For several days the Rhine crisis kept Europe in suspense. In view of the blatant violation of both the Versailles and Locarno treaties by Germany, the French premier, Pierre Flandin, urged on by Poland's foreign minister, Józef Beck, at first considered mobilization.[11] The British government of Stanley Baldwin, however, aborted the initiative to strike at the still unprepared Hitler. With the French only halfhearted about resistance, the crisis fizzled out in a series of verbal protests.

The hesitation of France to act profoundly altered both the material balance of power in Europe and the whole political climate in the West. The presence of strong German forces in a strategically vital region of Germany bordering directly on France drastically increased Germany's security in the west, while destroying French protection against a surprise attack. Moreover, German troops and fortifications in the Rhineland jeopardized France's ability to march unopposed into the western, most industrialized areas of Germany, in case of a German threat against either Poland or Czechoslovakia. These circumstances further degraded the value of the French alliance to Warsaw and Prague and made Poland and Czechoslovakia vulnerable.

The events of March 1936 compelled the Belgians to reconsider their position. After 1919 the Belgians had abandoned their neutrality, signed a defensive military alliance with France, and participated with France in the 1923 Ruhr intervention, as well as in the Locarno arrangements of 1925. On October 14, 1936, they declared that the presence of the German troops directly along their frontiers had placed them almost in the same position as before 1914, and thus they were forced to resume their previous posture of neutrality. By an agreement of April 24, 1937, both Paris and London released the Belgians from their obligations under the Locarno Pact and accepted Belgium's return

[11] L. B. Namier pointed out that "no one urged an immediate armed riposte as strongly as Beck," *Europe in Decay* (London: Macmillan, 1950), p. 162.

to a neutral status, in return for Brussels' promise to fortify its frontier with Germany. As a result of these arrangements, however, the French lost the advantage of having the opportunity to use Belgian territory in case of German aggression. But by far the most important effect of the remilitarization of the Rhineland was psychological. A vital question had been raised: If the French would not fight in defense of their own vital interests in a region close to their soil, would they do so to help the distant Poles, Czechs, or Russians?[12]

ITALIAN ADVENTURISM AND THE SPANISH CIVIL WAR

Meanwhile, disappointed in his hopes for a secret deal with Paris and London on Ethiopia, Mussolini launched his long-awaited offensive in October 1935 against that country. The vacillation of the Western powers toward Italian aggression and the weakness and failure of the League of Nations' sanctions contrasted with Hitler's boldness and his encouraging attitude toward Rome's adventuristic policy. This attitude was, of course, dictated by self-interest. Hitler saw Italy's Ethiopian involvement as highly advantageous to Germany for two reasons. First, it finally ended Mussolini's commitment to the Stresa front and thus lessened his will to act as a guarantor of Austria's independence. Second, Italy's diversion in Ethiopia rendered France and England less capable of reacting to Hitler's designs in Europe. Germany's benevolent neutrality toward Italy laid the basis for a rapprochement between Rome and Berlin.

Meanwhile, despite the League of Nations' sanctions and Britain's hollow threats of closing the Suez Canal, the war in Ethiopia ended with Italy's victory by the spring of 1936. On May 9 Mussolini proclaimed the establishment of the Italian-African Empire. Almost at the same time, the pro-Italian French premier, Pierre Laval, was defeated and the new Popular Front government was unwilling to continue his policy of conciliating Fascist Italy. This turn in France's Italian policy coincided with the presence of new voices in Rome, where the ambitious new foreign minister, Mussolini's son-in-law, Count Galeazzo Ciano, was pressing for closer ties with Germany. They were also favored by the events in Spain.

While the Popular Front coalition was settling down in Paris, a civil war had broken out in Spain. In July 1936 several army units revolted against the leftist government, which in February 1936 had won parliamentary elections by a narrow margin. Soon Spain was torn between the Republicans, or supporters of the government, and the rebels, led by General Francisco Franco. The Communist party of Spain, naturally, threw its support to the Popular Front government. Initially, this small sect, which counted about a thousand active Communists in 1931, expanded to over 100,000 members in 1936, and its membership skyrocketed in the course of the Spanish civil war to a million by June 1937. Through the "United Front" of all the leftist groups, the Communists exerted a powerful influence on the larger but much less dynamic Socialist movement, especially on its youth organization, which soon merged with its Communist counterpart.

The bloody and protracted Spanish civil war rapidly became an event of considerable international significance. Spain was an important source of vital strategic raw materials, such as copper, zinc, iron ore, mercury, and lead. Both France and Britain had considerable capital invested in Spain. Although suspicious of General Franco, they did not cherish the prospect of a Communist ascendancy there. Hence, France and England assumed an ambivalent and hesitant attitude toward the civil war.

Germany and Italy, on the other hand, were determined to see their Fascist kinsmen in the Spanish Falange movement win

[12]For a study stressing the importance of the first three years following Hitler's seizure of power see Gerhard L. Weinberg, *The Foreign Policy of Hitler's Germany: Diplomatic Revolution in Europe, 1933–1936* (Chicago: University of Chicago Press, 1970).

the war for both ideological and political reasons. Mussolini acted first, and under the guise of "volunteers," he sent to Spain some 50,000 men. In exchange for aid, Mussolini tried to secure from General Franco naval and air bases in the Balearic Islands. The German contingent counted a few thousand tank and aviation experts, including the crack "Condor" air force squadron.[13] Both Axis partners quite openly used the Spanish civil war as a testing ground for their newly produced war equipment, especially armor and planes. Thus, the civil war in Spain, like the wars in Korea and in Indochina in more recent times, was a trial conflict by proxy: The powers not only tested their new hardware but used smaller countries as pawns in their deadly game.

The approach of the USSR was ambivalent. Spain was the scene of the second experiment in popular-front governments, and Communists played a vital role in the coalition. Consequently, it was difficult for Stalin to allow a leftist government to be destroyed by the rightist rebels, brazenly supported by Germany and Italy. Thus, for ideological and military reasons, Stalin was duty bound to help the Spanish Republicans. Yet he was afraid to alienate his potential allies in a planned anti-Fascist coalition by too bold a policy of supporting the Spanish Communists. Finally, in October 1936 Moscow decided to lend military aid to the Republican side, but it was to be limited to military advisers and equipment only. At the same time, through the agency of the Comintern, foreign Communists were encouraged to recruit volunteers for several "international brigades" to fight for the Spanish Republic. The recruits were trained, equipped, and transported to Spain, where they were to bolster the sagging Republican resistance.[14]

Supported more consistently by their Axis sponsors, the rebels soon gained the upper hand. The more precarious the situation of the Loyalists grew, the greater became their dependence on their main source of military supplies, the USSR, and the firmer became the hold of the pro-Moscow Communists. By the spring of 1937, the Comintern agents came to manipulate most of the governmental and armed forces apparatus. Yet the Republican resistance, even bolstered by Soviet aid and the international brigades, could not counter the rebel military superiority. By April 1939 the Spanish civil war ended with the triumph of General Franco.

To Hitler, the Italian involvement in the Spanish civil war was a welcome windfall: By alienating France and Britain from Soviet Russia, it prevented the formation of a powerful anti-German coalition, and it pushed Italy deeper into his embrace. The war also allowed him to test some models of his new weapons, especially dive bombers and tanks, to correct their shortcomings. The high ratio of attrition of the German and Italian tanks, on the other hand, brought French and British experts to different conclusions and led them to believe in the superiority of defensive weapons over offensive ones. They declared tanks to be too fragile a weapon to be relied on as a decisive instrument of warfare because they had allegedly proved too dependent upon passable roads and too vulnerable to artillery fire. The next war would probably be long, and success would come to the side commanding superior resources. On the basis of this analysis, both the French and the British came to formulate their defense policies: steady and systematic efforts, not a crash rearmament of the German type. The most likely alternative to a prolonged stalemate of the 1914 to 1918 type would be the exhaustion of the attacking side and its

---

[13]Throughout the Spanish civil war some 19,000 Germans served in Spain; the average number at any one time was about 5,000. The Condor legion shot down 313 enemy aircraft and lost 72 of their own.

[14]One of those brigades was composed of American volunteers and bore the name of Abraham Lincoln. The international brigades attracted some prominent communists who were destined to play a significant role during and after World War II, such as Josip Broz, known as "Tito" in Yugoslavia, Palmiro Togliatti in Italy, and Laszlo Rajk in Hungary.

eventual collapse. The Soviet analysis of the Spanish civil war was much more perceptive: tanks were useful provided they were properly used in large formations. But the Soviet tank expert was suspected by Stalin of being a supporter of Leon Trotsky. Consequently, his report was shelved when the author was shot soon after his return to Soviet Russia.

THE AXIS AND THE ANTI-COMINTERN PACT

The Spanish civil war decisively altered the position of the Italians, who now were bogged down in a series of tasks far beyond their limited resources. They were simultaneously trying to maintain their position in the Mediterranean, where they were challenging France and Britain. In the Balkans they were working with Albania and Bulgaria to outflank Yugoslavia and Greece, in order to neutralize the French and British influences there. In the Danube valley Mussolini tried to preserve the protectorate over Austria as well as Hungary against a steady political and economic German infiltration. At the same time, he had to consolidate his still precarious hold on newly conquered Ethiopia, a difficult enterprise in itself. When in July 1936 Mussolini decided to intervene in Spain, he added a fifth demanding task, thus making the cumulative load truly unbearable. In view of Italy's limited strengths something had to be abandoned.

The decision to rearrange the Italian priorities was not easy for Mussolini. His planned Italo-German rapprochement faced severe obstacles, both ideological and political. The heritage of World War I had left a deep-seated suspicion of Germany among Italians. Most formidable was the problem of South Tirol, where some three hundred thousand German-speaking Austrians were longingly looking to Hitler, their compatriot, for help. Yet the comradeship in arms between the Italians and Germans fighting together in Spain, the ideological affinities between nazism and fascism, and Hitler's sympathetic attitude toward Italy's aspirations in Africa and the Mediterranean, rooted in a common hostility toward France and Britain, all played a part in the gradual rapprochement between Rome and Berlin.

In October 1936, during Ciano's first visit to Berlin, a German-Italian preliminary protocol was signed, delimiting respective spheres of interest between the two partners. According to the document, the Mediterranean basin was declared to be Italy's main area of influence. Although neither side was obliged to support the other in the event of a European war, each agreed to pursue a concerted policy in Spain and southeastern Europe. Although the protocol was meant to be secret, Mussolini, annoyed by his increasing isolation and eager for a spectacular diplomatic success, immediately revealed its contents, calling it the "Rome-Berlin Axis." In September 1937 he visited Berlin and easily fell under the spell of Germany's military might, skillfully displayed to him by his host in the form of a series of brilliant parades and maneuvers. Bewitched by the magnetism of German military strength, Mussolini began to lean toward a more intimate partnership with Hitler.

While gradually entrapping Italy, Hitler was also drawing closer and closer to Japan. The strategic significance of the Japanese as possible allies of Germany hinged largely on the question of whether Japan would face Russia or concentrate on expansion in China. Hitler in 1936 thought that Japan's value to him would consist in its willingness to divert Russia's military potential away from Europe. He was aware that Tokyo's continued expansion in China jeopardized Germany's friendship with that country, including considerable military cooperation with the Kuomintang. (At that time, a military mission was training the Chinese military cadres for their struggle against both the Japanese invaders and the local Communists of Mao Tse-tung.) Both Goering and Blomberg regarded China as a potentially more valuable ally against Soviet communism than Japan. But, as in many other cases, Hitler was not inclined to listen to advisers, trusting his own intuition. Eventually he shifted the center of gravity of Germany's interests definitely toward Japan. In June 1938, the German ambassador and military advisers were withdrawn from China to please Tokyo. Soon Japan was to become Germany's main partner in the Far East.

And indeed, on November 25, 1936, Germany and Japan concluded a treaty, the essence of which was a common stand against Soviet Russia and the Soviet-sponsored Communist actions. Italy acceded to this anti-Comintern pact on November 22, 1937. Immediately, however, a divergence in Italo-German interests manifested itself. Rome's primary wish was not for Tokyo to neutralize Soviet Russia but to expand southward, toward Hong Kong and Singapore, and thus embroil the Japanese in a conflict with Great Britain. This action, in the calculations of Mussolini and Ciano, would make London withdraw a segment of the Royal Navy from the Mediterranean for the defense of the Far East.

HITLER'S GRAND STRATEGY

While Italy and others pondered the real meaning of the anti-Comintern pact, Hitler concentrated on his grand strategy. German documents captured by the Allies after the war reveal beyond any doubt that both Czechoslovakia and Austria were, at that time, constantly on Hitler's mind, and that he derived a great deal of encouragement from Britain's attitude toward his east-central European objectives in general. This became quite clear during the November 1937 Berlin visit of Lord Halifax, then President of the Council, that is, second-ranking member of the British Cabinet. Ostensibly Halifax came as a sportsman to visit the International Hunting Exhibition, but he also held negotiations with top German officials. According to the German record of the interview, he gave Hitler to understand that the British government would be inclined to allow Germany a free hand in central and eastern Europe. In February 1938 the British ambassador in Berlin, Sir Nevile Henderson, conveyed to Hitler that Britain "had a keen sense of reality" and was essentially in sympathy with his desire for "change in Europe."

Meanwhile, Hitler's most secret plans for the future were revealed at a briefing held at the Reich's Chancellery on November 5, 1937. With Hitler and his adjutant, Colonel Friederich Hossbach, who was taking the minutes, only five other people were present: Field Marshal von Blomberg, the German war minister; Colonel-General von Fritsch, the commander in chief of the army; Admiral Raeder, the commander in chief of the navy; Goering, the commander in chief of the air force; and Baron von Neurath, the foreign minister.[15]

According to Hossbach, Hitler opened his briefing by saying bluntly that the aim of Germany's policy was to make secure and to preserve the racial community and to enlarge it. In other words, Germany needed territory, or space, for its people. Since Germany could never be fully self-sufficient in raw materials and could never supply its growing population with enough food from its own resources, its future, Hitler asserted, could be secured only by acquiring additional living space in eastern Europe.

Germany had to evaluate the potential of two rivals, Britain and France, who were not as strong as they appeared. There were weak spots in the British Empire, such as Ireland, India, the Far East (threatened by Japan), and the Mediterranean (threatened by Italy). In the long run, the British Empire could not survive in its current shape. France's situation was more favorable than that of Britain, but France was

[15]The text of the document, known as the Hossbach memorandum, is available in *Documents on German Foreign Policy, 1918–1945,* Series D, Vol. I, No. 19, (London: H.M.S.O., 1949).

confronted with internal political dissent. Nonetheless, Britain, France, Russia, and their satellites must be included as opponents in Germany's calculations. Despite his previous fulminations against Soviet Russia and communism, Hitler said little in his briefing about the USSR. In one enigmatic sentence he simply hinted at the possibility of Soviet cooperation against Poland: "Poland, with Russia in her rear, will have little inclination to engage in war against a victorious Germany."

"Germany's problem," Hitler concluded, "could only be solved by means of force, and this was never without attendant risk." There remained to be answered the questions *when* and *how*. As answers Hitler visualized three alternatives. First, the peak of German power would be reached between 1943 and 1945. And that its equipment would become obsolete, and the rearmament of the other powers would catch up with that of Germany. "One thing only was certain, that we could not wait longer." If he was still living, it was his unalterable resolve to solve Germany's problem of space at the latest by 1943 to 1945.

Germany's first objective must be to overrun Austria and Czechoslovakia and so secure Germany's eastern and southern flanks. Hitler believed that almost certainly Britain, and probably France as well, had already tacitly written off the Czechs. In any case, France would be very unlikely to make an attack without British support, and the most that would be necessary in that case would be to hold Germany's western defenses. The conquest of Austria and Czechoslovakia would greatly bolster Germany's resources and add at least twelve divisions to its army. Italy's neutrality would depend upon Mussolini; that of Poland and Russia, upon the swiftness of Germany's military action.

In the Hossbach memorandum Hitler for the first time faced squarely the possibility of confronting not only France and Russia but also Britain, thus putting into doubt his early axiom of winning the British over to the German side. The harangue implied a frank resolve to take any risks to reach his goals; the means, timetable, and the realizing of his final objectives were to remain flexible and depend upon circumstances.

One of the reasons for the briefing was probably to override the growing objections to his rearmament plans and his timetable on the part of his main expert advisers, especially Dr. Schacht and Marshal Blomberg, the minister of war. Both of them were opposed to another attempt at annexing Austria by force. The *Anschluss,* they argued, would mean a European war, for which Germany was not yet prepared. Hitler disagreed and began to look for a valid pretext to destroy this opposition to his views. In the meantime the rearmament drive proceeded at full speed. The vast increase in military spending was to produce considerable strains in the economy. A series of new warnings on the part of Dr. Schacht, commissioner for war economy since May 1935, were ignored. In December 1937 Hitler dismissed him, entrusting the entire rearmament program to Goering.

The firing of Schacht was soon followed by a bloodless but quite extensive purge of the army and the diplomatic corps. In February 1938 Blomberg was forced to resign on a charge, conveniently provided by the Gestapo, that his wife had been a prostitute. Soon sixteen other generals known to be skeptical toward either Hitler's goals or his timetable were also dismissed under various pretexts. The conservative minister of foreign affairs, Baron Konstantin von Neurath, was replaced by his rival, Joachim von Ribbentrop, a rabid Nazi and a foppish dilettante who had first been head of the party's foreign affairs section and then Germany's ambassador in London. When the generals insisted that Blomberg's job should be taken over by a resolute and independent-minded man distrustful of the Nazis, General Werner von Fritsch, commander in chief of the army, the Gestapo provided another trumped-up charge that he was a homosexual. With most potentially dangerous opponents of his plans out of the way, Hitler abolished the minister of war and created the Armed Forces High Command (*Obercommando der Wehrmacht,* or *OKW*). The OKW was to function under Hitler's strict personal supervision as his General Staff of all three services. As its chief he appointed his creature, the servile nonentity, General Wilhelm Keitel, whom one of his colleagues described as "Hitler's head clerk." With the Wehrmacht and the Ministry of Foreign Affairs under his control, Hitler was free to plan and carry out his adventuristic designs as previously outlined in the Hossbach memorandum. The constellation of international relationships favored his plans.

3

The Prelude

AUSTRIA: THE FIRST VICTIM

Absolute mastery at home signaled the beginning of a broader and bolder diplomatic game. Its first objective was the Austrian Republic established in 1918. For most Germans, Austria was a foreign country saddled with a host of economic troubles that they would have preferred to avoid. For Hitler, it was his native land, which he had deserted in 1914 and which he wanted to add to the Reich. The question of how to achieve his goal without precipitating a European conflagration had haunted him ever since the failure of the attempted Nazi *Putsch* in July 1934. The painful experience of that summer convinced him that a successful solution of the problem depended upon two factors: the neutralizing of Italy and the strengthening of the Nazi movement inside Austria.

All the time, Hitler was carefully watching the broader international scene. The French reaction to the occupation of the Rhineland convinced him that Paris would not wage a war for the sake of Austria. Neither would Great Britain. As late as February 21, 1938, Neville Chamberlain explained to Count Dino Grandi, the Italian ambassador to the Court of St. James, that London considered Austria lost. This washing of hands by Britain further weakened Mussolini's resolve to defend his shaky protégé, the Austrian chancellor Dr. Kurt von Schuschnigg, against his formidable Axis partner upon whom he increasingly relied in so many international issues.

Meanwhile the Austrian Nazis were systematically infiltrating the state apparatus and secretly arming their fighting squads. The showdown was precipitated by an incident in January 1938, when the Austrian police raided the Nazi GHQ in Vienna and captured a detailed plan of another Nazi uprising. To prevent the final liquidation of the Austrian Nazis, Hitler invited Schuschnigg to his Bavarian residence on February 12 to discourage him from carrying out further reprisals. When his guest arrived at Berchtesgaden, he was met by Hitler, surrounded by his generals who deliberately displayed military maps prominently marked with red arrows indicating German troop concentrations ready to pounce on Austria. Schuschnigg was immediately faced with an ultimatum: He should either share power with the Austrian Nazis or resign, or else. . . .

Schuschnigg accepted the ultimatum to gain time and outside support in Paris, London, and Rome. Meanwhile, however, the Austrian Nazis were already taking things into their own hands, terrorizing people, beating political opponents, and looting Jewish stores. At that time France and Britain, on whose backing Schuschnigg had counted, were nearly paralyzed by a double political crisis. France was flooded by a wave of strikes and the Popular Front government was disintegrating. In London, the foreign secretary, Anthony Eden, resigned; his office was now taken over by the appeasement-minded Lord Halifax.

Since both Paris and London ignored his appeals for help, in despair Schuschnigg tried to contact Mussolini by telephone. Il Duce was not to be reached, however. Seeing chaos submerging his country, on March 9 Schuschnigg took a last resort decision. A referendum was to decide the country's fate on Sunday, March 13: Its people were to be asked whether they wanted to preserve a "free, independent, social Christian and united Austria."

When Hitler learned about the referendum, he threatened Schuschnigg with immediate invasion unless he canceled his decision and handed over political power to the Austrian Nazi leader, Dr. Seyss-Inquart. In his predicament, Schuschnigg once more appealed for help to Mussolini, but the urgent telegram sent to Rome remained unanswered. On Friday evening, March 11, in desperation, Schuschnigg made a farewell radio address to the Austrian people. While he was making his speech, a gang of Nazis broke into the studio and arrested him. Next morning the first detachments of the German forces crossed the Austrian border. By midday of Saturday, March 12, Vienna was occupied. Hitler himself drove triumphantly into his native land that day and was greeted by Dr. Seyss-Inquart. Meanwhile, on Mussolini's order German and Italian troops, when they met at the Brenner Pass, exchanged friendly greetings.

Austria and Beyond

The Anschluss, Hitler's first venture outside the boundaries of Germany, added more than 7 million new subjects to the Reich. This peaceful conquest allowed Hitler to form seven new army divisions, some of them crack Alpine troops. Germany also gained impressive resources in iron, timber, waterpower, industrial potential, and the gold reserves of the Bank of Austria. The possession of Vienna provided him with vital controls over the river, rail, and road communications of the middle Danube and thus over the trade of Hungary, Czechoslovakia, Yugoslavia, and Rumania. This also had strategic implications. By the incorporation of Austria, the key country of the Little Entente, Czechoslovakia, France's and Russia's ally, was surrounded on three sides. Soon Austria was not only united with the Reich but fully integrated with it in every respect.

The occupation of Austria was, on the whole, a smooth affair but provided the German army with valuable experience in operating large-scale forces, especially its newly created armored divisions. The fact that a large number of German tanks and armored cars did break down on difficult Alpine roads confirmed the opinion of foreign opponents of mechanization who claimed that tanks were brittle and hence impractical weapons; the German experts, however, soon introduced the necessary improvements to the faulty equipment, thus

The Occupation of Austria, March 1938

updating it further. By that time they had evolved the basic model of a panzer division with which the Wehrmacht would begin the war. The panzer division, as a rule, had one tank and one motorized infantry brigade. Each division had a motorized artillery regiment with two battalions of howitzers; a reconnaissance battalion with motorcycle and armored car companies; an antitank battalion, an engineer battalion, a signal battalion, and rear trains and services. The average strength of a panzer division was approximately 12,000 officers and men, and 200 to 300 tanks. It would undergo many changes, but during the first phase of the war this model of a structured armored division would serve as an ideal to be emulated.

The control of Austria gave further impetus to the already formidable German economic offensive in southeastern Europe and the Near East. In 1936 Dr. Schacht visited the Balkan capitals and initiated a series of astute barter agreements. He contracted to buy Balkan goods at relatively high prices and gave long-term credits for the purchase of German machinery and armaments. Payment for the goods was to be made in blocked marks that could be used only to purchase German goods. The Balkan partners had to accept these conditions because the Great Depression had made them anxious to secure any conceivable market for their surplus goods. By this means, by 1937 Berlin had already cornered over one-quarter of the trade of southeastern Europe, including Greece and Turkey. The seemingly innocent barter agreements were the driving wedge that paved the way for a systematic penetration of the Danubian and Balkan countries, not only economically but also politically. Thus, on the eve of World War II, exercising its enormous economic ascendance, Germany was already close to monopolizing the trade of southeastern Europe. The strategic rationale behind the trade offensive was to foster Germany's economic self-sufficiency. It was in the interest of Germany, short of most raw materials except coal, to stimulate close economic exchanges with an area that would always be free from possible naval blockade by enemy powers and that contained not only vast food resources but also such vital raw materials as oil (Rumania), aluminum, copper, lead, and zinc (Yugoslavia).[1]

International Reaction to the Anschluss

The international reaction to the Anschluss was rather placid. Britain's Conservative government failed to condemn the annexation of Austria, which, as a member of Parliament put it, "is, after all, a German-speaking land." At the news of the invasion of Austria, the French proposed to mobilize some classes of their reservists, but again, when London objected, the plan was dropped. Mussolini, making virtue out of necessity, accepted the German invasion with outwardly lavish professions of satisfaction. To Hitler's telegram expressing his gratitude for Italy's acceptance of the German annexation, the Italian dictator replied, "My attitude is determined by the friendship between our two countries, which is consecrated in the Axis." While Germany's gains were most impressive, the main loser of the Anschluss was Italy. It lost its most important gains of World War I: its secure frontier along the Alps and its predominant position in the Danubian region.

The Anschluss was a masterpiece of diplomacy. Throughout the crisis Hitler acted with a sleepwalker's self-confidence and gained enormous advantages without firing a shot. The new bloodless victory raised his prestige both at home and abroad. Already by the spring of 1938 the Greater German Reich dominated the European continent and was well on its way to becoming the strongest military power in the world. Had he stopped at that moment, he would have gone down in history as the unifier of most of the German people into one powerful Reich—solid, secure, threatened by nobody. Hitler's hubris and the essentially criminal nature of his regime were still obscured by his dazzling economic and diplomatic successes, as well as by his pledge that the Anschluss fulfilled his last and ultimate territorial ambition.

FROM AUSTRIA TO CZECHOSLOVAKIA

The Anschluss extended the frontiers of the Third Reich some 400 miles to the southeast, making Czechoslovakia's strategic situation critical. Despite assurances given to Prague in March 1938, by May Czechoslovakia had become the next target of Hitler's concerted political offensive.

The Czech republic contained numerous national minorities, including more than 3 million Germans. These Germans lived mostly in compact industrialized areas along the Sudetes Mountains, and had belonged to the Habsburg imperial complex since the sixteenth century. The Versailles treaty had left them within the historic boundaries of Bohemia-Moravia, or the heartland of the Czechoslovak republic. Now in the spring of 1938 a vitriolic propaganda campaign by Hitler presented to the outside world the distorted image of the Czechs persecuting the Sudeten Germans. The Prague govern-

---

[1]On the eve of World War II there were some twenty basic products vital for warfare: oil, iron, coal, rubber, copper, nickel, lead, glycerine, cellulose, mercury, aluminum, platinum, antimony, manganese, asbestos, mica, nitric acid, sulfur, wool, and cotton. If one takes the British and the French empires together, they had most of these products except antimony and mercury. The trouble with most of the resources of the Western powers was that they had to be transported from their overseas possessions over dangerous routes.

ment protested against these absurd accusations and offered the German minority concessions amounting to home rule. But when Hitler supported his threats with massive concentrations of his armed forces on the borders of Czechoslovakia, Prague replied by mobilizing its impressively equipped army.

The confrontation alarmed Britain's Neville Chamberlain. He found the Nazi tyranny distasteful and felt its persecution of Jews to be odious, but he was not prepared to be publicly critical. A conservative businessman, he viewed Hitler's methods as brutal and crude, but he admired his anticommunism. In Chamberlain's view, nazism had sprung from the evil Versailles treaty, and he truly believed that should Hitler's legitimate grievances be satisfied, Germany would discard the worst aspects of nazism and return to the League of Nations. With a European war threatening, and aware of the British lack of preparedness, on September 13, 1938, Chamberlain telegraphed Hitler pleading to meet him in person. Hitler, flattered by the message and grasping its potentialities, accepted at once. The prospect of the British government's head coming to him as a supplicant delighted him beyond measure.

At the conference, on September 15, Chamberlain accepted Hitler's demand that the Sudeten Germans be accorded the right of national self-determination. The Reich would thus acquire all the Sudeten areas along the frontier, the population of which was more than 50 percent German. At midnight on September 21, President Eduard Beneš of Czechoslovakia, fearful of abandonment by the Western powers, bowed to the German-British proposal.

The crisis appeared to be solved, but Hitler wanted more. He was anxious to dismantle the Czechoslovak nation. Accordingly, when Chamberlain, elated by his apparently successful first mission, returned to Germany on September 22 to discuss the details for transferring the Sudeten regions, he was shocked by the Führer's new demands. Hitler wanted neither plebiscites nor

German armored cars are reviewed by Hitler in Vienna on March 14, 1938. National Archives

negotiations; he insisted rather on immediate and unconditional surrender of the disputed regions by October 1. This was his "last word."

CONFRONTATION

Meanwhile, the problem had assumed larger dimensions, because the Hungarian and Polish governments put forward their demands. They both argued that the Hungarian population of southern Slovakia and the Poles of Teschen Silesia southwest of the Olza River should not be treated less favorably than the Germans of the Sudentenland. President Beneš accepted Warsaw's claims as fully justified but was reluctant to agree to those of Budapest.[2] On September 23, when Chamberlain returned to London, British newspapers expressed fears that Europe was on the brink of a dangerous confrontation. The British and French governments rejected the German demands as an unacceptable ultimatum. Meanwhile, the British government gave support to its energetic First Lord of the Admiralty, Duff Cooper, who put the Royal Navy on alert. Along with the British, the French began reluctantly to mobilize their forces.

Two days later Hitler spoke in Berlin, repeating his categorical demands for the cession of the disputed regions by October 1: "This is my last territorial claim in Europe, but it is a claim from which I shall not recede. . . . I declare my patience is at an end." Europe found itself on the brink of war.

British and French military measures galvanized some German diplomats and generals, believing that the Third Reich was not yet fully prepared for a full-scale conflict on two fronts. Through a special envoy they urged the British government to stand firm because Hitler, a criminal maniac, had no support among the German people. The conspirators promised that, should the British government assume a firm posture, they too would be ready to act and would arrest Hitler and his associates, rather than plunge the world into a big war. The French ambassador in Berlin, François-Poncet, received similar signals from members of the anti-Hitler opposition, but he never reported them to Paris. Erich Kord, the secret messenger sent by the conspirators to London, was not granted a hearing by Chamberlain. The only prominent British politician who dared to talk to Kord was Winston Churchill, then out of power and generally regarded as an irresponsible warmonger.

THE MUNICH CONFERENCE

On September 26 Chamberlain made a radio speech to the British people. After outlining the frightening international situation, he concluded: "How horrible, fantastic, incredible it is, that we should be digging trenches . . . because of a quarrel in a faraway country, between people of whom we know nothing." At the same time, Chamberlain was in touch with Mussolini to urge him to moderate Hitler's demands. Mussolini knew that in case of a general European conflict, Italy, as a partner of the Axis, would be involved. His country's lack of military preparedness, its involvement in the still unfinished Spanish civil war, the burden of pacifying the newly conquered Ethiopia—all spurred him to vigorous action. On September 28 Mussolini personally appealed to Hitler to postpone the impending invasion of Czechoslovakia at least for twenty-four hours. To these pleas were added the urgent messages of Chamberlain, Premier Daladier of France, and President Roosevelt. Reluctantly, Hitler agreed to Mus-

---

[2]While condemning Poland's attitude toward Czechoslovakia during the Munich crisis, L. B. Namier points out that, despite foreign minister Joseph Beck's eagerness for prestige and attention, he would have preferred to be on the side of France and Britain. Namier also stresses that it was Józef Beck who, when Hitler remilitarized the Rhineland, "urged immediate armed response." Consequently, Namier concluded, had the Western powers taken a firm stand against Hitler in 1938, they would have had Poland on their side; see *Europe in Decay: A Study in Disintegration, 1936–40* (London: Macmillan, 1950), p. 162.

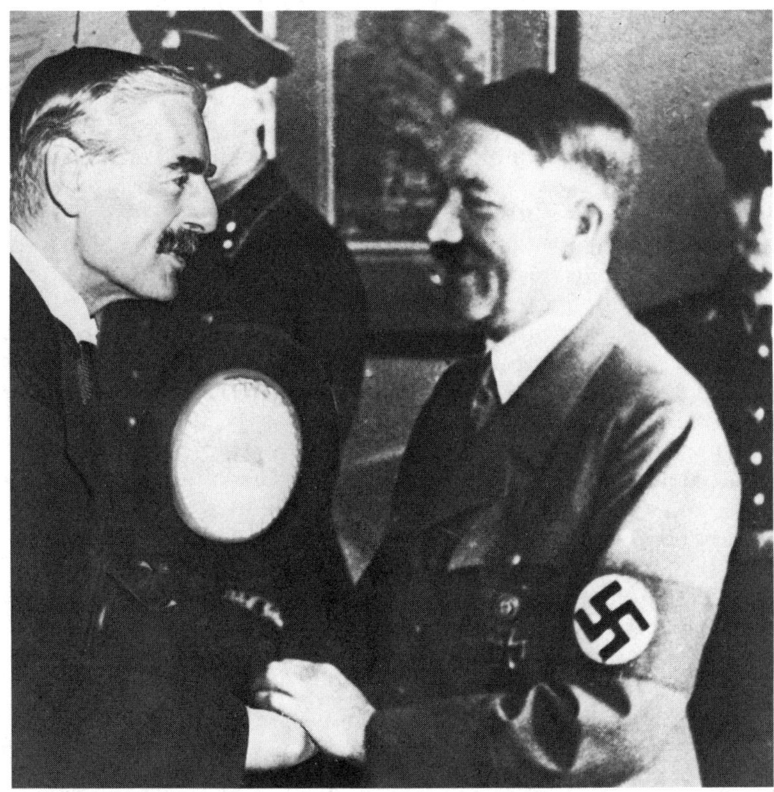

Hitler bids farewell to Neville Chamberlain after the Munich conference.
National Archives

solini's suggestion that the Sudeten problem should be submitted to an international conference of four powers—Germany, Italy, Britain, and France—to meet in Munich on September 29.[3]

To make the Czechs agree to the cession of the Sudeten territory without a plebiscite by October 1, the Western powers resorted to blackmail. The British minister in Prague bluntly warned President Beneš that if the Czechs rejected the new plan, they would be responsible for the war and their own inevitable destruction. For his part, the French minister intimated that should Czech stubbornness unleash an armed conflict, the French would not fulfill their treaty obligations.

The four powers gathered for the Munich Conference on September 29 at the "Brown House," the Nazi GHQ. The Axis powers were represented by Hitler and Mussolini, and Chamberlain and Daladier represented Britain and France, respectively. No Czechoslovak representative was admitted to the conference. Instead, an official delegation from Prague was left meekly waiting in an anteroom to be told eventually the decision of the four powers dismembering their country. The final terms of the Munich verdict incorporated the essentials of Hitler's demands of September 22. The Czechs were given from October 1 to 10 to complete their evacuation of the Sudeten areas that were inhabited by more than 50 percent Germans. Britain and France promised to guarantee the frontiers of the now mutilated Czechoslovakia against unprovoked aggression.

Under the concerted pressure of the Big Four powers, including its formal ally

---

[3]For a description and analysis of the Munich Conference see John Wheeler-Bennett, *Munich—Prologue to Tragedy* (New York: Duell, Sloan, and Pearce, 1963); and Robert Kee, *Munich* (London: Hamish Hamilton, 1988).

France, the Czechs were forced "in the interest of peace" to cede immediately to Germany the Sudeten borderlands. This area included most of the country's modern and powerful frontier fortifications, along with most of its industry, including numerous armament works and most of the country's natural resources. Dismembered, discouraged, and prostrate, Czechoslovakia was neither economically viable nor militarily defensible. The middle Danube was left wide open before the overwhelming presence of the Nazi Reich. The partition of Czechoslovakia, the pillar of the Little Entente, led to political erosion of this alliance. Yugoslavia and Rumania began to waver in their loyalty to the Western powers; Hungary tightened its association with Germany.

Hitler's plan for the destruction of Czechoslovakia was based on the assumption that Britain and France had written off that "faraway country" as a total loss and would limit their action to diplomatic face-saving protests. His judgment once more proved superior to that of his generals and diplomatic experts. The third successful bluff in a row, after the Rhineland and Austria, consolidated this prestige and strengthened his spell over the broad masses of the German people. Intoxicated with dazzling success, Hitler could initiate further ventures, employing the threat of war.

INTERNATIONAL REACTION TO MUNICH

The initial Western reaction to Munich was, on the whole, ecstatic. Its architect, Chamberlain, after his return to London, was greeted as a national hero. One of the few Western statesmen who immediately grasped the magnitude of the defeat was Winston Churchill. In a House of Commons speech he asserted that Munich was a craven surrender of a defensible position through mere cowardice and unwillingness to defend it.

To Soviet Russia, its absence from the four-power Munich conference amounted to exclusion from the European concert. Stalin resented bitterly the snub and his diplomatic isolation. Since May 16, 1935, Czechoslovakia had been bound by an alliance not only to France but also to the USSR. The Soviet alliance hinged, however, on a previous fulfillment of obligations by the French. Consequently, from a strictly legal point of view, the Russians were free from their duties toward the Czechs because of the French refusal to act. Nevertheless, Litvinov kept on repeating that the USSR was ready to discharge all its duties toward Czechoslovakia in accordance with the treaty of alliance and with the League of Nations covenant. Accordingly, despite the French refusal to aid them, the Czechs could have invoked Soviet aid. Yet they never did, either from fear of provoking Hitler or perhaps in doubt whether such a call would have been effective. Actually, President Beneš deliberately downplayed the Czech-Soviet alliance. The Agrarian party, the largest segment of the middle-of-the-road government coalition, was strongly anticommunist and dreaded the idea of Soviet troops setting foot on Czechoslovak territory.

Here the historian must ponder at least two questions. Would the Soviet armed forces, decimated by the purges involving some 30,000 officers whose loyalty Stalin suspected, have been able to protect Czechoslovakia against the Germans? Moreover, how would the Red Army have reached Czechoslovak territory over Rumanian and Polish territory? Not only the Poles but even the Rumanians, Prague's Little Entente allies, refused to let the Red Army pass. Disregarding these vital considerations, Moscow propaganda represented the Soviet Union as the only power willing to defend its Czechoslovak ally.

The Munich conference put additional strain on the already badly shaken Franco-Soviet alliance. Despite the terms of the 1935 treaty, the Russians were not consulted by Paris in the vital matters pertaining to their mutual ally. The sacrifice of Czechoslovakia to Hitler's appetites and the accommodating, even obsequious, attitude of the Western powers toward him, gave rise to further Soviet suspicions that France and Britain would welcome a continuing German expansion to the east. Presumably, Stalin then decided that his participation in what was originally meant to be a system of collective security no longer served Soviet purposes. While loudly blaming the Western powers for caving in to the Germans at Munich, he secretly probed for accommodation with Hitler.

As early as 1937 the Soviet ambassador in Berlin, Jacob Surits, a man of Jewish extraction, was removed from his post and replaced by an ethnic Russian, A. T. Merkalov, who went to Berlin with instructions to work for improved economic relations with Germany. This overture would furnish a stepping-stone toward a gradual relaxation of political tensions. In July 1938, at the peak of the Czechoslovak crisis, Merkalov achieved an oral agreement for ending mass-media abuse against the respective heads of state, Hitler and Stalin. Mutual polemics were also to be softened. The Soviet press denounced the Munich appeasement as a shameful betrayal of Czechoslovakia by the Western powers and as an attempt to isolate the USSR. Yet the Soviet media remained coyly restrained as far as Nazi Germany was concerned.[4]

Soon after Munich both France and Britain sped up their military preparations. But the strategic and logistic gains to Germany resulting from the dismemberment of Czechoslovakia far exceeded anything the sluggish western Allies could quickly achieve in armaments. This imbalance raises a series of crucial questions. Was the breathing spell of a year gained thanks to Munich worthwhile? Did France and Britain enjoy a materially improved advantage in the autumn of 1939 as opposed to the previous year? Would Hitler really have made war if Britain had stood firm? And if he had made war at that moment, would he necessarily have won? If a year was gained by Munich, what of the cost? Here, one must bear in mind that by 1938 the Third Reich was only in its third and crucial year of full-scale rearmament. Its military cadres were not yet fully primed, and its war industries were only nearing the capability of producing the weapons necessary for total warfare. Contrary to Western estimates, the Luftwaffe was as yet unprepared to stage its air raids on London because of a shortage of long-range bombers. Furthermore, the Siegfried line remained far from complete. Whatever the answer to these questions, the craven surrender at Munich marked the nadir of the policy of appeasing Hitler by means of unilateral concessions and western delusions that peace could be bought by throwing weaker countries to the Nazi and Fascist wolves and meekly paying the danegeld. Hitler's second bloodless expansion beyond the boundaries of the former Weimar Republic was bound to whet his appetite for further conquests. Again he disregarded the warnings of his advisers, especially Grand Admiral Erich Raeder, commander in chief of the Kriegsmarine, and Admiral Karl Doenitz, who commanded its submarine arm. Although the former had urged building a balanced fleet, the latter had insisted on a U-boat fleet of at least three hundred units as a necessary precondition of winning the war. In 1939 the Germans had only fifty-seven boats.

THE POLISH CRISIS

By the autumn of 1938, while giving an appearance of accommodation toward the French and the British, Hitler became rough with the Poles. The end of October brought the first rumblings of the thunder heralding another storm. On October 24 Ribbentrop invited the Polish ambassador, Józef Lipski, to present him with a plan that he called a "global settlement" of Polish-German issues. The essential points of the proposal were (1) a demand for incorporating Danzig into the Reich and (2) the con-

[4]The reorientation of Stalin's foreign policy is well described by Adam Ulam in his *Expansion and Coexistence: The History of Soviet Foreign Policy, 1917–1967* (New York: Praeger, 1968), pp. 234–279.

struction of an extraterritorial highway and railroad through Polish Pomerania to connect Berlin with Königsberg in East Prussia. In compensation Germany would extend the nonaggression pact of 1934 for twenty-five years and would guarantee the existing common frontiers. Ribbentrop also suggested that Poland should join the anti-Comintern pact and coordinate its policy with Berlin.

The astonished Lipski pointed out that the proposal was diametrically opposed to Germany's previous solemn pledges and assurances that it would respect Poland's rights in the Free City. It was clear to Warsaw that the surrender of Poland's rights to Danzig was tantamount to severing Poland's access to the Baltic and that joining the anti-Comintern pact would suck the country into Hitler's orbit, thus isolating it completely from the Western powers. Should Warsaw allow Danzig to be formally incorporated into the Reich, modern German guns installed on the territory of the former Free City would completely control Poland's access to the Baltic Sea. It was Frederick II of Prussia who said that "he who controls Danzig, rules Poland." (Recall R. H. Lord's observation that abandoning Danzig to Germany would have equaled the ceding of the mouth of the Mississippi River to a foreign power.)

Refusing the German demands, Warsaw nevertheless expressed its willingness to solve the existing differences by negotiation. As for Danzig, Beck suggested that "a solution could be found, based on a joint Polish-German guarantee," which would take full account of the national aspirations of its German population, as well as of Poland's vital interests. He also expressed his readiness to study jointly with Berlin the question of a new, simplified railroad and motor-transit traffic between the Reich and East Prussia; Hitler, however, rejected these concessions as insufficient.

Hitler himself admitted in his secret address to his military commanders on May 23, 1939, that Danzig was neither the main cause of his increasing pressure on the Poles nor his major objective. He placed the Free City in the foreground of his diplomacy and propaganda because he expected that the Western powers would think it too insignificant a piece of real estate to warrant either Poland's intransigent stand or their firm support of the Poles. Hitler simply considered Danzig a most favorable ground on which to divide France from Britain and both of them from Poland. Hence Goebbels' skillfully worded slogan spread in France and Britain: Why die for Danzig?

Within a few days the well-oiled propaganda machine of Dr. Goebbels was pointed at the Poles. Gradually the standard preliminaries of Nazi coups were set in motion against the Poles. All the inequities and atrocities that the Czechs were once supposed to have committed in the Sudetenland were now allegedly inflicted by the Poles on their innocent German minority. Like an octopus that darkens the water before striking its victim, Dr. Goebbels was trying to render the political atmosphere as murky as possible.

Germany Takes Czechoslovakia

While mounting a propaganda offensive against Poland, Hitler was closely watching a new crisis brewing in the Czechoslovak Republic. In March 1939, shaken by another Slovak crisis, Prague decided to reassert its dwindling control over the restless, autonomous Slovakia. This gave Hitler an excuse to complete the dissolution of Czechoslovakia. On March 10 Prague suspended Monsignor Tiso, the prime minister who had been elected by the Slovak assembly, and replaced him with a man loyal to Prague, with Czech troops ready to march to reassert their rule. Tiso refused to step down, while at the same time the Slovak assembly unanimously voted to secede from Czechoslovakia and declared Slovak independence.

On March 15 the Czech president, Dr. Hácha, was forced to appear in Berlin to explain his allegedly anti-German policy. Once there the elderly, ailing lawyer was confronted with Hitler's ultimatum: Either accept Germany's protectorate over Bohemia-Moravia, as well as Slovakia's independence, or see Prague razed to the ground. When the shocked Hácha collapsed, he was revived by injections of stimulants administered to him by Hitler's physician. Resuscitated, Hácha was ordered to sign the agreement. The same day, German troops entered Prague while Hitler proclaimed the Third Reich's protectorate over Bohemia and Moravia.

The German gains were again impressive. According to Hitler's speech to the Reichstag on April 28, 1939, the Czech booty comprised over 1,500 planes, 469 tanks, 500 antiaircraft guns, more than 43,000 machine guns, a million rifles, a billion rounds of rifle ammunition, and more than 3 million rounds of field-gun ammunition. To this must be added numerous armament works including that of Škoda. Some Czech tanks were used in the campaigns of 1940 in Norway and France. What Hitler failed to mention were the Czech uranium mines of Jachimova Dolina. At that time several prominent German scientists were conducting nuclear research and were ahead of their Western counterparts.

The next day, March 16, Hitler allowed his satellite Hungary to incorporate the easternmost tip of the former Czechoslovak Republic, the province of Carpatho-Ukraine. Hardly a week after the occupation of Prague, a German ultimatum compelled Lithuania to cede the port of Memel (Klaipėda) and the surrounding region, which had 149,000 inhabitants, among them 59,000 Lithuanians. Making one of his rare sea voyages aboard a German warship, a seasick Hitler proclaimed the incorporation of Memel into the Greater German Reich.

Before the spring of 1939, acting against his experts' advice, Hitler had won three successive gambles: He remilitarized the Rhineland, annexed Austria, and dismembered Czechoslovakia—all this without firing a shot and with only token opposition from the outside world. One of his claims at Munich had been that, once having united all ethnic Germans, he would have no new territorial demands. This claim was finally abandoned in March 1939. Now Hitler was caught in a flagrant breach of promise: Some 8 million Czechs were pressed into the Greater German Reich. Before 1939 Hitler, as Goebbels put it, acted not only with the force of a lion but with the guile of a snake. Now he threw away his mask. How many "last" territorial demands did he have up his sleeve?

Allied Pledges to Poland, Rumania, and Greece

Initially it seemed that the Ides of March 1939 would also pass away without lasting repercussions for Hitler. Chamberlain at first tacitly accepted the German protectorate over Bohemia and Moravia and quietly approved the annexation of Memel. Chamberlain's uninterrupted appeasement policy was not limited to Germany. On March 23 he sent a personal letter to Rome and appealed for Mussolini's help in reestablishing mutual trust between Britain and the Axis. The letter confirmed the Italian dictator's conviction that he could proceed with his expansion plans without provoking too much opposition from the Western powers. And indeed, on Good Friday, April 7, Italian troops landed in Albania. Weak local resistance was soon crushed. An appropriately manipulated Albanian Constituent Assembly on April 12 offered the country's crown to Italy's King Victor Emmanuel III. The annexation of Albania not only outflanked Yugoslavia, a French ally in the Balkans, but also threatened Greece, at that time nearly Britain's client.

The occupation of Prague and Memel, followed by the invasion of Albania, alarmed British military circles. According to their intelligence reports of mid-March, the occupation of Prague was merely a prelude to an imminent attack on Rumania and Poland, possibly by the end of March. A partition of Rumania would put at Hitler's disposal the oil fields of Ploeşti (the largest in Europe) as well as the country's considerable agricultural resources, and endanger Greece. What angered the prime minister most was the manner in which Hitler resolved the fate of the Czech state. Still bent on accommodation, Chamberlain sought to gain time and make sure that Hitler's expansionist drive would be diverted in the desired direction. Chamberlain's strategy during the crisis of 1939 was essentially not dissimilar to that taken during the Munich Conference. What changed was the mood of the British mass media and the British people at large, who clamored for tangible steps to cope with the aggressors.

Scorched by restless British public opinion, a reluctant Chamberlain had to act forcefully if only to save his tottering leadership of the Conservative party. On March 29 the government decided to double the Territorial Army, and on April 26 the Parliament voted to introduce conscription, a measure without precedent in time of peace. On March 31 the British leader stated in the House of Commons that "in the event of any action which clearly threatened Polish independence and which the Polish Government accordingly considered it vital to resist with their national forces, his Majesty's Government would feel themselves bound at once to lend the Polish Government all support in their power." Chamberlain added that he was authorized by his counterpart in Paris to state that France had adopted an identical position.

A fortnight after Chamberlain's momentous declaration concerning Poland, he announced on April 13 that similar pledges had been made by the British and French governments to two other prospective victims of Axis aggression: Rumania and Greece. These three unexpectedly strong joint diplomatic steps of Paris and London concerning Poland, Rumania, and Greece appeared to result in a dramatic change on the international chessboard. Were the British and French guarantees fully implemented, Rumania and Poland would then form a continuous barrier stretching from the Black Sea to the Baltic, a front separating Germany from the USSR. Germany could not attack the USSR without marching through Poland and Rumania—that is, without bringing about a Franco-British intervention.

While welcoming the British stand, Warsaw rejected a unilateral guarantee. The Poles insisted that they had a bilateral alliance with France and would be willing to negotiate a similar agreement with Britain. And indeed, two sets of negotiations were opened: one between Warsaw and London for a new defense alliance and one between Warsaw and Paris to revitalize and update the old ties dating back to 1921. In May a Polish delegation went to Paris to conclude a military convention, according to which the French promised the Poles five squadrons of their latest aircraft and immediate bombardment of key German objectives in case of Hitler's attack on Poland. The main assistance was to come, however, from French ground forces, which were to start their operations along the Franco-German border "on the third day after the end of the mobilization," and a full scale offensive on the fifteenth day of the mobilization. But immediately after having signed the convention, General Maurice Gamelin, chief of the General Staff, issued a secret instruction to his subordinates that considerably weakened its letter and spirit.[5]

In May Sir William Ironside, inspector general of overseas forces, visited Poland. In his diaries he admitted that he was given no formal written instructions by his boss, Isaac Leslie Hore-Belisha, secretary of state for war, who could hardly locate Poland on the map of Europe. Consequently, Ironside wrote his own instructions, which he did not reproduce in his diaries. Ironside, who had seen the Polish army in 1924, "was impressed by the troops but anxious about plans"; he pointed out that "the military effort that they [the Poles] have made is short of prodigious," but his conclusions about Poland's ability to put up a protracted resistance were vague. Meanwhile London

---

[5]As a British historian stressed, Gamelin agreed that the "bulk" of the French forces would take the offensive, if Germany attacked Poland. The Poles understood "the bulk" to mean that most of the French army would participate; see A. J. P. Taylor, *The Origin of the Second World War* (London: Hamish Hamilton, 1961), p. 238. Most historians believe that Gamelin deliberately misled the Poles.

dragged its feet in making available to the Poles the credits it had promised to Warsaw for purchasing military hardware, especially some 120 Hawker-Hurricane fighters, capable of intercepting German bombers.[6]

The Effects of the Franco-British Pledges

Although the Franco-British pledge to Rumania never took effect and the pledge to Greece was honored only by London much later, the eventual Polish-British alliance was to play a significant role in the drama of World War II. From the beginning the alliance was most controversial. Although over fifty years has elapsed since that time, no complete British documentation of the problem is available as of this writing. Hence it has been speculatively treated by most historians, who split into two schools of thought.

According to one line of reasoning, Chamberlain's dramatic gesture was motivated by a desire to bolster Poland's resistance to Hitler's encroachments and to warn him against attack on that country and thus avert an impending war. The Poles, if abandoned by the West, would sooner or later have succumbed to the mounting pressure and become Hitler's satellite, like Hungary or Slovakia. Hence there was a necessity for prompt action to reassure them that they were not alone in their resistance. This action also would make it plain to Hitler that, in case of an attack against Poland, he must fight a triple-coalition war on two fronts. The aim of the British-French move was to deter Hitler from another aggressive move. The intent was to defuse the crisis and provide time for a negotiated settlement for the German-Polish dispute, perhaps another Munich.

The second school of thought maintains that by making a virtual alliance with Warsaw, the British purposely played on Hitler's paranoic fear of "encirclement." In this view, they actually plotted to provoke him into an angry move eastward and thus divert his fury from western Europe by channeling his energies toward the east, where he was bound, sooner or later, to clash with his ultimate enemy, Communist Russia. The well-informed British military historian, Captain B. E. Liddell Hart, stated quite frankly in his analysis of the origins of World War II that

> in 1937–38, many [Western statesmen] . . . were frankly realistic in private discussion, though not on public platforms, and many arguments were set forth in British governing circles for allowing Germany to expand eastwards, and thus divert danger from the West. They showed much sympathy with Hitler's desire for *Lebensraum*—and let him know it. But they shirked thinking out the problem of how the owners could be induced to yield it except to threat of superior force.[7]

Whatever the accurate version, for Hitler the British-French declarations were obviously a shock that made him furious. He renounced the German-Polish nonaggression pact of 1934. He beat his fists on the table and shouted: "Now I'll make for them a devil's brew." Nevertheless, on the strength of his previous experiences with Paris and London, he still hoped that Poland would be abandoned to him as Czechoslovakia was. The Nazi leader wanted to isolate the Poles and bully them into a Czech-like submission by dealing with them alone.

Yet it is not correct to say that the British declaration precipitated the war. On March 25 Hitler in fact called General von Brau-

---

[6]Roderick MacCleod and Denis Kelly, eds., *The Ironside Diaries, 1937–1940* (London: Constable, 1961), pp. 81–82 and 88.

[7]*History of the Second World War,* Vol. I (New York: G. P. Putnam's Sons, 1970), p. 8. Reprinted by permission of The Putnam Publishing Group from *History of the Second World War* by B.H. Liddell Hart. Copyright 1970 by Lady Liddell Hart. It is impossible to draw definite conclusions on the subject because some sections of the Public Record Office have not yet been opened to the public; they include many parts of Winston Churchill's archives, some files concerning Polish-British relations, and those pertaining to Germany and Soviet Russia. They have been officially sealed until the 21st century. For a broad background of Poland's relations with France and Britain see Anna Cieńciała, *Poland and the Western Powers, 1938–1939* (Toronto: Routledge & Kegan Paul, 1968).

chitsch, commander in chief of his army, and told him that he had lost all hope of solving the Polish question by political means and was determined to destroy Poland so completely "that for the next decades there would be no longer need for her to be accounted as a political factor." Nine days later, Hitler ordered his armed forces to be ready for operations against Poland (code name Case White) not later than September 1, 1939. Accordingly, by the end of March, Germany and Poland were facing each other along an extended and complex frontier of over 1,500 kilometers. The outside world was wondering about the next move. Well aware that the Czech submission had merely emboldened Hitler, the Poles resolved not to yield an inch. Any retreat, they argued, would only encourage further concessions and result in another abject surrender resulting in slavery. Clearly overrating their military capabilities and the readiness of their Western allies to help them, the Polish leaders were still hoping that Hitler was bluffing. They also underrated Russia's strength and its readiness to come to terms with Hitler.

The stiff Polish posture toward Germany was greatly encouraged by the visit of the Soviet deputy-commissar for foreign affairs, Vladimir Potemkin. On May 10, Potemkin saw Józef Beck and in a highly misleading conversation reassured him about Moscow's full understanding of Warsaw's difficult position. He considered Soviet-Polish relations correct and favored their further improvement. Should Poland fall victim to German attack, the USSR would adopt a policy of benevolent neutrality toward Poland, he said.

THE STRENGTHENING OF THE ROME–BERLIN AXIS

In view of the stiffening stand of the Western powers, Hitler decided to transform the loose "Rome-Berlin Axis" into a formal alliance that could then blackmail France and Britain. Evidence suggests that Mussolini was aware of the dangers inherent in an association with a much stronger and more dynamic partner. Even at Munich he had realized the weakness of Italy's position within the Axis. He was frightened by the tempo of Hitler's progress and the possibility that his country might be drawn into a major conflict regardless of Rome's readiness for war. Mussolini's initiative on behalf of an international conference at Munich had been mainly dictated by his fear of a premature war for which his country was unprepared. At the end of October 1938 when Ciano saw Ribbentrop in Rome, Il Duce was frightened by the German thirst for war. In his diary Ciano noted that Ribbentrop "does not name either the enemy or objectives, but war in three or four years." For Mussolini this deadline was much too close; he wanted a margin of at least five years. It was during this meeting that the Axis partners divided their spheres of influence. Most of Europe was to go to the Germans, while Italy reserved to itself the Balkans, the Mediterranean, and Africa.

The sudden occupation of Prague and the establishment of German garrisons in Slovakia came as a shock to Mussolini. What Mussolini wanted was an immediate, tangible compensation to restore some balance, at least in the Balkans. This equilibrium was the rationale for Italy's invasion of Albania. Even the bolstered Italian control of the Adriatic at the narrowest point did not counterbalance the German gains north of the Alps and along the Danube. What was to be done? By 1939 Mussolini was already so alienated from the Western democracies, and so dependent on the Third Reich, that his freedom to maneuver was limited. By 1939, enmeshed in a net of his own making, he conceived a stratagem whereby he would tie himself closer to Hitler, to be able to moderate, at least to some extent, his adventuristic behavior.

Hitler's perspective was different. He was aware of the numerous weaknesses of the largely obsolete Italian army, and remembered well its poor performance during World War I. Yet he was rather impressed

Europe on the Eve of World War II, August 1939

by the *Regia Aeronautica*, with its 2,500 aircraft, as well as by the modern Italian navy. With its 4 speedy and highly maneuverable battleships, 22 cruisers, some 120 destroyers, and well over 100 submarines, it could play a valuable diversionary role by tying down both British and French naval forces in the Mediterranean, while he would wage his lightning war on the continent of Europe and score a decisive victory before the huge resources of the British and French empires could be thrown into the balance. Thus, the Italian fleet would make up for the smallness of his own naval forces.[8]

According to the Italo-German treaty signed May 22, "should it happen that, contrary to the wishes and hopes of the Contracting Parties, one of them was involved in war . . . the other will place itself immediately at its side, and support it with all its forces by land, on sea and in the air."

[8]For an introduction to wartime German-Italian relations see F. W. Deakin, *The Brutal Friendship* (New York: Harper & Row, 1962), chap. 1, p. 31.

The alliance was to bind both partners at once and forever in case of any involvement against any opponent. The text of the agreement lacked customary clauses limiting the validity of the treaty to a definite period or to "unprovoked attacks." This made the Italo-German pact into a frankly offensive alliance. Ciano called it "real dynamite."

The alliance was largely the work of the two dictators and hinged partly on the ideological affinity of the two totalitarian movements. Mussolini, however, never completely lost sight of the difference of political interests between Italy and Germany, which, despite numerous declarations to the contrary, did clash both in the Danubian region and in the Balkans. But having drawn his ambitious scheme of conquests, he knew that even its partial realization was possible only in close partnership with the erratic Hitler.

One may argue that the formalized Rome-Berlin Axis was inherent in the ideological affinity of the two totalitarian systems, as well as in the personal relationship of the two dictators. But while negotiating with Germany and signing a conspicuous pact with Hitler, Mussolini did not close the door on either France or Britain. On the contrary, he steadily maintained secret negotiations with Paris and London for possible concessions in the Mediterranean and Africa. As he stressed to Ciano in October 1938, "We must keep both doors open."

Disturbed by the war rumors, Ciano wanted to know what was really happening and met Ribbentrop at Salzburg on August 11. Ribbentrop, who until then had kept Hitler's bellicose plans secret, informed Ciano of the Führer's determination to settle the Polish affair immediately and at any cost. Ribbentrop, noted Ciano, "rejects any solution which might give satisfaction to Germany and avoid the struggle."[9] When Ciano, anxious to moderate Germany's demands toward Poland and thus avoid Italy's involvement in the conflict, asked Ribbentrop, "What do you want? The Corridor or Danzig?" he answered: "Not anymore—we want war!" Ciano further added: "I am certain that even if the Germans were given more than they ask for they would attack just the same, because they are possessed by the demon of destruction."

The Russo-German Pact

While formalizing his ties with Italy, Hitler was also groping for a rapprochement with Soviet Russia. The story of the German-Soviet deal is long and complex. The deep-seated mutual hostility was, of course, a major obstacle to political collaboration. For several years the two countries had proclaimed each other as the main enemies of humanity. From mid-1937 these polemics had been softened somewhat; the echoes of the respective propaganda campaigns, however, were still reverberating.

The ambivalent mood prevailing in Moscow in March 1939 may be sensed from the contemporary pronouncements of the Soviet leaders. While Hitler was preparing his annexation of Bohemia and Moravia, the Eighteenth Congress of the Communist party of the Soviet Union was gathering in Moscow on March 10, 1939. In his general report, Stalin restated his thesis that Britain and France, where he had highly placed spies, by sacrificing Czechoslovakia wanted to divert Hitler's attention from the West and to encourage his eastward expansion toward the USSR. He admonished France and Britain that the Soviet Union would not "pull the chestnuts out of the fire for them" and that it stood "for peace and the strengthening of business relations with all countries." He warned that the Soviets were ready to defend themselves against any aggression, but offered Berlin the benefits of expanded trade. While the Eighteenth Congress was still in session, Hitler occupied Prague on March 15 and forced the Lithuanians to cede Memel a week later.

Establishment of the German protectorate over Bohemia and Moravia, and the deployment of a German military base in

---

[9] Hugh Gibson, ed., *The Ciano Diaries, 1939–1943* (New York: Doubleday, 1946), p. 119.

Slovakia, moved German influence beyond the middle Danube. The incorporation of Memel bolstered the German position in the Baltic. Hungary had already been penetrated by the Nazis, and the Balkan countries had for years been under increasing economic as well as political pressure from Berlin. Thus, the German pincers were drawn inexorably toward the Soviet frontiers, along both the Danube and the Baltic.

Yet British guarantees to Poland, Rumania, and Greece, contrary to the expectations of the Western statesmen, were not welcome news at the Kremlin. The British-Polish ties especially provoked surprising Soviet comments. Litvinov spoke these ominous words: "Having pledged herself to render assistance to Poland without any reservations, England has, in fact, concluded a treaty with Poland against us. True, we do not intend to attack Poland, but nevertheless, by strengthening Poland's position vis-à-vis the USSR, the agreement with England cannot fail to be an inimical act." A definite shift of the Kremlin's stand was foreshadowed by a change in its foreign policy pilot. On May 2 Maksim Litvinov, whom the Germans had ignored and boycotted as a Jew, was replaced as commissar for foreign affairs by an ethnic Russian and Stalin's close co-worker, Viacheslav Molotov. For the first time since Trotsky's resignation from that post in 1918, Soviet foreign policy was in the hands of a full member of the Politburo. The change at the top of the Soviet foreign ministry had an immediately positive effect on the intermittent and secret talks that Soviet diplomats had conducted in Berlin since 1938.

While pursuing these negotiations, the Kremlin tried to probe for the exact extent of the unprecedented British commitment to eastern Europe. Did the British really intend to go to war in defense of Poland and Rumania? Overcoming their deep mistrust of Soviet aims (memories of the Great Purge still lingered!) British and French military missions were dispatched by boat to Moscow in July 1939. During the talks both sides seemed to dawdle because of mutual suspicion. One serious barrier impeded them at every step. It was the right of passage of the Red Army through Poland, Rumania, and the Baltic countries (Lithuania, Latvia, and Estonia). Not only Poland and Rumania but also the little republics firmly refused to accept Soviet guarantees in case of a German attack, for even "indirect aggression," argued their leaders, would allow the Soviets to establish their bases even in time of peace.

All the western neighbors of Russia interpreted this formula as a blanket consent for the establishment of Soviet troops on their territory and as an extension of a Russian protectorate that would lead eventually to annexation of the entire area into the USSR. This struck terror in the hearts of most of the people bordering the Soviet Union from Finland to Rumania except for hard-boiled Communists. The Polish ambassador in Paris said to the French foreign minister, Georges Bonnet: "What would you say if you were asked to leave Alsace-Lorraine guarded by the Germans?"

The Western powers were hesitant to impose such a drastic solution on sovereign states that they themselves had nurtured and supported. When the Western delegates promised to press Poland and Rumania, as well as the Baltic states, into submission, the Russians immediately put forward another issue: that of a foothold on Finnish soil. What Stalin demanded from Paris and London was really an alliance between the Soviet Union, France, and Britain in which Moscow would be able to dictate when and how to act.

The frustrating Moscow negotiations dragged on throughout most of the hot summer of 1939 until the end of August. It was clearly impossible for Paris and London to give Stalin a free hand to expand at will. Hitler, however, had no such scruples. By April 1, 1939, the Soviet ambassador in Berlin, Merkulov, had visited the German foreign ministry. Merkulov dwelt at some length on the fact that his country was deliberately fending off Anglo-French proposals for an alliance against Germany because they were offering too little. Should the Germans suggest better terms, Stalin would rather side with them. But when Berlin outlined generous proposals implying a Soviet free hand in Finland, the Baltic republics, Poland, and even Rumania, Stalin suspected a trap. Moreover, with both sides competing for his favors and with plenty of time to choose the highest bidder, Stalin was in no hurry. Hitler, however, anxious to strike at Poland during the last weeks of the warm, dry summer, was getting impatient. Increasingly eager to pounce on Poland before the autumn rains would curb his tanks, Hitler on August 2 decided to force Stalin's hand and ordered Ribbentrop to hold out as bait not only a new partition of Poland but also a German intervention in Tokyo to stop the ongoing Soviet-Japanese fighting in Manchuria and Mongolia. Stalin still remained reluctant to commit himself. Hitler became furious. On August 20 he insisted that Ribbentrop be invited to Moscow within twenty-four hours; otherwise the whole proposal would be withdrawn. This was a virtual ultimatum and Stalin accepted it at once.

On August 23 Ribbentrop, along with some thirty experts, flew to Moscow for a brief but momentous visit. That same evening, at the Kremlin, in an atmosphere of surprising cordiality, he and Molotov signed two important documents: an open declaration of nonaggression, friendship, and cooperation, and a secret protocol. The nonaggression pact provided that both parties would refrain from attacking each other should either of the signatories be attacked by a third party. The secret protocol divided eastern Europe into two spheres of influence: Estonia, Latvia, Poland (east of the Vistula), and Bessarabia were to be left to the Soviet Union; Lithuania and Poland (west of the Vistula) were to remain within the German sphere. Each side was given a free hand in its respective spheres. The agreement was to apply immediately.

The conclusion of the double deal was followed by a lavish banquet given by Stalin at the Kremlin. Ribbentrop and Molotov slapped each other on the back and called themselves "old revolutionary comrades" now finally struggling together against a common enemy, the "Western capitalists." Ribbentrop was in an especially exuberant mood and told Stalin a story circulating in the diplomatic quarters of Berlin: Soon the

Moscow, August 23, 1939: Molotov at the desk signs the Soviet-German pact. Stalin and von Ribbentrop stand and watch. National Archives

Soviet Union would join the anti-Comintern pact. Stalin refused to laugh. Nevertheless, he gave his "word of honor" that the Soviet Union would never betray Germany. He went as far as to raise his glass of champagne and drink a toast to Hitler: "I know how much the German people love their Führer."[10]

Why the Pact?

The Stalin-Hitler pact exploded with the force of a dynamite blast. The diplomatic about-face of both former mortal enemies had been vaguely suspected by only a few seasoned Western observers. Their warnings, however, were mostly met with ripples of laughter triggered by the skepticism of all those who had reasoned in purely ideological terms and continued to believe in the allegedly unbridgeable Communist-Nazi hostility.

For Hitler, to neutralize the Soviet Union and thus isolate Poland was of paramount and immediate importance. He was hell-bent on a short knockout war to be finished before the autumn rains. He was willing, therefore, to sacrifice on the altar of strategic necessity his most cherished ideological prejudices. Hoping that the Western powers would repeat their 1938 performance and leave Poland to his mercy as they had abandoned Czechoslovakia, he was now confident of dealing only with the isolated Poles.

The Stalin-Hitler pact was not the determining cause of the war, yet it considerably enhanced Germany's ability to wage the war: By securing Germany's eastern flank, Stalin removed the last obstacle to Hitler's attack on Poland. Now, a war on just one front seemed to be assured. As for Stalin, many factors contributed to his deal with Hitler. One of them was the uncertain situation in the Far East resulting from the undeclared war with Japan along the Manchurian and Mongolian frontier. Another motive was Stalin's growing disillusionment with the French and British and their reluctance to cooperate with him against Germany on his terms. While France and Britain seemed to be interested in bolstering an anti-German front in eastern Europe, Stalin's main aim was acceptance by the Western powers of a Soviet hegemony there. Forced to choose between an outwardly safe deal with Germany, for which he was to be handsomely paid, and cooperation with the West, which could drag his country into a war against Hitler, Stalin chose the former option.

Stalin drinks to Hitler's health on August 23, 1939, at the Kremlin banquet. National Archives

The pact with Stalin elated Hitler. This was reflected in one of the most revealing harangues he ever made after its signing. Speaking to a selected group of the Nazi party and military leaders, he was quite frank. He had ordered Ribbentrop to sign the Moscow agreement because he was in a

[10]For documentation of the Stalin-Hitler pact see R. J. Sontag and J. S. Beddie, eds., *Nazi-Soviet Relations, 1939–1941* and *From the Archives of the German Foreign Office* (Washington, D.C.: Department of State, 1948). For an early warning about the coming of the German-Soviet deal see Robert Coulondre, *De Staline à Hitler—Souvenirs de deux ambassades 1936–1939* (Paris: Hachette, 1950), pp. 262–74.

great hurry to begin the campaign before the autumn rains made the Polish roads more difficult for his tanks. "Our strength lies in our speed and our brutality; Genghis Khan has sent millions of women and children to death knowingly and with light heart. History sees in him only the Great Founder of State." Hitler expressed only a fear that "some S.O.B." (*Schweinehund* in German) might propose mediation and thus deprive him of the pleasure of crushing the Poles.

To cover his tracks Hitler staged a deliberate provocation in the form of a fraud. Inmates of German concentration camps led by S.S. men and dressed in Polish uniforms staged an attack on a German radio station at Gleiwitz, in Silesia, on August 31. After a trumped-up attack the inmates were shot and left lying on German territory as visible proof of an "unprovoked Polish aggression."[11]

On September 1, at dawn, the German troops launched their attack on Poland. World War II had started.

---

[11]The unleashing of World War II is described and documented by the Swiss historian Walter Hofer in *War Premeditated, 1939* (London: Thames & Hudson, 1955). For the Soviet view see Jane Degras, ed., *Soviet Documents on Foreign Policy,* Vol. III, pp. 315–81; for the Polish side see *Official Documents Concerning Polish-German and Polish-Soviet Relations, 1933–1939* (London: Hutchinson, 1940), especially pp. 53–130 and 182–222. For a recent discussion of the subject, see Gordon Martel, ed., *The Origins of the Second World War* (Boston, London, Sydney: Allen & Unwin, 1986).

4

World War II

The Overture[1]

THE POLISH CAMPAIGN

The Polish campaign was the first large-scale demonstration of the new doctrine of Blitzkrieg, or lightning, warfare. The Polish campaign opened a new era of military history, with its unprecedented use of large armored units, the panzer divisions, acting as the steel tips of conventional army units and working in close cooperation with massive air armadas. The plains of Poland became a testing ground for revolutionary innovations in the art of war in the twentieth century. The defeat of the Polish armed forces and the brutal occupation that followed were grim portents of the fate awaiting the other vanquished peoples under the Nazi New Order.

Poland Faces Hitler

Warsaw reacted to the signing of the ominous Hitler-Stalin pact of August 23 by ordering a general mobilization. The French and British ambassadors in Warsaw, however, intervened on August 29 and prevailed upon the Polish government to cancel the order so as "not to provoke Hitler." Napoleon used to say, "Order, counter-order, disorders." Due to the Allied pressure, the Polish general mobilization was not only delayed but had to be largely conducted under the enemy's guns and air bombardment, thus plunging the defensive preparations into chaos even before the official start of hostilities. Thousands of mobilized soldiers rushed to their units to be sent home

[1]For a background of World War II see Gerhard L. Weinberg, *The Foreign Policy of Hitler's Germany Starting World War II, 1937–1939* (Chicago and London: University of Chicago Press, 1980), especially pp. 595–640.

after a few hours, only to be recalled in a couple of days to make the same journey under wartime conditions in trains often attacked by the enemy. As a result the Polish armed forces were only partially mobilized.

The German invasion of Poland was launched at dawn on Friday, September 1, without a formal declaration of war, by the bulk of the German forces.[2] One of the factors that predetermined the outcome of the campaign was Poland's precarious geopolitical position. Poland's frontier with Germany stretched some 1,250 miles; another 500 miles were added by the establishment of Hitler's protectorate over Bohemia and Moravia and by Slovakia's subservience to Berlin; East Prussia was already one huge military bastion. Then came the Hitler-Stalin pact, which also made Poland's eastern approaches vulnerable. The country had no Maginot Line and no natural barriers to obstruct the enemy attack except for the Carpathian Mountains in the south. Before the start of hostilities, Poland was beset from all sides by overwhelming forces.

Surrounded, Poland also had fewer people and suffered from a technological lag in comparison with Germany. The Poles had striven to overcome the technical deficit and had made considerable sacrifices by allotting a lion's share of their state budget to national defense. In peacetime the Poles had slightly over 300,000 men under arms. During the spring and summer of 1939, by means of partial mobilization, they increased their forces by some half a million. A further 2 million trained reserves might have been mobilized, but last-minute Allied pressure had prevented it. Well trained and inspired with high morale, the Polish army remained deficient in modern tanks, heavy artillery, antiaircraft guns, and motorized transport. There were only two recently organized armored brigades, for instance, and only one of them was actually ready for combat. In general, the number of motor vehicles was insufficient, and for transport, the Polish forces relied mainly on railways. This was another major weakness, since the tracks and stations were a primary target of the Luftwaffe. In contrast, the Polish air force had only some 900 aircraft, of which only some 400 were modern and operational.[3]

On September 1 Poland's thirty-nine divisions faced some sixty German divisions, nine of them armored with about 3,000 tanks and supported by nearly 2,000 aircraft.[4] This deployment of some 960,000 men, the bulk of the Reich's armed forces, including practically the entire armor and air force, represented Hitler's gamble that neither France nor Britain would care to help their ally in the east.

The invading forces were organized into two army groups, Northern and Southern. The army group North was commanded by General Fedor von Bock and comprised the Third Army, operating from East Prussia and the Fourth, based in German Pomerania. The more powerful Southern Army group, commanded by General Gerd von Rundstedt, comprised three armies: the Eighth, Tenth, and Fourteenth. The Eighth and the Tenth operated from Silesia, and the Fourteenth had its jumping-off base in Bohemia, Moravia, and Slovakia. The Hungarians, although politically dependent on

[2]For three different approaches to the Polish campaign see the military analysis by Robert M. Kennedy, *The German Campaign in Poland* (Washington, D.C.: Department of the Army, 1956); Nicholas Bethell, *The War That Hitler Won* (London: Alten Lane, Penguin Press, 1972); and Walter Warlimont, *Inside Hitler's Headquarters, 1939–45* (New York: Praeger, 1964) pp. 22–65. For a Polish point of view see Józef Garliński's *Poland and the Second World War* (London and New York: Macmillan, 1985), pp. 11–39.

[3]The Polish General Staff had ordered from France 160 modern fighters (Morane 406s), but none arrived in time. Total personnel strength of the Polish air force was 6,300 officers and men (R. M. Kennedy, *Campaign in Poland,* p. 54).

[4]The Luftwaffe had altogether 4,303 operational aircraft available by the outbreak of hostilities. These included 1,180 bombers, 336 dive bombers, 1,179 fighters, 552 transports, 721 observation planes, 240 naval aircraft, and 95 miscellaneous craft (Kennedy, *Campaign in Poland,* p. 35). In 1939 the Polish army had 887 light tanks; except for one armored brigade, they were organized in company or battalion strength.

Germany, refused to participate against Poland, their traditional friend. With the Fourteenth Army was a small Slovak contingent, offered to Hitler by the pro-Nazi regime in Bratislava to prove its subservience to Berlin. Thus, Poland's only partially mobilized army of some 900,000 men had to face a much better equipped enemy force converging from three directions.

This numerical and technological superiority had the advantage of initiative and the new methods of Blitzkrieg warfare. A swift blow was to destroy Poland's fighting capacity before the French and British would decide to act. An essential feature of lightning warfare was to drive armored wedges deep into the enemy front, bypassing strong points of resistance without concern about flanks. Tanks and aircraft formed the backbone of the penetration spearhead. The motorized infantry and artillery supported the panzers, widening the wedge and making it secure against possible enemy counterattacks. Then followed the ordinary infantrymen on foot, further expanding and consolidating the penetrated territory. Once a deep penetration had been achieved and exploited successfully, defense could only have been restored by an armored and aerial counterattack of superior strength. The Luftwaffe continuously pounded the enemy defense: command posts, radio stations, supply depots, and railway lines. The success of the Blitzkrieg thus relied not so much on superior forces as on surprise and speed of attack. This new pattern of highly mobile warfare made the old concept of a "front" meaningless.

The German Invasion

On September 1 at 4:30 A.M. the battleship *Schleswig-Holstein* opened fire on the Polish military depot on Westerplatte near Danzig. At the same time, the German Third Army struck southward toward Warsaw, while the Fourth pounced on the "Corridor" to cut off the Polish forces operating there. In the center the Eighth Army moved toward the industrial city of Łódź. The Tenth Army pushed from Oppeln (Opole) toward Częstochowa, Piotrków, and Tomaszów, encircling Warsaw from the south. In the south the Fourteenth Army pressed toward Cracow.

From the first, the Luftwaffe not only attacked key military objectives but also terrorized the civilian population. The summer of 1939 was one of the most beautiful and sunny that Europe had seen in a long time. The weather provided the Luftwaffe with ideal conditions for action. The dive bombers, or *Stukas,* the noses of which were painted to resemble a shark's jaw, strafed objectives on the ground to the accompaniment of special whistles on the wings. When diving the *Stukas* produced piercing sounds that panicked prospective victims, even before any real material damage was inflicted. These howling sirens, called by the German airmen the Trumpets of Jericho, complemented the work of the machine guns and bombs. One of the pet objectives of the Luftwaffe was the long columns of civilians evacuated from large urban centers. From time to time, squadrons of *Stukas* would appear in the cloudless sky and dive on the marching crowd, forcing people to run for cover in the ditches beside the road or neighboring fields. The pilots would amuse themselves by machine-gunning at will the helpless evacuees.

Some members of the German minority in Poland acted as a vanguard of the Wehrmacht, or a "fifth column," and took an active part in helping the invasion. Espionage and sabotage were practiced on a large scale; parachutists dressed in civilian clothes or even wearing Polish military uniforms cooperated with the invaders.[5]

After a few days of desperate resistance along the frontiers, all the efforts of the Polish forces to stop the invaders proved unavailing. On the third or fourth day the German juggernaut broke through the Pol-

[5]For the use of the German minorities abroad for intelligence work see David Kahn, *Hitler's Spies: German Military Intelligence in World War II* (New York: Macmillan, 1978), pp. 97–100.

German fighter-bombers, *Stukas,* approach Warsaw.
National Archives

ish cordon and began to roll forward toward Warsaw. The Polish commander in chief, Marshal Edward Rydz-Śmigły, who had concentrated the bulk of his forces near the borders, found himself in a bind: He had few reserves left and could move them only with great difficulty because of constant air bombardment. After three days of fighting, the Polish front had been broken everywhere. Marshal Rydz-Śmigły lost contact with his armies in the field and overall control of the campaign. The commanders of each of the seven armies had to act on their own.

The largest of the remaining pockets of resistance was the Army of Poznań, commanded by General Tadeusz Kutrzeba. He had managed to carry out a credible withdrawal from western Poland toward Kutno without losing much of his original strength. By September 8 he noted that the German Eighth Army, flushed by its initial triumphs, had exposed its left flank. Kutrzeba grasped the chance and launched a sudden counterattack southward across the river Bzura. The sudden Polish thrust pierced the vulnerable lines of the Eighth Army at several points and stopped its advance. Forced to wheel around, the German forces faced the northeast to contain the unexpected threat. Thus opened the first large battle of the war, the battle of Kutno-Bzura.

Between September 10 and 16 the fate of the battle remained in doubt. On September 11 the German Army Group North threw all its resources into the battle, including its entire bomber contingent, to assist the Eighth Army in its unforeseen difficulties. After two days of incessant air assaults, the Polish counteroffensive was broken. Now, lacking adequate air cover, the Army of Poznań recoiled to retreat toward Warsaw during the night of September 18/19. The more mobile Germans were able to overtake it and sealed Kutrzeba's battered units into a massive cauldron in the fork formed by the Vistula in the north and the Bzura in the south around the town of Kutno. There the last phase of the battle was enacted. Only a segment of the contingents that had formed the backbone of the Poznań Army managed to break through the German ring to join the defenders of Warsaw.

Meanwhile the Polish capital had been encircled by the Third Army, descending from East Prussia, and the Eighth Army pressing from the west. The city resisted for nearly two weeks. On September 25, on Hitler's personal order, Warsaw was savaged by an armada of some 400 bombers, making repeated sorties. Large areas of the shattered city were reduced to blazing ruins. The hopelessness of further resistance compelled the garrison commander to open negotiations on the following day with the commander of the Eighth Army, General Johannes Blaskowitz. The city's capitulation was signed on September 27, but various elements of Polish resistance continued their struggle until October 6.

During the course of the Polish invasion, Hitler made no attempt to interfere with the conduct of operations, even though the entire war had been Hitler's personal adventure. Nevertheless, during the initial phases of the conflict, he remained inhibited by the professional authority of his generals and limited his interference to general directives.[6]

Through the sixteenth day of September the shattered Polish forces continued their delaying actions and even launched sporadic counterattacks. While fighting a series of desperate delaying battles, Marshal Rydz-Śmigły tried to establish another line of defense along the rivers Narew, Bug, and San. His plans were frustrated by the next decisive event of the campaign: the Red Army's invasion of eastern Poland.

The USSR and Japan

The secret protocol of the Hitler-Stalin pact did not specify active Soviet participation in the Polish venture but merely provided that, should Poland undergo a "territorial-political transformation," the line between the Soviet and German "sphere[s] of interest" would run along the Vistula. But from the beginning Hitler had been eager to associate Stalin in his aggression as visibly as possible. Hitler urged his partner on September 3 to join him in action. Through Ribbentrop he sent a message to Stalin suggesting that the USSR "mobilize its forces against Poland" and "occupy the territory which it had allotted in the secret protocol."[7]

While remaining aloof militarily, as early as September 9 Stalin warmly congratulated Hitler on the German "entry into Warsaw," although the Polish capital was not actually captured until September 28. Berlin's pressure on Moscow to enter Poland with Germany was repeated on September 10, but this call also was ignored. On that day Molotov complained to the German ambassador, Count von Schulenburg, that the Soviet Union was in a difficult position because of the continuing Soviet-Japanese fighting in Manchuria. At the same time, however, the Soviet mass media started to condition public opinion to a possible Soviet intervention in Poland by vividly describing the threat of German imperialism to the Soviet Union and the necessity of rescuing Ukrainian and the Belorussian brethren "from falling under the German yoke." This hostile and self-serving stand triggered a vigorous German protest on September 15, when Schulenburg pointed out that Soviet pronouncements contradicted the arrangements made in Moscow on August 23 and "would make the two sides appear as enemies before the whole world." Under this pressure Molotov eventually agreed to justify the impending Soviet military intervention on the premise that the Polish state had ceased to exist. Henceforth, Molotov argued that all previous Soviet commitments toward the Republic of Poland, notably the Riga Treaty of 1921 and the nonaggression pact of 1932, were annulled and that the Soviet Union was free to act to protect its interests.[8]

The Soviet stand in September 1939 has

---

[6]For Hitler's instructions for the Polish campaign and its aftermath see *Blitzkrieg to Defeat: Hitler's Directives 1939–1945,* edited and with an introduction and commentary by H. R. Trevor-Roper (New York: Holt, Rinehart & Winston, 1964), pp. 3–18.

[7]For the Soviet sources pertaining to the intervention in Poland see Degras, ed., *Soviet Documents on Foreign Policy,* Vol. III, pp. 363–81. For a Polish point of view see Garlinski, *Poland in the Second World War,* pp. 21–24.

[8]For the Polish point of view see *Official Documents Concerning Polish-German and Polish-Soviet Relations, 1933–1939, The Polish White Book* (London: Hutchinson, 1940), Part II, especially pp. 159–222.

to be viewed not only in the context of the relations between Moscow and Berlin but also against the background of relations between Berlin and Tokyo. The main reasons for Soviet hesitations were Stalin's uncertainty as to the West's stand and the conflict in the Far East. There, along the 4,000-mile frontier with Manchuria, Outer Mongolia, and China, an undeclared war had been smoldering since the spring of 1937. As a result of Japan's nibbling on Moscow's vassal, Outer Mongolia, the Soviet Far-Eastern troops, commanded by the Red Army's rising star, General Georgy K. Zhukov, became involved in 1937 in a series of clashes with Japan's Sixth Army operating from Manchuria. By July-August 1939 the fighting between the Japanese and Soviet troops was to reach a high pitch of intensity. By September, after weeks of careful preparations, Zhukov launched a crippling blow and knocked the Sixth Army back into its Manchurian bases.

This setback, as well as the shock of the unilateral and unexpected signing of the Hitler-Stalin pact, deeply affected the Tokyo warlords. Instantly, they had to reappraise their entire strategy. They were astonished that, despite the anti-Comintern pact of 1936, which had provided for mutual consultation between its partners, especially those pertaining to Soviet Russia, Hitler had failed to forewarn Tokyo about the impending pact with Stalin. Only at midnight on August 23 had the Japanese military attaché in Berlin, General Hiroshi Oshima, been summoned to the German foreign office and been told by Ribbentrop's deputy, Ernst von Weizsäcker, that his boss had just left for Moscow to conclude what appeared to be a partnership with the proclaimed common enemy, the enemy with whom the Japanese were then in open hostilities. Oshima's surprise was more like a shock. "From yellow [noted Weizsäcker in his diary] his face turned gray."

The Hitler-Stalin pact, combined with their military setbacks in Manchuria, had a profound influence on the Japanese. In Tokyo the cabinet fell, and Japan's long-range strategy was completely altered. Through the summer of 1939 the rivalry between Japan's army, advocating an overland expansion from Manchuria into southern Siberia, and its navy, which favored a drive toward Southeast Asia, grew heated. Events in August-September of 1939 tipped the balance in favor of the navy and its concept of a "Southeast Asian co-prosperity sphere." The Hitler-Stalin pact radically redirected Japan's subsequent behavior toward Germany and Soviet Russia. Thereafter the Japanese not only felt free to act on their own, without consulting the other Axis partners, but were also determined to repay Hitler in kind. If the Germans permitted themselves to make such a sudden, separate deal with Moscow, the Japanese would do the same.

On September 15 an armistice, signed in Moscow, ended Soviet-Japanese hostilities in the Far East and established a joint border commission to supervise its enforcement. France and Britain, despite their declaration of war on September 3, remained passive. In Stalin's eyes the immediate danger of a two-front war was reduced and left him free to act more aggressively in Europe. On the same day seven armies of the Belorussian and Ukrainian military districts, or nearly 500,000 soldiers, were ordered to march into eastern Poland on September 17.

The Balance Sheet of the Polish Campaign

On that day at dawn, the Red Army attacked Poland's eastern provinces along all their borders. Polish forces had already been badly mauled by the German onslaught and their resistance to Soviet forces was weak. The whole operation cost the Soviets 757 dead and 1,862 wounded, while they captured some 46 percent of Poland's territory along with 13 million people and took as POWs about 230,000 military personnel of all ranks, including some 15,000 officers. When the last traces of Polish resistance collapsed at the beginning of October, Stalin sent to Hitler a personal message that ended with the words, "Our alliance has been sealed in blood."

The German and Soviet Invasion of Poland, September 1939

Soviet leaders hesitated about following up their attack, but German troops proceeded to march beyond the Vistula, the original eastern limit of the Reich's sphere of influence. This advance created a temporary crisis in the relations between the two partners. Because of German gains in central Poland, the territorial clauses of the secret protocol of August 23 had to be renegotiated. According to the revised version of September 28, the Germans gave up their claim to Lithuania in exchange for the lands west of the rivers Narew, Bug, and San. Thus the bulk of ethnographic Poland fell under the control of the Third Reich, while the ethnically mixed eastern marches were occupied by the USSR. This was sealed by a joint communiqué published in Moscow, which also asserted that Paris and London were responsible for the continuation of the war. The announcement added that "it would serve the interest of all peoples to put an end to the state of war existing between Germany on the one side and England and France on the other."[9]

[9]*Nazi-Soviet Relations, 1939–1941. From the Archives of the German Foreign Office,* Department of State, Washington, D.C., 1948, p. 108; also Degras, *Soviet Documents,* Vol. III, pp. 379–80.

The price of the Polish campaign to the Germans was not high in human losses either, but costly in military hardware. The Wehrmacht lost 10,572 killed, 5,024 missing, and over 30,000 wounded. The Poles lost nearly 200,000 men killed, wounded and missing; they destroyed 582 planes and 674 tanks, or over one-fourth of all panzer forces engaged; some 600 armored cars and 285 planes were totally lost and 279 had been heavily damaged.[10] During the Polish campaign the German Army expended nearly 80 percent of its ammunition supplies. These losses could not be easily replaced before the beginning of 1940.

The opening campaign of World War II was over in thirty-six days. Immediately, a triumphant Hitler launched a peace offensive vigorously supported by Moscow's propaganda and diplomacy. Hitler celebrated the Nazi conquest of Poland in a speech to the Reichstag on October 6. He had no claims on France, he said, and none on Britain except for her colonies. "Why should there be war in the West? For the restoration of Poland?" He hoped that Britain and France would accept a compromise peace on the basis of the new status quo and would start negotiating for the return of former German colonies. On October 9, 1939, the Soviet newspaper *Izvestia* characterized Hitler's speech as a "realistic basis for peace negotiations" and blamed the Anglo-French alliance for the continuation of a "senseless war." In his speeches Molotov stressed Anglo-French efforts to embroil the Soviets in a destructive war with Germany.

German news reporting on the Battle of Poland was characterized by purposeful exaggerations. Carefully edited films, made during the campaign by Dr. Goebbels' propaganda ministry, were sent to German diplomatic and consular posts throughout the world with instructions to give them the widest possible distribution. The films dramatically portrayed the horrific aspect of the war, especially the allegedly decisive effect of the aerial bombardment. They stressed the hopelessness of any resistance to the superbly efficient fighting machine that could sweep away every obstacle in its path, and the inexorability of eventual German triumph. German propaganda also gave birth to many legends, such as the destruction of almost the entire Polish air force on the ground and the hopeless charges of Polish cavalry against German tanks. No such charges ever took place; nor was the Polish air force destroyed on the ground on the first day of the war. Actually, destruction of the first Polish aircraft on the ground took place on September 14.[11]

The Polish campaign finally convinced Hitler that his military gut instinct reflected a supreme strategic talent. He came to believe that his timid and hesitant generals, usually bogged down in technical matters, should be relegated to preparing only tactical details and logistical schedules, while he personally should direct the war along grand strategic lines.

THE BRITISH AND FRENCH RESPONSE

While Poland was fighting, its Western allies, despite their formal declaration of war on September 3, stood by and watched. As a matter of fact, for two days there were considerable doubts as to whether France would declare war at all, despite previous promises and resolutions. Although Britain

[10]For a German evaluation of the air losses see Cajus Bekker, *The Luftwaffe War Diaries* (London: Corgi Books, 1972), pp. 77–78. The Germans lost 285 aircraft totally destroyed and 737 airmen killed, while 279 Luftwaffe planes were so heavily used they had to be eventually scrapped; the Polish air force lost 333 planes.

[11]The German propaganda was right in emphasizing Poland's exaggerated trust in the power of the cavalry. On the other hand, during the early stages of World War II horses still formed an essential element of warfare, especially in the field of transport. The German ground forces had a cavalry division on horseback and used altogether well over a half-million horses on September 1, 1939 (Robert Goralski, *World War II . . . A Political and Military Record,* [New York: Putnam, 1981] p. 96).

had announced that it would honor its pledges to Poland, the Chamberlain government was reluctant to shake off appeasement. Only overwhelming pressure in the House of Commons and bitter attacks of the mass media forced Chamberlain's hand. Obviously, many M.P.'s came to the conclusion that Neville Chamberlain was trying to evade Britain's clear treaty obligations toward Poland, which they considered as incompatible with Britain's honor and prestige. But at the bottom of this moral indignation lay a simple "gut feeling" permeating politically conscious strata of British society after the seizure of Prague, which once more dramatized the abject cynicism of Hitler and the worthlessness of his word. The French government was even more sluggish. Britain declared war on Germany first on September 3 at 11 A.M., and the French followed reluctantly after serious hesitation. On September 2, when the Polish ambassador vigorously protested against the French's delay in carrying out their clear treaty obligations to give Poland immediate air support, the minister for foreign affairs, Georges Bonnet, indignantly replied: "You don't expect us to have a massacre of women and children in Paris." Yet no French government could afford to disassociate itself from its British ally and renounce its position as a Great Power. Finally, the French declared war on Germany after a delay of six hours.

The two formal declarations of war, however, were not followed by any significant military moves aimed at relieving the hard-pressed Poles in their desperate plight. Everyone expected that Poland would be mangled by the overwhelming German forces and that the fate of the war would be eventually decided on the western front, but no one had expected that the defeat would happen so quickly. It was not the morale of the Polish forces that cracked; they were simply crushed by sheer force of numbers combined with technical superiority. The Poles had an army large enough to hold perhaps up to a third of the German forces, but they could not cope with more than two-thirds of the entire Wehrmacht, including most of its tanks and planes, after September 17 supported by a considerable segment of the Red Army.

British and French declarations of war caused the Poles, naturally enough, to expect immediate land and air operations. Yet the French and the British did nothing to help the beleaguered Poles imploring their promised assistance. This was again contrary to the letter and spirit of both the Franco-Polish alliance of 1921 and the military convention of May 1939, as well as that of the British-Polish Mutual Assistance Pact signed on August 25. The pact had stated categorically that in case of aggression by a European power (which was defined as meaning Germany) "the other contracting party will at once give the contracting party engaged in hostilities all the support and assistance in its power." Article 5 emphasized that such mutual support and assistance would be given "immediately on the outbreak of hostilities." By the Franco-Polish convention of May 19, 1939, the French promised the Poles five squadrons of their bombers and immediate bombardment of key German objectives in case of Hitler's attack on Poland; the main assistance was to come, however, from the French ground forces, which were to start their operations along the Franco-German border "on the third day after the end of the mobilization" and then with a full-scale offensive with "the bulk" of their army on the fifteenth day of the mobilization.

British reaction was no better than the French. On September 5 the Polish military attaché in London went to the air ministry with an urgent request for the Royal Air Force to launch the promised bombing raids against Germany. Nothing came of it. The same day, a conservative M.P., Leopold Amery, saw the air minister, Sir Kingsley Wood, and urged him to set afire the Black Forest with incendiary bombs, as a reprisal for the German raids on Polish cities. "Oh, you can't do that," said Kingsley Wood, "This is private property." To save appearances the British Bomber Command was ordered to drop leaflets on Frankfurt, Mu-

A Polish antitank gun tries to cope with the German armor. The Pilsudski Institute, New York

nich, and Stuttgart, telling the people the facts about Hitler's aggression against Poland and thus attempting "to rouse the Germans to higher morality." As Sir Kingsley Wood put it in his parliamentary speech, these "truth raids" had caused the German authorities "great irritation."[12]

The French did launch a limited and timid diversionary offensive in the Saar and the Palatinate, and within a few days the French forces had occupied some 100 square miles of German territory. By October, however, when German resistance stiffened, the French forces had retired to their original positions. It was obvious that Paris and London had decided early to postpone any large-scale offensive in the west. But the Poles were told none of this. The declarations of war were intended as a mere gesture by the Western Allies; nothing would be done until Britain and France could either negotiate a compromise settlement with Germany or their economic blockade and "silver bullets" could bring Germany to its knees. In both cabinets their respective foreign ministers, Lord Halifax and Georges Bonnet, favored further negotiations with Berlin.[13]

CONTINUED BRITISH AND FRENCH PASSIVITY

Attacked from four sides, outflanked and overwhelmed, Poland collapsed, fighting to the last moment while abandoned by its Western allies. Could Poland have been rescued from its predicament? Great Britain had no army capable of intervention, but its navy and air force could have bombed and shelled German military installations and communication centers. General Gamelin had nearly a hundred divisions ready to fight. His forces could have broken through to the Rhine and threatened the Ruhr, which Hitler considered "the Achilles heel" of the Reich. But Gamelin refused to give the order. We know, from the depositions of General Alfred Jodl at the Nuremberg trial, that the Germans were astonished and relieved that the French did not attack them while the Siegfried line was still "little better than a building site." Another leading German general, Heinz Guderian, was also surprised that the French did not take advantage of their favorable situation in September 1939 to attack the Reich from the west while the bulk of the German

---

[12]For an exhaustive analysis of the lack of any effective Franco-British aid and its impact on the Polish campaign see Jon Kimche, *The Unfought Battle* (London: Weidenfelds, 1968). For a French criticism of Gamelin see Henri Michel, *La drôke de guèrre* (Paris: Hachette, 1972) and Pierre le Goyet, *Le Mystère Gamelin* (Paris: Press de la Cité, 1975), pp. 225–39. See also the article of Henri Michel, "La France devant l'écrasement de la Pologne, Septembre 1939" in *La Nouvelle Revue des Deux Mondes,* October 1979.

[13]For the secret negotiations conducted between Britain and Germany during the Polish campaign, see a work of a professor of Freiburg University, Bernd Martin; *Friedensinitiativen and Machtpolitik im Zweiten Weltkreig 1939–1942* (Düsseldorf: Droste Verlag, 1974), chaps. I and II. Even this extensive work, based largely on primary sources, is not complete because some sections of the Public Record Office have not yet been opened to the public. For instance, some files of Sir Winston Churchill's archives have been officially sealed until the 21st century. Outwardly, Germany's refusal to restore Czechoslovakia's and Poland's independence played a key role. Hitler's colonial ambitions most probably also hampered their negotiations.

forces, including the entire panzer force, was fighting in Poland.[14]

According to the later testimony of Field Marshal Wilhelm Keitel, the Germans in September 1939 had not more than thirty poorly prepared combat divisions in the west. Most of the German troops were raw recruits, many of whom had never fired live ammunition, and this was sufficient for barely three days of fighting. The better German troops, all tanks, and practically the entire air force were thrown into the Polish campaign. During the second week of the war, while the battle of Kutno-Bzura was still raging and the fate of Poland was not yet definitely sealed, German forces in the unfinished Siegfried line were in a critical situation.

In retrospect it is obvious that in 1939 the Germans were not ready for war on two fronts simultaneously. They had only ninety-eight divisions, of which only fifty-two were active. Of the remaining forty-six, only ten were fully fit for immediate action, because the remainder had only a month or so of training. Even in the air the Germans did not have a numerical superiority over their opponents. As of September 1939 the Allies in fact had more first-line, though not very modern, aircraft. There is no doubt that Germany's better planes were of more advanced design than those of the Allies, but the Luftwaffe's crushing superiority in the air was a myth, largely cultivated by Hitler to intimidate his opponents. In September 1939 the Germans had only 3,600 planes, of which, however, some 2,000 were engaged in Poland, thus leaving about 1,600 for the defense of the entire Reich, including a reserve of only 900 aircraft.[15] In 1939 the Germans had no strategic bomber force and the existing craft were suited more to tactical cooperation with land units than to long-range bombing.

German intelligence reports, uncovered by the Allies after the war, indicated deep anxiety about the Wehrmacht in the west. These reports expressed fear that should the Allies attack early in September, they could reach the Rhine with little resistance. Had Gamelin executed his breakthrough toward the Ruhr, it was the opinion of many senior German officers that he could not only have threatened the industrial heart of the Third Reich but might have trapped the hard core of the German army on the Saar front. The potential setback would probably have encouraged the sulking and conspiring generals to act against Hitler, while at the same time discouraging Stalin from committing himself more deeply to face eventually a vigorous Franco-British coalition.

What makes Allied passivity still stranger is the British lack of contingency plans for bombing Germany's vulnerable points. The RAF Bomber Command had prepared a plan for destroying nineteen power plants and twenty-six coking plants in the Ruhr by flying 3,000 sorties in a fortnight. But in September 1939, when it came to a decision, the entire scheme was postponed. Having built up a strategic bombing force, the British decided to wait until the French were attacked; the RAF would then bomb German points of concentration, communications, and airfields. Meanwhile, the French were told in effect, "that they must not expect much results from the assistance of British bombers."[16]

Some of the British Air Staff, like Air Vice-Marshal Sir Arthur Harris, felt angered at seeing an allied army and air force destroyed by indulging in a mere "confetti

[14]Heinz Guderian, *Panzer Leader* (New York: E. P. Dutton, 1952), p. 73; Guderian called the Poles "a tough and courageous enemy." The final report of the chief of the French military mission in Poland, General L. A. J. Faury, sent to Paris from Rumania at the beginning of October 1939, concludes his evaluation: "Les Polonais n'ont donc succombés que devant la superiorité écrasante en chars et en aviation; il n'y eut jamais de panique et de déroute, mais des replis commandés et dirigés" (French Army Archives of Vincennes, carton 19, dossier 7N3006); see also dossier 7N2516, "Bulletin de renseignements militaires . . . du 3 Sept. au Nov. 1939."

[15]A. J. Overy, *The Air War, 1939–1945* (New York: Stein & Day, 1981), p. 22 ff.

[16]Sir C. Webster and N. Frankland, *The Strategic Air Offensive Against Germany* (London: H.M.S.O., 1961), Vol. I, pp. 97 and 104.

German tanks break through in the Battle of Kutno-Bzura. Ullstein Bilderdienst, West Berlin

war." The opportunity to attack Germany while it was engaged on the Polish front was sacrificed by adhering to the accepted policy of caution and conservation of resources. Some leaders hoped that the prime minister still desired to negotiate with Hitler after Germany had destroyed Poland. Air Commodore Sir John Slessor, director of plans on the RAF, argued: "At present we have the initiative. If we seize it now we may gain important results; if we lose it by waiting we shall probably lose far more than we gain."[17] The opinion of the RAF was shared by Field Marshal Ironside, who noted in his diaries: "Militarily we ought to have gone all out against Germany the moment she invaded Poland. . . . We did not and so we missed the strategic advantage."[18]

SOVIET EXPANSIONISM IN EASTERN EUROPE

As France and Britain were reluctantly mobilizing their resources, the victors were dividing their spoils. Early in October 1939 Hitler incorporated not only Danzig but also Polish Pomerania, Posnania, Upper Silesia, and a fragment of central Poland, including the district around the industrial city of Lódź, into the Greater German Reich. Thus, the frontiers of the Third Reich were pushed beyond those of the old empire of 1914. The bulk of the annexed Polish lands were organized into a new *Gau* or province. The mutilated remainder of Poland, the area around Warsaw, Cracow, and Lublin as far as the Soviet border on the Bug, was decreed to be a general government with Cracow as the seat of its ruler, a rabid Nazi, Dr. Hans Frank. The Germans soon started the persecution and eventual extermination of Jews as well as the educated class of Polish society; the remaining strata were to be reduced to helots for the "Master Race."[19]

While the Germans were establishing their "New Order" in western and central Poland, the eastern segment of the country was suffering from the Stalinist policies of "social engineering." The Soviets proceeded to mass arrests of "politically unreliable elements" and their forcible deportation to distant parts of what later was to be called the "Gulag Archipelago." At the same time, Stalin turned his attention toward the three small Baltic republics, the existence of which

[17]Ibid., pp. 35–36. This is also the opinion of the French military historian Pierre Le Goyet (*Le Mystère Gamelin*, pp. 173–95).

[18]Roderick MacLeod and Denis Kelly, eds., *The Ironside Diaries, 1937–1940,* pp. 113–14. Actually he believed that Britain should make its main military effort in the Middle East!

[19]For a German study of the problem see Martin Broszat, *Nationalsocialistische Polen Politik, 1939–1945* (Stuttgart: Deutsche Verlag, 1961).

had hinged on Poland's independence. The Poles had insisted on adding to the British-Polish defensive alliance an additional protocol that extended the alliance to the Baltic states. According to this annex to the treaty, Great Britain would be obliged to assist Poland in defending Lithuania, Latvia, and Estonia against a German attack. Of course, neither the British nor the Polish negotiators realized that the fate of the Baltic republics had already been determined two days earlier in Moscow by the signing of the Molotov-Ribbentrop Pact and its secret protocol.

On September 20, three days after the Soviet invasion of Poland, Moscow accused Estonia of threatening the security of the USSR by allowing the interned Polish submarine *Orzeł*(Eagle) to escape from Talinn. Red Army units of the Leningrad military district were ordered to be ready to march into Estonia, while a squadron of the Soviet Baltic Fleet immediately sailed into Estonian territorial waters. On September 24, at the request of the Soviets, Estonia's foreign minister appeared in Moscow. Brushing aside the still-valid Soviet-Estonian nonaggression pact, Molotov threatened war against Estonia unless it agreed to sign a mutual assistance pact for ten years, which would include establishment of military, naval, and air bases on Estonian territory. The helpless Estonians submitted to this Soviet pressure; they were assured by Stalin and Molotov that Estonia's internal regime would not be infringed upon and that Soviet garrisons would be withdrawn immediately after the war.[20]

Then came Latvia's turn. On October 2 a Latvian delegation was summoned to the Kremlin to hear a similar ultimatum and similar soothing assurances. During the talks some sixteen Red Army divisions were ominously present along the Soviet-Latvian border. Next, Lithuania was requested to send a delegation to Moscow. To the Lithuanians Stalin offered the city of Wilno (Vilnius) to soften their fears of Soviet garrisons on their soil. For over two decades the city had been written into the constitution of the Lithuanian republic as its legal capital. Possession of Wilno by the Poles had been the main apple of discord between the two countries. Lithuanian patriots had desired nothing more than to regain Vilnius from Poland. Yet the Lithuanians refused Berlin's urgings to join in the attack on Poland at the coveted price. Now, faced again with the unexpected gift offered by Stalin, the Lithuanian minister hesitated. On October 10, after long soul-searching, the Lithuanian delegation, frightened by a mounting concentration of the Red Army along their eastern borders, complied with the menacing Soviet demands.[21]

Meanwhile, on October 22, 1939, the Soviet commander of the occupation forces in eastern Poland ordered elections for the selection of deputies to the local Soviets. The electorate, of course, had no voice in the nomination of the candidates, who came mostly from the Soviet Union and were often complete strangers to the voters. Voting was permitted only for the one candidate whose name appeared on the ballot; Soviet occupation troops were also given the right to vote. Chosen deputies were then elected to the Supreme Soviet by a show of hands. They proceeded to pass resolutions providing for the "admission" of their territories into the Soviet Union, for the confiscation of large estates, and for the nationalization of banks and industries. Shortly after these political actions, deportations of "undesirable" and "unreliable" elements started anew, affecting an even greater number of people than before.

Some have seen Stalin's decision to grab as much territory as he could, even in alliance with Hitler, as a rejection of the ideological premises of communism and a definite shift in the traditional Russian ap-

[20]For a background of the treaty see Albert Tarulis, *Soviet Policy Toward the Baltic States, 1918–1940* (South Bend, Ind.: Notre Dame Press, 1959) and George von Rauch, *The Baltic States: The Years of Independence, 1917–1940* (Berkeley: University of California Press, 1974).

[21]For the text of the Soviet-Lithuanian agreement see Degras, *Soviet Documents,* Vol. III, pp. 380–81; see also the *Polish White Book,* p. 193.

proach to territorial expansion. The loss of a broad belt of territory in the west to Russia's western neighbors at the end of World War I had been painful to all Great Russian nationalists, with whom Stalin by then came to identify himself. These losses, a humiliating reminder of Russia's defeats during 1914 to 1920, had also damaged the USSR's strategic situation by depriving it of Baltic ports in Lithuania, Latvia, Estonia, and Finland, thus making Leningrad a dangerously exposed frontier city.

These geopolitical considerations, however, do not necessarily demonstrate that nationalism was Stalin's main motivating force, or that he definitely rejected the ideological premises of communism. His appetite for former tsarist domains and his craving for international prestige, it can be argued, did not affect his basically Marxist analysis of the world situation. For Stalin, armed conflicts were natural and inevitable concomitants of capitalist societies. The war between Western democracies and Nazi Germany was merely a clash between two brands of almost equally dangerous systems. He hoped that a protracted, ruinous war between them would speed up the ongoing erosion of world capitalism, thus enhancing the chances for Communist Russia to impose its kind of peace on an exhausted world.

ENIGMA

Beyond the defeat of the enemy on the battlefield, the purpose of war is the achievement of political and other aims of the victor. The conqueror desires to consolidate the benefits of victory. Hitler, however, failed to establish meaningful advantages in Poland. No political party accepted German rule and no pro-Nazi government was ever formed, in contrast with all the other occupied countries of Europe. The terror and persecution that prevailed from the beginning in both parts of divided Poland produced uncompromising opposition drawn from a broad cross section of the population. Moreover, to preserve the continuity of Polish statehood, a government in exile was formed in France by General Władysław Sikorski, who became its prime minister, as well as commander in chief of all Polish armed forces, at home and abroad.[22]

[22]General Sikorski organized in France and Great Britain a force that by the spring of 1940 numbered 82,000 men. This Polish contingent included three infantry divisions, three brigades (one of them armored), eleven antitank companies, several air force squadrons, and a small but quite active navy. Most of these forces took an active part in the French campaign of 1940, refused to capitulate together with the French, and were partly evacuated to Britain to continue the struggle.

Soviet and German military delegations meet at Brest-Litovsk to delineate a new frontier. National Archives

In addition to the continued armed opposition against Hitler both in their homeland and abroad, the Poles made another vital contribution to the Allied war effort. This assistance concerned the crucial field of military intelligence, specifically signals and cryptology. In 1929 Polish counterintelligence intercepted an Enigma machine sent from Berlin to the German legation in Warsaw. While the package was being examined at the railway customs office, a Warsaw electrical company reconstructed an exact replica of the machine and proceeded to manufacture it. This technical accomplishment was followed by the intellectual challenge of breaking the German coding system through intricate mathematical theories of cycles. In 1932 three Polish mathematicians from the University of Poznań solved the patterns and finally unlocked the German secrets. By January 1939 most German messages were decoded by the Polish intelligence service.[23]

During the summer of 1939 the Poles decided to share their Engima secret with their Western allies as Poland's contribution to the common cause. At a meeting of leading Polish, French, and British intelligence officers in July of 1939 near Warsaw, the Poles turned over to their allies two of their fifteen reconstructed Enigma devices. Despite Poland's crushing defeat most of the cryptanalytic experts managed to escape from Poland to France. Some of the escapees brought with them a few more reconstructed Enigmas to the West. The remainder of these instruments had been destroyed so as not to fall into enemy hands. While French intelligence did not exploit all the possibilities inherent in this mechanical marvel, the British cryptologists had time to unscramble the new German code with the assistance of the Polish experts. Soon the British created a special ultrasecret intelligence net, or Ultra for short, to utilize the potentialities of the Enigma, the secret of which was later passed over to the United States.[24]

[23]For Enigma see Józef Garliński, *Intercept, Secrets of the Enigma War* (London, Milburn, and Toronto: J. M. Dent and Sons, 1980). The names of the three young mathematicians who broke the Enigma secrets were Marian Rejewski, Jerzøy Różycki, and Henry K. Zygalski. A vast documentation of the problem and a model of a reconstructed Enigma machine are available at the General Sikorski Institute in London.

[24]For the early revelations concerning the Polish-French-British deal and its aftermath see Gustave Bertrand, *Enigma* (Paris: Plon, 1973), especially pp. 23–69. For a recent study of the problem see Władysław Kozaczuk, *Enigma: How the German Machine Cipher Was Broken, and How It Was Read by the Allies in World War II* (Frederick, Md.: University Publications of America, 1983). For a practical and most effective application of Enigma and Ultra during various phases of the war, see Ronald Lewin, *Ultra Goes to War* (London: Hutchinson, 1978).

5

The Scandinavian Gambles

THE RIVAL CAMPS DURING THE "PHONY WAR"

In 1939 nothing dramatic was happening on the western front. After a fainthearted attempt at penetrating the Saar, the French had withdrawn to dig themselves in behind the Maginot Line. In some places the Maginot and Siegried lines lay only a few hundred meters apart, and troops from each side often watched each other at work and drill. Frequently, the German and French soldiers entertained each other by broadcasting music and propaganda through loudspeakers. Factories on both sides were increasing production, and they were seldom molested by air bombardment. Not all bridges on the Rhine were destroyed. Even a traffic in vital materials continued for a while. Months after the declaration of war, iron ore from Lorraine was exchanged for German coke through neutral Belgium and Luxembourg. While the Nazis continued drilling their troops, French morale rapidly dwindled because of enforced idleness. The "phony war," as this eventless period was called, continued without blood or tears until May 10, 1940.

The Maginot Line, the pivot of the Allied defenses, reached only from Switzerland to the Belgian border in the region north of Sedan. The Maginot Line was a vast belt of fortifications, whose depth in the southern and central sectors, between Metz and Belfort, attained 100 miles. By the spring of 1940 the system was hastily expanded from Sedan toward the English Channel with only pillboxes and blockhouses placed at kilometer intervals. This new section, stretching toward the coast with some antitank obstacles, lacked depth and strength. German attack in that direction, it had been assumed, would falter first in Belgium and eventually halt in the thickly wooded Ardennes mountains.

The British offered little prospect of immediate help for the French; conscription in Britain was delayed until March 1939. In September, when the war broke out, Chamberlain finally consented to plans for a fifty-five division army to be ready within the next two or three years. Meanwhile, the organization and transport of a British Expeditionary Force of ten divisions proceeded fairly efficiently but with no undue haste. The first armored division was not ready until the spring of 1940.

The Allies boasted that they would defeat Hitler with economic measures, or so-called silver bullets. Economically, both France and Great Britain were in an advantageous position. Besides their naval superiority of more than 12 to 1 and vast reserves of raw materials in their colonies, they enjoyed financial and economic security. Together they possessed gold reserves of more than $13 billion, with foreign investments of some $15 billion and a generous supply of foreign exchange. Trusting to their prosperity, the British and the French regarded economic warfare as the key to their eventual victory.[1]

The German economic situation appeared to the Allies as critical. Their opponents were deficient in most raw materials except for large deposits of coal. They produced some 453 million tons of coal, or at least 50 percent more than the combined output of France and Britain. But Germany had no domestic supplies of rubber, bauxite, mercury, platinum, or mica, so vital for modern war production. Germany's supplies of iron ore, copper, antimony, manganese, and nickel were severely limited. Still more critical was the Reich's lack of oil, essential for its motorized armed forces. In 1933/34 Germany produced about half a million tons of natural oil from domestic wells, but it needed 5 to 6 million tons in peacetime and at least double that amount for wartime needs. The conquests of Austria and Czechoslovakia improved the petroleum reserves only slightly. The German reserves of gold did not exceed $20 million, while the foreign investments were modest and supplies of foreign exchange were barely sufficient to pay for about one-third of Germany's normal imports.

The Germans, however, revealed extraordinary resourcefulness and soon again turned their abundance of coal into a near panacea. The Reich's annual production of oil during the war was to amount to between 7 and 8 million tons. Its stocks at the beginning of the war were low, and foreign imports, except during 1939 to 1941 (the years of the German-Soviet pacts), were never higher than 2 million. Germany's ingenuity converted its abundant supplies of coal into a variety of petroleum products. More than one-third of its fuel needs were met by synthetic gasoline made out of coal. Even more successful was Germany's production of synthetic rubber, called *buna*, its output rising from 22,000 tons in 1939 to 69,000 by 1942. This was more than was needed for its entire military and civil consumption. Domestic synthetic oil was to be supplemented by Rumania's resources, soon to reach some 7 million tons of oil a year. The conquest of the Balkans, especially Yugoslavia, was to provide Germany with sufficient bauxite and nickel, and trade agreements with Spain and Sweden supplied the Reich with mercury, copper, lead, and iron ore.

THE ALLIED BLOCKADE AND THE SEA WAR

The Allied economic blockade also relied on an overwhelming preponderance on the seas. Despite the naval agreement of 1935, Hitler had never increased his *Kriegsmarine*

[1] In this respect see W. N. Medlicott, *The Economic Blockade* (London: H.M.S.O., 1952), especially Vol. I. A great deal of insight on the problem has been provided by Patrick Salmon's "British Plans for Economic Warfare Against Germany: The Problem of Swedish Iron Ore" in Walter Laqueur's, ed., *The Second World War* (London: Sage, 1982).

to the permitted 35 percent of the Royal Navy. Accordingly, the German leaders most disappointed by the early outbreak of the war were Admirals Erich Raeder and Karl Doenitz. Hitler had once promised Raeder that he would have until 1944 to prepare his navy for "settling the old account with the British." The head of the submarine branch, Admiral Doenitz, cherished the same hope and swore that 300 U-Boats would be enough to humble proud Albion. Yet with the onset of war Germany manned only fifty-seven U-boats.

In 1939 the German fleet was composed of the battleships *Scharnhorst* and *Gneisenau,* three armored ships referred to as pocket cruisers, and two new heavy cruisers, the *Bluecher* and *Admiral Hipper.* The German navy also possessed six light cruisers and twenty-two destroyers. The *Bismarck* and *Tirpitz* were still a year from completion, and the Reich was outnumbered by the British 7 to 1 in battleships, 6 to 1 in cruisers, and 9 to 1 in destroyers. Only two aircraft carriers were under construction as against Britain's six. German U-boats constituted only one-fifth of the strength estimated as a necessary minimum for a war against Britain.[2]

During the "phony war" the Germans took the initiative. In the North Sea, for example, the fast pocket battleship *Deutschland* (soon to be renamed *Lützow*) sank several Allied ships of inferior strength and speed. One German submarine penetrated the British naval base at Scapa Flow and sank the battleship *Royal Oak,* the recently converted aircraft carrier *Courageous.*

By far the most dramatic naval incident of the "phony war" took place in South Atlantic waters against the *Admiral Graf Spee,* the sister ship of the pocket battleship *Deutschland.* The *Graf Spee* had sailed before the Allied blockade in order to spread havoc in the shipping lanes of the South Atlantic. A British naval squadron caught up with the Reich's "sea tigress" on December 13, 1939. Inferior in speed and firepower, the heavy cruiser *Exeter* and two light cruisers daringly gave battle and damaged the *Graf Spee* severely. By superior seamanship and battling maneuver the British squadron forced the German battleship to seek refuge in the harbor of Montevideo, Uruguay. There, the caged German battleship was eventually scuttled and its crew interned, while the ship's captain, Hans Langsdorff, committed suicide.

This first major British naval victory brought great relief to London. Meanwhile, both sides continued to brace themselves for a long naval struggle. The Allies tightened their blockade, and the Germans strove to break through it mainly by means of an intensified submarine warfare. A German Naval War Staff memorandum of October 15, 1939, stated clearly that "Germany's principal enemy in this war is Britain. Her most vulnerable spot is her maritime trade. . . . The principal target of our naval strategy is the merchant ship, not only the enemy's but every merchantman which sails the seas in order to supply the enemy's war needs."[3]

THE FINNISH CAMPAIGN

Throughout the winter of the "phony war" Hitler was busy. With the end of the Polish campaign, at the beginning of October 1939, he shifted his troops ominously toward the Dutch, Belgian, and French frontiers. The once puny German garrisons

[2]For an expert analysis of the naval balance of power in 1939–40 see John Creswell, *Sea Warfare 1939–1945* (Berkeley and Los Angeles: University of California Press, 1967), pp. 52–55; and S. W. Roskill's *War at Sea* (London: Kimber, H.M.S.O., 1954), Vol. I. The German perspective is well presented in the books of the German admirals Doenitz (*Admiral Doenitz Memoirs* [London: Weidenfeld and Nicholson, 1959]) and Grand Admiral Erich Raeder (*The Struggle for the Sea* [London: Kimber, 1954]).

[3]For Hitler's directives concerning the economic warfare against Britain see Trevor-Roper, ed., *Blitzkrieg to Defeat, Hitler's Directives, 1939–1945,* New York: Holt, Rinehart and Winston, 1964, pp. 18–21.

The *Graf Spee* scuttled in the Montevideo harbor. National Archives.

along the Siegfried line were reinforced. He ordered new units of armored and airborne troops to be formed. Before these plans could be perfected, however, a double crisis arose in Scandinavia with the sudden Soviet attack on Finland.

The Finnish republic had emerged out of the turmoil of the Russian revolution and the disintegration of the western edges of the old Tsarist Empire. Finland, like Norway, was among the most underpopulated countries in the world. Finland's population of 4.5 million people was scattered over a huge area of 130,000 square miles including numerous lakes and forests. One-third of Finland is situated above the Arctic Circle, kept warm only by the mellowing influence of the Gulf Stream swinging northward into the Arctic Ocean. Even such northerly ports as Petsamo are never ice-bound and provide ideal naval bases. Otherwise, most of Finland has a harsh northern climate.

Until the Russian Revolution of 1917, the Grand Duchy of Finland was an autonomous part of the Tsarist Empire. Soon after the Bolshevik coup d'etat on November 6, 1917, the Finns declared their separation from Russia. Lenin formally recognized the full independence of the Finnish republic in accordance with the principle of national self-determination. Nevertheless the Bolsheviks encouraged radical and pro-Communist elements in Finland to seize power in the name of the "dictatorship of the proletariat." By January 1918 Finland was beset by a civil war during which the Bolsheviks backed the "Reds" against the "Whites." The Whites were led by Baron Carl von Mannerheim, a former tsarist general. The war ended with a victory of the Whites. On October 14, 1920, the Peace Treaty of Tartu fixed the boundaries between the two countries. In the crucial Karelian Isthmus, a 90-mile strip of land between the Gulf of Finland and Lake Ladoga, the frontier ran only some 20 miles north of Petrograd (to be renamed Leningrad only in 1924, after the death of the Soviet dictator).

The strategically unfavorable boundary and the policies of a largely conservative Finnish government came to annoy the USSR. Moscow objected to the rejection of Communism by masses of the Finnish people, resented Helsinki's association with the other Scandinavian countries, Sweden, Norway, and Denmark, and suspected the Finns of sympathizing with other "bourgeois" forces. In October 1939, while the Soviets were establishing their bases in Lithuania, Latvia, and Estonia, negotiations were suggested by Moscow for similar arrangements with Finland. Unlike the three small Baltic republics, however, the more self-reliant Finns squarely opposed many, although not all, of the Soviet demands. The territorial claims focused on three main items. The first insisted on moving the Finnish frontier back along the Karelian Isthmus to give the USSR possession of the Finnish fortifications known as the Mannerheim line; the second request involved leasing the Hangoe Peninsula to Russia to complement its bases in Lithuania, Latvia, and Estonia and so give it firmer control over the Gulf of Finland; the third territorial demand would transfer the ice-free Finnish port of Petsamo on the Arctic Sea, situated just west of the Soviet naval base of Murmansk.[4]

The Finns were willing to make some territorial readjustments in favor of the Soviet Union, but they refused the cession of the fortified line of defense and the disbanding of the Finnish armed forces. Stalin rejected the Finnish accommodations. On November 30, after a trumped-up border incident in which a Soviet frontier guard had been killed under mysterious circumstances, four Soviet armies, comprising some forty-five infantry divisions, attacked the Finnish territory at eight points. At the same time, in Terijoki, a Baltic resort captured by the Red Army, the Finnish veteran of the Comintern, Otto Kuusinen, proclaimed the establishment of the Finnish Democratic Republic. The puppet government immediately acceded to all Soviet demands. Immediately after the Soviet attack, the Helsinki government appealed to the League of Nations. The league, on December 14, declared the USSR the aggressor and expelled it from its membership.

In the war between the Finnish David and the Soviet Goliath the sympathy of the non-Communist world was overwhelmingly on the side of the Finns. The United States expressed a special admiration for Finland, the only country in Europe which went on paying interest on its foreign loans even during the Great Depression. Eleven thousand volunteers arrived in Finland from all over the world, including some 8,000 Swedes.

The Winter War, as the Finno-Russian struggle was called, abounded in dramatic episodes. The Finns defended themselves with consummate skill and tenacity. The fighting raged in snows often 5 to 6 feet deep with temperatures not infrequently dipping to 30 to 40 degrees below zero centigrade. In such weather, engine oil would freeze. Murderous fighting lasted through December and January, and the Red Army managed to advance between 15 and 40 miles, depending on the sector. The USSR eventually committed to the Finnish campaign some 1.5 million men, or about half of its European army, along with 3,000 planes and almost as many tanks. Yet this huge force was bogged down for three months by a Finnish force of less than 230,000 men. There were many reasons for the effectiveness of Finland's resistance. Its soldiers were much more accustomed to the native climate than were those of the Red Army. Equipped with skis and sleds, the Finns were more functionally clothed; they wore layers of underwear, along with parkas, white capes, and hoods.

Another secret of the Finnish successes was their resourcefulness, which yielded some simple but imaginative inventions. For instance, the Finns, who had only a few antitank guns, perfected the weapon improvised in Spain in 1936–1939, namely gasoline, alcohol, and tar-filled bottles, wrapped

---

[4]For the diplomatic background of the Soviet-Finnish conflict see Max Jakobson, *The Diplomacy of the Winter War: An Account of the Russo-Finnish War, 1939–1940* (Cambridge: Harvard University Press, 1961); and Eloise Engle and Lauri Paanen, *The Winter War: The Russo-Finnish Conflict, 1939–1940* (New York: Charles Scribner's Sons, 1973).

Finnish soldiers at the Viipuri Front, December 1939. National Archives.

in rags. Thrown at air intakes or open hatches of enemy tanks, such bottles would instantly set them ablaze. These successful "Molotov cocktails," as they were called, were soon to be mass-produced, and special antitank units were created to use this unorthodox weapon.

The Finns had to cope with a crushing Soviet air superiority. Finland's 162 mostly antiquated biplanes with 200 trained airmen had to face some 3,000 Soviet aircraft. Foreign aid (including supplies from the United States, Italy, and Hungary) counterbalanced somewhat the overwhelming Soviet advantage in the air. The secret of the Finn's performance in the air, however, was again to be found in their resourcefulness. The Finnish campaign, perhaps more than any other, demonstrated that the human person is ultimately the most powerful weapon. Many of the Finnish planes were equipped with skis, but most of the Soviet aircraft had only nonretractable landing gear, which made landing in snow a treacherous affair and a virtual impossibility in heavy snow. This paralyzed many of the Soviet planes, thus drastically reducing their numerical superiority. The results were impressive. During the Winter War, 684 Soviet planes were definitely destroyed, and probably some 300 to 400 others were damaged beyond repair. The Finns lost only 62 of their aircraft.

Despite their bravery and ingenuity, the disparity in numbers and natural resources was so huge that Finnish resistance could not last. By February 1940 the Soviet offensive against the Mannerheim line involved some 600,000 troops. On the crucial Summa sector twenty-seven Soviet divisions with 104 batteries were pounding the line with some 300,000 shells daily. This barrage was the most massive since the German shelling of Verdun in World War I. By February 27, after ten days of murderous bombardment and constant mass assaults, the Russians had finally broken the Finnish defenses.

ALLIED INTERESTS IN SCANDINAVIA

For a while the war inspired some illusions among Allied leaders who hoped that the Soviet-Finnish struggle would generate serious strains between Germany and Soviet Russia. Hitler, however, adopted a hands-off policy toward the conflict as the price for Stalin's neutrality toward his plans in the west and for Soviet deliveries of vital raw materials. Public opinion in France and Britain, outraged by the Soviet aggression, pressed for help for the gallant Finns. This was especially true in France, where the political right wing was eager to punish Communist Russia for its aggression. But London and Paris faced a dilemma in regard to the role of Scandinavia in the war.

While Paris and London were pondering various options, the Finnish crisis became entangled with the problem of Swedish iron ore. The iron ore mines of Galivare, in northern Sweden, produced a high-grade product vital to Germany's war effort, particularly to the munitions industry. The German-Swedish traffic in iron ore could not legally be blockaded along with the rest of Germany's overseas trade. During the summer and autumn the ore could be loaded at Lulea, at the head of the Gulf of Bothnia, and shipped down the Baltic, out of range of possible attacks by the Allied navies. During the winter, however, the Baltic was frozen, and the ore had to be transported by rail across the Norwegian border to Narvik. Thanks to the Gulf Stream, this port was ice-free even during severe winters like that of 1939/40.

It was clear to London and Paris that the iron-ore traffic must be stopped as soon as possible. The Norwegian coasts allowed the cargo ships to sail within neutral Norwegian or Swedish territorial waters for most of the 800-mile route between Narvik and the Skagerrak. Intercepting the cargo ships, therefore, was nearly impossible without violating the neutral waters; the Allies were at a loss about what to do. But if troops were sent to the aid of the Finns, they reasoned, this presence would provide the Allies with a convenient pretext for stopping the flow of the Swedish ore to Germany. Winston Churchill, then First Lord of the Admiralty, suggested that the Allied Expeditionary Force might land at Narvik and then proceed across northern Norway to Sweden to seize the critical iron ore mines of Gallivare. Allied leaders were sharply divided, however, about Churchill's plan. Most of them made Norwegian and Swedish consent a precondition of launching the operation. Oslo and Stockholm, however, firmly rejected the scheme.

The most eloquent supporters of the plan were the French. For Paris, the Finnish venture was a serious necessity from the point of view of domestic policies. Prime Minister Daladier hoped to use the aid to Finland to enlist conservatives in his war effort. By coming to grips with "the Bolshevik aggression" against Finland, argued Daladier, France and Britain would be merely carrying out the League of Nations resolution calling all its members to help a victim of unprovoked attack. By striking Stalin, the Allies would hurt Hitler. Deep down, however, the French leaders, afraid to face imminent warfare in their homeland, sought to deflect the conflict as far from their frontiers as possible, while shifting the main burden of the expedition to the British.

After protracted and bitter debates, by the end of February 1940 the Allies had decided on a triple action. Mine fields were to be laid in Norwegian territorial waters and so placed as to force the ships involved in the coastal traffic into the open sea for a considerable distance, thus exposing them to attacks by the Allied naval blockade patrols. At the same time an expeditionary force was readied to land in Norwegian ports, whether invited or not. Simultaneously, a daring scheme was laid to disrupt

The Soviet-Finnish Treaty of Moscow, March 1940

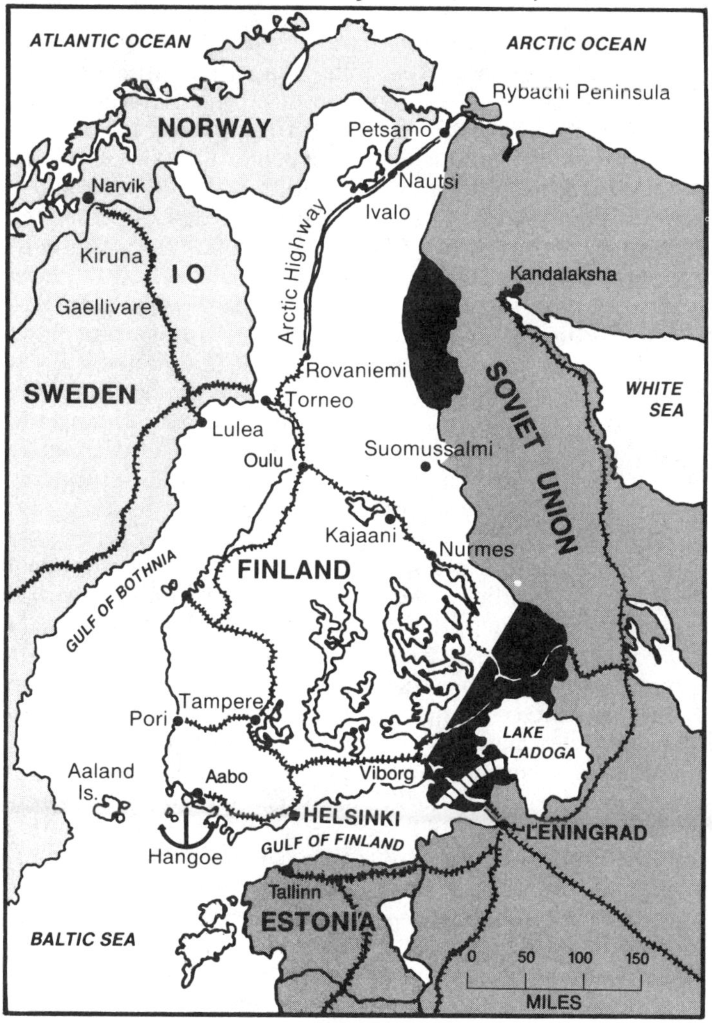

KEY:

- Soviet Union
- Territories Ceded to the Soviet Union
- Swedish & Norwegian Territories
- IO Swedish Iron Ore Mines of Kiruna & Galivare
- Soviet Navel Base at Hangoe
- Narvik-Lulea Railroad
- Mannerheim Line

iron exports to Germany by raiding one of the Swedish east-coast ports, so as to involve Sweden in the war on the side of the Allies by provoking a gross German infringement on its neutrality.[5]

The desperate Finns were hoping for assistance from their "Nordic brothers," especially the Swedes. When offered aid by Paris and London, the Helsinki government approached Stockholm requesting the right of passage for the Allied troops who would come as "volunteers." On March 5 the Swedish cabinet informed Helsinki that by unanimous vote it denied permission to foreign troops to cross Sweden's territory under any pretext. Should the Allied troops attempt such a passage, the cabinet ruled, not a single rail or highway would be left undestroyed.

At the beginning of March 1940 the head of the Finnish Defense Council, Marshal Mannerheim, presented the government with three choices. The first was to open peace negotiations with Moscow; the second, to ask Sweden for immediate military aid; and the third, suggested acceptance of the aid from France and Britain of some 100,000 "volunteers." He pointed out, however, that only a small segment of this Allied contingent would reach Finland, while many more troops would be needed to secure Norway and possibly Sweden from German attack. The Finnish cabinet was divided about what should be done. Finally, Mannerheim's opinion—to negotiate—prevailed.

HELSINKI NEGOTIATES

Finland's peace treaty with the Soviet Union of March 12, 1940, surrendered the Karelian Isthmus (including that nation's second largest city, Viipuri or Vyborg), the region north of Lake Ladoga, a peninsula to the north of Murmansk, and a group of small islands in the Gulf of Bothnia. The Finns also granted the Soviets a forty-year lease on the naval base of Hango, which guarded entry to the Gulf of Finland. On its part, the Soviet Union returned to Finland the port of Petsamo with its Canadian-American-controlled nickel mines. Altogether, the Finns lost over 22,000 square miles with 12 percent of their population (some 450,000 people). Finland had suffered some 23,000 casualties, while inflicting staggering losses on the Red Army: 68,000 killed, 200,000 wounded; nearly 1,000 planes and over 2,300 tanks were lost. The victory nonetheless strengthened the Soviet strategic position in the Baltic and made Leningrad more defensible.[6]

The spectacle of Soviet incompetence during the Winter War damaged the prestige of the Red Army. Hitler was confirmed in his conviction that Soviet Russia was nothing but a colossus with feet of clay, needing but a push to topple over. On the other hand, the humiliating setbacks in the Finnish campaign dramatized to the Soviet leadership the necessity for military reforms. One of the Red Army's obvious weaknesses was its cumbersome chain of dual command. At the time of the Finnish campaign every order of a field commander had to be approved by the unit's political commissar. This competition not only created delays but inhibited initiative and destroyed responsible leadership among Soviet officers to the point of inertia and even torpor.

Another defect of the Red Army lay in its senior commanders who relied not so much on imaginative tactics as on throwing masses of men and machines to decide the issue of battles by "gnawing through" enemy positions by the sheer weight of brutal force. Individual Soviet soldiers and junior officers were nearly as tough as the Finns, but they were inadequately led, trained,

[5]The British attempt proved a fiasco, ending with the arrest of two Britons, a German dissident socialist, and a young Swedish woman in February 1940; see Thomas Munch-Peterson, *The Strategy of the Phony War—Britain, Sweden and the Iron Ore Question, 1939–1940* (Stockholm: Militärhistoriska Förlaget, 1981), especially pp. 221ff.

[6]For the Soviet evaluation of the Soviet-Finnish War and its outcome see Nikita Khrushchev, *Khrushchev Remembers* (Boston: Little, Brown, 1970), p. 152; for the authoritative Finnish evaluation, Carl Gustav Mannerheim's *The Memoirs of Marshal Mannerheim* (London: Cassel, 1953), p. 332.

and equipped to fight a war in a strange environment.

The Winter War compelled the Red Army to change. First, unified command was reintroduced and political commissars were subordinated to field commanders. Field officers were made solely and unquestionably responsible for all military decisions. Second, cooperation among different branches and services of the armed forces was improved. Third, training of troops under various conditions was perfected, and field regulations were revised to make them correspond to the demands of modern warfare. The most important improvement was a vigorous effort at resupplying the Red Army and Air Force with modernized equipment and weapons, often through crash production programs. While adopting some of the Finnish innovations, such as Molotov cocktails and the wooden boxes to hide land mines, Red Army researchers promptly developed an array of new weapons, including massed rockets. Another improvement was application of newly developed lubricants that allowed their weapons, tanks, artillery, and aircraft to function in frigid temperatures. In Marshal Zhukov's words, 1940 was for the Red Army the year of "the great transformation."

Helsinki's decision to negotiate was of crucial importance for the future course of the war. Had the Finns accepted Allied aid, Norway and Sweden would have resisted the Allied landing. Accordingly, these two Scandinavian countries would have been forced into co-belligerency with the Third Reich and Soviet Russia. The partnership of Berlin and Moscow would have been consolidated and turned into a tight military alliance. The center of gravity in the early stage of the war would have shifted to the Far North, covering the whole of Scandinavia and extending to the Arctic Circle. Allied

Spring 1940: Soviet engineers examine details of the recently captured and now dismantled Mannerheim line. National Archives

intervention in Scandinavia against the USSR might have triggered the second segment of their anti-Soviet stratagem: The Allied Air Force in the Near East would have started bombing the Don industrial basin iron ore mines and the oil wells of the Caucasus region. Thus, France and Britain, unprepared even to face Germany alone, would have been forced to fight both Germany and Russia.

How the Scandinavian intervention might have affected the Rome-Berlin Axis is a highly speculative matter. Mussolini's ideological opposition to collaboration with Communist Russia was often voiced during the autumn of 1939; moreover, the pact with Stalin, allotting Bessarabia to the Soviets, was contrary to the previous Italo-German division of zones of interest, whereby the Balkans and the Danubian basin were to stay within the Italian orbit. By agreeing to Stalin's design on Bessarabia and the mouth of the Danube, Hitler encouraged the Soviet expansion in the direction of Italy's backyard at the expense of Rumania, Italy's "Latin sister." Mussolini, aware of the pro-Finnish feelings of his people, permitted some 150 Italians, mostly pilots, to volunteer and sent a considerable amount of war material to Finland, despite German objections.[7]

HITLER MOVES NORTH

Hitler knew a great deal about the Allied plans for Scandinavia and had to decide between the opinions presented to him by his generals and admirals. Ever since the conquest of Poland, Admirals Raeder and Doenitz had urged Hitler to carry out a preemptive occupation of Norway. They argued that it was necessary to deny its bases and resources to the Allies and to safeguard the right flank of the German forces preparing for a decisive blow in France through the Low Countries. Seizure of the long Norwegian coast would be invaluable for U-boats in the battle for the Atlantic; Bremen, Kiel, and Hamburg did not provide adequate bases for the expanding flotilla of German submarines. On October 10, desperately searching for a way of attacking Britain's supply lines, Raeder submitted to Hitler a detailed plan for capturing naval and air bases in Norway, which he considered ideal for winning the battle of the Atlantic. The Wehrmacht opposed these plans, however, because it considered them a risky overextension of German resources, which should be concentrated on one paramount task, that of defeating the Franco-British forces on land.

The land-minded Hitler, absorbed in his scheme of attacking the Low Countries and France, initially favored the Army's point of view. But, the specter of Allied troops reaching Finland through Norway stung Hitler into action. By December 13 he had ordered contingency plans for a military occupation of Norway and Denmark; on January 27, 1940, a small staff of experts was to plan the new venture.

Then on February 17 the British destroyer *Cossack* intercepted the German prison ship *Altmarck* in Norwegian territorial waters and liberated some 300 prisoners captured by the *Graf Spee*. This incident angered Hitler and pushed him toward immediate action. Elaborate amphibious training was imposed on all three services, and a fleet of invasion barges was assembled. Revenge on the British, especially Churchill, whom he came to regard as his personal enemy, became one of Hitler's obsessions.[8]

On February 20 General Nikolaus von Falkenhorst was summoned to Berlin and told by Hitler that the invasion of Denmark was to be carried out by two divisions,

[7]For Italy's ambivalent attitude toward the Russo-Finnish War, see *The Ciano Diaries, 1939–1943* (New York: Doubleday, 1946), especially pp. 172–3, 176–7, 180, 196, 201, 208, and 209.

[8]For Hitler's directive see Trevor-Roper, ed., *Blitzkrieg to Defeat*, pp. 22–24. For a military analysis see E. F. Zimke, *The German Northern Theatre of Operations 1940–1945* (Washington, D.C.: Department of the Army, 1959). The Allied side was presented in the official British military history: J. R. M. Butler, *Grand Strategy*, Vol. II (September 1939–June 1941) (London: H.M.S.O., 1957); and T. K. Derry, *The Campaign in Norway* (London: H.M.S.O., 1952).

including a motorized brigade. Seven other divisions, including two of mountain troops, were to concentrate on Norway. Falkenhorst, was to serve under the direct command of Hitler, as the Supreme Commander in Chief of his *Oberkommando der Wehrmacht* or *OKW.* Along with the invasion preparations Hitler undertook political measures to soften any possible Norwegian resistance. Goebbels directed his mass media to employ admonitory and then menacing tones toward all three Scandinavian countries, accusing them of conspiring with Paris and London against the Third Reich. After some hesitation, Hitler decided to use the services of Major Vidkun Quisling to split the Norwegian resistance from inside. Quisling was a former General Staff officer in the Norwegian army and military attaché in Moscow. After holding office as war minister in 1932/33 in the conservative Agrarian Party cabinet, Quisling formed his own National Unity party. The party preached Nordic solidarity, as well as Nordic racial superiority, and proclaimed its sympathy for Hitler's ideas. Hitler received Quisling three times between December 14 and 18 and promised him military help for his plans.

The German Invasion of Denmark and Norway, April 9, 1940

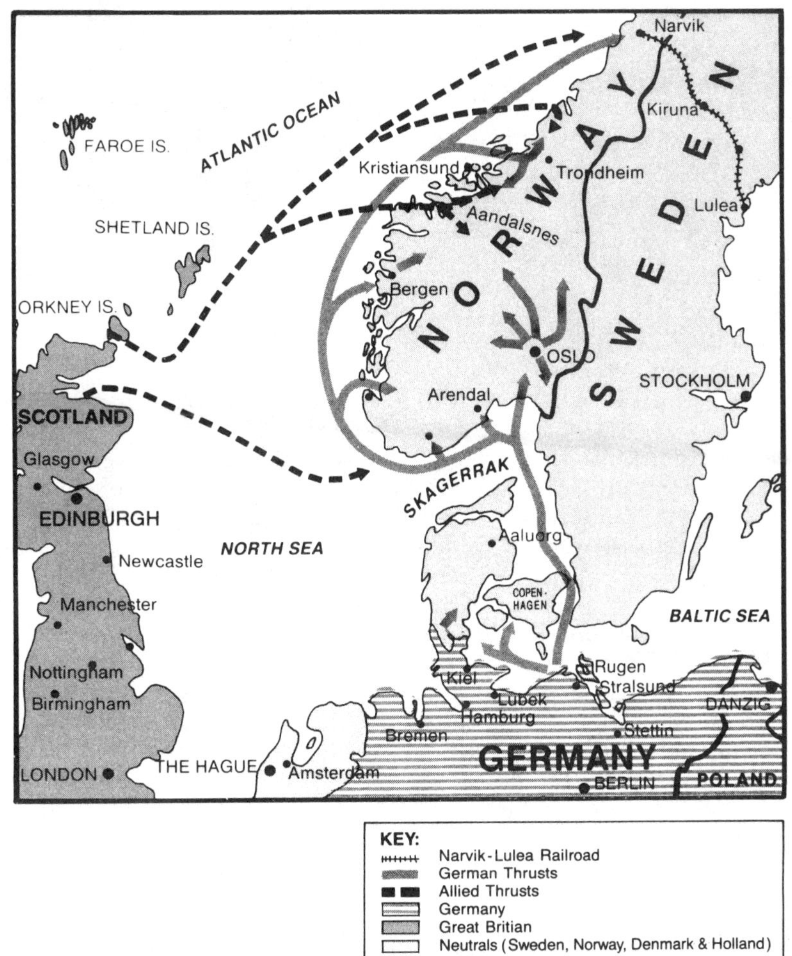

On April 5, 1940, the British and French ambassadors in Oslo presented the Norwegian government with two identically worded and strong protests against the placid toleration of German infringement on the countries' professed neutrality. The notes stated that Paris and London henceforth reserved the right of taking such action in Scandinavian territorial waters as would be necessary to protect their vital interests. Both the governments of Oslo and Stockholm feared that more far-reaching steps could be in store for them. Three days later, on April 8, Allied warships started to lay mines. In reply to this move, on April 9 the German ambassadors confronted the Oslo and Copenhagen governments with ultimatums that insisted on Norway's and Denmark's immediate acceptance of the Third Reich's protection of their sovereignty against the Allied encroachments. Meanwhile, the German amphibious forces were already on their way to occupy both countries. On April 9 the invading army crossed the Danish frontier, landed in five scattered points along the coast of Norway, and carried out two parachute drops. At the same time, Quisling proclaimed establishment of his government, which promptly accepted Hitler's offer to extend the Third Reich's protectorate over Norway.

The Danish invasion was practically a walkover. Inhabited by some 4 million people, mostly farmers and traders, Denmark possessed only a weak militia of 11,000 men and had little means and less will to resist. The whole operation was over within a few hours, and the King's proclamation to submit was obeyed by the Danes. There were only a few casualties, mostly from sporadic acts of uncoordinated, spontaneous resistance by some army detachments.

The Norwegians also realized the hopelessness and at first were undecided whether to surrender or not. Whatever doubts King Haakon VII and the government had about Hitler's demands were put aside by the rash and provocative behavior of Quisling. His proclamation of a pro-Nazi government was an affront to the King. He could have accepted the offer of the chancellor of the powerful German Reich, but he could hardly submit to a rebellious subject who tried to usurp political power. Quisling's arrogant proclamation thus boomeranged and finally determined the King's decision to resist.

A detachment of German infantry peacefully marching into Denmark. National Archives

Although the invasion of Norway had been a rather hastily improvised affair, luck and the Norwegian unpreparedness helped the attackers. The fact that to the last moment Oslo was not sure who was going to land, the Allies or the Germans, contributed to the general confusion. On April 9 when zero hour arrived, the German troops emerged from the holds of the seemingly harmless merchant ships that had been admitted into the key Norwegian ports a few days before. This stratagem, a maritime version of the Trojan horse, so surprised the Norwegians that they watched it in bewilderment. The gist of the invasion consisted of the dropping of German parachutists and landings at five points: Oslo, Trondheim, Bergen, Stavanger, and Narvik. After some confused skirmishes and a great deal of blundering, all five points were captured. Stiff resistance was put up by Norwegian forces at the Oslo airport and harbor. There, the fortress guns, which controlled the approach to the capital through a narrow fjord, sank or crippled several enemy transport vessels, including the cruiser *Bluecher* and the pocket battleship *Luetzow* (formerly *Deutschland*). The struggle around the capital lasted for some twelve hours, just long enough to allow the King and the government to escape northward to the region of Narvik. There, in a region initially outside the range of the Luftwaffe, the growing resistance proved more effective, largely because of the Allied aid.

THE ALLIES RESPOND

Paris and London had been warned about the assembly of menacing forces in northern German ports, yet the Allies continued to believe that these concentrations were only precautionary measures. When news of the German attack on Denmark and Norway reached London and Paris on April 9, both capitals were shocked. Although various contingency plans had been made and unmade in confusing succession to deal with probable emergencies, neither of the Allied General Staffs had adequate information even about the main harbors and airfields of Norway. Eventually it was decided to land troops at three points: two in central Norway, at Namsos and Andalsnes, and the third around Narvik. The rationale of the Namsos and Andalsnes bridge heads was to recapture Trondheim and slow down the German advance to the north where the King and government were trying to organize effective opposition and where the main Allied effort was to be concentrated.

Meanwhile, the German reinforcements crossing the Skagerrak were harassed by Allied submarines and mines. Nevertheless, German troops continued to pour across the Danish Straits. Here sea power revealed its limitations. With superior Luftwaffe squadrons using land bases, it was difficult to keep Allied surface ships operating. They were forced to withdraw. To interdict enemy communications, the British and French navies would have to establish control of the narrow and shallow Skagerrak and Kattegat straits, which were dominated by the Luftwaffe. Without an adequate number of long-range bombers the Allied warships were at hazard in such confined waters.

With Oslo and Stavanger firmly in German hands, the question that faced the Allies was, Could they recapture Trondheim, the key to central Norway? This might prevent the enemy from occupying the northern region of the country, which was still out of the reach of the Luftwaffe. If so, both Trondheim and Narvik would be denied to the invaders, and the crucial iron-ore traffic could be stopped. On April 14 the British landed two battalions of infantry of about 1,500 men at Namsos and Andalsnes, north and south of Trondheim. These troops had to operate, however, some 500 miles from their bases in Scotland, well beyond the range of their fighters. Moreover, the two battalions of rough recruits were dumped into the deep snow and quagmire of April slush without either field artillery, air cover, or antiaircraft guns. The British soldiers were not adequately provided with skis, parkas, and snowshoes; some ski bindings had been forgotten aboard the ships, thus making the skis useless. Within a few days the British contingent was cut to ribbons or captured by the Germans supported by strong units of the Luftwaffe.

In view of this, the Allies reembarked the battered remnants of their weak contingent and shifted their main effort to the chief iron-ore port of Narvik. The arctic town of Narvik was the grand prize of the campaign, for the Germans as much as for the Allies. For Hitler to lose Narvik while capturing the rest of Norway was, in effect, to lose the campaign. For the Allies to capture Narvik while losing the rest of the country was really to cut a single-track railway line which ran from Narvik into Sweden and its northern iron-ore fields. To deny this route had been an uppermost objective in Allied planning. French, British, and Polish forces, which managed to land in that region, had a tough time fighting the Alpine German division of General Edward Dietl, who defended it with skill and tenacity.

Narvik was the only spoke where the Allies resolutely employed their sea power. During the night of April 9/10 Captain B. A. W. Warburton-Lee, commanding the 2nd British destroyer flotilla, maneuvered his five ships into the long and narrow Narvik fjord. At the outset, his ships ran into ten enemy destroyers and engaged them at close range. In this daring encounter he sank or disabled three of the ten. But with the enemy superior in strength, withdrawal was most hazardous, and the captain lost two ships as well as his own life. Stronger naval forces were called for to finish the task. Three days later, the battleship *Warspite* and nine destroyers steamed up the fjord and sank all the remaining German ships. Narvik remained for the time in enemy hands, but no other German naval surface units survived in the northern waters to harass the Allied land expedition that attacked the German Alpine troops holding the town.

By May 28/29, Narvik had been retaken by the Allies at a heavy price. The Germans suffered 1,317 killed and 2,375 lost at sea. The Allies suffered heavier casualties. The British lost approximately 4,400 men on land and at sea; the Norwegian losses amounted to 1,335 men, and the French and Poles lost another 530 men. All this was in vain. The Allied naval losses in the Norwegian waters were also heavy; most of them were inflicted by land-based aircraft. Meanwhile, however, the Germans had succeeded in gradually extending their airfields northward. Narvik would soon be untenable unless far thicker Allied air cover was brought to the area. The communication line to Narvik engaged almost the entire available naval forces to keep it open. From Scapa Flow to Narvik was a distance of 800 miles by the direct route, and considerably more when making a detour to keep out of range of enemy airfields in central Norway. At the moment when the Third Alpine troops were about to be pushed into Swedish territory came the disastrous news from France about the German drive to the English Channel. Now every soldier was needed to reinforce whatever still remained of the tottering French front on the mainland. On June 8, the Allies decided to withdraw their soldiers from the ruins of Narvik and to transport them hastily to France. Norway was lost.

A column of German tanks copes with the snow-covered mountains of Norway, near Bergen.
National Archives

THE GERMAN VICTORY IN SCANDINAVIA

While King Haakon VII and his ministers were evacuated from Narvik to London, Quisling, whose name was to become a generic term for pro-Nazi collaborator, established his pro-German administration under the protection of its real rulers, Gauleiter Joseph Terboven and General von

Falkenhorst, appointed by Hitler as military governor of Norway.

Despite the crushing Allied naval superiority, the Germans were to be victorious because of their bold improvisation. As hasty as their planning was, it still resulted in the eventual coordination of their three armed services; the Germans demonstrated in Norway that Hitler's lightning war could work even in snowy mountains and blizzard conditions. The occupation of Denmark and Norway was the first large-scale combined operation of World War II, involving all three elements of modern warfare. Throughout the Battle of Norway the Luftwaffe dominated the skies and greatly helped both the army and the *Kriegsmarine*. One of the most striking lessons of the Scandinavian interlude was the vulnerability of ships sailing without adequate air cover. Most Allied naval losses were inflicted by the Luftwaffe, especially by the dive bombers; the much weaker German navy could often defy the much stronger Allied fleets, all because of German air superiority. But the most striking single feature of the campaign was the skillful handling of naval and air transport, mainly gliders and airborne troops.[9]

For the Allies, the balance sheet of the Norwegian campaign, the first direct and major encounter with the German forces, was definitely negative, despite their crushing naval superiority. Once more Hitler impressed the outside world with the daring of his tactical plans and the speed of their execution. Small, skillfully integrated teams were dispatched on fast warships to elude Allied surveillance; supplies and equipment had been sent on ahead, concealed aboard merchant vessels. These tactics completely fooled the Allies. They were outwitted, outmaneuvered, and outfought. Hitler was right in describing the Allied intervention in Norway as "frivolous dilettantism." Except for some daring actions by the Royal Navy and the rather creditable performance of British, French, and Polish troops around Narvik, the Allied forces displayed logistical unpreparedness as well as tactical confusion.

As a reward for their military successes in Norway and Denmark, the Germans captured large stocks of food, lumber, wood pulp, and oil. In both conquered countries Hitler secured a number of airfields and harbors, as well as a considerable number of merchant ships, which could be used in his further western drive. By conquering Norway Hitler acquired the only European commercial laboratories (at Vermork) that produced heavy water, essential for manufacturing nuclear weapons. Hitler had also secured his iron-ore supplies. But the most important gain of the Scandinavian conquest was the improvement in the German strategic position. The Norwegian fjords proved to be ideal submarine bases. The instant Danish surrender allowed German war planes to operate immediately from the Jutland airfields, located much closer to Norway than those in northern Germany.

Although German victory was swift and complete, it was costly in the long run, not only because of the naval losses but also because it tied down some 300,000 soldiers on a secondary front to which Hitler came to attach an exaggerated importance to the end of the war. The German navy had to pay heavily for the success of the Scandinavian gamble. In addition to the loss of the *Bluecher,* the light cruiser *Karlsruhe* was sunk by a submarine and the *Königsberg* was destroyed by British Fleet Air Arm aircraft from Scapa Flow. At the same time British and Polish submarines took a heavy toll of the transports crossing the Skagerrak to

[9] In October 1918 the U.S. General William ("Billy") Mitchell proposed to capture Metz by using parachutists, but the war ended before his scheme could be put into practice. During the 1930s the Red Army tried several experiments with airborne troops. In 1936, for instance, they parachuted 2 battalions, light field guns, and some 150 machine guns during the maneuvers near Kiev, and the airborne team swiftly occupied the city. The German military attaché was impressed by the operation and urged Hitler to emulate the Soviet performance and develop such airborne detachments on a large scale. For the combined operation in Norway see J. L. Moulton, *A Study of Warfare in Three Dimensions: The Norwegian Campaign in 1940* (Athens: Ohio University Press, 1967).

Oslo; they severely damaged many submarines and the pocket battleship *Luetzow.* Most German destroyers had been lost after the Scandinavian campaigns. By the end of June 1940, the *Kriegsmarine* consisted of only three cruisers, four destroyers, and three-dozen submarines. Further, many ships of the Norwegian merchant marine, the fourth largest in the world, went over to the Allies, thus bolstering their maritime transport.

The Norwegian campaign was a belated eye-opener that demonstrated how badly the Allies had underestimated their opponent. Their naval superiority meant little without adequate air support and close coordination between the two services. Soon the Scandinavian lesson would be confirmed by similar experiences in the Mediterranean and the Far East, where the Royal Navy was to lose the *Repulse* and the *Prince of Wales* because of inadequate air cover.

With German airplanes and warships firmly established in Bergen and Trondheim, the Allied task of defending the Atlantic trade routes became more difficult. If the enemy had also seized Iceland, it would have been more so. Because Iceland, Greenland, and the Faeroe Islands were crucial, British forces had to occupy them at once. On May 10, the day the Germans invaded western Europe, a brigade of British Royal Marines and Canadian forces performed the task, thus safeguarding not only a net of naval bases but also the creolite mines in Greenland. These mines were of great importance to the Canadian aluminum industry, vital for the Allied war effort. When the Battle of the Atlantic was at its height, the use of Reykjavik as a refueling station for escorts and the establishment of long-range aircraft on Icelandic airfields were essential factors in the contest for the Atlantic.

GAMBLES WON AND LOST

By the end of 1939 and the beginning of 1940 all participants in the Scandinavian contest had indulged in gambles. This raises a series of questions. The first question is why Stalin, a cautious man who would normally take two bites at a cherry, gambled on a surprise attack against Finland under most unfavorable winter conditions. It seems that, heartened by the recent victories over Japan's veteran troops in the Far East and the easy triumph in Poland, he exaggerated the potentialities of the Red Army, while underestimating the toughness and resistance of the Finns. But what probably determined the Soviet dictator's decision to invade Finland was a consideration of long-range strategy. Stalin knew that Hitler was already preparing his offensive against France and Britain. This venture would involve Germany in an exhausting struggle. Consequently, Stalin wanted to grab and consolidate whatever he could along Soviet Russia's western perimeter, as long as the Germans were getting ready to strike in the west. He paid dearly for his gamble in men, materiel, and international prestige. Yet eventually he did profit from the humiliating setbacks of the campaign at least partially. Thanks to its experiences in the Winter War the Red Army was better prepared to face the Wehrmacht during the crucial battle of Moscow, in October–December 1941.

Hitler, an inveterate high-stakes player, gambled once more by attacking Norway. He paid for his brilliant successes by losing most of his surface warships. While seemingly to improve his strategic position, he was unable to exploit it fully because of his resulting crippling naval losses.

The most significant gamble that failed was the Allied offer of direct military help to Finland. Had Helsinki accepted that offer, the whole of Scandinavia would have been plunged into the European war. Norway and Sweden, while defending their neutrality, would have been pushed into Hitler's arms, and the hitherto limited Soviet-German cooperation might have been turned into a tight military partnership. The consequences of such an alliance for the course and the outcome of World War II are imponderable.

6

A Decisive Victory in the West?

PLANNING THE WESTERN OFFENSIVE

On September 27, 1939, Hitler summoned his principal commanders to inform them of his plans in the west. As in World War I, Belgium would be invaded, but this time also Holland. All that the Führer required his commanders to tell him was how long it would take them to complete the transfer of troops and equipment from Poland to the west, so that he himself could decide on the date of the new offensive.[1]

The German military leaders, most of them veterans of World War I, were pessimistic about Hitler's assurances of a quick victory. They suggested that it would be better to wait until 1942 before launching a decisive offensive in the west. They still regarded France and Britain as formidable opponents and favored a prompt end to the untimely hostilities by negotiated settlement. Losses in the Polish campaign—especially in tanks, planes, and ammunition—were, they felt, too serious. In addition, a shortage of raw materials prevented the equipping of the fifty additional divisions that would be needed to achieve superiority over the Franco-British forces.

During the military planning some members of the German establishment were again making secret overtures to the Allies to arrange for acceptable peace terms. Throughout the autumn of 1939 and the spring of 1940, for instance, the chief of the German military intelligence service (Abwehr), Admiral Wilhelm Canaris, and

[1] For Hitler's plans for an offensive in the west see H. R. Trevor-Roper *Blitzkrieg to Defeat*, pp. 12–17; see also Erich von Manstein, *Lost Victories* (Chicago: H. Regnery, 1958), pp. 71–152.

his assistant, Colonel Hans Oster, conspired with leading officers in the Wehrmacht to bring about the overthrow of Hitler to prevent what they considered the imminent defeat of Germany by the superior Franco-British forces.

Brushing aside the objections of his military establishment, Hitler on October 9 issued his directives, which stressed that any further delay would "strengthen the military power of the enemy and reduce the confidence of neutral nations in Germany's final victory." When Hitler requested a definite plan for a western offensive, the General Staff submitted a plan that involved a rapid thrust through Holland and Belgium into northern France, employing a mighty German right flank supported by the bulk of the armored divisions. After a deep penetration of French territory, an enveloping drive would sweep southwest to surround and capture Paris and thus end the war. This scenario was tentatively accepted by Hitler.

From the start the plan of the General Staff was criticized by General Erich von Manstein, then Chief of Staff for Gerd von Rundstedt, who had been designated by Hitler to command the central sector of the western offensive. Manstein condemned the plan of the General Staff as too stereotyped and, therefore, one that deprived the Wehrmacht of an essential precodition for victory, namely surprise. By overwhelmingly focusing the main drive in the north, Manstein believed, the German troops would have to face the bulk of the British Expenditionary Force (B.E.F.), supported by the RAF, thus encountering the best segment of enemy troops. Should the British stop the German offensive, their counterattack might then endanger the industrial heartland of Germany, the Ruhr.

Manstein urged, therefore, a radical recasting of the plan. His scenario involved a feint attack through Holland and Belgium to divert the enemy's attention from the central sector of the front. This sector he considered crucially important, especially the area on the northern tip of the Maginot Line situated

Hitler surrounded by his staff, plots his conquests. On Hitler's left stands General Franz Halder the Army Chief of Staff (1938–1942). National Archives

at the juncture of France, Belgium, and Luxembourg, around Sedan on the Meuse. Vulnerable because of light fortifications, the area was also inadequately manned because the French valued the protection of Luxembourg's neutrality. The French also relied upon the defenses afforded by the wooded Ardennes mountains, which they considered impassable by heavy armored units. There, at Sedan, argued Manstein, the massed panzer divisions should strike; the Wehrmacht could cut off the B.E.F. from the bulk of the French army and then push on to the English Channel. The main objective of the plan should be not to capture enemy territory, with Paris as the chief objective, but to split and then destroy the enemy forces in the north, the B.E.F. first of all.

Von Manstein's project got a rather poor reception from most of the top German generals. Traditionalists, they shared with their French counterparts the belief that heavy armor could never cross the Ardennes. Although Hitler basically liked Manstein's strategy, he modified only slightly the old plan, in the spirit of Manstein's scheme, by adding a decoy: a thrust toward Sedan. Here, however, fate played a strange trick. In January 1940 a German staff officer, carrying a copy of the recently approved German order of battle, had been forced to land in Belgium because of stormy weather. He was unable to destroy all the documents and was interned; the captured fragmentary plan was promptly passed to Paris and London by Belgian intelligence.

The Allies were enraptured. They faced a repetition of an updated plan of World War I, with which they were familiar. Consequently, they decided to counter the German offensive by a well-prepared preventive thrust into Belgium, carried out by their best units, including the entirely motorized B.E.F. The counteroffensive would pin down the German forces there along the fortified Albert Canal, well before the enemy could unfold its expected enveloping sweep toward Paris. As a consequence of the captured documents, however, Hitler ordered a radical recasting of the original plan of invasion in accordance with Manstein's original outline. Thus, an accident actually resulted in a new scheme. While the Germans recast their operation to fit a bold strategy, the Allied leaders ignored the regrouping, convinced that they faced a slightly modified Schlieffen plan, which stressed the crucial role of the right wing and not of the center.[2]

THE ORDERS OF BATTLE

The new German order of battle was tailored for the task. Army Group North under Bock (or Group B as it was designated on the staff maps) possessed thirty divisions to cover the Dutch sector of the front. Army Group Center (or A) under Rundstedt would strike through Belgium and Luxembourg at the region of Sedan on the Meuse (Maas) and drive not toward Paris but toward the Channel, in order to isolate Dutch, Belgian, and Franco-British armies from the main body of the Allied forces in France. Since this was the pivotal task, Army Group Center had the strongest forces, no fewer than forty-five divisions, including seven armored. Army Group South (or C) under Leeb, was the weakest, since its task was merely to contain the French troops on the Maginot Line; thus, Group South had only nineteen, mostly weaker, reserve divisions with no massed armor. Supporting the German field troops were Air Fleets Two and Three, commanded by Generals Albert Kesselring and Albert Sperle. These air units had at their disposal some 2,750 aircraft of all kinds, including over 1,000 fighters.

The Allied order of battle entirely overlooked the German regrouping and their intentions. No fewer than fifty divisions

---

[2]In 1905 General Count von Schlieffen, chief of the German General Staff, completed an operational plan for a war against France. The plan assumed that the French fortifications were impregnable and should be outflanked by a scythelike attack through Belgium and Luxembourg to envelop and capture Paris.

(nearly half of all troops) were to be located behind the Maginot Line, which Hitler never intended to storm, while the crucial center sector was manned by only twenty-two French divisions, including three motorized and two light mechanized ones.[3] The northern sector, where the Allies still expected the enveloping swing toward Paris, was composed of twenty-six divisions (seventeen French and nine British), including one armored, one light mechanized, and two motorized. The Allied strategic reserves, grouped east of Paris, numbered twenty-two divisions, including three armored. These newly organized and not yet completely trained divisions were the best ones the French had. The five light divisions were actually the old-fashioned cavalry divisions into which motorized and lightly armored units were injected.

If one adds the Dutch and Belgian forces to the French and British armies, Hitler's opponents had a total quantitative superiority in two categories: in the number of men (156 divisions as against 136) and in tanks (over 4,000 Allied as against 2,750 of the German). But while the Allied tanks were dispersed, largely in battalion strength and attached to various infantry and motorized divisions, the German tanks were massed in two "armored fists": one in the north (three divisions) and another in the center (seven divisions). Only in the air were the Germans superior both in numbers and in the quality of their weapons. German superiority was due largely to the British failure to commit the bulk of the RAF to the Continent, keeping instead a large reserve of the most modern planes at home. Together with their expeditionary force, the British sent to the mainland approximately 200 of their bombers and as many fighters, mostly Hurricanes, while keeping their Spitfires for home defense. On May 10 there were altogether only 416 British aircraft in France. Despite urgent pleas by the French High Command, the British were reluctant to commit the bulk of the RAF beyond Britain's shores. Together with 1,200 French war planes the Allies had only slightly over 1,600 planes to duel with the 2,750 Luftwaffe aircraft. Moreover, the Germans used their massed aircraft in conjunction with their mobile armored spearheads, while the Allies uselessly dispersed their planes.

Use of their inferior aerial resources created ceaseless discord between the French and British. The British, for instance, wanted to focus their bombing operation on oil installations and dislocation of the war industry in the Ruhr, while the French insisted on operations closer to the front line, to assist the hard-pressed army units and to stem the speed of the German onslaught. Most of the best French fighters, and there were fewer than 800 of them, were slower than the German planes, the Messerschmitt 109. In 1939/40 German annual production of first-line aircraft was approaching the 3,000 mark, while France was manufacturing less than 600 planes a year, most of them outdated. Most French bombers were not equipped with radio communication. Ground equipment for loading them with bombs was antiquated, so that time was wasted in getting them off the ground. In addition, the French had few bombers and in this respect they relied on the RAF almost entirely.[4]

From the start, the attitude of the Low Countries appeared as crucial to the planned Allied counterthrust, yet a lack of coordination with the Belgians and the Dutch haunted the Allies. Despite mounting evidence of Hitler's aggressive designs against both countries, Belgium and Holland stubbornly stuck to their separate defense ar-

---

[3]Over 2,000 coded German messages had been intercepted and deciphered but ignored by General Gamelin, who neglected the recasting of the original German plan and stubbornly stuck to the evidence obtained from the documents captured in January 1940. For the failure of the French to exploit the evidence provided by Enigma, see Gustave Bertrand, *Enigma,* pp. 84–90; see also Le Goyet, *Le Mystère Gamelin,* especially pp. 220 ff.

[4]For an evaluation of the aerial strength of the two sides, see R. J. Overy, *The Air War 1939–1945* (New York: Stein & Day, 1981), chap. 2.

rangements. In 1940 Belgium, the key country of the area, could mobilize twenty-two under-equipped divisions and a small air force. The prospects of defending Belgium were much better if Franco-British forces were permitted to enter the country before the German invasion. Yet the Belgian government persisted in refusing such permission and stuck to its neutral position. Consequently the Allies were never quite sure that Belgium would defend itself if the attack came. This attitude, as well as history, played into German hands because the experience of World War I was not exactly encouraging. The heroic stand of King Albert in 1914 resulted in a period of four years of German occupation and devastation of the country. In 1940 the Belgians reasonably asked whether they would have fared better if the Germans had been permitted to enter with no more than a diplomatic protest.

The Dutch and Belgian defenses naturally formed a common perimeter. From a strategic point of view they were joined, yet both countries behaved almost to the last minute as if they were two distant islands. The Dutch defense, with its small army of ten divisions, was based on the Maas (Meuse) and Ysser rivers, which flow through both countries. But the Dutch relied for protection mainly on the intricate network of their canals, as well as on their ability to flood much of their land by opening dams, while the Belgians counted on their fortification along the Albert Canal. The long Albert Canal cut through the northeastern part of the country and connected the Middle Maas with the North Sea at Antwerp. The linchpin of the Belgian defenses was the powerful, modern Eben Emael fort guarding the city of Liège and situated at the junction of the Meuse and the Albert Canal.

The warnings of an imminent attack were not lacking. On May 1 the French military attaché in Bern informed Paris that Hitler would launch his attack in the west between May 8 and 10 and that it would go through the Ardennes and be focused on Sedan. Colonel Oster informed a senior Dutch intelligence officer that the invasion would come on May 10, 1940. The warnings were ignored, however. So were the numerous messages coming in by way of the Enigma decoding device. Most intelligence was never read by the French Commander in Chief, General Maurice Gamelin. Even the urgent report on May 8 by a RAF reconnaissance aircraft of huge German armored columns moving toward the frontier of Luxembourg was brushed aside by Gamelin as a false alarm.[5]

THE GERMAN ATTACK

The coordinated German attack against Holland, Belgium, and France was launched at dawn on May 10. At 6 A.M., with troops already engaged in actual fighting, the German envoys at The Hague and Brussels delivered two identical notes telling both governments that Berlin had been forced to act to forestall an impending Franco-British invasion of the Low Countries. The Dutch and Belgian governments had to choose either to submit or to face annihilation. The Dutch and the Belgians now made urgent appeals for help to London and Paris. The Allies replied by rushing the troops for their Northern Army Group into the Low Countries. Although the defense of Belgium had long been expected, Allied countermoves were hasty and disruptive. More important, gaps between the altered placement of forces dangerously exposed the left wing and the central sector of the Franco-British front, in the critical area of Sedan. Worse yet, the troops dispatched to Beligum included the most mobile segment of the

[5]Although there is no French official history of the 1940 campaign, the official British version was presented by Major L. B. Ellis in *The War in France and Flanders (1939–1940)* (London: H.M.S.O., 1953); for expert German opinions about the campaign in the west, see B. H. Liddell Hart, ed., *The German Generals Talk* (New York: Morrow, Quill, 1979), pp. 105–36; see also Guderian, *Panzer Leader,* pp. 89–139. For background and personalities see Edward Spear's (Churchill's personal emissary to France during the crisis) *Assignment to Catastrophe,* 2 vols. (A. A. Wyn, New York: 1954–1955).

Allied forces, the highly mechanized B.E.F., as well as three motorized and mechanized French divisions.

Manstein's plan, about which Gamelin should have learned from the Enigma reports as well as other sources, worked to perfection. The Allies were lured into an encounter battle which, under the circumstances, proved to be a trap. The French Seventh and First armies and the B.E.F. were soon bogged down in the maze of the Dutch and Belgian canals, dams, bridges, and twisted roads, even before seeing the enemy. In these most intricate battles the Germans enjoyed not only the advantages of initiative and aggressive momentum but also of assured planning, superior training, and a wealth of experience in the novel methods of warfare practiced in Poland and Scandinavia.

The invasion of both Holland and Belgium was spearheaded by well-trained and equipped paratroopers, followed by airborne detachments carried by either gliders or large transport planes. In the early hours of May 10 Holland's capital, The Hague,

The German Invasion of Holland, Belgium, Luxembourg and the Penetration of the French Northern Defense Line, May 10-20, 1940

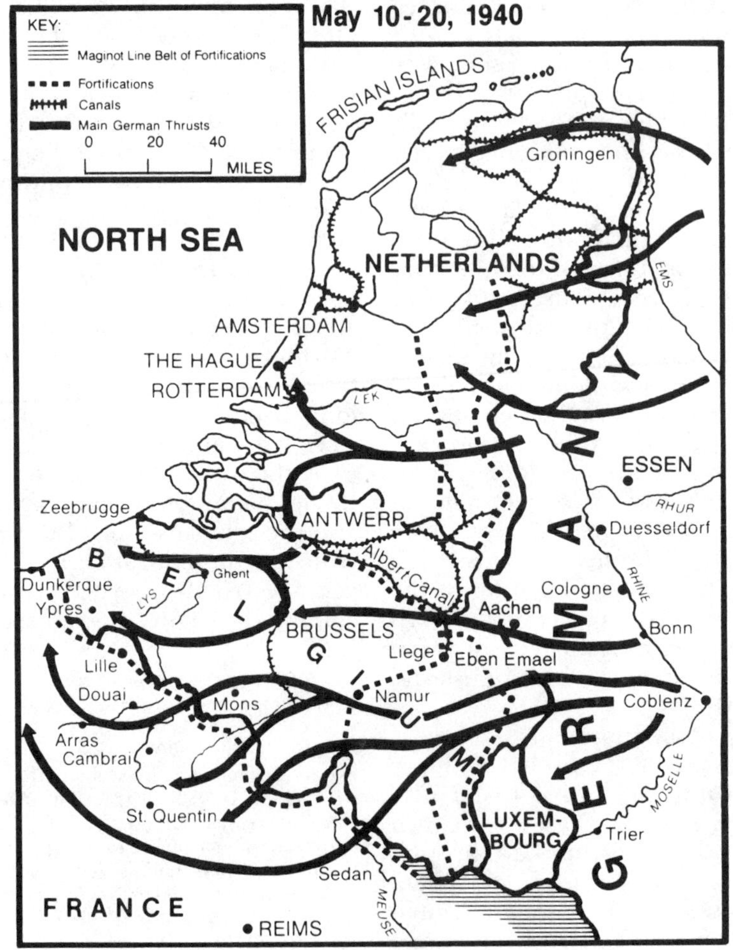

and the country's chief port, Rotterdam, were showered with five battalions of paratroopers, numbering some 4,000 soldiers and supported by an airborne infantry division of some 12,000 men. After the parachutists had captured the main airfields, the airborne troops landed and seized most of the bridges across the Rhine delta. German troops also captured the dams that could flood much of northwestern Holland. The bridges were kept intact long enough to allow the passage of the main body of the invading forces. The chaos generated by the powerful double blow from the air and on land momentarily paralyzed the Dutch defenses. The paralysis allowed the Germans to exploit the gap that was soon open to the south in the Maastricht area before Allied troops could reach it.

The remaining parachute battalion of the Wehrmacht was used in the attack on the southern end of the exposed junction of the Meuse and the Albert Canal, with its fort, Eben Emael. Here was the hub of the Belgian defenses. The storming of Verdun in World War I had proven that no fort could cope with enemy forces on its roof. Accordingly, on May 10, before dawn, fifty-five specially trained and equipped German engineers, transported by twelve gliders, landed silently with explosives on top of the Belgian fort and overwhelmed its sleepy sentries. Protected by the morning fog and smoke screens, German commandos pushed detonation charges into the barrels of the cannons and ventilation shafts. Then they dynamited all exits and observation posts. At the same time another commando team crawled from cupola to cupola to drop their explosives into the main ammunition dumps. As yet unhurt, most of the Belgian garrison of some 1,200 men became isolated, virtually blockaded in their own fortress.

The desperate commander of Eben Emael appealed urgently for assistance to the adjacent forts; he begged his colleagues to bombard the superstructure of his fort to chase away the intruders. When the two Belgian commanders obliged and opened fire it was already too late. By that time the German commandos had already moved away to other assignments.[6]

On May 11 around noon the main body of the invading Germans reached Eben Emael at the Meuse and the garrison of the fort had to surrender. The Belgian commander begged the Germans to release his men from their shelters to avoid suffocation. The seizure of the Eben Emael fort and the intact bridges on the Albert Canal cracked the Belgian defenses at their crucial points. Under the shield of airborne troops, two armored divisions of General Hopner's 16th Panzer Corps crossed the canal and drove a deep wedge into southern Belgium. The armored troops were followed by the bulk of General von Reichenau's Sixth Army. The road to Brussels lay open to the Germans well before the French and British forces could arrive there. Meanwhile, the Luftwaffe savaged the defenseless Rotterdam, turning its center into a heap of smoldering ruins.

Thus, the German invasion of the Low Countries was overwhelmingly successful. Luxembourg was also occupied within a few hours, without much resistance. The Dutch forces capitulated on May 15.

THE "IMPASSABLE" ARDENNES

During the attack on the Low Countries, Rundstedt's Army Group Center had been driving through Luxembourg and the hilly and forested edge of southern Belgium toward the northern tip of the French border, now denuded of some of its best troops. This 70-mile stretch around Sedan between the Ardennes and Luxembourg was highly vulnerable; the sector was an open space between the northern end of the Maginot Line and the southern fringe of the Belgian defense system. Rundstedt's Group Center possessed seven panzer and four motorized divisions, providing an armored battering ram of exceptional strength. Leading this juggernaut was Guderian's elite Panzer Corps, com-

[6]For a description and analysis of the operation see James E. Mrazek's *The Fall of Eben Emael* (published by the author, Washington, D.C., 1970).

posed of three divisions. After successfully traversing the 70-mile trip through the Ardennes, Guderian penetrated into French territory. On the fourth day of the offensive, May 13, his spearhead stood firmly on the banks of the Meuse, near Sedan.

During this furious rush of German forces the French Commander in Chief, General Gamelin, sat isolated in his GHQ at Vincennes, near Paris, in an office facing the moat in which the Duc d'Enghien and Mata Hari had been executed. Surrounded by books on the art of warfare, Gamelin lived in an ivory tower, distant and isolated from events at the front. As General de Gaulle, who visited him there, put it, Gamelin gave the impression of a scholar "testing the clinical reaction of his strategy in a laboratory." His GHQ did not even have a radio transmitter. He believed the attack was to fall on the strong Maginot Line defenses.[7] When the enemy was sufficiently weakened, argued Gamelin, he would then start a counteroffensive. The Ardennes, he believed, "were not good tank country." He discounted a French armored reconnaisance patrol's report of an advancing column of German tanks; Gamelin stuck to his opinion that it was a decoy and that the Ardennes were impassable. Even after their successful penetration, he continued to insist that the central sector and the Maginot Line would be the focal point of the attack. In retrospect, Gamelin's complacency bordered on treasonable arrogance.

General Gerd von Runstedt, Commander of the Army Group Center or "A."

THE GERMAN ADVANCE

Rundstedt's army group, spearheaded by the greatest concentration of tanks ever seen in war, had cut through Luxembourg and the Ardennes. By the evening of May 12 leading elements of the German armored divisions had reached the Meuse in two places. By May 13 Sedan, on the east bank of the river, had already been captured by the 1st and 10th panzer divisions. At the same time, Erwin Rommel's 7th "light division" (which contained only one armored regiment) had reached Dinant. On May 13 Guderian's engineers constructed a pontoon bridge so that his tanks could cross the Meuse. This was an opportunity for the Allies to launch a counterattack, but it was missed. The Germans crossed the Meuse early on May 14. On the morning of the same day, General Charles

[7] Trying to justify the fact in a letter to the editor of *L'Aurore* (Paris, Nov. 8, 1949), Gamelin wrote, "What would we, at this level, have done with a transmitter?" According to General Ironside, Gamelin knew a great deal about military theory and its history but little about strategy (*The Ironside Diary*, pp. 117–20). Gamelin's own elaborate story, presented in his *Servir* (3 vols. [Paris: 1946–47]), does not add much to our understanding of his failure as commander-in-chief.

Huntziger, French commander of the Second Army, telephoned GHQ that many of his troops were not holding under the enemy bombardment. Some of them were emerging from their pillboxes with uplifted arms. He ordered his troops to open fire on the defectors, but this proved of no avail. The panic spread and turned into chaos.

The Wehrmacht deliberately struck at the junction of two French armies (the Second and the Ninth), which contained several poorly trained reserve units. Most divisions of the Second Army had only begun to receive their antitank guns and had had no time to practice with them. One of the regiments, the 71st, had been recruited from the northeast, the largely Communist suburb of Paris. The entire 55th Division was undermined with defeatism: Long before the German offensive its soldiers refused either to work or drill and made a point of not saluting their officers. They reversed their helmets, a Communist sign indicating the determination of eventually turning against their "capitalist exploiters and oppressors," thus transforming the "imperialistic war into a civil war." The Ninth Army of General André Corap, which manned the sector north of Sedan, was also composed of units mostly below standard and of low morale. Only two of its divisions were regular ones.

On the evening of May 14 General Corap mistakenly ordered a general retreat to a new defense position about 10 miles west. This created a gap between the Ninth and the Second armies. That same day British and French forces lost about 85 out of 170 bombers vainly attempting to destroy the vital German pontoon bridge at Sedan. Because of the retreat of the Ninth, General Reinhardt's XLI Corps crossed at Monthèrme, and Rommel breached the new French defense line before it could be properly manned. The inept Corap was dismissed and replaced by the determined and resourceful General Henri Giraud, who tried to restore order, but he was captured a few days later.

The French endeavored to seal off the hole in their defenses between Dinant and Sedan. They threw into the battle some armored divisions hitherto kept in reserve, but the belated attempt failed. Heavy losses were suffered in tanks and planes, especially by the RAF. By the evening of May 15 the Germans had already gained a decisive advantage. Yet Hitler, who overrated Gamelin's ability to launch a counteroffensive and underrated the extent to which French morale had collapsed, stopped the further advance of the German armor. Guderian and Rommel, however, persuaded Hitler to cancel his order. Unleashed, by the morning of May 19 Guderian's 2nd Panzer Division was already at St. Quentin. By the evening of May 20 Guderian was in Abbeville on the English Channel.

Thus within ten days Rundstedt had driven a solid wedge into the gap between the Allied forces operating in Belgium and the bulk of the French forces now grouped south of the Somme and on the Maginot Line. "The Abbeville pocket," some 30 to 50 miles wide, created two battlefields. The elite of the Allied forces in more than forty divisions, including most of the B.E.F., were "like a cut rose in a vase," as a German officer said. South of the Somme there were still well over sixty divisions, but they did not contain much armor, and their morale had been shaken by the fast defeats and by the constant enemy bombardment. Gamelin's main hope, the Maginot Line, was never frontally stormed, and the large contingent of troops stationed there became useless.

CHURCHILL BECOMES PRIME MINISTER

The lightning German victories in northern and western Europe deepened the political crisis in Paris and London. In both capitals the conduct of the war was now attacked by mounting opposition. The humiliating setbacks suffered by the Allies in Norway had provoked a deep dissatisfaction and a sense of impotence in Paris, where the government of Daladier was replaced by that of

The German and Italian Invasions of France: May 10 - June 24, 1940

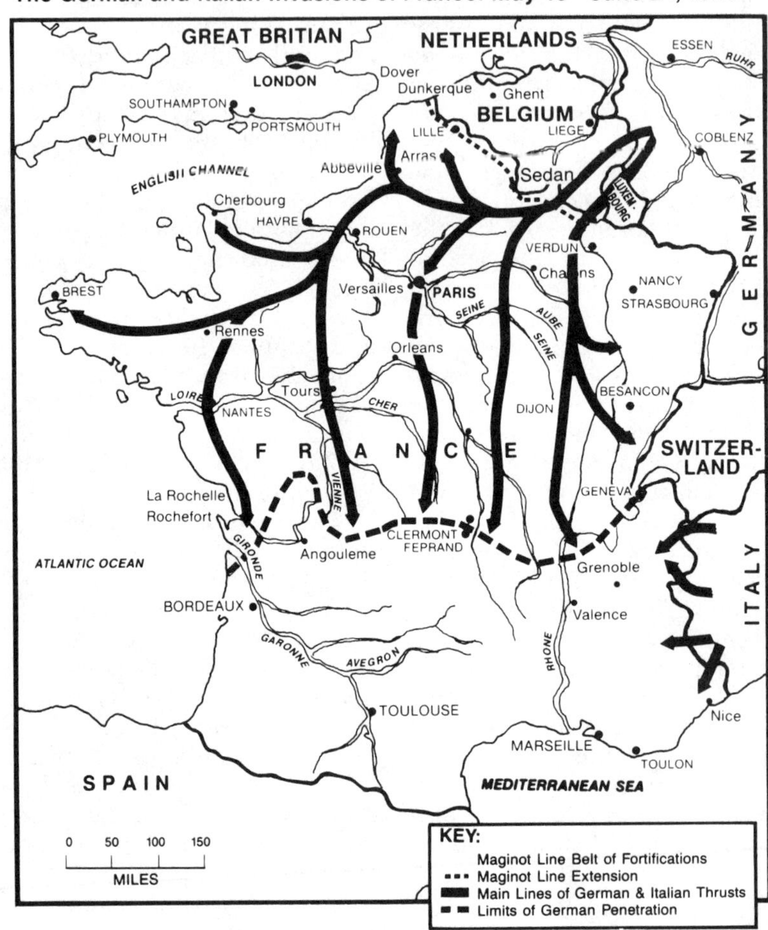

Paul Reynaud. In the House of Commons, Prime Minister Neville Chamberlain on May 7 faced a no-confidence motion by the Labour opposition. His Conservative party had a large majority, but at a critical moment forty Conservatives voted against Chamberlain, and another sixty abstained. Three days later Chamberlain resigned and Winston Churchill became prime minister.

On May 10, 1940, this short, stocky man of sixty-six, who looked like a cross between a bulldog and a giant panda, was chosen as Britain's prime minister at the moment of supreme danger to his country. His triumphantly somber return to power, after nearly two decades in the political wilderness, proved to be a major event of the war. Churchill had stood almost alone among the British Conservatives in warning against the Nazi peril and calling for speedy rearmament. During the House of Commons debate over the Munich agreement, he declared it to be an ignoble surrender to Nazi blackmail. Because of his broad and versatile experience as First Lord of the Admiralty (1911–1915), minister of munitions (1917–1918), minister of war and air (1918–1921), and as a battalion commander in France (1915–1917), he was uniquely qualified to lead Britain in this critical moment.

Churchill, whose mother was American, always urged a close association with the

United States. He had also anticipated a deal between Hitler and Stalin but continued to advocate a British-Soviet alliance against Nazi Germany should the transient partnership between Moscow and Berlin fall apart. For these reasons he did not actively oppose the acquisition by Russia of eastern Poland and of the naval base of Hangoe, or of islands in the Finnish Gulf, because he believed that such Soviet territorial acquisitions tended to sharpen the Russo-German antagonism and render an open conflict more likely. For him the alleged aid to Finland was merely a pretext for seizure of the Swedish iron ore mines.[8]

Five days after his appointment Churchill was already in Paris to confer with the new French premier, Paul Reynaud. When Churchill arrived, Paris was in the throes of panic. Clerks were burning the secret files of the foreign ministry. Reynaud told Churchill about the critical situation at the front; there was almost nothing, he said, to stop the Germans from swooping down on Paris. "Where is your strategic reserve?" Churchill asked Gamelin. "There is none," the latter answered, with a shrug.

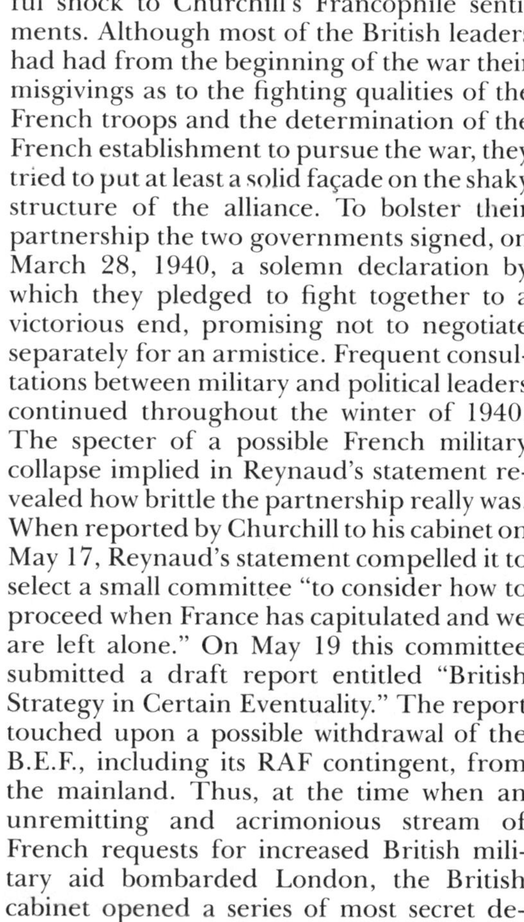

Reynaud's frank admission dealt a powerful shock to Churchill's Francophile sentiments. Although most of the British leaders had had from the beginning of the war their misgivings as to the fighting qualities of the French troops and the determination of the French establishment to pursue the war, they tried to put at least a solid façade on the shaky structure of the alliance. To bolster their partnership the two governments signed, on March 28, 1940, a solemn declaration by which they pledged to fight together to a victorious end, promising not to negotiate separately for an armistice. Frequent consultations between military and political leaders continued throughout the winter of 1940. The specter of a possible French military collapse implied in Reynaud's statement revealed how brittle the partnership really was. When reported by Churchill to his cabinet on May 17, Reynaud's statement compelled it to select a small committee "to consider how to proceed when France has capitulated and we are left alone." On May 19 this committee submitted a draft report entitled "British Strategy in Certain Eventuality." The report touched upon a possible withdrawal of the B.E.F., including its RAF contingent, from the mainland. Thus, at the time when an unremitting and acrimonious stream of French requests for increased British military aid bombarded London, the British cabinet opened a series of most secret de-

[8]For Churchill's perspective on the Battle of France, see the second volume of his memoirs, *Their Finest Hour,* pp. 27–241.

Winston S. Churchill, in an RAF uniform, surrounded by two of his close coworkers: Anthony Eden, War Minister (May–December 1940) and Foreign Secretary (December 1940–July 1945) and Sir Charles Portal, Marshal of the RAF and Chief of Air Staff (October 1940–December 1945). National Archives

bates on how to extricate its land and air contingents from a rapidly deteriorating war battlefield situation on the Continent.

NEW FRENCH LEADERSHIP AND THE BRITISH EXPEDITIONARY FORCE

The rapid race of German tanks to the Channel and the French inability to cope with them finally discredited Gamelin's leadership. On May 19 he was dismissed and replaced by General Maxime Weygand, a former Chief of Staff of Marshal Foch. Weygand, then seventy-three years old, was recalled from his post in Syria as commander of the Allied forces in the Near East and made commander in chief of all French armed forces.[9] As a former aid to Marshal Foch, he was supposed to possess the old marshal's secret. His task was to restore the rapidly deteriorating situation at the front. Weygand, however, was in the position of a doctor belatedly called to the bedside of a mortally wounded patient.

The French political establishment was now in a state of panic. On May 19, when German troops were entering Brussels, Paul Reynaud reconstructed his cabinet. He took over the ministry of defense and appointed the eighty-five-year-old hero of Verdun, Marshal Philipe Pétain, as vice-premier. Following the reshuffle, Reynaud made a fiery speech summoning his countrymen to a "sacred union" of all the patriotic forces. The same day, the notables of the officially agnostic and anticlerical Third Republic went to the cathedral of Notre Dame to pray for the miracle of a French victory.

Weygand's best hope of stabilizing the rapidly deteriorating situation at the front was to cut the Abbéville pocket by launching a vigorous counteroffensive. It would come from two directions: from the north, mainly from the region of Arras in Flanders where the bulk of the B.E.F. was operating, and from the south, from behind the Somme and Aisne, where there were elements of three French armies, the Sixth, the Seventh, and the Tenth. An attempt of this sort was undertaken on May 21, but two factors prevented its successful execution. First of all, the French troops, demoralized by a series of almost continuous setbacks, were rapidly losing not only their fighting spirit but even their coherence. The second factor was the inability of the B.E.F. to carry out the difficult undertaking alone.

General Gort's eventual decision as commander of the B.E.F. was governed by the situation in which his troops found themselves as a result of the German successes. On May 16—that is, the day after the Dutch collapse—advance units of the B.E.F. reached the region of Brussels. Before the British troops arrived at their planned positions on the Scheldt, however, the line had already been forced by the German panzers. At the same time, British communications had been cut off from the south by Guderian's march toward the Channel. In this crisis Lord Gort had two options. He could either counterattack southward to cut off the German wedge or he could continue delaying the relentless westward pressure of the enemy through Flanders. On May 20 Churchill, still eager to prove his loyalty to the French allies, ordered Gort to coordinate his thrust against the Abbéville pocket in accordance with Weygand's directives. But by then the situation in Flanders was already at variance with the information available to the British cabinet. Gort tried to carry out the order, but the obstacles were formidable. Shortages of food, fuel, and ammunition, combined with a mounting enemy threat to the remaining communications with the Channel ports, forced Gort to make a decision independent of the directives of London.

On May 25 Gort rejected another attempt at a hopeless joint Franco-British counter stroke. Instead, he continued his march straight toward Dunkirk as the last safe port of embarkation. On the same day, May 25,

[9]For Weygand's background see P. C. I. Bankwitz, *Maxime Weygand and Civil-Military Relations in Modern France* (Cambridge: Harvard University Press, 1967).

the King of the Belgians, Leopold III, aware of the British retreat toward Dunkirk, informed London and Paris that his country, most of which had already been overrun by the enemy, had soon to start negotiations for surrender.

Meanwhile, London's cabinet had prepared plans for the evacuation of the B.E.F. On May 24 Churchill came to believe that should the B.E.F. be destroyed, his country would be in a hopeless situation. With only one or two reserve divisions left, the British would not be able to resist any serious attempt at a German invasion of their shores. Churchill knew that while the RAF was losing in France an average of twenty-five fighters a day, British industries were able to produce only four per day. The loss of trained pilots was even more serious than that of aircraft. Britain's future was in extreme danger.

On May 28 King Leopold III of Belgium capitulated, thus freeing a large body of the German Army Group North to intervene more massively in the Battle of France. This strengthened Lord Gort's resolve to reach Dunkirk as quickly as possible, and it also sped up the Admiralty's preparations for the evacuation of the B.E.F. From May 28 the British exodus became a race to the sea to save the decimated ranks of the B.E.F.

When General Weygand was informed of the British decision, he was furious. He protested against it formally and denounced it as a breach of the alliance committed at a crucial moment of the battle. The British contribution amounted to only 10 percent of the French land forces, he argued, and this number of troops was almost six times smaller than the British contingent during World War I. At the same time Weygand charged the British with keeping their air forces at home for the defense of their island-fortress. To withdraw even their puny contingent from battle now, he said, amounted to more than a breach of the alliance. This was dishonorable. Faced with the fiendish Belgian capitulation and the British evacuation, as well as with mounting chaos in his own ranks, Weygand presented the French premier, Paul Reynaud, a memorandum urging him to open armistice negotiations.

THE EVACUATION OF DUNKIRK

The exodus of the B.E.F. from Dunkirk, which took place from May 27 to June 4, benefited from a variety of favorable factors. When the vanguards of the B.E.F. were approaching the Channel on May 24 and the bulk of the British forces were fighting the superior German panzers, Hitler gave an order to hold further advance. This provided Gort with an unexpected and most welcome breathing spell that allowed him to prepare the escape. The reasons for Hitler's decision are still shrouded in mystery. One factor may have been his admiration for the British Empire, which he was willing to preserve provided the British would accept his dominant position and restore the former German colonies. Total destruction of the B.E.F., Hitler may have believed, would have been too humiliating and hence an obstacle to future negotiations. Another factor, perhaps, was Hitler's experience in World War I. Hitler had fought in that war in the marshy fields of Flanders; he feared that it would be too dangerous to throw Guderian's heavy tanks into the boggy ground. He still remembered the French counteroffensive of 1914. He still did not trust in his luck and still feared a major counterattack by some sixty French divisions from behind the Somme. Another element in Hitler's decision was Goering's advice not to waste precious armor on a job that could be done more quickly and efficiently by the Luftwaffe.[10]

Whatever the ultimate motives of Hitler's order to stop Guderian's advance, the B.E.F. got two days of grace. When Hitler's order was rescinded, the weather became stormy. Vicious winds were followed by dense fog, thus preventing the Luftwaffe from attack-

[10]Hitler's reasoning is explained in Liddell Hart, ed., *German Generals Talk*, pp. 134–36.

French and British POWs captured by the Germans at Abbéville. National Archives

ing effectively the large masses of Allied soldiers rushing into the compact pocket around Dunkirk to wait for evacuation. Out of nine days, only two and a half were fully suitable for aerial operations. During those short intervals the Luftwaffe had to cope with the spirited intervention of massive sorties by RAF fighters operating from southern England. Hurricanes and Spitfires shot down 156 German planes, while losing about 100 of their own aircraft.

The evacuation was assigned to the Home Fleet, helped by the civilian population. Thousands of private craft and pleasure boats responded to the call and sailed to Dunkirk to rescue their soldiers. French and Belgian vessels also cooperated. Intermittent but fierce battles raged overhead. Artillery barrages provided by the Royal Navy gave some respite to the ground forces. British, Belgian, and French troops constantly streamed into the Dunkirk pocket. There was little protection on the open beaches. British and French infantrymen often turned their rifles upon the low-flying enemy planes. The ugly tensions brewed brutal scenes between the Allied soldiers for places in the waiting lines. At first the Royal Navy gave priority to the B.E.F. while neglecting the French and other Allied soldiers. To assuage the raging Weygand, Churchill issued an order on June 1 for a one-by-one evacuation of British and French soldiers and promised to send two divisions, then hastily assembling in Britain, to reinforce French defenses. One British and one Canadian division were indeed sent back to the Continent, but they too had to be evacuated because of the hopeless situation. Yet French troops in the Dunkirk area fought well; so did those in the garrison at Lille, which

June 1940: The evacuation of the Allied forces from France to Britain. The author of this book stands in the upper right hand corner and watches another transport ship, hit by a German torpedo and sinking. Author's Private Collection

pinned down several German divisions, gaining time for the withdrawal of the B.E.F.[11]

Of the 338,000 troops eventually rescued from the beaches, almost 190,000 were British and 109,000 French, with the remainder composed of various nationalities: Belgians, Dutch, and so on. Finally, the Germans overwhelmed the Dunkirk defenses on June 4. Manned largely by French troops, Dunkirk yielded some 60,000 prisoners, practically all of them French. The material cost of the Dunkirk evacuation was high. The B.E.F. had abandoned all its heavy equipment; 75 percent of the British soldiers returned home with their rifles only. The Royal Navy and the British Merchant Marine lost nearly 200 vessels of all kinds, including 6 destroyers sunk and 19 seriously damaged. The Luftwaffe had also sunk 7 French destroyers and torpedo boats.

The Dunkirk operation, which involved much imaginative improvisation, was glamorized by Churchill's fiery eloquence and became something of a national myth. The myth played its role in bolstering the British morale in the dark days between the French disaster and the upsurge of determination to resist Hitler at any cost.[12]

In retrospect the British withdrawal was a fully justified and farsighted move, but it was not then regarded as such by the French High Command and the French public at large. They condemned the evacuation as another deliberate treachery of "perfidious Albion," determined to fight the war "to the last Frenchman." A latent Anglophobia surfaced and deepened the mounting undercurrent of French resignation and outright defeatism. A countermyth was created, that of the downfall of France caused mainly by British betrayal. Hitler considered the removal of the British from the Continent as a great triumph. On June 2, the day the Dunkirk perimeter fell, he decreed that bells throughout the Reich should toll for three days to celebrate his victory in "the greatest battle of world history."

FRANCE'S DEFENSES FAIL

Weygand's objective was now to rally the army to stop the Germans along the Somme and Aisne and then to counterattack. He had ordered the French engineers to blow up all bridges across both rivers, preserving only two of them in view of the planned counteroffensive. These two bridges seemed to be of no use to the German armored forces. Each had a single line of railway tracks laid along two narrow embankments, running for about a mile through marshy meadows, a ground tricky for tanks. Both bridges also appeared to be well-covered by the French artillery massed on the southern banks of the Somme. Yet on June 5 General Rommel's light division managed to capture both bridges by surprise before dawn. German engineers promptly pulled up the rails, allowing Rommel to drive his tanks across the Somme, despite French bombardment.

By the evening of June 5 Rommel's tanks had penetrated 8 miles into the hastily improvised French defenses along the Somme. By June 6 the German bridgehead had been extended to 20 miles. From this pocket Rommel's troops swept further southward and split the French Tenth Army. On the fourth day of his drive, June 8, the Germans reached the Seine, south of Rouen. The river was crossed before the French had managed to rally and reestablish their defenses. Then on June 10 Rommel's panzers switched northward and pushed again toward the Channel, which they reached that evening at Le Havre. By this daring move Rommel cut off the retreat of the left wing of the Tenth Army, some five French divisions.

While Rommel was breaking the French defenses at their central sector, the two panzer corps under Kleist, operating on the right wing, also established bridgeheads

---

[11]For a recent study, based on some 500 interviews with the surviving participants see Walter Lord, *The Miracle of Dunkirk* (New York: Viking Penguin, 1982).

[12]For the British view of the B.E.F. in France see David Fraser, *And We Shall Shock Them. The British Army in the Second World War* (London: Hodder and Stoughton, 1983), pp. 25–82; see also David Gelb, *Dunkirk . . .* (New York: Marrow, 1989).

across the Somme, at Amiens and Peronne. From these points Kleist's tanks wheeled south toward the lower reaches of the Oise and pushed toward Paris. Simultaneously, the left wing of Rundstedt's army group broke through the defenses along the Aisne on June 9. The Maginot Line had been outflanked and bypassed. Weygand's master plan to stop the enemy along the Somme and Aisne collapsed, and the heartland of France lay open like a split oyster shell.

THE FALL OF FRANCE

After the piercing of the Somme line on June 7, the disintegration of the French army had reached such proportions that a coordinated defense was no longer possible. When the Germans crossed the Seine, General Weygand warned Paris: "The final break in our defensive line may take place any moment." If that happened, he said, the final disintegration of the French army will be "only a question of time. . . . The battle of France is lost." Weygand urged his government to seek peace. When Italy declared war on France on June 10, the French government left Paris for Angers and then for Tours. Paris was declared "an open city."

The French inclination to seek a separate peace revealed a profound mistrust in the Franco-British alliance, a deep animosity hitherto kept hidden. Winston Churchill flew to Tours on June 11 in a last-minute effort to dissuade the French cabinet from seeking an armistice. At the meeting of the Allied Supreme Council on June 12, he tried to persuade the French to carry on the war from North Africa, shoulder to shoulder with the British Empire. He went so far as to propose that the two countries establish a Franco-British union. This unprecedented offer roused, however, only indignation among most of the war-weary French leaders, who regarded it merely as a trap aiming at the British control of the French fleet and their overseas possessions. To Pétain and most of his colleagues the offer of a union with Britain must have seemed either monumental arrogance or a bad joke. They refused to believe that where they had failed so utterly, the British could succeed. Pétain was heard to mutter: "To make union with England was fusion with a corpse." A last-minute appeal for help by Premier Reynaud to President Roosevelt failed to produce expected results, and the Americans' encouraging words were insufficient. At that time the United States, shackled by neutrality legislation, was far from ready for intervention in Europe.

The Germans entered Paris on June 14, with military bands marching ahead of troops. During these festivities the bulk of the Wehrmacht's Group North pushed southward and northwestward toward the Loire valley and Brittany. Group Center, headed by Guderian's panzers, raced toward Lyons and the Swiss frontier. French organized resistance had nearly crumbled everywhere, and small isolated pockets of desperate fighters were wiped out without much difficulty.

The military collapse was paralleled by a bitter political crisis. In Bordeaux, on June 16, Reynaud resigned as premier and was replaced by Marshal Pétain, who reassembled the cabinet. The next day Pétain asked for an armistice with Germany. London declared it a break of the Franco-British alliance and reluctantly came to the conclusion that Marshal Pétain's government, soon to establish itself in Vichy, had to be treated as an enemy. Accordingly, the British now became absorbed with saving intact the French navy. The fall of France was an event of stunning importance for the British government and people, destroying the alliance on which Britain's entire strategy had been based. Henceforth, the nature of the war was transformed, and the British drastically revised their policies. They could rely only on their own forces and resources.[13]

---

[13]For an analysis of the disintegration of the Anglo-French alliance see P. M. H. Bell, *A Certain Eventuality . . . Britain and the Fall of France* (Liverpool: Saxon House, 1973); and Eleanor M. Gates, *End of the Affair, The Collapse of the Anglo-French Alliance, 1939–40* (Berkeley, Los Angeles: University of California Press, 1981).

HITLER'S TRIUMPH

The armistice was to be signed with great fanfare by Hitler himself on the afternoon of June 21 at Compiègne, near Paris. Here, on November 11, 1918, Marshal Foch had dictated terms of surrender to the German delegation in his private railway car. Hitler arrived at Compiègne well ahead of time in his customary brown uniform of an S.A. trooper with the Iron Cross below his left breast pocket. Behind him was Goering in his exuberant white, gold braided uniform and holding his bejeweled marshal's baton. With Goering were General Keitel (Chief of the High Command), General Brauchitsch (commander of the army), Grand Admiral Raeder (commander of the navy), Ribbentrop (foreign minister), and Rudolf Hess (Hitler's deputy for party affairs). They were faced by the French delegation, headed by General Charles Huntziger, minister of war of the new government. An Alsatian, Huntziger spoke fluent German, one of the few French top commanders to do so. Huntziger was accompanied by his diplomatic adviser, Léon Noel, the former French ambassador to Prague and Warsaw, as well as by a group of French military and civilian experts.

The triumphant Hitler announces the establishment of his "New Order" on the Continent of Europe. National Archives

Hitler, intoxicated by his hearty triumph had stage-managed the armistice ceremony with pomp as well as meticulous vindictiveness. The German guard of honor snapped to attention but did not present arms, a gesture of contempt toward the vanquished foe. The French and the German officers exchanged formal military salutes, but there was no handshaking. Hitler gave the Nazi salute. For him it was the greatest day of his life, the day of revenge over the despised French, the moment for which he had been waiting for more than two decades.

The French had suffered the most humiliating defeat in their history, far greater than those of 1815 and 1871. Taking into account the magnitude of the German victory, the armistice terms outwardly appeared not too harsh. The northern and western parts of France, including Paris, and the entire Atlantic coast down to the Spanish border were to be occupied by German troops for the duration of the hostilities. Most of the French army was to be demobilized; the French government (soon to be established in Vichy) was to retain only a skeletal force of 100,000 men for internal security. The French navy was to be demobilized and disarmed. Some 1.5 million French POWs were to remain in German camps to the end of the war as hostages of Vichy's loyal fulfillment of the armistice terms. Soon, Alsace-Lorraine was returned to Germany.

After publication of the armistice agreement, Hitler received numerous telegrams from all over the world. One of them came from the old Emperor William II from his exile in Holland, congratulating Hitler for achieving what had eluded the Kaiser. Another telegram, the most cordial and obsequious, came from Stalin. The day after the armistice, an official Soviet communiqué stressed the importance of "good neighborly relations" between the USSR and Germany and denied rumors of Soviet troop concentration along the Russo-German frontier. It was Stalin's benevolent neutrality that had allowed Hitler to concentrate most of his forces against the Franco-British coalition.

The end of the war seemed to be at hand. A segment of the German army was demobilized, the production of ammunition was cut back, and a large part of the war industry converted to civilian production. While praising the victorious German troops for their achievements, Propaganda Minister Dr. Goebbels ended his message with the words "You have just one more battle to win, then the bells of peace will ring." The German peace, stressed Goebbels, would soon be dictated in London.

ITALIAN OPPORTUNISM

During the signing of the Franco-German armistice, hostilities between the French and Italians continued. To the last moment Hitler suspected that Mussolini would repeat the Italian's trick in World War I of bargaining with the most likely winner. Consequently, when Ribbentrop visited Rome on March 10–12, 1940, he warned that Italy must enter the conflict "now or never." During a meeting between the two dictators at the Brenner Pass on March 18, Hitler repeated the warning while adding a bait: "Once France is disposed of Italy will be mistress of the Mediterranean and England will have to make peace." If Italy did not join the Germans in the war at once, it would become "a second-rate power." Mussolini, however, again pleaded for time. He needed at least three to four months to be ready to strike in the Balkans against Greece or Yugoslavia, not against France. Thus until the spring of 1940 Italy maintained its position of benevolent neutrality toward Germany while slowly preparing for entering the conflict by 1942/43.[14]

On May 30, with the Germans already in control of Holland and Belgium, as well as a strip of northern France, Mussolini assured Hitler that he was about ready to join him. Yet the formal declaration of war was still delayed until the French army had finally been crushed. As he explained to Ciano, Italy would not enter the war unless it had "a vast mathematical certainty of winning it." What he actually needed was "a few thousand dead" to be able to claim a proper seat for Italy at the future peace conference.

Italy entered the war belatedly on June 10, yet with ambitious plans for gains; its "postbelligerency" created all sorts of problems. Although the French had accepted their crushing defeat on the part of the Germans, they were determined to oppose the Italians as best they could. Defeated in the north, the French forces of six divisions, mostly crack Alpine units, were more than a match for thirty-two Italian divisions. During two weeks of fighting, before the Franco-Italian armistice was signed in Rome on June 24, the Italians managed to advance only a few miles. The offensive, as Ciano had warned Mussolini, proved to be a "howling failure" and confirmed Bismarck's well-known saying that "the Italians have such a big appetite and such poor teeth." Hitler desired to contain Mussolini's appetite for loot. The Führer was assisted in this aim by the poor performance of the Italian army at the front. Hitler's problem was now to reduce Italy's inflated claims and shift the discussion of Mussolini's grandiose colonial aspirations to the future peace conference. Even Mussolini's efforts to get Germany's backing for Italian occupation of the entire Rhone valley, Toulon, and Marseilles were brushed aside. Hitler approved only of Italy

[14]Italy's attitude toward the war is well-referenced in the *Ciano Diaries,* pp. 235–70; see also MacGregor Knox, *Mussolini Unleashed, 1939–1941. Politics and Strategy in Fascist Italy's Last War* (Cambridge, London, and New York: Cambridge University Press, 1982).

occupying the areas which it had actually conquered, that is, those of Nice and Menton, an area hardly over 800 square kilometers.

REASONS FOR THE GERMAN SUCCESS

Within nine months of the outbreak of the war, France had been crushed, occupied, and turned into a vassal state. As General Blummentrit, Rundstedt's operations officer, noted in his diary, Hitler considered the victory over France "a miracle." Yet the catastrophe had been developing for a considerable time. It had been prepared by a long list of fundamental blunders. Before their armies clashed with the enemy, the French had bungled four opportunities. The first was that of the rearmament; the second, the reoccupation of the Rhineland; the third was the abandonment of Czechoslovakia in 1938; the fourth resulted from the French failure to help Poland. To these blunders must be added the French performance in 1940. It was not the material strength and numbers that triumphed but superior strategy, better leadership, and the higher morale of the entire Wehrmacht. Throughout the whole campaign in the west, the Allied High Command, especially the French, suffered from a mental block created by their World War I experiences and a profound inertia that they could not transcend. The gap between the old and the new school of warfare was dramatic. The experiences of the Polish and Norwegian campaigns were ignored. So was the wealth of information flowing from Enigma, much of which indicated that the Schlieffen plan had been abandoned. The glaring weakness of the Allies was their leadership; on the French side it was essentially defensive, if not outright defeatist.

A fairly good analysis of the thinking of the upper level of the French military establishment has appeared in the diaries of perhaps the most intelligent of the British military leaders, General Sir Archibald Wavell.[15] In the winter of 1935/36 he attended with fifty French senior officers an advanced strategy course held by the French army at Versailles. It was a course for the elite of the French military. What struck Wavell and two of his British colleagues was not only the age and poor physical shape of their colleagues but especially their supreme pride and self-satisfaction. By that time the British army had begun to experiment with large armored units, but the French were far behind in this respect. Nevertheless, the French officers were completely uninterested in the problem. They refused to go beyond what had been achieved by November 1918.

The low morale of many French officers and soldiers throughout the campaign was in shocking contrast with the patriotism of their fathers who had fought at the Marne and at Verdun. It was especially true of the French air force.[16] The British troops had a much higher morale and fought with courage and resilience. Their leaders, however brave and resourceful they proved to be, were also rutted in the routine of the previous war and lacked experience in mobile mechanized warfare.

---

[15]For a more extensive summary of Wavell's report see his biography by John Connell, *Wavell: Scholar and Soldier* (San Diego: Harcourt Brace Jovanovich, 1964), pp. 171–72. For a postmortem of the French campaign as seen by the chief of the British military mission in France see PRO WO 208/624. For a British retrospective view and analysis of the French disaster see Sir Edward Spears, *Assignment to Catastrophe.* For a recent reassessment of the French collapse see Albert Seaton, *The German Army 1933–45* (London: Weidenfeld and Nicolson, 1982), pp. 122–44. See also the article by Henri Michel, *La Défaite de la France* (*Septembre 1939–Juin 1940*) (Paris: PVF, 1980); and his article on the subject in *La Revue de la Deuxième Guerre Mondiale,* no. 122 (April 1981).

[16]According to the on-the-spot observations of Churchill's liaison officer, one of the striking features of the French campaign was the low morale of the French airmen; for instance, according to the list provided by Paul Reynaud to General Edward Spears the French losses up to June 1, 1940, amounted to 700 planes, of which only 300 had been destroyed in air combat, with 200 destroyed on the ground in the army zone and 200 by accident (Spears, *Assignment to Catastrophe,* Vol. II, p. 3). See also Herbert Tint, *The Decline of French Patriotism* (London: Weidenfeld and Nicolson, 1964), p. 28ff.

Unlike their opponents, the German High Command and the Wehrmacht officers and soldiers had attained a high level of efficiency and professionalism. The German cadres had been meticulously trained for lightning operations, and their training was based on an interdependence of all services. They enjoyed the advantages of large-scale military operations from the occupation of Austria and Czechoslovakia and from the Polish and Scandinavian campaigns. The units that performed most brilliantly were the armored divisions. More than anybody else they were responsible for the swift decisiveness of the victory.

French casualties during the six-week campaign amounted to 90,000 killed, over 200,000 wounded, and some 1.5 million POWs. British total casualties came to 68,111, Belgian losses amounted to 23,350, and the Dutch had lost 9,779. The German dead totaled 27,000, with 111,034 wounded. Although total French losses in the air are difficult to assess because of confusing claims, the Luftwaffe lost 1,284 aircraft, and the RAF 931, half of them fighters.

BLOOD, SWEAT, AND TEARS

With most of Poland, Scandinavia, the Low Countries, and France under his control, Hitler was at the peak of power and prestige. Within less than a year he had conquered six countries, with an aggregate of well over 100 million people, an achievement without precedent in the annals of history. By the summer of 1940 he controlled most of the continent of Europe, from the Pripet Marshes to the Pyrenees, and from Narvik beyond the Arctic Circle to the shores of the Mediterranean. Italy was his ally; so were Spain, Hungary, and Slovakia. Rumania, Bulgaria, and Yugoslavia, undermined by German economic penetration and affected to a varying degree by Nazi propaganda, were seeking to ingratiate themselves with Berlin and its "New Order."

Nazi Germany was feared by her remaining opponents and admired by a considerable number of people who worshipped success for its own sake and were mesmerized by Hitler's recent triumphs. It is difficult to describe all the shifts and turns of the remaining neutrals during the days following the fall of France. Most of them behaved like scared rabbits hypnotized by a boa constrictor. Sweden promptly departed from its original neutral posture and granted German troops limited right of passage on Swedish trains to Norway. The Swedes agreed to this on June 18, some four days before the armistice. On June 25, 1940, the president of Switzerland warned his people that they ought to "adjust themselves" to the new European realities. The Swiss government soon followed with a measure curtailing access and protection to political refugees, including Jews. Greece and Portugal were the only European countries that did maintain their pro-Allied posture in those trying days.

While Marshal Pétain was establishing his new government in Vichy, General de Gaulle was raising the banner of protest against the planned capitulation. His rise from relative obscurity was dramatic. On June 5 de Gaulle left his armored division to become under-secretary of national defense in Paul Reynaud's cabinet. When de Gaulle's effort of shoring up the sagging determination of the defeatist cabinet to continue the war from North Africa failed, he flew to Britain. In the afternoon of June 18 the world heard from London two momentous speeches. One was by Churchill, another by de Gaulle. The British prime minister who had offered his countrymen nothing but "blood, sweat, and tears," now repeated his firm resolve to stand fast:

> Upon this battle depends the survival of Christian civilization. Upon it depends our British life, and the long continuity of our institutions and our Empire. The whole fury and might of the enemy must very soon be turned on us. Hitler knows that he will have to break us in this island or lose the war. If we can stand up to him, all Europe may be free and the life of the world may move forward into broad sunlit uplands. But if we fail, then the whole world, including the United States, including all that we have known

and cared for, will sink into the abyss of a new Dark Age, made more sinister, and perhaps more protracted, by the lights of perverted science.

Let us therefore brace ourselves to our duties and so bear ourselves that if the British Empire and its Commonwealth last for a thousand years, men will still say, "This was their finest hour."

De Gaulle in his speech declared himself leader of the Free French movement, then merely a small group of people dedicated to continue the struggle alongside the British. He stressed that "France has lost only a battle," while the global war was still on, and its ultimate outcome depended on the fate of Britain. Strangely enough, his speech was made on the 125th anniversary of the Battle of Waterloo.[17] Moreover, the speech was made by a man who had shared much of his countrymen's Anglophobia and who, in his private conversations, had often called England "the coldest of all cold monsters."

Another Allied leader who refused to capitulate was General Władysław Sikorski, Prime Minister of the Polish Government in exile and commander in chief of a contingent of some 82,000 soldiers fighting alongside the French. When he learned that Marshal Pétain had approached the Germans for a ceasefire, General Sikorski declared his determination to go on fighting. On June 18 he flew to London and, after learning from Winston Churchill that Britain would continue the war, asked the British Prime Minister for help in rescuing from France as many Polish soldiers as possible. The evacuation resulted in some 22,000 Poles being transported by British and Polish ships to Britain. Together with a few thousand determined Frenchmen who initially sided with de Gaulle and a handful of Czech, Norwegian, Dutch, and Belgian soldiers, these were the only Allied troops upon whom the British could count during the first critical months of the struggle for survival.

[17]For Charles de Gaulle's story of the fall of France and the origins of his movement, see his *War Memoirs,* Vol. I, *The Call To Honour, 1940–1942* (New York: Viking Penguin, 1955), pp. 53–166. The beginnings of the Free French movement were painfully slow; out of some 109,000 French soldiers evacuated from Dunkirk, only about 2,000 decided to stay in Britain and join General de Gaulle's armed forces; the rest insisted on returning to France. The Government of Marshal Pétain declared de Gaulle a "traitor."

7

Britain's Lonely Stand

HITLER'S VIEW OF BRITAIN

Hitler's unparalleled triumphs left him a somewhat dizzy master of the European continent. Britain, he reasoned, was weak, isolated, and helpless. He dismissed the notion that Britain might continue the struggle alone after the French capitulation. The logical consequence of his triumphs, he concluded, would be a compromise peace with Britain that would confirm Germany's hegemony in Europe, while leaving the British Empire alone.

Mussolini and the French government of Marshal Pétain, as well as many leading politicians, shared this view. Throughout Europe the pain and anxiety of the preceding weeks were quickly fading, and most yearned for peace. An after-battle pacifism was on the rise in a jubilant Germany, too. The mood of triumph and relaxation was encouraged by the demobilization of thirty-five divisions. Many war industries gradually shifted to production of consumer goods.

But Hitler himself, despite his arrogance and self-confidence, was troubled. Instinctively, he felt that all his victories were inconclusive as long as the incorrigibly cocky British refused to recognize his supremacy in Europe. Oddly enough, however, Hitler remained an Anglophile. His love-hatred of Britain was one of the paradoxes of his complex personality.[1] Yet his secret admiration for and desire to befriend England were at odds with his suspicion of "treacherous Albion."

Hitler blamed the British leaders for the war. After all, he argued, he had been

[1]For a background of the problem see Walter Ansel, *Hitler Confronts England* (Chapel Hill: Univ. of North Carolina Press, 1960).

determined not to challenge British naval supremacy by rebuilding a powerful German high-seas fleet. Hoping to avoid a clash with Britain, he ignored Admiral Doenitz's repeated pleas for 300 U-boats. In 1936 Hitler had sent to London his trusted adviser, Ribbentrop, to win Britain over to his vision of the world. Hitler wanted London to accept a division of respective spheres of interest: Germany was to be the main continental power, and Britain would remain the colonial one. According to him, there was a fundamental difference between Paris and London: Whereas the French were resolved to prevent Germany from becoming any sort of great power, the British feared only that kind of Germany which could project its might overseas and thus threaten Britain's world position. Ribbentrop's task was to persuade the London Conservative politicians not to stand in the way of a German hegemony over the continent of Europe in exchange for a promise to leave the British Empire intact.

Unlike Hitler, Ribbentrop was full of scorn for Britain, which he considered a bankrupt empire. Its leaders, he argued, were weak and indecisive. Returning from London full of condescension and contempt for the British, he said more than once to his co-workers: "England, such a little gray island, lost in the seas!" Hitler's personal contacts with appeasement-minded Ambassador Henderson tended to bolster Ribbentrop's point of view. The prevalence of such views among his advisers greatly influenced Hitler. Finally, the deplorable impression made by Neville Chamberlain convinced Hitler that all British politicians were "little worms." Britain would never dare to oppose Germany on the battlefield, the Führer felt, and would continue to yield concessions, provided they could be made at the expense of others.

BRITAIN REFUSES TO YIELD

Britain's declaration of war on Germany was an unexpected shock to Hitler. Following the announcement of war, he persisted in his efforts to conciliate London. On October 6 Hitler proposed a compromise on the basis of the new status quo. When no counteroffer was forthcoming from London, he renewed his overtures through the Duke of Windsor and Sweden, guaranteeing Britain its colonial possesions.

All these gestures by Hitler were greeted by London with scornful silence, thanks largely to the firm stand of one man, Winston Churchill. Speaking in the House of Commons on June 4, he warned his listeners about a possible invasion. Churchill as prime minister left no doubt about Britain's determination to fight, even alone, to the bitter end:

> We shall fight in France. We shall fight on the seas and oceans. We shall fight with growing confidence and growing strength in the air. We shall defend our island whatever the cost may be. We shall fight on the landing grounds. We shall fight in the fields and in the streets. We shall fight in the hills. We shall never surrender!

Churchill on several occasions said to his associates that he was prepared to die in his bunker. These fighting sentiments of the prime minister were not, however, shared by all his cabinet members. His foreign secretary, Lord Halifax, viewed Churchill's speech with skepticism and told the Swedish envoy in London that British common sense would eventually prevail over the prime minister's bravado. This attitude was shared by Halifax's close co-worker, his under-secretary of state at the Foreign Office, R. A. Butler, who believed that an opportunity to make a reasonable compromise should not be missed, while the Royal Navy was still largely intact and the RAF still an instrument of national defense to be reckoned with.[2]

Despite his numerous heroic denials even

---

[2]For the secret negotiations conducted between the Allies and Germany see Maurice Murin, *Les Tentatives de paix dans la Deuxième Guerre Mondiale* (Paris: Payot, 1949) and Bernard Martin's *Friedensinitiativen und Macht-politik im Zweiten Weltkrieg, 1939–1942* (Dusseldorf: Droste Verlag, 1974), especially chaps. III and IV.

Churchill himself must have had occasional moments of hesitation about the course to be followed under the circumstances. After all, one of his favorite sayings was, "You must look at the facts, because the facts look at you." And the facts of life of the fateful summer of 1940 were grim. To most observers of the international arena in the summer of 1940, Churchill seemed like a reckless gambler, determined to continue a poker game despite his ridiculously bad cards.

Yet slim as the British resources appeared at the moment, they were not negligible. There were some premises on which Churchill could base his daring decision to continue the war. He carefully appraised three trump cards. First of all, Britain's insular position was protected by some 20 miles of the choppy Channel, a formidable antitank ditch. The still largely intact Home Fleet, as well as the bulk of the RAF, was at Britain's disposal to interdict any German landing attempts. Second, Britain still headed its Commonwealth of Nations, commanding vast resources. Britain might eventually count on help from two powers whose interests were bound to be affected by the growing ambitions of the Third Reich: the United States and Soviet Russia.

In the short run the first asset was by far the most important. To overcome the English Channel would require a most elaborate and risky operation for which Hitler did not have sufficient resources. To stage a successful invasion of Britain, the Home Fleet and the RAF had to be destroyed. The intricate preparations for the invasion of the British Isles were bound to take time and thus allow the British to mobilize their own resources, as well as those spread throughout their Commonwealth, especially its English-speaking dominions: Canada, Australia, New Zealand, South Africa, and last but not least, India. And indeed, when Britain declared war on September 3, 1939, the dominions followed suit, although their response was neither as quick, automatic, nor as wholehearted as in 1914. This was especially true of the reluctant South Africa.

Nevertheless, Britain's dominions, mandates, and other imperial possessions in the Middle East and the Mediterranean provided vital strong points to serve as alternative bases for accumulating forces to eventually launch against the Axis dominated continent of Europe. Moreover, out of sixty divisions that the British Chief of Staff planned to deploy by mid-1941, one-third would come from the dominions and India. Already by 1940/41, the Commonwealth Air Training School allowed thousands of airmen, pilots, gunners, radio operators, and observers to undergo their training in Canada, Australia, New Zealand, South Africa, and Rhodesia.[3]

In the longer run, however, Churchill's hopes were staked mainly on two factors. The first was his conviction that the United States would eventually enter into the war because of its self-interest. Second, he counted on the probability of a German-Soviet rift, sooner or later. But these were the long-range conjectures overshadowed by the immediate anxiety created by the French capitulations.

THE DESTRUCTION OF THE FRENCH NAVY

Churchill's most urgent worry centered on the still-powerful French navy, the fourth largest in the world. At the armistice this fleet was composed of seven battleships, nineteen cruisers, one operational aircraft carrier, a powerful flotilla of seventy-one destroyers, seventy-six submarines, and a host of minor craft. Commander of this force was Admiral Jean François Darlan, an ambitious man who voiced strongly anti-British sentiments, which he shared with a large segment of his officers and crew. Darlan had assured Churchill that he would never allow the French fleet to fall into German hands, but despite Churchill's urgings, he had failed to order

[3] In this respect, see David Fraser, *And We Shall Shock Them, The British Army in the Second World War* (London, Sydney, Auckland, Toronto: Hodder and Stoughton, 1983), p. 113.

his ships to sail into British or neutral ports before the armistice was signed. A few days after the French capitulation, he gave his allegiance to Marshal Pétain and accepted a position as minister of marine in the Vichy government.

Under Article 8 of the Franco-German armistice agreement, the French warships were to be disarmed and stationed at their peacetime bases. Those ships moored in northern France, at Cherbourg, Brest, and Lorient, were in the occupied zone. The Germans, while pledging not to seize the French warships, reserved the right to use them for coastal surveillance and mine-sweeping operations. These were dangerous clauses. Could Hitler, who had broken all his previous pledges, be trusted in this case? The temptation to seize a powerful naval force that was within his reach was overwhelming. It was true that Admiral Darlan had issued an order than no French ship should be allowed to be captured intact and should be scuttled rather than surrendered. But the elasticity of Article 8 provided a variety of ways to allow the Germans and the Italians to seize the French ships; for instance, a sudden attack by Axis parachutists on the main Atlantic German controlled naval base at Brest could not be excluded.

After the failure of his offer of a Franco-British union, Churchill made an effort to persuade the government of Marshal Pétain to move to Algeria (at that time legally a part of metropolitan France). From there the French could continue the war with the aid of their overseas possessions and Britain's support. Following the rejection of this scheme, Churchill, essentially a Francophile, decided, with heavy heart, upon a most radical step. On June 27, 1940, only five days after the Franco-German armistice, the British cabinet ordered that the French ships based at the Mers-el-Kébir, near Oran, in Algeria, must be prevented from returning to their home port at Toulon. Darlan's personality, his bitterly anti-British attitude, as well as the ambivalent terms of the armistice pertaining to the French fleet, determined Churchill's actions. Should the French fleet fall into the hands of the Axis and join the German and Italian fleets, such a combination of naval forces would put the Royal Navy, spread thinly all over the world, in a most critical position.[4]

Fortunately for Britain, two of six French battleships were in ports under British control, but two battleships and two battle cruisers were anchored at the Mers-el-Kébir naval base and, after the armistice, not suspecting any attack, least of all on the part of the British. On June 28 Vice Admiral Sir James Somerville was given command of a strong task force of one aircraft carrier (*Ark Royal*), two battleships (*Valiant* and *Resolution*), and a battle cruiser (*Hood*) with orders either to force surrender of the French squadron at Oran or to destroy it. On July 3 all the French ships at anchor at Portsmouth and Plymouth were taken by Britain. That same day the French commander of the Mers-el-Kébir base, Admiral Marcel Gensoul, was confronted by Admiral Sommerville with two options: join the British with his squadron and allow his ships to be demilitarized at a British port, or scuttle his ships where they lay.

Admiral Gensoul proudly rejected the ultimatum and ordered his ships to be ready for action. The British task force replied by opening fire. After several salvos lasting some fifteen minutes, one French battleship

---

[4]For the story of the French fleet after the armistice see Raymond de Belot, *The Struggle for the Mediterranean, 1939–1945* (Princeton, N.J.: Princeton Univ. Press, 1951), pp. 3–32; and Churchill's *Their Finest Hour*, pp. 224–241. Unlike the army, the French naval service was composed almost entirely of regular, professional personnel commanded by a largely conservative officers corps; it was close-knit team, traditionally jealous of the more modern and progressive Royal Navy, so much superior in strength and efficiency. The persistence of these sentiments was public knowledge. For instance, Admiral Darlan did nothing to mitigate these feelings; quite the contrary, he stimulated them, even publicly boasting that one of his ancestors fought the Royal Navy at the battle of Trafalgar in 1805. In some cases French naval officers refused to speak in English to the British liaison officers. The coldly condescending attitude of the Royal Navy personnel toward their French counterparts did not help the Franco-British relations either.

(*Dunkirk*) was blown up, another (*Provence*) was beached, and one battle cruiser was severly damaged. Another battle cruiser (*Strasbourg*) managed to escape to Toulon. Five days later on July 8, British torpedoes immobilized another French battleship (*Richelieu*) lying at anchor at Dakar in West Africa. The French naval task force in Alexandria, Egypt, was interned without bloodshed. Thus, the core of the French fleet had been rendered useless to the Axis.

The British blows and peaceful seizures that had destroyed nearly one-third of the French fleet resulted in sharp diplomatic protests by the Vichy government and vitriolic accusations against "perfidious Albion" by both the French and the German mass media. Moreover, a wave of indignation rolled over France, both occupied and unoccupied zones. The Vichy government, especially its vice premier, Pierre Laval, even contemplated declaring war on Britain. This step was vetoed by Marshal Pétain, and the French limited themselves to a few rather ineffective air raids on Gibraltar.

The German Threat and British Defenses

The preventive crippling of the fourth most powerful fleet in the world reduced one of the major threats to Britain's survival. There were many more of them, however. Among others, there was the need to protect the British Isles against invasion and assure their communication lines and sources of supply. Then, of course, Italian entry into the war threatened Britain's position in the Mediterranean and the Middle East.

As early as the beginning of June, the possibility of invasion began to affect the British air and naval dispositions. Almost immediately after the fall of France, ominous preparations began to be made in northern France to launch operations against Britain. From newly acquired French airfields along the Channel, the Germans could now harass not only maritime traffic but also easily bomb military installations in southern England. Most of the British Expeditionary Force was back home, but without its heavy equipment; all its tanks and artillery had been abandoned. They were a "naked army." It would be some time before they could be re-equipped and reshaped into full fighting trim. Meanwhile, there were hardly two battle-ready infantry divisions in Britain and only 270 tanks!

To remedy, at least temporarily, the desperate situation, local militia, soon to be called the Home Guard, were hastily organized. The chief of the Imperial General Staff, General Ironside, believed that the army would put up a stout initial resistance behind the hastily fixed beach defenses. But it seemed doubtful whether any position could be held for long against a determined enemy attack, especially if supported by massed armor. Moreover, Ironside realized that the invader could not be destroyed effectively without a heavy counterattack by large mobile reserves. Yet such a counteraction could not be expected from the few ill-equipped British divisions. The best remedy would be to prevent the enemy from reaching the British shores at all. The still powerful Home Fleet and the RAF seemed like the only instruments capable of preventing any enemy landing.

The defection of France altered overnight the ability of the Home Fleet in the waters around the British Isles to defend the extensive shoreline. With the Germans holding the northern and western coasts of France from Dunkirk to the Spanish frontier, profound changes in the deployment of naval forces had to be made. British strategy in the years between 1914 and 1918 and at the beginning of World War II was to keep the enemy away from the French Channel ports. This had been the main task of the B.E.F., with the Home Fleet and the RAF behind it. After the French collapse, this strategy had to be reshaped.[5]

By August–September of 1940 the Germans had established their submarine bases on the Atlantic coast within a few hundred

[5] In this respect see Basil Collier, *The Defence of the United Kingdom* (London: H.M.S.O., 1957).

miles of the main British trade routes. From Le Havre, Brest, Lorient, St. Nazaire, and Bordeaux the German craft could even interdict Channel communications. This threat meant also that a much higher proportion of their submarines could be available for attacking Atlantic shipping. Moreover, the enemy could base its surface ships and U-boats in ports so placed that the British fleet in Scapa Flow was prevented from intercepting them while they were returning from their operations. By mid-June the English Channel could no longer be used except for a trickle of coasting traffic because of German mines, motor torpedo boats, and the presence of the Luftwaffe. The Germans had also been prompt in mounting radar-controlled long-range guns covering the Straits of Dover. Though British radar countermeasures eventually did much to reduce their effectiveness, the passage of the straits was hazardous for some time. The Channel was thus barred to overseas traffic, and the waters south of Ireland were also closed to shipping.

With no British bases in southern Ireland, it was too hazardous to pass even the South Atlantic and Mediterranean trade through these areas. If British forces had the use of a harbor in southwest Ireland, the position would have been much more favorable. But the mood of the great majority of the Irish people, supported by their brethren in the United States, ruled out such an option.

Thus, by mid-1940 vast distances were added to British trade routes. The minister of war transport estimated that the average round-trip time for ships carrying goods to Great Britain was about 90 days before France fell and 122 days thereafter. When Italy declared war and closed the direct Mediterranean route to merchant shipping, convoys heading from Suez had to steam 13,000 miles instead of the usual 5,000 miles.[6]

Already strained, the merchant marine and the Royal Navy had also to protect convoys with desperately scarce destroyers. Even in June of 1940 numerous British destroyers and corvettes were taken off their convoy duties to stand guard against an invasion threatening across the Channel.

Throughout the summer the waters of the western approaches and the British Isles were adrift with the rafts and lifeboats of merchantmen torpedoed by the U-boats, and the Royal Navy could do little to stop the slaughter in the Atlantic. On August 15 Hitler proclaimed a "total blockade of the waters around Britain," calling on neutral countries to keep their ships out of this "war zone." Immediately the sinkings rocketed, to peak in the final week of August 1940 at 110,000 tons, the most successful single week of the war for the U-boats. From July to October 1940, when the Admiralty was obliged to concentrate the bulk of its destroyers on antiinvasion tasks, the U-boats destroyed 217 merchant ships. Only two U-boats were sunk between July and October.

From the beginning Britain suffered from a shortage of the work horses of any fleet: destroyers. At the end of World War I the Royal Navy had 433 destroyers. In 1939 Great Britain began the war with 201 destroyers, many of them antiquated and thinly spread over the seven seas of the world. One hundred fifteen destroyers, sloops, and corvettes were based in home waters and another thirty-three were with the Mediterranean squadron. During the Norwegian campaign seven destroyers were sunk and another four severely damaged. During the evacuation of Dunkirk six more destroyers were sunk and nineteen damaged. The increased need to protect convoys made the demand for more destroyers one of Britain's highest priorities.

[6]On the eve of the war, the merchant marine was Britain's weakest point in its national defense. In September 1939 it had less than 18 million tons of merchant shipping. By June of 1944 the tonnage increased to 26 million tons because of the fact that most of the Norwegian and Polish and a part of the Belgian, Dutch, and French merchant ships went over to the British side. For the role played by the British merchant marine, see C. B. A. Behrens, *Merchant Shipping and the Demands of War* (London: H.M.S.O., 1955).

In his first telegram as prime minister to President Roosevelt on May 15, 1940, Winston Churchill asked for the loan of forty to fifty older destroyers to "bridge the gap" until a "large new construction" would supply them. In reply President Roosevelt requested a pledge that the British fleet would in no circumstances be handed over to the Germans. With this guarantee offered in August, the United States soon exchanged fifty World War I destroyers for a ninety-nine-year lease of British bases in Newfoundland, Bermuda, the Bahamas, Jamaica, Antigua, St. Lucia, Trinidad, and British Guiana. Churchill's diplomacy was skillful: He not only obtained the ships vital for Britain's defense, but he committed Washington to undercut its principles of neutrality in a challenge to the Axis.

The loan of the United States destroyers helped Britain but it was only a stopgap measure. There was a lot of trouble with the antiquated destroyers, which had to be refitted at considerable expense, but any vessel that could shoot and drop depth charges was worth its weight in gold during the strain of the Battle of the Atlantic in 1940 and 1941. Moreover, there were some 250,000 spare rifles; besides this there was nothing else the United States could send to Britain. At that time the U.S. Army had merely 200 tanks, and the Army Air Force had only 49 flying fortresses apart from a handful in the Philippines and at Hawaii, and 160 modern fighter planes.[7] Given the isolationist mood prevailing in the United States between 1937 and 1939, there was little that President Roosevelt could have done over and above what he actually did.

Reichsmarshall Goering talks to the Luftwaffe crews after their return from the great raid over Britain, August 12, 1940. National Archives

Another serious threat to Britain's security in the summer of 1940 resulted from the sudden bolstering of German aerial strength. With the Luftwaffe swarming in France, the English and Bristol Channel ports were subject to air attack. The usefulness of the main English dockyards, Portsmouth and Plymouth, was now much restricted. The specter of invasion had been in the minds of the British leaders since the fall of France, but it was not until July and August, when the Germans had firmly established their airfields in northern France, that the danger of landing became a palpable menace. London then feared that adequate shipping for an invasion was available to the enemy and that a vast number of barges from the Rhine and other inland waterways could be adapted to land troops. Some of these barges could be provided with self-propulsion and used to reach points from Devonshire to East Anglia.

---

[7] For the story of the destroyers against bases deal see Philip Goodhart, *Fifty Ships That Saved the World: The Foundation of the Anglo-American Alliance* (London: Heinemann, 1965); see also Churchill, *Their Finest Hour,* pp. 398–416. For recent documentation of the relationship between the two key Western leaders, see *Churchill & Roosevelt: The Complete Correspondence,* 3 vols.: *Alliance Emerging, Alliance Forged, Alliance Declining,* edited with commentary by Warren F. Kimball (Princeton, N.J.: Princeton University Press, 1984).

On the basis of Goering's assurances that the Luftwaffe could smash the RAF, Hitler formulated his directives for an invasion on June 30. Even then, however, he appeared hesitant and referred to the actual invasion as a measure to be undertaken not "for the purpose of overthrowing England militarily . . . but only to deal the death stroke, if still necessary."

After consulting his three service chiefs, Hitler decided on July 2 that the invasion was possible, provided that air superiority could be attained and certain other necessary conditions fulfilled. As yet, however, he made clear that "the plan to invade England has not taken any definite shape." Only two weeks later, on July 16, when all peace overtures had failed, he issued another of his curiously diffident directives: "I have decided to prepare a landing operation against England, and, if necessary, carry it out." The qualification "if necessary" indicated that he had not yet lost all hope for a compromise peace. The goal of the amphibious operation, called Sealion, was the elimination of Britain as a base from which war against Germany could be continued, before the end of September 1940.[8]

INVASION PLANS AND THE BALANCE OF FORCES

The strategic views of the three German services were divergent. Those of the *Kriegsmarine* were determined by Grand Admiral Erich Raeder. When it came to drawing up the more detailed invasion plans, Raeder quailed at the hazards of such an improvised operation without adequate amphibious capabilities and with a pitifully weak surface naval force.[9] The Norway gamble had cut the *Kriegsmarine* by half. Consequently, its role in the planned invasion was bound to be merely secondary. The navy's role had to be limited to assembling the necessary amount of landing craft, training their crews together with the army, and protecting them against the Royal Navy during the passage across the Channel. Raeder argued that "Operation Sealion" should be launched only as a last resort. He made it clear to Hitler that the undertaking might succeed only if the Luftwaffe had completely crushed the Royal Air Force.

Air mastery was an absolute precondition of success for the invasion, and the brunt of Sealion was to be borne by the Luftwaffe. Its task was to destroy the RAF, thus making the landing of at least twelve divisions possible. For this purpose the Germans assembled some 1.2 million tons of shipping, while massing the Second, Third, and Fifth air fleets of the Luftwaffe on the airstrips of France, the Low Countries, and Norway. The three air fleets together numbered approximately 2,669 aircraft, 1,800 of which were bombers.

The whole operation hinged on Goering's promise to destroy the defenses of southern England in some four weeks of continuous attacks. The Luftwaffe was to carry out its task of annihilating the British aerial defenses by, first, bombing all command posts, airfields, and radar stations in southern England so as to render them inoperative and, second, drawing as many RAF fighters as possible into dogfights so as to destroy them in the air.

Goering trusted that the superior numbers of his aircraft, as well as the experience of his pilots, would guarantee an easy triumph. With the destruction of Britain's air defenses accomplished, there would be little to oppose the landing of the German ground forces. The attacks would so shatter British morale, argued Goering, and create such havoc in the British supply and communication systems that the German landing would be easy.

This was an ambitious plan. But one has to bear in mind that in July and August of

---

[8]For the full text of the directive of July 16, 1940, see H. R. Trevor-Roper, ed., *Blitzkrieg to Defeat,* pp. 33–37.

[9]After the war Raeder admitted that, had he foreseen the acceleration of Hitler's ambitions, a naval program that put much stronger emphasis on submarines might have been sounder. For the German naval perspectives see Admiral Erich Raeder, *My Life* (New York: Arno Press, 1980), pp. 300 ff.

The Battle of Britain, July - December 1940

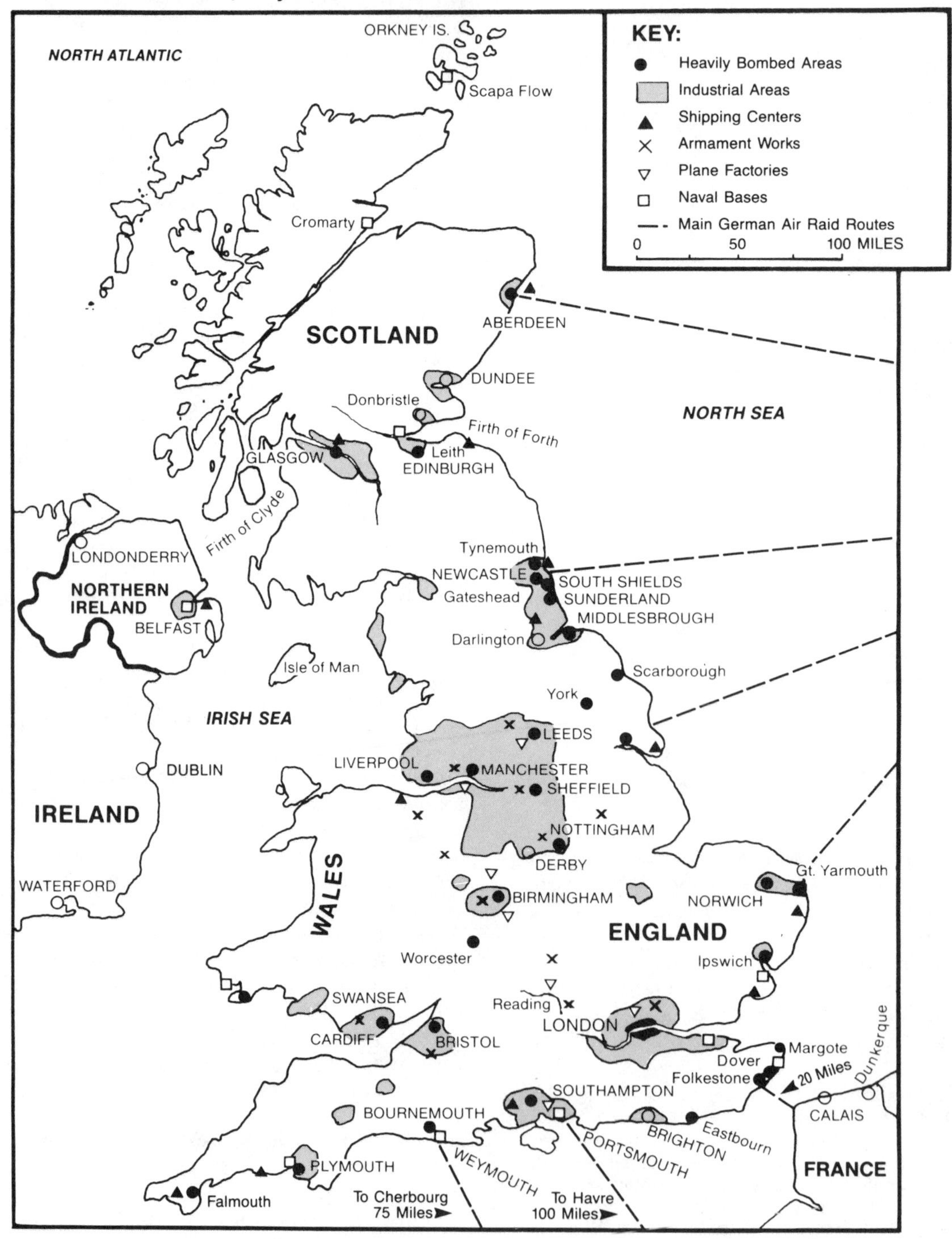

1940 British defenses were in a sorry state. In June 1940 there were only 1,204 heavy and 581 light antiaircraft guns in Britain, although the table of organization called for 2,232 of the heavy and 1,860 of the lighter variety. During the battles on the Continent all tanks and nearly 1,000 aircraft had been lost. By the beginning of August the RAF Fighter Command consisted of 1,434 pilots and 708 aircraft. Only about half of them were up-to-date Hurricanes and Spitfires, comparable to the Messerschmitt 109 or 110 fighters.

Yet the RAF had numerous basic advantages. Although the Germans had more aircraft and a greater reservoir of pilots, their reserves of planes were smaller. A strict and well-planned mobilization of all their resources by the summer of 1940 allowed the British to increase their aircraft production 250 percent within one year. German industries could produce only about 3,000 fighters per year while British output exceeded 4,500. Moreover, operating from its home bases, the RAF enjoyed numerous other advantages. Among them were two kinds of warning systems. One resulted from an efficient utilization of Enigma, through the "Ultra Secret" intelligence net. With prompt decoding of German radio messages by the Ultra people located in Bletchley Park, near London, the British leaders were warned about the time, strength, and direction of the intended Luftwaffe attacks. The second advantage was a superior integration of signals, ground control, and command organized well in advance by the RAF. The centerpiece of this system was radio detection and ranging, or radar for short. Radar reflected high-frequency radio impulses on a large cathode tube, not unlike our TV screens.

The German side also had radar facilities, but these were less advanced and less astutely used by the Luftwaffe.[10] During the late 1930s the Luftwaffe remained confident in its rapid numerical expansion and had ignored its own radar equipment. But the British, through growing fear of German bombers, not only improved their radar but by 1937 had installed a chain of early-warning stations along the shores of England.

By June of 1940 there were at least fifty-one such stations. By watching the position of radio echoes on the screen, trained operators could determine the location, direction, and height of any aircraft within the range of the radio impulses. As soon as a "blip" would appear on a radar screen, its operator would report it to the RAF ground control HQ. As a result of this, day and night, regardless of clouds, fog, or rain, the British radar posts could pick up any incoming plane at distances ranging from 50 to 120 miles, depending on the weather conditions. The radar system was connected with the two principal components of the RAF: its Fighter Command and Bomber Command. Thus, the whole ground control and command system of Britain depended on the work of "Ultra," on the one hand, and on the proper functioning of the early-warning systems, on the other.

Nevertheless, Goering also had some ingenious inventions up his sleeve. The most remarkable of them was a system of intersecting radio beams designed to locate targets for the Luftwaffe planes even in darkness and foul weather. The device was known as "Crooked Legs." Thanks to Enigma, however, the system was discovered as early as June 21, 1940, and the RAF managed to frustrate it by jamming the German radio waves. This confused the Luftwaffe pilots about their proper targets and, in fact, made the device live up to its name.

The Fighter Command, together with antiaircraft artillery and barrage balloons, was responsible for the aerial defense of the British Isles; the Bomber Command was in charge of the offensive operations. The commander of the former, Air Chief Marshal Sir Hugh Dowding, had at his disposal four fighter groups located in southern and south-eastern England. From his GHQ near

[10]For various technological aspects of the air war see R. V. Jones, *The Wizard War: British Scientific Intelligence, 1939–1945* (New York: Coward, McCann, 1978).

London, combining the Ultra bulletins with the radar reports, he could more easily decide where and how many of his craft to send skyward. At his underground GHQ, as well as at each of the four group HQs, the command posts contained gigantic color maps on which the location of all air units, friendly or enemy, could be plotted. Control officers on duty kept a constant eye on these maps and could anticipate each move fairly accurately to meet enemy threats. This effective defense system by the summer and autumn of 1940 placed the RAF far ahead of its opponent.

THE BATTLE OF BRITAIN

By mid-July of 1940, Hitler concluded that Britain would not surrender. After some sporadic air raids on Britain's defenses mostly for reconnaissance, Hitler decided on July 16 to launch his all out offensive. Goering ordered the launching of the long prepared "Operation Eagle" on August 8 by issuing his short order of the day: "From Reichs-marshal Goering to all units of Luftwaffe Two, Three, and Five. . . . Within a short period you will wipe the British Air Force from the sky. Heil Hitler!"

As if to mock his order, for the next three days the weather was so bad that no significant air operation took place. The first attack of any scale took place only on August 12. Aware of the German ploy of provoking as many RAF planes as possible into unequal air fights, Lord Dowding committed only just as many fighters as were needed to spread and confuse the attackers and make precision bombing difficult. The scattered enemy bombers presented easier targets to the RAF fighters. The Hurricanes and Spitfires, although slower than the enemy fighters, were more heavily armed and more maneuverable. Moreover, operating from home bases they could land on their own airfields and be instantly rearmed and refueled. The RAF had also carefully planned a dispersion of its squadrons away from permanent asphalt or concrete runways to improvised ones. Protected by sandbag banks and camouflage nets they were more difficult to spot by the enemy reconnaissance planes and bombers. And too, the holes in the turf were much easier to repair than those in the asphalt.

From the first, German losses were heavier than those of the RAF. Spurred by the toughness of the resistance, Goering increased his attacks. The most intense period of what came to be called the Battle of Britain was between August 24 and September 24. From August 24, an average of a thousand planes a day were thrown against southern England, damaging more and more airfields and disrupting the ground control and communication network. By the end of August the defenses of southern England were badly strained by the nearly constant raids of superior forces. Some RAF Squadrons were in the air five, six, or even ten times in a day.

By the beginning of September the attrition of skilled pilots, gunners, and observers became unacceptable. Between August 24 and September 6 the Fighter Command lost 103 pilots killed and 128 seriously wounded. Out of a total pool of about a thousand pilots, nearly a quarter had been lost. At the same time 466 Spitfires and Hurricanes were either destroyed or heavily damaged. Based on the average rate of attrition, the remaining reserve amounted to eleven days' supply. It was obvious that, should such attacks be continued another week or two with the same intensity, Britain would be unable to take any more.

The loss of planes could be countered by the rapidly mounting British aircraft output, but the loss of highly trained personnel was impossible to cure. The emergency situation required desperate measures. At the start of September nearly all the available pilots had been sent to the front-line fighter squadrons. Some of the pilots had incomplete training, leaving no more than 5 percent of able-bodied flying personnel with "convalescing squadrons." Even the Bomber and Coastal commands, as well as the Naval Air Army, had to lend their pilots to the

A "Spitfire" makes a pass at a Dornier, south of London. National Archives

hard-pressed Fighter Command. A crisis was reached at the end of August and gloom fell over Britain's leaders.

In this predicament, an incident caused by the frustration of the "Crooked Legs" beams by the RAF defenses resulted in a dramatic change of the situation. On the night of August 24/25, some of the massive German bomber formations lost their bearings and unloaded their bombs not on an airfield near London, but on the city itself. This was promptly declared by Churchill to be a terror raid on the civilian population. He immediately ordered a reprisal attack on Berlin. And indeed, on September 7 a handful of RAF bombers, defying the distance and the enemy defenses, bombed the German capital for the first time. Hitler exploded with mad rage. He had repeatedly promised the German people complete security from enemy bombs. Now he, in turn, ordered a series of savage mass counter-raids on British cities, especially on London. The next day 625 Luftwaffe bombers, protected by 648 fighters, again raided the British capital.[11]

Hitler's rash decision proved a blessing in disguise to the British. With victory in the air already in sight, the terror raids diverted German bombers from such vital installations as the radar stations and command posts, and thus interrupted the steady destruction of the vital infrastructure of British defenses. Now the bombers switched to potluck bombing of civilian dwellings or

[11]The bombardment of British cities posed numerous problems for the Home Office; for a comprehensive discussion see Terrence H. O'Brien's *Civil Defence* (London: H.M.S.O., 1955).

random buildings with little or no military importance. Consequently, the Battle of Britain turned mainly into the battle of London. London, a sprawling megalopolis of some 8 to 9 million people, could absorb, like a huge sponge, a great deal of punishment, leaving its vital functions practically intact.

Churchill's decision to launch a reprisal raid on Berlin was a masterpiece of psychological warfare. First of all, it raised the morale of the British people. Contrary to Hitler's hopes, the terror bombing, far from breaking the people's stamina, bolstered their determination and stiffened their will to win. Moreover, the reprisals against Berlin demonstrated to the Germans that Britain was far from defeated and that they were themselves vulnerable.

Fortunately for the British, Hitler knew little about the serious damage his Luftwaffe had done to many of the British defense installations. By the summer of 1940 his network of spies, planted mostly before the war, had been effectively destroyed by preventive measures applied by the British counterintelligence service, or MI5. Unknown to the public, even to most high government officials, British counterintelligence had established an elaborate network for surveillance and detection of foreign agents. By July and August of 1940 most German spies had been arrested, and many of them had been "bent" or "turned." Faced with long-term imprisonment or death, most of them agreed to serve the British or act as double agents, thus misinforming their former masters.[12]

The peak of the Battle of Britain was reached on September 14/15. For hours an immense armada of German bombers escorted by fighters darkened the skies, forming a huge air bridge. The RAF now had to commit most of its fast shrinking fighter force to the battle. Only 288 fully serviceable fighters remained available, and all of them flew into action, with no reserves left. This largest of the air battles so far ended with a clear disaster for the Luftwaffe: It lost seventy-six planes against thirty-four of the RAF. Since the German aircraft output was smaller than that of Britain, the Luftwaffe could not afford to continue attacks of this size any more. The crisis of the battle was over.

September 15 or the nearest Sunday is celebrated in Britain as Battle of Britain Day, a day of thanksgiving for the deliverance from the gravest peril Britain had known since Napoleon massed invasion troops at Boulogne in 1805.

The Defeat of the Luftwaffe

The balance sheet of the air battles of the summer and autumn of 1940 was definitely in favor of the British. Between July and November the Luftwaffe lost 1,733 aircraft and 643 damaged, while the RAF suffered 915 lost and 450 damaged. The proportion was still more advantageous as far as manpower was concerned. While the RAF lost 481 men killed and wounded, the Germans lost nearly 2,500 airmen; some of them perished while fighting, and some crash landed or parachuted in Britain. They were of no use to the Luftwaffe until the end of hostilities.[13]

By the middle of September the soaring losses began to affect the morale of the Luftwaffe flying personnel. Both the

[12]Some of the causes of the failure of German intelligence are discussed in J. C. Masterman, *The Double-Cross System in the War of 1939 to 1945* (New Haven and London: Yale University Press, 1972), especially pp. 46–190. See also David Kahn, *Hitler's Spies* (New York: Macmillan, 1978), pp. 11–12 and 525 ff.; for a broad background of the problem see F. H. Hinsley, *British Intelligence in the Second World War* (London: H.M.S.O., Vol. I, 1979), pp. 163–80. Besides effective counterintelligence service, the British managed to organize an aggressive spying network covering most of the world. One of the most successful examples of an effective intelligence net organized by the British was created by Sir William S. Stephenson, a British Canadian-born intelligence officer of World War I vintage. For his story see William Stephenson, *A Man Called Intrepid: The Secret War* (San Diego: Harcourt Brace Jovanovich, 1976).

[13]For an assessment of the Battle of Britain see R. J. Overy, *The Air War, 1939–1945* (London and New York: Stein & Day, 1981), pp. 33–59.

bomber crews and the fighter pilots were suffering mounting casualties from the RAF and the antiaircraft artillery. The strain on the fighter pilots was especially great for they were often compelled to fly five or more sorties a day without much rest. To physical exhaustion was soon added the frustration of constant defeats. Grumbling and even cases of open protest multiplied. Soon the Germans themselves began to doubt whether the invasion would ever come and whether it had any chance of success at all. The myth of their invincibility had been demolished. And indeed, on October 12, 1940, Hitler officially "postponed" Operation Sealion. This face-saving formula camouflaged its failure.

Contrary to popular opinion, the winning trump cards of the Battle of Britain were not the slim Spitfires. The myth of the Spitfires winning the air battle was spread by popular writers, film and TV serial makers, and even by the Germans themselves. For instance, Goering, disappointed with his pilots' performance, summoned one of his air aces, Adolf Galland, and chastised him for his comrades' poor showing. When he asked him what their most pressing needs were, the response was "Give me a squadron of Spitfires."

It was not the Spitfire, however, but the older and more sturdy Hawker Hurricane that played a crucial role during the Battle of Britain. This has been proved by one statistic: Four out of every five downings of enemy aircraft over Britain were by Hurricanes. When the Battle of Britain started, far more Hurricanes than Spitfires were available and in the key Number 11 Fighter Group, which was defending southeast England, there were fifteen squadrons equipped with Hurricanes and only six with Spitfires. The Hurricane had certain advantages over both the Spitfire and its main adversary, the Messerschmitt 109. Though slower at climbing and diving, the Hurricane could out-turn them both and was much more rugged than either.

The reckless effort of the Goering's Gamble in the Battle of Britain marked the high-water mark of German air strategy. After the winter of 1940/41, Hitler began to subordinate his air power more and more to the objectives of his land warfare. Night bombing was continued through the winter of 1940/41, but in those months the bulk of the Luftwaffe was transferred to the east and south to prepare for the planned invasion of Russia or to help the Italians. Hitler's directives of November 12, 1940, concerning "the preparatory measures of the High Command for the conduct of the war in the near future" contain an ominous formula: "Political discussion for the purpose of clarifying Russia's attitude . . . have already begun. Regardless of the outcome of the conversations, all preparations for the East . . . will be continued."[14]

WHY GERMANY LOST THE BATTLE

The Battle of Britain, the first major defeat suffered by Hitler, holds a distinctive place in the annals of warfare. It was the largest and the longest air contest ever fought. It was, too, the first aerial battle with long-range strategic implications: It interrupted Hitler's seemingly irresistible and victorious march and marked a major turning point of the war. The battle marked also the coming of age of the youngest service in modern warfare. Until World War II, air forces were regarded as auxiliaries and largely served the needs of their senior branches. This view did not change even after the conclusion of hostilities. Aircraft had remained until the end of World War I something of an extravagant curiosity, but now they became a major factor in tactics and strategy. Without completely validating the theories of Douhet, "Billy" Mitchell, the Udet, air power came a serious instrument which could, if not decide the outcome of a war, at least tip the balance of forces one way or another.

The failure of the German air attack on England and its abortive designs at an invasion were also due to remarkably defective long-range planning and sloppy intelli-

[14]Trevor-Roper, ed., *Blitzkrieg to Defeat,* p. 43.

Civil defense workers remove ruins of bombed out houses in London. National Archives

gence. A regime that hailed the fighting knight over the intellectual naturally tended to neglect its secret services as less "heroic" and less important. This bias toward archaic virtues and performance in the field resulted in poor training of the German intelligence agents. Moreover, imbued with a superiority complex, the Germans underrated their opponents. As a result, the overconfident German agents were often badly equipped to do their job.

For instance, the German manual in carrying out the air operations over Britain was a prewar guide known as the "Blue Study." This handbook set out the then available data about British harbors, roads, airports, and industrial plants. The manual was outdated; it did not include many newly built plants and emergency air fields and underrated the mobilization potential of British industries. Also, the Luftwaffe ignored intelligence concerning the newly established radar stations and the network of high-frequency radio stations. The Germans had known since 1938 that the British were experimenting with radar but either disregarded these efforts or underestimated their results. When the Wehrmacht captured a British mobile radio station on the beach of Boulogne in May 1940, Goering and his experts regarded it as too crude a device to merit close examination.

Operation Sealion was to be a closely coordinated team effort, involving all three services pursuing an ultimate goal. Such cooperation had been impressively achieved by the Wehrmacht during the Scandinavian campaign. As the war progressed, however, self-interest and vicious intraservice rivalry increased. The navy, jealous of the glory gained by the army and the Luftwaffe in the Low Countries and France, was sulking. Despite its limited capabilities, the admirals demanded a greater share in the planning of what appeared to be the final stages of the war. The navy's cautious plan for a narrow corridor clashed with the army's scheme for a broad-front landing necessary for the quick deployment of twelve divisions. Goering, who exploited his closeness to the Führer, managed to cannibalize the Naval Air Arm and started a feud with the navy that was never extinguished to the very end of the war.

Some have argued that Hitler's order to halt his troops' immediate attack on Dunkirk, thus allowing the trapped B.E.F. to escape, and his subsequent month-long hesitation to invade saved a defenseless Britain from disaster. Even an improvised landing of powerful German airborne and armored forces in July might have overcome a desperate resistance by what Field Marshal Ironside called Britain's "naked army," deprived of tanks and artillery.

These arguments lack factual basis; the Germans did not possess the requisite landing barges and amphibious equipment. Even in the autumn of 1940 the Germans were short of seaworthy transport. Surely they would have been unable to assemble a sufficient quantity in July. In addition, German naval forces were as weak in July as they were in October. A few submarines, completed in the interim by the shipyards of the Reich, had not changed the balance of naval forces to any marked degree.

At the root of Hitler's strategy was his original delusion that he could either woo or coerce the conservative leaders in London into cooperation with his global plans without going to war. Consequently, the Germans remained unprepared for a naval confrontation with Britain when his expectations were not met. Hitler was essentially a land animal. Although he once told Admiral Raeder that he kept a copy of *Jane's Fighting Ships* by his bedside, the proportion of the resources that the Führer was prepared to spend on his fleet was much too small to make it really effective.

At the end of May 1938 Hitler told a surprised Admiral Raeder to prepare for war against Great Britain; yet this conflict, he declared, would not take place for many years to come. In ten years time, Germany was to have six battleships of 50,000 tons, eight battle cruisers of 20,000 tons, four aircraft carriers of 20,000 tons, and a large number of light cruisers and 233 U-boats. This plan was regarded by Doenitz, the advocate of U-boats, as a major defeat. He declared that the minimum number of submarines he would need to bring Britain to its knees was at least 300. When Hitler precipitated the war in 1939, the Third Reich had only fifty-seven and a conventional fleet ridiculously small to cope with the worldwide task assigned to it by its Führer.

By 1939/40, Germany was scarcely prepared for a long range war in the air, either. In 1937 Hitler had halted development of heavy four-engine bombers necessary both for successful bombing of the British Isles and for enforcing, together with the U-boats, the sea blockade desired by Raeder and Doenitz. Hitler's views were supported by General Ernst Udet, chief of the technical office of the German air ministry. Udet, a former acrobatic pilot (his nickname was "the Flying Clown"), was a man of explosive temperament and great impatience. After World War I he became the chief pioneer and protagonist of the light dive bomber, or *Stuka.*[15] He argued that it was all Germany needed to win the short war of the future. He had no interest in heavy four-engine bombers for combat over long distances against, for example, enemy shipping in the Atlantic. Although German engineers had developed a prototype of such a bomber, Hitler, whose views about a short war coincided with those of Udet, had canceled their production in 1937. As a result of this policy, Germany was deprived of a strategic bomber force.

The available machines (such as the Dornier 17, Heinkel 111, and Junkers 88) were of medium range and unable to carry great loads at adequate distances and served mostly as auxiliary instruments of the army. Moreover, they were too slow and so poorly armed that they could not operate without strong fighter escort. During the Battle of Britain there were seldom enough fighters to accompany more than 300 to 400 bombers in a single mission. As well, the backbone of the German fighter force, the ME 109, had a limited range that did not go beyond London. The heavy twin-engine ME 110 was

---

[15]For a critical discussion of the German shortcomings in the air, see David Irving, *The Rise and Fall of the Luftwaffe,* especially pp. 72–74, 81–82, 144–45, and 197ff.

December 23, 1940: Prime Minister Churchill and General Sikorski inspect the First Polish Army Corps in Scotland. The Polish Institute, London

practically useless as an escort because it was too clumsy and not nearly a match for the more maneuverable RAF fighters. But by far the greatest German handicap was their radio equipment, rather primitive in comparison with that of the RAF planes, which were provided with radar, as well as with a superior radio ground-control system.

Although the Germans had more aircraft and a greater reservoir of pilots, their production capacity was smaller. The British, by a strict and well-planned mobilization of all their resources by the autumn of 1940, managed within one year to increase their aircraft production by 250 percent. German industries could produce only about 3,000 fighters per year, but the British output exceeded 4,300 per year.

To these technological and logistical factors one has to add human and psychological ones. Almost from its beginnings the RAF had attracted some of the most daring and imaginative young people in Britain and its dominions. The training of this elite was very exacting, and RAF spirit was superb. After the battles of Poland, Scandinavia, and western Europe, RAF squadrons were reinforced by the surviving airmen of the conquered countries. Thus, by the summer of 1940, the RAF was already a conglomeration of many ethnic elements. For all practical purposes it was an international contingent, including seven American volunteers.

Among the foreigners, the Poles, with 154 pilots, formed by far the most numerous group. The RAF, Britain's flower and pride, was now joined by those who came from all over the world to defend the last fortress of freedom. These resolute knights of the air spontaneously competed with each other not only in the name of the common cause but also out of national pride. Their backs to the wall, this elite fought with tenacity and bold skill. They were more than a match even for the Luftwaffe veterans. Determined to avenge their past defeats and humiliations, they inflicted a major defeat on their overconfident enemies. The triumph of this small band of Allied fliers fighting against heavy odds was epitomized by Winston Churchill who said, "Never has so much been done by so few for so many."[16]

The virtues of the RAF fliers were embod-

---

[16]Air victories by squadrons were:

1st—303 Polish squadron—117 air victories
2nd—501 RAF—87 victories
3rd—41 RAF and 603 RAF—69 air victories

See also *Destiny Can Wait: The Polish Air Force in the Second World War* (Melbourne, London, Toronto: William Heinemann, 1949), pp. 47–213.

ied in the person of Air Chief Marshal Hugh Dowding. Although he had successfully led a fighter wing in France in 1916, his World War I experience did not blind him to the necessity for constant improvements in old methods of air combat and technological progress. His self-effacing and frugal personality contrasted with that of his main opponent, Reichsmarshal Goering, a self-centered exhibitionist addicted to gluttony and drugs. In a way the Battle of Britain was a duel between these two leaders.

NEW ARMED FORCES IN THE MAKING

While fighting for their survival, the British had to look beyond the emergency facing them and prepare for eventual return to the continent of Europe. Despite the intra-service rivalries, the Wehrmacht was a formidable fighting machine, and throughout the summer and autumn of 1940 the British had little with which to oppose it. On land, almost everything had to be created from scratch. Sir Alan Brooke, former commander of the II Corps of the B.E.F., as chief of the Imperial General Staff since 1941, was the real begetter of the new army.

Brooke brought from France profound reservations about the stamina and training of the British soldiers as compared with those of the enemy. The only way to enhance them was by hard, vigorous, and systematic training. This was impeded for a considerable time by lack of equipment. Under Brooke's dynamic leadership and Churchill's often impatient supervision, the field army expanded eventually to some fifty divisions, including eleven armored and two airborne. In addition to that, some highly specialized and carefully trained units were organized to carry out unorthodox assignments dictated by the requirements of a new type of mobile warfare. They became known as "commandos."

In June 1940 the Director of Combined Operations was created; initially it had six independent companies and ten "commandos." The commandos were units of light battalion size, composed of volunteers and equipped for raiding an enemy-held coastline. By 1941 the British had begun to experiment with landing craft, training of crews for amphibious operations, mine sweeping, smoke screens, and other cooperative and intricately scheduled exercises.[17] Thus Germany's opponents, first the British and then the Americans, developed the skills of combined operations and gained a vital advantage over their enemies.

THE MOBILIZATION OF THE HOME FRONT

Behind the dash and bravery of the few there stood the great majority of the ordinary British people. Having entered the struggle hesitantly, shocked by a series of painful defeats, including Dunkirk, by the summer of 1940, British men and women were faced with a supreme test. The French catastrophe finally shattered the comfortable illusions of some British leaders that the war could be won by an economic blockade combined with only marginal and peripheral military operations. By the end of June Britain found itself on the brink of disaster. This galvanized all ranks of the people into action. Mobilizing every ounce of energy, they threw themselves into the war with all the grim determination for which they have been traditionally known.

During the last stages of the French campaign the British began to work out a national defense plan. While Dunkirk was evacuated, a group of military experts and economists assigned to the War Cabinet submitted to the prime minister a policy paper outlining the phases for an immediate shift to a war economy and an immediate total mobilization of Britain's resources. One of the main points of the plan was strict allocation of manpower and raw materials based on the

[17]For the reshaping of the British forces after the fall of France see David Fraser's *And We Shall Shock Them,* especially pp. 83–112.

priority of indispensable products over financial solvency. Everything was to be subordinated to the war effort. Sharp restrictions were placed on civilian consumption. This Spartan austerity meant severe rationing of food, fuel, and clothing. The shortages were immediately felt and were accepted with the spontaneous and patriotic cooperation of the people. Imports were to be reduced to a bare minimum, and exports were to earn as much foreign currency as possible. Price controls were imposed and, generally speaking, observed without much grumbling.[18]

On May 22, 1940, the Production Council, under the chairmanship of a prominent Labour party politician, Arthur Greenwood, minister without portfolio, was set up. Its main duties were to assess the manpower required by Britain's war effort and to assign a ranking among competing demands for materials and labor. In his task Greenwood was ably assisted by another Labour party leader, the courageous and imaginative Ernest Bevin.

Bevin had never sat in the House of Commons; his whole life had been devoted to furthering the interests and welfare of workers, and particularly those who were not craftsmen: the dockers, the vanmen, and the lorry drivers. With a passionate belief in social justice he had organized them into a single union and had won their confidence. Because he was their trusted leader, he managed to persuade the working class of Britain to submit to the stringency of the war economy with little opposition. Britain's sudden shift from a laissez faire economy to one planned for total war was achieved quickly and successfully by widespread popular consent rather than coercion.

At times, public opinion ran ahead of the officially decreed measures and insisted on a harsher rationing of consumer goods. Yet drastic measures and crash programs were, by and large, avoided. The only exception was the aircraft program. Between April and September 1940 delivery of fighters nearly doubled. The second priority was assigned to antiaircraft guns, rockets, and barrage balloons. In both of these efforts the mercurial friend of Winston Churchill, the Canadian-born Lord Beaverbrook, minister of aircraft production, a man of drive and determination, rendered signal service to Britain. Between January and April 1940 he increased the output of airplanes to 2,279, and from May to August the amount grew to 4,576, of which 1,875 were the urgently needed fighters.

The key problem in planning was manpower, especially highly skilled labor. Britain's population was considerably smaller than that of Germany, especially with the Reich's increasing utilization of slave labor from conquered countries. The vast human resources of the Commonwealth and British Empire, however, counterbalanced those of Hitler's continental domain. Moreover, aware of their handicap, the British government introduced a much more extensive and ingenious employment of labor, especially women.

The prime example of labor mobilization was the National Service Act of December 1941. This act provided for the drafting of all the able-bodied from eighteen to fifty years of age for either military or essential auxiliary services and empowered the authorities to shift manpower from nonessential to critical fields. By mid-1944 the age groups subject to either military or auxiliary service were further extended to include women up to fifty years old, or the so-called grandmother category. This exceeded anything Hitler, a traditionalist concerning the German family, would ever dare to do.[19]

---

[18]For an official view of the British economic effort see D. N. Chester, ed., *Lessons of the British War Economy* (Westport, Conn.: Greenwood Press, 1951) and W. Hancock and M. Gowing's *The British War Economy* (London: H.M.S.O., 1949 and 1957).

[19]For the British government study of the mobilization of human resources see H. M. D. Parker, *Manpower: A Study of Wartime Policy and Administration* (London: H.M.S.O. and Longmans, Green, 1957). Even in 1943, after Stalingrad, Hitler refused to mobilize German women to the last moments of the war because of his old-fashioned views about their role in society.

To reduce the import of food, the acreage of land under cultivation was increased to a maximum, and women were employed in agriculture to a hitherto unknown extent. An auxiliary organization known as "the Women's Land Army" was established. Its slogan was "Dig harder to beat the U-boats." The Land Army's song echoed the refrain:

Back to the land, we must all lend a hand,
To the farms and fields we must go,
There's a job to be done,
Though we can't fire a gun,
We can still do our bit with the hoe.

By 1941 Britain's imports were halved, as parks and private allotments were tilled and turned into "victory gardens." Initially, the Third Reich, with its systematic yet gradual preparations for war from 1933 to 1939, had a definite advantage over its complacent opponents. Although a considerable segment of the Reich's economy converted to war, Hitler failed to mobilize it as totally as did Britain until the last moment before his defeat. This instant and extensive economic mobilization allowed the British to overcome the most severe crisis in their history.

No other belligerent power achieved such results during World War II with such efficiency. All this was made possible largely owing to the impressive social discipline and patriotism of the British people. Of course, the American aid was also of crucial importance.

8

The Struggle for the Mediterranean

Throughout the critical year 1940 mortally imperiled Britain stood in isolation that was far from splendid. Valiantly coping with overwhelming odds, the British were not only defending their home island but faced lethal tasks in the Atlantic and in the Mediterranean. The dangers to their island home inherent in the battle of the Atlantic were more immediate, but defeat in the Mediterranean must also eventually spell disaster; an Axis victory there would mean the loss of the vital Suez Canal, thus cutting Britain's communication with India and Malaya, significant reservoirs of manpower, tin, and rubber. Moreover, an Axis victory in the Middle Sea would give them access to the oil-bearing fields of Iraq and Iran, without which Britain could hardly carry on the struggle. Finally, a German-Italian victory in the Mediterranean might encourage Japan to enter the war as an active partner of the Axis, thus opening another theater of operation in the Far East at the time when the British resources were already stretched to the breaking point.

THE NORTH AFRICAN AND MEDITERRANEAN THEATER OF OPERATION

Egypt with its Suez Canal was the key to the Mediterranean. Italy's entry into the war had endangered the vital Nile Valley from both the west and south: from Cyrenaica and Tripolitania (present-day Libya), and from Italian East Africa (as the newly consolidated colonies of Eritrea, Somalia, and Ethiopia were then officially called). Axis control of Egypt would, moreover, link Italy's Mediterranean possessions with those of Ethiopia,

Somalia, and Eritrea, thus subverting Britain's vulnerable position in Africa.

In June 1940 the British Mediterranean squadron, deprived of French support, alone confronted the numerically impressive Italian navy. The Italian fleet in the Mediterranean appeared initially to be a deadly menace to the Royal Navy. With 6 battleships, 19 modern cruisers, 120 destroyers and torpedo boats, as well as over 100 submarines, the Italian fleet looked formidable. So menacing did the situation first appear that the Admiralty contemplated in July 1940 abandoning the eastern Mediterranean and concentrating its power at Gibraltar. Churchill, however, vetoed this move. For Churchill retention of both eastern and western segments of the Middle Sea was essential for Britain's survival. He believed British sea power there should confound Axis attempts to control the Mediterranean, conquest of which could ultimately win the war for them.

The importance of the Mediterranean and the Suez Canal to Britain may be guessed from the following fact: On the eve of the Battle of France in May 1940 Churchill ordered 7,000 soldiers and nearly half of the available tank reserves sent to Egypt to reinforce the puny British garrison there. He also strengthened the Mediterranean squadron of the Royal Navy. By demonstrating Britain's determination to defend Egypt, he desired not only to warn Mussolini against any aggressive move but also to encourage Greece, Yugoslavia, and Turkey to join in a front against the Axis.[1]

For each of the Axis partners the importance of the Middle Sea was different. For Mussolini the Mediterranean was of primary strategic and psychologic significance, as Italy's mare nostrum and preferably the main theater of war. For Hitler the Mediterranean was merely a part of his "peripheral" strategy in the struggle against Britain, his main enemy. Diversion of Britain into the Mediterranean would drain its resources and thus facilitate Hitler's hoped-for negotiations for final surrender of Britain.

As for the Balkan countries, Hitler wanted to use their raw materials and to employ the region to secure his rear for the planned attack on Soviet Russia. Mussolini naturally wanted Hitler's "peripheral war" to be focused, not on Soviet Russia, but on the Mediterranean theater, thus preserving for Italy the right of strategic initiative there. In the Balkans Mussolini's main prospective targets were either Yugoslavia or Greece, and in North Africa the conquest of Egypt and the Suez Canal were his main strategic objectives. This outlook was the essence of Mussolini's "parallel war" designed to secure Italy's position in her "zone of influence," a war conducted in association with Germany, but essentially independent of his Axis partner.[2]

With Italy's entry into the war, Britain's strategic position in the Mediterranean, the Near East, and the Middle East became critical. The Near Eastern and Middle Eastern command alone covered the huge area from Iran to the Anglo-Egyptian Sudan. The British garrisons in these regions in 1940 numbered about 60,000 men and 300 planes; and troops represented a mixture of English and Scottish regiments, hastily reinforced with South Africans, Australians, Maoris from New Zealand, and various Indian units. The commander in chief of the Middle Eastern and Near Eastern regions, General Archibald Wavell, a quiet, scholarly

[1]For the British point of view on the Mediterranean and the Middle East see Winston S. Churchill, *Their Finest Hour,* pp. 417–72 and 507–51; I. S. O. Playfair, C. J. C. Molony et al., *The Mediterranean and the Middle East, Vols. I–III,* (London: H.M.S.O., 1954–64); Vol. I, covers the period up to May 1941. For a discussion of the travel problem see Raymond de Belot, *The Struggle for the Mediterranean, 1939–45* (Princeton, N.J.: Princeton University Press, 1951), especially pp. 3–134; see also Walter Ansel, *Hitler and the Middle Sea* (Durham, N.C.: Duke University Press, 1971).

[2]For a discussion of Italy's participation in the opening of the Balkan and Mediterranean phases of the war see MacGregor Knox, *Mussolini Unleashed, 1939–1941. Politics and Strategy in Fascist Italy's Last War* (Cambridge, London, and New York: Cambridge University Press, 1983), especially chaps. 5 and 6.

The Mediterranean Theater of Operations, 1940-1943

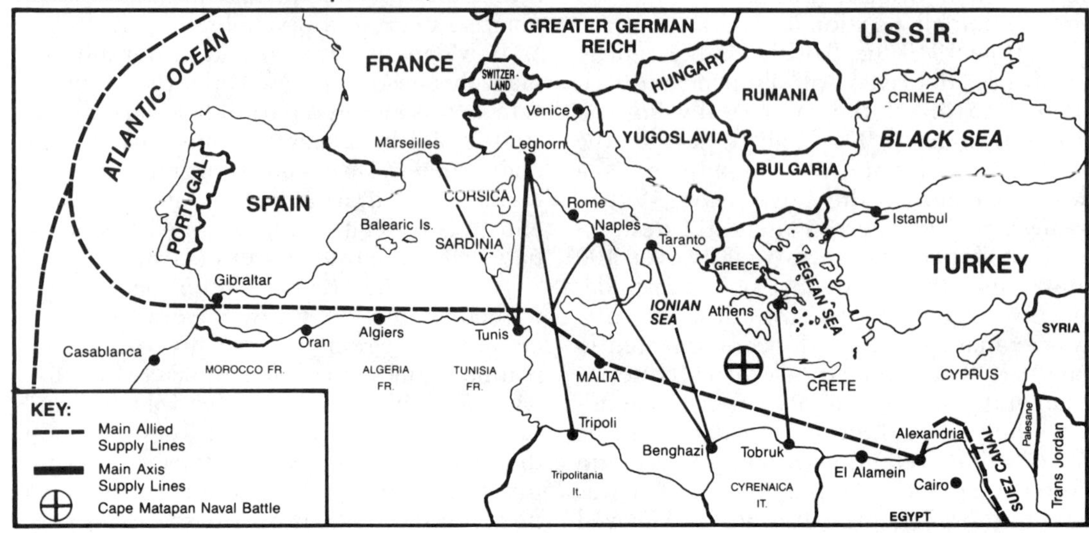

man who in his spare time wrote poetry, faced a set of nearly impossible tasks. His job was complicated by a delicate political situation because Axis agitation among the Moslem population was on the increase and represented a highly destabilizing factor.

The key country in General Wavell's command, Egypt, had regained independence from the British in 1936 but reluctantly recognized Britain's special interests in the region, including the Suez Canal and the right to maintain troops on Egyptian territory. The majority of the Egyptians, however, looked upon the British as intruders and as a reminder of the recent semicolonial past. At the end of May 1940, at the peak of the Battle of France, the Egyptian premier demanded that all British troops should move out of Cairo and that the city should be declared an open, unfortified town to assure its immunity from possible air attack. London's sharp rejection of the demand did little to appease the nationalistic sentiments motivating the young intellectuals, students, and army officers. Some of the leaders of conspiratorial cells among the military, such as Gamal Nasser and Anwar Sadat, were in touch with Axis agents.

Britain's position in the Mediterranean hinged on three bases: Gibraltar, Malta, and Alexandria. The Italian naval and air forces, based on Taranto, threatened to split the area into two isolated segments. In these circumstances the Malta archipelago was destined to play a crucial role.

Close to the center of the Mediterranean, Malta lies roughly midway between Gibraltar and Suez. With a population of under 300,000 (smaller than Staten Island, New York), Malta acquired a strategic importance entirely out of proportion to its size and the miniscule garrison guarding its five tiny islands. But unless the British could hold Malta, the Royal Navy would have to operate in two separate squadrons in the Mediterranean. Momentarily leaving only light naval forces, a few airplanes, and a small garrison in Malta, as well as a limited task force in Gibraltar, Churchill decided to concentrate his main effort in the eastern basin, to defend Egypt and the Suez Canal. Slowly, however, and despite overwhelming odds, the British kept on reinforcing the tiny bastion of Malta by all available means. Thus, the Maltese islands formed a composite aircraft carrier anchored in the middle of the western Mediterranean—a thorn in the paw of Axis power and a vital relay station for British convoys supplying their Middle East forces.

Spain's Role in the Mediterranean

In the struggle for the Middle Sea, the role of Spain held a special importance. The fall of France, which sent a tremor of fear throughout most of neutral Europe, did not affect Spain in the same way. Generalissimo Francisco Franco, the victor in the civil war and head of the Falange movement, was sympathetic to the Axis and looked forward to its eventual victory. Yet Spain was still recovering from its internal ordeal and Franco, a cautious politician, was determined to pursue one task before all others: to rehabilitate his half-ruined and nearly starving country. Hitler, however, after his failure to invade Britain, saw a unique chance of drawing Spain into the war against his main enemy by offering Gibraltar as an incentive. This rocky island-fortress, which the Spanish had lost to Britain in 1704, was sentimentally important to the patriotic Spaniards.

Hitler saw Spain's entrance into the Axis alliance as an almost magic solution to present and potential problems. Should Spain enter the war on the side of Germany and Italy, the French colonies in North Africa would be prevented from going over to the British side. Portugal would be neutralized and the western gate to the Mediterranean, Gibraltar, effectively closed, thus locking the British naval forces there. British supplies of raw materials from the Near East and Middle East, especially oil, would be threatened. With Spain, the whole balance of power in the Mediterranean would tilt against Britain and, Hitler hoped, push it toward surrender.

To wrest a positive decision from the Spaniards, Hitler met Franco at Hendaye in the French Pyrenees on October 23, 1940. The Spanish dictator was urged to enter the war on the side of the Axis by January of 1941 and help to capture Gibraltar. According to Hitler, Britain was already beaten and its formal surrender was only a matter of time. Spain should, therefore, follow the Italians and speed up the inevitable triumph of the Axis. General Franco, however, must have remembered an old Spanish proverb that one should think carefully before choosing whether to become the mere tail of a powerful lion or the proud head of a tiny mouse.

Victorious in the civil war largely thanks to German and Italian aid, Franco was in no hurry to repay his debt of gratitude. He procrastinated and tried to postpone his final commitment by putting forward impossible political demands that included acquisition of French Morocco. This request was not only contrary to the terms of the recently concluded armistice with the Vichy government but also to Hitler's desire to remain on good terms with the regime of Marshal Pétain. Franco also pleaded the sorry state of his country, especially its desperate economic situation. Spain, he said, needed time as well as a huge supply of weapons and raw materials to rebuild both its shattered society and its battered armed forces. In a conversation lasting nine hours, Hitler urged Franco to exchange his benevolent neutrality for an active belligerency. All of Hitler's rhetoric was useless, however. Hitler left Hendaye furious, saying he would prefer to have three or four of his teeth pulled than to go through such an exasperating experience again. To the end of the war, while constantly pressed with bold and urgent demands by the Axis powers, Franco would pay them in small coin only.[3]

The North African Environment

In September 1940, while the Battle of Britain was reaching its peak, another campaign was starting in Africa. The struggle centered around North Africa and East Africa, especially the North African deserts stretching from Cairo to Casablanca. Italy, as we remember, had entered the war on June 10, 1940, as a "postbelligerent," more eager to grab the anticipated spoils than to fight.

---

[3]For a study of the military aspects of German-Spanish relations see Charles B. Budrick, *Germany's Military Strategy and Spain in World War II* (Syracuse, N.Y.: Syracuse University Press, 1968).

The unexpectedly quick collapse of France caught the Italian forces in North Africa unprepared for an immediate offensive. Italy's forces had sufficient, if not abundant, resources. The Tenth Army, facing Egypt, numbered over ten divisions with some 300 aircraft and a large number of fast but very light tanks, only a few of medium size. But with the apparent end of the war in sight, the new head of the Tenth Army, Marshal Rodolfo Graziani, was not in a hurry to start full-scale hostilities. Consequently, only at the beginning of September, egged on by Mussolini, Graziani reluctantly launched his long-postponed offensive against Egypt and the Suez Canal. He was opposed by Britain's Western Desert Force, with its crack 7th Armored Division, the 4th Indian Division, and a few batteries of artillery, altogether a numerically weak army corps.

Although far smaller numerically than the Italian Tenth Army, the Western Desert Force was much better equipped: It was fully motorized and had more modern guns and tanks. The Italians had only seventy medium tanks of fourteen tons armed with 47-mm cannons and three machine guns. They were no match for the 270 British Cruisers and Matildas; even the lighter British tanks, the Cruisers, let alone the Matildas, were impervious to the Italian antitank guns. Unlike the Hurricanes and Spitfires, most of the Italian planes had no sand filters, which made them unsuitable for desert conditions.

The North African campaign, which was to last for nearly thirty months until May 1943, was fought in a hostile environment primarily in a vast desert zone, stretching over some 2,500 miles. At night the mercury would fall to freezing; by day, temperatures often passed 100 degrees Fahrenheit, when soldiers could fry eggs on the tops of their tanks. A hot Sahara wind, called the *khamsin,* blew sand as fine as talcum powder for days on end at speeds of up to 90 miles per hour. Brown sand storms drove grit into men's flesh, choking throats and coating nostrils. The sand buried supplies like drifting snow, jammed gun breeches, and set compasses whirling, while the *khamsin* traumatized the minds of the combatants. There were numerous cases of psychiatric disorders among men on both sides long after the winds had stopped. When the *khamsin* subsided, troops on both sides suffered from mosquitoes and from fly swarms so aggressive and persistent that it was often impossible to raise food to the lips before it became black with insects. The desert fighters despaired of any of the comforts of civilization; the shortage of fresh vegetables and the brackish water only served to aggravate thirst instead of quenching it. To the soldiers in the desert, it was "hell's own battleground."

The hostile terrain, a long stretch of waterless coastal desert, provided nothing. Every ounce of material had to be brought in from outside: food, water, ammunition, gasoline, and weapons had to be trucked over primitive and punishing roads. British and Axis supplies came from distant centers along highly vulnerable routes; logistics dominated all strategy and tactics.

In view of the large distances, another vital factor in the North African campaign was mobility. Roadless like the sea, the desert's flat surface was eminently suited for tanks and armored cars. Rapid movement on the desert created all sorts of opportunities for a war of feint, surprise, and ambush. Fortune favored the side commanded by more resourceful leaders, but ultimately the victory in the North African campaign would fall to those who were better supplied in the shortest time and at the decisive point.

Italian Defeat in North Africa

Graziani undertook the offensive only by the beginning of September. At that time Goering was turning the full weight of his bombers on London in the firm conviction that this "absolute air warfare" would bring the British to their knees and thus end the war. This opinion was shared by Mussolini and a large segment of his military establishment, including Graziani. Starting from Bardia, his troops moved across the Egyptian border at Sollum and then proceeded at a leisurely pace along the coast to Sidi Barani. Under the impact of the massive Italian push, the small Western Desert Force, commanded by General Richard O'Connor, retreated while fighting a successful delaying action. O'Connor stopped only 60 miles east of Alexandria, where he set a firm stand at the fortified line of el-Alamein, protected from the south by the Quattara depression.

While the Italians advanced, Mussolini was elated. His ambitious plans for conquering Egypt, with the Suez Canal, and for establishing an Italian protectorate over the entire Arab world seemed to be nearer fulfillment. To Ciano he declared that Graziani's drive afforded Italy "the glory she has sought in vain for three centuries." In Graziani's rear were trucks with marble slabs to mark the expansion of Italy's African empire beyond the Suez Canal.

By the end of September Mussolini was so sure of conquering Egypt that he made a series of reckless decisions in other areas. Considering a negotiated peace with Britain close at hand, he decided that 600,000 of the 1.1 million men under arms in Italy could be sent home. Eager to participate in the expected German victory over Britain, he ordered some of his submarines to cooperate with the U-boats in the Atlantic; 200 of his bombers and fighters were to be sent to Belgian bases to help the Luftwaffe in the last stages of the Battle of Britain. Il Duce even smugly refused Hitler's offer of a German armored division to reinforce Graziani's forces. As an official communiqué of the Stefani news agency declared, "We want to reach Suez with our forces alone." Ignoring the repeated advice of his military council, urging him to restrict his immediate designs on land to North Africa, Mussolini ordered the Italian armed forces to be ready to attack Greece.

Generals Wavell and O'Connor discuss their drive against the Italian forces. Imperial War Museum

The Italians, however, soon faced some hard facts. After having encountered stiff resistance along the fortified lines of el-Alamein, Graziani's troops had to stop. Begging Rome for more medium tanks and antitank artillery to cope with the heavily protected British armor, Graziani ordered his legions to await reinforcements, while constructing a net of improvised forts. This loss of nerve and momentum in the Italian advance was taken advantage of by General Wavell. He ordered O'Connor's Western Desert Force to throw a series of harassing forays against the nearest Italian outposts. The purpose of these probing raids was essentially to make Graziani believe that the Western Desert Force was much stronger than it actually was and to gain time for assembling the badly needed reinforcements that were, meanwhile, streaming to Egypt from all over the British Empire and the Commonwealth.

A weak point of the Italian defense line was that it stretched widely over more than 90 miles and that individual forts were not interconnected. Large gaps between the forts, especially in the southern sector, were not sufficiently guarded by mobile patrols. One of the British raids carried out by the 7th Armored Division, soon to be called the

Western Desert Force Offensive Against the Italians, December 7 & 8, 1940-February 9, 1941

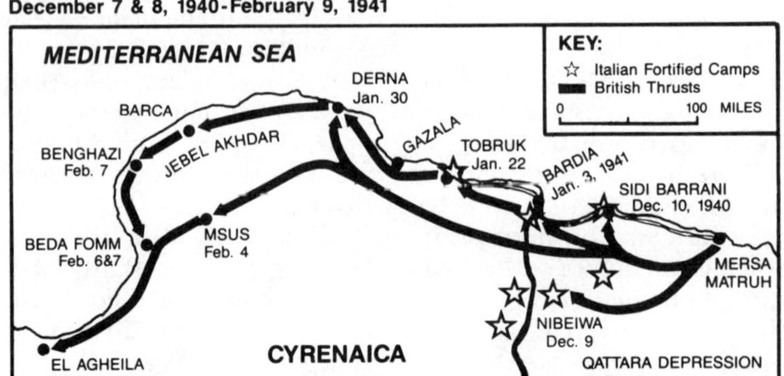

"desert rats," spotted a wide southern gap and penetrated it deeply.[4] The foray revealed such helplessness and passivity in the Italian troops that O'Connor continued to probe their defenses. By its own momentum the surprisingly successful raid soon carried the left wing of the Western Desert Force far behind enemy lines and into a series of clashes with the garrisons of the various Italian forts.

The first occurred on the morning of December 9, 1940, at the Nibeiwa camp. The appearance of British tanks so deep within their own perimeter took the Italian soldiers, many of them scurrying about in various stages of undress, completely by surprise. A few offered spasmodic resistance, but most of them surrendered. By the night of December 11, the Western Desert Force had captured 38,000 POWs and 73 tanks. Pushing westward, the advanced elements of the 7th Armored Division, with their Matildas fully protected from the enemy antitank artillery by their thick armor, reached the coast, and thus were astride the Italian line of retreat. What was initially a limited foray turned eventually into a piercing offensive operation that had enveloped the main Italian defenses from the south and had reached the sea.

The second battle took place on January 3, 1941, when O'Connor attacked the fortress of Bardia in the Gulf of Salum. There the resistance was stiffer, but after some fighting Bardia was captured. The booty was still more impressive: 40,000 POWs, 178 tanks, and a considerable number of transport vehicles. The third phase of the campaign took place on January 21, when the British stormed the major Italian defense post and supply base, Tobruk. Its capture resulted in over 25,000 POWs, still more armor, artillery, and a wide variety of supplies. The three successive British victories shattered the Italian Tenth Army and compelled its remnants to abandon most of Cyrenaica. All this was achieved at the price of fewer than 2,000 British casualties—killed, wounded, and missing.

O'Connor's next goal was to capture the capital of Cyrenaica, Benghazi. When he had learned that Graziani was already evacuating the town and heading toward Tripolitania, the British commander changed his mind and decided to cut off the Italian retreat. A furious race then commenced between the fast-retreating remnants of the Tenth Army and the Western Desert Force. Because of the acute transport shortage, O'Connor dumped most of his food, water, and ammunition supplies, except those in-

---

[4]The 7th Armored Division took as its emblem the Libyan desert rat or jerboa; this animal is quick and has a reputation for survival under most difficult circumstances. For an expert military analysis of the campaign see Liddell Hart, *History of the Second World War,* Vol. I, pp. 109–27.

British infantry forces attack an Italian fortified point. Imperial War Museum

dispensable for forty-eight hours of fighting. Had he not succeeded within this narrow margin of time, he would have been in a terrible predicament in the middle of the desert.

O'Connor's gamble was, however, crowned with another splendid success. This time O'Connor trapped most of the remainder of Graziani's Tenth Army and destroyed it in battle on February 5–7. Some 20,000 POWs, 120 tanks, 216 guns, and 1,500 trucks fell into British hands. O'Connor's dazzling victories were partly due to the superiority of his equipment and the fighting spirit of his troops, but largely to the shock produced by his daring moves. Graziani, in an abject report to Mussolini, pleaded nervous exhaustion; he was dismissed from his command and returned to Italy in disgrace.

Following his lightning triumphs, O'Connor was determined to press for a further march into Tripolitania. If successful, the offensive would complete his conquest not only of Cyrenaica, but also of Tripolitania, thus depriving the Axis of its last foothold in North Africa. Meanwhile, however, he received orders from Wavell to halt his advance. Most of the Western Desert Force, "except the barest defensive minimum," as Churchill put it, was to be dispatched to Greece. The Italian defeats in North Africa had been equaled by a series of still more humiliating blows inflicted on Mussolini's armies by the Greeks. Threatened with a German invasion, Greece, in Churchill's opinion, required immediate British aid.[5]

The Loss of Italian East Africa

The British scored no less dazzling successes in North East Africa. The considerable Italian possessions in the Horn of Africa included the old colonies of Eritrea and Somaliland; since 1936 they had been merged with the newly acquired Ethiopia into Italian East Africa. In these territories nearly a quarter of a million colonists from Italy lived and worked, guarded by over 300,000 native as well as Italian soldiers. Mussolini's imperial dreams had been most

[5]For a description of the British side of the Western Desert Force achievements, see W. F. G. Jackson, *The North African Campaign, 1940–43* (London and Sydney: B. T. Batsford, 1975), pp. 1–90.

ambitious. When the British hold on Egypt, British Somaliland, and British East Africa would be ended, these colonial provinces would be merged with the Italian possessions to form an immense sovereignty of Mussolini's empire emulating that of Rome.

The viceroy of Italian East Africa, Amadeo of Savoy, duke of Aosta, was almost as slow to take the initiative as Marshal Graziani. Afraid that he was unlikely to get further supplies of motor fuel and munitions through the British blockade, the duke failed to exploit his crushing superiority over the puny British garrisons in Sudan and British Somaliland, each of them numbering only a few battalions.

By the autumn of 1940, only a series of Italian raids had taken place along Italian East Africa and the strip of British possessions there. Some initial movements had given the superior Italian forces some success; they even managed to capture British Somaliland. Soon, however, the British and imperial forces, reinforced by General Wavell from Egypt after the easy triumph over Graziani, regained the initiative and counterattacked. Operating from Kenya in the south and from the Anglo-Egyptian Sudan in the northwest, British troops launched an offensive against the Italian East African garrisons. Quickly, British Somaliland was reconquered; on February 26, Mogadishu, the capital of Italian Somaliland, was captured. Cooperating with Ethiopian guerrillas, who had been supplied with 10,000 rifles, the British entered the capital of Ethiopia, Addis Ababa, on April 6, 1941. The rest of the campaign amounted mostly to mopping-up operations.

The swift British conquest of Italian East Africa was due, in part, to the desertion of a large number of native troops, who overwhelmingly preferred the British. More dangerous to the British than the Italian resistance were tropical diseases. The British suffered only 1,200 war casualties, but nearly 75,000 cases of tropical malaria and dysentery were recorded. Before the end of 1941 all of Italian East Africa was under British control. They had taken some 230,000 Italian POWs. Mussolini's dream of a new Roman Empire collapsed. "The chance of five thousand years," as Ciano had put it in his diary, had vanished overnight.

The End of the Italian Naval Threat

Graziani's and the duke of Aosta's passivity on land was paralleled by a similar attitude of the commander in chief of the Italian fleet, Admiral Angelo Iachino. Until the late autumn of 1940, Rome had taken it for granted that the invasion of England would either result in British collapse or at least in the redeployment of their forces from the eastern Mediterranean to the home island. If Italy was about to achieve naval supremacy in the Mediterranean by default, there was no sense in challenging prematurely so formidable an enemy. Also, like most of his officers, Admiral Iachino suffered from a profound inferiority complex toward the Royal Navy and was most reluctant to face its ships in an open battle.

The commander of the British Mediterranean naval squadron, Admiral Sir Andrew Cunningham, took immediate advantage of the lack of decisiveness of the *Regia Marina*. Far from intimidated by the Italian numerical superiority, he adopted Wavell's aggressive tactics from the very beginning.[6]

The first of Cunningham's attempts at nibbling at the Italian navy was made on July 10. Cruising the shores of Calabria, the reconnaissance planes of his old but recently modernized battleship *Warspite,* spotted an enemy squadron of two battleships, twelve light cruisers, and their destroyer escort. With one aircraft carrier, three battleships, five light cruisers, and several destroyers, Cunningham challenged the Italians at

---

[6]Cunningham was Commander in Chief, Mediterranean, from 1939 to 1943 and First Sea Lord from 1943 to 1945. He told his story in *A Sailor's Odyssey: The Autobiography of Admiral of the Fleet, Viscount Cunningham of Hyndhope* (London and New York: Hutchinson, 1951).

once. In the engagement one Italian battleship and a cruiser were severely damaged with little loss to the Royal Navy. Nine days later, the Australian light cruiser *Sydney* and four destroyers ran into two Italian cruisers off Crete and sank one of them.

These two successful encounters encouraged Cunningham to press further his aggressive approach. He resolved to reduce decisively the striking power of Italy's main naval base at Taranto in southern Italy, a permanent threat to British supply routes to Egypt and Malta which guarded them. On November 11 at 10:00 P.M., taking advantage of a full moon, twenty-one Swordfish biplanes suddenly dove on the Italian ships quietly at anchor in their home base; the attack was launched at the unusual altitude of 35 feet. Within a few minutes three enemy battleships were put out of action. The attackers lost only two planes, and two more were slightly damaged. This daring action resulted not only in crippling a large segment of the Italian fleet but in freezing the Italian fleet with a paralyzing fear of the Royal Navy.

The Taranto raid marked an important stage in the emergence of the aircraft carrier as the dominant factor in modern naval warfare. Moreover, the raid signaled the crucial role that Enigma and Ultra would play during the remainder of the war: Cunningham knew nearly all the vital details about the location of the Italian fleet and its incomplete protection. For instance, he was aware that at the Taranto docks the torpedo-defense nets reached only to the maximum draft of the battleships and not to the bottom of the harbor and that many barrage balloons sheltering the port had been swept away in a recent hurricane. Consequently, Cunningham decided to use torpedoes that could pass under the protective nets and detonate under the keels of the target vessels.[7] Now the British mastery of the Mediterranean was near complete.

[7]For the raid of Taranto see John Creswell, *Sea Warfare, 1939–1945*, chap. I, pp. 78–93.

CONSEQUENCES OF THE AFRICAN AND MEDITERRANEAN TRIUMPHS

The splendid African and Mediterranean victories, following the successes of the Battle of Britain, provided a badly needed boost in the morale of the beleaguered British people. The strategic situation in the Near East and Middle East was considerably altered. The Suez Canal, once blocked by the double Italian threat, could now function fairly normally. British, and later American, supplies were henceforth shipped through it to the "Army of the Nile," as Churchill liked to call the Western Desert Force. The pressure on Malta was partially relieved. Winston Churchill heralded the Battle of Britain and the desert victories of the year 1940 as "the finest hour" of the British people. He considered the triumphs scored in that fateful year more brilliant and significant than the victories over Louis XIV and Napoleon.

By the end of 1940 admiration for Britain's surprising and unparalleled achievements was widespread not only in the free world but also throughout most of Axis-occupied Europe. President Roosevelt sent Churchill a personal handwritten message enthusiastically lauding Britain's triumphs. His letter, dated January 20, 1941, ended with a stanza from Longfellow's "Building of the Ship," originally applied to the United States:

Sail on, oh, ship of State!
Sail on, oh, Union, strong and great!
Humanity with all its fears,
With all the hopes of future years,
Is hanging breathless on thy fate!

With Great Britain tested in the greatest air battle in history and revealed as daring in victories in Africa and the Mediterranean, there arose a new awareness of the solidarity of the English-speaking nations. United States spokesmen began to perceive an American self-interest in the destruction of the Axis. A new mood was generated in the

A British Matilda tank with a captured Italian flag.
Imperial War Museum

United States, which slowly eroded isolationist sentiments. Isolationism was, however, deeply rooted. Even the exchange of fifty antiquated destroyers for naval bases, so advantageous to United States security, was criticized. But the new mood created by recent British victories allowed President Roosevelt to launch an ingenious program of keeping Britain going "by all means short of war." The key to his scheme was the idea of getting rid of what he called "the silly old dollar sign" in transactions essential to Britain's struggle against the Axis. The President supported his argument for helping the British in their predicament with an example: "Suppose my neighbor's house catches fire and I have a length of garden hose. . . ." Would a refusal to lend the hose to one's neighbor be a sensible step? Such passivity would be not only unfriendly but also damaging potentially to the American house.

President Roosevelt's initiative was most timely. Britain began the war with some $4 billion in gold and had spent practically all of it by the end of 1940. The President wished to help by "eliminating the silly dollar sign," but his actions unleashed a lengthy debate among United States lawmakers that lasted two months. Finally, in March 1941 Congress conferred upon the President the power to lend or lease any equipment to any nation whose defense he deemed essential to United States security.

Under the Lend-Lease and its renewals, by the end of 1945 over $50 billion would be extended to the allies of the United States in World War II. Of this amount over 60 percent went to Great Britain. Approximately half of lend-lease was in munitions and petroleum products, about one-fifth in industrial commodities, and the rest in food and services. As provided in the act, "reverse lend-lease" accounted for raw materials, food, and quarters for American troops abroad, and the total for this would reach $17 billion.

Italian Weaknesses

Italy's defeats on land and sea were due as much to Mussolini's faulty strategy as to the country's material and psychological unpreparedness for a serious war. For the ill-advised war plans, Il Duce was largely responsible, since the dictator served as the self-imposed commander in chief of the armed forces, as well as War Minister.

Italy's main problem, however, was its economic backwardness, which the Fascist

A group of Italian, mostly happy, prisoners captured by the British in North Africa. Imperial War Museum

system—for all its high-sounding claims—was unable to overcome. The Italians lacked the economic potential to take full advantage of their Ethiopian conquests and enough military strength to defend their scattered colonial possessions. Even the intervention in the Spanish civil war had represented a gross overextension of Italian resources.

Although between 1935 and 1938 Italy had expended 11.8 percent of its national income on national defense (compared with 12.9 percent for Germany, 6.9 percent for France, and 5.5 percent for Britain), the Italian armament programs were ill-conceived and badly coordinated. The highly publicized "mechanization" of the Italian army remained largely on paper. Italy, a pioneer of motorization with the first armored division in the world, could not keep pace with the other powers. In 1940 Italy had antiquated artillery from 1918 and possessed merely a handful of medium tanks, the bulk of its armor being composed of light tanks and armored cars. This array had looked impressive in the early 1930s, but was no match for the tanks of Germany, France, and Britain by 1939/40. The Italian army was good enough to suppress the Sanusi or Amhari tribes but could not fight on equal terms with elite British units. To Italy's technological backwardness one should add bitter rivalries; factional intrigues raged between ranks of the regular officers and those commanding the Fascist militia. Some gallant exploits notwithstanding, none of the Italian armed services could cope with a task for which they lacked adequate tools and lines of command.[8]

Even in the field of aviation, the Italians, who had been its innovators in the 1920s, were by 1940 far behind their Axis partner as well as their British opponent. Italian fighters compared favorably with those of the French but did not match British or German craft. The Italian navy was large and modern but suffered from numerous handicaps. The fleet had hardly any air arm and no aircraft carrier, because Mussolini considered that Italy itself was a natural and unsinkable carrier. Excessively centralized command structure often stifled initiative at sea, while the naval officers on the spot were blinded by lack of adequate reconnaissance aircraft and radar. There were also such glaring technical shortcomings as defective

[8]The reasons for the backwardness of the Italian armor are discussed in John Joseph Timothy Sweet, *Iron Arm: The Mechanization of Mussolini's Army, 1920–1940* (Westport, Conn.: Contributions in Military History, no. 23, 1980), especially pp. 175–90.

torpedoes and fire-control devices. In addition to all these shortcomings, from the beginning the Italian navy suffered from an acute gasoline and oil shortage and was increasingly dependent on scarce German supplies. Thus, despite numerous cases of individual bravery the *Regia Marina* was hardly a match for its determined and much better equipped and brilliantly commanded British opponent.

The Italian defeats in Africa undermined not only Italy's but also Mussolini's prestige. By December 1940 Il Duce belatedly realized that without German military and economic aid, Italy could not even defend its North African possessions let alone expand them. On December 19 Mussolini was compelled to swallow his pride and ask Hitler for help.

9

The Balkans

The German offensive in the west in 1940 was greeted by Stalin with relief as the beginning of a long, exhausting war waged far away from Soviet frontiers. In Stalin's expectations, the capitalists would tear each other to shreds, he calculated, and the Red Army would wait for the outcome of the contest. Meanwhile, the Soviet dictator could take advantage of Hitler's involvement in the west by consolidating his position in the Baltic and Black Sea regions. He lost no time in taking action. In June 1940, while the French were capitulating, Soviet intelligence had conveniently discovered a secret plot allegedly hatched by the governments of Lithuania, Latvia, and Estonia against Moscow. This conspiracy gave the Red Army a needed pretext to march in and occupy all three Baltic states. The Soviet military brought along teams of trusted agents who, collaborating with the local Communists, established new governments friendly to the USSR. Soon, as a face-saving device, hastily prepared plebiscites ratified these political upheavals, and in July the three Baltic states were incorporated into the USSR as its fourteenth, fifteenth, and sixteenth republics.

At the same time, Stalin tried to stretch the terms of his 1939 deal with Hitler concerning Rumania.[1] In the note to Bucharest of June 26, 1940, Moscow insisted that "in the interest of justice" the provinces of Bessarabia and northern Bukovina be ceded to the USSR. The latter demand went beyond the secret protocol: Although Bes-

[1]For source material on the German-Soviet cooperation in 1940/41 see R. J. Sontag and J. S. Beddie, eds., *The Nazi-Soviet Relations*, pp. 100 ff.; for a discussion of the relations: Adam Ulam's *Expansion and Coexistence*, pp. 280–313.

sarabia had been a part of the deal, northern Bukovina had never been mentioned. The Soviet demands forced King Carol II to appeal to Berlin for help. Hitler, however, contemplating an invasion of Britain, advised compliance with both requests. Thus, Bessarabia was declared the Moldavian Soviet Socialist Republic, and northern Bukovina was incorporated into the Soviet Ukraine. The annexation of the two former Rumanian provinces extended Soviet frontiers up to the mouth of the Danube. With the occupation of northern Bukovina, Stalin for the second time had pushed beyond the old boundaries of the Tsarist Empire. The first case was that of eastern Galicia, which until 1918, like northern Bukovina, had belonged to the Habsburg Empire.

Angered by the Soviet violation of the secret protocol, Hitler decided to reassert German hegemony in the Danube region. In August 1940 Hitler summoned representatives of Rumania and Hungary to Vienna, as clients, and together with Ciano arbitrated their territorial disputes, which had threatened to explode into an open conflict. The Vienna award gave Hungary the northern half of Transylvania. This second spoliation of Rumania produced a storm in Bucharest amounting to a coup d'état. The discredited King Carol II had to flee the country, while an authoritarian dictatorship was set up by General Ion Antonescu, under the nominal kingship of Carol's son, Michael. Antonescu promptly submitted to Hitler's pressure and allowed a large team of German military and economic advisers to be sent to Rumania to reorganize its military forces and supervise its economy, especially the logistically vital oil fields of Ploeşti.

The Soviet Union was not invited to the Vienna conference. The exclusion of the Russians from decisions concerning the Balkan and Danube regions was followed by two anti-Soviet arrangements: the stationing of German troops first in Finland and then in Rumania. This created tension between Moscow and Berlin, and a series of sharp Soviet protests followed. Another snub to Moscow came on September 26, 1940, when the Berlin-Rome-Tokyo Axis was reconstituted with menacing overtones.

On that day, Germany, Italy, and Japan issued in Berlin a solemn declaration dividing the world into three "natural spheres of interest": Europe was to be Germany's sphere, the Mediterranean and Africa Italy's, and southeast Asia was allotted to Japan. The three anti-Comintern powers undertook "to assist one another with all political, economic and military means" should all of the contracting powers be attacked by a power "not at present involved in the European war, or in the Sino-Japanese war." This could mean either the USSR or the United States of America.

To relax the mounting tension, Hitler invited Molotov to Berlin on November 12/13. Molotov's visit was the first official trip of a Soviet statesman to the Nazi capital. At the meeting, Hitler and Ribbentrop suggested that, in view of the imminent downfall of the British Empire and Commonwealth, the Soviet Union should participate with the Axis in the partition of the world. The Soviets should redirect their interests away from the Balkan-Baltic area toward the Persian Gulf, the Middle East, and the Indian Ocean; that is, they would inherit a part of the traditional British sphere of influence.

While eagerly accepting the German recognition of the prospective Soviet position in the Persian Gulf and the Middle East, Afghanistan, Molotov repeatedly stressed the primacy of Russia's European interests from Finland to Turkey. He emphasized the vital importance of Rumania and Bulgaria for Soviet security. Molotov protested the increasing German military presence in Rumania and the ongoing infiltration of Bulgaria by the Axis. The Soviets would like to have their bases in the Bosporus and the Dardanelles. Against whom, asked Molotov, were the new Rumania borders guaranteed? And what about Soviet security in Turkey, Finland, and the Black Sea straits?

While Ribbentrop was making a speech on the benefits of the Soviets in joining the Axis powers in partitioning the British Empire

Rudolf Hess, Hitler's deputy for Party affairs, greets Viacheslav Molotov in Berlin. National Archives

and arguing that the defeat of England was certain, a massive British air raid took place over Berlin and an alarm was sounded. In the air raid shelter, Ribbentrop repeated his argument that Britain was finished as a great power. Then Molotov asked, "If Britain is finished, whose bombs are falling on us?" There was no answer. Molotov's visit merely revealed a widening gap separating Russia and Germany. He returned to Moscow angry and empty-handed.

Molotov's stubborn insistence on the primacy of Soviet interests in eastern Europe finally convinced Hitler that Stalin's price for continuing cooperation was too high. This conviction reconfirmed his July decision to prepare for a final military showdown with Russia. On December 18, 1940, Hitler issued his directives for operation "Barbarossa": a short campaign against Russia would open by May 15, 1941, and end by the autumn of that year; the purpose of this attack was to eliminate the Soviet Union as an ever-present menace to Germany in the east.[2]

THE ITALIAN CAMPAIGN AGAINST GREECE

While Hitler was making his momentous decision to march on the USSR, and while the Western Desert campaign in Africa was entering a critical stage, the Italian armies were fleeing from Greece and retreating back toward their Albanian bases. Mussolini's decision to attack Greece was a result of his inordinate thirst for military glory and his jealousy of Hitler's constant successes. Frustrated by the French armistice, Il Duce was determined to reassert his "parallel war," conducted simultaneously in Africa and in the Balkans and independently as far as possible of his Axis partner. The choice of his Balkan victim was, however, no easy matter for the Italian dictator. His initial choice was Yugoslavia, but here his appetite ran afoul of German vital interests.

Ever since the occupation of Albania in April 1939, both Yugoslavia and Greece lived under the threat of an Italian attack. Hitler, however, insisted on the integrity of Yugoslavia, because its economic resources were vital for the German war effort. By 1939 Yugoslavian mines provided most of the Reich's tin, about one-third of its aluminum, and smaller, but still vital, amounts of its supplies of copper, lead, and hemp. As a source of raw materials, Yugoslavia ranked second only to Rumania's 6 million tons of oil per year. Moreover, Yugoslavia was situated at the southern approaches of the Reich between the German and Italian spheres of influence, in a sort of buffer zone between the two Axis powers.

Consequently, Mussolini shifted his atten-

---

[2]For Hitler's decision to attack Soviet Russia see *Hitler's Table Talk,* pp. 31, 182–83, and 430; for the order of "Case Barbarossa" see Trevor-Roper, ed., *Blitzkrieg to Defeat,* pp. 19–52; for a monograph on the subject see Robert Cecil, *Hitler's Decision to Invade Russia, 1941* (London: Davis-Poynter, 1975).

tion toward Greece, thought to lie in the Italian orbit of domination. When Mussolini greeted Hitler in Florence on October 28, he boastfully informed him that Italian troops had crossed the Greek frontier at dawn and were on their way to Athens. Hitler, although unenthusiastic about the independent initiative, viewed the Italian venture against the Greeks as a part of his own "peripheral" strategy, which ultimately aimed at his main enemy, Britain. An Italian-controlled Greece could be helpful to Germany because it would threaten the entire British position in the eastern Mediterranean. Mussolini's plan to capture Greece thus seemed to complement Hitler's overall planning. Hitler merely questioned Italy's ability to execute the operation swiftly.

Mussolini's decision to pounce on Greece was not as sudden as it seemed at the moment. From the beginning of the war Italian intelligence had spotted numerous instances of Greek help to the British forces in the Mediterranean and the Near East. As early as July 1940 Rome had charged the Greeks with breaches of neutrality that enabled the British to carry out aerial attacks on Italian submarines. To punish the Greeks and prevent further encroachments, the Italians argued that they should be allowed to occupy the coveted Greek islands in the Ionian Sea.

When the Greek premier and dictator, Ioannis Metaxas, refused even to discuss such concessions, Mussolini ordered his highly skeptical and reluctant General Staff to make contingency plans for a short campaign to subdue the arrogant British vassal. Il Duce's military experts protested, arguing that the African war was enough to tax Italy's limited resources. Mussolini brushed aside their argument and insisted that Greece, a backward and small country of 8 million people, could be subdued by some twelve Italian divisions concentrated in Albania. He considered Greece as important to the Mediterranean as Norway was to the North Sea; Greece's conquest was a vital step toward realization of his dream of the Mediterranean as Italy's *mare nostrum*.

When General Metaxas refused to renounce the British guarantee of April 1939, Il Duce arranged a provocative incident on August 15: An Italian submarine torpedoed a Greek cruiser in the Aegean Sea. On October 28, before dawn, the Italian minister in Athens presented an ultimatum to General Metaxas, demanding that the whole of Greece be opened to Italian troops. The reason given by Mussolini was that the Greek government, contrary to their promised neutrality, had granted air and naval bases to the British. Metaxas rejected the ultimatum. At the same time, the Italian army in Albania invaded Greek territory at several points.

An Italian Breda bomber over Greece. National Archives

Greek resistance was stiff. Equipped with French cannons and tanks, the well-commanded Greek army was more than a match for the invaders. They fought splendidly, while Italian morale rapidly vanished. For the average Italian troop the war was a strange adventure; for the Greek fighter the conflict meant defense of his homeland.

After some initial Italian successes, their opponents stopped the advance and counterattacked with vigor and skill. While the Greeks pursued their counteroffensive, Admiral Cunningham struck at the Italian fleet at Taranto on the night of November 11/12. The British, moreover, immediately occupied the island of Crete and sent several RAF squadrons to the mainland to bolster Greek air defenses. Greek troops entered southern Albania on November 22 and took Koritsa. Large quantities of Italian equipment were destroyed and many Italian POWs were captured. By December 4 the Greeks had broken through the enemy lines of defense. Metaxas and the commander in chief, General Alexandros Papagos, publicly proclaimed that the Greeks fought "for the liberation of Albania." Gambling that his troops could drive the Italians into the sea before spring, Metaxas feared that German help for Italy might then be available. A prompt and decisive Greek victory, he reasoned, might induce Yugoslavia and Turkey to join a common front.

YUGOSLAVIA'S PREDICAMENT

Privately Hitler expressed admiration for the Greeks and compared them with the heroic Finns. He referred to them as "two small nations who knew how to defend themselves." On the other hand, the Führer could not tolerate Italy's defeat by a British client. The plight of his Axis partner in both Africa and the Balkans threatened Mussolini's Fascist regime at home and hence Italy's participation in the war. In turn, such a collapse would endanger his strategy of a series of peripheral wars against Britain. To Italy's three successive setbacks in North Africa, Greece, and the Mediterranean, the Führer reacted by making a twofold decision. He gave orders on December 13 to prepare plans for a German intervention in Greece to aid his routed Italian allies; next, his units trained for colonial service were to be ready to depart for North Africa immediately.[3]

Hitler's rescue operation in Greece was preceded by a careful buildup of German manpower and equipment in Rumania and Bulgaria in order to protect the southern flanks of his troops then concentrating for his planned offensive against the Soviet Union. Since Bulgaria was reluctant to participate in a war against Russia, Hitler's Balkan plans focused on Rumania, which had just been despoiled by Russia's annexation of Bessarabia and northern Bukovina and was, therefore, thirsting for revenge. Threatened on three sides by Soviet Russia, Hungary, and Bulgaria, the Rumanian dictator, Marshal Antonescu, placed his country under German protection and invited German troops onto Rumanian soil. Hitler now possessed a launching point for his planned thrust toward the Ukraine and Greece.

Vital also for Hitler's attack on Greece was Yugoslavia, rich in raw materials and promising as a location from which to invade Greece. Hitler planned to woo the Yugoslavs into a close association with the Axis, thus assuring at least a secure passage for his troops. Here Hitler's scheme clashed with Churchill's. The British prime minister had urged Belgrade to resist Berlin's pressure in order to ensure that the Greek flank could not be turned. By the end of 1940 Belgrade became a diplomatic cockpit with Axis spokesmen competing with those of Britain who, in turn, were secretly supported by Washington's diplomats.

Yugoslavia's position was precarious not only in the international arena but also at home. Ethnic and religious tensions, especially the Serb-Croat conflict, had not been resolved by the establishment in 1929 of

[3]For Hitler's war directives in the Mediterranean and the Balkans see Trevor-Roper, ed., *Blitzkrieg to Defeat*, pp. 52–58 and 60–74.

King Alexander's personal dictatorship. Croatian autonomists denounced his government as another attempt to turn Yugoslavia into a "Greater Serbia." After the King's assassination in Marseilles in 1934 by a Bulgarian terrorist acting on behalf of the Croatian Fascist terrorists, Alexander's first cousin, Prince Paul (serving as Regent for the young king Peter) sought in vain to alleviate the ethnic conflicts. The Croatian irredentists, however, constituted a thorny internal problem.

Oxford educated and basically pro-Western (he considered himself "an honorary Englishman"), the Regent was painfully aware that his country bordered on both Germany and Italy and was not prepared for war. After the destruction of Poland Prince Paul tried to keep Yugoslavia out of the conflict by a carefully contrived policy of neutrality. After the fall of France the Regent loosened his country's previous pro-Western ties and tried to convince Hitler and Mussolini that they had nothing to fear from Belgrade's policy of nonalignment. Secretly, however, after the beginning of the war the Regent, looking for an ally who could make Germany and Italy think twice before attacking Yugoslavia, established secret contacts with Moscow.

This overture to the USSR was a delicate operation in view of the Yugoslav government's persistent and militant anticommunism. During the early 1920s Belgrade had welcomed some 300,000 White refugees, victims of the Russian civil war; until the autumn of 1939 tsarist Russia still had a quasi-diplomatic representation in Belgrade. Although excluded from the second Vienna award of August 1940 and eager to reassert his influence in the Balkans, Stalin was not yet ready to turn the initial economic exchanges into a partnership with the inveterate protector of the White Russian emigres.

Not until after the fall of France, on June 24, 1940, did Prince Paul manage to establish diplomatic ties with Soviet Russia. Yet all attempts of the first Yugoslav ambassador in Moscow to open negotiations for an alliance between the two countries were ignored by Molotov. Such a formal tie would naturally worry Yugoslavia's neighbors. Consequently, to assuage at least one of them, the Regent signed the Treaty of Eternal Friendship with Hungary on December 12, 1940.

THE POLITICAL STRUGGLE FOR AND IN YUGOSLAVIA

Meanwhile, Yugoslavia's diplomatic and military situation was rapidly deteriorating. On March 1, 1941, Bulgaria signified its adherence to the Axis. On the next day German troops crossed the Danube causing considerable anxiety in Belgrade. By that time Yugoslavia was nearly surrounded by the Axis except for the small Greek sector of the frontier in the south. German and Italian pressure to join the Tripartite Pact was mounting. The Regent tried to procrastinate by setting a high price for joining the Axis. His conditions included a specific territorial guarantee against Italian encroachments, exemption from the obligation of active military cooperation against the western Allies, a promise that Yugoslav troops would not be dispatched across their country's frontiers, and last but not least, direct access to the Aegean Sea through the Greek port of Thessaloniki (Salonika). All these conditions were eventually granted.

When the Yugoslavs still hesitated, Hitler on March 1, 1941, raised the question of the future ruler of Russia, hinting that it might be a member of the house of Karageorge. Prince Paul would then be considered a likely candidate for the imperial crown. When the Regent still vacillated, Ribbentrop presented an ultimatum for a decision within twenty-four hours. On March 25 the long-delayed adherence to the Tripartite Pact was signed in Vienna by the Yugoslav delegation.

All this time British diplomacy was working frantically to abort the negotiations by all means available. British propaganda tried to influence the country's public opinion against the pact, representing it as an abject surrender and a humiliating blow to

The Invasion of Yugoslavia and Greece by the Axis, April 6, 1941.

Yugoslavia's national honor. Opposition to the pact was orchestrated by Britain's Special Operations Executive (SOE), which spread its point of view by means of pamphlets, leaflets, rumors, and a number of secret radio stations. Churchill instructed the British ambassador in Belgrade to be aggressive: "Continue to pester, nag and bite."[4]

President Roosevelt was also persistent in his attempts to convince the Yugoslavs that it was in their interest to resist Hitler. A special emissary, Colonel William Donovan, arrived in Belgrade on January 23 with the President's personal warning that if Yugoslavia allowed the passage of German troops, the United States would not intercede on Yugoslavia's behalf at the peace table. The British-American exhortations found a wide-

[4]The official British sources about the activity of the staff of the British legation in Belgrade in those days are not available at the Public Record Office; for the official British point of view: Sir Llewellyn Woodward, *British Foreign Policy in the Second World War* (London: H.M.S.O. 1970), pp. 22 ff.; and W. S. Churchill, *The Grand Alliance,* pp. 156–75.

spread echo in Serbia, although much less so in Croatia or Slovenia.

Interestingly enough, on March 26 the British air attaché in Belgrade visited the Yugoslav air force headquarters and had a long conference with some of the leading Yugoslav generals. During the night of March 26/27 a military coup took place in Belgrade led by the generals in question. The conspirators, supported mostly by young officers, occupied the ministry of war, the prime minister's office, the ministry of foreign affairs, and the main post office of Belgrade. In this way the insurgents gained control of all communications within the country. Premier Cvetković was arrested. Prince Paul was on the way to his summer residence in Slovenia when his train was stopped; two officers informed him that the regency had been overthrown and that he was to be exiled. By 4:00 P.M. on March 27 the revolutionaries were in complete control of the capital and announced that young King Peter had come of age and was now the ruling monarch.

The new government, headed by General Dušan Simović, immediately declared that Yugoslavia would maintain its current international relations; it simply wished to "renegotiate" the conditions of its adherence to the Tripartite Pact. Protestations of friendship toward Berlin and Rome were aired, but against a background of wild demonstrations throughout Serbia in favor of Britain and the United States. The most popular slogan was "Better war than the pact." The windows of the German tourist bureau in Belgrade, which served as Gestapo headquarters for the whole of Yugoslavia, were broken and the swastika flag was torn to pieces.

When Hitler was told what had happened in Belgrade, he first regarded it as a joke. He viewed the conditions granted to Yugoslavia as most magnanimous and more than sufficient to satisfy the country's wildest national dreams. But when his ambassador and military attaché in Belgrade confirmed the seriousness of the situation, he went into a rage. He feared that Stalin would exploit the Yugoslav coup to further his aims in the Balkans, advance toward the Turkish straits, and ruin his "Barbarossa" scheme at the last moment. The Führer acted with vengeance. He ordered the Ober Komando der Wehr-Macht to "punish" the Yugoslavs by destroying the country "both militarily and as a state." The Second and the Twelfth Armies were to be the main executors of the order.

April 1941: The Ruins of Belgrade. National Archives

The left wing of the Twelfth Army operating from Bulgaria and Rumania was to sever connections between Greece and Yugoslavia. The Second Army was to attack Yugoslavia from Austria and Hungary. The Italians were to strike from Albania, Venice, and Trieste and to occupy Yugoslavia's Adriatic ports.

For a time, however, the Hungarians created some obstacles. When the regent, Admiral Horthy, received a message on March 27 that Hitler had asked for military cooperation while promising Hungary a revision of the hated Treaty of Tranon, he was delighted. Initially, Horthy was all "fire and flames" in favor of the project. But his civilian advisers then reminded him that Hungary's Treaty of Eternal Friendship with Yugoslavia had been signed only four months before.

With some effort, Premier Pál Teleki persuaded the Regent to return an evasive answer to Hitler. Meanwhile, however, General Werth, chief of the Hungarian General Staff, in conversation with the Germans, accepted Hitler's request that the Hungarian army join in the attack on Yugoslavia. When he heard of these arrangements, Teleki challenged them in the name of the recent friendship treaty. But he was alone in his protest. Meanwhile, the Hungarian minister in London reported that Britain would declare war if the Hungarians cooperated in an assault on Yugoslavia. Unable to stop the passage of German troops, Teleki shot himself on April 2.

THE AXIS ATTACKS

The Axis launched their drives on Yugoslavia and Greece simultaneously on April 6, 1941.[5] Their offensive against Yugoslavia came from four directions: from Austria and Hungary, and Rumania and Bulgaria, while from the west the Italian forces attacked from their Istrian and Albanian bases. The bulk of the German forces operated from across the Bulgarian frontier. In return for his compliance King Boris had been offered most of Yugoslavian Macedonia as his share in the venture, as well as Axis indulgence in his nonparticipation in Barbarossa.

Yugoslavia's geopolitical position was almost as ragged as that of Poland's in 1939. Moreover, while embarking upon a bold course in foreign policy, the new Yugoslav government of General Simović failed to take adequate measures for the defense of the country.

Warnings of the approaching storm were not lacking. On April 2 the Yugoslav military attaché in Berlin reported to Belgrade that the Germans would attack Yugoslavia on April 6. Twice on April 5 the British warned that the German invasion would arrive the next morning. In both cases General Simović dismissed the information as unduly alarmist. No preparations were made to repel the German attack. So certain was Simović of Yugoslavia's security that the date for the wedding of his daughter was set for the morning of April 6. Instead of immediately proclaiming a general mobilization, he delayed it until April 7, a day after Hitler's invasion.

Yugoslavia's leaders had formed an exaggerated picture of the strength of the British forces sent to Greece and implicitly relied on British aid. The British, having skillfully avoided any binding promises, could allot to the Yugoslavs only a small number of aircraft from the limited contingent already stationed in Greece. The rifle strength of the Yugoslav Army was nearly equal to that of the invaders, but it was desperately short of antiaircraft and antitank guns, and its air force was no match for the Luftwaffe supported by the *Regia Aeronautica.* London suggested that General Simović attack at once the Italian garrisons in Albania and establish contact with the Greeks through

---

[5]For an analysis of the Yugoslav and Greek campaigns see Martin L. Van Creveld, *Hitler's Strategy 1940–41. The Balkan Cue* (Cambridge: Cambridge University Press, 1973); and G. Blau, *The German Campaign in the Balkans (Spring 1941)*, Washington, D.C.: Department of the Army, 1953.

the Monastir gap, but Belgrade failed to follow the suggestion and remained passive to the last moment of the Axis invasion on April 6. By April 7 the Germans had captured Skopje and pushed through the Monastir gap toward northern Greece. Yugoslavian passivity was such that the Italians captured a large part of their navy anchored in their ports.

Born in a burst of rage, "Operation Punishment" was executed with murderous vengeance. Belgrade was savaged in a manner similar to the sackings of Warsaw and Rotterdam. Like the Poles in 1939, the Yugoslavs conceived themselves bound to defend their whole frontier and refused to abandon Slovenia and Croatia for political reasons. The four Yugoslav army corps in the north were rapidly split by the German armored columns and their remnants were driven southward. At the same time, Hungarian and Italian troops advanced toward Zagreb and occupied most of Croatia. Already by April 10 the German troops occupied Zagreb. On April 13 they entered Belgrade. Meanwhile, the Twelfth Army, operating from Bulgaria, swung through Serbia and Macedonia, cutting contacts between the Yugoslavs and the Greeks. The Italian troops occupied Lubljana and a part of the Adriatic coast. The Hungarians entered the war as late as April 12 and limited their operations to their former province Bachka with its capital Novi Sad. In eleven days the entire country was occupied by the Axis and their clients. King Peter and his cabinet were evacuated and taken by British sea plane to Egypt. Eventually the government established itself in London, like those of Czechoslovakia, Poland, Norway, Belgium, Holland, and the Free French Committee of General de Gaulle.

Crushed Yugoslavia was partitioned. Croatian autonomists, many of whom had aided the Germans and the Italians, were rewarded with a quasi-independent state, the Kingdom of Croatia, headed by a junior prince of the Savoian dynasty (who never appeared in his capital at Zagreb!). The native Fascist government, led by an agent of Mussolini, Anté Pavelić, ran the country in the name of the Italian prince. Meanwhile, Germany annexed most of the province of Slovenia, and Hungary regained its former lands of Banat and Backa-Baranya, the fertile plains north of Belgrade. Italy expanded its territory to the east of Fiume (Rijeka) and annexed a part of the Dalmatian coast and Montenegro. Bulgaria grabbed Yugoslavian Macedonia and even a slice of southern Serbia. The Serbia heartland was reorganized as a German puppet state with General Milan Nedić as its prime minister.

Mussolini's nominal gains in Yugoslavia could not overshadow the defeats that the Italians had suffered in Greece. These proved a humiliating blow both to Mussolini and to Italy's aspirations to be regarded as a great power. The defeats in Africa and in the Balkans ruined Mussolini's original idea of a "parallel war." His strategy was predicated on the prompt German triumph in the battle of Britain, followed by a peace conference that would give him a chance to claim his slice of victory.

Each of Mussolini's independent military ventures deepened Italy's dependence on its Axis partner. By 1941 he realized that without German aid—military and economic—Italy could not pursue any meaningful large-scale operations outside its metropolitan territory. The German conquest of Yugoslavia and Greece resulted in the takeover of the crucial tin, copper, aluminum, and bauxite mines of those countries. The Rumanian oil fields of Ploeşti were under firm German control, while the Italian economy was suffering increasingly from the shortage of fuel, further undermining Italian morale and making the war increasingly unpopular.

The African setbacks, as painful as they were, could be explained away by domestic propaganda as inflicted by the crack troops of the British Empire, the ineffective Graziani, and the especially trying circumstances of desert warfare. But the series of successive victories scored by tiny Greece over Italy's troops were beyond any explanation. As Mussolini complained to Ciano, the Italians, who had been "an anvil for sixteen centuries, could not, in a few years, become a hammer." By 1941 Italy was reduced to the rank of a senior vassal of the Third Reich.

BRITAIN AIDS GREECE

Simultaneously with the Axis attack on Yugoslavia, the German Twelfth Army invaded Greece from Bulgaria. The rapid collapse of Yugoslavia had further exposed the northern frontier of Greece. The Greeks, long reluctant to accept Britain's aid against Italy, now asked for help. The British leaders were divided as to the scope of the aid to be sent to Greece. A British guarantee had indeed been given by Neville Chamberlain on April 13, 1939, but the means for its implementation were hard to find by the spring of 1941. The small Western Desert Force was then about to finish the mopping-up operation in Libya. The British knew that if Tripoli were not captured and the last Axis foothold in North Africa destroyed, the Germans and the Italians would reinforce the remnants of Graziani's Tenth Army and with German aid resume their offensive against Egypt. Consequently, the liquidation of the last Italian base in Tripolitania seemed like a most urgent task. This would make it impossible for the Axis to threaten Egypt again without first undertaking a major seaborne invasion. Moreover, Tripoli would be an excellent base from which RAF bombers could attack Sicily, the South of Italy, and German-occupied France.

Nevertheless, there were weighty political considerations arguing for helping the embattled Greeks. If Britain forsook Greece, this display of weakness might have a negative effect on great potential allies: the United States and Soviet Russia. Winston Churchill thought Britain was honor bound to help the Greeks and saw in the appearance of a British Expeditionary Force in the Balkans the best way of encouraging the Turks to abandon their neutral position and actively side with Britain. He realized that the British might be driven out of Greece, as they had been out of Norway, but the cause for which he stood might suffer an even heavier blow if Britain reneged on its solemn pledge to aid an old and loyal ally. The dilemma he faced was whether to attempt and fail, or not to attempt at all.[6]

Thus far, British military aid to the Greeks against the Italians had been limited to a few RAF squadrons. Now, with the Germans about to march into Greece in full force, more substantial aid was urgently needed. Despite General Wavell's hesitations, a large part of the Western Desert Force, reinforced by freshly arrived Australian, New Zealand, and Indian units, was ordered to embark for Greece. Only a tiny force was left to watch the remnants of the Tenth Italian Army in Tripolitania.

Transporting some 56,000 men over 200 miles of water was a daring operation in the teeth of the large Italian Naval squadron. Indeed, on March 27, RAF reconnaissance planes spotted a concentration of the Italian fleet off Cape Matapan, the southernmost point of the Greek mainland. This was duly reported to Admiral Cunningham in Alexandria. To protect the supply route to Greece, Cunningham had to act with both cunning and boldness. Because the harbor of Alexandria was under constant surveillance by Axis spies, he must lead his large task force, composed of one aircraft carrier, three battleships, and nine destroyers, without alerting a net of enemy agents.

To deceive the enemy Cunningham left his flagship, the *Warspite,* and went ashore with his suitcases as if to stay in Alexandria at least for the night of March 27/28. He then played golf at his country club, patronized by the local diplomats, including the Japanese consul, who was also the chief Axis intelligence agent in Alexandria. The presence of the British admiral at the club was immediately reported to Admiral Iacchino. After making reasonably sure that his enemy had been lulled into a sense of false security, Cunningham left the club unno-

[6]For Churchill's view on Greece see *Their Finest Hour,* pp. 440–506 and 531–51.

A British 17 pounder crew in action. Imperial War Museum

ticed. Hidden in a dense fog fallen upon Alexandria, he headed straight toward the harbor; in darkness Cunningham sailed with his squadron toward the Greek mainland. A few hours later, using radar-directed guns and aircraft of his fleet air arm, he pounced upon the unsuspecting Italian squadron. Three of its cruisers and three destroyers were sunk, and heavy damage was inflicted on one battleship and other units. The only loss the British suffered was two aircraft.

The crippling damages inflicted at Matapan, following upon the Taranto raid of the previous November, destroyed Italian numerical superiority. Moreover, the blow made the Italian fleet battle shy to the end of the war and gave them the nickname of Timid Leopard. From then on it cleaved to its bases and seldom engaged in anything more ambitious than convoy duties. After Matapan, safe transport of the British Expeditionary Force was assured, despite some occasional harassment by the Luftwaffe operating from Italian bases. When the Battle of Matapan was analyzed by the Axis intelligence experts, they concluded that Cunningham must have had the advice of a highly placed spy. The British knowledge of the Enigma secret was never even suspected.[7]

[7]For an analysis of the Battle of Matapan see Geoffrey Bennet, *Naval Battles of World War II* (London and Sidney: B. T. Ratsford, 1975), pp. 112–34.

THE INVASION OF GREECE

In the German campaign in Greece there were two distinct stages: first, the offensive on the mainland and, then, the capturing of Greek islands, chiefly Crete. Each phase required different tactics and application of different methods. When the Germans invaded the Greek mainland, the bulk of the Greek army, some fourteen divisions, was engaged in pursuing the Italian invaders back into Albania. Only a small segment of the Greek forces, some six divisions, were aligned behind the "Metaxas line" facing Bulgaria, where the main German forces had concentrated. What remained amounted to not much more than eight divisions, which were now reinforced by the British Expeditionary Force from Egypt, under General Maitland Wilson.

In Greece the Germans promptly carried out several well-planned tasks. First, they captured the Monastir gap; this action separated the Greeks operating in southern Albania from their forces at home and also severed the Yugoslav armies in Macedonia. Second, the right German wing pushed the Greek troops westward toward the Ionian Sea. Next, the left German wing broke through the Metaxas line. Then both wings joined forces and turned south. From April 14 the British Expeditionary Force and its Greek allies gathered at a position around Mount Olympus were assailed by the advancing Germans. After cutting through these forces, the Germans pushed toward Salonika. The main natural obstacle between central Greece and the Peloponnesus was the Corinth Canal. Passage southward over this obstacle was assured by German parachutists, who instantly captured the canal. Pushing the combined Greek and Allied units further southward, the invaders rapidly approached Athens and captured it on April 27. The retreating Greek and Allied forces fought a series of bitter delaying encounters, but the Germans occupied the remaining southern Greek mainland by April 28.

The British, after consultation with the Greeks, decided to cut their losses by speedily evacuating the remnants of their troops to Crete and to Egypt. Before the Germans captured the last embarkation port of Kalamata, General Maitland Wilson managed to save the bulk of his 43,000 troops. Unfortunately, some 11,000 soldiers, Greek as well as British, and most of the heavy equipment were left behind. The evacuation was possible because after Taranto and Matapan the Italian navy had grown battle-shy and did not dare to intervene in force. The Luftwaffe, however, exacted a heavy toll by attacking the vulnerable port, inadequately protected by its few antiaircraft guns and fighter planes. The cost to the British was heavy in ships and planes as well as men. Altogether, the losses to the B.E.F. in Greece amounted to 15,000 men (dead, wounded, and POWs) as against 5,300 for the Axis.

The Greeks, despite their victories over the Italians, were thus eventually crushed by the German intervention. The defeat in Greece and the "second Dunkirk" at Kalamata were harsh blows to British prestige. The pain was especially sharpened because the North African campaign and the situation throughout the Middle East had at that moment taken an unfavorable turn.[8]

Throughout the Yugoslavian and the Greek campaigns the role of the Italian contingents was marginal. By that time the contempt of the German military establishment for their Axis allies was so deep that Marshal Siegmund List, commander of the German Twelfth Army, refused to admit an Italian unit to take part in the planned victory parade in Athens. Only Hitler's personal intervention compelled List to drop that veto.

For a brief period Hitler agreed to share control of Greece with Mussolini, but he soon changed his mind. While maintaining a fiction of a condominium, the Germans rapidly extended their administration over the entire country. Nevertheless, Italy was allowed

[8]For two British points of view on the Greek campaign see Charles Cruickshank, *Greece, 1940–1941* (London: Davis-Pointer, 1976); also Churchill, *Their Finest Hour*, pp. 531–51 and *The Grand Alliance*, pp. 3–21 and 94–110.

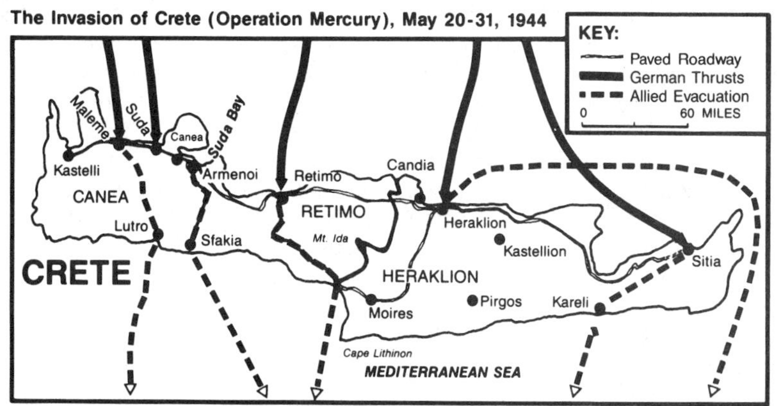

to annex the Ionian Islands as a consolation prize. Germany's Bulgarian ally took its revenge on Greece for defeats in the Second Balkan War of 1913 by incorporating Greek western Thrace (considered by the Bulgarians a part of their Macedonia). Salonika remained under German occupation.

THE BATTLE OF CRETE

Now, however, the British leaders felt the increasing urgency of another task: the defense of Crete. Separated by more than 100 miles of water from the Greek mainland, Crete stretches some 160 miles long, with a breadth varying from 35 miles in the middle to 89 miles at its eastern end. Crete's northern coast has long stretches of smooth, sandy beaches and three excellent ports, Canea, Suda Bay, and Heraklion, whereas its southern coast is mostly rugged and abrupt with no natural harbors. In 1941 most of the airfields were also on the northern side of the island. With the loss of the Greek mainland, the island acquired a new importance in Allied military planning. Initially, Crete had been considered merely a support base and depot for the British Expeditionary Force in Greece. Now the island served not only as a crucial evacuation station but also as a defense bastion sheltering Egypt and the Suez Canal.

For the Axis, however, control of Crete could provide a convenient point for an attack against the Suez Canal, as well as valuable air and sea bases that, in conjunction with the Dodecanese islands, could further the eventual mastery of the Mediterranean and, perhaps, the entire Near East. Precisely this notion inspired one of the most daring of Hitler's military experts, General Karl Student. A pioneer of parachuting, he had masterminded the capture of the Belgian forts and the Corinth Canal. He now commanded the newly created Airborne Corps. It was largely due to Student's persuasion that Hitler decided to use airborne troops to conquer Crete.

The original Greek garrison on Crete had consisted of one infantry regiment, a few coastal defense and antiaircraft batteries, and only twenty-four obsolete planes. By the end of April this puny force was bolstered by the remnants of various Greek units and nearly 27,000 British, Australian, and New Zealand troops evacuated from the mainland; the reinforcements included thirty-five aircraft and nine tanks.[9] This motley force of slightly over 30,000 men was commanded by Major General Bernard C. Freyberg. Born in Britain but educated in New Zealand, he had been one of the most celebrated heroes of World War I; wounded five times and mentioned six times in the dispatches, Freyberg was decorated with the highest British military award, the Victoria Cross, as well as with the Distinguished Service Cross.

Full of spirit and determination, General Freyberg used his boundless energy to prepare the shaky defenses of the island. The odds, however, were against him. His men, a ramshackle crowd composed mostly of fresh evacuees, many of them shellshocked and all suffering from battle fatigue, were desperately short of equipment, especially aircraft and tanks. Against them were arrayed German veterans of several victorious campaigns who enjoyed the benefit of greatly superior air cover.

General Student's scheme was based on the concept of a massive, simultaneous use of all three principal methods of airlifting troops: dropping parachutists with light equipment directly on the selected targets, landing troops with heavier equipment in transport planes, and airlifting soldiers by gliders. The parachuted spearhead was to include the veteran Seventh Airborne division of about 13,000 men; they were to be followed by 9,000 soldiers of the Alpine division. Student had at his disposal 700 transport planes and 80 gliders, to be escorted by 180 fighters and 430 bombers. His plan envisaged the dropping of the airborne

[9]For a monograph about the battle of Crete emphasizing the role of Student's parachutists see David A. Thomas, *Nazi Victory—Crete, 1941* (Briarcliff Manor, N.Y.: Stein & Day, 1972).

A German parachutist lands near the Maleme airport. National Archives

troops at the three main airfields on the island: Meleme, Retimo, and Heraklion; they would capture and hold these fields until the arrival of the main body of invaders arriving by the sea. General Freyberg had been forewarned by Ultra about the gist of the German strategem. Yet, an old-style warrior, he was skeptical of it and actually paid more attention to the prospects of amphibious landings on the beaches than to airborne attacks on airfields.

On the morning of May 20, after several hours of sustained bombing of all three of Crete's airfields, the enemy airborne units began to drop from the sky. The invaders met stiff resistance and most of the first wave of the Seventh Airborne division was nearly wiped out. But the German planes and gliders, well protected by the Luftwaffe, kept on coming, landing more and more reinforcements. The German engineers who followed promptly repaired the damaged airstrips, which, in turn, allowed for landing more and more heavy transport planes and gliders. A fierce battle of attrition was waged, and German air superiority proved decisive. Within twenty-four hours the Germans had 30,000 troops on the island of Crete.

The Maleme airport was the first to fall. By May 26 all three aerodromes were in German hands. As more enemy troops landed, they pushed the defenders out of the crucial airfields and toward the south of the island. Seeing the hopelessness of the situation, the British ordered an evacuation. The departure from Crete was carried out from the island's southern beaches and fishing harbors. About half of the defenders, mostly British and imperial troops, were evacuated by the Royal Navy mainly to Egypt. The Navy was vigorously backed by its tiny Fleet Air Arm, but since this air support was severely limited, the losses were huge. More than 3,000 Allied soldiers were killed, nearly 2,000 were wounded with an equal number missing, and 12,000 became POWs. The Royal Navy alone lost 1,823 killed and 180 severely wounded; 1 aircraft carrier, 3 cruisers, and 6 destroyers were sunk, and 3 battleships, 6 cruisers, and 7 destroyers were heavily damaged. In addition, the RAF had lost 16 medium bombers and 23 fighters. Counting the evacuations from Norway, France, and the Greek mainland, this was the third "Dunkirk" of the war for the British.

The Battle of Crete, a major three-dimensional operation in the war, represented a Pyrrhic victory for the Luftwaffe and the German airborne troops. Both of them, however, had to pay a heavy price for their triumph. The Seventh Air Fleet was decimated: it lost 170 troop-carrying planes and gliders, and 220 other aircraft were destroyed and 130 heavily damaged. Altogether the invaders lost 17,000 men, most of them highly trained parachute fighters. These crippling losses to such elite detachments compelled Hitler to reject Student's plan to capture the Suez Canal by means of another airborne operation. No similar large-scale use of airlifted troops was to be attempted by the Germans until the end of the war.

THE SIGNIFICANCE OF THE AFRICAN AND BALKAN CONFLICTS

The Balkan involvement of the two main protagonists, Britain and Germany, has been a subject of bitter and still largely unresolved controversies. The collapse of the entire Greek expedition profoundly affected Britain's prestige. This defeat, in turn, led to a resurgence of pro-Axis agitation throughout the Arab world and in Persia, thus threatening Britain's oil supplies. Finally, Turkey's entry into the Allied cause was rendered most unlikely.

By mid-1941 Hitler had won for Germany and the Axis another series of brilliant victories. They were scored, however, on the front he considered secondary. Nevertheless, the achievement possessed great potential. The Italian Dodecanese archipelago, combined with Crete, could be interlocked to form a powerful aero-naval base for operations against Egypt. Such a venture would help the Axis to chase the British from the Mediterranean and the entire Middle East. Yet, after achieving his Balkan and Mediterranean successes, Hitler turned his back on the Balkan-Mediterranean arena. The victories had been spectacular, but led nowhere.

In retrospect, one sees that Hitler's ideological phobia, his hatred of communism, blinded him in regard to his strategic priorities. If Britain was Germany's primary enemy, the "peripheral strategy" should have been pushed to its logical conclusion, with Egypt, the Suez Canal, and the oil-bearing fields of the Middle East as main objectives. The Russian plans should have been shelved. Stalin had refrained from stabbing Hitler in the back when he was fighting the Franco-British forces and thus would never have dared to challenge Hitler at the peak of his power after the 1940 triumph. If the destruction of Soviet Russia was for Hitler a more weighty priority, however, the Balkan and Mediterranean campaigns should have been designed to secure only the rear of the German forces ready to march eastward.

The Balkan-Mediterranean involvement, of course, also had its Italian aspects. Hitler could not afford to permit his Axis partner to be defeated and risk the downfall of the Fascist regime in Italy. For Hitler, strategic and ideologic motives were interconnected in his "brutal friendship" for Il Duce, the idol of his early political career. Yet, by the end of 1940, hardly half a year after their entry into the war, the Italians were a millstone on Hitler's neck.[10]

---

[10]For a German point of view concerning the Rome-Berlin Axis see Burkhart Mueller-Hillebrand, *Germany and Its Allies in World War II: A Record of Axis Collaboration Problems* (Frederick, Md.: University Publications of America, 1980), especially pp. 11–146.

10

Toward Cairo and Moscow

GERMAN PREPARATIONS FOR ENTERING NORTH AFRICA

The humiliating defeat of Italy in the western desert, followed by its simultaneous rout in Greece, shocked Hitler profoundly. For strategic and psychological reasons he had to back his Axis partner on both fronts. The North African front seemed to be the more urgent need. German intervention there was much less of an improvisation than it might have appeared. For a long time Goebbel's propaganda ministry had been preparing German public opinion for recovery of its lost German colonies in Africa. Soon after the Nazi seizure of power, the Party Colonial Office and two experimental military centers had been founded: one in Schleswig-Holstein and another in Bavaria.

These sites were training grounds for colonial units adapted to tropical conditions. By a mixture of steam and heated air, the soldier was acclimatized to desert conditions. Special diets were developed by the medical staff of the Hamburg Tropical Disease Institute. Experiments with vitamin pills and other medicaments led to development of special food lozenges for desert warfare. Soldiers were forced to subsist on a minimum of drinking water; the sand dunes of eastern Pomerania and East Prussia provided the terrain for maneuvers under sumulated conditions. Artificial dust and sand storms were created; sandproof casings for the engines and the interior of tanks were eventually designed. On January 11, 1941, Hitler ordered this experimental group expanded into an army corps and appointed General Erwin Rommel as commander of what now became the *Deutsches Afrika Korps*, or DAK for short. Its

General Erwin Rommel. National Archives

soldiers were issued sun helmets and light tropical uniforms with a sleeve brassard decorated with a silver palm tree and one word, *Afrika*.

Rommel played a remarkable role in the annals of both world wars. He was born in 1891 as a son of a schoolmaster and chose a military career only under the pressure of his father, who practically compelled Erwin to join the army. He fought with distinction in the German infantry during World War I, both in the western and on the Italian fronts. After the armistice, Rommel was not initially included in the shrunken cadres of the Reichswehr but became a military instructor for the Hitler Youth and in 1933 of the S.A. squads. In the rapid expansion of the Wehrmacht after March 1935, he was appointed full colonel and put in charge of the Führer's headquarters. At his request Rommel was appointed commander of the Seventh Light Panzer Division on the eve of the great offensive in the west. Although his division comprised only one panzer regiment, instead of the standard two, Rommel's division played a brilliant part in the French campaign; it fought as the vanguard unit of the Army Group Center, which played a decisive role in breaking up the enemy front at Sedan. It was Rommel's light panzer division that spearheaded the race to the English Channel. Among the exploits of Rommel was the capture of eight British generals and 25,000 men, the majority of whom belonged to the B.E.F.[1]

With Italy's disastrous defeat at the hands of British General Wavell, German plans for Africa had to be updated. A leading tank expert, General Wilhelm von Thoma, sent to North Africa in October 1940, was of the opinion that only a large German contingent of four armored divisions would assure a decisive victory in North Africa. Hitler, however, preoccupied with the preparation for the Russian campaign, could not spare such a body of armor. His plan for the Mediterranean was simply to bolster the Italians enough to keep them in the war and thus to disperse the British forces as much as possible. This was the original task of the DAK, initially composed of a mere two divisions (Fifteenth Panzer and Fifth Motorized). Rommel was to be subordinated to the Italian High Command and act purely defensively.[2]

The appearance in Libya of a crack German force led by a dynamic commander who had at his disposal considerable units of the Luftwaffe was bound to alter the situation not only militarily but also politically. By contributing to Italy's war effort in what had been hitherto regarded as Italy's exclusive bailiwick, Hitler acquired a considerable influence on the strategy in that area. With this step, Mussolini's original idea of a "parallel war" collapsed altogether. A new chapter was opened in the struggle for North Africa.

---

[1]For Rommel's standard biographies in English see Desmond Young, *Rommel the Desert Fox* (New York: Harper & Row, 1950); and David Irving, *The Trail of the Fox* (New York: Thomas Congdon Books, E. P. Dutton, 1977).

[2]For Hitler's directives see Trevor-Roper, *Blitzkrieg to Defeat*, pp. 52–55 ff; for the British side see Playfair et al., *The Mediterranean and the Middle East, Vol. II, The Germans Come to the Help of the Ally, 1941* (London: H.M.S.O., 1956).

ROMMEL LANDS IN AFRICA

Advanced elements of the DAK landed at Tripoli on February 14, 1941. According to Rommel's own account, by the time he reached Tripolitania and surveyed the situation, he decided to depart from Hitler's instructions that he must engage in only defensive operations. Rommel's World War I experiences on the Italian front had inspired him with contempt toward his Italian allies. He tried to camouflage his feelings, and he instructed his subordinates to do the same, but Rommel acted in accordance with his innermost conviction that the Italians were a negligible quantity. Knowing that the British troops facing him were extremely thin because of the aid to Greece, Rommel refused to give Wavell time to prepare his reinforcements, streaming in from all over the British Empire, for training and acclimatization to the desert conditions. Theoretically, he was supposed to be subordinated to the Italian High Command, but he ignored these instructions and acted on his own.[3]

Rommel disembarked most of his units in a hurry. Working day and night, not even waiting for all his supplies to arrive, he pounced on the unsuspecting British at El Agheila (where the coast swings north from the Gulf of Sirte and the great bulge of Cyrenaica begins). Wavell, who had been warned by Ultra about Rommel's arrival, did not expect the DAK to be ready for battle before May. When by the end of March the enemy's vanguard had wiped out the British at El Agheila, Wavell was flabbergasted. By April 4 the advanced elements of the DAK were already in Benghazi. The shattered and confused British troops were routed and had to abandon Cyrenaica. On April 13 Tobruk was encircled and Bardia was evacuated.

Brilliant at the opening gambit, Rommel shattered his opponents and captured a number of British POWs, including three generals, headed by the commander of the Western Desert Forces, Richard O'Connor. Only shortages of food, fuel, and ammunition prevented Rommel from pressing further eastward. By the end of May, after a spectacular dash of some 500 miles through the hot and dusty desert, the exhausted DAK halted exactly where Graziani's Tenth Army had stopped, that is, at the fortified lines of el-Alamein. There, protected by the sea in the north and the Quattara depression in the south, the prudent and resourceful Wavell scrambled enough reinforcements to make Rommel's further advance more difficult.

This dramatic reversal of fortune in North Africa was due to a variety of factors. Not the least important was Rommel's leadership and his acute tactical sense. He rejected the standard assumption that the prime purpose of tanks was to fight tanks

[3]Rommel openly disregarded these instructions; he trusted his luck and hoped that the distance from Berlin would protect him from Hitler's direct interference with his activities. For Rommel's view see B. Liddell Hart, ed., *The Rommel Papers,* and Liddell Hart, *German Generals Speak,* pp. 155–56.

Rommel's First Lightning Offensive, March 24-April 25, 1941

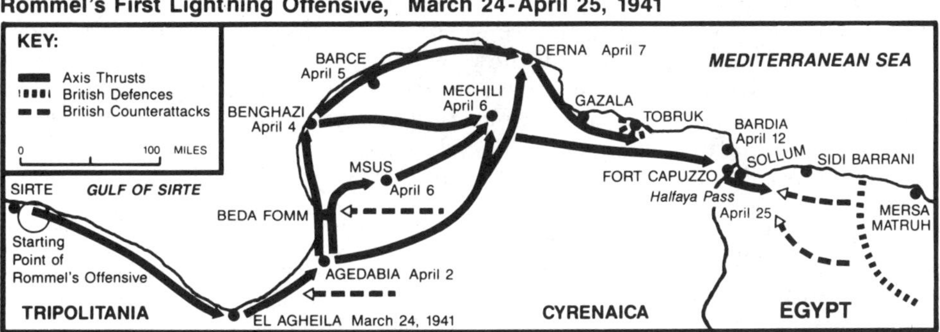

A victorious British Crusader tank is passing a burning German Mark IV. Imperial War Museum

and perceived that antitank gun batteries should be the primary tank killer; enemy armor must be drawn toward his massed antitank batteries and destroyed. The panzers, thus freed to attack the weak points of the enemy's formation and to deal with the infantry and artillery, could finally penetrate and overrun the opponent's rear areas.

Rommel vindicated the value of the "defensive-offensive" method in mobile mechanized warfare. Most eager to exploit the offensive potentialities of armored units, he also grasped the concept of the defensive counter to such attacks. In this Rommel in fact readapted the traditional "sword and shield" theory. In addition, Rommel fully exploited his superior equipment, especially dual-purpose antiaircraft and antitank and longbarreled 88-mm guns. Rommel's strafing Messerschmitt fighters and screaming Stuka dive bombers were far more numerous than RAF craft, the reserves of which had been depleted by the requirements of the Greek campaign.

Rommel was an unusual phenomenon. Trained as an infantry officer, he had all the dash and daring of a cavalry commander. A born gambler, he was willing to take both tactical and personal risks. More often with his soldiers than at his headquarters, he possessed an intuitive knack of turning up at critical moments, often to exert a decisive impact on his men. Rommel's stratagems were numerous. One of them involved transforming simple Volkswagen jeeps into wood-and-canvas dummy tanks; he earned the nickname of the Desert Fox. Always close to the front line and his fighting troops, he shared most of their hardships and privations. Unlike the Italians, who had a double standard, one for officers and one for men, Rommel insisted that he and his staff share the same rations as the enlisted men. Respect for their leader's austere and comradely ways created solidarity between the rank and file and their commander.

The lull resulting from Rommel's shortage of tanks, fuel, and ammunition lasted through the summer of 1941. This interlude gave the British time to reinforce and resupply their troops, drawing on the resources of the Commonwealth and on increasing American aid. The hitherto puny Western Desert Force was bolstered with fresh men and better equipment and expanded to comprise two full army corps. The new formation was retitled the Eighth Army, although Churchill, fond of picturesque names, still called it the Army of the Nile.[4]

---

[4]For Churchill's views of the second phase of the North African campaign see *The Grand Alliance,* pp. 3–21, 196–217, and 333–51.

THE POLITICAL SITUATION IN THE MIDDLE EAST

Meanwhile, however, British preparations for a counteroffensive were disrupted because of the volatile political situation in the area. The Arabs, as well as the Persians, had long resented British domination in the Middle East. Jewish migration to Palestine, a trickle prior to 1933, had increased considerably after Hitler's seizure of power. This irritant in the already strained Arab-British relations spread pro-Axis sympathies throughout the Moslem world. In Palestine the British had to maintain a considerable garrison in order to prevent Arabs from slaughtering the increasingly restless local Jews. The propaganda took full advantage of this enmity. The hatred of the Arabs for Jews was not limited to Palestine but spilled over to Transjordan, Egypt, Saudi Arabia, and Iraq.

The situation in the region, so vital for the British, worsened in the spring of 1941. Turkey, the guardian of the Black Sea straits, was much impressed by Hitler's easy Balkan and African triumphs. After the fall of France, the Turks tried to distance themselves from London and proclaimed their nonbelligerency. Worse yet, on June 18, 1941, Ankara signed with Berlin a treaty of "mutual trust and sincere friendship." Basically pro-British, Turkey was militarily weak; Churchill's persistent efforts to draw that nation into the war failed. The price Ankara put on a possible alliance with the British included at least two armored divisions and fifty air force squadrons, a commitment far beyond the capacity of the British.

The second weak point for the British in the Levant was Syria and Lebanon, both were controlled by Vichy and flooded by the Axis and pro-Arabic propaganda. A third and related weakness involved the nominally neutral, but actually pro-German, Iran. A fourth and deeply troublesome concern was oil-rich Iraq. In April 1941, after Rommel's first spectacular successes, Iraq's pro-Nazi ruler, Rashid Ali, sent to London an ultimatum that insisted on the end of the British protectorate and an immediate evacuation of their garrisons from Iraq.

Iraq's pro-Axis policy forced the British to act; the British ambassador in Baghdad engineered a coup d'état that toppled Rashid Ali and replaced him with a pro-Allied ruler. This intervention precipitated a series of riots and acts of sabotage organized by Axis agents, affecting not only the oil-bearing fields of Mosul and Kirkuk, but also those in northern Iraq. This serious threat to the pipeline ending at Haifa in Palestine endangered fuel supplies for the Mediterranean squadron of the Royal Navy, as well as the needs for the Western Desert Force. Pressed by Churchill, Wavell rushed a small task force from Palestine, some 400 miles across the Arabian Desert. British troops entered Baghdad on June 1 and crushed the revolt. This vigorous action in Iraq enabled Wavell to protect Britain's strategic position.[5]

There still remained the problem of Syria and Lebanon. By 1941 it was feared in London that Marshal Pétain, acting under strong pressure from Berlin, might hand over both these French protectorates to the Axis. To prevent this, on June 8, 1941, British imperial and Free French forces operating from Palestine and Iraq marched into Syria and Lebanon and overwhelmed the local pro-Vichy garrisons. On June 21 Damascus was captured by the Free French troops, and by mid-July both provinces were under Allied control.[6]

Axis agitation in Iran was led by the pro-Nazi father of the last Shah, Reza Pahlavi. The German invasion of Russia on June 22, 1941, made it a vital necessity for the British to remove him as soon as possible in order to open a southern route for Allied supplies to the embattled Soviet forces. This deposition was accomplished by a simultaneous British

---

[5]Playfair, *The Mediterranean,* Vol. II, pp. 177–98.

[6]The British side of the Syrian and Lebanese problem during the war is presented by Major-General Sir Edward Spears in his book *Fulfillment of a Mission* (London: Leo Cooper, 1977); for the French point of view of the British-French controversies in the Near East and Africa see Charles de Gaulle, *War Memoirs, Vol. II, Unity 1942–1944,* especially pp. 15–77.

and Soviet action in August. The Shah was overthrown and replaced by his minor son. Until the end of the war, and even for a short period after it, northern Persia was to be occupied by Soviet troops, while the southern segment of the country remained under British control. In December 1943 the United States signified its adherence to this convention. Thus, by a series of swift moves, the Allies slammed the door against Hitler and Mussolini in this strategic area of the Near East and Middle East, with its vital oil fields.

INCREASING RUSSO-GERMAN TENSIONS

While the Rome-Berlin Axis was about to lose several of its pawns in the Middle East, another significant alteration took place within the Tripartite Pact. The change resulted from Japan's growing disillusionment with Germany's increasingly independent policy, which Tokyo considered as incompatible with the principles underlying the Axis alliance. From the very start, Tokyo had been offended by the unilateral and quite unexpected signing of the Hitler-Stalin pact while Japanese troops were fighting the Red Army in the Far East. As a consequence of their growing resentment and despite the gestures of outward loyalty to the anti-Comintern pact, the resentful Japanese also resolved to pursue their own independent policy.

During his visit in Moscow on April 13, 1941, the Japanese foreign minister, Yōsuke Matsuoka, signed with the USSR a neutrality pact. According to it, should a third power attack either Japan or the USSR, they were to preserve neutrality toward each other. The Soviet-Japanese agreement freed Moscow from the risk of a two-front war in case of a future conflict with Germany and allowed Stalin to start withdrawing a large portion of Soviet troops from the Far East.[7]

Strangely enough, Hitler ignored the importance of the neutrality pact. While Matsuoka passed through Berlin at the end of March, Hitler and Ribbentrop had been informed about the Japanese efforts to arrive at such an arrangement. Yet both of them did not protest and merely tried to persuade Matsuoka that now was the moment for an attack on Singapore. There was no question of associating Japan in the invasion of Russia. On the contrary, the Russo-Japanese neutrality pact was considered by Hitler as advantageous to Germany because it seemed to indicate that Tokyo was ready to turn its expansive drive against the British. The Japanese attack against the United States was not something that Hitler had bargained for. It came to him as a complete surprise.

At the same time, relations between the Soviet Union and Germany were becoming strained. The growing concentration of Germans along the western approaches to the USSR was an open secret. Soviet intelligence and many outside sources, including President Roosevelt as well as Prime Minister Churchill, sent repeated warnings about an impending German attack on Russia. German reconnaissance aircraft made more and more frequent forays over Soviet territories; German deliveries of vital machinery were increasingly delayed, while the Russians kept on sending their prescribed quotas and even exceeded them in some cases. Yet the "callous, crafty, ill-informed giant," as Churchill called Stalin, resolutely chose to disregard the warnings and apparently continued to trust Hitler's assurances of good-will.

This reliance placed by Stalin on Hitler's word was reflected in the relaxation of defense preparations along the new Soviet-German borders. With the territorial changes of 1939/40, Soviet supply lines were extended some 250 miles westward. Before the Stalin-Hitler pact, Soviet frontier forces, which were under NKVD juris-

[7]For the impact of the Soviet-Japanese nonaggression pact see George Alexander Lensen, *The Strange Neutrality: Soviet-Japanese Relations During the Second World War, 1941–1945* (Tallahassee, Fla.: The Diplomatic Press, 1972).

diction, had been maintained in a state of instant readiness, with a three-week supply of ammunition, fuel, and food always available. After the pact the frontier forces were ordered to stand down from immediate readiness, and only three days' supplies were finally allotted to them. Work begun on the new frontier fortifications in August 1940 was suspended until the spring of 1941. Measures of partial mobilization were undertaken by the Soviet armed forces, but they were carried out slowly in order not to provoke the Germans.

At the same time, a remarkable effort was made to observe the terms of the trade treaty with Berlin. For example, until the very moment of the German attack, Soviet supplies of large amounts of raw materials were, as a rule, more scrupulously dispatched than those coming from Germany. More was to come in September 1941. The highly unbalanced Soviet-German trade pact obliged the Russians to deliver 1.4 million tons of grain from the coming harvest, and deliveries were to be completed by the end of September; it was more than the Central Powers had extracted from the defeated, prostrated Russia by the Treaty of Brest-Litovsk of March 1918.

It was obvious that Stalin was terrified of Hitler. To placate him Stalin was ready to pump dry his own country, already short of food, in order to further appease the German Moloch. This line of policy was accompanied by a series of servile gestures toward Hitler's diplomatic representatives. For instance, after bidding farewell to Matsuoka, Stalin put his arms around the shoulders of the German ambassador in Moscow, Schulenburg, and embraced him. Then he went to the assistant military attaché, Colonel Hans Krebs, shouting, "Ah, a German officer. We will stay friends with you under all conditions."

While turning a deaf ear to the western warning, Stalin suspected British intentions in furnishing data about a coming German attack. He believed that the British wished to embroil Russia and Germany in a conflict and to profit by the ensuing war. Referring to the constant western warnings about the impending German invasion, Stalin said to General Georgy Zhukov: "You see, *they* are trying to frighten us with the German menace, while the Germans are being scared with the Soviet menace. They want to pit us against each other." Nevertheless, Stalin must have been inwardly worried about the growing symptoms of the German massings along the western Soviet perimeter. One of the few visible signs of Stalin's concern was his assumption from Molotov on May 6 of the premiership of the USSR, while remaining the party's secretary general. Thus the two supreme offices in the country were officially united in the hands of its actual master.

GERMANY STRIKES

The German attack on Soviet Russia had already been launched at dawn on June 21/22, 1941, before the German ambassador in Moscow actually handed Molotov the official declaration of war. Berlin's note justified the invasion on the pretext that the Russians "were about to attack Germany from the rear," while Germany was getting ready for the final blow at Great Britain. The unpreparedness of Soviet forces at the time of the invasion and Stalin's obsequious helpfulness toward Hitler were the best refutations of the German claims. The shocked Molotov's reaction was most revealing: "Can it really be that we have deserved all that?"[8]

Russia was to become the largest and the most ferocious campaign of World War II. The general shape of this gigantic struggle was largely determined by geography. The border between the Soviet Union and the German sphere of influence stretched more than 1,800 miles across the European continent from the Baltic to the Black Sea. This gigantic front was divided into a northern and a southern sector by the Pripet Marshes, some 250 miles long and 120 miles wide.

[8]For the documents on the breakdown of the German-Soviet relations see Sontag and Beddie, *Nazi-Soviet Relations, 1939–1945* pp. 178 ff.

German tanks crossing the Dnieper north of Kiev over a pontoon bridge. National Archives

The final plan adopted by OKW foresaw the commitment of three German army groups, supported on both wings by their vassals. The attack was planned as a three-stage operation. The first phase, the frontier-zone battle, had the goal of reaching the general line of the Dnieper. The second stage and objective were to destroy the bulk of the Soviet forces west of the Dnieper and to capture Moscow. The third element of the plan envisaged the final phase: a drive up the line formed by the Archangel-Ural-Volga line, where Hitler is reported to have indicated the frontier of his future empire with a pencil line on a military map. Hitler intended to crush Soviet Russia in one swift blow before the close of 1941 and then, with the resources of the USSR at his disposal, return to the West and deal the final blow to Britain. The German dictator hoped that the Soviets would stand firmly and fight so that they could be surrounded and annihilated west of the Dnieper, before the Wehrmacht lines of communication became too extended.

Hitler wanted to represent his attack on Russia as a great European crusade against communism. Italy and Rumania declared war on the USSR on the same day as Germany; Hungary and Slovakia followed suit on the following day. Although not members of the Axis, the Finns joined the offensive on June 25.

Hoping for a quick success, Hitler's plan hinged on the speed of advance and the rapid destruction of the enemy forces during the Summer of 1941. Of the 3.8 million men available to Hitler, 3.2 million were deployed on the eastern front; they were organized into 148 German divisions, including 19 armored and 12 motorized; 3,350 tanks, 7,184 pieces of artillery, 60,000 lorries and nearly 700,000 horses, most of them in light artillery batteries and baggage trains. These forces were supplemented by Rumanian, Hungarian, Finnish, Slovak, and Italian contingents; eventually they were to be augmented by various voluntary legions: Dutch, Flemish, Valonian, Norwegian, Ukrainian, Baltic, French, Spanish, and so on. Altogether the invading forces numbered at least 154 divisions.[9]

---

[9]For an evaluation of the respective OBDs see John Erickson, *The Soviet High Command* (New York: St. Martin's Press, 1962), pp. 565–87; and his *The Road to Stalingrad: Stalin's War With Germany,* Vol. I (London: Weidenfeld and Nicolson, 1975), pp. 98, 133, and 143–73.

German Invasion of Soviet Russia, June 22-December 6, 1941

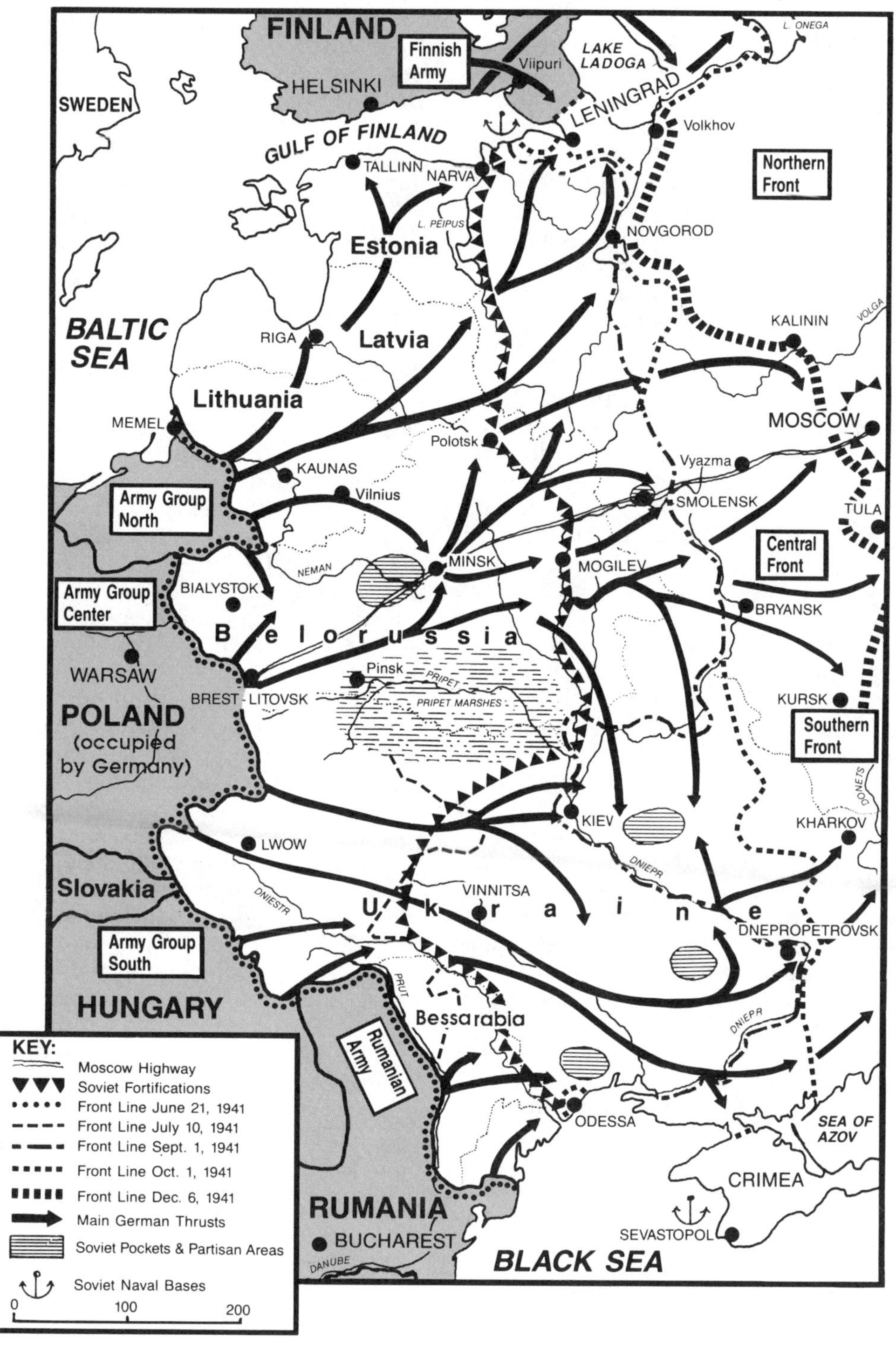

The German and vassal forces, organized and directed by the OKW, were to advance along three main directions. The Army Group North, under Field Marshal Ritter von Leeb, was to march through the former Baltic States with the objective of taking the vital industrial area of Leningrad. In this first, or northern path, the main target was the cutting of the Murmansk-Moscow railroad in order to block Soviet supplies from abroad. Leningrad was to be conquered in cooperation with the Finns.

With qualms and hesitations, the Finns joined in the general offensive, while focusing their energies on the reconquest of their lost lands. Before and during the war Hitler tried repeatedly to bind Finland to Germany with a formal treaty. The Finns, however, always evaded these requests; they regarded the campaign as a defensive war, a continuation of the one started by the Russians in November 1939. The official Finnish term of their intervention was "the Third War of Independence."

The second direction followed by the Germans in Russia involved Army Group Center, under Bock, which was to drive through Belorussia to take Minsk and Smolensk and, after the anticipated destruction of the bulk of the Soviet forces, to push on toward Moscow and beyond. The third route of the attack taken by Army Group South under Rundstedt, had the primary goal of securing the grain resources and mineral wealth of the Ukraine, as well as the subjection of the Crimean peninsula with its naval base at Sevastopol, a stepping stone toward the Caucasus and the main repository of Soviet oil, Baku.

Soviet forces on the western front were numerically superior to those of the attackers, amounting to 170 Russian infantry divisions, with 6,000 planes and 54 armored brigades of about 200 tanks each. Like the invaders, the Soviets were organized into three army groups (or "fronts" in Soviet terminology): northern, central, and southern. These were commanded by Marshals Kliment Voroshilov, Semyon Timoshenko, and Semyon Budenny, respectively. Although the Soviets were numerically superior to the invaders, the equipment of the Red Army was of uneven quality; except for some categories of tanks (like the T-34), rockets, and submachine guns, Soviet armaments were inferior to those of the Wehrmacht. Moreover, the Red Army was deployed in linear, static defense groups and lacked not only depth but also an overall strategic plan.

THE BATTLE OF RUSSIA

The German offensive achieved tactical surprise along most of the front. This linear alignment of the Soviet forces gave the invaders the advantage of strategic initiative as well as options in attacking weaker sectors of the cordon. Soviet troops were caught in their barracks, and aircraft were trapped on the ground. The surprise was nearly complete: Bridges over the Bug, a frontier river since September 1939, were left intact and undefended. German Army Group Center intercepted a desperate Russian wireless signal: "We are being fired on. What shall we do?" Soviet headquarters wired back a stern reprimand: "You must be insane. And why is your signal not in code?"[10]

German spearheads by the beginning of July had everywhere penetrated and pierced the Soviet lines, dispersing them into small groups that were then rolled up by the slower-moving infantry formations. The German infantry by early July had destroyed nearly half of the estimated Soviet air strength and the Wehrmacht had taken an

[10]For the Russian campaign see Robert Cecil, *Hitler's Decision to Invade Russia, 1941* (London: Davis-Poynter, 1975); John Erickson, *The Road to Stalingrad: Stalin's War With Germany*, Vol. I (London: Weidenfeld and Nicolson, 1975); for the opening phase see especially chaps. 3–7. For the main descriptive stories of the war: Alexander Werth, *Russia at War, 1941–45*, 4th ed. (New York: E. P. Dutton, 1964); Barton Whaley, *Codeword Barbarossa* (Cambridge: MIT Press, 1973); Albert Seaton, *The Russo-German War, 1941–1945* (New York: Praeger, 1970); and Alan Clark, *Barbarossa: The Russian-German Strategy Against Russia, 1939–1941* (London: and New York: Oxford, Clarendon Press, 1973).

unprecedented number of prisoners, 1,200 tanks, and 600 guns. All of Lithuania and most of Latvia were in German hands by mid-July, as well as large tracts of the Ukraine. Enemy inroads were especially deep in the south; there the mostly Ukrainian units, commanded by the old and incompetent Marshall Budenny, were either surrendered in large masses or were in retreat at great cost. Smolensk was the first point at which the German advance was checked for a week through dogged persistence. Nonetheless, German forces had covered some 400 miles in eighteen days, and had advanced within 200 miles of Moscow.

When Stalin had awakened on the morning of June 22, he refused to take seriously the report of the enemy attack and called it a "rumor spread by *agents provocateurs*" whose aim was to spoil Moscow's relations with Berlin. By midday, when he realized that the invaders had achieved resounding successes, he lost his nerve: Convinced that everything was lost, for ten days Stalin experienced a near breakdown and plunged into a prolonged drunken orgy.

The first official war appeal was made on his behalf by Molotov. Only on July 3, 1941, did Stalin recover from his fit of depression; he then addressed the Soviet people in a broadcast which he opened in a trembling voice with the words: "Brothers, sisters, I turn to you my friends!" He attempted to justify the pact with Hitler, as having provided both time and space necessary "for preparing our forces to repulse Fascist Germany," and summoned his subjects to an all-out war against the invaders. Contrary to the previous official announcements, which had attempted to minimize the disaster, Stalin admitted that the enemy had made deep inroads on all three sectors and continued its eastward drive. This speech was the first occasion on which the Soviet people could learn about the magnitude of the military defeat suffered by the Red Army. Throughout the address, Stalin de-emphasized Marxist ideology and appealed to traditional Russian sentiments. He called on the Russian people to "fight our patriotic war of liberation against the Fascist enslaver"; he tried to resuscitate "the spirit of 1812" by urging the

July 1941—The Red Army in retreat.
Soviet Embassy Washington D.C.

formation of partisan detachments and by calling for scorched-earth tactics if necessary.

From the beginning of July the Soviet war effort was directed by the State Defense Council, presided over by Stalin himself. He was assisted by the rising star of the Red Army, General Georgy K. Zhukov, chief of the General Staff since January 1941. Viacheslav Molotov was given supervision over diplomatic issues; Lavrenty Beria was made responsible for security problems, while a younger member of the Politburo, Gregory M. Malenkov, was entrusted with the supply and equipment problems of the armed forces as well as with the liaison with the Communist apparatus.

The Wehrmacht again applied the well-tested methods of lightning warfare, which combined the use of armor with devastating air raids not only against military objectives but also against the civilian population, thus causing a disruptive panic to movement of troops and supplies. These combined strikes along selected points of least resistance broke Soviet defenses. Once through the largely linearly disposed Soviet forces, the Wehrmacht would encircle the Soviet troops, make them capitulate, or destroy them piecemeal.

To slow down the onslaught, Stalin ordered Soviet troops to engage the enemy piecemeal, in brigade and division increments. When these Soviet units were surrounded by the enemy they were ordered to stand fast to the bitter end. The young and inexperienced Soviet commanders, mostly survivors of the purges of 1935 to 1938, remembering what had happened to their predecessors, had to operate under the brooding eyes of the political commissars, whose powers had been reinstated just a few weeks before the attack. Both the field commanders and their political supervisors blindly obeyed the orders from Moscow and seemed to fear Stalin more than they feared the Germans.

Although the Red Army had superiority in troop numbers and masses of equipment, the Germans initially enjoyed a great advantage in superior organization and leadership. It was true that by 1941 the Russians theoretically had 14,000 tanks, or more than all other armies of the world put together, but most of them were obsolete and lacked spare parts. The superb T-34 tank, which proved impervious to most of the German antitank guns and was more mobile than the German Panzers, was only recently made available to a few units; by June 1941 there were only 1,475 of the T-34s at the front and they were delivered only by April–May; most of their drivers had less than two hours of actual tank-handling experience. Moreover, many of the modern tanks were integrated into newly formed conscript infantry divisions. The huge Soviet air force of 6,000 aircraft, nearly twice as large as the Luftwaffe, also suffered not only from obsolescence but also from vague concepts about operational functions. In practice, the planes were used mostly for cooperation with the ground forces.[11]

After destroying the Soviet divisions defending the Baltic area, the Germans besieged Leningrad by the beginning of September.[12] They promptly cut the city from the rest of the country; access to Leningrad was limited to the route through Lake Ladoga, which mercifully for the defenders froze earlier than usual and thus allowed the Red Army to consolidate its defenses and stop the enemy advance. The Germany Army Group Center pushed through Minsk and Smolensk toward Moscow and took some 300,000 POWs. It seemed that Moscow might fall by September–October. The panic that swept the Soviet capital would have facilitated its rapid conquest.

Meanwhile the Army Group South swept like a tornado through the western Ukraine. The Wehrmacht took masses of POWs and

---

[11]The problem of responsibility for the Soviet lack of preparedness has been discussed in the book by Vladimir Petrov and A. M. Nekrich, *June 22, 1941: Soviet Historians and the German Invasion* (Columbia: University of South Carolina Press, 1968).

[12]For the story of the longest siege in modern history see Dmitri V. Pavlov, *Leningrad, 1941: The Blockade* (Chicago: University of Chicago Press, 1965); Leon Gouré, *The Siege of Leningrad* (Stanford, Calif.: Stanford University Press, 1962).

pushed irresistibly toward Kiev and then beyond the Dnieper, thus achieving huge territorial conquests. Superiority in mobility and command there allowed the Wehrmacht to triumph. When the pincers finally closed on September 15, Kiev was surrounded and then abandoned on September 19. The Germans took some 600,000 Soviet prisoners; mounds of captured equipment and supplies were piled up at staging areas. The spectacular triumph at Kiev further turned Hitler's head: He proceeded to weaken the armor of the central sector and reinforced the southern wing, which was to play the decisive role in the conquest of the Soviet breadbasket and eventually open to the Germans access to the coveted oil of the Caucasus.

Significantly, many Red Army units withdrew to the east or lingered behind the front, some of them to fight later with Soviet partisan units. The main German objective, the decisive destruction of the Red Army's main forces, was beyond the Wehrmacht's grasp. Ominously, Odessa and Sevastopol kept up their resistance with the valiant aid of the Soviet Black Sea squadron.

THE GERMAN DRIVE FALTERS

Throughout the summer it seemed as if Soviet Russia was facing an imminent catastrophe. The southern, Ukrainian, sector of the front was especially critical. There, many soldiers deserted their units and threw away their weapons. The Soviet system seemed to be disintegrating; in numerous villages the peasants dissolved the collective farms, pillaged the barns, and divided the land, cattle, and implements.

The unprecedented advances along all three sectors made Hitler overconfident. He took it for granted that he could capture Moscow any time he wished. In August, Propaganda Minister Goebbels ecstatically announced to the world, "We have smashed the Red Army to splinters. Russia lies like a limp virgin in the arms of the German Mars." By that time, however, certain problems resulting from the haphazard preparation of the campaign began to surface. German intelligence on Russia was scarce and often faulty. German units, for instance, were often provided with obsolete maps; some of them showed paved roads where none existed or represented marshy cattle tracks as roads. Occasionally, the maps bore little relationship to the terrain they purported to chart, and so the German forces had to feel their way through totally strange areas, losing valuable time and wasting precious fuel. German progress was thus slowed, and tactical and operational planning was disrupted.

Another complication was the difference in gauge between the German and Soviet railroads, making it even more difficult to get supplies to the front. This variation was especially vital in the case of tanks: Instead of being transported to the front line by train, they had to be driven, which resulted in tanks reaching the battlefield in poor shape. Supply problems were worrisome even during summer and became critical by the autumn: mud and snow meant that the toughest equipment began to break down from excessive wear.

The experience at Smolensk, where the first real Soviet resistance jelled, had rudely disabused the Germans of the notion that the Red Army had lost its fighting capacity. Further, the Northern Army Group, after reaching Novgorod on August 16, also encountered stiff opposition around Lake Ilmen, on the approaches to Leningrad. Yet by mid-August Bock declared himself ready to continue his advance toward the Soviet capital, the political hub of the Soviet empire and its main communication center. Guderian also advocated an immediate, vigorous offensive on Moscow. He argued that the best way to keep the enemy off balance was to drive forward relentlessly with the panzers in the vanguard, without bothering about numerous pockets of Soviet resistance left behind.

Now, however, Hitler's huge war machine, operating largely on costly synthetic fuel and on limited European oil supplies, was getting dangerously low on reserves. Consequently, he began to wonder whether the oil of the Caucasus would not be more vital than capturing Moscow, which he had taken for granted anyway. The Führer decided to halt the offensive on Moscow in order to strengthen the southern wing of the advance by dispatching a large segment of the German armor to the Ukrainian sector. This decision provoked a prolonged debate about strategy lasting nearly six weeks; these valuable weeks were lost while the Central Group, without much of its armor, lost a great deal of its momentum.[13]

Finally, by the close of September, Hitler ordered his squabbling and sulking generals to mount two drives simultaneously. One was to be launched on September 30 against Kharkov, the industrial Don basin, and beyond, in order eventually to capture the oil-rich Caucasus. The other, to be launched on October 2, was a decisive drive toward Moscow.

The push toward Moscow started too late, when the autumn rains turned the ground into a quagmire. Yet despite abysmal weather, the offensive at the central front achieved an initially impressive progress: It broke through the Soviet linear defense, reduced most of the Soviet large units into small pockets and then destroyed them methodically. Soviet losses were so severe that for the first time on these local fronts the Germans actually outnumbered the defenders.

[13]For a retrospective German view see Liddell Hart, *The German Generals Talk,* pp. 166–87.

STALIN'S RESPONSE TO THE CRISIS

The beginning of September 1941 represented the nadir of the Soviet army's predicament. On September 3 Ivan Maisky delivered to Churchill Stalin's gloomy personal letter in which the Soviet dictator begged for the opening of a second front, "this year somewhere in the Balkans or in France, one that would divert thirty to forty German divisions from the Eastern Front." The letter ended with an ominous conclusion: "Without these two kinds of aid the Soviet Union will either be defeated or weakened to the extent that it will lose, for a long time, the ability to help its Allies by active operations at the front against Hitlerism." Ten days later, in another personal message to

A Soviet propaganda poster urging workers to produce more weapons. National Archives

the British prime minister, Stalin went as far as to agree to the landing of twenty-five to thirty British divisions at Archangel or shipping them to the southern areas of the USSR.

A few weeks earlier, on July 30, Stalin begged President Roosevelt's special envoy, Averell Harriman, for the sending of American troops to any sector of the Soviet front to fight under American command. These pleas resulted from a desperate lack of Soviet reserves. The only well-trained troops Stalin could possibly spare at that time for the defense of Moscow were the Far Eastern garrisons facing the still-powerful Japanese contingents stationed in Manchuria. Despite the Soviet-Japanese neutrality pact, Stalin was not quite sure about the ultimate intentions on the Tokyo warlords. But by mid-September his master spy in Tokyo, Richard Sorge, sent him a series of soothing messages to the effect that Southeast Asia, and not Siberia, was Japan's goal. Only then did Stalin order a large-scale withdrawal of nearly half of the Siberian Army.

The first months of the ordeal proved to be a good school for many Soviet commanders, who now had to learn the tricks of modern warfare the hard way. During the summer Stalin tried to undo the most disasterous consequences of his purges of the late 1930s by releasing their surviving victims from the concentration camps. Rehabilitated, many of them were put into a number of key jobs, civilian as well as military. Under the experienced eye of the veteran commander of the Far Eastern Army, General Zhukov, the Red Army soldiers began to use effectively their reinforcements and their weapons.

THE ATLANTIC CONFERENCE

Parallel to the battle of Russia, important events were taking place in the Far East. Ten weeks after Japan's neutrality pact with Soviet Russia, Japanese troops on July 2, 1941, seized French Indochina. Fear of further aggressive moves led President Roosevelt to warn Tokyo to keep out of the Dutch East Indies. Following this, the United States and Britain froze all Japanese assets under their control. Hitler's invasion of Russia and Japanese expansion in Southeast Asia pushed the United States still further away from its posture of benevolent neutrality toward Britain. British diplomacy skillfully continued to maneuver the United States into a closer association with the anti-Axis coalition. These efforts resulted in a meeting between the leaders of the two countries in the mid-Atlantic in August 1941.

The Atlantic conference was unprecedented because it produced a joint formal declaration by the leader of a belligerent power (Churchill) and the leader of a non-belligerent one (Roosevelt), outlining the principles for which the war was to be fought. The statement, dated August 14, 1941, soon to be called the Atlantic Charter, promised "a better future for the world . . . after the final destruction of Nazi tyranny." The declaration also formulated in eight points the basic principles on which the future peace should be based. Both powers renounced territorial or other aggrandizements and declared their desire to see "no territorial changes that do not accord with the freely expressed wishes of the peoples concerned."

In this Atlantic declaration both powers promised to respect the right of all peoples "to express their wish to see sovereign rights and self-government restored to those who have been forcibly deprived of them." Both countries "hoped to see established a peace which will afford to all nations the means of dwelling in safety within their own boundaries, and which will afford assurance that all the men in all the lands may live out their lives in freedom from fear and want." During the meeting of Roosevelt and Churchill the most fundamental issue was the United States' entry into the war. Although Roosevelt was most willing to help both Britain and the USSR in their war effort, he made it quite clear that the United States had no intention of making any commitment of joining the two countries as an active participant. Nevertheless, throughout the talks the two sides treated each other as if they were virtual allies.

During their exchanges of views, Churchill unveiled to President Roosevelt Britain's strategy for defeating the Axis powers in Europe. The essential points of the plan were (1) to maintain a tight naval blockade of Germany, Italy, and their vassals; (2) to conduct intensive bombing of key points of Germany and Italy; (3) to assist resistance groups in all Axis-occupied countries; and (4) to carry out a "closing and tightening of the ring" by thrusting powerful forces in amphibious landings all around the Axis periphery. After these preparatory operations aimed at weakening the Axis resistance, a full-scale strike against Germany and Italy was to take place.

Meanwhile, an undeclared naval war was going on between the United States and Germany. Although Hitler had issued an order not to attack American merchant ships outside the blockade area, which was also recognized by the United States as being out of bounds, numerous mistakes and acts of disobedience were bound to occur. For instance, on May 21, 1941, a German submarine sank the U.S. freighter *Robin Moor* en route to South Africa and at a place well outside the German blockade zone. Two more U.S. merchant vessels were torpedoed toward the end of the summer. On September 4 a U-boat fired two torpedoes at the U.S. destroyer *Greer.* A week later, on September 11, President Roosevelt announced that Axis warships entering the American defense zone did so "at their peril" and ordered the U.S. Navy to "shoot on sight" in case of need. Thus, step by step, the United States was driven increasingly closer to actual belligerency, and President Roosevelt was not very much worried about it.

The Atlantic meeting devoted a great deal of attention to the situation created by Hitler's attack on Russia. From the start Russia's position within the alliance was ambivalent. Stalin did not join the coalition against Hitler as a willing partner, but rather as his betrayed accomplice. Having committed acts of aggression in collaboration with the Nazis, the Soviet dictator had been guilty of numerous violations of international law and those basic human rights so much stressed by the Atlantic Charter. Soviet entry into the anti-Axis alliance posed, therefore, a set of intricate problems: Would Stalin subscribe to the Charter? And if so, would he respect its principles in practice?

Despite these doubts President Roosevelt was determined to supplement the British assistance to Russia with that of the United States. Yet all this aid was considered insufficient by Moscow. Stalin loudly and repeatedly insisted on a prompt opening of the "second front" in Europe as the best, most direct form of aid. Disregarding the North African campaign, the British and American effort on the seas, and the ongoing bombardment of the Axis powers, as well as their material aid to Russia, he urged them to land immediately and in force on the continent of Europe to divert from the eastern front at least thirty to forty divisions.

The British argued that they were barely able to cope with the Atlantic and Mediterranean operations, as well as with the worsening situation in the Far East, and that they simply did not have enough manpower and resources to mount a full-scale invasion for at least another year or so, even with the American aid. Occasionally the British leader was quite blunt and reminded Stalin that he was fighting for his own survival and that Russia had had a chance of establishing the second front while the Franco-British armies were fighting desperately against the Wehrmacht in May and June of 1940. Stalin decried this stand as not only evasive but even downright treacherous: Refusal to open a second front immediately was a sly trick to bleed Soviet Russia white in order to diminish Communist influence in Europe after the war.[14]

All these queries and problems were eventually somehow patched up in the name

[14]In this respect see Churchill, *The Grand Alliance*, pp. 383–88.

of "Allied unity." Yet from the beginning it was rather obvious that Stalin would manipulate the slogan of "Allied unity" for his benefit, while pursuing an independent line of policy. Britain and the United States, for their part, were so relieved by Hitler's overwhelming eastward thrust and were so clearly delighted to see the Soviets bearing the brunt of Hitler's fury that, in their euphoria, they did not attach any conditions to their aid to the Soviets. Unable to match Russia's massive contribution to the land war and to satisfy Stalin's requests for immediately establishing a second front in Europe, President Roosevelt and Prime Minister Churchill were only too happy to buy Stalin's cooperation not only with military and economic aid but also with political concessions in matters considered by them to be of secondary importance. Here Poland was a classic test case.

SOVIET-POLISH RELATIONS

From the start of the Russian campaign, the problem of Soviet-Polish relations loomed large in the exchanges of views between London and Moscow. For the purpose of forming a united front of all countries threatened by Germany, the British government put strong pressure on the Polish government, an ally of Britain since 1939, to ease relations with the USSR. Winston Churchill admitted that Soviet Russia from the start of the war had essentially pursued a policy of cold self-interest and only tried to qualify that opinion by expressing a wish that the Soviet armies should be standing on the Ribbentrop-Molotov line as friends and allies of Poland instead of as invaders. Churchill seized the opportunity of Hitler's attack on Russia to step forward as a mediator and tried to bridge the gap between the Polish government in London and the Kremlin.

As a result of Churchill's efforts, on July 30, 1941, the Polish premier and commander in chief, General Władysław Sikorski, and the Soviet ambassador in London, Ivan Maisky, signed an agreement that provided for a resumption of diplomatic relations between the two governments. By the agreement, the Soviet Union renounced the 1939 Stalin-Hitler pact. The two governments mutually agreed to render each other aid and support of all kinds in the war against Germany. The Soviets consented to the formation on Soviet soil of a "Polish army under a commander appointed by the Polish government in accord with the Soviet government." The army was to be made up of Polish prisoners of war and deportees from eastern Poland to be released from their places of detention scattered throughout the USSR. The Polish army in Russia was to be subordinated, in an operational sense, to the Soviet Supreme Command, in which the Polish officers were to be represented.[15] Thus Poland, an ally of Great Britain since August 25, 1939, became also a war partner of the USSR. On July 18, 1941, the Czechoslovak government in London also resumed diplomatic relations with the USSR and started to form a nucleus of an armed force on Soviet territory.

Relations between the Polish government in London and the Kremlin were bedeviled from the outset by numerous controversial issues. They included territorial questions, as well as a host of minor problems pertaining to the organization of the Polish forces on the Soviet territory and the fate of the civilian deportees there, not all of whom were immediately released and returned to Polish citizenship. Last but not least, there was the bitter and highly explosive question of some 15,000 Polish officers who had been captured by the Red Army in 1939 and imprisoned in three main POW camps. After March–April 1940 these officers had mysteriously vanished without a trace. Questioned about their fate, Soviet authorities gave a series of conflicting answers. Despite these thorny problems the prime minister of the Polish government in London, General Sikorski, went to Moscow and in December 1941 signed an agreement with the USSR

[15] For the Polish army in Russia see Władysław Anders's *An Army in Exile* (London: Macmillan, 1949).

that bound both sides to fight together against Nazi Germany.

THE BATTLE OF MOSCOW

While lend-lease protocols were being negotiated in Washington, on the Russo-German front both invaders and defenders were mustering their forces for the battle before Moscow. The Germans were brimming with self-confidence. On October 12, 1941, the *Völkischer Beobachter* ran the headline "The German Hour Has Arrived—The Eastern Campaign Is At Its End." Yet the Red Army, while seriously weakened, was not quite annihilated. Hitler's morbid preoccupation with physical destruction of all major Soviet units gave Stalin and Zhukov time to improve new lines of defense west of Moscow and to throw into the battle the reinforcements meanwhile constantly arriving from Siberia.

Weather conditions worsened dramatically. On September 11 the first snow fell on the Russian front. The October mists and rain mixed with heavier snow turned the vast zone of the front into a sea of mud. Tanks, artillery, and transport vehicles sank deep into the quagmire. This vast sea of mush deprived the Wehrmacht of one of its chief advantages: mobility. By November extremely heavy snows fell throughout the northern and central sectors, and the mercury began dropping dramatically—ten, twenty, thirty degrees centigrade below zero. German soldiers, equipped only for a short summer campaign, were now victims of frostbite and other winter ailments. Horse meat, frozen potatoes, and beet roots were the standard diet. Many detachments were riddled with dysentery, but to squat in the open to perform natural functions was most dangerous; there were numerous reports of men dying as a result of freezing.

In these conditions the Wehrmacht had to face Soviet forces now reinforced by over twenty Siberian divisions with seven armored brigades, numbering 1,400 tanks, 1,000 aircraft, and several cavalry regiments. By December 1941 every third defender of Moscow came from the Siberian units. Whereas German communications and transport were often paralyzed because of deep snow that proved too much for motorcycle dispatch riders or automobiles, the Red Army maintained their communications lines thanks to the small, tough, and

Soviet artillery on the front line. National Archives

shaggy Siberian horses, used to such conditions; moreover, the animals' phenomenal capacity for survival, even when they were given nothing to eat except conifer twigs or root straw, allowed such cavalry units to penetrate deep behind enemy lines, causing havoc among the unsuspecting German rear echelons. In peak conditions, dressed in white, quilted uniforms, with felt boots and fur caps, the units withdrawn from the Far East now faced the shivering, exhausted German soldiers of Bock's central army group.

On December 2, when Hitler ordered an all-out assault on Moscow, the mercury dropped to 40 degrees below zero. This temperature rendered dynamos dead and made it impossible to start engines. Oil in the tanks and trucks acquired the consistency of tar; breechblocks of rifles froze solid; cylinder blocks were split and axles refused to turn. Complex weapons were unusable; the grenade and the bayonet were the only available tools. In hand-to-hand fighting the Red Army soldiers, mostly tough and resourceful country boys, proved superior to their enemies.

The forested areas around Moscow increased the effectiveness of the Soviet partisan detachments now increasingly active. The Soviet air force, decimated mostly on the ground by the early German raids, was now resupplied and, numerically far superior to the Luftwaffe, began to provide significant aid to the Red Army.

During the battle of Moscow instances of individual heroism were frequent. For instance on December 6, 80 miles to the east on the highway connecting Volkolamsk with Moscow, twenty-eight soldiers of the Panfilov division held up the enemy advance on the capital for a whole day. Only three of the twenty-eight warriors survived, but they had destroyed eighteen out of fifty German tanks before being overwhelmed. After repeated and bitter attempts to break through the Moscow front, the German Army Command announced on December 8 suspension of military operations "because of the severe weather conditions"—clearly a face-saving device for the failure to capture the Soviet capital as initially planned.[16]

The hitherto invincible Wehrmacht, which had knocked over the armies of Poland, France, Greece, and Yugoslavia and driven the British from the Continent, came to a dead halt before Moscow. Yet, during the winter of 1941/42 the German war machine had been deeply shattered but did not collapse. On the whole, the frostbitten and exhausted Wehrmacht warriors, their weapons frozen solid, seldom panicked and managed to stage orderly retreats, fighting sternly the advancing Soviet troops. None of the local German withdrawals turned into a rout. The losses in men and materiel were most painful, however. Tanks that had never been designed for this sort of continuous campaigning now littered the countryside. The German supply service sagged precariously under the tremendous strain.

Though appallingly mauled, the Soviets went over to the offensive. The Red Army's counteroffensive pushed the German vanguards some 100 miles away from the gates of Moscow. Leningrad could now be resupplied by way of Lake Ladoga. This repulse went some small way toward alleviating the horrid winter siege of the city.

Now the Wehrmacht had to withdraw along some segments of the front, and only Hitler's display of determination prevented a general retreat. Despite the advice of his military experts and in complete disregard of the cost to his soldiers, he ordered the Wehrmacht to stand and fight to the last where they were. He refused categorically all requests for withdrawal. It is generally agreed that his orders to stand fast, which he kept on repeating throughout the winter of 1941/42, helped to save the Wehrmacht from an even more disastrous defeat, similar to that which Napoleon had suffered in 1812. The order was enforced with utmost ruthlessness. Officers who disobeyed it were dismissed or court-martialed. Even Marshal von Rundstedt was ordered to hand over his

[16]For an analysis of the causes of the German defeat see Liddell Hart, *The German Generals Talk,* pp. 166–87.

command for withdrawing his troops after the failure of the offensive on Rostov. Guderian, who had led one of the panzer armies on the Moscow front, was relieved of his command for failing to press the attack on the Soviet capital. On December 19 Hitler removed Marshal von Brauchitsch from his post as Commander in Chief of the army and directly assumed the responsibility for this post himself.

The stopping of the German march on Moscow was the first major defeat on land suffered by the Reich's armed forces in the war. It was, therefore, an event of inestimable military and psychological importance. The myth of German invincibility was shattered.

REASONS FOR THE GERMAN FAILURE

Behind the Soviet military achievement there was a great deal of meticulous intelligence work on a most impressive scale. In barring the way to Moscow, Stalin and his chief military adviser, General Zhukov, were greatly aided by vital information bearing on enemy plans. Knowledge of enemy intentions allowed the Soviets to shift available weapons to those formations operating on decisive sectors of the front. From Tokyo, Richard Sorge furnished Stalin crucial intelligence on the German and Japanese war plans; from Berlin, a Soviet intelligence network, known as "the Red Orchestra," manned by well-placed Germans, had begun to supply data from authoritative sources on Hitler's intentions. A German Communist sympathizer, Rudolf Roessler in Lucerne, Switzerland, served as another agent under the cryptonym of Lucy.

Another reason for the failure of the 1941 campaign was German attitudes toward the Soviet POWs as well as the civilian population of the occupied territories of the USSR. Much of the disastrous racialist policy must be laid at Hitler's door. Hitler had entered the Soviet Union with the slogan of smashing its Communist system and liberating its oppressed national minorities, especially the Baltic peoples—the Ukrainians, Belorrussians, and the peoples of the Caucasus. Numerous national committees were formed in Germany for that purpose. That is why, at the start of the campaign, the German soldiers were often greeted by the population of the western borderlands with the traditional welcoming symbols: bread, salt, and flowers. At the same time, many Soviet units, composed of soldiers recruited from among these nationalities, deserted or surrendered in large masses. Yet Hitler instantly reneged on his promises. None of his original pledges were actually carried out.

After the first triumphs he systematically suppressed all the various national committees he himself had established before the campaign as instruments of his political warfare. Contrary to the earlier promises of the German propaganda, some of the hated Soviet institutions, like the collective and state farms, were preserved. They were now used by the German authorities as instruments of exploitation, to milk the resources of the occupied areas for the benefit of the Nazi Reich. Most of the inhabitants of these conquered provinces of the USSR were treated like colonial slaves. Numerous workers were forcibly conscripted to work in German factories and mines. Finally, some 3.8 million Soviet POWs, who had surrendered to the invaders in 1941, were mistreated; some of them were surrounded by barbed wire, where they were either allowed to starve or deported to Germany to work under inhuman conditions. Altogether, the Germans took over 5 million Soviet POWs, most of whom perished one way or another. An especially cruel treatment was reserved for political commissars of the Red Army. Hitler personally ordered them to be shot on the spot.

Soon it became obvious to the people in German-occupied areas that Hitler's policy of "liberation" was a hoax. He had nothing to offer the Soviet people but oppression and exploitation in a worse form than that under Stalin. When news about German terror and exploitation in the conquered territories penetrated back behind Soviet lines, the resistance to the invaders began to stiffen dramatically, especially in the Belorussian and Russian areas. This opposition was reflected in the attitude of both the Soviet front-line soldiers and the populations in occupied areas. Nuclei of spontaneous resistance began to form throughout the occupied territories. As early as the autumn of 1941 instances of terror, sabotage, and even organized armed opposition to the Germans became more and more frequent. Clearly, the oppressors were sadistically cruel foreigners contemptuous of everything native. Soon passive resistance turned into a bitter popular war of unheard-of ferocity.

As the German occupation continued, the first guerrilla bands were formed by local Communist party activists and by Red Army soldiers caught behind the lines by the German advance. Often the partisans could communicate with the unoccupied areas of the country by radio and so could coordinate their activities with those of the regular Soviet army. Although the partisans essentially lived off the land, they were increasingly supplied with arms and munitions by airdrops provided by a special organization soon set up in Moscow to equip the guerrillas with weapons, wireless sets, and other necessities. Partisans began to harass the Germans quite effectively and to disrupt their lines of communication. Eventually a large-scale guerrilla movement developed. Guerrilla fighting at times during the Russian civil war of 1918 to 1921 had been impressive, but Soviet partisans in World War II covered still vaster stretches, hundreds of miles behind the enemy lines, from the Arctic Circle to the shores of the Black Sea and even into the Caucasus.[17]

One of Hitler's basic assumptions while invading Russia was the necessity of destroying the bulk of the Red Army and most of its industrial supply base prior to the capturing of the three vital political communication centers of the USSR, Leningrad, Moscow, and Kiev. None of these objectives were achieved. During the summer of 1941 about two-thirds of the Luftwaffe was engaged on the Russian front, but only a small part of it was devoted to strategic raids aimed at destruction of the Soviet armament industries. This prompted the Soviet authorities to stage a rather impressive eastward evacuation. Many Soviet factories and some rolling stock were totally moved beyond the Volga to the Urals and even to central Asia. This gigantic operation, often paralleled by superhuman sacrifices by numerous ordinary Soviet citizens, by the spring of 1942 enabled most of these factories to restart production on their new sites. In some cases the relocated factories were retooled and increased their production. Together with British and American aid, which was growing as time went by, the Soviet armed forces could be gradually resupplied with new weapons and equipment by the autumn of 1942.

[17]The role of guerrilla warfare has been covered in a symposium by John A. Armstrong and others, *The Soviet Partisan Movement in World War II* (Madison: University of Wisconsin Press, 1964).

THE UNITED STATES ENTERS THE WAR

The halting of the German onslaught on Moscow coincided almost to the day with another major turning point in World War II. As the Red Army was forcing the advanced Wehrmacht units to retreat at the Moscow front, half a world away, at the Hawaiian naval base of Pearl Harbor, Japanese aircraft on December 7, 1941, smashed in one sudden blow the bulk of the U.S. Pacific Fleet. The Japanese attack was greeted both in London and in Moscow with a sigh of relief. Now pushed into war by Japanese aggression, the United States became an ally of Britain, as well as of the USSR. The entry of the United States into the war created a triangular coalition commanding resources far superior to those of the Axis. The United States, with its lend-lease assistance to both its partners, soon became the arsenal of the "Grand Alliance."

The Japanese attack on the United States presented the Grand Alliance with numerous challenges: Almost until the end of the war it involved its Western partners and not

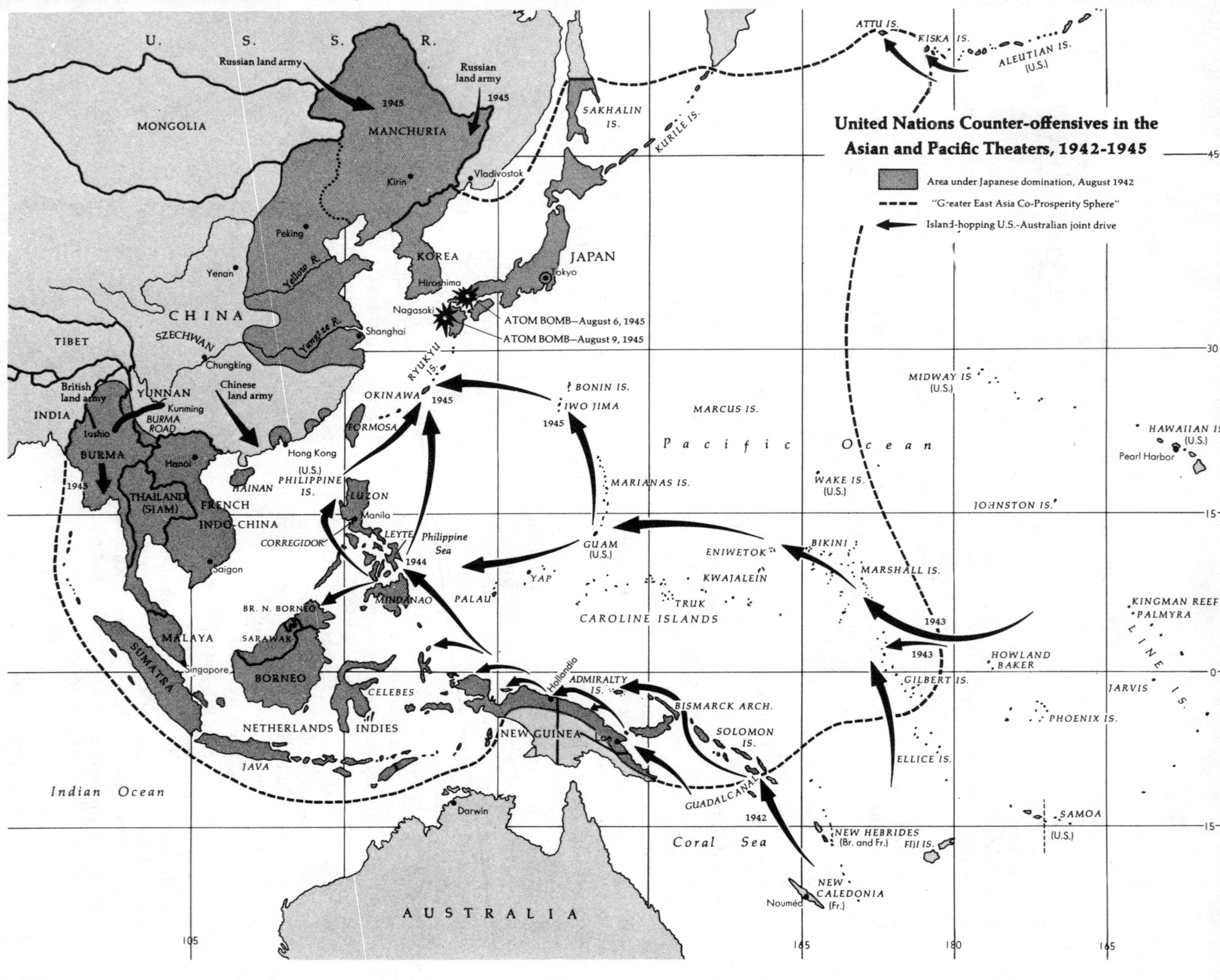

United Nations Counter-offensives in the Asian and Pacific Theaters, 1942-1945
Area under Japanese domination, August 1942
"G-eater East Asia Co-Prosperity Sphere"
Island-hopping U.S.-Australian joint drive
U. S. S. R.
Russian land army
Russian land army
1945
1945
MONGOLIA
MANCHURIA
Kirin
Vladivostok
SAKHALIN IS.
KURILE IS.
ATTU IS.
KISKA IS.
ALEUTIAN IS. (U.S.)
Peking
Yellow R.
KOREA
JAPAN
Tokyo
Hiroshima
Nagasaki
ATOM BOMB—August 6, 1945
ATOM BOMB—August 9, 1945
Yenan
CHINA
SZECHWAN
Yangtze R.
Shanghai
TIBET
Chungking
Chinese land army
British land army
YUNNAN
Kunming
BURMA ROAD
INDIA
Lashio
BURMA
1945
Hanoi
Hong Kong
THAILAND (SIAM)
FRENCH INDO-CHINA
Saigon
HAINAN
RYUKYU IS.
OKINAWA
1945
FORMOSA
(U.S.) PHILIPPINE IS.
LUZON
Manila
CORREGIDOR
LEYTE
Philippine Sea
1944
MINDANAO
BR. N. BORNEO
SARAWAK
BORNEO
MALAYA
SUMATRA
Singapore
CELEBES
NETHERLANDS INDIES
JAVA
Indian Ocean
BONIN IS.
IWO JIMA
1945
MARIANAS IS.
GUAM (U.S.)
YAP
PALAU
MARCUS IS.
Pacific Ocean
CAROLINE ISLANDS
TRUK
KWAJALEIN
ENIWETOK
BIKINI
MARSHALL IS.
WAKE IS. (U.S.)
MIDWAY IS. (U.S.)
JOHNSTON IS.
HAWAIIAN IS. (U.S.)
Pearl Harbor
KINGMAN REEF
PALMYRA
LINE IS.
HOWLAND
BAKER
JARVIS
GILBERT IS.
1943
1943
ELLICE IS.
PHOENIX IS.
SAMOA (U.S.)
Hollandia
ADMIRALTY IS.
BISMARCK ARCH.
SOLOMON IS.
NEW GUINEA
Lae
GUADALCANAL
1942
Coral Sea
NEW HEBRIDES (Br. and Fr.)
FIJI IS.
NEW CALEDONIA (Fr.)
Nouméa
Darwin
AUSTRALIA
105
165
180
165
45
30
15
0
15

the USSR. Initially, the Japanese drive seemed to be irresistible. The Indochinese colonies of France had been captured in the summer of 1941, and now it was to be Britain's turn to feel Japan's might. The attack on Pearl Harbor was accompanied by almost simultaneous Japanese onslaughts against Hong Kong, Malaya, the Philippines and on the Asian mainland. Most of the native populations proved to be a willing audience for Japanese anticolonialist propaganda. Hong Kong was entirely isolated and fell on Christmas Day. The vaunted island citadel, Singapore, with all its guns and fortifications facing seaward, thus lay open to the Malaysian land side from which the Japanese attack was launched. Within six weeks Japanese troops had conquered the Malaysian peninsula and captured Singapore on February 15, 1942: More than 70,000 British troops surrendered.

Even before the capitulation of Singapore, Britain was to suffer a heavy blow on the seas. The battleship *Prince of Wales* and the heavy cruiser *Repulse* were sunk on December 11, 1941, by Japanese bombers and low-flying torpedo planes. As Winston Churchill declared in the House of Commons, "In my whole experience I do not remember any naval blow so heavy and painful. . . ."

Despite the Japanese attack on the United States, Washington refrained for a time from declaring war on Germany and Italy. Initially, Hitler's attitude toward the United States was hesitant and cautious. This attitude changed only on December 11, 1941, when Hitler proclaimed war on the United States as a gesture of solidarity with Japan. On December 12 he issued an instruction that declared "the United States of America and those states of Central and South America who join the U.S.A. or Allies in their attitude toward Germany are henceforth to be treated as enemies." This gratuitous step was soon followed by a similar one on the part of Italy. By that time all Great Powers were involved in the war. Thus, by mid-December of 1941 the war became global and lived up to its name as a world war.

Maxim Litvinov, Soviet Ambassador in Washington, discusses U.S. aid to Russia with General George Marshall. National Archives

Hitler obviously underrated the industrial and military potential of the United States to an extent that boggles the mind. For him, the Americans were a decadent nation "half Judaized, half negrified" and thoroughly corrupted by materialism and incapable of producing soldiers to match his own veterans of so many campaigns. On January 7, 1942, he said, "I don't see much future for the Americans. It's a decayed country. And they have their racial problem, and the problem of social inequalities. . . . My feelings against Americanism are feelings of hatred and deep repugnance. . . ."[18]

---

[18]For Hitler's diatribes against the United States see H. R. Trevor-Roper, ed., *Hitler's Table Talk, 1941–44: His Private Conversations,* 2nd ed. (London: Weidenfeld and Nicolson, 1973).

TIMING AND RESOURCES

The year 1941 was critical for the outcome of the entire war. During that year the Germans had captured large stretches of land in the Balkans, in North Africa, and in Russia, where they had inflicted painful losses. Nevertheless, the Reich was unable to win decisive victories and failed to reach any of its planned goals. Germany captured neither Moscow nor Cairo, neither the Caucasian oil fields nor the Suez Canal. The Western Desert Force remained intact, and the Red Army was building its manpower and resources with astonishing speed.

By the summer of 1941 Hitler was not only fighting two widely separated land campaigns—one in North Africa and another in Russia—but was also engaged in the Battle of the Atlantic and facing the beginnings of a British air offensive on his main industrial centers. By the end of 1941 Hitler was already stalemated on both land fronts, and the Battle of the Atlantic was still undecided, with the entry of the United States into the war multiplying the antisubmarine resources of the Royal Navy. Hitler challenged the United States, a sleeping industrial giant with a potential far surpassing Axis resources, and he would find himself overmatched.

Hitler's setback in Russia cannot be fully understood without taking into consideration his Balkan and Mediterranean involvements. Hitler missed capturing Moscow by only a narrow margin. His Balkan and North African ventures had a serious impact on the Russian campaign. In weighing these factors, one has to differentiate between two aspects distinct and yet interconnected: timing and resources.

The prevalent approach by historians on these issues has been to stress timing to the neglect of the second factor, that of the available resources at the start of the Russian campaign. Originally, Hitler had planned to launch Operation Barbarossa on May 15, 1941, yet the offensive started only on June 22. Most experts agree that the unforeseen Yugoslav campaign had a greater impact here than the intervention in Greece that the German General Staff had anticipated since December 1941. The effect of the spring 1941 rains, which made the muddy Soviet roads impassable for the German tanks and transports until the end of June, may be controversial. Timing can be a matter for ceaseless speculation.[19]

Available resources, however, raise a topic of cold facts and figures—a matter of allocation of limited manpower and materiel. As a result of the Balkan and Mediterranean ventures the German forces invading Russia were short by at least a dozen vital divisions. Some of them would be engaged to the end of the war in the mountains and forests of the Balkans, trying to cope with some of the toughest guerrilla fighters of Europe; some of the best panzer troops would be fighting until May 1943 in the North African campaigns. There is no doubt that both the Balkan and North African divisions were badly needed on the Russian front.

Moreover, the German troops who were eventually redirected from Greece and Yugoslavia to Russia arrived there exhausted and with their equipment in poor shape. For instance, the Army Group South started the campaign with only 600 tanks and had to face the 2,400 tanks of Budenny. Superior German leadership prevailed, but partly as a result of the lack of armored troops, Budenny's forces escaped complete annihilation around Kiev. The losses in aircraft and airborne troops suffered during the capture of Crete were also acutely felt on the eastern front. Throughout the battle in Russia, German commanders complained of inadequate air support.

The cumulative impact of both timing and resources spelled Germany's eventual doom. Who knows what would have been the outcome of the battle of Moscow had the Wehrmacht appeared at its gates a few days earlier, and with forces a few panzer divisions stronger?

---

[19]For a discussion of the problem see Martin L. van Creveld, *Hitler's Strategy, 1940–41: The Balkan Clue* (Cambridge: Cambridge University Press, 1973), pp. 69–101 and 170–78. For the German point of view see Liddel Hart, *The German Generals Talk,* pp. 167–80.

11

The Turn of the Tide in the West

The Battle of the Atlantic and El Alamein

ALLIED STRATEGY

The United States and Britain Plot a Course

During the first months after Pearl Harbor, the United States might have been compared to a rudely awakened giant groping for the best ways of dealing with a critical two-front struggle: one in the Far East, another in the European theater of war. From the very beginning, agreement on priorities concerning Allied strategy was a major problem for the United States and Britain. To coordinate Britain's plans with those of its new ally, Winston Churchill went to Washington at the end of 1941.

At the British-American conference that took place December 22, 1941 to January 14, 1942, serious disagreement arose between the two partners about how to defeat the Axis powers. Both realized that the Soviets had to be supported to the best of the Allied ability—that the Red Army's stand must somehow or other be maintained. Both sides also concurred that the burden of the Red Army, fighting its murderous battles, should be alleviated by establishing the "second front" as soon as practicable. The main difference centered around the timing and the location of the front. Both partners further recognized that a massive invasion of the continent of Europe across the English Channel was eventually inevitable.[1]

The British believed, however, that while Italy was already tottering, the Third Reich still remained most powerful. Consequently,

[1]For the British-American strategies in 1942/43 see Churchill, *The Second World War, The Grand Alliance,* pp. 419–50 and 624–98, respectively.

before an invasion of northern France could be launched, a long and bloody struggle must first disperse Germany's forces and sap its strength at various less well-defended points in Europe. In one of these discussions with Roosevelt, Churchill sketched on paper a map of Nazi Europe shaped like a crocodile, with France representing its hard snout and the Mediterranean its soft underbelly. The Allies were unprepared as yet to attack the hard segments, he stressed, but they were ready to cut into the vulnerable soft spots, namely Italy and the Balkans.

Churchill's "soft underbelly" strategy was based on two assumptions: First, the Axis faced a crucial strategic problem with communications in that region; second, the Balkans—especially Yugoslavia, Albania, and Greece—were seething with unrest, and widespread resistance movements were ready to assist the Allied forces. According to the prime minister, by striking across the Mediterranean the Allies could fatally strain the enemy's inadequate north-south communications and take advantage of strong local resistance movements. Because of the Alpine ranges and the Balkan mountains, the Axis' capacity to move its troops and supplies was reduced to a seventh of its ability to transfer its fighting power from east to west. Allied landings in southern Europe would compel the Axis to deploy large elements to defend an immense stretch of coastline, while continuing to hold down the restless peoples of the Balkans, where strong guerrilla movements were already challenging Axis control. This was especially true of Yugoslavia.

The Americans, however, considered this indirect approach to be too slow. They argued that a peripheral strategy would prolong the European war for several years, thus delaying the final showdown with Japan. The Third Reich, they were convinced, could be defeated only with a powerful frontal attack from England against northwest France, thus diverting at least thirty to forty German divisions from the critical Russian front. Central to this dispute was a plan originally conceived by General George C. Marshall, Chief of Staff of the United States Army, and his head of the War Plans Division, General Dwight D. Eisenhower. According to them, to save the Red Army from possible disaster, the invasion should take place in the late summer or early autumn of 1942.[2]

Churchill and Sir Alan Brooke, chief of the Imperial General Staff, insisted that the best way America and Britain could lose the war was by suffering a defeat by landing prematurely in France. The overwhelming strength of at least twenty-five German divisions then stationed in France, protected by strong fortifications, spelled a potential disaster for the Allies. Moreover, only three or four American divisions were ready for the venture, and the British had no more than a dozen large army units operational. Churchill and Brooke considered forty-eight divisions to be a minimum requirement for a northern invasion. Churchill bluntly warned President Roosevelt that if such an expedition was attempted in 1942 the Channel would be soon transformed into a "river of blood."

Solid historical reasons were responsible for the cautious British attitude toward the "second front." Britain had long and successful experience with peripheral strategy during the Napoleonic period and the Crimean War. Further, while attempting to stage massive direct offensives on the Continent during World War I, Britain had suffered terrible losses amounting to almost a million men. Consequently, British leaders were determined to avoid a similar bloodletting. In World War I, they argued, British forces landed easily at docksides in France, but now they would have to fight their way across the English Channel while storming a

[2]This early overzealous American stand was criticized by the leading U.S. strategists; see, for instance, Dwight D. Eisenhower, *Crusade in Europe* (New York: Doubleday, 1948), pp. 49–252. For another admission that a cross-Channel invasion in 1942 with limited forces and a grossly inadequate number of landing craft would have spelled a full-scale disaster, see Omar Bradley and Clay Bruce, *A General's Life. An Autobiography* (New York: Simon & Schuster, 1983), p. 159.

wall of steel and concrete saturated with guns. The British also remembered well the beachheads of Norway and the nightmares of Dunkirk, continental Greece, and Crete from which they had only recently been driven by the Germans in 1940/41. After their traumatic, humiliating experiences, Churchill and his military advisers had no intention of running the risk of another bloodbath. Moreover, by the time the United States entered the conflict, Britain had been in the war for well over two years and its resources were already nearing depletion.

The clash of opinions led to bitter debates. President Roosevelt and his military advisers were threatened to shift the main American effort from Europe to the Far East. Such a strategy had been strongly advocated by General Douglas MacArthur and Admiral Ernest Joseph King. At this critical moment the new Grand Alliance was close to splitting, with consequences only too easy to anticipate. The crisis ended with the President's decision to seek a compromise and to reaffirm his original decision that the European theater of war had primacy over the Pacific front. A full-scale invasion of Hitler's "fortress Europe" was to be delayed until 1943 or perhaps even the spring of 1944.[3]

There were at least four justifications for the Allied resolve to tackle Germany and Italy before Japan. First, the main opponent of Axis domination in Europe, Britain, was fully engaged in a life-and-death fight and had to be assisted immediately. Britain needed 30 million tons of imports a year but was receiving only 25 million, and the U-boat campaign threatened it with starvation.

Second, Germany possessed a greater military potential than Japan and could at any time unleash some secret weapon of devastating power that could definitely win the entire struggle.

Third, Germany already controlled the entire western coast of Europe (except for Spain and Portugal) and thus threatened the routes on the Atlantic that were crucial for both the United States and Britain.

Fourth, both the distances and the logistics of a large-scale invasion of Europe promised to be easier than an invasion of the Japanese islands. What also helped to continue the "Europe first" strategy was the stunning American naval victory at Midway Island on June 4, 1942; United States forces crippled no fewer than four Japanese aircraft carriers, and the Japanese navy was reduced overnight to mere parity with the faster-expanding United States Pacific Fleet. With Midway, the initiative in the Pacific passed to the Americans.

The conference ended with the compromise decision to demolish quickly the remnants of the Axis forces in Libya, to deny Germany control of the western coast of Africa, and to give the Allies a base for eventual operations against the Axis' "soft underbelly" in southern Europe.

Allied Planning for a North African Landing

Unable to open a second front by invading France, the Western Allies decided to lighten the Soviet burden by landing powerful forces in the French North African possessions of Morocco and Algeria. The invasion of North Africa, called Operation Torch, was to take place toward the end of October or at the beginning of November 1942; the operation would have an American Supreme Commander, General Dwight D. Eisenhower, and a combined Anglo-American staff. Formation of this Combined Chiefs of Staff Committee represented a crucial step in the future task of managing the overall Allied war effort.

Great hopes were placed on this armed landing in North Africa; well-equipped, fresh troops would here oppose poorly armed French colonial forces whose morale and political mood would be softened by psychological warfare. The next step would

[3]For the memorandum by the United States and British Chiefs of Staff, January 1942, at the Washington War Conference (Arcadia), see Keith Sainsbury, *The North African Landings 1942: A Strategic Decision* (London: Davis-Poynter, 1976), pp. 178–79.

be eliminating Italy from the war, and forcing Germany to replace Italian troops not only on the Apennine peninsula but also in the Balkans. This drain of Axis fighting men would certainly aid the Russians. The Russians, however, were not to be represented on the committee.

The conference had far-reaching consequences for Allied strategy. The commitment of massive resources and troops for a large-scale landing in French North Africa, and the subsequent difficulty of transporting them back to the United Kingdom, led inevitably to their deployment in further operations in the Mediterranean instead of using them in a cross-Channel attack. The conference marked the last time that a fully mobilized Britain would be able to impose its strategic concepts on a United States only then gearing up for war. From the start the vast resources of the United States dictated Britain's eventual status as a junior partner in the alliance. But for the first two years American unpreparedness ensured that a British stamp would be put on Allied strategy in the European theater of war.

Aside from the plans for the North African landing, the conference produced the joint declaration of twenty-six nations in the anti-Axis coalition, which pledged their resources for the final goal of destroying the Axis. This so-called United Nations declaration bound the participants to continue the war to the end together without making a separate peace.

Probing the Atlantic Wall

The conference, while shifting the assault on "fortress Europe" to the back burner, did not abandon the concept altogether. Quite the contrary, the Americans insisted that preparations for the invasion of the Continent should be intensified. The intricate planning for the eventual invasion of northern France demanded laborious and cooperative effort, however. A precondition of such a venture was the destruction of the U-boat force, which could stymie large-scale transport of some forty American divisions and their supplies to Britain. A trans-Atlantic crossing, in turn, required at least 10 million tons of additional shipping yet to be built.

Meanwhile, the Allies tested enemy defenses along the Atlantic wall and perfected operational skills by staging a series of amphibious forays. Soon after the fall of France the British organized some 5,000 specially trained soldiers into ten battalions of raiders known as commandos. They were to be led by a young Royal Navy captain, one of the heroes of the battle of Crete, Lord Louis Mountbatten. On March 4, 1942, he was appointed chief of combined operations and sat as the fourth Chief of Staff with an acting rank of vice-admiral, as well as lieutenant general and air marshal. This unprecedented appointment, which elevated a young captain not yet forty-two to one of the most responsible posts, created a great deal of bitterness and jealousy, but proved most beneficial.

Mountbatten had an instinctive feel for modern combined operations, and he brought zest and skill to his immediate objectives: trial raids on the coast of occupied Europe and preparation for an eventual invasion. Some argued that petty forays were a futile diversion of effort. But Mountbatten, supported by Churchill, remained convinced that such pinprick raids maintained an offensive spirit in the troops, compelled the enemy to deploy considerable forces along the vast coastline, and raised public morale at home. Moreover, the destruction of vital enemy facilities and the capturing of its newest equipment would also be valuable gains. When enough men were trained and provided with enough up-to-date landing craft, Mountbatten staged a series of major probes along the German defenses along the Atlantic shoreline.

THE BATTLE OF THE ATLANTIC

The preparation for both the North African landing and the projected reconquest of Europe required an intensified struggle

The tanker SS *Dixie Arrow* burning in the Atlantic, March 26, 1942.
National Archives

against the fast-multiplying U-boats in the Atlantic and the Mediterranean. Yet, after Pearl Harbor, the United States found itself with heavy responsibilities also in the Pacific. In both theaters of operation the United States Navy initially experienced a shortage of surface craft and airplanes.

The Germans took full advantage of American unpreparedness and tried to win the Battle of the Atlantic before the United States attained full mobilization. In late December 1941 some thirty U-boats nosed out of Wilhelmshaven, Cuxhaven, and St. Nazaire to a new hunting ground in the western Atlantic. Avoiding the few escorted convoys, the U-boats focused their interest on the zone along the east coast of the United States from Maine to Florida. These shallow waters were known among the German crews as "the U-boat paradise." Nearly forty Allied ships, almost half of them tankers, fell victim to the U-boats in little more than two weeks.[4]

An initial lack of experience in the American fleet put extra strain upon the beleaguered Royal Navy ships and personnel. The Royal Navy stretched its resources to the limit in this effort. Back in the spring of 1941 the United States had helped Britain by all means short of open warfare. Now, in February 1942, the Royal Navy rushed ten corvettes across the Atlantic to be manned by American crews, and also sent twenty escorts to assist in clearing the eastern coastline of German underwater raiders.

The North Atlantic was the scene of the longest naval battle of the war. This cold, merciless struggle grew progressively more brutal. The attacked vessels were first rocked by torpedo salvos and, if still afloat, hit by shell fire. At first, when crews escaped in lifeboats, they were questioned about their cargoes and destination by U-boat commanders and occasionally offered pro-

[4]For the naval aspects of the American entry into the war see Croswell, *Sea Warfare*, pp. 107–19. Samuel Eliot Morrison, *The Battle of the Atlantic, Sept. 1939–May 1943* (Boston: Little, Brown, 1963). Even before entering the war, the United States helped British ships by repairing them in American shipyards and shared vital intelligence with London. Moreover some U.S. citizens joined the British armed forces as volunteers.

Battle of the Atlantic, 1940-1943

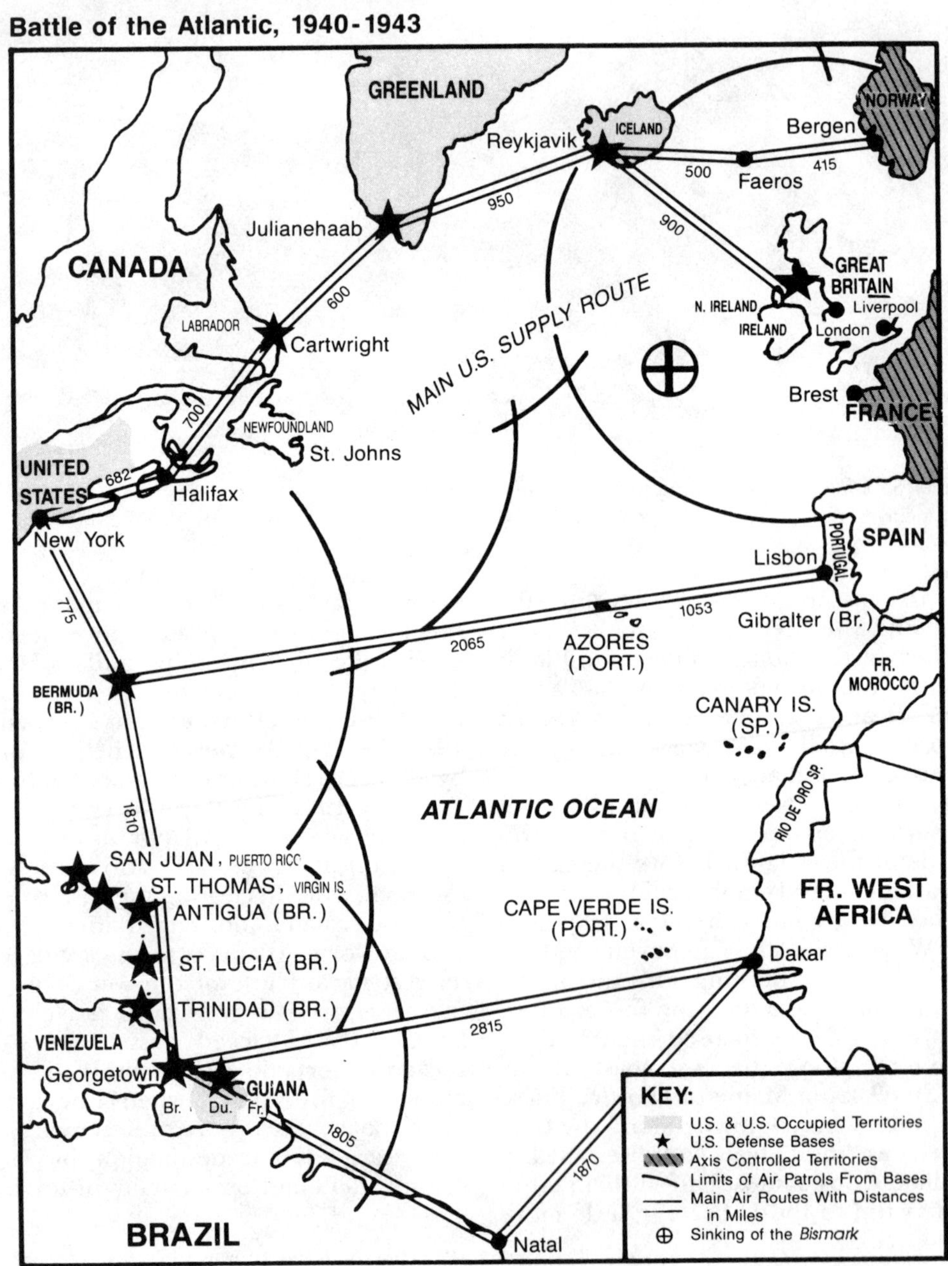

U-boat 118 under fire of a convoy destroyer. National Archives.

visions and water. But soon this gave way to ruthlessness. Rescuing the survivors of sunken ships was abandoned.

German naval forces were too weak to bid for mastery in the Atlantic, and therefore Admiral Erich Raeder avoided all opportunities to fight a major sea battle.[5] Instead, Raeder used his heavy ships as commerce raiders and thus compelled the Allies to commit ships of equal strength to serve as convoy escorts. Between 1939 and 1941, the larger German ships—including the pocket battleships *Deutschland* (later named *Lützow*) and *Admiral Scheer,* the battle cruisers *Scharnhorst* and *Gneisenau,* the battleship *Bismarck,* the heavy cruisers *Admiral Hipper* and *Prinz Eugen,* and several armed merchant cruisers—hit Allied merchant vessels and caused heavy losses to the Allied merchant marine. The newly built 42,500-ton German battleship *Tirpitz,* stationed in Norway, was consigned to such a raider role. The *Tirpitz* posed a deadly threat to Arctic convoys sailing close to Norway. Together with its sister ship *Bismarck,* it outclassed any Allied warship then in existence. The bloodletting suffered by Allied convoys, the strategic importance of Scandinavian waters, and the presence of the *Tirpitz* would combine and conspire to draw Britain into perilous and remarkably significant operation.

In 1940 Britain lost 4 million tons of shipping, mainly to U-boats; in 1941 yet another 4 million tons were destroyed. Thanks to Enigma the British had repeatedly broken the codes of the Wehrmacht and the Luftwaffe, but the *Kriegsmarine* retained a separate and more complex cipher that the Royal Navy experts were unable to read. In May 1941 British cryptographers began to solve the current cipher used by Doenitz for communication with his U-boats at sea. Yet mastery of the German U-boat code was to last only two months before it was changed again and the crippling maritime losses in the Atlantic continued.[6]

Now Hitler placed the submarine in the forefront of his naval effort. Doenitz organized combat groups of submarines, known as wolf packs, who operated under one commander and coordinated their tactics. The cruising range of the wolf packs was still further increased by new and better

[5]For his story of World War II see Erich Raeder, *My Life* (New York: Arno Press, 1980), pp. 300 ff.; he insists that the *Kriegsmarine* was ordered to help the crews of the torpedoed enemy merchantmen.

[6]For the role of Enigma during the North African campaign see Ronald Lewin, *Ultra Goes to War,* pp. 179–82 and 262–68. For the British view of the near disastrous Allied shipping losses see Churchill, *The Grand Alliance,* pp. 111–35.

supply, including specially equipped U-boat bases, know as "sea cows," which carried ammunition, oil, replacement crews, and experts who could undertake any but major repairs at sea. In addition, they were now provided with special devices, known as *Schnörkels,* that allowed them to recharge their batteries while submerged.

In addition to the fast-growing number of submarines, the Germans had four most formidable warships. Besides the *Scharnhorst,* the *Tirpitz,* and the *Prinz Eugen,* another of Germany's most modern battleships, the *Bismarck,* was about to enter in full action. Armed with eight 15-inch guns and protected by thick, massive armor plates, the 42,000 ton sea monster had a top speed of 30 knots. Destruction of the *Bismarck* became a high priority of the Royal Navy.

On May 18, 1941, the *Bismarck,* together with the heavy cruiser *Prinz Eugen,* sailed to Bergen, Norway, to harass the Allied convoys to Russia. The Royal Navy and the RAF were ordered to abort this interference. On May 21, RAF reconnaissance aircraft spotted the two German ships putting to sea in foggy weather and heading north through the Danish straits toward Bergen. On May 23, the cruisers *Suffolk* and *Norfolk* recognized them and radioed a report to the battle cruiser squadron that included the *Hood* and the barely completed battleship *Prince of Wales.* In the morning of May 24, despite its inferiority, the *Hood* engaged the *Bismarck.* A shell from the *Bismarck* plunged through the *Hood*'s deck armor into one of its ammunition magazines. The *Hood* was ripped apart and only three of its 1,500-man crew survived. The *Bismarck* also scored several hits against the *Prince of Wales.* But one of the British battleship's 14-inch shells did hit the *Bismarck,* causing a streak of fuel to leak from a ruptured tank.

The damaged *Bismarck,* still protected by the *Prinz Eugen,* turned south to seek shelter in Brest. Although the *Prinz Eugen* succeeded in evading the Home Fleet's surveillance to reach the French harbor by June 1, the *Bismarck* failed to do so because of leaking fuel. The RAF, which had spotted the *Bismarck* on May 26, never relinquished its watch and, helped by Ultra, kept the Royal Navy informed of the slow meanderings of the wounded "sea tigress." A British naval squadron, dispatched from Gibraltar, included the aircraft carrier *Ark Royal.* This carriers's Swordfish aircraft hurled torpedoes at the *Bismarck.* The battleship's rudder was jammed, thus immobilizing the *Bismarck.* The next morning (May 27) the battleships *King George V* and *Rodney* joined the attackers and began pouring heavy shells on the German giant. Set ablaze, the *Bismarck* continued to fight. Finally, the cruiser *Dorsetshire* closed in and torpedoed it, and the *Bismarck* began to sink. All but 110 of its 2,300-man crew perished.[7]

[7]For a dramatic description of the fate of the *Bismarck* see Churchill, *The Great Alliance,* pp. 305–20; and Geoffrey Bennett, *Naval Battles of World War II* (London and Sydney: B. T. Batsford, 1975), pp. 135–49. For the German side of the story, see Raeder, *My Life,* pp. 338–40. For the role of Enigma, see Ronald Lewin, *Ultra Goes to War,* pp. 200–203.

The *Bismarck* hit by the British battleship *Hood* off Greenland. Bildarchiv Preussischer Kulturbesitz

Throughout 1942 new U-boats were produced much faster than the Allies could destroy them; for every U-boat lost, the Germans sank eight or nine Allied ships;. In August alone, German U-boats had destroyed over a hundred ships in wolf-pack attacks against the North Atlantic convoys; in September almost another hundred Allied vessels were sunk. Admiral Doenitz's construction program yielded impressive results. Victory in the Battle of the Atlantic seemed to be within Hitler's grasp. Four and a half million tons of Allied shipping disappeared during the first six months of 1942 (70 percent of it to submarines); losses continued thereafter at the same rate, and the North Atlantic grew into a murderous test and its outcome was in grave doubt.

The convoy system seemed a failure, and the Atlantic battle a defeat. There was the constant danger that Britain would be eventually starved into surrender. Meanwhile, however, months of hard work by the Admiralty Submarine Tracking Room, closely cooperating with Ultra technicians, resulted in the cracking of the new German naval cipher; the same time, the Admiralty introduced a new code of its own, replacing the old one that the enemy had been able to read regularly.[8] Finally, too, United States shipyards began to float an increasing number of warships, tankers, and transport ships. But meanwhile, Britain's position was near desperate.

In the Mediterranean, because of its narrower confines, the naval situation was also critical. In the summer of 1941 the Royal Navy, decimated during the Battle of Crete, temporarily lost control of the Mediterranean; enemy air superiority inflicted severe damage on convoys, and until the close of 1942 most supplies for the British Eighth Army had to be carried around the Cape of Good Hope. Malta was beleaguered and, although never invaded, could only be relieved by infrequent and desperate runs from each end of the Mediterranean.

[8]For the breaking of the German naval cipher see Ronald Lewin, *Ultra Goes to War,* pp. 211–19.

BRITAIN'S DESPERATE MEASURES

As a result of these events, the British experienced their most critical moment four months after the United States' entry into the war, before the aid of a fully productive America could reach the British Isles. By March 1942, Atlantic losses had reduced British oil reserves to almost nothing. Now, at Britain's most dangerous moment, the *Tirpitz,* then anchored at St. Nazaire on the western coast of France, made ready to rejoin the U-boat packs. Also by March of 1942 three of Germany's most formidable warships—the *Scharnhorst,* the *Gneisenau,* and the *Prinz Eugen*—were poised to combine in convoy attacks in the North Atlantic for a final blow at Britain's ship lanes. All three warships had been in Brest at the northwestern tip of France for repairs. In fact, these vessels were bottled up; to take station for battle they had to escape from what amounted to a blockade.

On March 11, in order to break through the narrows of the English Channel—the most feasible way of reaching their North Sea home bases before sailing for the Atlantic—the ships risked a hazardous dash. Accompanied by a protective force of six destroyers, an array of smaller ships, and a powerful air umbrella, the German vessels departed from Brest. On March 12 five Royal Navy Swordfish bombers attacked the ships; nevertheless, the *Scharnhorst,* the *Gneisenau,* and the *Prinz Eugen* arrived safely into German harbors. This escape marked a resounding victory for the Germans and caused a deadly fright among the British. Desperate measures were contemplated and eventually carried out in a hurry since the Allied Atlantic losses were not sustainable in the long run.

With German battleships threatening supply lines, it became imperative to find and sink the *Tirpitz* then at St. Nazaire, which boasted the only dock on the Atlantic coast large enough to shelter a ship as large as the *Tirpitz.* With the dock destroyed, the battleship would be trapped. Lord Mountbatten decided to launch a raid on St. Nazaire at once. The raid, it was realized, might result in the loss of most of the sailors and soldiers participating in it. Such almost suicidal losses would have to be accepted because of Britain's desperate situation.

The plan involved sending an old destroyer, the *Campbelltown,* laden with explosives and escorted by seventeen small wooden coastal boats, on a perilous passage. At 12:30 A.M. on March 28, 1942, a task force of some 260 commandos successfully entered the gateway to St. Nazaire, the Loire estuary. Although the *Campbelltown* was repeatedly hit by gunfire, it managed to ram into the great Normandy dock harboring the *Tirpitz.* Despite the murderous fire, the commandos demolished the machinery and working parts of the Normandy dock in less than half an hour. The dock was never used again during the war.

The Allied losses, however, were appalling. One hundred fifty-nine army and navy men were killed and nearly 200 were taken prisoner. But even the desperate St. Nazaire raid did not make the Atlantic sea lanes secure.

Consequently, another measure designed to cope with the most critical situation was the raid on Dieppe on August 19, 1942. A specially trained Canadian brigade (some 5,100 strong), together with 1,000 British commandos and 50 American rangers, was ordered to make a daring assault force; 252 ships and as many as 69 RAF squadrons (more than had fought in the Battle of Britain) supported the attackers. The commandos and rangers were to silence enemy coastal batteries located east and west of Dieppe, but the town itself would be captured by the Canadians.

The German resistance was far more fierce than anticipated. Despite careful planning and the gallantry of the raiders, the main force failed to cross the Dieppe seawall. Many Canadians were slaughtered while still in the landing craft; altogether, 68 percent of the Canadian soldiers were listed as killed, wounded, or missing; the Germans took 2,000 of them prisoner. The RAF lost 106 aircraft, but German losses totaled only 48 planes.

The entire venture had the look of a full-scale disaster, yet for the British it served a purpose. The Dieppe venture demonstrated clearly the impossibility of a cross-Channel invasion in 1942. Moreover, the British and their American allies learned valuable lessons in amphibious warfare; these experiences furnished precious indications about how to arrange the coming African invasion.

Another important lesson of Dieppe was that even a large-scale invasion could not be expected to capture a major, well-defended port in any swift manner. This awareness generated the concept of the future artificial portable harbors. The Dieppe raid also demonstrated that a far more powerful preliminary bombardment of the enemy coastal defenses by capital ships must be combined with extensive sabotage of rear areas by local resistance teams, reinforced by Allied paratroops and commandos. The third and in some ways the most important lesson of the Dieppe raid was the conviction that a scheme of deception to mislead Hitler concerning the locale and timing of the main Allied landing would be essential for its success.

With the destruction of the *Bismarck* and the temporary neutralization of the *Tirpitz,* the Germans lost the main power of their surface fleet. This disaster sharpened the lingering disagreements between Hitler and Raeder and brought about the decline of the *Grossadmiral* who still advocated maintaining a "balanced fleet." Hitler tended increasingly to favor Raeder's rival, Admiral Doenitz, who had preached the primacy of a powerful submarine force. As its commander, Doenitz further organized the U-boats into packs and launched another fierce undersea offensive against Allied shipping.

THE WAR IN AFRICA

The British Counteroffensive in North Africa

During 1942, with the battle of the Atlantic raging, the situations both in Russia and in North Africa were also critical. When

Rommel first arrived in Tripoli in February 1941, the Italian army was in full retreat and the British Western Desert Force was rolling westward as fast as its supplies would permit. Rommel changed this promising prospect in little more than two months; by June 1941 he stood at the frontier of Egypt and threatened the Suez Canal.[9]

During the same period Hitler was launching his renewed effort to capture the oil of the Caucasus, and throughout the summer of 1942 the Wehrmacht scored a series of brilliant successes. Thus, in both land campaigns the Germans were victoriously pushing forward and seemed to be close to decisive victories. Should they capture the Suez Canal, the Allies' road to another major source of oil, Iraq and Iran, would be in great danger.

To defend the threatened Suez Canal, Churchill insisted on a counteroffensive as soon as possible. He replaced Wavell with General Claude Auchinleck as commander in chief in the Middle East. This was not a fortunate choice. Auchinleck, who had devoted most of his life to the Indian army, had little experience with modern mechanized warfare; moreover his operational views were not much different from those of his more experienced predecessor. Auchinlech also wished to pause to gather more resources in order to cope with Rommel.

By the autumn of 1941, Auchinleck's obduracy had at least produced a quantitative British advantage. The rapidly expanded old Western Desert Force now numbered two Army corps; renamed the Eighth Army, it now had 700 tanks, 600 field guns, and no fewer than 34,000 supportive vehicles. But this British armored force was impressive only on paper; it represented a miscellany of tanks too many of which were obsolescent and mechanically unreliable, and certainly no match for Rommel's Mark III and Mark IV tanks. What is more, the tactics of mechanical warfare had not been sufficiently mastered by the British. The Germans and Italians for their part were also able to make good use of the period from August to November for adding reinforcements. The modest Afrika Korps had gradually expanded into a powerful Panzer Army Africa. In spite of his professional judgment that an attack would be premature until his troops were properly trained, Auchinleck, like Wavell, finally succumbed to Churchill's pressure and on No-

[9]For the German commander's point of view see *The Rommel Papers,* pp. 91–153; see also *The German Generals Talk,* pp. 154–65.

June 21, 1942: Tobruk captured by the Germans.
Imperial War Museum

vember 18, 1941, he opened the offensive known as Operation Crusader.

The British attack had the objective of relieving besieged Tobruk and recapturing the Cyrenaica. But Auchinleck forfeited the advantage of an enveloping movement by trying to smash the enemy's armor in a series of head-on tank battles. He still believed that tanks should fight tanks. Rommel countered the superior numbers of the British mechanized forces with a skillful use of his powerful antitank artillery. The British assault was repelled; worse, they allowed the panzers to counterattack, who thereby inflicted crippling losses and crushed the British offensive. The unreliability of British armor, the low standards of tactical command, and the absence of a coherent doctrine for mobile war were exposed once more. Operation Crusader stood revealed as a duel between a master and an apprentice.

Rommel Pushes toward Egypt

Japan's entry into the war in December 1941 had beneficial consequences for Rommel. Suddenly, the Far Eastern segment of the British Empire was in danger, and available reserves had to be withdrawn from Egypt and dispatched to the opposite side of the military chessboard. As a result, almost immediately two Australian divisions left for New Guinea, and a British division, on the way to reinforce the Eighth Army in Africa, had to be diverted from Suez to Singapore. An Indian division, also marked for service in Africa, went straight off to Rangoon. In this way both the actual and potential strength of the Eighth Army was reduced. The garrison at Tobruk was also weakened because of the removal of most of the Australian contingent. By the spring of 1942 Tobruk's garrison consisted only of the 70th British Division, the Polish Carpathian Brigade, and a mixture of tanks in the 32nd Army Tank Brigade.

At the same time additional forces arrived to support the Panzer Army Africa. The Luftwaffe's Second Air Fleet was also now stationed in Sicily, and Kesselring began orchestrating from Rome an air and sea offensive against Malta. Two packs of eighteen U-boats commenced their havoc with Allied convoys in the Mediterranean. By November 1941 they had sunk the aircraft carrier *Ark Royal* and the battleship *Barham.* On December 18 a British cruiser and a destroyer disappeared among mines. Next morning, two Italian frogmen penetrated the harbor at Alexandria to put out of action the two battleships *Queen Elizabeth* and *Valiant.* This was Italy's greatest triumph in World War II naval warfare. Within a few weeks, then, the Royal Navy had again lost its previously dominant position in the eastern Mediterranean.

The main Allied obstacle to the free flow of supplies to Rommel in Africa was British control of Malta. From the start of the Mediterranean campaign the naval-minded Churchill had realized the vital importance of Malta for his desert forces. Consequently, the British kept the island bastion alive, losing hundreds of planes and vast shipping tonnage in the process. But the sacrifices proved worthwhile. Rommel's need for reinforcements and supplies could not be fully satisfied as long as Axis convoys were smashed by the planes and ships operating from Malta.

Mussolini also attached great importance to Malta. Yet the lack of coordination in Axis plans was to cripple his obvious intention to capture the island. By the end of April 1942 the Italian scheme of taking Malta by a full-scale airborne and amphibious assault (Operation Hercules) had been laboriously worked out between Rome and Berlin. The attack on Malta was to be launched early in July, before the start of Rommel's offensive against Egypt. But soon after this agreement Hitler developed doubts about the Italian ability to carry out their part of the assault. He was convinced that the Italians had no guts for such a risky venture. They would not be punctual and persistent enough in supporting the German parachute troops; their Navy would not face the British, and they were thus likely to leave the German airborne contingent stranded without supplies. So, on the 21st of May, Hitler decided that Operation Hercules was to be suspended at least until Rommel succeeded in taking Tobruk, a major obstacle in his planned push toward Cairo.

Meanwhile, the impatient Churchill again ordered Auchinleck either to stop the Axis forces and recapture Tobruk or to resign. Rommel, however, preempted the planned British Operation Battle-Axe by another sudden leap. On May 26, 1942, he pounced on the Eighth Army and broke through its defenses. On June 10 he captured the fortress of Bir Hakeim, valiantly defended by the Free French brigade commanded by General Marie-Pierre Koenig. In one of the most gallant actions fought by the French during World War II, half of Koenig's brigade was lost; the rest had to be evacuated. Then Rommel stormed in and captured Tobruk on June 21, after thirty-three weeks of siege.

Tobruk, strategically important as the largest and best harbor in Italian North Africa, also constituted a treasure house of loot that delighted both Germans and Italians. Taking Tobruk represented a great triumph for Rommel personally, and his order of the day had a Napoleonic ring to it: "We have taken in all over 41,000 prisoners and destroyed or captured more than 1,000 armored fighting vehicles and nearly 400 guns. During the long hard struggle of the last few weeks you have, through your incomparable tenacity, dealt the enemy blow upon blow. . . ."

Five days after the conquest of Tobruk, before the Eighth Army could recover from an almost constant series of blows, Rommel launched another thrust. Combining cunning, audacity, and speed, he again routed the British in a confused battle at Mersa Matruh on Egypt's frontier. Now Rommel was poised for a push on the Nile Delta.

After capturing Tobruk and reaching el-Alamein, Rommel was at the height of his career. He was now promoted to field marshal. On October 2 he left his troops and went to Germany to receive his baton from Hitler's own hand.

By the end of June the demoralized British in Cairo believed that Egypt would fall to the Axis at any moment. Evacuation preparations were undertaken at full speed. Throughout July a black pall of smoke hung over the city as officials burned their files and secret codes. At Alexandria the Royal Navy put to sea quickly. In Palestine the British authorities hastily distributed arms to Jewish guerrilla units, mostly to the Hagana, arms never to be returned. The elated Mussolini flew from Rome to Rommel's headquarters to be ready for a triumphant entry into Cairo. With him Il Duce brought a white Arabian stallion and "the Sword of Islam."

Rommel's success in June 1942 profoundly altered the strategic perspectives of the Axis. Such experts as Halder and Raeder now advised Hitler to furnish full logistic support to Rommel and redesign overall German stragegy to make the Middle East, Iraq, and Iran his major targets. Oil in these regions could be more easily captured than that of the Caucasus. But Hitler, obsessed with the dream of quick victory in Russia by the end of 1942, ignored these suggestions. Supplies to Rommel were pinched off. The Panzer Army Africa was still regarded as of marginal importance.

The Eighth Army Regroups and Rearms

The shattered Eighth Army was meanwhile recovering from the blows it had suffered in Operation Battle-axe. With his army's remnants back in el-Alamein, Auchinleck's first concern was to stop Rommel's head-on rush toward Alexandria. Since the bulk of the British armor had been lost during the earlier fighting, Auchinleck withdrew the remnants of the Eighth Army back to the old defenses stretching 40 miles from el-Alamein at the coast to the edge of the Quattara depression. Below steep cliffs, the vast bed of the depression was a mass of trackless waste, much of it an impassible soft salt marsh; the temperature of the depression in summer was like that of a Turkish

General Montgomery in his command tank. Imperial War Museum

bath. Now he decided to make his stand in the fortified passage to defend the Nile Delta and Cairo.

Rommel's lightning triumphs had a shattering effect on the British, once more deeply humiliated by having had their crack troops routed by the Desert Fox. There were fears that India might be invaded. Churchill's cabinet was threatened with a vote of no confidence. Britain's prestige throughout the world dropped disastrously.

On the day of Tobruk's surrender Churchill had been in Washington again conferring with President Roosevelt and had to plead for help. The President, deeply alarmed at the defeat of the only western force then fighting the Axis on land, immediately ordered 300 Sherman medium tanks to be shipped to Egypt to replace British losses in Operation Battle-axe. Together with previous shipments of Grant tanks, these were invaluable gifts. Finally, the Eighth Army had received a full division's component of tanks that were more than a match for Rommel's dwindling force of Mark IIIs and Mark IVs. Weighing 30 tons, the Sherman had a high-velocity 75-mm gun and two machine guns; its engine allowed for a speed of 26 miles per hour and 115-mile range. Together with other reinforcements rushed in by the British, the Eighth Army finally collected the resources necessary for a showdown with its formidable opponent.

The Eighth Army's defeats in the spring of 1942 precipitated another alteration in the British Middle Eastern command. In August, on his way to Moscow to talk with Stalin, Churchill stopped in Cairo to relieve Auchinleck of his command. Now the commander in chief of the Middle East was General Sir Harold Alexander, a gallant but modest soldier with vast experience in France and Burma. But the Eighth Army's commander was to be Alexander's antithesis, the flamboyant and eccentric General Bernard Montgomery.

Montgomery was a small, hawk-faced man of strict puritanical habits and infinite self-confidence. Son of a bishop of Tasmania, he neither drank, smoked, nor played cards, and he read the Bible daily.

Churchill selected Montgomery because of his brilliant military record. In 1940/41, out of the wreckage of the British army after Dunkirk, Montgomery had trained first a division, then a corps, and finally an army to the highest standards of effectiveness. He combined military skill with methodical preparations and packaged these approaches with remarkable showmanship.

British infantry takes surrender of German tank crewmen. Imperial War Museum

Montgomery carefully staged all his public appearances and meticulously memorized all his pronouncements.

The failure to capture Malta had ruined any hope for an unimpeded logistical link with Axis forces in Libya. Between January 1941 and May 1942, submarines operating from Malta sank no fewer than seventy-five Axis ships with a tonnage of nearly 400,000 tons. Germany's ally, Italy, was slow to provide adequate maritime transport; air transportation often had to be resorted to. In July and August 1942, 300 aircraft were used to transport 36,000 men and their equipment. As early as August Rommel had been stopped at el-Alamein as much by exhaustion of his resources as by Auchinleck's stubborn resistance.

By this time the Eighth Army had grown into a mighty colorful and cosmopolitan body. In addition to British units, it included Australians, New Zealanders, Indians, Poles, Czechs, Free French, and South Africans. This medley of soldiers required firm leadership to integrate it into one body and endow it with a new spirit of self-confidence and determination. The new commander knew instinctively how to weld this crowd into a firmly disciplined team. Montgomery inspired an intense devotion especially among enlisted men. His soldiers admired this stern and stoic leader, whom they came to call Monty.[10]

While granting to Rommel the permission to dash into Egypt, Hitler, preoccupied with the capture of Stalingrad in the Russian campaign, failed to sustain Rommel with adequate supplies. Meanwhile all the advantages had shifted to his opponent. The German-Italian force was 370 miles from Tobruk, while the Eighth Army was only 70 miles from Alexandria. Obviously, then, Rommel was removed from his supply center and was unquestionably weaker than his adversary. His force was 16,000 men below strength; his full complement of equipment lacked 210 tanks, 175 troop carriers and armored cars, and 1,500 other vehicles. Virtually everything Rommel needed had to be shipped across the Mediterranean, which made deliveries erratic. Even the acquisition of Tobruk did not significantly improve his situation. Whereas the British had the convenience of a railway running some distance forward from their base, the Panzer Army Africa, with no railway between Tripoli and

[10]For a recent sympathetic study by Nigel Mailton, see segments of his three-volume biography, *Monty, the Making of a General, 1887–1942* (New York: McGraw-Hill, 1982) and *Master of the Battlefield: Monty's War Years, 1942–1944* (New York: McGraw-Hill, 1984).

Cyrenaica, could not enjoy this alternative means of transport. This was compounded by a shortage of transport vehicles, since the Afrika Korps never had enough lorries.

While Rommel's forces were starved for necessary supplies, the Eighth Army was getting stronger and stronger. Besides material reinforcements it benefited from superior sources of intelligence. A special liaison unit of Ultra was established at headquarters of the Middle East command soon after DAK arrived; from that moment until the close of the campaign Rommel's opponents were receiving transcripts of his reports and his cries for supplies as well as his plans. These reports enabled the British naval and air forces to strike with accuracy against Axis shipping. The RAF and the Allied submarines, both benefiting from Ultra intelligence, began to destroy an increasing percentage of Axis convoys. By the end of August, Rommel was short some 6,000 tons of fuel.

Reinforcements to the Eighth Army were at the same time flowing in from all over the world, including the United States. By October Montgomery had unified the various components of his army and had prepared individual units for their special tasks. Minefield clearance, for example, was dutifully practiced by special teams; rank and file as well as junior officers underwent physical training and drilling in teamwork. Montgomery was convinced that battles could be won only by the combined efforts of infantry, tanks, artillery, and engineers integrated into an "all arms" pattern of combat. These integrated tactics and his meticulous management of rapidly expanding resources made the Eighth Army a truly potent force. In under three months Montgomery, working with single-minded dedication, retrained the rearmed Eighth Army, and inspired it with a new offensive spirit. There would be no talk of retreat when Rommel attacked—the British would stand and fight.

By the close of October 1942, the Eighth Army possessed 1,029 tanks, 2,311 guns, and 81 battalions of infantry, amounting to 195,000 men in all. Although the Eighth Army was far superior to the enemy forces even at the time he assumed command, Montgomery resisted London's pressure to launch a counteroffensive at once. He waited until the end of October when his superiority had grown so overwhelming that the showdown seemed to involve a minimal risk.

Since the inevitability of his offensive was obvious, Montgomery sought to achieve surprise about the time and the place of the attack. He mounted a deception scheme to persuade the enemy that the main effort would be made in the south. Montgomery would feint an attack in the south, but strike in the northern sector at the juncture of the German and Italian forces. To mislead the enemy he placed hundreds of dummy vehicles, laid mimic pipelines, and generated an intense spurious radio traffic between simulated units.

The Battle of el-Alamein

The Eighth Army's attack opened on the northerly front on October 23, 1942, with a massive artillery barrage from 456 guns reminiscent of World War I. With Axis defenses shattered by a four-hour pounding, the British infantry moved forward. After the enemy outposts were pinned down by the heavy weapons, the engineers, under cover of smoke, uprooted mines and cleared two broad lanes for the British advance. Despite the Eighth Army's materiel superiority a breakthrough had not been completed during the first night. Everywhere enemy resistance was fierce, and even the Italian divisions, sandwiched between the German units, fought bravely along with their better-trained and more heavily armed allies.

During the first two days of the attack the Eighth Army merely struggled to maintain momentum, trying to open an adequate breach through the mine fields for its armor. By the start of November, however, after a week of nearly continuous assaults by the superior British forces, the weight of numbers prevailed. Axis defenses sagged at

The Battle of el-Alamein, October 24-November 4, 1942

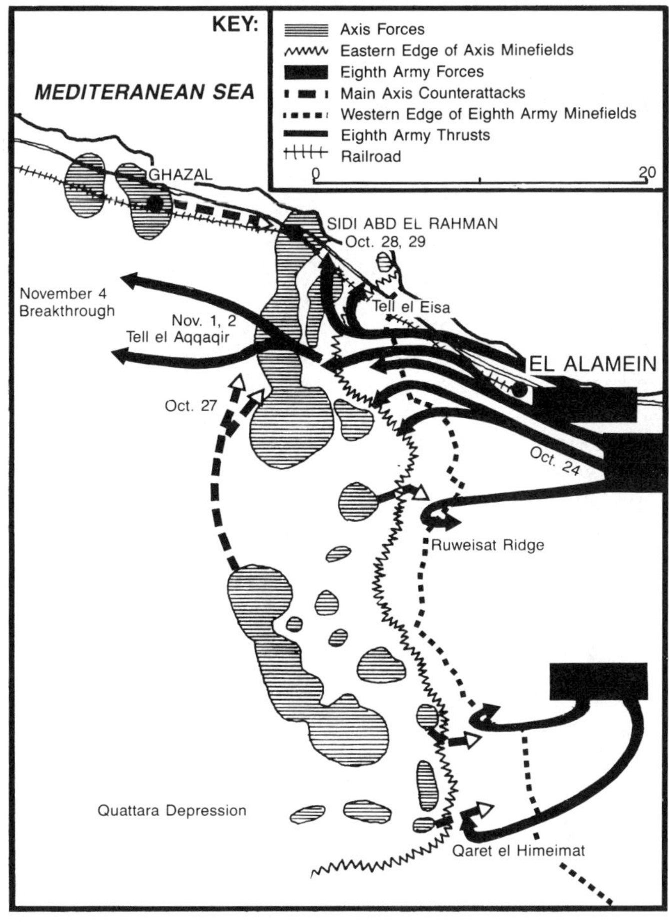

a number of points, and Montgomery's armor poured through several openings. The infantry followed and challenged the Italian and German positions at bayonet point. Savage hand-to-hand fighting crushed German resistance.

When the battle of el-Alamein began, Rommel was in Germany on sick leave. General Georg Stumme, who had taken command in Rommel's absence, died during the fighting on the morning of October 24 from heart failure. Hitler immediately ordered the convalescing Rommel back to Africa. But even his reappearance at the front could not restore the deteriorating situation. On November 2, realizing that the battle had been lost, Rommel requested from Hitler permission for a limited withdrawal. The next day, the Führer replied: "Yield not a yard of ground and throw every gun and every man into the battle. . . . As to your troops, you can show them no other road than to victory or death."

By November 4, however, the Axis condition had grown so desperate that, in defiance of Hitler's orders, and abandoning the Italian contingent to its fate, Rommel gathered all the available transport and moved the remainder of the battered German units westward toward Fuka. This move was dictated because of the mounting danger of encirclement. The retreat was made over a broad front, mainly through open desert, since the coastal road was continuously flooded by the brilliant light of British flares and rocked by intense nonstop RAF attack.[11]

By the night of November 4, British pursuit forces were in the rear of Rommel's ragged army. Only the downpour that began on the evening of the sixth saved the Germans from annihilation. While Rommel's troops were spurred on by desperation, Montgomery's were numbed by the exhaustion and stupor that usually follow a prolonged, murderous battle. Moreover, Rommel's reputation, particularly his magic for surprising table-turning ripostes, suggested caution. Yet, even though his panzer army was now a tattered skeleton, Rommel's achievements in retreat were almost as astonishing as his skill in advance. Time and again Rommel slipped from traps and somehow managed to rally his men and to stem again the Eighth Army growing pressure.

The Allied pursuit was resumed soon after the rain stopped. In twelve days, forward elements of the Eighth Army—the Seventh Armored division—had reached Msus, thus covering a distance of 560 miles. They had passed Sollum (270 miles) on the eleventh of November, and the next day were at Tobruk (360 miles). The vanguard of the Eighth Army, the Seventh British Armored division, the now famous "Desert Rats," entered Tripoli on January 23, three months to the day after the start of the battle at el-Alamein. They captured 30,000 Axis POWs, including nine generals. Montgomery by then had been promoted to a full general and made a Knight Commander of Bath for distinguished service in the field.

Montgomery's unhurried movements after the el-Alamein victory resulted not only from his native caution and bad weather but also from his awareness of what was about to take place on the western end of North Africa. He knew that on November 8 American and British troops were to land in force on the territories of the French possessions of Algeria and Morocco.

---

[11]For Rommel's point of view on the decisive phase of the North African campaign see *The Rommel Papers,* pp. 272–425.

12

The North African Landing

The Allied North African landing of November 8, 1942, was an involved political as well as military operation. The appointment of General Dwight D. Eisenhower and three other Americans as commanders of the task forces was of great psychological importance: It aimed at diminishing expected French resistance to the Allied landing. Long study, longer negotiations, and meticulous rechecking finally produced a plan. The Allies would land at Casablanca, Oran, and Algiers, with the American units everywhere in the vanguard. The Western Task Force, commanded by General George Patton, would protect Morocco, and the British First Army, under the command of General Kenneth A. Anderson, would rush as rapidly as possible from Algiers to Tunis to forestall its occupation by Axis forces retreating from Libya or landing from Sicily and southern Italy. Torch, as it was termed, represented a combined British-American operation, although for political reasons the Allies tried to stage it as an overwhelmingly United States venture.

THE POLITICS OF TORCH

But crucial questions remained: Would the French forces of Morocco, Algeria, and Tunisia, numbering nearly 200,000 men, resist? Would local French leaders accept the authority of General Henri Giraud, whom the Allies planned to slip secretly into North Africa to lead the renewed struggle against the Axis? Especially enigmatic was the possible attitude of French naval personnel. Still smarting from the deadly stroke the British had dealt them at Oran, the French fleet seethed with anti-British feelings. The remaining French forces would also resist any

British landing, and there was no guarantee that the Americans would fare any better. The civilian population in both metropolitan France and French North Africa was apathetic toward the war and wished to avoid any bloodshed. Americans, it was assumed, were at least less unwelcome to the French. Consequently, the plan called for advanced teams of GIs upon landing to wave their tricolored flags and carry loudspeakers shouting: "Don't shoot! Long live France!" The American landing troops were to carry mortars that shot fireworks in a joyous display of the coming liberation.

The deputy commander in chief under General Eisenhower for this Torch operation was General Mark Wayne Clark; he was sent as a secret emissary to confer with the pro-Allied French prior to the landing.[1] From the beginning of the planning for Torch the British and Americans considered including General de Gaulle in the secret. Yet past experience warned against this. Units under de Gaulle's command had taken part in the ill-fated Dakar expedition in September 1940, where the landing forces had to retire in the face of local Vichy French resistance. The British always believed that this fiasco had resulted from leaks in de Gaulle's London headquarters. This unfortunate experience, combined with President Roosevelt's dislike for de Gaulle, brought about his elimination from the planning of Torch. De Gaulle's presence in the initial landing, it was also feared, would incite determined opposition on the part of the largely pro-Vichy officers' corps.[2]

General Mark W. Clark (top right) embarks an amphibious landing craft. National Archives

Eisenhower's provisional command post was located in a dark tunnel in the rock of Gibraltar. When the United States came into the war, neither the State Department nor the armed services had a single expert on North Africa familiar with the Arabic language and its dialects. The Americans thus relied heavily on the intelligence collected by the British and their French agents. Despite this lack, a successful ruse deceived the enemy; for instance, Canadian troops were issued arctic clothing for a supposed operation in Norway, and American troops were told that their tropical clothing was intended for use in the Persian Gulf. As a result of this deception, the Axis navies were surprised and failed to redeploy their fleets before the landing began; only a few Allied assault and supply ships were sunk by them. Thanks to the Enigma, moreover, the Allies managed to destroy no fewer than fourteen Axis submarines during the Torch operation. As Eisenhower aptly put it, "The Allied

---

[1]After Torch was under way Clark handled the negotiations, which ended in the securing of French cooperation. For his story: Mark W. Clark, *Calculated Risk* (New York: Harper & Row, 1950), especially pp. 39–132.

[2]For a political background of the North African landing see Arthur L. Funk, *The Politics of Torch: The Allied Landings and the Putsch, 1942* (Lawrence: Regents Press of Kansas, 1974). For de Gaulle's views, see the second volume of his war memoirs, *Unity 1942–1944* (New York: Simon & Schuster, 1959), especially pp. 45–114.

invasion of Africa was a most peculiar venture of armed forces into the field of international politics; we were invading a neutral country to create a friend."[3]

To soften possible French resistance, General Henri Giraud had been rescued from virtual imprisonment in southern France and brought by a British submarine to Gibraltar on November 7, 1942. Laboring under the misapprehension that he was to assume command of the whole Allied expedition, Girard first assumed a haughty and unyielding posture. Believing his honor was involved, he felt disinclined to accept any post in the venture lower than that of complete command. Fortunately, after a night's sleep, he changed his mind and decided to participate on the condition that if he were successful in winning French support, he would become the administrator of French North Africa.

Despite the American propaganda and Giraud's appeal for cooperation the French troops did resist the Allied landing. Yet Algiers was taken by nightfall on November 8. French resistance at Oran, however, was more protracted and determined. But the stiffest opposition was encountered at Casablanca. There, one task force lost 64 percent of its landing ships (242 boats) in establishing a solid beachhead, while the French troops suffered some 7,000 casualties. Despite this, the Allied material superiority and persistence prevailed: By November 11, only three days after the landing, all the main French bases in northern and northwestern Africa from Bône to Safi were safely in Allied hands.

A decisive role in stopping the fighting was played by Admiral Darlan, commander in chief of the French armed forces and Pétain's right hand, who happened to be in Algiers at that time on a visit to his ailing son. No doubt, Darlan had collaborated with the Axis, but that cooperation probably represented no more than Darlan's assessment of power relationships. In the circumstances created by the armistice, Darlan believed, collaboration with the Axis then served the best interests of France. Secretly, however, Darlan worked to maintain contacts with the Allies and tried to preserve the French fleet intact and even to expand its elements. As Germany became immersed in Russia, Darlan continued to make overtures to President Roosevelt's man in Algiers, Robert Murphy; Admiral Darlan intimated an interest in exploring the new possibilities created by the American participation in the war. Faced with the possibility of prolonged

[3]*Crusade in Europe,* p. 88.

November 8, 1942: US troops land on a beach near Casablanca. Imperial War Museum

turmoil and possible civil war, an agreement with Darlan was struck on November 13. Darlan became head of the civil government, while General Giraud led the armed forces.

Forty days after the deal, on December 24, 1942, Darlan was killed by a young French royalist. This assassination opened again the question of French political leadership in Africa. Suspicion of de Gaulle in the French army and in all echelons of civil government was at that time intense. Consequently, Eisenhower and Murphy turned to the only course open to them; they asked General Giraud to step into Darlan's place. Giraud, uninterested in politics and civil administration, was by no means anxious to become the new French leader in defiance of Marshal Pétain. Yet, under the circumstances, Giraud felt compelled to agree.

HITLER RESPONDS TO THE ALLIED LANDING

Though the Allied landings had taken Hitler by surprise, he took instant action. He ordered an immediate takeover of unoccupied France, and he dispatched reinforcements to the Axis contingents retreating toward Tunis, which the French surrendered without resistance. The Vichy government, now under control of Berlin, broke off diplomatic relations with Washington without, however, declaring war. From the third day after the Allied landing Hitler rushed troops from Italy to Tunis in all available aircraft and vessels. But the great prize, the French Mediterranean naval squadron anchored in Toulon, eluded Hitler. French naval commanders ordered the fleet scuttled immediately after the crossing of German troops into the unoccupied zone.

The German invasion of the unoccupied zone of France had, by and large, negative consequences for the Axis. Hitherto the bulk of the French people had been remarkably loyal to the Vichy government and rather indifferent to de Gaulle's effort to induce them to resist German overlordship. The shock of German occupation of the whole of France galvanized many formerly passive elements in French society. Scattered nuclei of resistance began to spring up. Toward the close of the war they came to represent a fairly important factor in the calculations of both the Allies and the Axis occupiers.

Although they now faced a rapidly deteriorating situation in North Africa, both

THE ALLIED PINCERS IN NORTH AFRICA

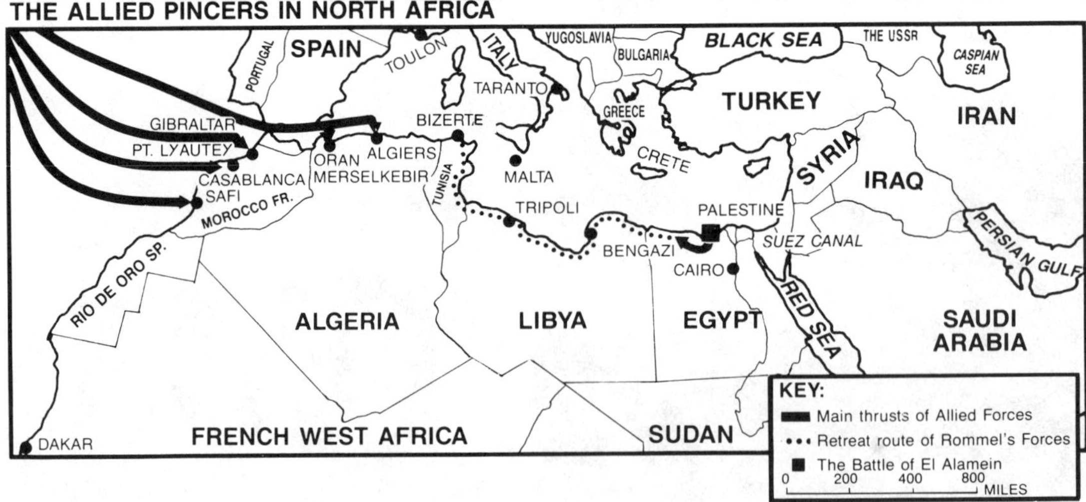

A German Messerschmitt (ME-*110*) fighter refueled at an improvised airfield in Tunisia. National Archives

Hitler and Mussolini resolved to defend their newly gained outpost in Tunisia. At Hitler's order the best that German arsenals could spare now sped across the narrow 80-mile route from Sicily to Tunis and Bizerte. A number of new tanks and aircraft were included. Eventually, some of the best Axis units were sent on to bolster the war-weary garrison in Tunisia. The Hermann Goering Regiments, the German parachutists, the Tenth Panzer division, and other crack units—all these were to arrive, and for the first time the Axis armies in Africa were predominantly German.

Although limited by shortages in transport, these supplies were sufficient to check the advanced units of the Allied First Army when they reached the boundaries of Tunis, two and a half weeks after the initial landings. By the beginning of 1943 the Axis had in Tunisia an entire Army Group, commanded by General Juergen von Arnim. A year before a mere half of the forces thrown by Hitler into Tunisia in 1943 would have given Cairo and the Suez Canal to Rommel.

Meanwhile Rommel's forces were rapidly streaming into Tunisia. He had with him remnants of the Fifteenth and Twenty-first panzer divisions and the Nineteenth Light Infantry. When he reached Tunisia, he found Arnim's Fifth Panzer Army already well established in its defense positions. But the two men were bitter enemies and each tried to spike the other's plans. Until March 8, 1943, nobody knew who was really in command. Instead of pooling their resources and coordinating their actions, each of them willfully conducted his own private war.

By this time Rommel was a sick and discouraged man. Yet with his usual zeal he set to work trying to save what he could in this most difficult of situations. The best defensible position in eastern Tunisia, the Mareth line, was composed of a series of old French fortifications, which could be held long enough for supplies coming in through Bizerte and Tunis. Few shipments arrived, however, and Rommel lacked artillery and enough petrol, since many of the Axis tankers were sunk on their way to Tunisia. This shortage hampered Rommel's mobility. Retreating from el-Alamein, Rommel had succeeded in bringing back a great quantity of antiaircraft guns, especially the 88-mm all-purpose cannons, but there was an absence of field artillery. The British Eighth Army alone had 500 guns and also greatly outnumbered the Axis in tanks and aircraft. German bombers could no longer operate from the last remaining patch of Tunisia held by the Axis, and it was becoming increasingly difficult for fighters to use restricted air strips.

THE CASABLANCA CONFERENCE

With the fighting in North Africa about to enter its decisive stage, President Roosevelt, Prime Minister Churchill, and their staffs met at Casablanca on January 13, 1943, to chart the course of future joint operations. The Casablanca conference (January 13–24) was also attended by the Combined Chiefs of Staff, including Generals Eisenhower, Harold Alexander, and Giraud. De Gaulle, who had learned about the Allied landing from a BBC communiqué, at first refused to come, but eventually turned up after heavy British pressure forced his arrival. He was bluntly told that if he did not come, he would be replaced by someone else. Stalin had also been invited to participate, but he refused to leave his country, claiming that his duties as supreme military chief required his presence in Moscow. He was to be informed about the decisions to be taken, especially those concerning the second front.

Before tackling the wider strategic plans, the two Western leaders had to deal with the political mess in Algiers. President Roosevelt, who saw himself as a keen judge of men, again wanted to ignore de Gaulle; he favored the more pliable and less politically experienced Giraud. Roosevelt had a low opinion of de Gaulle, whom he considered "a narrow-minded French zealot with too much ambition for his own good and some rather dubious views on democracy." The U.S. secretary of state, Cordell Hull, supported the president and referred to de Gaulle's followers as "the so-called Free French." Roosevelt's low estimation of de Gaulle turned to profound dislike when the Free French occupied the islands of St. Pierre and Miquelon off Newfoundland, after the United States had concluded an agreement with Vichy guaranteeing the status quo of French possessions in the Western Hemisphere. Roosevelt prodded Churchill to break up his partnership with the cantankerous Frenchman. Churchill refused, and despite de Gaulle's genius for infuriating his allies by calling Britain "the coldest of all cold monsters," he continued to sponsor him.

De Gaulle was somewhat quixotic in personality. With the sad face of a Harlequin and a head too small for his tall body and an enormous nose, he cut a somewhat strange figure. Full of passionate love for his native country—that sacred plot of land inhabited by a brilliant race predestined to lead the world toward a higher civilization—he was a prickly man, a master of intrigue and passive resistance.

The pressure of Roosevelt and Churchill compelled de Gaulle to join Giraud and to establish together a stable civil and military authority over the freed African territories. Allied-occupied Africa was thus to serve as a stepping-stone toward conquering metropolitan France. Eventually Giraud and de Gaulle announced that they had compromised on their differences. The shotgun marriage did not last long. In practice it amounted to a victory for de Gaulle; his agents had skillfully infiltrated the North African administration and armed forces and gradually took them over.

By this time de Gaulle had begun to show less interest in military operations as such and had turned decisively toward politics. Henceforth, he devoted himself to sustaining the fighting spirit of France, safeguarding its sovereignty, and preserving the integrity of the French Empire. The beginning of de Gaulle's emergence as a statesman of international significance dates to these days, when he etablished himself after the Axis defeat in Tunisia as the leader of the liberated segment of the French domains.[4]

The ten days of the Casablanca conference gave definite shape to Allied strategy for the future conduct of the war in Europe.

[4]For de Gaulle's point of view, see the second volume of his *War Memoirs: Unity*, pp. 115–66. For his activities at that time see Francois Kersaudy, *Churchill and de Gaulle* (London: Collins, 1981), especially pp. 161–257.

Despite urgent demands from General Douglas MacArthur and Admiral Ernest J. King for more troops, ships, and aircraft for the Pacific, President Roosevelt reaffirmed the primacy of the European theater of war. Planning at Casablanca determined that after the liberation of the whole of North Africa, Italy was to be the next target. General Mark Clark, appointed as commander of the U.S. Fifth Army, was to spearhead the invasion of Italy. Looking ahead, the conference prepared for a final blow, an invasion of the northern coast of France, tentatively planned for 1943 and certainly for 1944. More immediately, the target now was the western segment of the Axis' "soft underbelly," Italy. This next step was again Churchill's choice, earned as a result of the victorious advance of the Eighth Army and the successful American-British landing in Morocco and Algeria.

The strong British voice in strategy was also due to its more massive presence. The six British divisions of Montgomery's desert force, plus the four divisions of Anderson's First Army, outnumbered the Americans. French colonial troops were underequipped and, at that time, counted for little. Under the circumstances, the British, who momentarily possessed more sizable forces, once more managed to impose their strategic concept on their American partners.

On January 24, 1943, at a press conference immediately following the Casablanca conference, President Roosevelt first enunciated the doctrine of unconditional surrender by all Axis powers. The doctrine was mainly Roosevelt's idea, and Winston Churchill had agreed to it rather reluctantly. The principle of unconditional surrender bolstered Allied resolve and unity, but its impolitic rigidity excluded negotiation even with Hitler's opponents inside the Third Reich. One of the main objectives of this proclamation of complete surrender was to reassure Stalin that the Allies would not secretly plot a separate deal with the Axis powers. Yet the declaration probably stiffened German resistance and prolonged the bloodshed.

Unconditional surrender had historical antecedents. The Allied leaders lived with the memories of President Wilson's Fourteen Points and all the complications that had followed, including the German myth that they had been tricked into an armistice. President Roosevelt, even more than Churchill, was determined to achieve decisive victory with no residual obligations. The doctrine was not meant to suggest that the Allies intended to impose draconian conditions on the defeated Axis peoples; it signified rather that they were not prepared to bargain with the present governments of Germany, Italy, and Japan until they admitted defeat. Unfortunately, the declaration was a blanket ultimatum and did not exclude the satellite states; this oversight was a blunder, for by this time most of them, starting with Finland and Hungary, were sending various peace feelers to London and Washington.

The manifesto of unconditional surrender was immediately exploited by Goebbels, who loudly proclaimed the Allied declaration as proof that the Allies desired to wage a war of extermination. In a speech on January 30 he called upon the German people to rally around Hitler. Goebbels warned that since the enemies of Germany were fighting to "enslave the German nation," the war had become an urgent struggle for national preservation in which no sacrifice was too great.

The Casablanca conference further decided that, apart from decisions on overall strategy, the British Eighth Army and the Desert Air Force would both come under Eisenhower's command upon entering Tunisia and that General Alexander was to become his deputy as commander of the Allied forces in North Africa. Admiral Cunningham remained the naval commander in chief of the joint air forces. Thus, practical command of all the forces on the two fronts became British under Eisenhower as Supreme Commander of the entire war theater. The choice was a judicious one, for while Eisenhower's strategic talents may be open to question, his ability to inspire and coordinate his colleagues' efforts was above debate. His brilliant success in this task during the last stages of the North African campaign was soon to be rewarded by a much more responsible assignment.

THE BATTLE OF TUNISIA

The Tunisian theater formed roughly the triangle enclosed by the coastal road from Constantine, in Algeria, through Bizerte and Tunis to Gabes, and then the road running through Tebessa back to Constantine. Two mountain ranges ran through the region, forming its dorsal spikes. Tunisia's eastern approaches were protected by the line of fortifications known as the Mareth line, which the French had constructed against a possible Italian invasion from Libya.

By the beginning of 1943 the relatively small Tunisian defensive perimeter was saturated by Axis forces. Yet their strategic position was far from enviable: The victorious Eighth Army was pushing from the east, while the American, British, and French forces were advancing from Algeria. The Tunisian airfields were inadequate for the Axis aircraft, especially bombers. Allied air superiority, moreover, was unchallenged. Rommel's defensive plan was to prevent the uniting of the superior forces approaching him from both Libya and Algeria and toward their joint offensive. By engaging the enemy forces separately, he had hoped to beat them one by one.[5]

The Battle of Tunisia, December 1942-May 1943

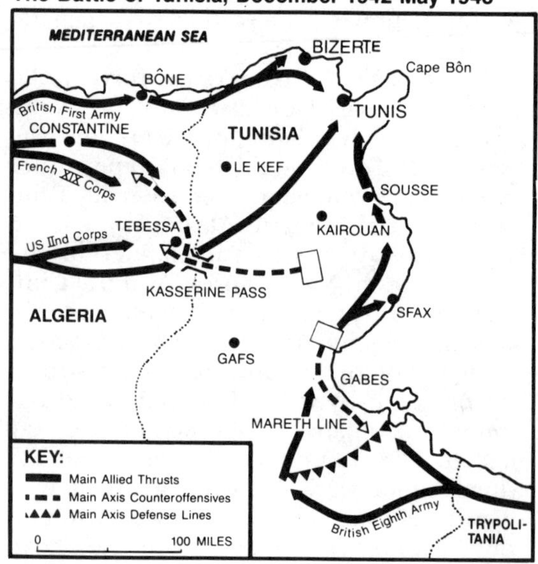

The Battle of Tunisia marked the war's first encounter of American land forces with the Germans. Outwardly, the American troops looked very impressive. Their equipment was first-class and superior to the British equivalents. The Sherman was certainly the best tank of its class in the West. The jeeps, the command vehicles, the signaling sets, the bulldozers, and the electrical workshops all functioned marvelously. The self-propelled guns of the Americans, for example, were some of the best artillery along the whole front. The American rations were lavish to the point of extravagance. The American GIs had arrived on the scene with exuberance and bravado. German intelligence immediately spotted that the GIs were not as well trained as the British, that their discipline was rather slack, and that the Americans were suffering command problems. Moreover, the Americans were spread out in a straggling line through the gap in the Tunisian mountain chain called the Kasserine Pass. Toward the middle of February Rommel and Arnim gathered the best of their hard-bitten veterans, along with their new tanks and guns, to inflict a stinging blow on the unbloodied GIs.

On February 14 the Germans pounced upon the American sector at the Kasserine Pass, where the U.S. infantry had not prepared proper defensive positions. The panzers cut through the thin line at Sbeitla and Sidi Bou Zid. American guns were captured before they could fire a shot. American tanks were forced back as the Germans overran the pass. Many GIs panicked and fled, either to be taken as prisoners or slaughtered. Throughout the area large

[5]For Rommel's evaluation of the strategic situation of Tunisia, see *The Rommel Papers*, pp. 370–424.

numbers of destroyed Grant, Lee, and Sherman tanks lay scattered.

The German breakthrough at Kasserine, and the resulting threats upon Thala in the north and Tebessa in the west, threatened the whole Tunisian front line. The Tebessa area was the geographical point of the junction of the American with the British Eighth and First armies and therefore the Allied weak link. This point also served as the administrative center for the whole of this region. If the Germans captured Tebessa, they could prevent cooperative efforts by the two Allied forces for months. Much worse results would follow the collapse of Thala, for, from there the Germans could advance straight to le Kef and then toward Algiers and might easily encircle it entirely by running through to the coast at Bône. Something like 100,000 Allied troops could be trapped. General Alexander, just now assuming field command, was confronted with a critical situation. He knew that the slow-moving, extra-cautious Montgomery would not be likely to attack for a month.

At the news of the Kasserine Pass disaster, Alexander quickly left his headquarters near Constantine to gather every available soldier, tank, and gun to bolster the retreating Americans in the Kasserine area. After some of the bitterest fighting of the campaign, the Allies rallied and retook the Kasserine Pass on February 25. Yet Arnim and Rommel had inflicted painful losses, especially on the U.S. Second Corps; the Americans lost up to 10,000 casualties, as against only 2,000 Axis troops. Over 200 Allied tanks had been destroyed. American pride and prestige had suffered badly.

The Kasserine action stirred discussion in Britain about the fighting qualities of the American troops, their courage, and their willingness to fight. Most of these accusations were greatly exaggerated. The United States troops then were at the same stage of war preparedness as the British were during the Norwegian campaign: insufficiently trained, untested, and apt to be thrown off balance on facing veteran enemy forces for the first time. The Americans, nevertheless, were much more adaptable than the British, and would learn more quickly. The rout at the Kasserine Pass was in no way on the scale of Dunkirk, but it had the same electrifying effect on the Americans as Dunkirk had had on the British. The humiliated GIs were fighting mad; they now realized what they were up against and had behind them the most powerful war machine the world had ever seen.

Nevertheless, some purging, reorganizing, and bolstering of American force had to be accomplished. After Kasserine, General Eisenhower appointed a new commander of the U.S. Second Corps, General George S. Patton, Jr., known for his unbounded courage and stern discipline. Patton's buoyant leadership rapidly brought the Second Corps to a high fighting pitch. Almost instantly the Americans rallied and displayed their drive and dash until the end of the campaign. Indeed, the United States forces fought not only with an uninhibited vigor that astonished both friend and foe, but also with rapidly increasing skill. Britain's Chief of Staff, Sir Allan Brooke, observed: "The Americans had a lot to learn. . . . But in the art of war . . . when they once got down to it they were determined to make a success of it." A certain amount of tact was required in educating the American newcomers in the realities of modern warfare. Such diplomacy was not always sufficiently applied by all British commanders, especially by Montgomery.[6]

The North African campaign pushed to center stage the remarkable team of military men who would eventually help to break the power of the Axis in Europe. These included Generals Eisenhower, Patton, and Omar Bradley, each of them a remarkable individual. Eisenhower was not a great strategist, yet he was a skillful coordinator of the inter-Allied effort, whereas both Patton and Bradley were first-class fighting gener-

---

[6]In this respect see David Irving, *The War Between the Generals* (New York: Coudon and Lattes, 1981), especially pp. 235 and 244.

General Omar Bradley. National Archives

als. All of them won their spurs in the Tunisian campaign. Bradley was a schoolmasterly and meticulous strategist, with a rather shy and lackluster personality, but Patton was an extroverted showman.

A former cavalryman, Patton always wore perfectly tailored breeches, highly shined boots, and a pair of ivory-handled six-shooters. A scowl on his stern face and his jaw straining against his helmet strap, he was a daring commander roaming just behind the first line of his troops. His most frequent command was "Forward." One of his most quoted wartime sayings was, "We won't just shoot the sonsabitches—we're going to cut out their living guts and use them to grease the treads of their tanks." He himself was like a heavy tank or a bulldozer pushing everything aside to reach his goal. Acknowledged by both his supporters and detractors to be a brilliant leader of men, Patton was often an arrogant and abrasive character who eventually antagonized almost as many people as he fascinated.[7]

[7]For an attempt to unravel Patton's complex personality see Martin Blumenson, *Patton: The Man Behind the Legend, 1885–1945* (New York: Morrow, 1985).

The Tunisian Triumph

At the beginning of March General Alexander, serving as Eisenhower's deputy, commanded the Eighteenth Army Group. From that time onward the Allied forces in Tunisia—the First and Eighth British Armies, the French XIX Corps, and the U.S. II Corps—were for the first time grouped effectively for operations.

Rommel, meanwhile, struck in the far north among the rough hills of the Sedjanane sector in order to achieve the limited goal of disrupting Allied concentrations in that sector. Then he turned suddenly south. His lightning blow threw the Eighth Army's imminent offensive momentarily into confusion. Rommel's position was highly advantageous: He sat behind the Mareth line and could wait behind it for the Allied attack. When Montgomery's storm against the line failed, Rommel advanced to meet the Allies in the open field. On March 8, 1943, his tanks charged across the hard flat ground against the fixed British position, straight into the powerful British gun batteries. Fifty German tanks were blown up in their tracks, and the remnants drew off in disorder. Why

General George Patton. National Archives

Rommel deliberately broke his own fundamental principle, never to attack fixed positions with tanks, is difficult to explain. His determination to settle old accounts with Montgomery may be a possible explanation.

On March 20 Montgomery finally broke through the Mareth line and proceeded up the coast to take Sfax, Sousse, and Enfidaville. The Germans were now squeezed in a relatively small perimeter south and west of Tunis and Bizerte. Despite an urgent plea to Hitler, Rommel failed to obtain permission to evacuate as much of his battered forces as possible. After the defeat at Mareth, Rommel surrendered his command to Arnim and left Africa for good.[8] Meanwhile, Hitler refused to surrender Africa; he continued to pour troops and weapons into Tunisia. But the German soldiers had lost their offensive spirit. The news of the capitulation of the crack Sixth Army at Stalingrad demoralized the African troops. Increasingly, the opinion that what awaited them was a "Tunisgrad" spread among them.

In April the spring rains stopped and, especially in the south, the terrain was drying quickly. By mid-April the Allied First and Eighth armies linked up and compressed the Axis perimeter in Tunisia from three sides. By the end of the month, the Allies launched a full-scale coordinated offensive against Arnim's skillfully fortified positions. Tunis was captured on May 7, just six months after the landing in North Africa. The remnants of the Axis African Army Group, some 252,000 German and Italian troops (far more than had capitulated at Stalingrad), laid down their arms on May 17, 1943. After three years, the war in Africa was over.

The Tunisian triumph, following the victories at el-Alamein and Stalingrad, ignited the spark of the Allies. For the German people, however, the capitulations of the elite army group and the collapse of the entire front in Tunisia was a heavy shock. Moreover, a considerable segment of German war production now fell into disarray. The already strained German industrial machine had been geared to a significant extent for production of highly specialized desert equipment and materiel for the forces fighting in Africa. Some of the equipment could be used only in tropical conditions, and its production engaged a disproportionate amount of Germany's production capacity. After the capitulation in Tunisia, many factories became temporarily useless until they could be retooled and shifted to other types of equipment, and a mounting campaign of Allied bombing delayed these changes. If Hitler had been prudent he would have cut his losses in North Africa and would have met the Allied invaders in France with double the strength he had in 1944. The outcome of such a decision would be incalculable.

THE SIGNIFICANCE OF THE ALLIED VICTORIES

The victorious Allied war effort in North Africa and the Mediterranean was paralleled by a still more decisive triumph in the Atlantic. By mid-1942, the United States had begun to build transport ships and oil tankers faster than the German submarines could sink them. These transports were mostly the easily built "Liberty" ships. Moreover, the Allies were gradually developing a range of new devices designed to offset the advantages enjoyed by the wolf packs of the new types of U-boats equipped with *Schnörkel* tubes, which allowed them to remain submerged while recharging their batteries. Long-range aircraft, especially Liberator bombers, were arriving in sufficient numbers to patrol almost the entire Atlantic sea lane. Regular convoy escorts were bolstered by clusters of a dozen vessels specializing in hunting the U-boats. A new microwave radar installed in Allied search planes greatly helped to locate U-boats; microradar, unlike the old longer-wave models, gave the Germans no warning of the approach of searching aircraft. This massive surge of technology came at the last moment. In March 1943 the Allies lost ninety-seven ships. What made

[8]For Rommel's point of view see *The Rommel Papers*, pp. 416–22; see also David Irving, *The Trial of the Fox* (New York: E. P. Dutton, 1977), pp. 264–86.

May 12, 1943: German and Italian POWs taken by the Allied Forces in Tunisia. Imperial War Museum

the sinkings more serious was that two out of three were lost on convoys, which were considered to be the main answer to the U-boat threat. After the war the British Admiralty concluded that the Germans never came so near to disrupting communications between the New World and the Old as in the first twenty days of March 1943. Defeat stared the Allies in the face.

Thanks to these technological advances, by April Allied shipping losses had been cut in half. In May the statistics were dramatically reversed: The Germans lost an unprecedented fifty-six U-boats, almost a third of their total at sea—a major catastrophe! As a result, Admiral Doenitz had to call all U-boats operating west of the Azores into port. By May the Allies had thus won mastery of the Atlantic.[9] This and the Axis capitulation in Tunisia made May 1943 the "month of the thunderbolt." Seldom in the history of warfare has the reversal of the situation come so suddenly.

With the North African victory and the defeat of the U-boat menace, Allied convoys could now sail in relative safety through the Mediterranean, as well as across the Atlantic. These capabilities were major preconditions for the invasion of the European continent. After May 1943 the Allied navies lifted some 1.5 million American troops to Britain without losing a single man to U-boat attack. The danger to Egypt and the Suez Canal had been averted. The opening of the Mediterranean to Allied shipping meant also that the Allies could establish a new front along the southern floor of Europe and build a net of new airfields from which to attack Germany. The Italian navy had been, for all practical purposes, blockaded in its Taranto base and in the Adriatic Sea. Malta, until then in constant danger, was now fairly safe, except for an occasional air raid. Turkey and Persia, with its vast oil resources, were out of danger of an Axis invasion. Spain, until the close of 1942 under constant Axis pressure to join, now

[9] For the reasons for the German naval disaster see Crewswell, *Sea Warfare*, pp. 138–50 and 232–39. "The redeeming of Africa" has been described in the fourth volume of Churchill's war memoirs, *The Hinge of Fate;* for the official British account: Major-General I. S. O. Playfair and others, *The Mediterranean and Middle East, Vol. IV: The Destruction of the Axis Forces in Africa* (London: H.S.M.O., 1966).

began to resist and gradually to resume a posture of classic neutrality.[10]

One consequence of the North African victory was that the attack across the English Channel was postponed until 1944. Meanwhile, the Allies were to spend most of their resources for operations in the Mediterranean. By the spring of 1943, the Eighteenth Army Group of Field Marshal Alexander represented a powerful force that had to be used where it was located without transporting its bulk back to Britain, an enormous logistic effort.

The battle of el-Alamein, followed by the Axis capitulation in Tunisia and the victory in the Atlantic, represented a major triumph of the Western Allies over the Axis. In Britain the sense of relief was dramatic. After the successful North African landing, Churchill ordered the bells of the London churches to ring for the first time since the war. In the battle of el-Alamein, Churchill detected the turning of the hinge of fate. He wrote: "It may almost be said, 'Before Alemein we never had a victory. After Alamein we never had a defeat.' "

The full strategic meaning of these successes may only be fully appreciated, however, in conjunction with the almost simultaneous and similarly overwhelming victories by Soviet forces, first at Stalingrad and then at Kursk.

---

[10]To assure that Spain would remain at least "nonbelligerent," the United States appointed as their ambassador in Madrid a conservative Roman Catholic historian, Carlton J. H. Hayes. In his book *Wartime Mission in Spain, 1943–1945* (New York: Macmillan, 1945), he described his mission in Spain from May 1942 to January 1945.

13

The Turn of the Tide in the East

Stalingrad and Kursk

The successful defense of Moscow turned Stalin's head. Disregarding his military experts, the Soviet dictator ordered an offensive for the spring of 1942 in the Ukrainian sectors in order to wrest from German hands the industrial region of Kharkov. The Soviet assault, launched by Marshal Timoshenko on May 12, recaptured Rostov-on-Don. A German counteroffensive quickly blunted this thrust, however, and Kharkov remained untaken. By May 17 the Germans had the Russians trapped. Timoshenko begged Stalin to allow him to stop the attack, but Stalin refused. The Red Army was so weakened by this premature and ill-prepared spring offensive that it could not hold against the Fourth Panzer Army, which broke out toward Voronezh on June 28. The Soviet position grew so dangerous that Stalin finally granted a belated permission to withdraw. By that time the Red Army had lost some 240,000 men.

A NEW GERMAN OFFENSIVE IN RUSSIA

The 1942 German campaign was largely planned by Hitler. Since the winter of 1941 he had ceased to listen to professional military advice and relied overwhelmingly on his own "intuition." Dismissing Brauchitsch, Halder, Bock, Rundstedt, Guderian, and Hoeppner, as well as thirty-five divisional commanders, Hitler directed the war personally as commander in chief. His initial success gave permanence to his management of strategic and tactical war making.

Hitler's driving concept was to capture the Caucasus up to the line of Batumi–Baku

Soviet tanks and infantry counterattack near Sevastopol. Soviet Embassy, Washington, D.C.

before the end of 1942 and thus acquire the Caucasian oil fields to supplement his dwindling reserves of fuel. Simultaneously, to cover the thrust on the Caucasus and to interdict the region's communication with the Russian heartland, Stalingrad and the lower course of the Volga River were to be secured. To achieve these aims, the Soviet front was to be pierced in the sector between Kursk and Taganrog, while the remnants of resistance in the Crimea were to be dealt with in a piecemeal fashion. The Crimean peninsula controlled the Black Sea, as Hitler saw it, and thus Sevastopol, the main naval base of the Soviet Black Sea fleet, represented the key to control the Crimea. Axis divisions had overrun most of the peninsula by November 1941, but Sevastopol itself remained in Russian hands and served as a base of operations for surface ships and submarines operating in the western segment of the Black Sea.

The Soviet Black Sea fleet constituted a powerful threat to the German Eleventh Army and the Rumanian Third and Fourth armies supporting Manstein's forces. Only Stalin's lack of understanding of offensive naval strategy, his mistaken belief that the main function of the navy was to support the army, to be an arm of the land flank at sea, prevented the Soviet fleet—composed of one battleship, five cruisers, some thirty destroyers and a number of smaller craft—from smashing the weak Axis naval forces in the Black Sea.

In their lack of understanding of naval problems Stalin and Hilter were very much alike. The Russian campaign was essentially a land operation on both sides.

In 1942 Hitler shifted the main weight of the German drive from Moscow farther to the south. Capitals, he felt, could always wait until the destruction of the main enemy forces; what was needed, Hitler believed, was a brilliant flanking encirclement and not another frontal attack. Napoleon, his predecessor, had erred in taking Moscow in 1812; it merely burdened him. In the north Hitler planned a local operation on the Leningrad front to establish direct contact with the Finns. On the remainder of the eastern front, the Wehrmacht was to remain on the defensive. Thus, in 1942, stress was laid on the strategy of exhausting Russia by means of conquering the areas vital for its war effort, while encircling Moscow from the south by means of a huge enveloping sweep.[1]

The late spring and summer of 1942 opened with a series of new spectacular German successes. In July, after heavy fighting, Field Marshal von Manstein captured the Crimea, including the naval base of Sevastopol. One strange feature of Hitler's plan for Russia was his scheme for annexing the Crimean Peninsula directly into the Reich after it had been settled with Germans. To Hitler the peninsula represented a future summer resort for his war veterans, a potential "land of milk and honey. . . ." Then, pressing his Crimean gains, Manstein reoccupied the "gateway to the Caucasus," Rostov-on-Don (momentarily recovered by the Red Army in the spring) and continued his daring sweep to the southeast, toward the northern Caucasus.

Manstein's drive on the oil fields involved the great risk of dispersing available forces; it stretched German and other Axis forces from Kursk beyond Stalingrad, a distance of some 360 to 400 miles. The overextended northern flank of the front became especially vulnerable to attack by Soviet forces then concentrating north of the Don River. Moreover, the southern offensive excessively lengthened the German lines of communication, with only three railways to rely on and with a vulnerable junction at Rostov as their hub. There was a danger that the Red Army could recapture Rostov from the north, thus cutting off the German forces engaged in pushing toward Stalingrad and the Caucasus. Finally, to get the critically necessary oil from the Caucasus, the Germans had to negotiate a most formidable obstacle, the ridge of the Caucasus Mountains.

The initial German successes in their 1942 summer offensive were almost as spectacular as those of the summer of 1941. By the summer of 1942 the Soviet defenses in the northern Caucasus, as well as those around Stalingrad, seemed to be collapsing sector by sector. By the end of August the Nazi red flag with a black swastika was proudly planted on the top of the highest mountain in Europe, Mount Elbrus. The petroleum fields of Grozny and Batum seemed to be within the reach of List's army group. At the same time, during July and August the rout of the Red Army units, especially on the southern sector of the front, assumed epidemic proportions. The specter of a total Soviet collapse again appeared on the horizon. The summer of 1942 was, indeed, the Red Army's second "Black Summer."

Desperate, Stalin resorted to a series of draconian reprisals on his military leaders and troops, combined with tactical concessions on the home front. An antiespionage organization was created under the code name Death to Spies, known by its Russian abbreviation *Smersh.* Special internal security detachments were assigned to follow front-line units and shoot on sight all those retreating or hesitating. Summary executions for disobeying orders, for cowardice, or simply for lack of zeal now became standard procedure in the Red Army, applied not only to combat soldiers and officers but even to incompetent or timid generals. Hitler observed these despotic measures with admiration and envy. Why couldn't he deal in the same way with his generals?

To cope with the danger of a general Soviet collapse, patriotic slogans continued to overshadow Communist propaganda. The old military oath pledging the soldier to struggle for the emancipation of workers throughout the world was dropped and replaced by a new one requiring him to fight "for the Soviet Motherland" above all. As early as January 1942 a Panslavic magazine, *Slavyanye* (Slavs), was established in Moscow to present the war as a Slavic crusade against Hitler's Teutonic invasion. The hate campaign against the Germans, orchestrated by a popular writer, Ilya Ehrenburg, was

---

[1]For Hitler's directives of April 5, 1942, for the spring campaign in the east see *Blitzkrieg to Defeat,* pp. 116–20; see also Warlimont, *Inside Hitler's Headquarters,* pp. 226–40 and Hellmuth Gunther Dahms, *Geschichte des Zweiten Weltkriegs* (Tübingen: Rainer Wunderlich Verlag, Hermann Leins, 1965), pp. 430–57.

stepped up and reached unprecedented intensity. A series of Slavic congresses and conferences were held; concessions were made to the religious sentiments of the soldiers and atheistic propaganda was reduced. The dual command of officers and political commissars was finally abolished. Political commissars were now turned into simple political and educational officers in charge of ideological indoctrination, propaganda, and welfare and were strictly forbidden to interfere with the military decisions of their field commanders.

The Battle of Stalingrad

Meanwhile, south of Voronezh the crack Sixth Army, commanded by General Friedrich Paulus, was marching toward Stalingrad. Hitler considered Stalingrad not only an important industrial and communication center but also a symbol of the Soviet dictator's rule over Russia. The task of General Paulus was to interdict the oil transports between the Caucasus and Moscow and thus starve the Red Army and Soviet industry of its fuel. Russia's loss was to be Germany's gain. "There, 30 million tons of traffic on the Volga," Hitler said, "can be cut off, including 9 million of oil shipments," thus overnight paralyzing the Soviet war effort. The Sixth Army had the help of Italian, Hungarian, and Rumanian allies, all of them inferior in equipment, training, and morale to the Germans. Hitler took the capture of Stalingrad for granted. Yet he was most anxious also to capture the oil fields of Grozny as soon as possible, and so Hitler shifted some of Paulus' best armored and motorized units to the southern army group of Field Marshal von List, aimed at the Caucasus. As a result, the Sixth Army, stripped of a large segment of its motorized vehicles, found itself overwhelmingly dependent on horse-drawn transport; the marching infantry could not keep up with the armor of the Fourth Panzer Army in the vanguard of Paulus' forces. With the Sixth Army thus weakened, sizable pockets of Soviet resistance were bypassed and left to annoy Paulus' rear later on. The German double push did not fulfill Hitler's expectations. Both of the great prizes that had seemed easy to capture a few weeks before now presented perils not only from an unexpectedly strong Red Army stand around Stalingrad but also from Soviet partisans operating behind the German lines.

These delays enraged Hitler, yet he ordered both operations to continue. For prestige reasons the Stalingrad operation was given priority. Some of the reserves of men and materiel that had initially been denied to Paulus now were shifted back from the Caucasus to reinforce the Sixth Army. List's army group, already on the northern slopes of the Caucasus and holding a front of some 500 miles, had to give up not only a large part of the armored forces but also all of its antiaircraft artillery, along with all its aircraft except for some reconnaissance squadrons. Thus List, now poised on the ridge of the Caucasus Mountains, lacked air support to fight off the Soviet air force, which sent some 800 bombers to defend the oil fields of Grozny.

These shifts in troops and equipment destabilized German operations. One of the major reasons for the failure of the Caucasus offensive was a shortage of fuel caused by the Rostov bottleneck through which most supplies passed, since the Black Sea route was considered unsafe because of Soviet submarines. This fuel crisis stalked some of the armored divisions for weeks; a trickle of fuel arrived on the backs of camels to avoid using gasoline in the supply trucks. Paradoxically enough, all this was happening with millions and millions of tons of oil hidden just a few hundred feet below! This strange fuel shortage, together with the exposed position of the Germans, presented a growing danger to their own eastern flank.

Hitler's failure to grasp the gravity of the situation along the southern sector of the front was compounded by his underestimation of Stalin's reserves. The seemingly irreplaceable losses of Soviet manpower in 1941 had been made good from the large pool still available in the central Asiatic and Far Eastern provinces of the USSR. Recruits from those parts of the Soviet Empire were

Stalingrad in flames.
National Archives

possessed of matchless endurance and, being primitive, required minimal logistic backing. In many ways they were ideal for another winter campaign, which Stalin had in store for Hitler. As for the equipment, the Red Army was finally provided with large quantities of the T34 tank, simple to the point of crudity, but, again, ideally suited for the rough Soviet conditions. Thus, by the autumn of 1942, the Red Army not only had unmerciful superiority but was better equipped with armor and artillery than its Axis opponents.

In September and October the struggle for Stalingrad reached its climax. Vacillating strategy and the dispersal of forces, coupled with delay in attack, spelled disaster for the Germans. Moreover, the Soviets strengthened their defenses around Stalingrad before the Germans reached its outskirts on August 20. On August 25 Hitler issued a personal order to capture the city of Stalin, the symbol of his opponent's authority. The bulk of the Sixth Army reached the city's suburbs only on September 4 in a weakened condition; it failed to take the city by storm and got bogged down in its streets. From then on the advance was measured not by miles but by yards. Murderous street-to-street, and even house-to-house, fighting ensued. Bombardment by aircraft and artillery soon turned Stalingrad into a heap of smoking ruins. The battle raged almost without interruption for eight days and nights. The ferocity of the combat peaked in the period from mid-September to mid-November.

After the first two or three weeks the center of the city was beaten into a midden by artillery fire and air bombardment. One of the strong points of the Soviet defense position was that most of their air, artillery, and supply bases were located on the high left bank of the Volga, beyond the German reach. The Red Army was quick in adapting its tactics to circumstances. To neutralize the enemy advantage the Soviets usually counterattacked at night when neither the Luftwaffe nor the panzers could operate. In the battle's last stages small teams of opposing soldiers met each other in mortal hand-to-hand combat amid the petrified sticks of blackened chimney stacks. They fought with grenades and bayonets for each street, each doorway, and even for every foot of ground in sewers. In the end, some 85 percent of the city was destroyed. From mid-September Soviet attacks coming from the Kalmuck steppes on the right bank of the Volga ripped the German lines. The German attackers were several times a mere step away from capturing the headquarters of the Soviet commander of the Sixty-second Army, General Vasily I. Chuikov. Yet on each occasion they were frustrated by the dogged resistance of the Red Army soldiers and by the lack of available reserves. Paulus had committed to battle every unit of his dwindling forces. By November 19 the exhausted Sixth Army had to stop its offensive because of intolerable losses and the onset of a killing winter.[2]

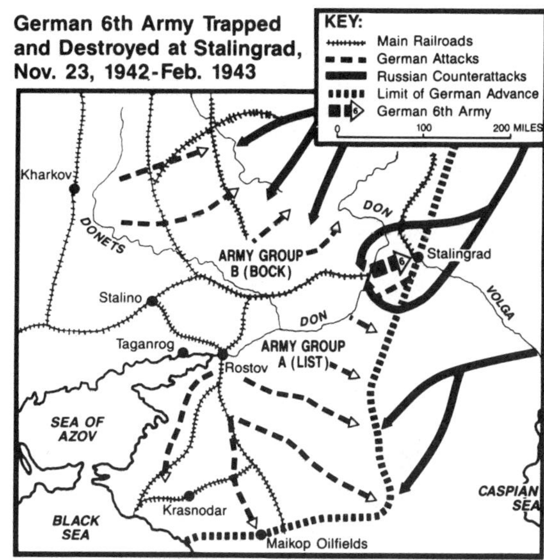

A German Defeat

While the remnants of the German Sixth Army sat decimated and exhausted in the smoking debris of Stalingrad, the Red Army prepared a mighty counteroffensive. Ably assisted by Deputy Supreme Commander Zhukov, Stalin planned this counterstroke, involving three army groups (or fronts) amounting to some eighty divisions of nearly 1 million men, supported by 13,500 guns and mortars and 1,100 aircraft. Despite the evident steady buildup of Soviet forces to the east of Stalingrad that posed a threat of encirclement to the Sixth Army, Hitler still determined to take the city of Stalin and forbade Paulus to retreat from even the farthest extremity of his holdings.

The Soviet counterattack started on November 19. First, the army group of General Nikolay Vatutin hit the poorly armed and trained Rumanian troops on the Don covering the northwestern approaches to Stalingrad. Overnight, the flimsy Rumanian contingent collapsed, and their divisions surrendered. At the same time, from those Don bridgeheads that still remained in Soviet hands, Red Army tanks pounded on the remnants of the German Sixth Army. Simultaneously, the mechanized forces of General Fyodor Tolbukhin carried out a broad enveloping movement from the south. The Soviets then moved swiftly from north and south through the breach to exploit their gains. Within four days the German Sixth Army, with its 200,000 men, was cut off by this brilliant envelopment. With the outflanking of the Sixth Army by November 23, the German position in the northern Caucasus had become untenable.

Again Paulus proposed the withdrawal of the Sixth Army to the west in order to join with the rescue expedition then forming under Manstein. Hitler seemed inclined initially to follow his advice. Paulus felt so certain of Hitler's consent to the withdrawal that without waiting for a final reply he issued instructions to prepare first for a retreat. On November 25, to quicken the withdrawal, all equipment that could not easily be evacuated because of its weight or for lack of fuel was to be dumped in the Don or destroyed. Tanks and armored cars with thin plating were thus disposed of, along with a considerable quantity of guns, radio stations, engineering equipment, and uniforms. Soon, however, they were to learn Hitler's encouraging order: "Hold out. Aid will come from outside."

Paulus warned Hitler that to hold out, the Sixth Army needed at least 700 tons of supplies daily. Hitler arbitrarily lowered the

[2]For the battle see William Craig, *Enemy at the Gates: The Battle for Stalingrad* (New York: Reader's Digest Press, E. P. Dutton, 1973); also Geoffrey Jukes, *Stalingrad: The Turning Point* and Werth, *Russia at War,* pp. 441–84; Book 2, vol. 1, of John Erickson's *The Road to Stalingrad,* pp. 343–475.

Sixth Army's minimum needs to 500 tons per day. To Hitler's query whether the German air arm would be able to deliver 500 tons of supplies to the Sixth Army, Goering replied in the affirmative. On the strength of Goering's word, Hitler reaffirmed his order of no retreat. Now the fate of the German soldiers trapped in Stalingrad hung on the promise of the chief of the Luftwaffe to deliver the needed supplies. To bolster the morale of the Sixth Army, Hitler promoted its commander to the rank of field marshal.

Hitler also ordered a strong relief force sent to the aid of the Sixth Army. Picked for this duty was Field Marshal von Manstein and his veteran Eleventh Army, now reinforced and expanded into an Army Group Don. At first the relief force pushed victoriously eastward, but was stopped some 23 miles from Stalingrad by fierce Soviet resistance. By December 24, the exhausted German rescue expedition had been pushed back. By the end of the year every German formation east of the Don had been severed from contact with forces to the west by the broad sweeps of the three Soviet armies. The position of Paulus' troops grew desperate; they were encased in a cauldron tightly surrounded by Soviet forces. Ammunition became so scarce that only twenty or thirty cartridges were distributed daily to each German soldier. For a month or so the defenders lived mostly on a diet of horse meat and a few slices of bread.

On January 30, 1943, the tenth anniversary of Hitler's coming to power, he failed to deliver his traditional triumphant speech. By that time the Red Army was closing in on central Stalingrad from all directions. The Germans, starving and half-paralyzed by cold, were still putting up a desperate yet hopeless resistance. The agony of the Sixth Army grew so severe that finally on February 3, 1943, Paulus felt compelled to agree to surrender. Some 91,000 frostbitten and half-starved survivors of the once-elite Sixth Army trudged into Soviet POW camps. The captured numbered one field marshal, Paulus himself, 23 generals, and 2,500 other officers. More than a decade later, in 1955—only about 6,000 of these survivors finally returned to their homeland. Some 140,000 German and satellite soldiers had died fighting and from hunger and disease.

The Soviets took enormous booty. The captured equipment included 5,762 guns, 1,312 mortars, 156,987 rifles, 10,722 automatic weapons, 10,679 motorcycles, 750 planes, 1,550 tanks, 480 armored cars, 230 ammunition dumps, 240 tractors, 2,569 bicycles, 933 telephone sets, and 397 kilometers of signal cable. In the captured food magazines the Russians discovered large quantities of champagne, which the far-sighted German command had shipped to celebrate their conquest of the city of Stalin.

A major problem facing the victors concerned the enormous piles of corpses; spring was coming and with it the danger of an epidemic, and the frozen soil precluded burial. To dispose quickly of these bodies the Soviets gathered thousands of corpses and stacked them in layers alternating with rail-

The triumphant General Vasily Chuikov, commander of the 62 Army awaits the German capitulation. Soviet Embassy, Washington D.C.

road ties. These huge piles of dead bodies were then ignited in ghastly pyres.

An atmosphere of victory pervaded Soviet Russia in the early weeks of January 1943. In those weeks, Stalin assumed the title of marshal of the Soviet Union and generalissimo. Stalin distributed awards and decorations to the brilliant constellation of military stars that had emerged.

The most gifted of them was Gregory K. Zhukov, who had received his appointment as marshal of the Soviet Union already in January 1943. The meteoric rise to fame of this stout, square-jawed son of a peasant and a former tsarist NCO started in the summer of 1939 as a result of his crushing victory over the Japanese along the Mongolian border. As chief of the General Staff in 1941, he masterminded the counteroffensive that drove the Germans back from the gates of Moscow. Appointed deputy supreme commander in August 1942, he was largely responsible for mastering the chaos that threatened the Red Army with collapse and turned the near chaos into another successful upsurge. The victory at Stalingrad made Zhukov into a national hero and the number one Soviet military commander. Also, Generals Konstantin Rokossovsky, Alexander Vasilevsky, and Leonid Govorov received promotions as marshals.

At the same time, Stalin introduced new badges of rank and reinstated the stiff golden shoulder boards, which in 1917 the revolutionary soldiers had torn off the shoulders of the officers of the Imperial Army as symbols of the old regime. A special factory was opened in Moscow to produce the new emblems. New military decorations, to be awarded to officers only, were now created, among them the orders of Suvorov, Kutuzov, and Alexander Nevsky. New parade uniforms were designed and distributed to the men of the Red Army and Navy.

The Consequences of Stalingrad

Experts have long pondered the significance of the battle of Stalingrad. Was Stalingrad worth the price Hitler was willing to pay for it? The city was an important communications center and posed a considerable danger to German forces protecting the left flank of the Caucasus drive. Yet strategically Stalingrad was no more important to the Germans than Voronezh, for example, which they decided to leave in Russian hands. Stalingrad did not control use of the Volga waterway, on which oil and Anglo-American war aid were shipped northward. Moreover, the Germans had several other more worthy targets than Stalingrad. Stalingrad represented a five-month long bloodletting that should never have occurred. But Hitler wanted Stalingrad; obsessed with its destruction, he even forgot his main goal, the oil of the Caucasus. Stalin was almost equally determined to hold the city bearing his name. Thus the battle for this middle-sized city on the Volga was, in a way, a personal prestige contest between the two dictators.[3]

In this contest, Stalin proved more flexible and imaginative. To defend Stalingrad he expended his most abundant resource, manpower, in order to grind down Hitler's shrinking reserves. Through awesome and stubborn sacrifice, the Red Army successfully drew the vast bulk of German resources on the southern front into the Stalingrad meat grinder. Psychologically, Stalingrad spelled an end to the myth of the Third Reich's invincibility, and a start for another myth: that of Stalin's military genius.

The battle of Stalingrad was second only to the battle of Moscow as a major turning-point of the war and particularly of the German-Soviet campaign. The Wehrmacht suffered a great shock to its morale and never recovered from it. The crack Sixth Army was destroyed along with entire auxiliary contingents of Italians, Rumanians, and Hungarians. The Luftwaffe, exhausted by the use of its squadrons for supply duties at

[3]For a discussion of the battle of Stalingrad see Włdyław Anders, *Hitler's Defeat in Russia* (Chicago: Regnery Gateway, 1953), pp. 81–158. For the German critical analysis of Hitler's handling of the battle see *German Generals Talk,* pp. 188–209 and Warlimont, *Inside Hitler's Headquarters,* pp. 248–305; see also Clark, *Barbarossa,* pp. 187–302.

Marshal Gregory K. Zhukov, victor in the Battles of Moscow, Stalingrad, and Kursk. Soviet Embassy, Washington D.C.

Stalingrad, never regained its control of Russian skies. Fuel supplies fell so low that air operations increasingly depended on current production. The Luftwaffe remained often on the ground, and German forces, imitating the enemy, often reverted to the use of horses on an increasing scale. The hope of a German victory faded.

In the spring of 1943 Soviet authorities organized the National Committee for Free Germany, made up of German Communists who had lived for some time in Russia and of officers recruited from prisoner-of-war camps. Old German Communists were assigned leadership roles: Wilhelm Pieck and Walter Ulbricht. To the Free German Committee another body was soon added: the League of German Officers. Headed by the captured General von Seydlitz, it eventually included Marshal Paulus himself. Both groups aimed propaganda appeals to the German people; troops were urged to desert and generals urged to overthrow Hitler in order to save Germany from total disaster. The League of German Officers obviously hoped that a military coup d'état might save Germany from a profound social upheaval and allow the junta to negotiate a tolerable peace that would save at least some of the territorial gains of Hitler. Their propaganda produced, however, little discernible effect.

The victorious Russian offensive that followed the victory at Stalingrad forced a German withdrawal from the northern Caucasus and most of the Ukraine. On the northern sector of the front, the Russians relieved the siege of Leningrad by cutting a seven-mile-wide gap between Lake Ladoga and the German lines. This made the life of the remaining 600,000 inhabitants easier. The relief of Leningrad made the central sector of the front more secure.

The castastrophe on the Volga and the subsequent German retreat presented the Nazi propaganda with a most serious problem. Goebbels decided that it could be explained only by fabricating another myth. He refused to admit that the Sixth Army had surrendered. Instead, he claimed that the entire army had been destroyed to the last man fighting. On February 3 he instructed the mass media: "The heroic battle for Stalingrad will become the greatest of all the heroic epics in German history. The German nation, inspired by the eternal heroism of the men of Stalingrad, will demonstrate even more nobly than before those spiritual and material qualities which assure the nation of the victory it is now more fanatically than ever resolved to win." Germany's mission was to protect the west from a "Jewish-Bolshevik-Mongol inundation."[4]

Some months before the battle of Sta-

[4]For a discussion of the Stalingrad problem see Baird, *The Mythical World of Nazi Propaganda,* pp. 188–90.

lingrad, Russia's American and British allies had won a series of victories. First, the battle of Midway on June 1942 thwarted the Japanese advance in the Pacific. Japan lost all of its four carriers, several other vessels, and about 330 airplanes. Then came the triumphs of the British Eighth Army at el-Alamein, followed by the successful American-British North African campaign of the autumn and winter of 1942. In May 1942 an entire German-Italian army group in Tunisia had been crushed and its remnants, more than twice the size of the Sixth Army's, marched into Allied POW camps. This continuous series of defeats rocked the Axis. From the spring of 1943 the Axis was on the defensive everywhere, even on the Atlantic. The cumulative effect of these Allied triumphs, including Stalingrad, constituted the decisive turning point of World War II—"the turn of the tide," as Churchill put it. The battle of Moscow had indicated that Hitler could not expect to conquer the Russians instantly, while the battle of Stalingrad and the Allied successes elsewhere raised the specter of Axis defeat. But Mussolini's logical arguments that Hitler should cut his losses in Russia and focus on the defense of the western European fortress were rejected once more.

The German Rearmament

Now facing the clear possibility of defeat, Hitler ordered a total mobilization of all the Third Reich's resources. On February 9, 1942, he named Albert Speer as his armaments minister. Speer's predecessor, Dr. Fritz Todt, had died in a mysterious plane crash in East Prussia after taking off from Hitler's headquarters at Rastenburg. Hitler's personal architect, Speer had directed the construction of most of the party buildings at Berlin, Nuremberg, and Munich. He knew little about armaments and war, but he had a flexible mind, great energy, and a brilliant talent for improvisation.

Speer set to work immediately and his wartime achievements constituted another economic miracle of Nazi Germany. Within six months armaments production increased 27 percent in guns, 25 percent in tanks, and 97 percent in ammunition. By December 1943, despite the mounting Allied air offensives, overall output of arms and ammunition would be higher than it had been in February of the previous year. The production of armored equipment rose markedly. Tanks, assault guns, and self-propelled guns mounted in number; tanks increased from some 4,512 in January of 1942 to nearly 11,000 two years later. By the middle of 1943 the Wehrmacht was well supplied with heavy Panthers and Tigers, which were more formidable than any Allied armored vehicle. The Tiger became, by far, the heaviest and most formidable German tank. The first series weighed 52 tons each; the second, 70 tons. The main armament of the Tiger was an 88-mm gun; the Panther mounted a 75-mm gun. This vast manufacturing program necessitated an increased use of forced labor and POWs. By 1944 Speer was utilizing a work force of 14 million; four out of every ten prisoners of war were employed by him on weapons and munitions work.

Within one year Speer managed to achieve something very close to a miracle; he more than tripled the overall output of armaments in the period from 1941 to 1944.[5] Almost as incredible is the fact that at the beginning of 1944 the German army was better armed than at the start of the Russian campaign. Had Speer's total mobilization been ordered before the start of the Russian campaign, both its outcome, and indeed that of the war as a whole, might have been different.

---

[5]For his own story see Albert Speer, *Inside the Third Reich* (New York: Avon, 1970), pp. 257–305. The aftermath of Stalingrad saw an emphasis on the S.S. divisions; their number was increased, and they were substantially larger and better equipped than regular army divisions. Wehrmacht divisions mustered up to 15,000 men, whereas S.S. divisions, about 20,000. Moreover, the S.S. divisions were provided with more tanks and guns of the latest model available: Tigers and Panthers, as a rule.

Despite the crash rearmament program decreed by Hitler, in the spring of 1943 Germany possessed less relative strength than Soviet Russia, which by that time was mobilizing the resources of its vast empire. The 1942 campaign had weakened the Wehrmacht considerably, whereas the Red Army had emerged stronger and better equipped, thanks partly to American lend-lease, 22 percent of which went to Russia.[6]

In 1943 the Wehrmacht was too weak to undertake an offensive on a major scale, but remained powerful enough to apply an elastic defense to wear out its opponent. Manstein fathered this tactical concept, employing alternately well-calculated local retreats and sudden counterstrokes. The retreat avoided the blows of the attacker and drew him on, while sudden counterthrusts held out the chance of defeating the aggressor at the moment when his drives and thrusts waned. With the Wehrmacht's superiority in mobility, it is quite probable that had the Germans applied the method of flexible, flowing defense in 1943, the Red Army might have been exhausted before reaching the frontiers of the Reich.

Manstein recommended this military policy, but Hitler remained deaf to common sense and once more gambled on another offensive. Determined upon offsetting the humiliation at Stalingrad, Hitler resolved upon a decisive blow to take place in the spring of 1943. The planned offensive aimed at smashing the Soviet central front by annihilating the exposed Red Army forces between Voronezh and Kursk. The Wehrmacht was thereafter to resume the drive toward Moscow. Hitler chose the Kursk sector because there a bulge jutting deeply westward seemed to present favorable conditions for a sudden onslaught. This design on the "Kursk salient" found support from most of Hitler's military advisers; most of them, however, wanted this operation, named Citadel, to be launched early in the spring in order to surprise the enemy, still mostly preoccupied with the southern sector of the front and with the defense of Leningrad. Hitler insisted on a maximum concentration of forces, and this resulted in delaying the offensive from May to July. Fifty divisions, including sixteen panzer and motorized formations with 2,200 tanks, 10,000 pieces of artillery, and 2,000 aircraft, were finally concentrated for the Kursk breakthrough to begin on July 5, 1943.

The Battle of Kursk

Soviet intelligence had been forewarned by its numerous agents—especially "Lucy"—about the Kursk operation as the next major enemy offensive. Taking advantage of the delay, Marshal Zhukov had just enough time to organize his defenses in overwhelming force and considerable depth. Over 20 percent of the Red Army's soldiers, 27 percent of its aircraft, and more than 36 percent of its tanks were concentrated on a sector of some 400 miles to defend the Kursk salient, which represented only 13 percent of the entire front. Some 300,00 people of the Kursk, Orel, and Voronezh districts, largely women, were enlisted to dig huge battle stations. No fewer than eight defense lines were constructed, each protected by strong mine fields. The average density of mines numbered 3,000 for every square mile, or some six or seven times as many as during the battle for Moscow. Civilians and soldiers also built a maze of trenches, reinforced underground bunkers, and machine gun nests; clusters of dug-in tanks and multiple-barreled guns and massed *Katiusha* rockets were rooted into key positions.

Zhukov's plan permitted the Germans to exhaust themselves by storming eight successive lines of defense, after which they would face a counteroffensive. The intelligence obtained by the Zhukov permitted the Soviets to fight the battle of Kunsk fully prepared and enjoying superiority in troops, in guns and mortars, and in tanks. The timing of the battle of Kursk represents another failure of Hitler's intuition:: By 1943 he was

---

[6]For the Western aid see Erickson, *Road to Berlin*, pp. 83–84.

Soviet artillery in the Battle of Kursk. Soviet Embassy, Washington, D.C.

like an alarm clock out of order, striking at the wrong moment.[7]

The Germans prepared their thrust meticulously and preceded it with an unusually heavy air barrage. On July 5 a southward assault by the Ninth Army followed the bombardment on a 35-mile sector along an Orel–Kursk axis. At the same time, to the south of Kursk, the Fourth Panzer Army carried out a powerful surge along a 30-mile sector westward of Belgorod. By the end of the day the Soviet front had been deeply penetrated and split in both spots. But these represented only the first lines of a defense organized in great depth. The concentration of the Soviet artillery appeared heavier than ever: As a German tank officer noted in his diary, "We are racing into a ring of fire." Moreover, the weather seemed to be conspiring against Hitler; a sudden heavy thunderstorm put an end to the successful German advance. The Kursk battle also revealed a full range of technical deficiencies in the new German equipment, largely produced in a crash program. The new Panther tank and the Ferdinand mobile guns suffered from serious structural problems; immobilized at the most inopportune moments, they served as ideal targets for Soviet antitank gunners.

[7]For a description of the battle of Kursk see Erikson, *Road to Berlin,* pp. 86–146; Clark, *Barbarossa,* pp. 277–302. For the German point of view see Erich von Manstein, *Lost Victories* (Chicago: Regnery Gateway, 1958), pp. 443–49.

The Battle of Kursk, July 1943, And The Subsequent Soviet Offensive

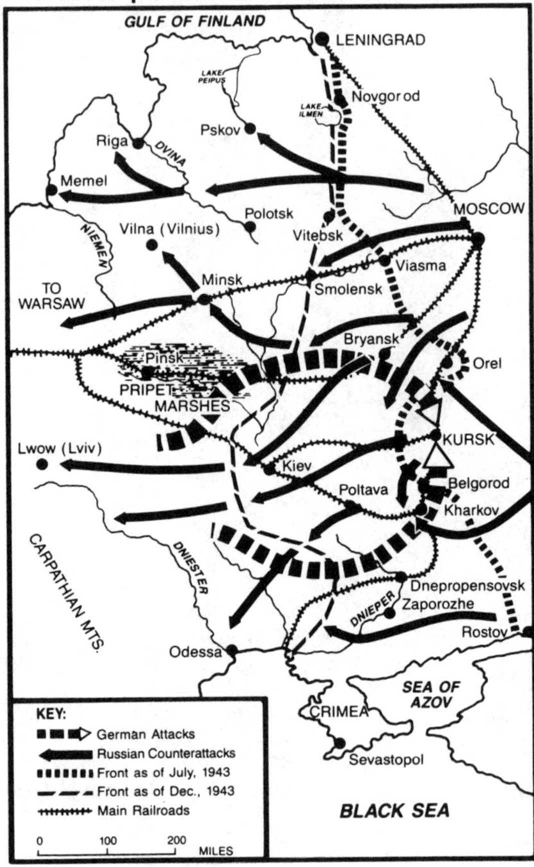

Meanwhile, the Soviet High Command dispatched to the two penetrated sectors additional artillery reinforcements. By July 8 the Soviet antitank guns, together with the heavy mine fields, managed to slow down and almost stop the enemy advance. Marshal Zhukov then launched his counteroffensive on July 12. This mighty thrust focused on the Orel sector in the north. The German drives ground to a halt both in the north and in the south.

At this crucial moment, Hitler received news about the successful Allied landing in Sicily and the fast disintegration of the Italian defenses there. Consequently, on July 13 he decided to stop the Kursk operation in order to save Italy. The withdrawal of the elite Second S.S. Panzer Corps from the front line further slowed down the German offensive on the southern Belgorod sector of the bulge, where Manstein's forces had scored the greatest progress. The battle of Kursk dragged on until August 17 with neither side capable of scoring a decisive success. The German losses, however, were so crippling that the German High Command ordered a gradual withdrawal northward toward Bryansk and in the direction of Kharkov to the south. Soviet pressure was so strong at Kharkov that Manstein had to evacuate it on August 23 and retreat further south toward the Dnieper.

The battle of Kursk constituted one of the greatest battles of all time: Over 2 million men were thrown into the fighting. Kursk certainly represented the greatest battle of armored vehicles, with nearly 6,000 tanks and an equal number of mobile armored guns supporting them. The initial German gains were won at crippling, unacceptable losses; even the mounting production of tanks, planes, and guns could not replace these losses in due time. Hitler's decision to postpone the assault to July gave the Red Army time to prepare an almost impenetrable wall around Kursk. Stalingrad followed by Kursk put an end to Hitler's hopes of winning the war in the east. These two battles ripped apart the Wehrmacht's vitality; strategic initiative thenceforth went to the Russians. This was especially true at the central sector of the front, particularly severely weakened by the exhausting effort made around Kursk.

Soviet Political Strategy in Eastern Europe

The advance of the Red Army toward east-central Europe broached a series of highly sensitive political problems. As long as the Russians were fighting a life-and-death struggle, military issues overshadowed everything else. But with the military climax behind and with the Red Army approaching the contested areas of east-central Europe, political problems began to loom larger and larger. In April 1943, for example, the Germans had discovered in the Katyn forest near Smolensk the graves of some 4,000 Polish officers who had been executed by pistol shots in the back of their skulls. According to medical experts the Polish officers had apparently been killed in the spring of 1940, a year or so before Hitler's occupation of Smolensk. When the Polish government in London asked the International Red Cross in Geneva to investigate the crime and to determine the date of the massacre, Moscow angrily broke off diplomatic relations with the Polish government in London, accusing it of slandering the Soviets.[8]

Following the break, the USSR created a "Union of Polish Patriots in Russia" in June 1943 to rival the Polish government in London. At the same time, Stalin began to gather the surviving veterans of the old, once-dissolved Communist party of Poland and other pro-Soviet elements from all over east-central Europe. The Soviets commenced to coach them for their future role in that geographical area. Important political issues were accumulating for Stalin: The future of Germany, Poland, Yugoslavia, and Czechoslovakia had to be discussed, and there was the problem of the second front. Top-level consultation was essential, but several attempts to invite Stalin to meetings, like that at Casablanca in January 1943, had failed. Stalin usually excused himself by referring to military emergencies at home.

The Soviet leader was careful to cultivate a reputation as an indefatigable freedom fighter. In May 1943, for example, Stalin dissolved the Comintern as apparently no longer needed; he delegated its work to an institute discreetly located in a distant suburb of Moscow. By appearing to abandon the worldwide ambitions of militant communism, he hoped the West would be more trusting toward his future intentions. By 1943 Moscow had achieved such a far-reaching control over other Communist parties that the cumbersome machinery of the Comintern seemed no longer to be needed. Leaders of the Communist underground movements in all Axis-occupied lands were ordered to achieve rapprochement with the local anti-Fascist resistance.

A captured German "Tiger" tank. Imperial War Museum

Germany on the Defensive

After Kursk, the Wehrmacht resigned itself largely to defensive operations. The thrilling sweeps, the daring thrusts, were absent throughout the summer and winter of 1943. The Germans now waged desperate battles against the mounting material superiority of the Red Army. In these battles a thinly stretched German infantry, bolstered with some antitank guns, acted mainly as a warning system to signal the few remaining German panzer teams to render assistance. These panzer teams constantly hopped from one spot to another, blunting thrusts and rescuing Wehrmacht units. The Red Army gradually reconquered the area around Leningrad and the Ukraine, and by the first half of 1944 the frontiers of the

[8]For a scholarly monograph on the subject see Janusz Zawodny, *Death in the Forest* (Notre Dame, Ind.: University of Notre Dame Press, 1962).

pre-1939 USSR had been crossed and the conquest of east-central Europe began.

Military defeats brought political disadvantages for the Germans and the Axis. Hitler's grand coalition began to crumble. After Stalingrad, practically all his allies (the Italians, the Rumanians, the Hungarians, the Slovaks, and the Finns) had secretly initiated negotiations with enemies of the Axis.

The mood of the captive people of Europe was reflected in a story coined in a Warsaw café: "What is the difference between Hitler and the sun? The sun rises in the east and sets in the west, while Hitler rises in the west and sets in the east."

14

The Invasion of Italy, the Air Offensive, and the Teheran Conference

The final liquidation of the Axis front in North Africa freed considerable Allied forces in the Mediterranean war theater and thus put extraordinary pressure on Italy. The Italians fully shared in the Tunisian capitulation, and it affected them more severly than was the case of Germany itself; they had lost the remnants of their mobile mechanized units capable of defending their homeland; their morale had been much lower, their resources much scarcer, and they were now fully exposed to Allied attacks from the air and sea. The Italian forces had suffered defeat in the Balkans, in the Mediterranean, in North Africa, and in Russia, where the Italian Eighth Army was practically annihilated at Stalingrad. By the spring of 1943 nearly a million Italian soldiers had been stationed on foreign soil in Albania, Yugoslavia, Greece, Tunisia, and Soviet Russia. By 1943 Britain held over 300,000 Italian POWs, including some 100 generals. Adding to the Italian military near-collapse was the domestic situation. In March 1943 a series of strikes shook the industrial cities of Lombardy, and a prevailing atmosphere of defeatism stalked the peninsula. The Italians felt the war to be dragging and spreading with no end in sight for them.

The almost uninterrupted series of disasters had also revealed the growing strains within the Axis. In Italian eyes the rationale for the alliance with Germany had been the hope of achieving historic objectives in the Balkans and in the Mediterranean basin. By the spring of 1943 all these Italian aims had failed to materialize, and Italy was no more than a vassal of the Third Reich. In a meeting with Hitler near Salzburg on April 7, 1943, Mussolini tried to persuade the Führer to patch up a truce with Russia and to concentrate on the battle for the Mediterranean and western Europe. Hitler refused; deeply involved with the planning of his Kursk offensive (Operation Citadel), he bluntly declared that he had few troops to spare for the defense of the Italian mainland. By that time all but the most fanatical pro-Nazi Facists began to feel bitter frustration.

THE "MAJOR MARTIN" RUSE

Italy's mounting crisis was closely observed by the Allies. Since the autumn of 1942, Prime Minister Churchill had constantly thought about the Mediterranean as the "soft underbelly of the Axis" and toyed with plans for taking Italy out of the war. The joint British-American sea power provided them with superior flexibility in shifting the point of gravity of their attack. Another Allied advantage in their planned reentry into Europe lay in the wide variety of options open to them: The immense stretch of coastline from Greece to Spain was ideally suited for staging a variety of landings. The presence of Field Marshal Harold Alexander's powerful army group in North Africa furnished the rationale for using these tough veterans in the Mediterranean theater of war. But should this army group be directed toward Corsica and southern France or perhaps to Sicily and the Italian peninsula? Should they land on Sardinia or leapfrog from Crete to the Greek mainland and then to Yugoslavia? Eventually it was decided at Casablanca to move against Sicily, the capturing of which would finally clear the sea passage through the Mediterranean and thus save a considerable amount of shipping.

To keep Hitler guessing, British intelligence devised an ingenious deception. The fraud was conceived and carried out by a young British naval officer, Lieutenant Commander Ewen Montagu. His strategem was to deliver into the hands of German agents operating in Spain a faked plan of projected Allied operations. For this purpose he suggested using a corpse of a supposedly dead courier carrying top-secret operational documents from one Allied commander to another. The first task in this deception operation was to find a suitable body whose condition would match that of a man who had perished at sea after a recent airplane crash. A pneumonia victim was located in a London morgue, placed in cold storage, and dressed in an appropriate uniform. The cadaver thus became Major William Martin of the British Royal Marines. Personal letters, an overdrawn bank account, documents concerning a fictitious fiancée—all were placed upon the corpse. Meticulous care was then used to produce three false military documents. The most important document was a personal letter from the vice-chief of the Imperial General Staff in London to General Alexander, commander of the Fifteenth Army Group in North Africa. The spurious letter, which began "My dear Alex," went on to discuss, not one, but two contemplated operations in the Mediterranean theater of operation. Plainly mentioned was a projected invasion of Greece; the target of the other operation was not mentioned, but it implied that it could be Sicily.[1]

A second letter was designed to establish "Major Martin's" credentials and explain the reason why an obscure Marine officer was being flown to North Africa. It also explained why the "vital letter" was not being sent through normal channels and went on to call the enemy's attention to Sardinia as the target in the western Mediterranean. The third document was a bulky official pamphlet with a request signed by the chief of the Allied Combined Operations, Lord Mountbatten, for General Eisenhower to write a foreword for inclusion in the American edition. It was added to provide the justification for the use of a briefcase. The briefcase containing the three documents

---

[1]For the story of the strategem see Ewen Montagu, *The Man Who Never Was* (London: Lippincott, 1953); the book ignores the Ultra aspects. Montagu's later work, *Beyond Top Secret Ultra* (New York: Coward, McCann, 1978), includes the role Ultra played in the scheme; see also Anthony Cave Brown, *The Bodyguard of Lies* (New York, London: Harper & Row, 1975), pp. 282–86.

was chained to the belt of "Major Martin's" trenchcoat.

The body was then packed in dry ice and placed in a steel canister. The canister was then delivered to a British submarine. Only its commander was told about the contents of the canister. At the time of the launching of "Operation Mincemeat," thc body was removed from the canister and the dead "William Martin" was put into an inflated life preserver and dropped off the shore of the Spanish town of Huelva on April 30, 1943. Rescued and examined by the Spanish security agents, the contents of the briefcase were passed, as a matter of routine, to the German and Italian military attachés in Madrid. The German High Command accepted the documents as genuine and acted accordingly. That is, the German garrisons in Sardinia and Greece were strengthened, while those in Sicily, Calabria, and even northern France were greatly reduced.

In due course the Spanish government informed the British government that the body of "Major Martin" had been located. There was no mention of the briefcase, however, which precipitated a series of mock protests. After some delays and varying explanations, the briefcase was handed over to the British ambassador in Madrid, with its contents apparently still intact. After learning that the seals of the documents had been tampered with, the chief of British intelligence flashed the following message to Winston Churchill, who was then in conference with President Roosevelt in Washington: "Mincemeat swallowed whole."

The ingenious ruse worked well. Hitler ordered the First Panzer Division to be rushed from France to Greece, while the newly organized Ninetieth Panzer Grenadier Division reinforced the four Italian divisions in Sardinia. The crack Eleventh Airborne Corps of two parachute divisions was moved to the south of France to be ready to help the Sardinian garrison in case of need.

THE ALLIES STRIKE

When the Germans had completed their redeployment of troops, the Allies attacked. The Italian island-fortress of Pantelleria, between Tunis and Sicily, was neutralized by heavy bombardment and surrendered with

British infantry attacks Catania defenses. Imperial War Museum

little resistance on June 11. Allied air attacks from North Africa also pounded Axis airfields and concentrations in Sicily and southern Italy. This aerial hammering continued with great vigor for a whole month up to the time of the actual invasion of Sicily (Operation Husky). The task of invading the island was handed to General George S. Patton's Seventh Army and General Montgomery's Eighth. Transported to Sicily in some 3,000 vessels, the largest amphibious operation in the war thus far, the invasion took place on July 10 on a front of almost 100 miles. Montgomery's Eighth Army landed south of Syracuse, and Patton's Seventh Army went ashore in the Gulf of Gela. Some 150,000 soldiers were landed on the first three days; the ultimate total was 478,000 (250,000 British and 228,000 Americans). These overwhelming Allied contingents were faced by some 195,000 Italian troops, mostly Sicilians, reinforced by four German divisions, or slightly more than 60,000 troops; they included the Herman Goering and the Fifteenth Panzer Grenadier divisions.

This first big seaborne assault on a European coast held by the enemy erred on the side of security by massively throwing four British and four American divisions on the Sicilian beaches, practically shoulder to shoulder, instead of using the two Allied armies to form a pincer and cut off the enemy retreat toward the Italian mainland. Thus the Allies failed to trap the Axis troops inside the island. If Patton's Seventh Army had landed near Palermo, it could have cut the German-Italian route of withdrawal toward the Strait of Messina. But the Allies, overconfident after their Tunisian triumphs and relying on their overwhelming air support, expected to crush the Axis troops in a series of swift, decisive blows by a frontal attack.

Sicily's defense had been entrusted to the

The Italian Campaign, July 1943 to the End of 1944

Fascist Grand Council: Mussolini (on the right) presiding. National Archives

Italian Sixth Army, bolstered by German reinforcements. From the start, many Italian units surrendered to the Allied contingents without much resistance. In view of the threat of a wholesale Italian collapse, the command of Axis forces was taken over by a German, General Hans Hube, who ensconced the remaining, mostly German, forces in a net of formidable positions around Mount Etna.

The small German force put up an unexpectedly tough resistance. Montgomery's initial attempt to take Catania failed. Patton advanced on Messina. Only after August 5 was Montgomery able to resume his progress against Catania. The Italians evacuated Sicily in disorder between August 3 and 16, leaving the Germans to fight a tough campaign up until the seventeenth, when Patton finally occupied Messina. The Allied commanders failed to use their amphibious capabilities and most of the enemy troops were evacuated to the mainland, and there was no significant sea and air interdiction. Now only a narrow strip of water separated the Allies from Reggio di Calabria, toe of the Italian boot.

Hitler snorted with indignation at the poor performance of the Italians in defense of their own soil. General Vittorio Ambrosio, chief of the Italian General Staff, blamed the Germans for weakening their Sicilian contingents for the benefit of Greece, Sardinia, and the Russian front. His memorandum of July 4 made it clear to Hitler and Mussolini that the Axis now faced the prospect of a second front on the Italian mainland; Ambrosio made it clear that the Italians lacked the resources to meet such an invasion. "If we cannot prevent the setting up of such a front," he wrote, "it will be up to the highest political authorities to consider whether it would not be more expedient to spare the country further horror and ruin, and to anticipate the end of the struggle, seeing the final result will undoubtedly be worse in one or more years." The Germans must shift their air and land forces toward the Mediterranean, Ambrosio declared, even if that meant suspending operations in Russia. Hitler disregarded this advice.

The Allied landings in Sicily unleashed a political avalanche. On July 24 the Fascist Grand Council, led by the former ambassador in London, Count Dino Grandi, voted for the Crown to reassume the constitutional power that had been usurped by Mussolini. The next day the King dismissed Mussolini from his posts as premier and commander in chief. The King's memory was long and the firing of Il Duce was performed with a vengeful spirit: The monarch spitefully recalled that Mussolini in May 1940 had threatened to "boot (the King) in the butt." Now the king dismissed Mussolini, while remarking, "You are the most hated man in Italy." The discarded dictator was immediately arrested and spirited away in an ambulance to the island of Ponza and then to a place of military detention in the Abruzzi mountains.[2]

Mussolini's downfall threw Hitler into a rage. The huge German intelligence net had neglected to warn Berlin in time about the impending crisis, and this failure added to Hitler's fury. How could nearly 10,000 German agents scattered throughout Italy have overlooked the impending crisis? Hitler, however, was determined to save both his friend and the Fascist regime in Italy. He ordered an S.S. commando squad to rescue Il Duce from his imprisonment. The raid succeeded brilliantly; Mussolini was brought to Germany; Hitler settled him at Solo, in the North of Italy, in nominal charge of a Fascist republic entirely controlled by the Germans.

The more important task for Germany, however, was the defense of the now threatened peninsula. Distrust of the Italians by Hitler made the OKW prepare a takeover of the peninsula years before. Mussolini's collapse, however, was so sudden and so complete that most of Hitler's military experts expressed doubts whether anything south of the river Po could be effectively defended. This view was strongly opposed by Field Marshal Albert Kesselring, who was since October 1942 commander of all German forces on the Mediterranean except for North Africa. He considered that leaving to the Allies untrammeled freedom of movement in southern and central Italy would have meant sacrificing the Reich's southern defenses in depth by giving the enemy an unbidden opportunity of bombing Austria and southern Germany. To have evacuated most of the peninsula and held the Po valley and the Alps only would not result either in any appreciable saving of men and materiel or lessen the danger of an Allied invasion of the continent of Europe. Quite the contrary, defending every inch of Italian soil would be Germany's most economic strategy. This corresponded to Hitler's view. Consequently, he ordered Kesselring to implement his scheme cautiously but firmly. Kesselring was instructed to conduct his relations with the Italian High Command in such a way that the planned penetration of German divisions into northern Italy would proceed unobtrusively. He intended not to provoke Italian hostility nor to hasten a collapse but to be ready to cope with either. Meanwhile, a new Army Group B began to assemble under Field Marshal Rommel; his headquarters were to be at Munich. The defense of Italy was to bear the symbolic code name Axis.[3]

Field Marshal Albert Kesselring. National Archives

[2]For the Italian crisis see David W. Ellwood, *Italy 1943–1945* (Bath: Leicester University Press, 1985), especially pp. 19–67.

[3]For a detailed description and analysis of the Italian campaign see Liddell Hart, *History of the Second World War,* Vol. II, pp. 433–76. For the German point of view see Albert Kesselring, *A Soldier's Record,* pp. 189–267. For an American point of view see Mark W. Clark, *Calculated Risk* (New York: Harper & Row, 1950), especially pp. 183–215.

ITALY CHANGES SIDES

On July 28, 1943, the new Italian government headed by Marshal Pietro Badoglio decided to make peace overtures to the Allies. Diplomatic and military envoys were secretly sent to Lisbon and Tangier, but the Allies did not immediately take full advantage of the Italian domestic crisis. President Roosevelt, in a speech delivered on July 28, still insisted that "our terms for Italy are still the same as our terms for Germany and Japan—unconditional surrender." The inflexible stand of the Allies, along with other misunderstandings, made abortive all attempts to effect a prompt Italian capitulation. Fearing the advancing Germans, the royal family, the government, and most of the key figures of the High Command escaped hurriedly from Rome to Brindisi aboard a cruiser. The fleeing authorities failed to issue clear orders to the Italian troops. As a result, most units permitted themselves to be disarmed by the Germans, in many cases without a shot. Moreover, the Germans acted promptly and put Operation Axis into effect with brilliant efficiency. Most of Italy was soon under German control.

Kesselring had rightly reckoned that the Allied conquest of Sicily would soon be followed by a landing in Italy. Events were to prove him right and give him a chance to display his remarkably versatile talents. Originally an artillery officer, he joined the Luftwaffe in 1933, before its official establishment, to serve as its administrative head. In 1936 he became its Chief of Staff and commander of Air Fleets One and Two in Poland and France, respectively. In June 1940 he was raised to the rank of field marshal. His air fleet took part in the battles of Britain and Russia and then transferred to the Mediterranean, where he acquired the additional duties of Commander in Chief South. In October 1942, shortly before the Allied landings in Morocco and Algiers, he was given command of all German forces in the Mediterranean except those in North Africa. In March 1945 he would rise to be commander of all German forces in the west. No other Axis commander had such a variety of major tasks.

The Allies signed an armistice with Italy on September 3 in Sicily. According to the agreement, Italy was to deny all facilities to Germany and transfer all aircraft, warships, and merchant shipping to the Allies. The day of the armistice, the British Eighth Army made the leap from Sicily to the city of Reggio di Calabria on the toe of the peninsula. The conquest of Italy was to be carried out by two Allied armies: the U.S. Fifth Army, commanded by General Mark Clark and comprising one American and one British army corps, and the British Eighth Army, commanded by Montgomery. The British landed at Reggio on September 8, and the Americans struck farther northward at Salerno, south of Naples. The British landing at Messina was practically unopposed. This created a sense of unwarranted optimism. As a Canadian observer recorded, "The stiffest resistance of the day came from a puma which had escaped from the Zoological Gardens in Reggio. . . ."

The bulk of the German forces were concentrated around Naples, because their intelligence had learned about the Allied scheme of landing there well in advance. When they did so at Salerno, Kesselring was ready. He had at his disposal eight divisions, six of which were stationed in the south, mostly around the Anzio beaches. Despite the Allied superiority in all categories of weapons, especially in the air, the German resistance was stiff from the start and persisted for a full week. At one moment the situation around Naples seemed so desperate that reembarkation appeared imminent. Only the Royal Navy battleships *Warspite* and *Valiant,* which had meanwhile arrived from Malta, saved the situation with massive pounding of their 15-inch guns. Nevertheless, the *Warspite* was badly damaged by German heavy bombs, guided by radio, and the American cruiser *Savannah* and the British cruiser *Uganda* were also severely hit. On September 15/16 the situation was mastered, contact established with the British,

A U.S. infantry squad about to land in Italy at Salerno. National Archives

and a painfully slow Allied advance begun. The near disaster at Salerno had been avoided, but the unimaginative planning of the campaign was bound to produce plenty of trouble for both Allied commanders Clark and Montgomery.

The Allied invasion of the Apennine peninsula suffered again from an overcautious doctrine: no amphibious landing without full air cover. Benefiting from overwhelming naval superiority and hence flexibility, the Allies should have trapped the German leaders, confused by the Italian armistice, by staging two separate yet coordinated landings, one in the south of the peninsula, another around Rome. As the German generals pointed out after the war, the landing of the British Eighth Army should have taken place not on the toe of Italy, where it had to push up the entire length of the foot to the assigned Adriatic coast, or at Salerno, but in the exposed heel of Italy, preferably in the Taranto sector. The sector was defended by one parachute division only. No appreciable reinforcements could have been brought down in time either from the Rome region, because they were not available, or from the Po valley, because of the distance involved. Had the Allied contingent employed in the landing at Salerno been used around Rome, where there were only two German divisions, the results could have been decisive. According to General Siegfried Westphal, Kesselring's Chief of Staff, a combined sea and air landing would have captured the Italian capital, including the German GHQ at Frascati near Rome, within seventy-two hours or so. Besides the obvious political repercussions of such a victory, it would have resulted in cutting off the supply route of the six German divisions retreating from the south of Italy and ended the campaign in a few weeks.[4]

The Allied timidity and their reluctance to use their available airborne contingents (the British First and the U.S. Eighty-second airborne divisions) to capture Rome brought significant compensations for the Germans: They were allowed to regain their calm, disarm the five Italian divisions abandoned by Badoglio near Rome, master the situation around Naples and Salerno, and prepare for a series of masterly delaying operations that prolonged the Italian campaign far beyond the Allied calculations. The price paid by the Allies for their failure to profit from their most valuable advantage, amphibious power, was very high. It produced stagnation of the whole campaign and several humiliating stalemates that delayed the final victory. By the end of 1943, in four months, the Allied forces had advanced only 70 miles beyond Salerno and were still 80 miles south of Rome; their losses in men and materiel were far higher than those of their enemy. Eight months elapsed before the Allies captured Rome and another eight passed before they reached the Po valley.

---

[4]Liddell Hart, *The Other Side of the Hill* (London: Cassell, 1951), pp. 464–65.

The Allied Advance through Italy

Finally the Allies consolidated the Salerno positions, and their superior power forced Kesselring to withdraw northward. The time gained at Anzio allowed him to entrench his two armies along a series of strong defense positions mostly based along the mountain rivers that dissect the peninsula flowing from the Apennine mountains in two directions, eastward and westward. These rivers, swollen by the autumn rains and with their bridges demolished and their northern banks skillfully fortified by the Germans, were the first major obstacle facing the U.S. Fifth Army when it resumed its offensive on October 12, 1943. Nevertheless, General Clark managed to get both his corps across the swollen Volturno by October 15 but then made painfully slow progress over the roadless, rugged mountains north of the river.

On the eastern side of the Apennines, Montgomery resumed the advance on October 22 and forced a passage over the Trigno River. On both sides of the Apennine mountains the Germans continued to hamper the Allied advance with skillful delaying actions. Kesselring, meanwhile, had been using the time won for him by his rugged men to complete the Gustav line. Its elaborate defenses, in places 10 miles wide, ran along the Garigliano and Rapido rivers, then over the central mountain chain and finally just north of the Sangro River to the Adriatic. On the western end, the Gustav line was particularly strong, backed up as it was by the mountains on either side of the Liri River. The line was held by the tough German Tenth Army under the resourceful general Heinrich von Vietinghoff.

It was this sector of the Gustav line that the U.S. Fifth Army attacked on November 20. Again, slow progress was made, but at enormous cost in men and materiel. At the end of the year 1943, the Fifth Army had been brought to a halt in severe winter conditions some 5 miles south of the Rapido. In the east the British had slightly better fortune; by switching two divisions from his left wing, Montgomery formed a powerful right wing and forced the Sangro on November 15. The Eighth Army then broke through the Gustav line east of Lanciano and took Ortona on December 27. Then until the early spring both sides settled down to a position warfare, similar in many ways to that of World War I. While Montgomery was transferred to Britain to cooperate with Eisenhower in preparing for the invasion of northern France, the command of the Eighth Army was taken over by General Sir Oliver Leese.

On January 22, 1944, the British and American troops made an attempt at outwitting the Germans by making a sudden landing at Anzio, behind the Gustav line. The purpose of this belated move was to seize Rome, only 20 miles away. At first, the Anzio landing took the Germans by surprise, leaving them bewildered. The Sixth U.S. Army Corps was unopposed and could have

Field marshal Sir Harold Alexander inspects the Anzio beach. National Archives

reached Rome within a few hours, but General John Lucas, instead of driving straight toward the Eternal City, settled in comfortably on the beachhead waiting for fresh troops that he did not need anyway. This gave Kesselring a chance to dispatch reinforcements. Kesselring rapidly moved troops toward Anzio from as far afield as distant Genoa. In farm carts, civilian coaches, trucks, and anything they could lay their hands on, the Germans were streaming to bolster the cordon around Anzio. Again the Germans fought with tenacity, and by April 1 the Anzio bridgehead was sealed off. Three months after the landing began, the Allies, in total command of the air, had suffered twice as many casualties as the Germans. "I hoped," Churchill said, "that we were throwing a wildcat on the shore, but all we got was a stranded whale."

The Gustav line also saw a painful stalemate. Since the Allies had failed to take Rome by a stratagem, they had to settle down to a slow, methodical offensive. The hub to the German defenses south of Rome was the steep hill, Monte Cassino, crowned by a Benedictine monastery protected by the fast-flowing Garigliano River. Commander of the crack First Parachute Division, General Frido von Senger and Etterlin, a bona fide anti-Nazi and a devout Roman Catholic, was in charge of defending the monastery. At first he refused to use the building itself and entrenched his troops around the monastery. Only after the allies had started to treat it as a military objective and reduced it to rubble, he ordered his soldiers to occupy the ruins. Soon they turned them into a bastion by setting their artillery and machine guns there.

During the weeks that followed the heavy bombing, a fierce struggle for Monte Cassino developed. The Germans valiantly defended the ruins, while the Allies, again overlooking various alternatives, kept on launching stubborn frontal attacks. Was the storming of the monastery justified? Could the German garrison be simply isolated and neutralized, while the drive to Rome would continue, thus speeding up its fall? The question has been endlessly debated ever since.[5] Whatever the answer, the fact remains that the Allies made the capturing of Monte Cassino a precondition of their further advance and committed disproportionately large resources to the battle. In February the French Expeditionary Force, under General Alphonse Juin, and the New Zealand Corps, under the defender of Crete, General Bernard Freyberg, tried to storm the hill, but both made only limited advances and suffered extremely heavy casualties. The next attempt was made by the British troops after six weeks of reinforcing and regrouping on May 11, but the Germans managed to contain the attacks. Eventually the task was entrusted to the Second Polish Army Corps, commanded by General Władysław Anders. After a murderous struggle the Poles managed to capture the hill and the ruins of the Monte Cassino monastery on May 18.[6]

With the capturing of Monte Cassino, the road to Rome was open. But professional competition and jealousy between the generals Clark and Leese hampered the Allied advance. This helped the Germans in the withdrawal of the bulk of their forces to the north in good order. Allied plans had originally envisaged trapping the German army at Cassino by cutting off any chance it had to retreat northward as the Allies pushed toward Rome and beyond. At the last moment General Mark Clark, determined to capture the glittering prize, shifted his troops from

---

[5]For a discussion of the Monte Cassino battle see M. W. Clark, *Calculated Risk*, pp. 216–38; see also Fred Majdalany, *The Battle of Cassino* (Boston: Houghton Mifflin, 1957); Dominick Graham, *Cassino* (New York: Ballantine Books, 1971); and Władysław Anders, *An Army in Exile* (London: Macmillan, 1949). For a more recent account on the battle of Monte Cassino, see David Hapgood and David Richardson, *Monte Cassino* (New York: Congdon & Weed, 1984).

[6]General Patton, who inspected the Second Polish Army Corps, was very much impressed with its commander as well as with the Polish troops, and noted in his memoirs: "His troops are the best-looking troops, including British and American that I have ever seen" (George S. Patton, Jr., *War As I Knew It* [Boston: Houghton Mifflin, 1947], p. 80).

May 18, 1944: Polish flag on Monte Cassino. Polish Institute, London

an encircling maneuver and raced them straight toward Rome. His troops entered the city on June 5, 1944, just ahead of the British soldiers.

Thus the race to the Eternal City, by splitting the forces and confusing the original plans, prevented the Allied linkup north of Rome, thus helping to save two battered German armies from encirclement and possible annihilation. Buttressed by reinforcements from western Europe and the Balkans, they were able to hold a new mighty defense position, the Gothic line, north of Florence. Thus, a Stalingrad south of Rome did not materialize and the Italian campaign was prolonged by several months.

Until the invasion of northern France in June 1944, the campaign in Italy represented the most important land operation waged by the Allies in Europe. The operation tied down to the end of the war about twenty-five German divisions, while the Allies themselves committed some twenty-one divisions. The defense of Italy cost the Germans 556,000 casualties, and the Allies 312,000 killed or wounded. In retrospect it appears that the invasion of Italy, although rather ineptly conducted, did serve as a diversion of German troops away from the Russian front and the beaches of Normandy, but it dragged on too long and cost too much in men and materiel. In addition, the advance up the Adriatic coast enabled the Allies to support more effectively the guerrillas in the Balkans and especially the partisans in Yugoslavia and Greece.

Meanwhile, however, the Italian campaign was shifted to the back burner. After the battle of the Sangro in November 1943, troops and landing craft began to be drawn away from Italy to England in preparation for the Normandy landing.

THE ALLIED AIR OFFENSIVE

The Allied advance up the Italian boot also won for the Allies a capability of supplementing the ongoing bombardment of the main military and industrial targets in Germany that the British air offensive carried out at heavy cost and limited mostly to northwestern Germany. The capture of the large Foggia airfields east of Naples brought Allied bombers within striking distance of targets in southern regions of the Greater Reich. As early as 1940, when the British were still fighting with their backs to the wall, a small British bomber force had made modest attacks on Berlin, Mannheim, Bremen, Wilhelmshaven, and Kiel to curtail the concentration of the growing submarine force. In March 1941 the RAF repeatedly attacked with some success the battle cruisers *Scharnhorst* and *Gneisenau* anchored at Brest. From the beginning the British Bomber Command faced the choice of attacking either by day or by night.[7] Daylight bombing was likely to be more accurate, but early experience in raiding naval bases, such as Kiel, showed the British that their bombers were defenseless against enemy fighters. Therefore, if major bombing raids were to be continued by day, these would require long-range fighter escorts, and these the RAF did not have. Even if such fighters could be produced in adequate numbers, they would be at a disadvantage toward the Luftwaffe because the German aircraft would be operating over their own territory, close to their home bases and under direct control from the ground. Consequently, the British decided from an early date that it could afford night raids only when German fighters would experience difficulty in locating the attackers.

The British air offensive was masterminded by Sir Arthur Harris, who took over Bomber Command in February 1942. A colorful and highly independent man, Harris had bold ideas concerning aerial warfare. A veteran of World War I, his knowledge of the complex operational, technical, and meteorological factors affecting bombing was unique. Harris saw the bomber offensive not only as a way of striking directly at the enemy but also as a means of obviating the slaughter of men as had taken pace in those stalemated land battles of World War I. Harris brought scientific and operational research to bear upon development of a fearsome instrument of war, the strategic bombing force, utilizing an able group of advisers, headed by the imaginative scholar Richard V. Jones. By 1942 Harris had at his disposal an average of about 340 heavy bombers. By that time the Lancaster bomber, with four engines and capable of taking the 22,000 pound "Grand Slam" bombs, was already in service. The development of path-finder techniques and of various methods of saturation bombing were largely Harris's work; soon he earned the nickname "Bomber Harris."

Gradually the RAF intensified its air offensive, and by May 1942 the first of the thousand-bomber raids on the soil of Germany was mounted. British bombing compelled the Germans to redeploy much of their aircraft from the eastern front and elsewhere to defend their vital industries, including the factories producing their synthetic fuel. This reassignment of aircraft was a considerable help to the Russians, then passing through their "Black Summer" of 1942.

ARRIVAL OF THE U.S. AIR FORCE

In the summer of 1942 the U.S. Eighth Air Force started to operate from British bases and supplemented the strained resources of the RAF. The Americans, with their powerful B-17 bombers that carried a bombsight, introduced new methods of precision day bombing; thus British night attacks were now combined with day-light bombardment by the Americans. This continuous danger to German military objectives was a considerable drain on the enemy's diminishing resources. In August 1942 the U.S. Eighth Air Force, commanded by General Ira Eaker, launched its first bomber mission by raiding the railroad marshaling yard near Rouen in France. General Eaker believed in daylight precision bombing by the powerfully armed Boeing B-17 "Flying Fortresses" operating without fighter escort. This tactic proved an expensive proposition. The great raid on a German ball-bearing factory at Schweinfurt on October 14, 1942, demonstrated that adequate escort was a must. Once past Aachen the Flying Fortresses were beyond the range of fighter cover and at the mercy

[7]For the standard official work on the air offensive see Sir Charles Webster and Frankland Noble, *History of the Second World War: The Strategic Air Offensive Against Germany*, Vols. I–VI (London: H.M.S.O., 1961) and W. F. Carven and J. L. Cate, eds., *The Army Air Forces in World War II*, 7 vols., (Chicago: University of Chicago Press, 1951–54); see also Anthony Verrier, *Bomber Offensive* (New York: Macmillan, 1959). For a short treatment of both British and American retrospective views of the air warfare see Frankland Noble, *The Bombing Offensive Against Germany* (London: Faber and Gaber, 1965) and DeWitt S. Copp, *Forged in Fire* (New York: Doubleday, 1982).

A Berlin street after an Allied bombing raid. German Information Center

of German aircraft. Sixty Flying Fortresses were shot down and 138 damaged out of 291 aircraft taking part in the mission. In the long run, these were unacceptable losses.

To provide escort for the American bombers, a long-range fighter became an urgent necessity. United States industry astonished experts by producing a new version of a long-range fighter known as the Mustang in two months. The P-51 Mustang could fly 435 mph at 30,000 feet; by adding an extra disposable fuel tank, the operating range of the Mustang was extended to 900 miles. Now the U.S. Air Force had an effective fighter escort over a longer segment of their runs to Germany. Superior to the German fighter in speed and maneuverability as well as in range, the P-51 was available in numbers even Albert Speer's resourcefulness could not match.

The Casablanca conference of January 1943 outlined the strategy for the combined round-the-clock bomber offensive. The plan postulated "the progressive destruction and dislocation of the German military, industrial, and economic system, and the undermining of the morale of the German people to the point where their capacity for armed resistance is fatally weakened." The size and effect of the raids mounted accordingly in the early months of 1943. On the night of March 5, 1943, for example, 442 aircraft made a severe and successful attack on Essen. On the night of May 16, a RAF squadron breached the Moehne and Eder dams and sent some 330 million tons of water flooding through parts of Kassel. On July 9, 196 tons of bombs were dropped on Hamburg, inflicting 80,000 casualties, destroying 6,200 acres of built-up area, and severely damaging the great ship-building yards, which produced U-boats. The city was knocked out economically, severely damaged, and a million of the inhabitants had lost their homes. Albert Speer, the minister for war production, expressed the view that six more such attacks could bring Germany to its knees.

Yet his overall aircraft production rose despite these raids because of the astonishingly disciplined behavior of the German workers, and also because of a mass utilization of forced labor, most of which was deportees from eastern Europe. The Allied bombers tried to hit the German research and development complex at Peenemuende, which manufactured the V-1 and V-2 rockets. As a result, the development of these "secret weapons" was slightly delayed. A huge attack by 597 RAF aircraft on August 7 and 8 only managed to kill some of the staff and cause limited material damage. Yet the team of scientists, including the leading German rocket expert, Wernher von Braun, would continue working at Peenemuende until the arrival of the Red Army in 1945.

Precision bombing: Two bridges destroyed on the Seine. National Archives

Despite mixed results, the RAF continued its night bombing. Sixteen attacks on Berlin were made by Bomber Command in the winter of 1943/44. Up to 14,000 people were killed, most of them civilians, and 3 million made homeless, and some 5,000 acres of the city were devastated. Humanitarian considerations were brushed aside; the British argued that not they but the Germans had unleashed such inhuman methods of warfare by savaging the civilian populations of Warsaw, Rotterdam, London, and Coventry.

Obviously, the days of the Luftwaffe's superiority were over by 1943/44. By that time combined British and United States air power covered Germany from both the United Kingdom and Italy. These twin round-the-clock blows forced the Germans into a continuous combat that could not be sustained by the Luftwaffe because of a constantly shrinking industrial base and a growing lack of fuel. Nevertheless, mobilizing all available resources, Albert Speer introduced a series of desperate measures for the expansion of aircraft production. Responding to the challenge, the Allies had to match their unique capability of forcing combat where the Germans dare not refuse it: in defense of the vital armament factories and fuel distilleries, thus destroying the roots of the enemy recovery by the continuous air bombardment. By speedily dispersing his plant facilities, Speer managed to save about 80 percent of Germany's aircraft production. But this effort that might earlier have made Hitler's Europe impregnable was frustrated by the Allied air forces round-the-clock capacity to pulverize factories and fuel plants by a combination of precision and carpet bombing. These efforts drained the lifeblood of the Luftwaffe.

While German patriotic ardor and resilience made possible the production of a large number of aircraft, especially fighters, the shortage of time resulted in a lack of properly trained crews to man these machines.

THE TEHERAN CONFERENCE

As the war reached the point of military crisis, the necessity for discussing its political objectives by the three main leaders of the anti-Axis Alliance grew increasingly clear. President Roosevelt had been eager to meet Stalin personally for a long time, hoping to establish an intimate relationship with the Soviet dictator; this friendship Roosevelt considered essential for closer coordination of Allied military planning, as well as for postwar cooperation. Stalin, on his part, had temporized, arguing that his constant presence at his GHQ in Moscow was a vital necessity. The Soviet leader obviously wanted the tide of the war to turn decidedly in his favor before discussing the future in any formal meeting with his Western partners. Eventually he asserted his prestige by making Roosevelt as well as Churchill come, if not all the way to Moscow, at least to Teheran, then under joint Allied military occupation.

By the autumn of 1943 the almost uninterrupted series of Soviet victories that had carried the Red Army from Stalingrad to Kiev and close to the prewar Soviet boundaries formed the background to the first summit conference at the Iranian capital. The Western Allies could not match the spectacular Soviet successes, and thus Stalin could negotiate at Teheran from a position of strength. The lack of the second front imbued both President Roosevelt and Winston Churchill with a guilt complex, which Stalin exploited. The Soviet dictator was determined to exact high political pay-offs for his military victories.[8]

The Teheran conference had been most carefully prepared by Stalin in every way, psychological and political. For instance, on Saturday, November 27, immediately after the arrival of the two top Western delegations, Molotov announced the discovery by Soviet secret agents of a German plot to assassinate President Roosevelt. Molotov suggested that the President should move to the compound of the Soviet embassy, as otherwise there might be a "scandal"; Molotov insisted that security in the Soviet embassy was foolproof because it was surrounded by specially trained NKVD troops. Anthony Eden offered the President accommodations in the British legation, but the President opted for the Soviet sanctuary. This action, he argued, should show Stalin, to whom he often referred as "good old Uncle Joe," that the President trusted him completely. What is more, on Monday morning, November 29, when Churchill asked Roosevelt to lunch, the President refused. Again his argument ran that he "did not want Stalin to know" that he and Churchill "were meeting separately"; there must be no intimation of a common Anglo-American front. Anything that might arouse Soviet suspicions was to be avoided, the President insisted. The President hoped that with this show of trust the Russians would shed their fears and eventually open their doors to the West for trade, cultural exchange, and full cooperation within the framework of a future international organization to replace the League of Nations. The President's tendency to talk with Stalin alone, to the exclusion of Churchill, left Churchill bewildered and isolated. He was surprised at the President's attitude because "I thought we all three should treat each other with equal confidence."

The Teheran conference lasted just four days, from November 28 to December 1, 1943. At the first meeting Stalin stated that after Germany's defeat the Soviet Union would declare war on Japan. This declaration delighted the President. During the extensive discussions of future operations against Germany, Churchill emphasized all over again the advantages of the Mediterranean strategy in anticipation of a major invasion of France. Stalin, suspecting the British of trying to reach Belgrade, Bucharest, Budapest, and Vienna ahead of the Red Army, categorically vetoed the Balkan plans. Roosevelt, whose military experts for the most part strongly favored an invasion of northwest Europe, supported Stalin. This Soviet-American bilateralism, visible from the beginning, lasted to the end of the Teheran conference.

One of the crucial issues of the conference was that of the second front on the European mainland. Although the Soviets were eager to see an earlier Allied strike at Germany, they had to accept May 1944 as

[8]The collection of documents on wartime conferences was published by the Department of State in the series Foreign Relations of the United States: Diplomatic Papers (Washington, D.C.: United States Government Printing Office, 1947–68). For a recent narrative of the first summit conference see Keith Eubank, *Summit at Teheran* (New York: William Morrow, 1985).

Teheran Conference: Churchill's 69th birthday. National Archives

the target date for the British-United States landing in northern France, or Operation Overlord. Marshal Voroshilov questioned Admiral Leahy concerning the scale of the American buildup in England. Voroshilov seemed to believe that Overlord was comparable to the crossing of a river. General Marshall pointed out that "the failure of a river crossing is a reverse, while the failure of a landing operation from the sea is a catastrophe." As a result of this debate, Stalin promised that the Soviets would launch an offensive at about the same time with the object of preventing the German forces from transferring from the eastern to the western front.

At the conference an informal agreement was reached about the eastern frontier of Poland, which was to run essentially along the Ribbentrop-Molotov boundary, euphemistically called the Curzon line.[9] Informally, it was decided that Poland was to be compensated for the loss of the eastern marches to the Soviet Union at the expense of Germany. Stalin's claim to the northern segment of East Prussia, including Koenigsberg, was also accepted. All the time President Roosevelt avoided any written commitments concerning Poland, that is, its government and frontiers. Defending this, he tried to explain to Stalin the facts of American political life by saying he had a presidential election campaign coming up in 1944. The State Department was against any wartime territorial settlements, but the President intended to accept Russia's territorial demands with no strings attached. Although "personally he did not wish to run again, if the war was still in progress, he might have to." There were in the electorate from 6 to 7 million Americans of Polish descent, Roosevelt explained, and as a practical politician, "he did not wish to lose their vote." The President personally accepted the necessity of shifting Poland's eastern frontier to the west and establishing its western frontier on the Oder and Neisse rivers. He hoped, however, that Stalin would understand that he could not "publicly take part in any such arrangement at the present time." Stalin "understood."

Then the President went on to say that there were also "numbers of persons of Lithuanian, Latvian and Estonian origin . . . in the United States." He said that American public opinion would want some expression of the right of self-determination on the part of the peoples occupied by the advancing Red Army. He "fully realized" that the three republics had in tsarist times and "again more recently been a part of Russia." He added "jokingly" that when the Red Army "reoccupied these areas, he did not intend to go to war." Agreement was also reached on a shift of Allied support in Yugoslavia from the

[9]For a discussion of the problem see George Kacewicz, *Great Britain, The Soviet Union and the Polish Government in Exile (1939–1945)*, (The Hague: M. Nijhof, 1979); Sarah Meilejohn Terry, *Poland's Place in Europe: General Sikorski and the Origins of the Oder-Neisse Line, 1939–1943* (Princeton, N.J.: Princeton University Press, 1983).

royalist General Draža Mihajlović and his *Chetniks* to Marshal Tito's Communist partisans; this was done largely because Churchill considered that the partisans were "killing more Germans" than the Chetniks. President Roosevelt handed Stalin a highly laudatory report on Tito, which described the partisans as resembling George Washington's army at Valley Forge. Surprisingly enough, Stalin felt little enthusiasm about Tito.

Other discussions at Teheran included the outlines of the international organization to replace the defunct League of Nations; the new body was to be called the United Nations Organization, with the United States, Great Britain, the Soviet Union, and the Republic of China as permanent members of the Security Council, the highest executive body. The conference adjourned on December 1, 1943. Its end was preceded by a dinner held at the British legation in celebration of Churchill's birthday. The Americans and Russians were happy; their joint stand had prevailed over the British point of view. The banquet ended with many toasts, and Stalin complimented the American industrial machine "without which victory could not be won." Roosevelt toasted the unity of the Big Three with the words, "We can see in the sky, for the first time, that traditional symbol of hope, the rainbow." Churchill toasted that "worthy figure, Stalin the Great."

Supported by President Roosevelt, Stalin dominated the Teheran conference; his command of facts and the agenda was superior to that of his partners. Assuming a posture of moderation, he did not seek a formal recognition of all his territorial claims in eastern and central Europe. Patiently, he exploited the growing estrangement between the two Western leaders and Roosevelt's tendency to side with him rather than with Churchill. Through his promise to help the United States against Japan and to support Roosevelt's idea of a new international organization, the United Nations, Stalin won the President's gratitude. The President even suggested compensation for the Russians in Manchuria, at the expense of Chiang Kai-shek's China, for the Soviet entry into the war against Japan; the Chinese, like the Poles, were not consulted.

By frustrating the Balkan landing and obtaining firm assurances of an invasion of western Europe, Stalin created a situation in which the Red Army's advance, and hence Soviet political claims, would not be hindered by the Western Allies. Although final decisions concerning many problems discussed at the conference were not formalized, the cordiality of the discussions may have inspired Stalin with confidence that his western partners would eventually accept most of the Soviet territorial and political objectives. Decisions taken at Teheran were kept so secret that even the United States secretary of state, Cordell Hull, was not informed about some of them.[10] The way in which the Americans and British treated their Polish and Yugoslav allies strengthened Stalin's conviction that eastern Europe was of marginal importance to Washington and London. The Western Allies were apparently more interested in the façades of the future European governments in the Soviet sphere of operations than in their real content. The Atlantic Charter proved to be a convenient flag to sail under but a difficult rudder by which to steer the Grand Alliance.

The Teheran conference marked the high point of Allied wartime cooperation. Neither Yalta nor Potsdam, but Teheran was the source of decisions that shaped the subsequent phases of the war, as well as its aftermath. Consequently, the Teheran conference was one of the most momentous events of the war. By the time Churchill, Stalin, and Roosevelt left Teheran, the conflict had been transformed. The United States had translated its industrial potential into a surplus of military power. The anti-Axis coalition enjoyed the strategic initiative practically everywhere, but especially on the eastern front. The Red Army was driving the invader from its territory and about to

---

[10]For a discussion of the Teheran conference see Feis, *Churchill, Roosevelt, Stalin,* pp. 237–90.

cross the 1938 boundaries of the USSR. The U-boat menace had been defeated. Italy had surrendered. The United States and Great Britain had created a unique instrument of wartime cooperation, the Combined Chiefs of Staff. The Allies were practically masters of the air over Europe, a precondition of a successful invasion of France in 1944.

15

The New Order

The principle of "unconditional surrender," proclaimed by the Allies at the Casablanca conference in January 1943, has often been criticized as dictated by emotions and ultimately counterproductive. The principle was too rigid, and consequently it became responsible for the prolongation of the war with dire consequences not only for the Allies but also for the suffering conquered peoples of Europe, especially the inmates of the concentration camps, thousands of whom died every day. The call for unconditional surrender has to be viewed, however, against the contemporary perception of Hitler and his henchmen and their actual practices within the framework of what they called the New Order of Europe.

One has to bear in mind that by the beginning of 1943 Hitler already stood waist-deep in the blood of his victims and was viewed as the nearest personification of absolute evil ever to appear in Western history. The incredible criminality of the Nazi regime was regarded by his opponents as a deadly menace to the entire civilized world. Destruction of this "evil empire" root and branch, by all means available, was regarded as a sacred mission of the free world. Consequently, no negotiations with Hitler or his vassals ought to be undertaken by any of the Allies. All opponents of the Axis were convinced that they fought as just a war as had ever been waged. The only serious objection to the moral principles underlying the war was the fact that one totalitarian regime was fought in alliance with another cruel dictatorship. It was no accident that Dwight Eisenhower entitled his memoirs *Crusade in Europe*.[1]

[1]While reading recent attempts in memory harvesting by Studs Terkel (*The Good War: An Oral History of*

THE NATURE AND STRUCTURE OF THE NEW ORDER

The term *the New Order* was launched early during the war by the chief Axis slogan maker, Joseph Goebbels. The slogan was used often, but seldom was it defined with any precision because its content changed with the changing situation. The original essence of the Nazi battle cry was to be unification of Europe under the leadership of the Third Reich and its reorganization in accordance with Nazi authoritarian and racial principles. Every since the beginning of the war German propaganda was persistently arguing the thesis that Germany was engaged in a great constructive enterprise: a crusade to achieve the unity of Europe.[2]

After the fall of France, when Hitler became the master of most of the Continent, the stress was on the economic advantages that the Berlin-Rome Axis would provide to a Europe organized under its leadership. Germany's resources alone would obviously not suffice to win a protracted war against a great coalition commanding an enormous economic potential. It was essential for Germany to build an economy covering large geographic regions. Such a structure would not only ensure political stability but also provide for free flow of trade, harmonize the complementary economies of industrial and agricultural countries, and finally free the European continent of its dependence on overseas supplies. Here the Italian participation in the Axis was to be helpful. Italy, which had been conceded hegemony over the Mediterranean basin, including a great part of North Africa, the Adriatic littoral, and the Arab Near East, was to give access to many vital raw materials, especially oil. Later on these resources were to be supplemented by the supplies to be provided by the reconquered German colonies.

The heyday of the New Order slogan based on economic premises lasted one year, from the fall of France to the beginning of the Russian campaign. During this period the "Order," Goebbels stressed, was to be based "not on the principle of a privileged position for individual nations, but on the principle of equal chances for all." This was an old European ideal to which even the anti-Nazis could rally, and indeed many of them did. Mussolini supported this approach, which deemphasized the racial aspects of the Nazis' propaganda. Italy's military weakness, revealed right from the start, rendered his representations practically meaningless; in practice, the Nordic peoples were offered preferential treatment, while the other allies of the Third Reich were merely tolerated. To associate the Nordic peoples with the New Order, Henrich Himmler was willing, as early as the beginning of 1940, to recruit to the newly formed S.S. units Danes, Norwegians, Dutch, Flemings, and Finns. By mid-1941 Italian defeats on all fronts relegated Rome to the role of a vassal, and from that time the New Order was identified with Hitler's Reich and its Führer.

With the attack on Russia, the content of the New Order shifted from the emphasis on economic advantages to be derived from it to the slogan, protecting Europe against the Bolshevik menace. The growing shortage of manpower compelled the Germans to abandon the strictly racial approach and recruit non-Nordics to their armed forces. Most nationalities of occupied Europe provided volunteers to the German military and paramilitary formations, including even the elite Waffen S.S. Poland was the only country that provided no volunteers to the German military formations.

Behind the verbal façade of the New Order as a European commonwealth, however, the reality was different. When Hitler spoke of Europe, he obviously meant an extended Greater German Reich to which would be attached various vassals in the west

---

World War Two [New York: Pantheon Books, 1984]), one gets a strong impression that a great majority of the 120 people of various nationalities interviewed by the author regarded the struggle as a "just war."

[2]For a discussion of the essence of the New Order see Norman Rich, *Hitler's War Aims, Vol. II: The Establishment of the New Order* (New York: W. W. Norton, 1974), especially pp. 420–26.

and south and a purely colonial realm in the east. In practice, from the beginning, the mirage of the mutual economic advantages of the New Order was replaced by the policy of arbitrary annexations of the conquered lands into the Third Reich and subordination of all economies of the conquered countries to the interests of the Third Reich. These policies were enforced by means of extortion and outright plunder. In 1943 Himmler frankly told his S.S. leaders: "How the Russians or the Czechs fare is absolutely immaterial to me. . . . Whether nations live in prosperity or starve to death interests me only insofar as we need them as slaves for our culture, otherwise it is of no interest to me." Goering ordered his officials: "Whenever you come across anything that may be needed by the German people, you must be after it like a bloodhound. It must be taken out . . . and brought to Germany." And indeed, a great deal was taken out, not only in goods and services but in banknotes and gold. Whenever Hitler occupied a country, one of the first things his agents grabbed was the gold and foreign holdings of its national bank.

The royal castle of Cracow, seat of the Governor General of the occupied Poland, Dr. Hans Frank. Author's Private Collection

Economic exploitation, as well as genocidal practices, took its starkest form in eastern Europe, especially in Poland, Yugoslavia, and the German-occupied parts of the USSR. Goering ordered the use of "colonial methods" in all conquered territories of that region except for Lithuania, Latvia, and Estonia. The Germans descended on the conquered countries of eastern Europe like ravening wild beasts, like starved wolves, robbing, terrorizing, torturing, and killing the people they considered either "inferior" or "dangerous." As Professor Theodor Oberlaender, one of the German "experts" on the eastern problems, was bluntly told by Hitler in July 1941: "Russia is our Africa and the Russians are our Negroes."

One ample resource available in the conquered countries was manpower, and the Nazi leaders took ruthless advantage of this commodity. Soon after the fall of Poland, the German authorities began to ship Polish civilians and prisoners of war to Germany, primarily for farm work. From 1940 onward, the western European countries and Italy provided a considerable number of volunteer workers. The Russian campaign provided millions of Soviet POWs.

By 1942/43, after Stalingrad, it was clear that Germany was committed to a protracted war. Yet there had been no systematic planning for such a contingency. The rather vague goal of making Germany "the industrial and manufacturing center of Europe" was obviously not sufficient as a framework for the mobilization of all the resources necessary for a total war effort. The increasing demands of the armed forces for more soldiers and military hardware dictated desperate measures. The crash armaments program directed by Albert Speer tried to cope with the emergency by mass mobilization of slave labor. Fritz Sauckel, the head of a new office of labor allocation, scoured all of occupied Europe for manpower, utilizing press-gang methods, and rounded up some 2.1 million foreign workers. This raised their number in Germany to more than 6 million by the end of 1943. France and the Low Countries provided a great many, but the largest proportion came from the Soviet Union and the General Government of Poland. The peak figure of more than 7 million foreign workers, some 20 percent of Germany's total labor force, was reached in mid-1944.

At the end of the war, nearly 8 million half-starved foreigners (civilians and prisoners of war) were treated like draft animals and employed in Germany in terrible sanitary conditions without adequate housing or clothing, often kept in dog kennels or abandoned factories. Of the 5 million Soviet POWs only slightly over 1.5 million survived. Another 7 million workers, who remained in their native countries, were employed in producing munitions or other goods for the German war effort or were laboring to build the Atlantic wall.

The economic effects of the German occupation of Europe were on the whole negative. The "New Order" was no order at all: It was extortion and robbery. The total extent of the Nazi plunder of Europe is beyond computing, especially for eastern Europe, where administrative chaos reigned supreme. The figures available for western Europe from German sources show that by the end of February 1944, the total "occupation costs" at some 48 billion marks. At the official rate of exchange (2.5 Reichsmarks to the dollar) this would amount to roughly $19 billion of which France alone furnished more than half. By the end of the war, receipts from occupation assessments amounted to an estimated 60 billion marks (roughly $24 billion). France alone was forced to pay 31.5 billion of this total, its annual contributions of more than 7 billion coming to over four times the yearly sums which Germany had paid in reparations after World War I. In addition, the Bank of France was forced to extend "credits" to Germany totaling some 4.5 billion marks and the French government to pay a further half billion in "fines." At Nuremberg it was estimated that the Germans had extracted in occupation costs and various "credits" two-thirds of Belgium's national income and a similar percentage from the Netherlands. Altogether, according to a study by United States sources, Germany extracted in tribute from the conquered nations a total of at least 104 billion marks, or about $40 billion.

In addition to regular contributions, arbitrary confiscation and outright looting of private property was rampant; it started but did not end with Jewish property. Disregard for the orderly legal process and confusion over the legal ownership of property were a general hallmark of the New Order. For instance, early in the war most private motor vehicles were confiscated. Ludicrous corruption created open season for German businessmen and ordinary crooks who profited from unbridled confiscation of private enterprises in order to build up large industrial empires or small private fortunes. Here many Nazi leaders often set up the worst example; for instance, Goering would grab without hesitation art treasures he came across and happened to fancy. Human beings were treated like chattel. Inflation reduced consumption standards often to subsistence levels; shortages of essential raw materials brought about a generalized black market that favored the rich at the expense of the poor. All these factors created throughout most of occupied Europe the law of the jungle where corruption coexisted with coercion.

THE EXPANSION OF THE THIRD REICH

Next to the exploitation and outright spoliation of the conquered countries, another striking feature of the New Order was annexation of large chunks of their territories into the constantly expanding Greater

German Reich. In accordance with the Nazi slogan "Blood and Soil," acquisition of what the Nazis labeled *Lebensraum,* or the living space required by the Germans to thrive and multiply, was Hitler's fundamental war aim in eastern Europe.

The heartland of the Nazi realm was, of course, the Greater German Reich, expanded by means of a series of annexations. Large Polish areas adjacent to the Greater German Reich, well beyond the 1914 frontiers, were annexed into the Third Reich. After the end of the September 1939 campaign, the rump of Poland, or the triangle around Warsaw, Cracow, and Lublin, was organized as the so-called General Government and entrusted to the governorship of a ruthless Nazi satrap, Dr. Hans Frank. Hitler at first spoke of establishing some sort of Polish puppet state, but there was neither a Nazi party in Poland nor a candidate for a Quisling, and Stalin opposed any such idea.

By the end of 1939 Hitler had decided to make the General Government "the first colonial territory of the German nation." The German occupation of Poland was also the most severe of all the conquered lands. The German regime established in the General Government of Poland was geared overwhelmingly to a full-scale exploitation of the subjugated populace and the extermination of the educated strata of Polish society, as well as of all Jews. The Soviets in their occupation zone tried to abort the incipient passive resistance by large scale deportations to distant parts of the USSR, but the Germans resorted to outright executions and herding actual and potential resisters into labor and extermination camps.[3]

In addition to the annexation by the Third Reich of all western, and a segment of central Poland, after the victories in western Europe in 1940, Germany reannexed two border areas (Eupen and Malmedy) that had been given to Belgium by the Treaty of Versailles. Norway and the Netherlands also came under direct German civilian administration. Belgium and the northern and western two-thirds of France received German military administrators; two French departments adjoining Belgium were cut off from the rest of France and placed under the German officials in Brussels. What would have been the eventual fate of Norway, Holland, Belgium, and northern France is a matter of speculation. Only a final Nazi victory could have provided an answer to the question of the Third Reich's future frontiers. There are indications that Hitler wanted to absorb the Low Countries and eastern France (the old realm of Burgundy) to convert them into a dependent Flemish state.

Immediately after the fall of France, the grand duchy of Luxembourg, Alsace, and part of Lorraine were also administratively merged with the adjacent German provinces across the Rhine. When Yugoslavia fell in 1941, two-thirds of Slovenia was annexed. The invasion of Russia brought the de facto annexation of eastern Galicia and the Białystok province.

Besides annexation and direct rule, the Germans implemented various more subtle forms of indirect control. Before the war, two forms of indirect rule had already been applied in partitioned Czechoslovakia. In March 1939 Hitler had converted the western half of the country into the so-called protectorate of Bohemia-Moravia, and the eastern half into the vassal state of Slovakia, headed by the pro-German Catholic priest, Father Josef Tiso. In the protectorate of Bohemia-Moravia, a nominal Czech government was preserved throughout the war. President Hácha remained in office. The cabinet included not only some Czech rightist politicans but also one Reich German; collaboration was a rule, and resistance, mostly passive, was an exception. The Czech rightist party was small but vocal. All

[3]For a scholarly discussion of the problem see Martin Broszat, *Nationalsozialistische Polenpolitik, 1939–1945* (Stuttgart: Deutsche Verlags-Anstalt, 1961) and Jan Gross, *Polish Society Under the German Occupation: The General Government, 1939–45* (Princeton, N.J.: Princeton University Press, 1979). For a good background picture of the German occupation of Poland see Jan Nowak, *Courier from Warsaw* (Detroit: Wayne State University Press, 1982).

this was a façade to preserve the appearance of Czech self-rule. In Hitler's long-range plans Bohemia-Moravia was earmarked for annexation.

HITLER'S VASSALS

Unlike Bohemia-Moravia, Slovakia could claim such attributes of sovereignty as its own army and its own diplomatic representatives in pro-Axis capitals. In practice, however, it was an annex of the Third Reich. Tiso was a clerical corporatist, a pupil of Mussolini rather than of Hitler, and was harassed at times by more thoroughgoing Slovak Nazis who kept pushing for power and immediate extermination of all the local Jews. But Berlin preferred Tiso and provided him with favored treatment to build up his country's economy.[4]

In Norway the Germans eventually established the leading local Nazi, Major Vidkun Quisling, in the post of minister-president, with authority strictly limited to domestic matters only. But Quisling's rule was so unpopular among his countrymen that the Germans quickly shelved him in an effort to find other more reputable officials willing to collaborate. Their failure in this enterprise eventually led them in 1942 to fall back on Quisling, who was made a nominal minister-president.

Denmark enjoyed a special status; although the country had been occupied by German forces, King Christian chose to remain with his people and a regular Danish government was allowed to function until 1943. The Germans tried to preserve the appearance of Danish independence. Gradually, however, the Danes were subjected to steady German pressure to align themselves with the Nazi New Order. They were compelled to join the anti-Comintern pact and declared their willingness "to collaborate, in the most positive and loyal manner," in the building of a continental Europe led by the Third Reich. But in March 1943, when the occupiers permitted parliamentary elections (the only ones held in German-occupied Europe during the war!), the Danish people overwhelmingly repudiated the candidates engaged in collaboration. The Danish Nazi party won only 2 percent of the popular vote. Six months later, strikes and increased sabotage in Copenhagen gave the Germans an excuse to declare martial law, dissolve the parliament, suppress the cabinet, and resort to direct military rule.[5]

In the Netherlands the Germans hoped

Vidkun Quisling makes a Nazi salute. National Archives

[4]For a monograph on Slovakia during the war see Yeshayahu Jelinek, *The Parish Republic: Hlinka's Slovak People's Party, 1939–1945* (Boulder, Colo.: East European Monographs, 14, 1976). For Bohemia-Moravia see Vojtech Mastny, *The Czechs Under Nazi Rule* (New York: Columbia University Press, 1971).

[5]For the German rule of Denmark and Norway see Richard Petrow's *The Bitter Years: The Invasion and Occupation of Denmark and Norway, April 1940–May 1945* (London, Sydney, Auckland, Toronto: Hodder and Stoughton, 1974), especially pp. 118–327.

that the Dutch might be won over to collaboration with the New Order. For a time that hope seemed justified. Holland provided more recruits for the Waffen S.S. than any other western European country; Anton Mussert's Dutch Nazi party attained a membership of 110,000, and its members helped to make the liquidation of Dutch Jews one of the most thorough in Europe. But the Germans had little enthusiasm for Mussert's National Socialist movement; they preferred direct rule, and by 1941 the Dutch Nazi party was dissolved. The German Reich commissioner, Artur Seyss-Inquart, ran the country through his agents and the pro-Nazi high-ranking Dutch civil servants.

Belgium's situation was especially complex. While King Leopold remained in a castle near Brussels throughout the occupation, after the Belgium capitulation his cabinet escaped to London. The King described himself as a voluntary prisoner and refused to exercise his royal prerogatives. Nevertheless, the Germans found it convenient to use him as a screen behind which they could rule the country through a direct military administration. As in the Netherlands, many high civil servants kept their posts and obeyed German orders. Pro-Nazi groups were strong in Belgium but were sharply divided by the old ethnic conflict between Walloons and Flemings. Probably for racial reasons, the Germans leaned toward the Flemish party, some of whose members favored outright absorption into the Reich. Both groups successfully recruited for the Waffen S.S. A former Walloon Catholic Action activist, Léon Degrelle, was lured into collaboration and with his S.S. contingent took part in the "anti-Communist crusade." The Walonie S.S. Division of Degrelle fought to the bitter end, and their commander escaped to Franco's Spain only after the German capitulation.

France was a special case. Marshal Pétain, who in July 1940 became the head of the Vichy state, was no ordinary Quisling, like many other puppets. Pétain was one of the most illustrious Frenchmen of his generation and the object of great veneration as "the Victor of Verdun." Together with Marshals Foch and Joffre, he rode his white horse up the Champs Élysées in the first Bastille Day military parade after World War I, on July 14, 1919. Consequently, for an average Frenchman, he was a living symbol of their glorious recent past. Most men around Pétain were not merely French exponents of National Socialism but supporters of various authoritarian movements, monarchists, and conservative opportunists. Their ideal of a corporate state was based on the old social elites and resembled the systems of Franco and Salazar rather than those of Hitler or Mussolini.

On the other hand, there were around the Marshal some unsavory pro-Nazi doctrinaires and rabid anti-Semites, such as Pierre Laval, head of the government at Vichy in 1940 and again between 1942 and 1944, and they largely determined the policy of the increasingly senile marshal. In October 1940 Vichy excluded Jews from posts in the government and public media. In July 1942 the Vichy militia started transportation of Jews to the death camps. In its desire to restore a modicum of French control and autonomy to occupied France, Vichy tried to adopt anti-Semitic legislative measures that would rival those of the Nazis and ordered French police participation in anti-Jewish activities.[6] Some 10,000 Frenchmen served in various pro-Nazi military formations, such as the Anti-Bolshevik Legion, the French units of the Waffen S.S., or the Charlemagne Division. Some of the last defenders of Hitler's chancellery in Berlin were the remnants of that division; they continued to fight to the bitter end, even after Hitler's suicide.

Generally speaking, Hitler's policies in occupied Europe were highly differentiated. In northern and western Europe, Hitler imposed only such controls as were necessary for effective conduct of the war. In the German-occupied countries of eastern Europe, Nazi rule was colonial in its

[6]Michael R. Marrus and Robert O. Paxton, *Vichy France and the Jews* (New York: Basic Books, 1981).

most cruel sense. Nowhere in the west did the Germans install a new government made up of local Nazis, even though there were aspiring candidates everywhere. The only exception was Norway. Everywhere in Europe where the Germans decided to accept the native instruments of rule, Hitler preferred conservative and nationalist leaders to Fascist fanatics. The Vichy regime of Marshal Pétain in France and the rules of Marshal Antonescu in Rumania and of Admiral Horthy in Hungary are here good illustrations.

In dismembered Yugoslavia, three puppet regimes of varying types were established. A large new state of Croatia was placed under Italian supervision; its leader was the Croat Fascist Ante Pavelić, one of those few vassals of Hitler who could compete with him in ruthlessness. Some 2 million Serbs who had been included within the boundaries of the inflated Croat state were persecuted, and thousands were tortured and massacred. Outwardly Pavelić was regarded as a protégé of Mussolini, and Croatia was handed over by Hitler to Italian control. Pavelić agreed to accept an Italian prince, the duke of Spoleto, as king of Croatia, but the duke in fact never came to Zagreb. Some Ustăsa leaders began to seek German support as a counterweight to Italian control, and Berlin responded with alacrity. Soon the Germans had gained an economic foothold in Croatia, even before Mussolini's fall, and thereafter they extended their rule over the whole country.

A small rump of the Serbian state was entrusted to an old soldier, General Milan Nedich, who tried to cope as best he could with a hopeless situation. Nedich put the responsibility for the war and collapse upon the Simović government and the officers behind it. Their reckless action in overthrowing the Cvetković government provoked Hitler and caused the invasion, which was followed by the defeat and disintegration of the country. Had there been no coup, Yugoslavia could have stayed outside the conflict, because the Axis had pledged in Vienna to respect its neutrality. Then, after the tide of the war changed and the Axis began losing, Yugoslavia, whose sympathies were always with the Allies, could have entered the war on the Allied side when it was ready and thus have been on the winning side and in a position to gather its share of the fruits. Except for the coup, there would have been no invasion and no partition of the country and no civil war.

After their Balkan victories the Germans found in General Nedich a man who was willing to work under their aegis. Nedich had fought as a soldier against the invader. Taken prisoner, he finally agreed on August 30, 1941, to act as premier of Serbia; like Pétain, he felt that someone had to assume the responsibility of dealing with the Germans. Like Pétain, Nedich was convinced that Yugoslavia had been betrayed by the British. Both Pétain and Nedich originally acted out of patriotic motives; each hoped that he would be able to make the lot of his people somewhat easier. But having placed themselves at the disposal of the enemy, they found themselves making concession after concession until at last they became almost completely subservient.

The tiny mountainous region of Montenegro was run by a council of local Fascist sympathizers under Italian supervision. In Greece, a collaborationist cabinet provided a convenient façade for German and Italian control, with Berlin almost invariably having the final say in all important matters.

Bulgaria was the queerest of Hitler's vassals. Although King Boris permitted German forces to cross Bulgarian territory in 1941 to invade Yugoslavia and Greece in exchange for most of Macedonia, he avoided further commitment. Although he joined the anti-Comintern pact, he refused to declare war on Russia and managed to preserve considerable domestic autonomy, despite the presence of German troops on Bulgaria's territory. He did declare war on Great Britain and the United States, but avoided sending his troops to fight against them. He never declared war on the USSR despite German pressure. The Soviet Legation remained in Sofia until September 1944, when Moscow declared war on Bulgaria. The King's evasiveness irritated Hitler, but he was too busy to retaliate.

In Hungary and Rumania Hitler also discovered willing collaborators within the old governing elite. Hungary was peculiarly vulnerable to German pressure; for the regent, Admiral Miklós Horthy, collaboration was more a necessity than a choice. Within Hungary's borders lived a large German minority who might be used as an effective fifth column. Moreover, Hungary had one of the largest and most active Fascist parties in eastern Europe, led by Ferenc Szálasi's Arrow Cross movement, which Hitler used to blackmail Admiral Horthy to comply with his demands. Most of Hitler's demands were met, though with occasional quibbling; for instance, German troops attacking Poland in 1939 were not allowed to cross Hungarian soil; the Hungarians sheltered a large group of Polish military internees and civilian refugees and protected their Jews as long as circumstances permitted it.

In Rumania a bitter struggle between the old authoritarian right wing and the pro-Nazi and rabidly anti-Semitic Iron Guard movement headed by Horia Sima (after its founder, Corneliu Codreanu, was murdered in 1938) culminated in a victory for the old authoritarian, non-Nazi clique. Marshal Ion Antonescu, leader of the traditional rightist concept of the state, after a palace revolution in 1940, broke with the Iron Guard early in 1941 and drove its leaders into exile. Hitler kept Horia Sima on ice in Germany for possible future use, should Antonescu's regime prove disloyal. The Rumanians sent thirty divisions to fight in the east—more than any Axis state except Germany—and provided Hitler with much of his oil supply.

EASTERN TROOPS

After the conquest of the Baltic states, Belorussia, and most of the Ukraine, Hitler imposed on the conquered areas his own highly centralized administration, which ran them with an iron fist for the sole benefit of the Third Reich. Two large Reich commissariats, headed by Nazi officials, were carved out: the *Ostland* (the former Baltic states, plus Belorussia) and the Ukraine. Two additional Reich commissariats were created on paper: one to include the bulk of European Russia north of the Ukraine, and another for the Caucasus.[7]

In the *Ostland* and the Ukraine exploitation was cruelly colonial. On the whole, although Hitler's strategy was to demolish the Soviet system, his policies in the occupied territories in the east were diametrically opposed to this objective and tended to bolster the system.

The story of those Soviet soldiers who under various guises and pretexts fought alongside the Wehrmacht represents a peculiar form of collaboration. The number of the Soviet POWs was so large that to cope with them became a serious problem for the German authorities. With the failure of the 1941 offensive and the enormous subsequent casualties, the idea of trying to use Russian POWs to supplement the German and satellite manpower began to gain new momentum. Hitler was against dressing foreigners in German uniforms, particularly the Slavs. His initial principle was, "Only the Germans can bear arms." Various German commanders, however, had already begun to utilize large numbers of Soviet POWs and civilians who volunteered to work. Some more enlightened German intelligence officers were still pressing for the creation of a regular Russian liberation army and a government in exile; they tended to accept the slogan coined by the captured Soviet general Andrei Vlasov: Russians can be beaten only by Russians. Hitler considered this to be an insult to the Wehrmacht's honor; he mellowed only in 1944, faced with a desperate shortage of manpower. But then it was already too late to save him from disaster.[8]

---

[7]For a comprehensive discussion of Nazi occupation policies see Alexander Dallin, *German Rule in Russia, 1939–1945* (New York: Macmillan, 1957).

[8]Their story has been told by George Fischer, *Soviet Opposition to Stalin* (Cambridge: Harvard University Press, 1952), still a basic book on the subject.

The best-known group of the Soviet POWs who agreed to fight alongside the Wehrmacht is known as the Russian Liberation Army; the Army was founded in German-held Prague in November 1944 by General Andrei Vlasov, with the approval of Himmler. Through 1943 and most of 1944, Vlasov was kept in confinement in a Berlin suburb and displayed publicly only for propaganda purposes. Meanwhile, various units of Soviet volunteers, known as Eastern Troops, were used in various auxiliary capacities, including combating the local partisans. Because of their unreliability, most of them were transferred to the western front for use in coastal defense late in 1943.

Vlasov insisted that his volunteers, or legionnaires as they were called, be treated as full-fledged allies and not mercenaries, hired to avoid the shedding of "more valuable" German blood. He was aware of the appalling conditions prevailing in most of the camps where his volunteers were trained. These camps, mostly situated in Poland, were run by German officers, largely posted to the Soviet legions as a punishment. Despite their willingness to collaborate with the Germans, they were treated as "subhuman" creatures. For instance, throughout Poland trains and trams bore notices: Poles, Jews and Legionnaires—Last Coach. While Hitler wanted only a few mercenary troops as a propaganda weapon to encourage Soviet desertions, Vlasov insisted on political guarantees for Russia's future. Hitler was reluctant to grant them to the last moment.

Soviet POWs in a German camp. National Archives

Despite his stubbornness, his subordinates, pressed by the urgent necessity of finding new "cannon fodder," were constantly recruiting more and more Soviet POWs to the German ranks, first for auxiliary service and eventually for front-line duties. By October 1944 the "Eastern Troops" numbered over 800,000 eastern volunteers in the army and about 100,000 in the navy and Luftwaffe. The volunteers of the Vlasov Army wore on the German uniforms a blue cross on a white field, a symbol of the Russian patron, Saint Andrew. The purely military significance of the army was actually minimal; it saw exactly three days action in World War II: two against the Soviet army on the Oder River front and one against the German army and S.S. units in Prague, in reprisal at the end of the war. The Vlasov Army never had more than one combat-ready division, and that not until late January 1945; its total strength of 56,000 men constituted a minor fraction of the roughly 2 million former Soviet soldiers who served with the German forces in the war.

Most of the volunteers in the Vlasov Army and other military formations of this type were animated by hatred of Stalin's totalitarian machine, but otherwise their motivation was as varied as their nationality and individual political views. Contingents of various sorts of volunteers began to spring up under various names late in 1941 and early in 1942. By then, the units composed of Ukrainians, Belorussians, Georgians, Cossacks, Tartars, and even of Moslem soldiers coming from as far away as

Azerbaijan and Turkestan were already serving in various capacities, despite Hitler's specific orders to the contrary. There were also detachments composed of Great Russians, and others of mixed nationality. Each group had its own political objectives. Most Great Russians wanted to preserve the Soviet empire intact, although they were against its Communist ideology and structure. Others, especially the Ukrainians and the Moslems, desired to establish their independent states.

Hitler's policy of starving most Soviet POWs and his delay in forming large regular units of "Eastern Troops" must be considered as one of the factors contributing to his eventual defeat.

THE "RESETTLEMENT" OF THE JEWS

Besides territorial expansion and economic exploitation, the third feature of the New Order was the use of mass terror and genocidal policies applied to selected ethnic groups. As Hannah Arendt pointed out in her seminal work *The Origins of Totalitarianism,* the concentration camp was the essential institution of the Nazi regime—its basic prop. Although the Nazi genocidal policies affected many ethnic groups—mainly Slavic—the mass killing focused primarily on the Jews. All the Jews, together with the Gypsies and homosexuals, were to be exterminated as soon as possible and by all available means.[9]

The wartime program of extermination of all European Jews within the reach of the Third Reich was the culmination of a series of measures undertaken by the Nazis in the prewar years in Germany. Step by step the German Jews were stripped of their property and their livelihoods so as to compel them to emigrate. Until 1936 Hitler showed some restraint, partly for foreign policy and partly for economic reasons, to gain various concessions from world Jewry, mainly from its Zionist branch. By the end of 1938 many Jews—an estimated 170,000—had left, nearly 60,000 of them for British-controlled Palestine. On January 30, 1939, the sixth anniversary of the Nazi takeover, Hitler told the already solidly Nazi Reichstag that the Jewish race would be exterminated in Eu-

[9]Since the war, an extensive literature on the Holocaust has developed. One of the most comprehensive is the work of Raul Hilberg, *The Destruction of the European Jews,* revised and definitive ed., 3 vols. (New York: Holmes & Meier, 1985).

German concentration camp of Dachau, near Munich. National Archives

rope "if international Jewry were to plunge the world into another war."[10]

At the close of the Polish campaign, at the end of September 1939, Reinhard Heydrich, head of the S.S. Action Groups of the S.S., submitted plans to deport all Jews to Poland as the largest repository of European Jewry. Hitler may at that stage have thought for a while in terms of a Jewish state under German administration in the province of Lublin, then forming a border region between the German and Soviet occupation zones. After the fall of France he toyed with the idea of settling them on the island of Madagascar. But these projects were promptly abandoned and proved merely a stepping stone toward total physical extermination of the Jewish people. Why Hitler changed his mind is a controversial problem, open to all sorts of wild speculations.

Meanwhile, into the overcrowded ghettos in Poland the Germans sent most Jews from Germany, Czechoslovakia, Austria, the Baltic states, and Russia. They were forced into tiny, run-down sections of 200 towns and cities, surrounded by guards and barbed wire, deprived of their property and other assets, and their rights as citizens. In the ghettos they lived in a state of nightmarish limbo, awaiting an uncertain future. In the ghettos those able to work were employed at near starvation wages, mainly in the production of various items of equipment for the German armed forces. Conditions within the ghettos were sufficiently disturbing, however, that many people looked forward to "resettlement in the country," where, they mistakenly believed, they would be employed doing agricultural work.

Outwardly the official aim was "resettlement," which was a vague phrase used by the German authorities to obscure their true aims. With the attack on Soviet Russia in June 1941, the Nazi racial mythology and the anti-Bolshevik crusade became increasingly intertwined with anti-Semitism. Goering declared in Berlin in October 1942 that "this is not the Second World War, this is the Great Racial War. The meaning of this war, and the reason we are fighting out there, is to decide whether the German and Aryan will prevail or if the Jew will rule the world." The war was the appropriate moment to deal the final blow to the double-headed monster: "Jewish Bolshevism." The term "subhuman creatures," applied to Jews as well as Slavs, became part of the official propaganda and eventually of the common language. Soldiers as well as civilians were deluged with pamphlets and periodicals that purported to demonstrate the inferior nature of the Jewish and Slavic peoples. Carefully selected photographs and films of Russian prisoners tried to reinforce this message. The Russians, noted Goebbels in his diary, "are not people, but a conglomeration of animals."

German soldiers round up the Jews of the Warsaw ghetto. Polish Institute, London

[10]For a work on the subject see Edwin Black, *The Transfer Agreement: The Untold Story of the Secret Agreement Between the Third Reich and Jewish Palestine* (New York: Macmillan; London: Collier Macmillan, 1984), especially pp. 226 and 379.

THE FINAL SOLUTION

In her book on Adolf Eichmann, Hannah Arendt has rightly stressed that it was quite logical that occupied Poland was selected as the main place for the Holocaust. Poland was the largest repository of the Jewish population: some 3.3 million Jews resided on Polish territory in September 1939; moreover, Poland was a country far away from the eyes of Western observers. Consequently, it was the most convenient place for the construction of death camps. There were, finally, logistic reasons: Transport was in short supply, and killing could be most efficiently done on the spot. By 1941/42 Germany's resources were stretched thin, and Hitler could not divert many of them to transport the bulk of the Jews to distant places; therefore, Poland was to be provided with most of the extermination camps.[11]

Late in July 1941 Goering instructed Heydrich to prepare a detailed plan for the "final solution" of the Jewish problem in Europe. At an interministerial meeting in the Berlin suburb of Wannsee in January 1942, Heydrich's plan was approved. At his trial in Jerusalem in 1961, Adolf Eichmann, head of the Office of Jewish Affairs, recalled well the Wannsee conference, held on January 20, 1942, at which Third Reich bosses agreed on plans for the "final solution" of the Jewish question. The matter was discussed rather casually while orderlies made rounds with one cocktail after another. "It lasted an hour and a half," Eichmann recalled during his trial at Jerusalem in 1961. This 90-minute meeting was enough to set the stage for settling the fate of millions of human beings, or the "final solution of the Jewish question."[12]

By 1942 the concept of "final solution" needed no further definition. As part of Hitler's euthanasia program, carried out mostly by means of injections of deadly drugs, lethal gases had been developed. The first concentration camps had been established in Germany, at Dachau, Sachsenhausen, Buchenwald, Flossenburg, and Ravensbrueck. With the outbreak of the war, however, they were overcrowded and new ones were organized in most occupied countries. The largest and the most infamous was Auschwitz, situated at the junction of the German, Polish, and Czechoslovak territo-

[11]Hannah Arendt's *Eichmann in Jerusalem: A Report on the Banality of Evil* (New York: Viking Penguin, 1963), p. 68.

[12]For an analysis of the Wannsee conference see Arendt, *Eichmann in Jerusalem,* pp. 99–119. For a systematic discussion of the Eichmann trial see Iochen von Land with Claus Sibyll, eds., *Eichmann Interrogated: Transcripts from the Archives of the Israeli Police* (New York: Farrar, Straus & Giroux, 1983).

Two German soldiers escort a group of Warsaw Jews to be "resettled." The Pilsudski Institute, New York

Four Jewish freedom-fighters captured by the Germans during the Warsaw ghetto uprising. The Piłsudski Institute, New York

ries. Auschwitz was chosen as the main death camp largely for logistic reasons. Extensive research of the communication factor revealed that transport of a huge number of people to Auschwitz would present the least obstacles. Gas chambers were already available at Chełmno, near Łódź, and at Bełżec, near Lublin. The Wannsee gathering expressed approval of the existing facilities but ordered their expansion. The Auschwitz facilities were enormously extended. In the first half of 1942 construction of concentration camps mushroomed: A new death camp was built near Sobibor, and the labor camps at Majdanek, near Lublin, and Treblinka and many other establishments were converted into death camps.

Within the various ghettos in cities of east and west, Nazi-appointed councils of Jewish elders were to help the German authorities to administer the captive communities and see to it that the orders of the Nazi satraps were meticulously carried out. In their tasks the councils were to be helped by the Jewish militia, who were forced to select enough victims to fill each successive quota of human cargoes to be "resettled."[13]

Almost until the end of the war, trains of cattle cars from almost every part of Europe hauled their cargo to the extermination camps. A squeamish and cowardly man by nature, Heinrich Himmler was sickened to the point of fainting while witnessing some early mass shootings of Jews. Hence his decision to use gas in extermination chambers. Amply provided with the new Zyklon B gas, previously a standard chemical in exterminating domestic pests, hundreds of gas chambers were to achieve a grim record of efficiency. After a prisoner had arrived in the camp, the whole process of undressing and the walk down to the gas chambers lasted for men eight or ten minutes and for women some fifteen minutes. The processing of women took more time because they had to have their hair shaved off before they went to the gas chambers; the hair was to be used in the manufacture of mattresses for German women. In all extermination camps high standards of efficiency were strictly observed. Auschwitz alone operated at the rate of 12,000 victims per day. Himmler in a speech in October 1943 urged his S.S. followers on to greater exertions: "Not only Jewish men but every Jewish woman and child must

[13]In Israel, under the Nazis' and Nazi Collaborators' Law, enacted in 1950, some ghetto militiamen and camp *kapos* were brought to trial (Lucy S. Dawidowicz, *The Holocaust and the Historian* [Cambridge, Mass. and London: Harvard University Press, 1981], p. 136).

be destroyed," he cried, "so that no Jews will remain to take revenge on our sons and grandsons."

In the camps, survival meant for some a ruthless application of the law of the jungle: cheating fellow prisoners of their food ration, terrorizing them, or even turning spy for the Gestapo. For most it meant painful muddling through the incredible horrors of privation and degradation. How many people died in the concentration camps from disease, privation, and overwork can never be calculated exactly because only partial records have survived. As many as 7 to 8 million persons passed through the camps, and at least two-thirds did not survive. At least 3 million were Jews. In addition, about 2 million Jews were killed before arrival at the camps. Only a small percentage of the concentration camps' inmates were lucky enough to see the eventual liberations. When the war ended in 1945 some 80 percent of all European Jews, including virtually all German and east-European Jews, had been annihilated. In 1939, nearly 9 million Jews lived in Europe. Only a million remained alive by the end of the war in the spring of 1945.

THE ALLIED RESPONSE AND JEWISH RESISTANCE

Reports of the genocidal Nazi policies began to filter to the West in 1942 mainly through Polish resistance channels. The first eyewitness of the genocidal Nazi policy, Jan Karski, a secret messenger of the Polish resistance, submitted ample documentary evidence of the mass extermination of Jews as early as 1941. Many leaders abroad found it difficult to accept the available evidence about the Holocaust. Later on, the Polish government in exile provided additional gory details about the process of extermination in a radio speech in July 1942 and summoned Britain and the United States to apply severe reprisals. The Polish government's reports were again discounted by most Westerners, including many prominent Jews, as mere war propaganda. A declaration by the Western powers, formally accusing the Germans of genocide, was issued only in December of that year; no adequate measures, however, were undertaken to stop or mitigate the progressing genocide. The Allied leaders were determined to subordinate everything to the ultimate aim, that of winning the war promptly, and refused to divert their limited resources to an objective that they considered marginal.[14]

The destruction of most of Europe's Jewish population was not motivated by the Reich's military requirements. Quite the contrary; it proved to be counterproductive and contributed to Germany's eventual defeat. Among the millions killed there were thousands of highly qualified specialists, employed in war industries that were desperately short of skilled labor. By 1944 the shortage of manpower, caused inter alia by the genocidal practices, amounted to 4 million people. And at a time when German troops at the front awaited badly needed weapons, supplies, and ammunition, thousands of railroad cars and locomotives were tied up hauling Jews to the gas chambers. One of the reasons why Germany never developed the atom bomb, despite frantic efforts, was Hitler's mistrust of what he called "Jewish physics" and the emigration of most of Germany's nuclear physicists to the West. So determined was Hitler to murder all Jews that he was prepared to pay for it, quite literally, with the lives of German soldiers. He was bent on the total destruction of the Jews at any price. In his order of priorities, warped by his phobia, total exter-

---

[14]Walter Laqueur in his seminal work mentions the Polish underground couriers Jan Karski, Jan Nowak, Jerzy Lerski, and Tadeusz Celt, who brought to the West ample details about the extermination of Jews but were disbelieved by Allied statesmen, such as President Roosevelt, and their advisers, such as Justice Frankfurter (Walter Laqueur, *The Terrible Secret: An Investigation Into the Suppression of Information About Hitler's 'Final Solution'* [London: Weidenfeld and Nicolson, 1980], especially pp. 11, 107, 199, 208, and 229–38).

The gate of the Auschwitz concentration camp with the slogan "Arbeit macht frei"—"Work makes one free." Polish Institute, London

mination of the Jews took precedence over the war effort itself.

Some Jewish historians of the Holocaust have charged their brethren with complete passivity. Yet not all the Jews became passive objects of German bestiality and went to the death camps "like sheep to the slaughter." Sporadic resistance appeared here and there.

Jewish valor shone also in the heroic uprisings at the Warsaw ghetto in April 1943. In 1940, the Germans herded like cattle 400,000 Jews into one district of Warsaw and sealed it off with a high wall from the rest of the city. The area, approximately 2.5 miles long and 1 mile wide, was terribly overcrowded and systematically starved. Forbidden to leave the walled and guarded district, on pain of being shot on sight, the inmates had to work like slaves for a few factories run by the Nazi authorities. Since the Jewish population did not die fast enough and starvation limited efficient work, Himmler ordered the Warsaw ghetto to be liquidated by the spring of 1943. The liquidation was executed with terrible efficiency. Some of the 60,000 surviving Jews resisted their final liquidation. With a handful of revolvers and grenades, the youth of the ghetto fought for forty-two days to the bitter end.[15]

Other dramatic illustrations of Jewish resistance were the lesser uprisings in Auschwitz, Kovno (Kaunas), and Wilno (Vilnius). In Auschwitz, for instance, a revolt of the special team, made up mostly of Jews, who operated the gas chambers and crematoria took place in 1945. When a mass escape was attempted, one prisoner-trustee of the Nazi supervisors was assassinated, three guards were killed, and a total of twenty-seven other S.S. men were injured. One crematorium was also blown up altogether. Sadly, the revolt failed, but the Jews manifested that they were hardly sheep waiting to be butchered passively. Jewish partisans who fought against the Germans in the forests of

[15]An early eyewitness account of the Jewish resistance was received by the World Jewish Congress and published as "The Battle of the Warsaw Ghetto" in *The Extermination of 500,000 Jews in the Warsaw Ghetto* (New York: The American Council of Warsaw Jews and American Friends of Polish Jews, 1944). The report was later reprinted in the anthology by Nathan Ausubel, ed., *A Treasury of Jewish Folklore: Stories, Traditions, Legends, Humor, Wisdom and Folk Songs of the Jewish People* (New York: Crown, 1948; 24th printing, October 1965).

Poland and Lithuania, Belorussia, and the Ukraine are further examples of active Jewish resistance.[16]

ATTEMPTING TO UNDERSTAND THE HOLOCAUST

There are two basic schools of thought about the Holocaust: the functional and the revisionist. The functional school stresses the premeditated and almost "scientific" character of the plan for the "final solution," as well as the decisive role of Hitler himself. The revisionist theories, originating mainly in Germany but not entirely absent in Britain and America, set out to prove that the final solution resulted from chaos rather than planning, and that Hitler himself was not aware of the magnitude of the crimes committed in his name. A good example of this type of apologetic writing, which tends to absolve Hitler from full responsibility for the mass extermination of the "inferior" races, is that of David Irving, who claims that the Führer gave no explicit orders that Jews were "to be liquidated," but instead "evacuated to the east" and resettled in labor camps. Irving maintains, moreover, that Hitler knew nothing of the mass extermination of the Jews until the fall of 1943 and the man mainly responsible for the Holocaust was Himmler. Yet Irving does admit that Hitler often requested reports on the activities of the special task teams assigned the task of slaughtering not only the Jews but also other "inferior" people.[17]

Pragmatic evidence and pure logic belie the revisionist approach. Of course Hitler was not omnipresent or omniscient. During the war he concentrated on a few major, mostly military and foreign policy issues, and delegated vast powers to a host of henchmen in matters that he considered of secondary importance. But it is equally true that nothing of any real significance could take place against his will. Himmler was often at pains to invoke "the Führer's wish" while carrying out what he himself called "a horrid assignment." In the Third Reich any plan or decision was valid only if it corresponded to Hitler's view and only as long as Hitler did not utter a contrary opinion.[18] One of the arguments of the revisionists about the final solution rests on the fact that no one has ever discovered a written order for mass murder signed "Adolf Hitler." This is legalistic casuistry. No such document has been found and may never be located in the future. Whatever his faults, Hitler was not a pedantic bureaucrat, and many of his vital instructions were passed on orally.

OTHER HOLOCAUSTS

The Nazis tried to win over the Western peoples to make them junior copartners in the task of building the New Order, but those eastern Europeans who did not submit to it were treated as serfs and slaves of the Third Reich. This was especially true of the Poles, Yugoslavs, and Russians. These different attitudes were reflected in German terminology. While the west Europeans who refused to collaborate were usually referred to as "opponents" (*Gegner*), the eastern Slavs were called "hereditary enemies" (*Erbfeinde*).

An indication of the highly differentiated attitude toward various peoples was reflected in the human equation the Nazi

[16]As a Jewish historian of the Holocaust stated, there is a tendency to strain the term *resistance* beyond its usual meaning and include even telling jokes against Hitler as a form of resistance (Dawidowicz, *The Holocaust and the Historians,* p. 133). For various cases of Gentile as well as Jewish resistance see Józef Garliński, *Fighting Auschwitz: The Resistance Movement in the Concentration Camp* (London: Julian Friedmann, 1975), passim.

[17]David Irving, *Hitler's War* (London, Sydney, Auckland, Toronto: Hodder and Stoughton, 1977), pp. 12–16; see also his *Goering. . . .* (New York: Morrow, 1989), p. 344. Most of the "revisionist" writing about the Holocaust is based on forged or highly distorted evidence.

[18]Albert Speer, *Infiltration* (New York: Macmillan, 1981), p. 28. Speer makes it quite plain that all major decisions, including the program of genocide, were planned and willed, or at least approved, by Hitler himself.

masters computed for reprisals. German punishment in occupied Europe was often collective, applied at random, and determined by their general political objectives and their racist scale of values. A Pole caught publishing illegal literature, hiding a Jew, or indulging in any form of sabotage or diversionary activity was sure to be shot on the spot, but a Dane, a Norwegian, a Dutchman, or a Frenchman would only be sent to a concentration camp. In 1943 Hitler ordered that five Danes should be shot for every assassination of a German carried out by the local resistance. In Holland the rate was to be ten to one, and in Poland a hundred for one. On Soviet territories reprisals were entirely arbitrary. Human life was cheaper the farther one went east.

Although all Jews were actual or potential victims, not all victims were Jews. The next targets of the genocidal policies of Hitler were Gypsies and the Slavs, especially those Slavonic peoples who opposed him with greater determination than the others; these were mainly the Poles, Yugoslavs, and Russians. In the Nazi racial doctrine the Slavonic peoples were regarded as inferior "subhuman" creatures—a "conglomeration of animals." Moreover, their lands were coveted by the Germans as a prospective eastern extension of the Greater German Reich. That is why they had to be conquered and their political and intellectual states exterminated, with the rest of the population turned into serfs and servants of the "master race."[19]

Nine million to 10 million eastern European Gentiles died together with the almost 6 million Jews under the Nazi terror in World War II. Hitler viewed the war as an anti-Slavic crusade. The first Slavonic people who were the main target of the Nazi genocidal policies were the Poles; then came the Yugoslavs, the Russians, the Belorussians and the Ukrainians. In the Nazi scheme of things the Slavic peoples were an inherently inferior

[19]Bohdan Wytwycky, *The Other Holocaust: Many Circles of Hell* (Washington, D.C.: Novak Report Publishers, 1980). The book covers the fate of the 9 to 10 million eastern European Gentiles who died alongside the 6 million Jews under the Nazi terror in World War II; see also Richard C. Lukas, *The Forgotten Holocaust: The Poles under German Occupation, 1939–1944* (Lexington: Kentucky University Press, 1986).

A group of Auschwitz inmates dumped on the ground while awaiting allotment to overcrowded barracks. National Archives

breed of subhumans destined to serve as slaves of the Teutonic people.

The Slavonic Ukrainians are a special case: Initially they greeted the Germans with enthusiasm, yet by his treatment Hitler quickly disappointed them. Eventually, they turned against the German occupation authorities. Regarded as especially dangerous were those who, after their frustrated collaboration with the Germans, turned against them and fought for their independence as partisans.

The Nazi genocidal policy in Poland was the most ruthless, systematic, and consistent: It called for the gradual elimination of the native populations from these territories, so that the German *Lebensraum* could be increased. In the General Government the extermination policy started with the educated strata. In October 1939 professors of the ancient University of Cracow were among the first to be sent to a concentration camp where many of them died. Only primary schools were allowed to the indigenous population. In the part of Pomerania annexed to the Reich, 96 percent of the Catholic clergy were either killed on the spot or sent to various concentration camps.

The Jewish inmates of the extermination camps were promptly disposed of, whereas the Gentiles were either worked to death or treated as human guinea pigs and subjected to all sorts of experiments and abuse. These experiments were medical and, in the case of many women, often sexual. The whims and proclivities of the S.S. guards largely determined whether the women suffered occasional sexual abuse, were relegated to the camp brothels, or were sent to the Wehrmacht "rest centers." For instance, at the notorious Ravensbrueck camp, the German doctors deliberately infected Polish girls with gas gangrene or germs of various disease or practiced vivisection.[20]

[20]There is no consensus on casualty figures for another major target of the Nazi genocidal policies, the Ukrainians and the Belorussians, where the atrocities committed by the German troops and the occupation authorities were equally monstrous (Wytwycky, *The Other Holocaust*, pp. 64–70).

For all practical purposes no limits were set to the perverted imagination of various types of sadism. For instance, Ilse Koch, known as the Bitch of Buchenwald, developed a hobby of collecting the tattooed skin of the inmates. Those younger prisoners who appeared to have better skins free of defects were tattooed and then either killed by injections or shot in the neck, so that their skins would remain uninjured. Ilse Koch would then make lamp shades or book bindings of their hides; one which particularly pleased her had the tattooed title *Hansel and Gretel.*

Mass executions of prominent citizens were carried out in all other German occupied countries of eastern Europe, such as Yugoslavia and later in the Ukraine and Belorussia. (The Babi Yar ravine near Kiev

A group of children behind barbed wires of the concentration camp of Bełżec. Polish Institute, London

swallowed 130,000 Gentiles, in addition to 70,000 Jews.)

Nazi genocidal policies were not merely a spontaneous outburst of savagery of men at war; they were preceded by extensive, meticulously planned, scientific research and executed with a premeditated cruelty seldom, if ever, equaled in human history. The Nazi genocidal practices, with the enormity of their horrors that exceed imagination, have confronted humanity with unprecedented problems. History records a number of large-scale massacres, but all of them involved at least a shade of human passion. The Turkish massacres of the Armenians during World War I were savage but, on the whole, spontaneous outbursts of racial hate. The Nazi mass killing was different: Certain categories of people were carefully selected to be systematically exterminated because of a set of pseudoscientific anthropological and biological laws, or an alleged historic necessity that labeled some ethnic groups—mainly Jews, Gypsies, and Slavs—as inferior. The selected people were massacred in cold blood without emotion, in the same way that cattle are slaughtered in stockyards or vermin are exterminated by pesticides.

The incredible criminality of the Nazis' genocidal policy tends to overshadow the fact that during the war Soviet Russia also engaged in ruthless mass repression measures directed both against groups regarded as dangerous and against certain ethnic minorities considered as disloyal. After the fall of Poland, the Soviet occupiers matched the Germans in trying to exterminate the native elite of the newly annexed provinces, while deporting some 1.5 million people to various labor camps and settlements in the distant, forbidding parts of the Soviet empire. Some 14,000 Polish officers were killed one by one with pistol shots in the back of their skulls. The motivation in this case was, however, political, not racial: they represented a considerable segment of the politically conscious strata of the Polish intelligentsia, considered by Stalin a threat to his plans for Poland.[21]

Mass deportations also took place in the Baltic states in 1940/41 and again in 1944/45. Also the Ukrainians were subjected to harsh reprisals at the close of the war and after it. The Soviet deportations and atrocities are considerably less documented than the German ones largely because the Western Allies tried to keep them obscure, and at the Nuremberg trial the Soviet members of the international tribunal did everything possible to prevent their being mentioned. Of the people deported to Siberia and central Asia, many never returned. The Soviets' forcible shifts of population were not limited to the annexed territories but also affected some non-Russian minorities within the USSR. Shortly after the German invasion of Russia, the Soviet government deported eastward some half-million "Volga Germans" who had lived for two centuries north of the Black Sea; Stalin feared that they might make common cause with the invader and preferred to take no chances. Later on, the same fate befell the Soviet POWs and displaced persons returning from the west, as well as the Crimean Tartars and some ethnic groups of the northern Caucasus.[22]

In assessing the Nazi New Order, one should conclude that it failed miserably in its objectives. The conquest of the *Lebensraum* to ensure the security of the Germanic race ended in the shrinking of the Germanic diaspora in east-central Europe, and in the division of the German heartland into two states. The alleged defense of Europe resulted in its partition into two spheres of influence. The racial purification, which

---

[21]For the Katyń problem see J. K. Zawodny, *Death in the Forest: The Story of the Katyń Forest Massacre* (Notre Dame: Notre Dame University Press, 1962).

[22]For Soviet genocidal policies see Robert Conquest, *The Nation Killers: Soviet Deportation of Nationalities* (New York: Macmillan, 1970), passim.

had provided a rationale for the cold-blooded murder of millions of human beings, proved to be an unworkable anthropological absurdity and a cruel monstrosity. The regimentation of minds and bodies, inherent in the Nazi concept of society, stifled the very cultural creativity that Hitler had so boastfully declared to be the main objective of his allegedly regenerative policies. The "New Order," while contributing nothing whatsoever to human culture, undermined its fragile foundation. Nazi genocide shattered whatever illusions humanity may have had about its moral progress and revealed how thin the veneer of our civilization really is.

16

The Resistance

Initially, at least in western Europe, the New Order did not provoke a widespread active resistance. At the beginning the German triumphs of war greatly impressed some Europeans, not all of them Fascists or proto-Fascists. Even many firm anti-Nazis in western Europe were shocked and temporarily stunned by the fall of France and the withdrawal of the British to their island fortress. Everything seemed to be lost. Apathy and anger at the democratic political leaders who had failed in the crisis predominated. Some depressed people believed that Nazism was indeed the wave of the future and that it would eventually sweep away the old, bourgeois, liberal, plutocratic civilization. The admirers of the Nazi and Fascist systems were jubilating and making new converts to the gospel of success.

Moreover, at first the behavior of the German occupation troops and civil authorities in western Europe was disciplined and "correct." Yet the mounting economic exactions became increasingly severe and caused growing resentment. Finally, the activities of the German secret police, who tried to penetrate all political and social bodies, while making arbitrary arrests, eventually enraged even the most passive citizens. Gradually the opposition crystallized and small nuclei of resistance began to form, and clandestine leaflets began to appear. Everywhere little groups of patriots soon began to be drawn together to discuss the possibilities of opposing the invaders.[1]

[1]For general studies of the active opposition to German and Italian occupations see M. R. D. Foot, *Resistance: European Resistance to Nazism, 1940–1945* (London: H.M.S.O., 1976); Stephen Hanes and Ralph White, eds., *Resistance in Europe, 1939–1945* (London: Pelican Books, 1976); and Jorgen Haestrup, *European Resistance Movements, 1939–1945: A Complete History*

EAST AND WEST

The scope and intensity of the opposition varied from country to country, if only because the occupation policy was highly differentiated. Except for Poland and Yugoslavia, large-scale active resistance surfaced only gradually. The British, who after the disastrous spring of 1940 found themselves in a desperate situation, were determined to encourage all sorts of resistance in Axis-occupied Europe. Here, the Battle of Britain and the autumn of 1940 were turning points. The continuing courageous and effective British stand impressed most Europeans, even those who were ordinarily far from being pro-British, such as the Irish or the Spaniards.

The countries that produced the largest and most militant resistance movements and continued the fight throughout the war were Poland, Yugoslavia, and Greece. All of them, Poles, Serbs, and Greeks, had a long history of opposition by armed struggle against foreign invaders. Some 400 years of Greek and Serbian resistance against the Turks and over 120 years of Polish fighting against the partitioning powers had better conditioned them for clandestine activities than the peoples of western Europe.

In Poland as in Serbia armed resistance began immediately after the 1939 and 1941 campaigns and reached a level of effectiveness matched by no country in occupied Europe. Shortly after the defeat of 1939 a Polish government in exile was established in Paris under the leadership of General Sikorski. In June 1940, the government moved from Paris to London, whence it continued to send directives to the emerging underground in Poland in both German- and Soviet-occupied sectors of the country. Hitler's policy of indiscriminate terror, to be sure, left the Poles few options. Yet to resist actively meant to risk still more savage mass reprisals; on the other hand, to submit meant not only continuing ruthless exploitation but also national degradation. The choice was made immediately after the fall of Warsaw, and gradually the Poles organized an elaborate network of clandestine institutions that some Poles described as an "underground" or "secret state."[2]

The provinces annexed to the USSR were more tightly and skillfully controlled by the NKVD and permitted less active resistance. An underground movement had attempted to operate in the Soviet-annexed provinces, but its effectiveness was soon crippled by the Soviet deportations of Polish political leaders to various distant labor camps, and by the installation of an administrative net imported from the USSR with which Polish Communists collaborated willingly. In the German-controlled General Government, on the other hand, the lower administrative echelons continued to be staffed by Poles, and those officials often became, in one way or another, connected with the resistance.

Late in 1940 a variety of small, spontaneously established groups fused into a united movement which shortly came to be called the Home Army, operating under orders from the London government. The Home Army achieved some spectacular successes in the field of active and passive sabotage, intelligence gathering, and guerrilla fighting. At its peak in 1943/1944, the Home Army came to number about 300,000 men. Although its spirit was good, it lacked arms, equipment, and ammunition.

The Polish underground press also proliferated; more than a thousand clandestine periodicals were circulated, 300 of them on a regular schedule. The underground even managed to establish and operate clandestine universities to replace those closed down by the Germans; degrees were granted; a number of scholarly works were published.

(Westport, Conn. and London: Meckler, 1981); see David Stafford, *Britain and European Resistance, 1940–1945: A Survey of the Special Operations Executive, with Documents* (London: Macmillan, 1980).

[2]Jan Karski, *Story of a Secret State* (Boston: Houghton, Mifflin, 1944); Stefan Korbonski, *The Story of the Polish Underground State, 1939–1945* (New York: Minerva Press, 1956); and Tadeusz Bór-Kormorowski, *The Secret Army* (London: Macmillan, 1953).

A detachment of Polish resistance fighters, known as the "Home Army," being reviewed by its commander (first on the left) in a forest near Lubin. The Piłsudski Institute, New York

By contrast, in the neighboring protectorate of Bohemia-Moravia, where the German occupation was relatively mild, the resistance movement was weak throughout the war. Eager to manifest that opposition to the German occupation in the protectorate was alive, in May 1942 the Czechoslovak government in London parachuted a team of British-trained Czech agents to assassinate Reinhard Heydrich, the top S.S. official in Prague and the "Protector" of Bohemia-Moravia since September 1941. Prior to the attempt, in Czechoslovakia as a whole only 3,000 people had been arrested, but after Heydrich's death the terror intensified. In Prague alone, 1,700 Czechs were executed; at Brno, 1,300. On June 10 all the men and children of the little village of Lidice were exterminated, and the women were deported to the notorious concentration camp of Ravensbrueck.

The repression that followed the assassination of Heydrich on May 29, 1942, emasculated the Czech resistance movement. Those members who survived operated henceforth in small groups without much national direction and confined themselves to factory slowdowns and individual acts of sabotage. Guerrilla activities remained practically nonexistent.[3]

[3]Vojtech Mastny, *The Czechs under Nazi Rule: The Failure of a National Resistance, 1939–1942* (New York and London: Columbia University Press, 1971).

COMMUNISM AND THE RESISTANCE MOVEMENT

The front of European resistance was broadened in June 1941 after Hitler's attack on Soviet Russia made the Communists free to

Colonel Draža Mihajlović in his uniform of the Royal Yugoslav Army. National Archives

join the active opposition to the Third Reich. Hitherto the Communist parties had maintained a neutral position, actually denouncing French and British "capitalistic imperialists" with more vigor than "the Fascist imperialism" of the Axis. Before 1941 only a few individual Communists had joined resistance groups in defiance of Comintern instructions, and they were often censured for these acts of defiance. After June 1941 their participation was officially encouraged. Now the Communists were instructed to create in each Western country broad "national fronts" that would unite all anti-Fascist groups under their indirect guidance. In many movements, such as in those in Yugoslavia, Greece, Germany, or France, the Communists excelled in practical underground experience and ruthlessness in the struggle.

The Communist participation in the struggle against the Axis movement, although broadening the resistance front, involved considerable disadvantages. Being subservient to Moscow, they were considered bad security risks; any important intelligence available to them was bound to be transmitted eventually to Moscow. Moreover, to most non-Communist freedom fighters it was clear that the Communists did not share the same goals. All resistance groups were agreed on one point: the determination to destroy Axis power. But what were the Communists planning after its defeat?

Everywhere it became apparent that the Communists' attempt to create a national front was merely a tactical move—a stepping stone for giving them control of the entire resistance movement, to catapult them eventually into power. Nowhere was this tactic more obvious than in Yugoslavia. Immediately after Yugoslavia's defeat in April 1941, a General Staff officer of the Royal Army, Colonel Draža Mihajlović, took refuge in the hills of central Serbia and began to rally not only those soldiers who escaped captivity but the entire population to fight the invaders. His guerrilla force was known as *Chetniks* (the traditional label for bands of local self-defense against the Turks).[4] The response to his call was limited to Serbian patriots, traditionally pro-Russian but overwhelmingly anti-Communist.

Mihajlović conceived of his Chetniks as a military force at the disposal of the government in exile. He was determined to be sufficiently active to cause constant embarrassment to the enemy and, by preventing any reduction of the Axis contingents in Yugoslavia, to be of service to the Allied cause. He was also resolved to postpone any attempt at a large-scale uprising that could only result in severe reprisals and thus in unnecessary damage to his already half-ruined country. The legitimate government of King Peter in London was the only authority to give the signal when the final struggle for the country's liberation should begin. After June 22, 1941, however, this essentially military concept of resistance was challenged by a rival faction.

After Hitler's attack on Russia the leader of the Yugoslav Communist party, Josip Broz, known as Tito, set out to reorganize the activists of his party for underground work. Soon he formed a movement not only independent of Mihajlović's but also radically opposed to his objectives and methods of warfare. Tito soon managed to carve out a small area in western Serbia and to attract a following of fighters, known as Partisans, that included some non-Communists and non-Serbs.

At first, the two rival resistance movements observed a kind of cautious neutrality toward each other, but before the end of 1941 it degenerated into violence. Mihajlović was a monarchist committed to the idea of a Serb-dominated Yugoslavia; Tito was a Croat and a Communist who advocated a federal state and drastic reconstruction of the socioeconomic structure of the country in a radical Marxist spirit. The Tito-Mihajlović rivalry was one of the great controversies of

[4]The term *Chetnik* derives from the word *cheta,* a detachment of soldiers or a group of men engaged in guerrilla warfare.

the war and is still an emotionally loaded issue.[5]

Until 1943 Mihajlović was widely acclaimed as the most daring guerrilla leader in conquered Europe. The Yugoslav government in exile made him General and Minister of War as well as commander in chief of all resistance forces. First the British and then the Americans assigned liaison officers to his headquarters and promised to send arms when they could. Initially even Stalin advised Tito to accept Mihajlović as national leader and King Peter as the legitimate ruler.

Tito meanwhile was acting with considerable independence and he was clinging stubbornly to his reckless line of action. By his savage guerrilla tactics he often provoked the Germans and Italians into sizable counterinsurgent campaigns, which cost the inhabitants of Yugoslavia very dearly, causing devastation of entire regions of the country. In 1942 and again in 1943 Tito's army was driven far back into the mountains of Bosnia but never destroyed. Until mid-1943 Mihajlović and Tito were regarded by both the Axis powers and the Allies as more or less of equal caliber.[6]

Meanwhile, in the areas held by Tito, his Partisans set up a provisional administration. This was based on a People's Anti-Fascist Front under Communist leadership. In order not to alienate non-Communists in the ranks and amongst the civilian population, a relatively moderate line was followed, the Communists being careful not to dwell more than necessary on their ultimate aims. But everywhere the key posts were held by Communists and policy was in practice dictated by them. Liaison between the Partisan civil and military authorities was maintained by Communist political commissars who also closely supervised the ideological loyalty of the troops. By 1944 Tito's Partisans, supported first by the Western Allies and only later on by Moscow, emerged as the decisive element in Yugoslavia to establish their brand of communism in that country.

Josip Broz-Tito with his shepherd dog. National Archives

The Tito-Mihajlović rivalry was one of the major controversies of the second phase of the war and still generates a great deal of emotion because of the mutual accusations of various "parallel accommodations" with the enemy. Both contenders in the civil war were so embittered against each other that they often accepted Axis aid in order to exterminate each other. The Partisans wanted a Communist Yugoslavia affiliated with the Soviet Union. All those who were opposed to this were to be ruthlessly annihilated. The Chetniks wanted an independent and royal-

[5]For a pro-Tito British stand see Fitzroy Maclean, *Eastern Approaches* (London: Jonathan Cape, 1950), pp. 303 ff.; and W. F. Deakin, *The Embattled Mountain.* For an opposite point of view see David Martin, *Ally Betrayed: The Uncensored Story of Tito and Mihailovich* (Englewood Cliffs, N.J.: Prentice-Hall, 1946).

[6]For the methods and tactics of the Axis powers in their fight against the Chetniks and Partisans see Paul N. Hehn, *The German Struggle Against Yugoslav Guerrillas in World War II: German Counter Insurgency in Yugoslavia, 1941–43* (Boulder, Colo.: East European Quarterly, 1979); distributed by Columbia University Press, 1979 (New York), especially pp. 12–15 and 142–44.

ist Yugoslavia; they were prepared to resist to the death any attempt on the part of the Communists to establish their regime. For both sides the ends justified the means. This produced a savage struggle, ferocious even by Balkan standards.[7]

By the Spring of 1943 the Allied victory in North Africa had renewed Churchill's hope of piercing the Axis' "soft underbelly" and landing a considerable force in the Balkans with the assistance of the local resistance movement. Overnight the Yugoslav and Greek civil wars escalated in international importance. As for Greece, there was never any doubt whom the British would support. Then the question arose, who, Mihajlović or Tito, would be more useful for the planned venture?

For a considerable period of time the British military opposed the suggestions of the Foreign Office to drop Mihajlović and recognize Tito. As late as February and March 1943 the head of the military mission with the Chetniks reported that they were better organized and controlled more vital areas containing the principal copper and chromium mines. Moreover, the Chetniks held the main lines of communication between Serbia, Bulgaria, and Greece. The reports concluded: "On a short-term basis, i.e., who is doing most at the moment, the Partisans are, perhaps, the more valuable. On longer term considerations on all counts the answer is in favor of Mihajlović."[8]

By mid-1943 Churchill had come to the conclusion that Tito "was killing more Germans" than Mihajlović and switched the bulk of the British aid to the Partisans. Churchill's objectives in the Balkans were both strategic and political. He was convinced that with the entry of Turkey into the war, combined with the action of the Greek, Yugoslav, and Albanian guerrillas and the defection of Hungary, Rumania, and Bulgaria, the war might be shortened and the Soviet expansion in that area held back.

All these hopes were dealt a heavy blow at the Teheran conference. They were finally destroyed by the remarkable staying power of the German forces in Italy and the unwillingness of the western Allies to disregard the principle of unconditional surrender and negotiate separate capitulation agreements with Hungary, Rumania, and Bulgaria, all of them eager to disengage themselves from Hitler. But in September 1943 Churchill still believed that his "soft underbelly" stratagem would work and that a great deal, including momentary ideological considerations, should be subordinated to it.[9]

The Greek resistance bore some resemblance to that of Yugoslavia, though its outcome was different. Six months after the country was overrun in April 1941, two rival underground movements emerged in the rugged mountain country of the north: The National Liberation Front (E.A.M.), dominated by the Communists, and the National Greek Democratic Union (F.D.E.S.), headed by a democratic colonel, Napoleon Zervas. Although not a royalist, he loyally fought for the monarchy and its government in exile, both tarnished by their association with the Metaxas dictatorship and increasingly unpopular among the masses of Greek people.

As in Yugoslavia, numerous British liaison missions were sent to Greece to help the guerrillas, provide intelligence to London, and to encourage coordinated action between the rival groups. Despite these ef-

---

[7]It has been a Partisan contention that only the Chetniks had contact with the Germans and the Italians. Djilas confirmed that the Partisans did also collaborate with the enemy. As early as 1943, for example, the Italian command provided supplies to the Partisans in Montenegro—ostensibly for Italian prisoners of war; Milovan Djilas, *Wartime* [San Diego and London: Harcourt Brace Jovanovich, 1977], pp. 154, 198 ff., and 229 ff.).

[8]For British controversies see Report of February 19, 1943. Public Record Office, London, WO, 208/3102; see also similar reports of February 20, 21, and March 3, 1943; unfortunately most of the SOE as well as OSS archives are still closed to historians.

[9]For secret negotiations with Germany's "reluctant satellites" see Elisabeth Barker, *British Policy in South-East Europe in the Second World War,* (London: Macmillan, 1976), pp. 204–65.

forts, armed clashes, in which the Communist partisans were usually the aggressors and often the victors, occurred sporadically through 1943 and 1944. Because of their superior organization and ruthlessness, the Communists might have triumphed had it not been for the vigorous support accorded to Zervas by the British. In view of the crucial importance of Greece for the British Empire, Churchill was unwilling to see a key country of the Mediterranean subjected to the same fate as Yugoslavia.[10] Thanks to British aid, the remnants of the Communist bands were driven back into the northern mountains, where they vainly waited for Soviet aid to help them renew the fight.

THE RESISTANCE IN EASTERN EUROPE

The German attack on Russia in 1941 affected the Polish resistance movements differently than those of Yugoslavia or Greece. Unlike in the Balkans, the Communist underground movement in Poland was weak and its impact on the struggle limited. Moreover, in Poland the resistance had been almost as much anti-Soviet as anti-German, for until June 1941 one half of Poland's territory had been subjected to Soviet rule, almost as ruthless as that of Nazi Germany. The German attack made the Russians allies of Poland's main ally: Great Britain.

In July 1941 diplomatic relations between the USSR and the Polish government in exile in London were restored; many Poles who had been prisoners of war in Russia since 1939 were released to fight alongside the Russians on the eastern front. The Polish Communists now joined the active resistance—though rather as rivals of the Home Army than as its partner. In June 1943 the Union of Polish Patriots, made up of émigré Communists, was established in Moscow under Soviet patronage. The union shortly sent its agents into Poland to reestablish the Communist party under the new label Polish Worker's party. The Communist partisans, far less numerous than the Home Army, proposed fusion with the Home Army. The proposal was rejected because of the fear that the Soviets would subvert its rival from within. Thereafter, the two forces operated as increasingly hostile competitors for power.

The tension between the Polish government in London and the Soviets grew worse after April 1943 as a result of the discovery by the Germans of a mass grave of murdered Polish POWs in the forest of Katyń, near Smoleńsk. After Moscow had broken off diplomatic relations with the Polish government in London in April, 1944, the Union of Polish Patriots was converted into the Polish Committee of National Liberation.

The struggle against the German occupation of the Soviet Union is a special chapter of the European resistance movement. Because only the western fringes of the USSR were occupied by the enemy, the opposition to the German domination had the direct support of Moscow. In his first wartime order of the day addressed to the nation on July 3, 1941, Stalin called on all Soviet citizens to engage in partisan action and sabotage wherever possible. Irregular warfare had been an integral part of the Soviet military doctrine; now Moscow put it into practice and sought to encourage its partisans systematically and by all available means, including parachuting of trained instructors and supplies of arms. Soon liaison was established with various large pockets of Soviet resistance behind enemy lines, and the partisan movement was integrated and functional as a part of Moscow's total military effort. Already by the close of 1941

---

[10]When Brigadier Maclean pointed out that Tito was a Communist and that the system which they would establish would inevitably be on Soviet lines, Churchill asked him: "Do you intend to make Yugoslavia your home after the war?" "No sir," he replied. "Neither do I," Churchill said. "And, that being so, the less you and I worry about the form of Government they set up the better. That is for them to decide. What interests us is, which of them is doing most harm to the Germans?" (Maclean, *Eastern Approaches,* pp. 402–3; see also Churchill's *The Second World War, Vol. V, Closing the Ring,* pp. 308, 312, and 358.

the partisans had been placed under orders of the Soviet High Command.

In the autumn of 1941 Moscow set up the first special training camps for guerrilla fighters and began to send in these specialists by parachute, along with political agents and trained propagandists. By the summer of 1942 the number of partisans had risen to about 150,000 and continued to grow until the end of the war. The partisans were grouped in small bands, most of them not exceeding a few hundred people, operating in the swamps and forests behind the German front; they were particularly strong in Belorussia.

In the northern and western Ukraine, on the other hand, scattered detachments of anti-Soviet nationalist Ukrainian guerrillas clashed with the Soviet partisans. Some Ukranian leaders hoped for their land's independence and, trusting Hitler's promises, fought the Red Army. Sometimes the Germans supported these nationalist bands; more often, they found it hard to distinguish one variety of guerrilla fighter from another and suppressed even the initially pro-German freedom fighters.[11]

For the Soviet government, its loyal partisans served a double purpose. Not only did they harass the German troops, but they also served to remind the population in occupied territory that the Soviet regime would return one day, reassert its rule, and punish collaborators. This demonstration of the Soviet presence was essential in areas where much of the rural population had been deeply alienated by the collectivization drive of the early thirties, and in the newly annexed lands of Lithuania, Latvia, and Estonia, the areas which had been under Soviet rule from 1939 to 1941. The partisan units, by threatening reprisals against both the local Quislings and genuine freedom fighters, could put fear among those citizens whose loyalty to the regime was lukewarm. The partisans tied down Axis forces about equivalent to their own strength and accounted for numerous casualties in enemy ranks; their military contribution was real, but relatively incidental to the accomplishments of the regular Red Army. In the end, the political value of the partisans exceeded their actual military contribution.

THE FRENCH RESISTANCE

As has already been mentioned, for a variety of reasons the western European armed resistance emerged later than that in eastern and southeastern Europe and never reached the scope and intensity of the latter. Each country of western Europe eventually produced its resistance movement, and each contributed, in one way or another, to the gradual erosion and undermining of German rule.

In a book devoted to World War II as a whole and not to the specific role of the resistance, one has to emphasize the importance of the country that was to play the key role in the Allies' plans of reconquering the European continent. Immediately after its defeat, the French people remained passive, and only a few lonely voices were raised in dissent. These isolated individuals were encouraged by the activities of a small group of people who proclaimed themselves "the Free French," led by General Charles de Gaulle. He had been flown to London by the British and on June 18, 1940, issued a radio appeal to his countrymen urging them to carry on the fight in order to make up for the lost battle by contributing to the eventual winning of the war. Although de Gaulle was declared a traitor and condemned in absentia by the Vichy government, he continued his work from Britain despite the initial coolness and even hostility of most of his countrymen, who did remain loyal to Vichy.

The birth pangs of the Free French movement were acute. Initially the forces commanded by General de Gaulle were very

---

[11]The role of the guerrillas has been covered in Kenneth Macksey, *The Partisans of Europe in World War II* (London: Jart-Davis, 1975) and in a symposium by John A. Armstrong and others, *The Soviet Partisan Movement in World War II* (Madison: University of Wisconsin Press, 1964).

modest. Most French soldiers evacuated one way or another to Great Britain refused to join de Gaulle and insisted on being repatriated. In August–September 1940, the Free French army numbered only 140 officers and 2,109 men, and the navy comprised 120 officers and 1,746 ratings. In the summer of 1941, after the surrender of the French garrisons in Syria and Lebanon to the British and Free French forces, most of the French POWs also opted to return to their home country rather than join de Gaulle's contingents.[12]

As in other countries, also in France the Communists sided with the forces opposing the Axis only after June 1941. Fortunately, the impressive strength of the French Communist party was offset by de Gaulle's politically astute maneuvers and by the Axis occupation of all of metropolitan France. His Free French movement had been steadily gaining adherents since November 1942 and had won support in a considerable segment of the French Empire. His pro-Soviet gestures facilitated the subordination of the Communist clandestine movement to his leadership, probably on the instruction of Moscow, eager to split France from "the Anglo-Saxons." To please the French Communist party, for instance, de Gaulle went as far as to rehabilitate its general secretary, Maurice Thorez, who had deserted the French army and fled to Moscow in 1939, soon after the signing of the Stalin-Hitler pact.

By the spring of 1943 de Gaulle was able to transfer his headquarters from London to Algiers and to establish himself as head of the French Committee of National Liberation, a virtual unofficial government in exile. Largely against the opposition of the SOE, jealous of its own influence, General de Gaulle established his own intelligence network; his agents in 1943 managed to federate all the major French resistance groups into a single movement headed by the National Resistance Council and the Military Action Committee; most underground leaders, including the Communists, with varying degrees of reluctance, submitted to General de Gaulle. The growing toughness of the German occupying authorities in France after November 1942 gradually pushed an increasing number of patriotic people into the arms of the resistance, which became known as the *Maquis*.[13]

Admiral Jacques Trolley de Prevaux, head of the network Anne (F2) in his 1939 uniform. Author's Private Collection

On February 1, 1944, the military arm of the resistance was officially proclaimed by General de Gaulle as the French Forces of the Interior. While outwardly merging their units, in fact, the Communists kept their armed detachments separate. Nevertheless, on the eve of the Allied invasion of the Continent, the French resistance, lavishly

[12]For Charles de Gaulle's story of the origins of his movement see his *War Memoirs, Vol. 1, The Call to Honour, 1940–1942* (New York: Viking Penguin, 1955), especially pp. 81–304.

[13]The term *maquis* originally meant bush or dense growth of small trees and shrubs dotting a hillside; by 1943/44 it became a blanket term covering all sorts of underground resistance groups that fought the Axis forces, referring to undergrowth as their major hiding place.

supplied with arms by the Americans and the British, represented a respectable force, which by sabotaging German military and transport installations contributed to the success of the operation.

THE SOE AND THE OSS

The role of outside assistance in fostering the resistance was crucial. With the fall of France, Britain had to continue its struggle alone. All available means had to be used and one of them was irregular warfare; political subversion, underground propaganda, and guerrilla fighting. Attempts to act against the enemy in this way had been used earlier in the war, especially in the Balkans, but had not been officially acknowledged. This changed after the catastrophic spring of 1940. In July an official organization, the Special Operation Executive, or SOE, was formed. Churchill described the SOE as a "ministry of ungentlemanly warfare." The mission of the SOE was to encourage subversion and sabotage, "to set Europe ablaze" by all possible means, fair or foul. When Lord Halifax, the foreign secretary, suggested that his department should sit on a controlling committee, Lord Lloyd, the colonial secretary, told him bluntly: "You should never be consulted, because you would never consent to anything. You will never make a gangster!"

Initially the British High Command exaggerated the potential of the irregular warfare, such as sabotage and subversion. At the start some British leaders suggested that the Axis might be beaten by a combination of economic pressure, air attacks, and "the creation of widespread revolt in her conquered territories." Before long, however, sounder estimates prevailed, and the SOE was seen only as a contributory factor in weakening the enemy before the Allied landing on the Continent. From late 1940 onward, the SOE sent a growing number of well-trained agents into various European countries. More than a thousand eventually went to France, alone, to cooperate with the local resistance movement and various intelligence networks.[14]

One of the main instruments of Britain's wartime propaganda was the British Broadcasting Corporation, or BBC. Winston Churchill, with his spirited speeches broadcast to the Continent by the BBC, beamed rays of hope for eventual liberation of the Continent from the Axis tyranny. The Morse code equivalent of *V,* three short strokes and a long one, became the signal of the broadcasts of the BBC to occupied Europe. Churchill, by holding up his index and middle fingers in the "V for Victory" sign, became a symbolic figure of British self-confidence.

During the years of their lonely struggle, 1940/41, the British encouraged on the Continent the formation of a network of clandestine groups and intelligence agents who collected military information, circulated anti-German leaflets and newspapers, carried out sabotage assignments, and aided in the escape of refugees and Allied POWs who wanted to rejoin the fight. In 1942 the Americans, emulating the British, established an organization modeled partly on SOE called the Office of Strategic Services, or OSS for short. The OSS was the predecessor of the present-day Central Intelligence Agency (CIA).

At the head of the OSS was put Colonel William J. Donovan. Donovan had performed brilliantly during World War I, in which he rose rapidly to the rank of colonel of the famous Sixty-ninth Division, known as the Fighting Irish. For his valor in combat, he earned the nickname Wild Bill. He spent the years before the outbreak of World War II studying military affairs and planning the type of intelligence organization the United States would need in case of war. In the 1930s he had anticipated that unconventional and psychological warfare would have a major place in the battles of

---

[14]For a semiofficial story see Hugh Dalton, *The Faithful Years* (London: Muller, 1957) and M. R. D. Foot, *SOE: An Outline History of the Special Operations Executive, 1940–46* (London: British Broadcasting Corporation, 1984).

the future. He made a special trip to Ethiopia during the Italian Ethiopian campaign in 1935/36, and to Spain during the civil war in 1936/37. When World War II broke out, he was one of the few Americans with insight into the nature of modern warfare.

On assuming his duties as head of the OSS, Donovan was promoted to general. Independent by nature, he was respectful but not overawed by the British expertise in secret operations. The SOE and the OSS were so fused together that they operated in Europe hand in hand, although in a few cases cooperation turned into rivalry. The British were dubious of any operation not supported by local resistance movements, while the Americans were more daring. By the end of the war 524 highly trained men and women had been infiltrated into occupied Europe by the OSS.[15]

The SOE's expertise came from the rigorous training of its agents. In some of Britain's most stately homes in secluded parts of the country, agents were initiated into the cloak-and-dagger world of espionage and sabotage. This was a cruel world that knew no mercy. The Allies had to respond in kind to German ruthlessness. On December 7, 1941, Hitler issued his decree ordering his subordinates to eradicate every trace of opposition by all available means. The decree that launched the widespread and carefully planned operation known by its code name *Nacht und Nebel* (Night and Fog) instructed that "in the occupied territories, all measures are permissible in obtaining information from those responsible for crimes against the Third Reich. Such persons may be executed without appearing before a tribunal."

In view of this Nazi policy the Allied agents had to undergo a most rigid and versatile training before they could cope with their enemies on the Continent. The initiation of the individuals who volunteered for such duties started with conventional physical training and inoculation with some basic rules of behavior. The main principle was: Try to be inconspicuous, but watch everything and everybody. During preliminary courses the potential agent's behavior and reactions were closely observed. They were tempted into heavy drinking to establish whether they became boisterous, quarrelsome, aggressive—or above all, talkative. They were even watched in the bedrooms to see if they talked in their sleep.

Next came the training with weapons. This started with simple knives. The potential secret agents were to be instructed: "Any household has a knife. If you have a knife, you can get a pistol. If you have a pistol, you can get a rifle. If you get a rifle you can get a machine gun." The future guerrillas were to be taught to fight expertly; that meant silently. Would-be operatives were instructed that killing was only a last resort. As an instructor emphasized to his SOE recruits, "A knife should be used as delicately as an artist uses his paint brush. A knife stroke should be upward, from the testicles to the chin. Avoid killing an enemy. Put him in a hospital for six months. Alive an enemy would be more bother to his countrymen than dead."

Parallel with the training with conventional weapons came the development of a panoply of "dirty tricks" including "booby traps", for use in the field. From secret laboratories a flow of equipment streamed out; incendiary "cigarettes"; a match that hid a microfilm; toothpaste tubes and shoelaces with secret narrow hollows; and explosives camouflaged to look like loaves of bread, lumps of coal, fireplace logs, or even horse and camel droppings.

One of the basic aims of the resistance movements was to sabotage all fields of the enemy war effort. For instance, on the walls of a German factory in France the secret agents would paint a turtle to remind the workers to work slowly. Many half-starved foreign workers deported to Germany silently practiced the turtle principle even

[15]For a work on the subject based on the declassified OSS files and interviews with 122 survivors of the secret operations; see Joseph E. Perisco, *Piercing the Reich: The Penetration of Nazi Germany by American Secret Agents during World War II* (New York: Viking Penguin, 1979).

without outside encouragement. Eleven 20-millimeter shells once penetrated the gas tanks of a Flying Fortress during a raid over Germany in 1943 but did not explode. Armorers extracted the shell and found one that was not filled with explosives but contained a carefully rolled piece of paper with a scrawl in Czech: "This is all we can do for you now."

DARING EXPLOITS

Besides passive and active sabotage of the Axis war effort, members of the local resistance, often helped by SOE agents, organized some of the most daring, as well as elaborate, exploits of the war. One of the most dramatic examples was the raid of the Norwegian freedom fighters on the Vermork laboratories. By capturing Norway the Germans acquired the most important laboratories manufacturing heavy water in Europe. The hydroelectric plant and the laboratory where the heavy water was processed were located in Vermork, northwest of Oslo, in a deep, narrow valley very difficult to reach.

There was a fear that the Germans, who were researching an atomic bomb, might succeed, partly owing to the Norwegian stocks and laboratories. This led to a series of RAF raids on Vermork. The first attempt ended in disaster, when the British glider-borne raid crashed into a neighboring mountain. The second similar expedition ended in a similar way. Yet, somehow, Germany's lead in nuclear research had to be offset at any price. After these two failures, in February 1943 nine Norwegian parachutists, trained by the SOE, were dropped near Vermork. The parachutists broke into the plant and blew up its heavy water section without suffering a single casualty. Thus a half-ton of heavy water was denied to the Germans. The German commander in Norway, General von Falkenhorst, described the Vermork raid as "the best coup I have ever seen." After this, the last consignment of the precious stuff, some 14 tons, was dispatched to Germany in steel drums by a ferry. The Norwegian underground organization, known as Milorg, blew a hole in the bow of the ferry taking the drums across the Tinnage Lake while the boat was over the deepest water. The ferry sank in three minutes and so did any further prospect of a German atomic bomb in the near future.[16]

The Polish resistance also had a number of remarkable achievements to its credit. Perhaps its most significant feat in the field of intelligence was the discovery of the German experiments with the V1 and V2 flying rockets, with which the Germans had been practicing in Poland at an S.S. artillery range in a remote forest zone between the Vistula and San rivers. The news about the launching pads at Peenemuende, on the Baltic Sea, was also signaled by the Poles to London and led to a raid of 579 RAF bombers on the night of August 17–18, 1943.

In May 1944 an unexploded experimental V2 rocket without wings was rescued from a swamp near the Bug River, some 80 miles east of Warsaw, hidden from the German search, and carefully dismantled. The nearly 25,000 parts of the rocket were examined, measured, and photographed by Home Army experts. The results of the research, together with corresponding photographs and the most important parts of the bomb, were dispatched to London to help British engineers in devising their defensive measures against the "flying rockets."[17]

Not all was light and sweetness between the SOE and the underground movements. The often autocratic tendencies of the SOE leaders, who tried to run most clandestine activities in their own way, frequently led to acute tensions and numerous misunderstandings with various resistance groups and their respective governments in exile,

---

[16]For the full story see Thomas Gallagher, *Assault in Norway: Sabotaging the Nazi Nuclear Bomb* (San Diego and London: Harcourt Brace Jovanovich, 1975).

[17]For a detailed description of these operations see Józef Garliński, *Poland, SOE and the Allies* (London: George Allen and Unwin, Ruskin House, 1969), pp. 148–53.

who at times suspected British motives. For instance, the Free French GHQ in London bitterly resented SOE's practice of recruiting its own agents, and its monopoly of aircraft and supplies used by de Gaulle's agents. There was also considerable friction between the SOE and the Dutch, Norwegian, and Polish High Commands, anxious to preserve their autonomy in dealing with their respective countries.

ALLIED INTELLIGENCE NETWORKS

Another vital aspect of the clandestine activities was collection of intelligence for the benefit of the Allies. The war produced a bewildering variety of spy rings. Here only those of special significance for the outcome of the war will be discussed.

As a result of the fall of France, Britain's elaborate spy net collapsed. Its rebuilding represented considerable difficulties because, after Dunkirk and Oran, the British were extremely unpopular and generally mistrusted by the masses of French people. This hampered recruitment of local agents, who, as a rule, constitute the broad foundation of any large scale intelligence operation. This necessitated using Polish allies as instruments of such recruitments.

And indeed, the first Allied network was established in July 1940 by two Polish officers; acting first only on the territory of metropolitan France, they soon extended their activities to North Africa. German arrests, however, crippled their activities. In September the Polish Admiralty in London, urged by the British (who were reluctant to use their own agents), sent to France one of its officers, the naval engineer Tadeusz Jekiel, who had studied there before the war and had good contacts with his former colleagues. His task was to organize an intelligence network from among the French patriots. The purpose of the network was to keep the British Admiralty informed about Axis activities—mainly, but not exclusively, about naval matters. Together with a young artillery lieutenant, Leon Śliwiński, Jekiel re-

Leon Śliwiński, one of the leaders of the Allied intelligence network "F2." Author's Private Collection

cruited many Frenchmen willing to defy both the Axis authorities and the Vichy regime. Later on, Śliwiński also recruited Poles who became the backbone of the network. Eventually the organization, known as Reseau F2, gathered up well over 2,000 courageous amateurs in the art of collecting vital information about enemy activities on the European Continent.

Throughout the next four years the resourceful F2 network provided London and Washington with a vast amount of valuable intelligence sent by radio and microfilms dispatched to the Allies by the boats secretly circulating between the French Mediterranean coast and Gibraltar, or by special messengers. The information was supplied not by the professional spies but by civilians—dockers, railway men, factory workers, civil servants—for patriotic reasons. In turn, they were supervised by these two highly talented amateurs who often were envied by their professional colleagues because of their imagination, flexibility, and talent for improvisation. No information was considered too insignificant: Many vital details of military training, troop disposition, and naval convoys were duly reported to London. Unlike many other intelligence networks, F2 was never destroyed and operated from September 1940 until the end of the war.

One part of F2 was a network known as Reseau Anne, headed by Admiral Jacques Trolley de Prevaux, helped by his wife. Reseau Anne specialized mainly in the naval intelligence concerning the Axis activities in the Mediterranean. The high merit of the work of F2 and its partner Anne was recognized and rewarded by General de Gaulle's resistance as paving the way for the liberation of France.[18]

Even the smallest details that could be of possible importance were carefully noted, meticulously logged, and transmitted to the Allies. Consequently, throughout most of the war there was rarely a shortage of reliable reporting about the Axis in London or Washington. Taken in conjunction with information obtained from individual agents and the interceptions of German radio signals, the resistance reports made the Allies well informed throughout the war.

In the field of espionage Soviet Russia was much more farsighted and enterprising than the Western Allies. The Soviet intelligence networks were numerous, well organized, and some of them had been established well ahead of time. Among them one should point out the crucial role of the *Rote Kapelle,* or "Red Orchestra." The cryptonym *Rote Kapelle* was coined by German security agents to designate the Soviet espionage network in western Europe aided by local Communists and their sympathizers. The Orchestra was not a wartime creation but had grown directly from a variety of prewar Soviet networks in Europe. Several of the Soviet agents in the wartime networks were recruited and became active years before World War II.

The activities of the Red Orchestra were not limited to the Axis-occupied countries. Several ramifications of the *Rote Kapelle* were felt also in England. In the course of the war the Red Orchestra had become the principal segment of Soviet military intelligence. The Orchestra was directed by an old Communist activist, Leopold Trepper. The reports from agents were transmitted primarily by radio, and the Gestapo called it "music." The "music" on the air had its pianists (radio operators), a maestro in the field ("the Grand Chef," Leopold Trepper), and its conductor in Moscow ("the Director").

The Orchestra benefited from information provided by several high officers and officals of the Abwehr and had informants at fairly high levels of the Wehrmacht's High Command. The Red Orchestra transmitted about 500 messages before it was smashed by the German anti-espionage in October 1942. As a result of the breakup of the Red Orchestra, forty-six people were sentenced to death.

Although after that Trepper did continue his activities from Paris and Brussels, his effectiveness greatly diminished: The Red Army primarily needed information from behind the eastern front and not from western Europe. Fortunately for Moscow, another network, led by Sandor Rado, a Hungarian born geographer active in Switzerland, also paid rich dividends. Still another anti-Nazi master spy, Rudolf Roesler, who had fled his native country to Switzerland, was able to continue the intelligence work after the destruction of the Red Orchestra. Acting as Rado's agent, Roessler eventually created an effective information-gathering network in Lucerne, hence his cryptonym Lucy. From a radio station near

[18]An arbitrary hand had removed most source material from the F2 folder at the French military archives at Vincennes; consequently, the above description of the network's activities has been based on interviews with some of its former members, mainly with one of its leaders, Colonel Leon Śliwiński. The story of Reseau F2 was also summarized by its two organizers in their joint paper: Leon Śliwiński and Thadée Jekiel, *Historique du Réseau F2* (mimeographed 1977, rectified in June 1980, Paris: Polish Historic and Literary Society, 1984).

Lucerne, Roessler sent to Moscow over a hundred most valuable reports.[19]

Lucy's reports included, for instance, a detailed plan of Hitler's offensive against the Kursk salient. The precision and speed of his messages were astonishing. Roessler also had links with the Swiss and British intelligence services, and that is the reason his spying for the Soviet Union remained unpunished. Roessler's motivation was not so much ideological as mercenary. The sources of his information were extensive and reached the higher echelons of the Abwehr. Toward the end of 1943 Soviet Russia was receiving messages from more than a hundred radio transmitters that were sending reports from Communists and their sympathizers behind the German front line. Moreover, Soviet intelligence had by then cracked most German codes. General Franz Halder, the former chief of the German General Staff, expressed the opinion in an interview published by the journal *Der Spiegel* in January 16, 1967, that "almost every offensive operation of ours was betrayed to the enemy even before it appeared on my desk."[20]

Not all Allied spy and sabotage rings were successful. In some cases German counterespionage was more than a match for them. For instance, the liquidation of the *Famille-Interalliée* network in France and of the Red Orchestra in Germany and Belgium were masterly operations. Another example of the high caliber of some of the German counterintelligence agents was the deep penetration of the Dutch underground movement. During 1942 and 1943 the Netherlands was the scene of a silent duel between the SOE and the German counterespionage service. The SOE spared no effort to make German counterintelligence believe that London relied on a giant underground net of over 15,000 agents and saboteurs. The Abwehr, however, managed to infiltrate the net. In nearly 200 flights the Dutch section of SOE dropped agents and vast quantities of arms and explosives—most of them intercepted by German reception committees pretending to represent the Dutch underground movement. The BBC sent out code messages, giving details in their Dutch news reports about agents and materials to be dropped. The RAF, which supplied aircraft for the drops over Holland, lost several valuable machines (mostly four-engined) in such operations. For two years the Germans kept on sending fictitious messages to London concerning activities and successes of Dutch SOE agents—when dozens of them were already in German prisons and concentration camps.

ESPIONAGE IN THE NEUTRAL COUNTRIES

All neutral countries of Europe—Switzerland, Sweden, Portugal, Ireland, and Turkey—were significant centers of international espionage. The most important of them, however, was Switzerland. Situated at the heart of the Continent and adjacent to Germany and Italy as well as to France, it occupied a key role in many strategic contingency, as well as espionage, plans of all warring powers.

The Swiss position was extra cautious and hence ambivalent. Switzerland had long been secretly banking on an ultimate Allied victory, but tried to appease both sides. Despite the surveillance of the Germans, the Swiss had continued to mail to London large quantities of spare parts for watches, which could also be used as explosive mechanisms. This did not satisfy the Allies, however, and

[19]For the memoirs of the Grand Chef see Leopold Trepper, *The Great Game: Memoirs of the Spy Hitler Couldn't Silence* (New York: McGraw-Hill, 1977), especially pp. 87–316. For a study see *The Rote Kapelle: The CIA's History of Soviet Intelligence and Espionage Networks in Western Europe, 1936–1945* (Frederick, Md.: University Publications of America, 1979).

[20]For insights into the functioning and structure of the Abwehr see the memoirs of General Reinhard Gehlen, *The Service* (New York: World Publishing, 1972): For the role of the anti-Nazi opposition inside the Abwehr see Bernd Gisevins, *To The Bitter End* (New York: Houghton, Mifflin, 1947); see also Karl Heinz Abshagen, *Canaris* (London: Hutchinson, 1956), pp. 122 ff.

the blockade of Switzerland continued. The British criticized the Confederation for continuing to trade with the Germans, obtaining from them iron, coal, mineral oil, gasoline, sugar, and alcohol. In exchange Switzerland supplied Germany with cheese, butter, and meat, as well as with certain industrial products, such as machine tools, weapons parts, and munitions. Many Jewish refugees trying to enter Switzerland were turned back. All this did not satisfy Hitler, who several times contemplated an invasion of that country. Only the fear of a determined and well-prepared Swiss resistance made him abandon his plans.[21]

Because of its geographic location, Switzerland came to play an especially important role in the Allied contacts with the opposition movements in both Germany and Italy. In the Swiss capital, Bern, was active one of the most effective co-workers of General Donovan, Allen Welsh Dulles. Son of a Protestant clergyman, Dulles was educated as a lawyer and soon acquired wide diplomatic and espionage experience in Switzerland during World War I. Later on Dulles was a member of the American delegation to the peace conference of Paris, 1919/20. His solid knowledge of Europe led Donovan to send him again to Bern in 1942 to set up a major American espionage center.

Dulles officially joined his embassy as a legal assistant to the ambassador, but in fact he was in Switzerland in charge of the work for the OSS. His crucial task was to find out what was going on in Germany, Italy, and their vassals. His main interest was to discover who was really opposed to Hitler and to help those who tried to overthrow him. Dulles, who was personally opposed to the principle of unconditional surrender, tried to impress upon the German conspirators that Hitler's removal was absolutely essential and that the Western powers would refuse to give the conspirators any binding promises until Germany had gotten rid of its dictator. A coup d'état would provide tangible proof that the German opposition was a force to be reckoned with.

OPPOSITION AND CONSPIRACY IN GERMANY

For obvious reasons, active German opposition to the Nazi regime developed more sluggishly than in the Axis-occupied countries. Until the end of the war the German opposition to Hitler was timid, scattered, limited in scope, and thus had little effect on the outcome of the war. There were several reasons for this phenomenon. In the occupied countries resistance to an alien invader was regarded as a patriotic duty, but active opposition to one's own government, even a tyrannical one, in wartime was regarded by the overwhelming majority of the Germans as treason. Moreover, the preventive purges of the period 1933 to 1939 resulted in imprisonment of about 200,000 Germans and the exile of at least twice as many. Finally, the tradition of obedience to established authority also inhibited the average German, a poor conspirator by nature, from indulging in anything that might possibly damage the national war effort. Consequently, there was practically no guerrilla activity in the territory of the Third Reich, and the acts of sabotage committed there were mostly the work of secret agents, foreign laborers, or Communists who formed a considerable segment of the German resistance.[22]

The most vital task of the German opposition was to remove Hitler by means of a military coup d'état. The idea had been discussed already, during the Munich crisis in September 1938. At that time a few anti-Nazis, grouped around General Ludwig Beck, who had resigned on the eve of the crisis from the post of chief of General Staff, formed the nucleus of a conspiracy. Beck and his associates sent secret messages to

---

[21]For a study of Switzerland as an espionage center see Józef Garliński, *The Swiss Corridor: Espionage Networks in Switzerland During World War II* (London, Melbourne, Toronto: J. M. Dent & Sons), p. 198.

[22]For a general treatment see Allen Dulles, *Germany's Underground* (New York: Macmillan, 1947).

General Ludwig Beck, the last peacetime Chief of German General Staff and the military leader of the conspiracy against Hitler. German Information Center, New York

London to win British support for such a scheme. Prime Minister Chamberlain, however, was dubious about the genuineness of the plot and refused to talk to its emissaries. Hitler's smashing triumphs in Poland in 1939 and in the west in 1940 put an end to talk of a coup for the next two years.

Nevertheless, General Beck, an officer with great authority, managed to persuade many of his army friends, as well as some politicians, to form a conspiratorial cell to work actively for Hitler's overthrow. His belief that Hitler had to be removed if Germany was to be saved from a catastrophe was shared by the quartermaster of the General Staff. General Karl Heinrich von Stülpnagel; chief of the General Army Office, General Friedrich Olbricht; commander of the Berlin area, General Erwin von Witzleben; commander of the Twenty-third Division in Potsdam, General von Brockdorf-Ahelfeld; commander of the Fiftieth Infantry Regiment in Berlin, Colonel Paul von Hase; Colonel Claus von Stauffenberg, of the organization section of the General Staff; and chief of communications in the land army, Colonel (later General) Erich Fellgiebel. Despite its impressive composition, the group took no action for almost five years. Merely words, words, words. . . .

The most determined anti-Axis opposition centered around the top echelons of the German military intelligence service. Both its head, Admiral Wilhelm Canaris, and his deputy, Colonel (later on General) Hans Oster, were determined to overthrow Hitler, whom they considered "the destroyer" of Germany. Oster was actually far more consistent and effective; he organized a tight circle around himself and utilized the potentialities of the Abwehr to establish a network of confidential agents—an intelligence service of his own. He kept intimate conspiratorial links with Generals Ludwig Beck, Georg Thomas (head of the economics and armaments branch of the OKW), and Fritz Thiele and Erich Fellgiebel (chiefs of communications for the army and the OKW, respectively). One of the key men of the conspiracy was General Olbricht, permanent deputy to the commander in chief of the Home Army, or the main disposable force that could be used in case of a successful coup.

Besides the military opposition, there was a mixed bag of German politicians—

Claus von Stauffenberg. German Information Center, New York

Social-Democrats, conservatives, liberals, and Communists—opposed to Hitler for various reasons.

The Gestapo, aware of the existence of the military and political opposition, was carefully monitoring all conspiratorial groups. While the Communist spy ring was usually referred to as the Red Orchestra, the conspirators of a different hue were called the Black Orchestra (*die Schwarze Kapelle*). Nevertheless, the anti-Nazi plotting continued.

The largely aristocratic German military establishment had many grievances against Hitler. From the very beginning he treated them with suspicion. His dazzling military successes of the first two years of the war turned this suspicion into scorn. His conviction of his unique strategic genius made him belittle the spade work that had preceded the war and the innumerable services of his military experts, without which those successes would be unthinkable. The excessive concentration of power in Hitler's hands and his determination not to allow his field commanders any discretion imposed upon his marshals and generals a system of rigid control that was humiliating to senior professional officers. The disastrous consequences of Hitler's method of command were revolting to many of his senior officers, but the habit of blind obedience was so deeply ingrained in them that they accepted his stern control with little demur.

The main reason for their discontent about Hitler's conduct of the war was not its immorality but rather its ineffectiveness. Most of them were guilty of at least tacit complicity in his genocidal policies, with few discernible qualms. The marshals and generals complained bitterly to each other, but they seldom challenged his decisions to his face. They were inhibited by their oath from taking any active steps. Moreover, they realized that the rank and file of the Wehrmacht and the mass of civilians still had a great deal of confidence in the Führer's leadership, and that his authority on the home front had been strengthened by the threat of Soviet invasion of the homeland. Finally, the Allied demand of unconditional surrender and the British and American mass bombings of the German cities tended to play into the hands of the Nazis.

All these factors diminished in importance as soon as disaster became obvious. Already by 1943 the conspirators had planned several attempts to assassinate Hitler, but all of them went awry for one reason or another. Efforts to get in touch with the Allies in hope of arranging a negotiated peace were cold-shouldered because both London and Washington firmly stuck to the principle of unconditional surrender and were afraid that any leakage might endanger their relations with the Soviet allies.

Initially, Canaris and Oster provided the conspirators with various valuable covers and pretexts to travel abroad to contact the Allies. On March 30, 1943, however, Oster, the nerve center of the plot, was driven from office. The same happened to Canaris in February 1944; his Abwehr was now subordinated to the military office of the S.S. or *Milamt.* With their disappearance the conspirators had to redouble their efforts to achieve their plan at once. The successful Allied landing on the Continent dealt the final blow to the hopes of overthrowing Hitler before a decisive victory of the Allied powers. This forced the reluctant conspirators to act promptly.

The task of assassinating Hitler was finally undertaken on July 20, 1944, by Colonel Claus von Stauffenberg, a severely wounded war hero who had joined the plot in 1942. He volunteered to place a bomb in Hitler's headquarters because he was the only member of the plot to attend the top-secret staff conferences without being searched, because of being a crippled war hero; he had lost his right hand and his left eye in Tunisia. A time bomb was deposited by Stauffenberg under the map table at Hitler's staff conference at his GHQ at Rastenburg, in East Prussia. The bomb exploded as planned, but failed to kill the Führer, inflicting only slight injuries on him.[23]

---

[23]See "The Anti-Hitler Plot—As Seen From HQ in the West," *The German Generals Talk,* pp. 259–71; see also Warlimont, *Inside Hitler's Headquarters,* pp. 461–65.

The conference room at Rastenburg, Hitler's "wolf's lair," after von Stauffenberg's attempt. Göring and Borman (second and first from the left) inspect the wreckage. German Information Center, New York.

When the plotters attempted to seize control of Berlin, they were promptly arrested by General Friederich Fromm, commander of the Reserve Army, who remained loyal to Hitler. The attempt was a failure because the support the generals had lent to it came too late and was too hesitant.

Over and over again they found excuses to postpone the plot, and even when they finally did decide to act, their action was half-hearted, their resolution being inhibited by their oath as soldiers. The roundup of the conspirators followed the failure of the plot. Seven thousand were arrested, most of them senior officers. Most were tried not by customary military or civilian law courts but by "people's courts." Over 200 plotters were executed. Some conspirators committed suicide. The reprisals were so thorough that they decimated the resistance movement.

The elite aristocratic and conservative composition of most of the conspiratorial groups limited the appeal of their programs to the masses of the German people, who did remain loyal to Hitler and his regime. The military plotters, as courageous as they proved to be at the end, suffered for most of the time from Hamletic hesitation and followed more the dictates of desperation than of prudence.

Perhaps nobody personified the contradictions, ambiguities, and dilemmas of the Germanic nationalistic opposition to Hitler better than Martin Niemoeller. Commander of a U-boat at the end of World War I, he took an active part in the plotting that helped to undermine the infant Weimar Republic; considering it too conciliatory toward the victorious powers, he welcomed Hitler's accession to power in the belief that the Nazis would regenerate Germany. When Hitler tried to infiltrate the Lutheran chuch of which Niemoeller had meanwhile become pastor, he protested and accused the Führer of paganism and was imprisoned for eight years on Hitler's personal order. Yet in 1939 from prison he offered to volunteer for submarine service. While opposing the exclusion from clerical office of Jews who had converted to Christianity, Niemoeller never condemned anti-Semitism. He preached many expansionist concepts common to the entire German conservative right, including the return to the frontiers of 1914.

The German anti-Nazi opposition, except the compact and disciplined Communist group, had neither a common program nor a unified leadership. For the most part these were people less disgruntled by the crimes of the Nazi regime than fearful of a military defeat.

THE OPPOSITION IN ITALY

In Italy an opposition had existed ever since Mussolini proclaimed his dictatorship at the close of 1922, but expulsion of anti-Fascist leaders and reprisals practically silenced the voices of domestic dissent. Nevertheless, the opposition lingered among some intellectuals as well as workers of leftist proclivities. During the first months of the conflict, many anti-Fascists were reluctant to hamper their country's war effort for patriotic reasons. The building of a vital underground in Italy was also impeded by the passive stand taken by the Communists during the years of Stalin's pact with Hitler.

Field Marshal Erwin von Witzleben tried for treason in the Nazi People's Court and sentenced to be hanged on August 8, 1944. National Archives

After June 22, 1941, freed from the instruction of the Comintern inhibiting their opposition to the Axis powers, the Italian Communists revived the activities of the underground cells. For instance, they sponsored a series of strikes in the Turin region during the autumn and winter of 1942/43. Underground newspapers began to appear in large numbers from 1942 onward and found avid readers in a population that resented the rationing of food as well as the increasing domination of the Germans. In 1943 the Christian Democratic party was resurrected and set to work after an interlude of almost twenty years.

The overthrow of Mussolini in July 1943, however, was not the work of the opposition but a palace revolution engineered by dissident Fascists, supported by the King and the armed forces. Once the new Badoglio government had signed an armistice with the Allies in September 1943, the Italians split into three groups: the majority who did not wish to continue the war in anyone's behalf and who surrendered to the Germans, a minority who sided with Germany, and a minority who joined the Allies. Ideology and patriotism now often merged; the anti-Fascists launched partisan warfare, and any patriotic Italian could join the struggle.

Meanwhile, most of Italy, from Naples to the Alps, was immediately taken over by the Germans. In central and northern Italy, partisan bands took to the hills and began to harass the Germans, anticipating a rapid Allied advance from the south to liberate the whole peninsula. Nevertheless, the split between the Communists and non-Communists persisted. The rift ended only in April 1944, when the Communist party leader, Palmiro Togliatti, returned from wartime exile in Moscow proclaiming his willingness to cooperate with Marshal Badoglio, thus postponing the question of the monarchy's future until after the war. Only then the various resistance groups united and entered the Badoglio government.

OTHER RESISTANCE ACTIVITIES

Besides supplying the Allies with most valuable intelligence, fighting as partisans, and sabotaging the Axis war effort in a variety of ways, passive and active, the resistance movement also provided some less spectacular but very useful services. Among them was shelter given to the persecuted minorities, especially the Jews, as well as to Allied secret agents and soldiers escaping from POW and concentration camps. There are no exact statistics as to how many of them were given assistance by the clandestine organizations of occupied Europe. According to the latest conservative estimates, the number exceeds 30,000. POWs were saved and dispatched to Britain to continue the struggle. At least 500 people involved in helping the POWs paid with their lives for these activities.

By far the most important role played by the resistance was psychological. The courageous activities of dedicated groups of people willing to risk their lives to challenge the totalitarian tyranny gave back to the people their self-respect and self-confidence, thus keeping up their morale throughout the war.

By June 1944, when the Allied forces landed in northern France, the western European resistance movements were strong enough to provide them with a great deal of valuable active support. Their sabotaging of roads, harbors, and communications centers seriously hampered German troop movements, while guerrilla bands harassed enemy troops. The Dutch resistance, for instance, warned the British and the Americans of considerable German forces around Arnhem. In Belgium, it was the resistance groups that seized intact the invaluable port facilities of Antwerp. The fact that the Allied commanders often underestimated and even totally overlooked the efforts made on their behalf by the underground movements was another matter. Here the story of Arnhem was a classic example.

In eastern and southeastern Europe the resistance movement from the start assumed the form of fierce opposition to Axis rule. This opposition was far stronger and more widespread than the initially timid resistance the Axis powers encountered in western Europe. The eventual fate of the non-Communist resistance was complicated by the Soviet conquest of all the countries of the area, with the exception of Finland and Greece. The fate of the leaders of the non-Communist underground movements of that part of Europe, however, was, by and large, tragic. Those who did not submit to the new rulers were accused of cooperation with the enemy or with Western intelligence,

A slogan painted by the Polish Resistance on the Warsaw embankment of the Vistula: "Deutschland kaputt 1918–1943"—"Germany finished 1918–1943." The Piłudski Institute, New York

were incarcerated, deported, or even shot by the ruthless Communist masters of the region.

Yet throughout most of Europe the resistance movements had restored national dignity and moral unity and had ensured a smooth transition to the postwar era. Not the least important here was the intellectual effort of some of the best minds of Europe. Among those who joined the ranks of the resistance were such noted writers as Jean-Paul Sartre, Albert Camus, and Simone de Beauvoir in France; Günter Grass, Hans Richter, and Heinrich Boell in Germany; Cesare Pavese, Carlo Levi, and Ignazio Silone in Italy, and Czesław Milosz in Poland. Many of them not only produced anti-Axis propaganda but wrote several literary masterpieces, as well as some seminal works concerning the future of Europe. Most of these works were published only after the war. The role of the intellectuals in maintaining the morale of the respective countries should not be underestimated.

17

The Reconquest of Europe

PREPARING FOR D-DAY

While the Red Army was relentlessly driving toward Königsberg, Warsaw, and Bucharest, the western Allies were getting ready for the long-prepared landing in France. As a result of the Dieppe raid and several other lesser ventures of this kind, the Allies got a better idea of how to break through the German defenses. They devised new kinds of landing craft to disembark heavy equipment, including amphibious flail tanks to beat out mines with whirling chains. Because the intended landing area lacked deep-water ports, two artificial harbors, called Mulberries, were constructed, one each in the American and British attack zones. They also prepared a transchannel fuel pipeline called PLUTO (Pipe Lines Under the Ocean) and landing platforms made of frozen sea water and sawdust. Throughout 1943 and the spring of 1944 the concentration of the Allied forces in the British Isles continued. By June 1944 nearly three million soldiers, sailors, and airmen were ready for the storming of Hitler's Fortress Europe.[1]

Although at the eastern front the German position was getting increasingly weaker, Hitler's position was still strong in the west. With about sixty divisions deployed in France, the Low Countries, Denmark, and Norway, protected by formidable west-wall fortifications, he calmly awaited the Allied invasion. How to counterbalance this advantage and mislead

[1]For the Allied preparations for the Normandy landing see Dwight D. Eisenhower, *Crusade in Europe* (New York: Doubleday, 1948), especially pp. 227–32; and Frederick Morgan, *Overture to Overlord* (London: Hodder and Stoughton, 1950). See also Omar Bradley and Clair Blair, *The General's Story* (New York: Simon & Schuster, 1983), pp. 216–35; and Churchill, *Closing the Ring*, pp. 80–97, 482–96.

Hitler as to the time and place of the invasion was a major problem for the Allied strategists. With thirty-six German divisions concentrated in France alone, there was a danger that the Allied landing units could either be crushed before landing on the beaches or, even if successfully landed, be pushed back into the sea with incalculable consequences for the outcome of the war. To forestall either of these dangers Western intelligence conceived an elaborate deception plan.

At the Teheran conference Winston Churchill said, "In wartime, truth is so precious that she should always be attended by a bodyguard of lies." That is why the deception scheme bore the name *Bodyguard*. The first task of Allied intelligence was to make the German High Command believe that the Allied forces were much larger than they really were. The multiplication of bogus armies was to contribute to this task. Owing to rumors spread by the Allies and false leaks conveyed to Berlin by double agents, Berlin had a distorted picture of the American-British capabilities and plans. On the evening of the invasion Hitler credited the Western Allies with the equivalent of sixty-seven combat divisions, including eight airborne, all ready to strike from Britain. In reality they had fifty-two divisions, of which only thirty-seven were ready for immediate action on the Continent. To keep the Germans guessing and to multiply the apparent options as to the main landing place, and to disperse the enemy forces, two phantom armies were created. One was the First U.S. Army allegedly located in southern England and facing the Pas de Calais; another army was supposedly deployed in Scotland, facing Norway. Two more similar concentrations of troops were conjured in North Africa: one in Algeria and Tunis, facing southern France, and another in Egypt, pretending to be ready to invade Greece.

The well-advertised presence in Devon and Kent of General Patton and his phantom First Army was fundamental to the entire deception scheme. It was this ghost force that constituted the bulk of the contingent allegedly ready to invade the Pas de Calais area. A carefully simulated wireless traffic between Patton's HQ and various Allied Command posts was conducted all the time without too much camouflage, to allow the enemy to intercept the messages rather easily. The presence of another bogus army in Scotland led Hitler to believe that, simultaneously with the attack on France, his enemies would strike against Norway or Denmark or both. This made him retain in those two countries no fewer than seventeen German divisions, while twenty-four divisions were kept in Greece, Bulgaria, and Yugoslavia to face a possible invasion from Egypt.

The Allies had two main options for a landing in northern France. The first was to cross the English Channel at its narrowest point, starting from the Kent-Devon area and landing at the Pas de Calais–Boulogne region. There the main advantage was the short distance, about 20 miles of sea crossing. On the other hand, the disadvantages of this scenario were numerous. First of all, southeastern England had no large, modern harbor suitable for embarkation of a large number of troops with their heavy equipment. Second, the strongest enemy defenses, including the bulk of the Luftwaffe, were concentrated in the Pas de Calais–Boulogne sector, because this was the area that most of the German military leaders considered the likeliest spot to be chosen by the enemy for the invasion.

The second option available to the Allies was to strike from the region of Southampton and Portsmouth to Normandy and land between Cherbourg and Le Havre. There the distance was more than three times longer, but the other disadvantages were remarkably lesser. First of all, the sector east of the mouth of the Seine was not so strongly fortified and was garrisoned with inferior troops. Moreover, this sector was much further from the main supply bases in Germany. Finally, both Portsmouth and Southampton were fairly large, modern harbors and with some improvements could serve as an embarkation and supply base for a large invasion force. That is why the second option was eventually accepted by the Combined Chiefs of Staff.

Besides the strength of the invading forces and the place of their landing, the third vital element of the deception scheme was the timing. Anglo-American intelligence made an enormous effort to advertise through double agents and whispering propaganda the alleged unreadiness of the Allied forces to launch a successful landing before mid-July of 1944. The Germans eagerly swallowed these rumors, because they corresponded to their wishful thinking; Hitler himself grossly underestimated the ability of the Anglo-American leaders to cope with such an enormous undertaking before summer.

General Dwight D. Eisenhower, Supreme Commander of Allied Forces in Europe. National Archives.

GERMAN PREPARATIONS

One of the few German military leaders who was fairly immune to the Allied propaganda and deception schemes was Rommel. After his Tunisian defeat and recovery from his illness, he was in Italy throughout most of 1943. On November 5 Hitler ordered Rommel to France and charged him with the mission of inspecting the anti-invasion preparations. As commander of Army Group B, he would be subordinated to Field Marshal von Rundstedt, Germany's senior serving field marshal and commander in chief of all forces in the west.

The contrast between the two men could not have been greater. While the quickly aging, fatalistically inclined Rundstedt was passively awaiting the imminent blow, immersed in Karl May's adventure stories, Rommel was bursting with energy. Eager to take revenge for North Africa, he now invested all his renewed energy in improving the German defenses. After having inspected the "Atlantic Wall," he at once perceived its weakness and concluded that it represented little that could stop a determined attacker.

On his own initiative Rommel then proceeded to bolster the shore fortifications of that area with all possible obstacles that could abort any attempts at landing. He laid nearly 4 million mines in the shore zone and installed all sorts of traps, including concrete stakes and steel spikes in the coastal waters. Behind these obstacles were a vast network of barbed wire on the beaches and then the bunkers and gun shelters of the Atlantic Wall. Rommel reasoned that at the time of the invasion the German supply lines would be under heavy air bombardment and would not be able to bring forward much gasoline, tanks, guns, or ammunition. Consequently as much as possible should be stored on the spot. At the same time, contrary to Hitler's intentions, Rommel secretly moved some units of his elite Fifteenth Army from the Pas de Calais area to the sector north of Paris; from that region they could be thrown either toward the Channel or toward Normandy.

Rommel's preparations were handicapped, however, by a variety of obstacles.

First of all, the German forces in western Europe had no unified, effective chain of command. Theoretically, Field Marshal von Rundstedt was commander in chief in western Europe. Hitler, however, had excluded from his command Rommel's Army Group B, with its powerful mobile reserves, including the most seasoned armored divisions. Army Group B was to be stationed north of Paris and intervene wherever it would be needed, but on Hitler's personal order only. This dual command was complicated still more by Hitler's habit of bypassing Rundstedt and issuing direct orders to his subordinates, the individual army commanders. To muddle things still more, Goering reserved to himself the exclusive right of controlling the Third Air Fleet deployed in northern France. To top the confusion one must add the fact that Rundstedt and Rommel had completely different perceptions of the enemy's intentions and clashing concepts about how to defend northern France. Rommel was convinced that the Allies would try to land in Normandy; Rundstedt opted rather for the Pas de Calais–Boulogne sector.

Rommel, normally an exponent of extreme mobility, this time was ready to abandon this type of warfare because he was afraid that the overwhelming Allied air superiority would prevent the German armor from moving quickly from one critical point to another, at least in daylight. He reasoned that once the enemy had secured a firm foothold, the German defenders would be at a great disadvantage because of the lack of air support. He argued that the only way to stop the intruders was to prevent them from landing at all. Consequently, he suggested concentration of most of the available reserves along the rugged coastline of Normandy.

OPERATION OVERLORD

The landing in Normandy, or Operation Overlord, was a gigantic undertaking. The first invading wave of twelve divisions was to be transported with their supplies in 702 warships and over 9,000 craft of all kinds. Technical ingenuity made important contributions to the success of the operation. Tanks were provided with devices to clear paths through mine fields; two artificial harbors compensated for the lack of a major natural port at the outset, and oil was carried across the Channel by PLUTO. Airborne troops were to be in the vanguard. Frogmen were to reconnoiter the landing beaches; specially designed landing craft were to ferry men and tanks ashore.

No successful invasion was possible without establishing complete air superiority. The amphibious landings in North Africa and Italy, as well as in the Pacific, proved that a dominant sea power had not lost its old advantage of providing mobility on the condition that naval forces were adequately supported by air power. In Normandy the Allies tried to fulfill all the requirements. They were to prove capable of landing strong forces in any one of a number of different places, to prevent enemy interference by sea, to give close support from the guns of the fleet both on the beaches and further inland, and to provide adequate air cover to the entire operation.

Beginning in March 1944, the Allied strategic air force was ordered to shift part of its bombers to the transportation system of northern France. The purpose was to destroy, as much as possible, the German supply and communications lines behind the forces defending the Western Wall. The round-the-clock bombardment was so intense that by the spring the Germans could move their troops only at night. Even high-ranking German commanders, traveling to their staff conferences, avoided daylight. One of the notable achievements of the Allied air offensive on the eve of the invasion was the destruction of railways, bridges, and roads. Meanwhile, the systematic bombardment of synfuel factories also continued to destroy German oil reserves. In May 1944 Albert Speer observed in a memorandum submitted to Hitler that "the enemy has struck us at one of our weakest points. If they persist this time, we will soon have no longer any fuel production worth mentioning." The total reserve of aviation fuel in May 1944 was only 400,000 tons.

The fatal lack of oil, combined with the crippling of the French communication network, affected mobility of every branch of the German forces. Although nearly 800 propeller-driven fighters were supplied to the western front in the first fortnight of the invasion, Air Fleet III was never able to challenge the Allied command of the air. Besides its numerical inferiority and the shortage of fuel, the Luftwaffe was hampered by the disruption of its ground organization; it was partly due to the Allied bombing and partly to the activities of the French resistance movement bolstered by considerable supplies of weapons and explosives from Britain. By the spring of 1944 the Allied air mastery over the French skies was far advanced. The same was true of the adjacent waters.

Another absolute precondition of a successful invasion was control of the English Channel and the waters west of it. Within a month or so after D-day, eighteen out of forty-three German submarines that had taken part in the attacks on the invasion forces were sunk. To protect the shores of northern France, von Rundstedt had deposited a broad belt of mines along the English Channel; Rommel multiplied their numbers. Thanks to Enigma, however, the Allies were well informed about the structure of the belt and the gaps left in it by the Germans for their own traffic and coastal convoys.

Another vital precondition of a successful invasion was favorable weather conditions. A storm or even a gale wind could wreck the whole enterprise within a few hours. By mid-May Eisenhower had decided that the landing would have to take place either on June 5, 6, or 7, because of the late-rising moon and a low tide on those days. The moon and the tide were both vital for a successful invasion. Consequently, to combine these two meteorological preconditions was one of Eisenhower's major preoccupations. The paratroopers of the 82nd and 101st U.S. divisions and the 6th British Brigade were to be dropped at night, to act as pathfinders for the main landing force; the airborne troops needed moonlight for a successful airdrop, but they also required darkness until they were right over their respective drop zones. Thus, the need for a late moon was of vital importance. At the same time, the seaborne landing had to be

June 5, 1944: General Eisenhower chats with paratroopers of the 82nd US airborne division about to be dropped in Normandy to act as pathfinders of the main Allied invading force.
National Archives

done at low tide so the underwater German beach obstacles would be exposed. If the invasion were to be postponed again, it would be delayed until there was a favorable tide. The next possible date, June 19, was a moonless night, and this would greatly handicap the airborne troops.

The first days of June were stormy. The data from the North American continent and Greenland showed the weather dissolving into a series of disturbing low-pressure centers that were unmatched in the historical records of the past fifty years. As a result, the Normandy beaches, ravaged by tidal waves, were rendered unusable for landing. The Allied meteorological officers were unable to agree on how the lows would develop. By June 4, data from observers in the Atlantic convinced them that the weather would not be suitable for the fifth but possibly acceptable for the sixth. Yet Eisenhower's meteorological adviser ventured an optimistic prediction for June 6. A series of decoded Ultra messages convinced Eisenhower that the Germans were anticipating continued bad weather and would not expect the invasion before the end of June or the beginning of July. Eisenhower staked his decision on this opinion and on June 5 issued the historic order: "Let's go!" This was a momentous decision, probably one of the most important ever taken in modern history. The die was cast.

HITLER TAKEN OFF GUARD

For Hitler, the invasion of western Europe was both his great danger and his great opportunity, a decisive moment in the war. He calculated that if he could push the invaders back into the sea, they would not try again for a very long time, if ever. A decisive victory on the beaches would free at least fifty German divisions for the Russian front. This could allow him to stop the Soviet westward drive and, perhaps, turn threatened disaster into a German victory, or at least a stalemate. Such a double success might force the Allies to forget the unconditional surrender and negotiate a compromise peace.

Yet from the very beginning everything seemed to be conspiring against Hitler. Because of persistent bad-weather reports for the next few days, a number of high-ranking German officers went on leave. Rommel, for instance, took leave on June 4 and went home, near Ulm, to attend his wife's birthday party, while General Speidel, his Chief of Staff, was left in charge of the crucial Army Group B. The two officers at the next level of command below were also absent from their posts on the night of the invasion: General Friedrich Dollman, commander of the Seventh Army stationed in Normandy, was attending the war games at Rennes; Joseph "Sepp" Dietrich, commander of the crack fifteenth S.S. Panzer Corps, was in Brussels visiting his girlfriend. Consequently at the most critical moment of the invasion, the German chain of command was thoroughly dislocated.

On the morning of June 6, just before the Allied landing, Hitler went to bed at his Berchtesgaden retreat, after having issued a strict order not to be disturbed until mid-afternoon. Consequently, when the Allies struck barely one hour later, the confusion that followed in the high echelons of the German High Command was extreme. Rundstedt kept on believing that the Normandy landing was merely a decoy and decided to wait for the real thing. Even if he wanted to rush the mobile reserves of Army Group B to Normandy, he could not do it without Hitler's personal order. Such an order was impossible to obtain as long as Hitler was asleep and nobody dared to awaken him. When General Guenther Blummentrit, Rundstedt's Chief of Staff, asked the GHQ to release Army Group B, General Jodl, Hitler's Chief of Staff, refused either to do so on his own responsibility or to awaken the Führer.[2]

When Hitler finally got up around 4 P.M.

[2]For the German point of view see B. H. Liddell Hart, *The German Generals Talk,* pp. 227–58; see also Warlimont, *Inside Hitler's Headquarters,* pp. 222–460.

and learned about the Normandy landing, he concluded that it must be a decoy—a trap designed by the Allies to commit the bulk of his forces at the wrong spot. When he wanted to consult Rommel, he was told that he had left his command post on home leave. When Rommel finally got in touch with Hitler, the Führer allowed only a part of Army Group B to be rushed toward Normandy, retaining the rest in case of the expected main Allied landing in the Pas de Calais area. Trying to contact the commander of the Normandy defenses, Rommel learned that he was attending military exercises in Brittany. When Rommel telephoned the commander of the Fifteenth Panzer Corps, the main battering ram of Army Group B, it was revealed that the latter had gone to Belgium. Thus, the Allies benefited from an almost incredible series of favorable coincidences.

The fatal blow fell where Hitler least expected it and earlier than he had anticipated, and the attack came at a time when the German chain of command was in chaos. Consequently, all major preconditions of strategic surprise were present. The Allies, fighting for a toehold on the beaches of Normandy, instead of facing three armored divisions, had to cope with little more than a few panzer battalions and fortress troops, supported by scattered reserve units.

THE BATTLE OF THE BEACHES

The Allied invasion of western Europe had three distinct phases. The first was the battle of the beaches, or the attempt to establish a foothold in Normandy; this phase lasted for a week or so, until mid-June. The second phase consisted of the successful breakout from the narrow bridgeheads in order to destroy the Seventh German Army defending the Normandy peninsula; this stage occupied most of June and July to mid-August and ended with the battle of Falaise-Avranche. The third phase was to include a sweep around Paris and finish with the drive toward the Rhine, to be achieved by September 1944.

The first wave of Allied landing forces consisted of two armies: the First U.S. and the Second British, altogether twelve divisions. Assembled offshore, they sailed from the embarkation harbors and then landed on June 6 on a sector of some 50 miles west of Le Havre and east of Cherbourg, on five beaches: Utah, Omaha, Gold, June, and Sword. The first two beaches were assigned to the United States forces, the last three to the British. The first stage was the most crucial: Without establishing themselves firmly on these beaches and expanding their bridgeheads to allow the reinforcements to land, the Allied troops could not survive for long.

Despite their overall inferiority, the Germans, protected by their fortifications, fought with unexpected vigor and skill. Consequently, the vital battle of the beaches, which the Allies had expected to last only a day or two, dragged on for at least four days until June 10. German tenacity clashed against Allied superiority in practically everything—firepower, tanks, and planes. The Wehrmacht soldiers, however, continued to fight as savagely as a wounded animal at bay. They were helped by the storms that followed the landing and destroyed many Allied installations, including the artificial harbors. The German soldiers were taking pride in their reputation as indomitable fighters who did not surrender without firing the last round of ammunition. The fierceness of the German resistance was reflected in high casualties on both sides. The Germans were infused with a sense of desperation by Dr. Goebbel's propaganda, which identified the unconditional surrender and the postwar plan with the alleged Allied resolve to destroy the German nation as such.[3]

---

[3]In September 1944 the U.S. secretary of the treasury, Henry Morgenthau, presented to President Roosevelt an economic plan for Germany after its defeat. The plan called for either destruction or removal, as war reparation, of most of the country's heavy industry to make any German rearmament impossible. Germany was to become an agricultural or "pastoralized" nation.

June 6, 1944: unloading of supplies for the Allied forces. National Archives

Despite technical inferiority, the Germans succeeded in causing a near disaster on Omaha beach. Overlooked by cliffs and bluffs, this most arduous sector was assigned to the United States troops. At other much easier beaches, the resistance was less tough. Yet, in one day the Allied losses totaled roughly 10,000 killed and injured and the Germans lost up to 9,000 men. Winston Churchill's gloomy visions of the Channel "awash with corpses" failed to materialize thanks only to the surprise effect and the formidable material superiority of the Allies.

By the end of June more than half the fighters sent by Goering to France were destroyed, and the supply of replacements was drying up because of the resumed bombing of German aircraft factories. In the middle of June, the U.S. Eighth Air Force also renewed its day attacks against the synthetic oil plants. A week after D-day the third largest synfuel plant, in Gelsenkirchen, ceased operations as a result of night raids by RAF bombers. Total production of aviation gasoline for June came to 53,000 tons compared with 175,000 in April. Despite this warning about the impending offensive against oil, German fighters offered no resistance whatever when the Americans bombed the several oil refineries on June 18. Goering's night fighters were now increasingly grounded for want of fuel. Subsequent attacks were opposed, but with little success. By the spring of 1945 the once formidable Luftwaffe was practically helpless.[4]

Finally, thanks largely to the overwhelming Allied air superiority, the British and American troops, after four days of the most bloody of struggles, did manage to break out of the narrow coastal zone and expand their foothold. This allowed their aviation to operate from French soil and thus provide more effective close support for further land operations. After having established themselves on the beaches, the Allies proceeded to push toward the capital and chief port of Normandy, Cherbourg. This opened the second phase of the invasion: the fight against the Seventh German Army defending Normandy.

---

[4]For the story of its dramatic development and decline, woven around the life of one of its architects, Marshal Erhard Milch, see David Irving, *The Rise and Fall of the Lufwaffe* (London: Widenfeld and Nicolson, 1973).

THE BATTLE OF NORMANDY

The task was to be executed by the U.S. First Army, under General Omar Bradley. The conquest of Normandy was facilitated by the fact that Hitler and Rundstedt still continued to believe that the Normandy landing was a decoy—merely a prelude to the main assault that was still to come in the Pas de Calais area. Both of them stuck to their preconceived notion that the landing was merely a trap—a simulated attempt to threaten Cherbourg and to divert German attention from the ultimate goal of the whole operation, Paris. They calculated that the forces now ashore in Normandy must eventually link up with the main invasion yet to come in the Pas de Calais. To meet the Allied blow at that area Hitler was determined to keep the Fifteenth Army north of the Seine to guard Paris, the launching pads of the V-weapons, and finally the road to the Ruhr. The Seventh Army must deal with the landings in Normandy with its own resources, only slightly strengthened by whatever Rundstedt could share from his reserves. Eventually, only one battalion of Tiger tanks and an anti-aircraft brigade were sent to reinforce the Seventh Army in Normandy.

Although the Seventh Army had only one panzer division, the American progress in Normandy was painfully slow because of the difficult terrain favoring defense and the toughness of the German resistance. The intensely cultivated small plots of land, often separated by stone walls and high hedgerows or thick dirt banks with thorn bushes growing on the top, placed the burden of fighting on the infantry. In the *bocage* country American tanks and infantry became snarled among the hedgerows, which forced the tanks to operate only on the roads. The enemy fiercely defended every inch of ground. Daily gains were often measured in yards. Not until the Allied tanks were provided with new hedgerow-cutting devices could a more rapid advance be made.

The crucial port of Cherbourg was enveloped by the Americans only by June 21. When its German commander, General Dollman, asked Berlin for permission to withdraw, he received an order typical of Hitler's mentality: "Even if worse comes to worst, it is your duty to defend the last bunker and leave the enemy not a harbor but a heap of ruins." After six days of siege, Cherbourg fell on June 27. This finally gave the Allies a natural deep-water port from which to unload supplies.

Because the British on the west faced fairly open country more favorable to tanks,

Tanks of the US First Army of General Bradley push toward Cherbourg. National Archives

the Germans concentrated the bulk of the panzers against them. Caen, capital of the province of Basse-Normandie and seat of the duchy from which William the Conqueror had started his campaign against England in 1066, was Montgomery's main target. On June 25, even before the fall of Cherbourg, he moved on Caen from the south. The enemy resistance proved too strong, and the attack was repelled. In early July, after the RAF and the U.S. Eighth Air Force carpeted Caen with bombs, the British made another attempt to take the historic city but succeeded only partially. Only the third attack, launched on July 18, was crowned with success, and the rest of the ruined city was finally captured. Soon, however, the British advance bogged down when heavy rain turned the ground into a sea of mire.

A CHANGE OF COMMAND

By the end of June it became obvious that the Germans had lost the vital battle of the beaches. On June 29 Rommel suggested to Hitler that the Seventh Army should withdraw to the Seine, and that the armies in southern France should be redeployed to create a new line along the Seine and across to the Swiss border. If the Wehrmacht did not begin to withdraw from Normandy immediately, Rommel argued, the remnants of the Seventh Army would be destroyed, and the Fifteenth Army would be powerless alone to repulse any further Allied offensive. Yet Hitler ordered them to fight for every inch of soil.

His plans outran his resources, however. General Hugo Sperrle, commanding Air Fleet III, pointed out that he would need "an additional 1,200 to 1,400 fighters, if the supply routes to Normandy were to be defended." The total day-fighter strength of the Luftwaffe on all fronts was only 1,523, and only one-third of these were stationed in France. Nevertheless, Hitler stuck to his plan, with promises about miraculous weapons and repeated his standing order to "hold out in all circumstances." After this conference, Rundstedt and Rommel returned to France angry and disgruntled; reluctant as they were, they were committed

Allied Invasions of Europe, 1944-1945

to a policy of unyielding defense, the futility of which was more apparent than ever.

On July 1 Rundstedt warned Keitel that the situation was hopeless and advised opening peace negotiations. Hitler's reaction was not surprising. He dismissed Rundstedt and replaced him with the robust and hitherto more aggressive Field Marshal Hans Gunther von Kluge. In 1940 Kluge had commanded the Fourth Army first in the brilliant breakthrough to the Channel and in 1941 in the daring drive to Moscow. In the next two years, as commander in chief of Army Group Center, he had gained Hitler's confidence by accepting his orders without hesitation. By 1944, however, even Kluge doubted whether victory was possible. At this crucial moment Rommel was badly injured when an Allied fighter machine-gunned his staff car and he was taken to a hospital. Hitler replaced him by General Walter Model, "the Führer's Fireman" on the eastern front and another of his most trusted men, endowed with talent for improvisation. With this new team and several aces up his sleeve, Hitler was still hopeful of mastering the critical situation.[5]

HITLER'S SECRET WEAPONS

Hitler's hopes were based not only on his expectations of a split in the Grand Alliance but also on a series of "secret weapons." Among them were new jet-propelled fighters and, above all, two types of V-rockets.

The *V* stood for *Vergeltung,* which meant vengeance. The V1 rocket was actually a jet-powered pilotless plane loaded with a ton of explosives; it carried a one-ton warhead 152 miles at about 400 miles per hour. In flight it produced a characteristic noise, so that it was known also as the buzz bomb. The V2 rockets were much more sophisticated forerunners of the long-range ballistic missiles of our day; they carried a tank of liquid oxygen, which allowed them to fly above the earth's atmosphere, and were aimed from fixed positions, like long-range artillery. There was no effective defense against the V2 rockets once they were launched. With these two "secret weapons" Hitler planned to turn Britain into a heap of ruins and then chase the Allied armies from the Continent.

On June 13, seven days after the Normandy landing, the first four flying bombs hit London destroying several buildings and killing nine civilians. Soon thousands of them followed, causing temporary panic. The V1 was plagued, however, by an unreliable guidance system, and fewer than one-fifth of the 8,340 fired on England ever reached their intended target. Only 2,340 hit the Greater London area, while about 4,000 were destroyed by the Allied air forces or their artillery. The V1 frightened the civilian population but didn't break its morale; nor did it stop the progress of the Allied troops in France. Only some 1,100 of the V2 missiles hit Britain because of their faulty launching mechanism. They caused a great deal of destruction, killing over 2,000 people, but this was not sufficient to break the morale of the British people.

The main trouble with both V-weapons was that they came too late. By granting priority to conventional weapons, with which Hitler hoped to win the war quickly, he delayed assembly-line production of the rockets. This was especially true of the potentially very dangerous V2s, against which the Allies had few defenses. Yet when they were eventually hastily mass produced, they could have no decisive effect on the war's final outcome.

In September 1944 another of Hitler's secret weapons appeared on the front line. It was the world's first jet fighter, the Messerschmitt 262, some 120 miles per hour faster than the best Allied planes and more maneuverable than anything his enemies had at their disposal. But the jet fighter also came too late and was not produced in sufficient quantity. Even the devastating Allied raid on Hamburg, at the end of July 1943, failed to jolt Hitler into giving priority to the new fighter planes.

---

[5]For Hitler's strategy in France in 1944 see Trevor-Roper, *From Blitzkrieg to Defeat,* pp. 161–80.

He still insisted that offense, not defense, was the Luftwaffe's main task and ordered the Me262 to be converted into a high-speed bomber. Had Hitler used all his secret weapons and most of his tanks at the time of the Normandy landing, all of them concentrated on the invading force, the course of history might have been reversed.

AN ATTEMPT ON HITLER'S LIFE

The second phase of the battle of Normandy was profoundly affected by the July 20 attempt on Hitler's life. The plot was overwhelmingly the work of a small group of senior army officers, mostly of aristocratic origin. The *Kriegsmarine* and the Luftwaffe were not involved at all. The investigation of the plot revealed that the Abwehr, or military intelligence, had provided the plotters with most of the elements necessary for carrying out their task. The extensive purges that followed gave to Himmler an opportunity not only to get even with his competitors, such as Admiral Canaris and General Oster, but also to finally extend S.S. control over all branches of military intelligence. In general, the army's upper echelons were radically purged. Several thousand Wehrmacht officers were arrested and tried; those convicted of treason were executed. There were also numerous cases of suicide among the senior officers involved in the conspiracy. They included Generals von Kluge and Ludwig Beck. Rommel was a special case. He was neither aristocratic nor as deeply committed to the plot as the other conspirators. Himmler, who hated him, conveniently provided Hitler with additional incriminating evidence that definitely implicated Rommel in the plot. Hitler, who wanted to avoid executing a popular hero, gave Rommel the choice of a cyanide capsule or facing trial and execution. Rommel took the capsule.

Despite the mental and physical shock resulting from the injuries he suffered on July 20, Hitler remained determined to continue the war. Now he controlled Ger-many's destiny more firmly than ever. T mass of German people still failed to see the ruin at the end of the road down which they were being marched. Actually, his popularity was enhanced by the plot. His position was unchallengeable. Most party leaders knew that their fate was bound to his. Most generals knew that the war was lost, but they had no power to end it. Frightened by the aftermath of the plot, they tried to outdo each other in obsequiousness and tried to carry out his orders with slavish obedience. As an outward symptom of their loyalty they promptly replaced the traditional military salute with the Nazi "Heil Hitler!" shout, accompanied with an outstretched right arm.

The decline of the military was paralleled by the rise of Himmler. In the wake of the July 20 plot, his power mushroomed. In addition to being head of the S.S., the secret police and the state police, head of the entire intelligence apparatus since April 1944, supervisor of the Nazi racial policy as "Reichskommissar for the Strengthening of Germanism," and master of many sections of the armaments industry, he commanded thirty-eight Waffen S.S. divisions. Now Himmler was the second most powerful man in Germany.

THE LATTER PHASES OF THE BATTLE

The capture of Cherbourg the end of June
was another stepping ie in the second
battle of Europe. By nents the beaches were
secure, and reinfo were steadily
flowing to north rance for a push toward Paris. A western end was the
British Secon ny, commanded by General Sir Mile empsey; at the eastern end
was the U Army under General Omar
Bradley der these two armies made up
the T rst Army Group under Mont-
gom overall ground forces com-
m r the invasion. On July 23 the
First Army was created, composed
Canadian divisions and one Polish
d division, to come under Montgom-
army command. On August 1 the U.S.

Third Army under General Patton became operational and with the First U.S. Army formed the Twelfth Army Group under Bradley. Since the American divisions were bigger and better equipped than the rest of the Allied forces, the United States contingent represented by far a more formidable Allied force. The overall command was still firmly in the hands of General Eisenhower.

On July 26 Bradley launched an offensive along St. Lo-Perrier road, promptly achieving a breakthrough. Now, using the newly arrived Patton's Third Army, the Americans raced past Avranches and broke into open country. Thus, the gateway to the heart of France would be opened, provided the Allies could destroy the remnants of the German Seventh Army, meanwhile reinforced by various elements, especially Army Group B, finally sent there by Hitler. The hard core of the German forces was formed by four crack panzer divisions. Elementary strategy required a prompt German withdrawal from Normandy and Brittany eastward, toward Paris, in order to shorten and consolidate a front too extended to be defensible. Establishment of a more solid line somewhere in the center of France, perhaps on the Seine, was by then an urgent necessity. This was the opinion of most German military experts. But the Führer instead ordered the reinforced Seventh Army to counterattack westward through Mortain to Avranches. His objective was to cut the United States corridor in two, and then inflict another Dunkirk on his enemies. This was sheer folly in view of the decisive overall Allied superiority, especially in the air. The German generals, however, intimidated by the aftermath of the July 20 plot, hardly dared to protest against another folly of the Führer.

Trying to upset Bradley's offensive, the Germans launched a desperate counterattack in the direction of Avranches on August 7. They persisted for five days, yet succeeded only in slightly penetrating the American lines. The main body of the U.S. First Army absorbed the brunt of the German drive at Mortain and eventually managed to repel all the enemy attacks. Meanwhile, around the German wedge a trap was being formed. While the British Second Army contained the enemy on the west, the Canadian First Army moved southeast from Caen toward Falaise. By August 16 the British and United States forces in the north and Patton's troops from the south had squeezed the Germans into a pocket between Falaise and Argentan. From August 16 to 21 the Allies tightened their grip on the pocket, which contained the remnants of nearly twenty enemy divisions, but failed to capture or destroy all its forces. The enemy

Tank crewmen of the First Polish Armored division capture German soldiers at the battle of the Falaise gap. The Piłsudski Institute New York

units were still pouring through the gap around Falaise, and then westward toward Paris.

The First Polish Armored division was chosen to plug the Falaise gap. The division fought bravely to halt the retreating Germans but could not cope with the overwhelming pressure of the elite enemy units. The proud German veterans struggled with fury, skill, and the desperation of people fighting for their survival. Although thousands of Germans were killed and wounded and over 50,000 captured, some of the badly battered remnants of trapped divisions did escape westward to rejoin their comrades still entrenched in central and southern France.

The reasons for the escape of a considerable number of Germans through the Falaise gap have been one of the major controversial problems of World War II. American historians lay a good share of the blame on Montgomery's sluggishness and his reluctance to press with more vigor against the trapped enemy. British historians have tried to shift the blame onto Bradley, who had allegedly failed to explain to Montgomery his decision to send General Patton with most of his forces on a long drive against the Germans' ultimate line of escape rather than concentrating on the Germans in the pocket. The dispute is still on and is likely to remain unresolved.[6]

TOWARD PARIS

Meanwhile on August 15 the Allied forces had also landed in southern France (Operation Anvil). The U.S. Seventh Army, commanded by General Alexander Patch, struck between Toulon and Cannes against weak enemy opposition. With the French contingents in the vanguard under General de Lattre de Tassigny, the invading forces captured Toulon and Marseilles, taking 47,000 POWs. On August 29 Patch embarked on the trek north to establish contact with Patton's Third Army, which was pushing toward the Rhine. There was a long and bitter strategic argument over Operation Anvil. Eisenhower insisted on Anvil for two main reasons: first, to capture the ports of Toulon and Marseilles, vital for the logistic supply of his armies; and second, to get General Patch's Seventh Army, deployed on his southern flank for a vigorous drive toward the Rhine.

The British Chiefs of Staff opposed the American scheme because troops for Anvil would have to be taken from the Italian front, which they considered vital; they still hoped to pursue the Allied offensive to Trieste and then through the Ljubljana gap to Budapest and Vienna to be there ahead of the Russians. To save east-central Europe from the Red Army and enlarge a buffer of independent states on the Continent was still Churchill's pet idea. Eisenhower ignored Churchill's high-strategy considerations and stuck to his "purely military" reasoning and won once again. The American materiel preponderance made Eisenhower's points of view increasingly influential.

Meanwhile General de Gaulle, who had been denied by Washington and London the right of being the first of the leaders of the free world to set foot on his native soil, did land in France soon after D-day. The reaction of the French people was unmistakable: Most of them, whatever their previous opinions, welcomed the General and his Free French contingents enthusiastically. Both President Roosevelt and Prime Minister Churchill considered him a "self-appointed Joan of Arc" but had to respect the will of the French people. The President had declared: "I am perfectly willing to have de Gaulle made president, or emperor, or king or anything else so long as the action comes in an untrammeled and unforced way from the French people themselves."

Paris was originally regarded as a mar-

---

[6]The American point of view was most strongly stated in Bradley, *A General's Life,* pp. 294–95 and 293–306. For the British argument see John Keegan, *Six Armies in Normandy, From D-Day to the Liberation of Paris, June 6th–August 25th, 1944* (New York: Viking Penguin, 1982), pp. 249–80.

General Charles de Gaulle leaves the Notre Dame cathedral in Paris after a thanksgiving service.
National Archives

ginal military target. Eisenhower's original plan had not been to liberate it by battle but to surround it and then to force the Germans to surrender the city and capture it intact if possible. His plans were upset, however, by the impatience of the leaders of the French resistance. An uprising that had erupted in Paris on August 19 as a result of a series of riots and strikes gathered force day by day. "Citizens, take up arms," proclaimed the leaflets distributed by the local resistance leaders. Soon street fighting broke out in Paris and reached such proportions that a change of operational plans was urgently requested by General de Gaulle. Eisenhower agreed reluctantly, and General Jacques Philippe Leclerc, with his Second French Armored Division in the vanguard, was dispatched toward Paris to rescue the embattled city. "Hold on, we're coming," Leclerc wired to the leaders of the uprising.

Paris was liberated on August 25 by the Leclerc division, supported by United States troops. Despite Hitler's orders to the contrary, the German commander of Paris, General Ditrich von Choltitz, surrendered the French capital without destroying the city's historic monuments. Of those who died in the liberation of Paris, 901 were members of the organized resistance squads and 582 were civilians. Soon the French provisional government, headed by de Gaulle, began to lay down the foundation of a new administration and new French armed forces.

THE SOVIET DRIVE WESTWARD

While the Western Allies were storming Hitler's European fortress, the Russians were continuing their relentless drive westward. In 1944 the German army in the east suffered another series of catastrophes. In January the Russians struck at the Wehrmacht's thirty divisions at the Leningrad and Novgorod sectors and smashed the enemy's defenses on the northern sector of the front. By the end of the month the Red Army was already heading straight toward the Baltic, thus isolating the heavily outnumbered Finnish contingents in the north. In June the weight of the Soviet assault was shifted northward, and the Mannerheim line was broken. The Finns, once more, were compelled to sue for peace. By September 1944 Finland was out of the war. Since the armistice terms provided for Finnish military cooperation with the Red Army, they were compelled to chase the German contingents from their territory. After Italy, Finland, Rumania and Bulgaria also changed sides.

South of the Baltic-Finnish sector of the front, timing its offensive to coincide with the third anniversary of Hitler's attack, the Red Army had hurled its massed 118 infantry divisions, supported by 43 tank brigades, against Army Group Center. Within a few days the German front was riddled along the upper Dnieper. By the end of June the German defenses of the central front had cracked wide open. When the Red Army smashed Army Group Center, it achieved its most spectacular single military success of the war. For the German front in the east it was a catastrophe greater than that of Stalingrad or Kursk. On July 4, when the battle of Belorussia ended, the Red Army had torn a 250-mile gap in the hub of the German front, and Army Group Center was left with eight scattered divisions. The three German armies defending the hub of the front had lost over 130,000 men killed, 66,000 taken prisoner, 900 tanks, and thousands of motor vehicles. The way for the Red Army into Poland lay open.[7]

As Army Group Center practically collapsed, the reverberations made themselves felt across the eastern front, from the Baltic to the Balkans. By that time Soviet manpower was overwhelming: The Red Army facing the Wehrmacht had nearly 5 million men organized in more than 300 divisions, with 31,000 field guns, 5,200 tanks, and 6,000 aircraft, whereas all the remaining Axis soldiers on the eastern front numbered some 2 million men organized in fewer than 200 divisions, most of them decimated and with few tanks or artillery. The Red Army was now in a position to ram the German forces as far back as Warsaw and even beyond.

While the Western Allies were making slow progress in Italy and France, the Red Army rapidly pushed through eastern and central Poland and by the end of July reached the Vistula. All the time the Soviet propaganda had urged the Poles to rise to help the Red Army. When an uprising did break out in Warsaw, on August 1, 1944, the commander of the First Belorussian Front, Marshal Konstantin Rokossovsky, on Stalin's order, stopped the advance toward the Vistula.[8]

While the uprising in Warsaw went on for sixty-three days, the Red Army remained almost inactive, passively watching as the flower of the Polish resistance movement was crushed and the city utterly ruined.

[7]For the discussion of the collapse of the German defense system of the central front see John Erickson, *The Road to Berlin,* pp. 224–30.

[8]For the Warsaw uprising see J. M. Ciechanowski, *The Warsaw Rising* (Cambridge: Cambridge University Press, 1974) and J. K. Zawodny, *Nothing but Honor: The Story of the Warsaw Uprising* (Stanford, Calif: Hoover Institute Press, 1978); see also Henri Michel, *Et Varsovie fut detruite* (Paris: Albin Michel, 1984), especially pp. 249–351.

Three Warsaw insurgents with weapons captured from the Germans. The Piłsudski Institute, New York

Meanwhile the Soviet Army advanced in a spectacular way on other sectors, especially in the Balkans. By deliberately delaying his offensive on the utterly shattered central sector of the front for political reasons, Stalin missed a great strategic opportunity: The opportunity to march toward Berlin and capture it by the autumn of 1944 was skipped to make sure that the bulk of the non-Communist forces of Poland were destroyed. This would facilitate the task of the Communist-dominated "Polish Committee of National Liberation" to dominate the country.

When, after the war, General Eisenhower visited Poland, Arthur Bliss Lane, the United States ambassador in Warsaw, noted in his memoir: "I showed General Eisenhower through an arch which was still standing, a magnificent view of the Vistula River below and Praga beyond. I explained to him that during the insurrection of 1944 this part of town had been initially held by the Polish Home Army, which was daily expecting the Soviets to join forces with them from the other side. Emphasizing that he was speaking purely as a soldier, the general observed, 'What a perfect bridgehead!' "[9]

In September–October 1944, an uprising in Slovakia broke out. It was directed as much against the Germans as against the local Fascist regime. Like the Warsaw insurrection, the Slovak upsurge had also been encouraged by Moscow but was eventually let down by the Russians; in both cases they were eager to see the non-Communist resistance forces exterminated by the Germans, which would facilitate the future Soviet takeover of Czechoslovakia. The Soviet encouragement of the Warsaw and Slovak uprisings and the subsequent double inaction of the Red Army were reflections of Stalin's determination to deal only with people subordinated to him. Although Washington and London resented the increasingly independent, highhanded, and even occasionally openly hostile Soviet behavior, they bent over backward to patch up the mounting obstacles to the preservation of at least a façade of Allied unity.[10]

THE BALKANS

The Soviet drive toward the Balkans was highly successful. The first German vassal state to be occupied by the Red Army was Rumania. There the Fascist and pro-Nazi regime of Marshal Antonescu had been overthrown by a domestic revolt with encouragement from King Michael. He not only surrendered his country to the Russians on August 23 but also declared war on Germany. The traditionally pro-Russian Bulgarians, who had never been in a state of war with the USSR, were not anxious to capitulate to the Western Allies. To prevent the possibility, Moscow declared war on Bulgaria on September 5, 1944. Thus the reluctant Bulgarians were compelled to surrender to the approaching Russians alone.

The Bulgarian capitulation jeopardized the German garrisons in Greece, and they had to be hastily evacuated. Pushing rapidly westward, the Red Army had achieved a linkup with the Yugoslav Partisans of Marshal Tito, who had meanwhile liberated most of their country by their own efforts. On October 20 the Soviet troops of Marshal Fyodor Tolbukhin and Yugoslav troops of Marshal Tito jointly entered Belgrade. Soon the triumphant Tito established a Communist-dominated administration throughout the country, disregarding King Peter and his government in London.

In Hungary the Soviet progress was less impressive because of stiff German resistance. There, on October 15, the regent, Admiral Miklós Horthy, tried to surrender his country first to the Western Allies and

[9]Arthur Bliss Lane, *I Saw Poland Betrayed: An Ambassador Reports to the American People* (Indianapolis: Bobbs-Merrill, 1948), p. 177.

[10]For an illustration of outright Soviet hostility toward the United States Air Force unit stationed on Soviet soil see Glenn B. Infield, *The Poltava Affair. A Russian Warning; An American Tragedy* (New York: Macmillan, 1973), passim.

only then to the Soviets. His attempts were frustrated, however, by the local Fascist movement known as the Arrow Cross. With German support the Arrow Cross staged a revolt, and Horthy was imprisoned. The Arrow Cross made a desperate, ruthless effort to bolster the country's defenses by terror and by forced mobilization of all the remaining resources of Hungary.

Despite this, during the late autumn and winter of 1944 the Red Army pushed relentlessly to the heart of Hungary and besieged Budapest. Meanwhile a pro-Soviet Hungarian coalition government was set up in Debrecen with the participation of local Communists. On January 20, 1945, the new government signed an armistice with Moscow and declared war on Germany. Thus by the close of 1944 Hitler had lost all his vassal states. Now he stood alone fighting a desperate delaying struggle on three fronts, preparing to defend the German heartland of his former continental empire.

THE END OF THE SECOND BATTLE OF FRANCE

By the end of August 1944, after the liberation of Paris, four Allied thrusts raced eastward toward the Low Countries and the Rhine. In the extreme north the Canadian First Army trapped the Germans in a pocket below Le Havre and Rouen and sealed off the garrison of Dieppe on August 22. To the south of the Canadians Montgomery's Second Army moved northeast across the Seine between Rouen and Paris and captured Amiens on August 31. Meanwhile in the central sector the U.S. First Army also advanced across the Seine and then drove eastward across the Marne and Aisne, taking Laon and Sedan. Advancing at a pace of 20 to 50 miles a day, the Allies bypassed many sealed-off enemy pockets. This was especially true of the ports of Bordeaux, St. Nazaire, Boulogne, Calais, and Ostend. All of them were stubbornly defended by their German garrisons. By August 31 the Americans had crossed the Belgian border and continued to keep moving with great speed. Bypassing Paris from the south, Patton's armor overran Rheims and Châlons and captured Verdun of World War I fame. By the beginning of September Patton was already on the Rhine in Alsace and Lorraine.

Meanwhile, after having crossed the Somme, the British took Arras and then pushed on to Lille and Brussels. Without stopping at the Belgian capital, captured jointly with the United States on September 3, Montgomery's troops raced some 30 miles torward Antwerp. Although the city was successfully stormed, the Germans managed to retain some parts of the port controlling the north bank of the Scheldt, thus preventing the Allies from effectively utilizing the valuable harbor facilities. By September 12 detachments of the U.S. First Army were already on German territory near Eupen. Patch's Seventh Army, advancing up from the south of France, joined the bulk of the Allied forces in their march toward the Rhine.

Thus, September 1944 marked the end of the Second Battle of France. The struggle was much more protracted and bloody than the first. The balance sheet of the second French campaign was overwhelmingly in the Allied favor. While the Germans lost more than 500,000 as killed, wounded, and captured—altogether more than twenty divisions, five of them armored—the Allies sustained 224,000 casualties. Moreover, Hitler forfeited the whole of France, his most coveted prize, with its considerable industrial and agricultural resources, its bases and reserves of manpower. The Allies lost little time starting the rehabilitation of France to put its resources to their advantage for the last battles of the war. These were to be the battles for Germany itself.

The Allied successes in the summer of 1944 opened unexpected vistas of ending the war before the end of the year. How to finish off the apparently moribund enemy became a subject of sharp controversies in the higher echelons of the British-American Supreme Command. The debates centered around two problems: First, should the

Allies attack Germany along a broad front or on a selected sector; second, who would deal the final blow to the mortally wounded enemy?

TWO STRATEGIES

Here national prestige was closely intertwined with personal ambition. Montgomery favored joining his own Twenty-first Army Group and the U.S. Twelfth Army Group into a single powerful battering ram under his command to drive toward the Ruhr. A concentrated force, amounting to some forty divisions, would strike through Belgium, capture the estuary of the Scheldt, and thus make the supply base of Antwerp fully available to the Allies. With Antwerp behind them, the Allied force would then swing around the northern flank of the Siegfried line, overrun the launching pads of the V2 rockets, and drive deeply into the vital industrial basin of the Reich, the Ruhr. By promptly capturing the main German arsenal, argued Montgomery, the proposed drive would bring the Third Reich to its knees by Christmas 1944.[11]

The ambitious plan was opposed by General Bradley. He was convinced that his better equipped and more mobile Twelfth Army Group should become the center of gravity of the final offensive. One of his armies, Patton's Third, he argued, was consistently the fastest advancing segment of the Allied forces. Montgomery's record of slow progress, his love of cautious "set battles," automatically disqualified him from commanding strategic moves involving improvisation. The U.S. Twelfth Army Group should be the battering ram of the Allied offensive. It should, therefore, be authorized to advance along a broad front due east across the Rhine, south of Frankfurt, and then envelop the Ruhr from the south.

General Jean-Marie de Lattre de Tassigny, Commander of the First French Army.

Both thrusts, "concentrated" and "broad," reflected as much the rivalry between the two outstanding Allied commanders as between the British and American concepts of the war in general. Eisenhower, as Supreme Commander of the Allied Forces in Europe, was in a difficult position. He had to adjudicate in favor of one of those plans without appearing partial to either. Although he was inclined to support Bradley's broad-front strategy as the only one politically acceptable to American public opinion, the arguments put forward by the British side could not be brushed aside easily because of its potential for a quick end to the war. Consequently, Eisenhower, as a good diplomat, tried to procrastinate and compromise.

Unable to win his wholehearted approval for the British plan, Montgomery submit-

[11]For an analysis of Montgomery's role during the invasion see Richard Lamb, *Montgomery in Europe, 1943–1945: Success or Failure?* (London: Buchanan & Enright, 1983), especially pp. 228–303.

ted to Eisenhower a bold stratagem; its essence was in launching a coordinated airborne and ground blow to capture the lower Rhine delta. This was to be accomplished by throwing into that area the massive and hitherto largely unutilized reserves of the Allied paratroopers. The Allied airborne contingent was impressive indeed. It amounted to three and a half divisions: the U.S. 82nd and 101st Airborne Divisions, the British 1st, and the Independent Polish Parachutist Brigade. This well-trained and well-equipped First Airborne Army had only been partially utilized during the invasion of Sicily and the Normandy landing. The commander of the First Airborne Army had an American general, Lewis Hyde Brereton, a former member of General "Billy" Mitchell's staff. Brereton's deputy was General Frederick Browning, originally an officer of the British Grenadier Guards, whose restless temperament made him join a parachutist regiment and eventually become the father of his country's first large airborne units.

Operation "Market Garden," September 17-25, 1944

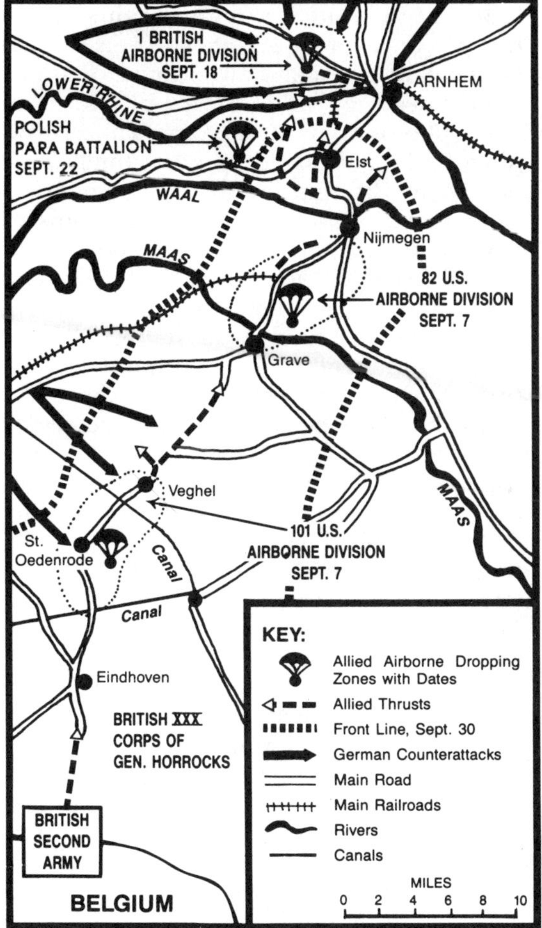

Throughout the summer of 1944 these elite troops were kept in England in constant readiness as a strategic reserve. They were ordered to be prepared no fewer than eighteen times for mass drops, to act as a vanguard for different Allied drives. Up to mid-September various airborne units had been alerted, briefed for action, and even loaded into transport planes and gliders. In each case, however, their respective missions had been canceled at the last moment.

According to Montgomery's plan, the airborne troops were to be used as a spearhead to the Allied ground troops by capturing the five bridges over three rivers, the Maas, the Vaal, and the lower Rhine (Operation Market). The control of these Dutch bridges would allow Allied ground troops to advance into northwest Germany (Operation Garden). Hence the code name of the whole operation, Market-Garden. The operation's main objective was to outflank the German defenses from the north and capture the Ruhr, while destroying the launching pads of the V-rockets. The First Allied Airborne Army was to lay down a 64-mile long carpet and seize the five key bridges, as well as several towns in between. This would create a large hole in the German defenses. Through the hole Horrock's XXX Army Corps would advance some 60 miles over eight water obstacles and a single narrow road. The airborne contingent and Horrock's force were to be promptly reinforced by other units to capture the industrial area along the Rhine. Without firmly controlling the five key bridges on the Rhine—including its branch, the Vaal—as well as on the Maas, the Allied ground forces could not advance quickly through the difficult Dutch countryside, dissected by hundreds of canals and dikes.

Impressed by the daring scheme of achieving four vital objectives at one stroke without abandoning the broad-strategy plan, Eisenhower put the First Airborne Army at Montgomery's disposal as early as September 5. Believing that the enemy was in a state of near collapse, Montgomery enthusiastically promoted the plan; should the scheme succeed, he would play a decisive role in the final stages of the war at least. The actual commander of the operation, General Browning, was also supremely self-confident. He assured Montgomery that a strong airborne force would open the route from Eindhoven to Arnhem long enough for the tanks of General Horrock's XXX Army Corps to capture a bridgehead on the eastern bank of the Rhine.

Browning was perturbed by only one factor: the extreme depth of the planned penetration of enemy territory. Staring at the map displayed on the wall of his study and pointing at the bridge over the lower Rhine at Arnhem, he remarked to Montgomery: "But I think, Sir, we may be going a bridge too far." Reassured by Montgomery that this was a mere detail, that the war was practically won and that this was the supreme moment to deal the final blow to the enemy, Browning plunged headlong into implementation of the plan.[12]

THE BATTLE OF ARNHEM

The Market-Garden operation was undertaken on the assumption that there were no substantial enemy forces capable of defending the lower Rhine delta. And indeed, at one moment, the confused Germans themselves wondered whether the delta could be defended at all in view of the lack of adequate forces. In reply to the desperate requests for reinforcement made by Field Marshal Model, commander of Army Group B, Berlin was able to send only a few battalions, hastily formed from sailors without ships, some scattered Luftwaffe ground troops, police officers, and ambulatory wounded recently dismissed from hospitals. Model, however, always a brilliant improviser, was able to integrate these motley elements with the remnants of the units retreating from France, Belgium, and Holland into a fairly coherent amalgam that was soon bolstered by the arrival of the Ninth Panzer and First Parachutist divisions and by the II S.S. Panzer Corps.

These considerable reinforcements did not go unnoticed by Dutch resistance agents on the spot. Between September 11 and 14 they sent to London several warnings about the presence of a "significant number" of German armored and airborne troops. The Dutch message was confirmed by a series of aerial photographs. Montgomery and Browning, both bent on carrying out their ambitious plan, disregarded these warnings. Despite the vocal protests of General Stanisław Sosabowski, commander of the Polish Parachutist Brigade, Operation Market-Garden was to proceed as scheduled.

Preparations for the landing of the airborne contingent were most impressive. Before dawn on September 17 some 1,400 Allied bombers began to pound the region of Arnhem. Then 2,023 troop carriers, transport planes, and gliders took off from twenty-four airfields in southern England; they were protected by 1,500 fighters as they streamed toward Holland. This was the largest airborne operation of the war, involving more than three airborne divisions and nearly 36,000 men.

Initially all went well. On September 17 the U.S. 101st Airborne Division, commanded by General Maxwell Taylor, landed outside the Dutch cities of Veghel and Eidenhoven, capturing their communications centers and the bridge over the Maas River. Then the Americans linked up with the vanguard of the British XXX Army Corps. The 82nd U.S. Airborne Division,

[12] This remark inspired what is probably the best-known book on the Market-Garden operation: Cornelius Ryan, *A Bridge Too Far* (New York: Popular Library, 1974).

commanded by General James Gavin, was also successful: It landed at Broive and Nijmegen and seized both towns and the bridge at Broive on the Waal; the other bridge, that of Nijmegen, was so strongly defended by the Germans that it was captured by the United States paratroopers only after a murderous four-day fight. On September 20 the Americans made a most daring assault across the Waal in canvas boats and captured the northern end of the bridge by September 21.

The most difficult task, however, was assigned to the British First Airborne Division commanded by General Brian Urquart. His paratroopers were known as the Red Devils because of the bright red berets that they recklessly wore instead of the standard steel helmets, and the reckless courage they had displayed in the past. The Red Devils were dropped at Arnhem, the farthest end of the airborne carpet, that is, at the point deepest inside the enemy held territory. The main objective was to capture the Arnhem bridge spanning the lower Rhine to allow the passage of the main body of the XXX Tank Corps. Because the mission was so important and so risky, General Browning eventually decided to reinforce his contingent with the Polish Parachutist Brigade of General Sosabowski. The Brigade was to be dropped at Arnhem on D-day plus two, that is, on September 19.

General Brian Urquart, commander of the British First Airborne division, in his HQ at Oosterbeck near Arnhem. National Archives

From the beginning, the neglect of the available intelligence and a series of accidents began to play havoc with Browning's bold plan. The choice of the main landing area proved to be a monumental blunder because the headquarters of both Army Group B and the II S.S. Panzer Corps were located at Oosterbeck, less than two miles from the main drop zone. As a result, Marshal Model could actually watch from a window of his headquarters the descent of the British paratroopers. Although at first shocked by the sudden attack, Model soon regained his composure and sent tanks of the Second S.S. Panzer Division into action. As a result, the lightly armed British parachutists, with no adequate artillery, had to face enemy armor. This was a hopeless fight from the beginning. British paratroopers, firing their light machine guns, rifles, and even pistols against the enemy tanks, presented a pathetic sight. At 3 P.M. the second half of the First Airborne Division landed near the Arnhem bridge, but they were equally helpless against the tanks and artillery of the S.S. panzer corps.

The struggle around the Arnhem bridge was among the most bitter and bloody of the entire war and involved extremely high casualties. The Germans quickly annihilated a small British force that did momentarily gain the northern end of the bridge. In view of the fierce enemy resistance and his intolerable losses, on September 18 General Urquart decided to withdraw the remnants of his rapidly melting contingent into a small, compact defense perimeter around the original landing near Oosterbeck and await reinforcements. Here, however, the bad weather, as well as faulty communication, again began to play havoc with Browning's plan. According to the original scheme, the Polish Parachutist Brigade was due to land in two days, on September 19. A hurricane, raging for two days, frustrated and aborted the scheme, however. Out of 110 planes carrying the Polish contingent, only 53 were able to drop their paratroopers on the left bank of the Rhine. The remainder was forced to return to England.

During the night of September 20, despite fog, rain, poor visibility, and heavy enemy fire, fifty Poles got across the Rhine in small canvas boats with some ammunition and supplies for their beleaguered British comrades. By the time a segment of the Polish Brigade had reached the exhausted remnants of the British battalion on the southern bank of the Rhine, the Red Devils had been reduced to a handful of mostly wounded and exhausted men fighting more for their honor than for the Arnhem bridge. Their food and ammunition had been exhausted, and their position had become untenable. The Germans were already in full control of the opposite shore and the bridge, and the British were squeezed into a small perimeter in the Oosterbeck area. They managed to hold on despite overwhelming odds until September 24, hoping for the arrival of the XXX Tank Corps. Here, however, another fatal mistake ruined the Allied plans. Because of a lack of communication and the single, narrow road open to them, Horrock's tanks began their advance toward the Arnhem birdge only on September 22, that is, after the withdrawal from it of the parachutists of the First British Airborne Division.[13]

All these mistakes, mishaps, and misunderstandings allowed the Germans to regain complete control of the battlefield and rush toward Nijmegen to deal with the Americans, fighting fiercely, but ultimately also helpless against heavy armor and artillery. The Market-Garden operation was a bloody failure of Montgomery's reckless strategy, which disregarded both the warning of the Dutch resistance and the initial hints of his co-workers. The master of the "set battles" gambled and lost, thus validating Bradley's argument that he was not well suited for any large-scale improvised schemes.

The Arnhem operation was one of the costliest defeats suffered by the Allies during the war. A large number of the elite Allied airborne contingents were wasted. The main objective, the Arnhem bridge, was not secured. The subsidiary objectives, although attained, could not compensate for the failure to hold the main passage over the Rhine. Of the 10,000 British airborne soldiers who had landed in Oosterbeck on September 17, after a week or so of fighting, only 2,000 remained, most of them wounded and utterly exhausted. The American and Polish losses were also intolerable.

The British catastrophe at Arnhem was, to some extent, countered by the American successes at Eindhoven and Nijmegen, but they were paid for by too high a price. The United States units lost 3,542 killed, wounded, or missing; the Poles paid with nearly one-fourth of their contingent left dead on the battlefield or drowned during the crossing of the Rhine to help their British comrades on the right bank of the river. The operation was vitiated from the beginning by the fixing of overambitious objectives and disregard of the available intelligence. Market-Garden proved to be a bravely executed but most lightheartedly planned operation that either should never have taken place, or should have been launched earlier, at the beginning of September when the disorganization of the retreating Germans was indeed at its nadir. The Allies underestimated the amazing German capacity to recover from the defeats of the previous summer and score their last victory of World War II. The winding up of the war had to be postponed until 1945.

---

[13]For the Arnhem battles see Gerard M. Devlin, *Paratrooper! The Saga of US Army and Marine Parachute and Glider Combat Troops During World War II* (New York: St. Martin's Press, 1979); Stanisław Sosabowski, *Freely I Served* (W. Kimber, London: 1960), especially pp. 118–50; and Charles Whiting, *A Bridge at Arnhem* (White Lion, London: 1976).

THE GERMAN COUNTEROFFENSIVE

At the close of 1944, although the bulk of the German forces had not been destroyed west of the Rhine, and although the Allies suffered a most painful setback at Arnhem, the optimistic mood at Supreme Allied GHQ persisted. Most high commanders continued to underestimate the German fighting ability. While the Allies kept on daydreaming, Hitler made a supreme effort to reverse the wheels of fortune by breaking the western front at the Ardennes. He trusted that a major setback to Allied arms would exacerbate the existing tensions within their camp, which, as he said, was "composed of such heterogeneous elements with such divergent aims." According to Hitler, a few heavy blows "would be enough to cause this artificially bolstered front" to collapse "with a gigantic clap of thunder."

Behind the shield of the Siegfried line, he secretly massed three armies, altogether some twenty-four crack divisions, including ten armored ones. Some of them were equipped with King Tiger Panthers, inspired by the Soviet T-34 tank but bigger and more heavily armed. Another surprise Hitler had prepared for his opponents was the Messerschmitt 262 jet fighters; with their superior speed and powerful armament, they were a deadly threat to the Allied propeller-driven aircraft, including the Mustangs and Flying Fortresses, the most advanced models of fighters and bombers at the disposal of the Allies. By mid-1944 Germany had over 500 of the world's first jet aircraft. The idea of a surprise breakout through the Ardennes toward Antwerp was Hitler's own brainchild. He insisted on repeating his Ardennes stratagem of May 1940. He was then to seize the Allies' largest supply base, Antwerp, and stage another Dunkirk.

By the autumn of 1944 various factors had come to favor the Third Reich. While the Allied lines of communication were getting dangerously long, those of the Germans were shortened. Moreover, the German soldiers were now fighting in defense of their native land. The Ultra reports, which had rendered such valuable service during the invasion of the Continent, were now of lesser use, since the Wehrmacht, now using secure wire lines, cut down radio communication to a minimum. Several weeks before the Ardennes offensive, Hitler imposed a total blackout on his military plans. All orders were to be delivered not by radio or telephone but by special messengers. Troop movements were to take place only by night. No officers with knowledge of the plan were permitted to fly west of the Rhine, for fear of capture by the Allies. Inclement weather during the late autumn reduced photo reconnaissance, and the German retreat from the occupied territories resulted in the drying out of this sort of intelligence also. Nevertheless Ultra intercepted a message to Tokyo from Baron Hiroshi Oshima, Japan's ambassador in Berlin, that revealed Hitler's plan to launch a major offensive in the west after the beginning of November. This and various other German decoded messages were ignored by the Allied headquarters.

Despite the severe setback recently suffered at Arnhem, most Allied leaders were inclined to disregard the danger of a significant enemy counteroffensive for the rest of the year. At the beginning of December Field Marshal Montgomery, for instance, had written General Eisenhower requesting leave in England over Christmas to visit his son. The conviction that the Wehrmacht was in no position to launch any major offensive seeped down to lower echelons and made both officers and soldiers rather overconfident and relaxed.

In mid-December, while Ike was being promoted to the rank of a five-star General of the Army and his staff were cracking bottles of champagne to celebrate the occasion, three powerful German armies lashed out against the unsuspecting feeble American forces, most of them new troops covering the Ardennes. The rolling hills and pine forests of the sector, the same which served as the focal point of the attack on France in May 1940, were the scene of Hitler's final gamble: to split the British-American front. The attack started on December 16, 1944. The few major roads crossing the Ardennes were vital for the success of the plan. The town of Bastogne, the focal point of the German drive, was an important junction and was the first target of the attack. Both foggy weather and strict secrecy helped to conceal the whole intricate stratagem.

Opposing the twenty-four German divisions, which included the Sixth S.S. Panzer Army, were about four U.S. infantry divisions and one armored one. The American units consisted partly of inexperienced troops and partly veterans recovering from wounds or shell shock. In the first day of the offensive, December 16, 1944, taking advantage of very bad weather, the Germans succeeded in disrupting the Allied front and made considerable progress in many sectors especially toward Bastogne. Confusion was spread in the rear areas by infiltrating small groups of specially trained English-speaking soldiers dressed in United States uniforms and well equipped to perform various sabotage missions.

Defense of Bastogne by the 101st U.S. Airborne Division was a pivotal point of the struggle, which went down in history as the Battle of the Bulge. The German armor encircled Bastogne on December 20, and the position of the American pocket seemed hopeless. Two days later the German commander of the besieging forces sent emissaries to the acting commander of the 101st Airborne Division, General Anthony C. McAuliffe, demanding surrender. To this the general replied with one word in American slang: "Nuts." Bypassing the stubbornly defended Bastogne pocket, the Germans pushed deeper into Belgium. By December 24 they penetrated to within 5 miles of the river Meuse. At one moment it seemed that the Allied front would be broken.

Eisenhower had to throw into the battle every available unit to prevent a full-scale catastrophe. The main rescue force was Patton's Third Army, which included the 82nd Airborne Division, commanded by the youngest United States general, James Gavin. His soldiers were completely unprepared for winter fighting and had to take white

The German Offensive in the Ardennes, December 16-31, 1944 ("The Battle of the Bulge")

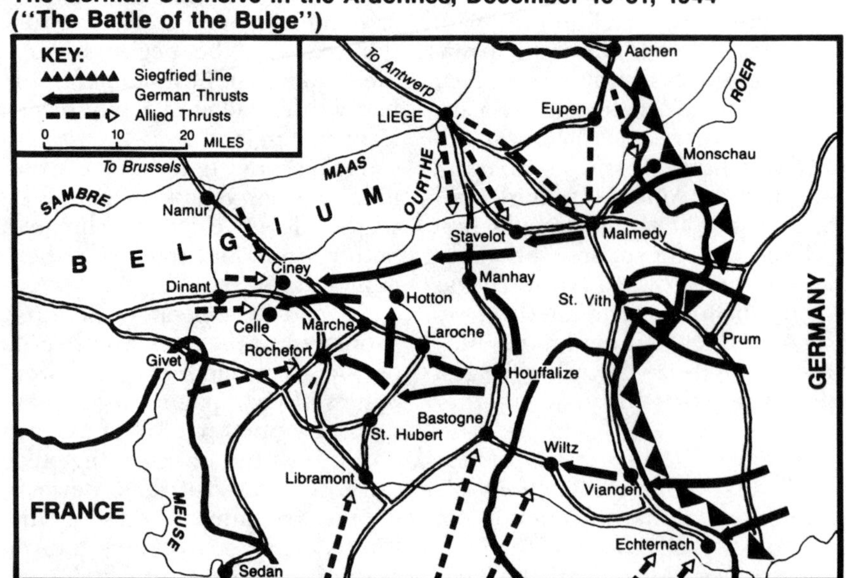

sheets and blankets from Belgian villagers to fashion makeshift snow-camouflage cloaks. The Allied counteroffensive was hampered by the fact that for more than a week most of the RAF and U.S. "Mighty 8th" Air Force had been grounded by deadly dense fog that blanketed England and the battleground on the European continent. For eight days the Allied planes were unable to break through the weather barrier and provide air support for the American troops on the ground. By December 24, however, the so-called Russian high had cleared the skies over the Continent and was moving westward. This allowed the resumption of air operations over the Continent. More than 2,000 four-engine bombers, Boeing B-17s and Consolidated B-24 Liberators, launched their largest single attack. Forty-four planes were lost, but the German momentum was broken, and their resources, especially gasoline, were exhausted.[14]

What finally saved the situation was the prompt arrival of Patton's Third Army. At the time of the Ardennes counteroffensive, the Third Army was successfully advancing along the Saar River. When the news of the German breakthrough reached Eisenhower's headquarters, he ordered Patton to rush to the rescue of the threatened sector of the U.S. V and VI corps. When asked how long it would take him to get to Bastogne, Patton replied, "48 hours." This first seemed like a boast in view of the distance separating the Saar region from the Ardennes and the icy roads that had to be used. But to the amazement of Bradley and the others, Patton kept his word. He moved the largest army the longest distance in the shortest period of time in the annals of World War II.

By December 26 Patton's 4th Armored Division had broken through the enemy encirclement and relieved the 101st Airborne Division valiantly holding Bastogne. The Third Army, operating in the south, was reinforced by a brigade of the British XXX Armored Corps in the north, the only British ground unit in the battle. Slowly the concerted Allied counteroffensive began to push off the most advanced German units, which had retreated to the outskirts of Dinant and the area west of St. Hubert. By that time Rundstedt advised Hitler to halt the offensive in view of the heavy losses and increasing shortages of gasoline. As usual, Hitler refused. Blindly obeying his "no retreat" order, most German soldiers desperately stood their ground, only to be overwhelmed by increasingly superior Allied forces.

After forty-three days of some of the most savage fighting of the war, Hitler's last gamble was defeated. As a result of this failure, Hitler lost most of his strategic reserves that might have either checked the coming Soviet spring offensive or delayed the British-American crossing of the Rhine. By the end of 1944, the Wehrmacht was finished as a coherent combat force. At the same time, its record was further tarnished by massacres of about 300 United States POWs as well as some hundred Belgian civilians in Malmedy. The entire battle was fierce, and the casualties were high on both sides. The Germans lost 100,000 killed, wounded, and captured; the Allies 81,000, 77,000 of them Americans, the heaviest battle toll in United States history. Yet it was the ultimate triumph of the American soldiers. Despite their initial setbacks, they bounced back and fought the crack German troops with a resilience and stubbornness that surprised the enemy. The British help on the ground was limited and slow; on the other hand, the RAF squadrons fought magnificently throughout the battle.

It was obvious that Hitler's gamble had failed. Nevertheless, the American-British victory was purchased at a heavy price, military as well as political. At the beginning of January 1945 the situation at the western front seemed so serious that on January 6 Churchill had sent a personal message to

[14]For a monograph of the Battle of the Bulge see John S. D. Eisenhower, *The Bitter Woods;* (New York: Putnam, 1969) and Bradley, *General's Story,* pp. 272, 293, and 354–60.

Sherman tanks of the US 4th Armored division rush toward Bastogne. Imperial War Museum

Stalin, urging him to speed up the planned Soviet offensive. And indeed, in response to his plea, on January 12, the Red Army's steamroller moved westward all along the central sector of the front. Warsaw was captured on January 17 by Soviet and Polish troops and the Communist-dominated Provisional Government of Poland, brought with the Red Army, was now planted amidst the ruins of the capital city. Considerable Soviet advances were also made in Hungary, where Budapest was besieged. This rapid Soviet advance in the Danube valley menaced the stability of Germany's entire eastern front. In view of this, on January 22 Hitler ordered the elite Sixth S.S. Panzer Army to be diverted from the Ardennes and sent to Hungary to defend the last source of oil available to him. This spelled the end of his last desperate gamble to regain the initiative on the western front.

On January 29, on the eve of the twelfth anniversary of Hitler's seizure of power, the massive Soviet juggernaut crossed the pre-1939 Polish-German boundaries. Berlin lay beyond the last natural and heavily defended obstacle, the river Oder. Meanwhile the Red Army also victoriously pushed toward Bratislava and Vienna. On the other hand, the Western Allies, while recovering from the Ardennes setback, were bogged down in Italy. It was against this background of a practically uninterrupted series of Soviet triumphs, temporarily paralleled by serious difficulties in the west, that the second summit conference gathered at Yalta in the Crimea at the beginning of February 1945.

THE YALTA CONFERENCE

Before the Yalta conferences, Winston Churchill visited Moscow at the beginning of October 1944. On the night of October 9, after a long wrangle about the future zones of influence of the two powers, the British prime minister scribbled on a scrap of paper the following suggestions for the Russo-British division of their respective zones of influence: Rumania—Russia 90 percent, the others 10 percent; Greece—Great Britain and the United States 90 percent, Russia 10 percent; Yugoslavia–50-50; Hungary–50-50; Bulgaria—Russia 75 percent, the others 25 percent. Then Churchill pushed the sheet across the table toward Stalin. "There was a slight pause," Churchill noted in his memoirs. Then Stalin "took a pencil and made a large tick upon it, and passed it back. . . . After this there was a long silence." Finally Churchill said: "Might it not be thought rather cynical if it seemed we had disposed of these issues, so fateful to millions of people, in such an offhand manner? Let us burn the paper." "No, you keep it," Stalin replied.[15] Later on, in view of the rapid advance of the Red Army, on Molotov's insistence, the Hungarian formula was revised to 72-25 and the Bulgarian to 80-20, both in Soviet favor. Thus the Soviet position in eastern Europe was established in

[15]The session of October 9 at the Kremlin was colorfully described by Churchill in his *Triumph and Tragedy*, pp. 226–28.

advance of the second summit conference of the war.

The second Big Three meeting gathered on February 4, 1945, in a set of summer palaces and villas at Yalta in the Crimea, near one of the battlefields of the Crimean War, where the British Light Brigade had vainly charged the Russian defenses ninety years before. President Roosevelt and the American party were located in the Livadia Palace, a fifty-room, six-bathroom summer palace built by Tsar Nicholas in 1911. Prime Minister Churchill and the British delegation were housed in a big estate nearby, named Koriz, a set of villas rather than palaces. This was a symbolic reflection of the Russian attitude toward the ally whose role was rapidly diminishing. Still more symbolic was the fact that Stalin occupied the palace located just between the dwellings of the American President and the British prime minister.

Throughout the conference the Russians tried to dazzle their guests by lavish hospitality often going to the extreme. One of Churchill's co-workers, Sir Gladwin Jebb, noted in his reminiscences about Yalta: "We arrived very late and tired, and we were asked what we wanted for breakfast the next day. We said: a boiled egg. The next morning there was caviar, a whole beautiful fish and a suckling." When the British delegation asked for a lemon for their gin, a lemon tree was immediately planted in the garden of their villa. In a mood of jubilation, throughout the conference champagne was flowing in sparkling cascades.

At Yalta, while Stalin negotiated from strength, the Western powers were hampered not only by their recent setback at Ardennes and the wrangles over the European strategy but also by the uncertainties of the Far Eastern war theater. A memorandum presented at the Quebec conference in 1943 had already stressed the point that "the most important factor the United States has to consider in relation to Russia is the prosecution of the war in the Pacific." Secretary of War Stimson revealed later that he had been informed by the military that an invasion of the Japanese home islands "might be expected to cost over a million casualties to American forces alone." When Roosevelt met Churchill on the island of Malta, en route to Yalta, the President expressed his fear that the war against Japan "might continue until 1947." Consequently, the President's decisions at Yalta were largely influenced by these grossly exaggerated apprehensions. Since Soviet aid seemed more important than that of Britain, the President continued his policy of supporting the Soviet point of view more often than that of Britain.[16] At Yalta, President Roosevelt was also preoccupied with the problems of the United Nations, which he considered as a guarantee of lasting world peace.

The Yalta conference confirmed the results of the largely informal Teheran summit and acknowledged the Churchill-Stalin deal of October 1944 concerning the division of the zones of influence in east-central Europe, where Soviet troops were in control anyway. The conference also restated the joint resolution to enforce the unconditional surrender of Germany and its occupation by the three Great Powers: the Soviet Union, the United States, and Great Britain. At Yalta, Great Britain looked for a France restored to its traditional place as a counterweight to Germany and a buffer against Russia. Despite de Gaulle's previous efforts to flatter and cajole him, Stalin fought against any idea of giving France access to the Inter-Allied Control Commission, which, as he stressed, must be confined to those powers which had stood firm against Germany. France was finally allowed to share in the occupation regime only after the war. Germany was to be not only split but also disarmed; its society was to be de-Nazified, its war industries dismantled,

---

[16]The essential documentary collection on Yalta are *Foreign Relations of the United States: Diplomatic Papers: The Conference at Malta and Yalta, 1945* (Washington, D.C.: U.S. Government Printing Office, 1955). The two most complete memoirs of the conference are Edward Stettinius, *Roosevelt and the Russians: The Yalta Conference* (New York: Doubleday, 1949); and the fragmentary, but colorful, accounts by James Byrnes, *Speaking Frankly* (New York: Harper & Row, 1947), pp. 29–90; see also W. S. Churchill, *Triumph and Tragedy,* pp. 329–402.

President Roosevelt's arrival at the Yalta airport; Vyacheslav Molotov and Edward Stettinius walk to the left of the jeep's driver.
National Archives

and its General Staff abolished. The Germans were to pay reparations to the victorious powers to the amount of $20 billion, half of the sum to go to the USSR. Those responsible for war crimes were to be tried by an international tribunal and punished.

Next to Germany, Poland was the most critical political problem of the conference. Churchill said to his colleagues: "Poland is the most important question before the Conference and I don't want to leave without its being settled." "Britain," the prime minister said, "declared war on Germany in order that Poland should be free and sovereign. . . . Our interest in Poland is that of honor. Having drawn the sword on behalf of Poland against Hitler's brutal attack, we could never be content with any solution that did not leave Poland a free and independent sovereign state." Churchill's passionate statement was then confronted by Stalin's brilliant sophistry. He replied: "For the Russian people, the question of Poland is not only a question of honor but also a question of security. Throughout history, Poland has been the corridor through which the enemy has passed into Russia. Twice in the last thirty years our enemies, the Germans, have passed through this corridor."

Had the two Western statesmen done their homework as thoroughly as their Soviet ally, they could have rebuked Stalin's twisted argument with ease. In the first case of the German aggression against Russia, that of August 1914, Poland did not exist, and its central provinces, "the corridor" through which German offensive was launched, belonged to Russia. In the second case, that of 1939, Poland was not a "corridor" for a German attack but a barrier that Stalin destroyed by allying himself with Hitler and then stabbing the Polish army in the back while it was still fighting the Wehrmacht on September 17, 1939.

But Churchill and Roosevelt either did not remember these facts or did not dare to mention them—did not want to drag the skeleton of the Stalin-Hitler partnership from the Allied closet. They meekly accepted Stalin's sophistry of a "friendly Poland," to serve as a Soviet buffer state.

Poland's fate had been informally settled at Teheran, but important details were yet to be worked out. The two crucial issues of the Yalta conference were those of Poland's boundaries and its government; the eastern frontier along the "Curzon line" was reaffirmed, and as "substantial compensations" for cession of nearly half of Poland's prewar territory to the Soviet Union, the Poles were to be allotted the southwestern part of East Prussia and territories east of the Oder-Neisse line. The capital of East Prussia, Königsberg, as well as the northeastern segment of the province, was to be annexed by the USSR for strategic reasons. When

Churchill and Roosevelt tried to object to these changes on the ground that they would necessitate moving 6 million Germans, Stalin said, "When our troops come in, the Germans run away."

As for the future regime of Poland, the Yalta conference, disregarded the Polish government in London, a faithful ally of Great Britain, and decided to reorganize the Communist-dominated provisional government established in Warsaw by the Red Army. The government was to be reorganized on a broader democratic basis; it was to hold "free and unfettered elections" in the near future. President Roosevelt pointed out to Stalin that the Polish elections "should be like Caesar's wife. I do not know her, but they say 'she was pure.' " Stalin replied with cynical frankness that proved to be prophetic: "They said that about her, but in fact she had her sins."[17]

Similar elections were to be held in other countries of eastern Europe, including Yugoslavia where the addition of some "democratic leaders" from among the local resistance leaders and from those residing abroad was also recommended. In practice, in both countries, the Communist elements were already in control, and most of the recommendations were never fulfilled. Meanwhile the Polish democratic forces, starting with most of the leading underground fighters, were being eliminated by the Red Army and the NKVD. The most shocking example of the high-handed Soviet methods was the arrest by the Soviet secret police of the sixteen Polish resistance leaders by granting them safe conduct to lure them to Moscow in February 1945 under the pretext of coordination of the struggle of the Polish resistance with that of the Soviet forces. Once the Polish leaders arrived in Moscow, they were imprisoned. Soon a show trial was staged and the sixteen were condemned as traitors and saboteurs. Protests of the embarrassed Western powers were ignored by Stalin.

CONCESSIONS AND AMBIVALENCE

The Yalta agreement also dealt with a provision concerning the terms under which the USSR would join in the war against Japan. The Soviet entry was to be carried out no later than three months after the end of the war in Europe. In exchange, Stalin was assured generous benefits; the status quo in Outer Mongolia, formerly a segment of China but by then already a vassal of the Soviet Union, was to be maintained. Moreover, Southern Sakhalin, lost to Japan in 1905, was to be restored to Russia, and the hitherto Japanese Kuril Islands, never a Russian possession, were added for good measure. The Chinese port of Dairen (Dalny) was to be internationalized, and Soviet interests there were to be recognized as preeminent. Finally, Generalissimo Chiang Kai-shek was to be persuaded to lease to the USSR a naval base in Port Arthur; the Chinese-Eastern and Southern Manchurian railroads were to be jointly operated by a Soviet-Chinese company. At Yalta the Russians were ready to pursue a coordinated Big Three policy in China: They forgot all about their Chinese Communist comrades and were ready to accept the regime of their foe, Generalissimo Chiang Kai-shek. Molotov went so far as to declare a lack of Soviet interest in the fate of the party led by Mao Tse-tung, who was not a Communist anyway, but leader of a bunch of "agrarian reformers." Thus, the Chinese allies, whether Communist or not, were treated as the Poles: Their destinies were to be settled behind their backs and without their consultation.

At Yalta the Big Three issued the "Declaration on Liberated Europe." While invoking the Atlantic Charter, they announced that in any country "where in their judgment conditions require," the Soviet Union, the United States, and Great Britain would "jointly assist" the people concerned to estab-

[17]Byrnes, *Speaking Frankly,* p. 33. Throughout the book there are many direct quotations; serving as an adviser to President Roosevelt, but not taking direct part in the debate, Byrnes made a complete stenographic record of the conference.

lish domestic peace, to set up "interim governmental authorities broadly representative of all democratic elements," and to hold free elections. The declaration made no distinction between friendly Allied countries, such as Poland, Czechoslovakia, Yugoslavia, and Greece, and Axis countries, that is, Germany and Italy and their vassals, Hungary, Rumania, and Bulgaria. Both categories of countries were to be treated alike, as wards of the victorious Great Powers, who arrogated to themselves the right to establish their governments and draw their frontiers. As Stalin put it, "Small birds should be careful how they sing."

President Roosevelt's decisions at Yalta were greatly influenced by his determination to win Stalin over to his pet concept: the United Nations Organization. This the worn-out and impatient President wanted to achieve as soon as possible by being kind and generous toward the Soviet dictator. After President Roosevelt had agreed that the United States would support the Soviet proposal that the Soviet republics of the Ukraine and Belorussia be admitted to the United Nations Organization, the President's friend and director of the Office of War Mobilization, James Byrnes, suggested that Puerto Rico, Alaska, and Hawaii also be given United Nations' memberships. The President ignored the remark.

Throughout the Yalta conference the President sided more often with Stalin than with Churchill. With all of his sympathy for the British people, Roosevelt reflected the complex sentiments of most Americans toward them at this time: a mixture of inferiority and superiority, envy and condescension. He had come to the aid of Britain and of the cause of freedom at a critical moment. Their cause and the cause of Britain were essentially the same in the hour of the common danger. But America's and Britain's ultimate long-range objectives were different in the face of the approaching victory. At Yalta, President Roosevelt was quite frank about these differences. "You see, Winston," he said to Churchill, "there is something here that you are not capable of understanding. You have in your veins the blood of tens of generations of people accustomed to conquering. We are here at Yalta to build up a new world, which will know neither injustice nor violence, a world of justice and equality."

The President made repeated, persistent attempts to prove that there was no collusion between Churchill and himself. The President constantly lectured the prime minister and played the role of arbiter between him and Stalin. "I have a hunch," he said to adviser Harry Hopkins, "that Stalin doesn't want anything but security for his country, and I think that if I gave him everything that I possibly can and ask nothing from him in return, *noblesse oblige,* he won't try to annex anything and will work for a world of democracy and peace." The euphoria that prevailed among the American leadership immediately after the Yalta conference was shared also by Harry Hopkins: "We believed in our hearts that this was the dawn of a new age we had all been praying for."[18]

As we have seen, many vital issues that were only informally outlined at Teheran were formalized and put into writing at Yalta. In retrospect, it is quite clear that the Yalta Declaration on Liberated Europe was merely a face-saving device—a fig leaf that covered the handing over of east-central Europe to the Soviets. To expect a country that had been massively and brutally violating democracy and human rights at home to respect them in the newly conquered countries was either naive or hypocritical. At Yalta as at Teheran, of the three major coalition partners, Stalin was the best prepared to bargain, the most determined and clearsighted. He had entered the war with a definite political purpose in mind and skillfully utilized his military advantages to achieve his ultimate objectives.

---

[18]The main American historians who had analyzed the Yalta conference are Herbert Feis, *Churchill, Roosevelt and Stalin: The War They Waged and the Peace They Sought* (Princeton, N.J.: Princeton University Press, 1957); John Snell, *The Meaning of Yalta* (Baton Rouge: Louisiana State University Press, 1956), and in a "revisionist" book, Diane Clemens, *The Yalta Conference,* (New York: Oxford University Press, 1970).

18

The Last Battles

Throughout 1944 German morale held fast. Exposed almost daily to the lash of Allied air forces, often short of ammunition, food, and water, German soldiers fought with a courage and resilience that continued to amaze their opponents. The Western Allies were at a loss about how to soften the German resistance before storming the Rhine and the Siegfried line. Here they were helped by an accident. Late in 1944, when the Germans suddenly evacuated Luxembourg, they left intact the powerful transmitter of Radio Luxembourg. The Allied forces took it over, renamed it Radio Annie, and turned it into an effective instrument of psychological warfare.

Radio Annie went on the air in December 1944 and functioned for almost two months, broadcasting military and civilian news of the war "in the unmistakable accent" of the Rhine region. Annie created a bogus German resistance movement calling for the destruction of Nazi rule and for immediate peace. To undermine German morale, Annie did not hesitate to spread wild rumors. For instance, it reported that Field Marshal Goering had evacuated his farm and given tons of excess produce and domestic animals to the local farmers. Right after that broadcast many civilians, infuriated that Goering had accumulated so much, began looting German trucks carrying foodstuffs to the front. Annie caused panics in Nuremberg and Ludwigshafen by reporting British and American tanks to be on their way when there were none.

THE BOMBING OF DRESDEN

While trying to undermine the enemy morale by psychological warfare, the Allies continued their bombing offensive against

Germany.[1] By the close of 1944, Allied air superiority was crushing. The Allies not only had many more aircraft and more ample fuel supplies but their airmen were far better trained. Toward the end of the war, Luftwaffe airmen received only about 110 hours of flight training whereas American airmen got as much as 360. Toward the end of the war, Allied superiority in the air was so pronounced that the idea of speeding up the end of the war by means of bombing was haunting the minds of the Allied leaders. One of the results of this frame of mind was the full-scale American cooperation with the RAF in the bombing of Dresden.

During the night of February 13–14, 1945, RAF bombers opened the attack on Dresden by descending on the city in two waves approximately three hours apart; 234 four-engine Lancaster bombers formed the first wave, and 538 of the same type of aircraft followed in the second. Just past noon on the fourteenth, 311 American Eighth Air Force B-17s unloaded their bombs on the city. Yet, by the time the second wave of RAF Lancasters attacked the city, it was already in the grips of a firestorm. As a result of the two assaults, the center of the city was gutted, and some 35,000 of its inhabitants were killed.

The devastation of Dresden has been the most controversial air attack of World War II in Europe. The reasons for the savaging of Dresden during the final three months of the strategic bombing offensive against Fortress Europe were complex. Because the city received such a powerful blow so close to the final German military collapse, it has naturally caused many to question its necessity. Dresden was of rather secondary strategic importance, full of refugees, mainly from Silesia, fleeing the terror of the Red Army. Was it morally justified and strategically worthwhile in view of its rather marginal military importance? Was it simply a supreme effort to club Germany into a quick surrender by all available means? Wasn't Marshal Konev and his First Ukrainian Front the main beneficiary of the Dresden bombing? Wasn't that like flogging a dead horse, and the wrong one at that?

February 15, 1945: Dresden after the Allied air raids. German Information Center, New York

The debate was opened by David Irving, whose *The Destruction of Dresden* first appeared in 1963 in London and declared the raid as the most devastating of the war. Three years later, however, in a correction to the London *Times* of July 7, 1966, Irving corrected the estimate of the fatalities caused by the bombing that appeared in his own book downward from 135,000 to 35,000.[2]

[1]Between 1942 and 1945 the RAF dropped on Germany alone altogether over 1 million tons of bombs, and the U.S. Army Air Force unloaded some 600,000 tons. The results of the bombing are still controversial. For a recent evaluation of the Allied air offensive see R. J. Overy, *The Air War, 1939–1945* (Briarcliff Manor, N.Y.: Stein & Day, 1980), pp. 131–62 and 262–71.

[2]This figure has been confirmed by Melden Smith, Jr., in his typescript Ph.D. thesis based on his research in the East German archives: *The Bombing of Dresden*

THE VALUE OF STRATEGIC BOMBING

The evaluation of the Dresden raid brings us to the entire question of the value of strategic bombing. Was the Allied bombing of European Axis powers worth it? Many historians tend to evaluate the World War II Allies' air offensives against the background of the Douhet-Mitchell theory of "victory through air power." It is true that at the beginning of the war many airmen, including the British and American air force leaders, basically agreed with this theory and believed that the struggle would be won in the air with "the barest assistance from antiquated admirals and paddlefeet." This rather narrow, monistic approach to strategy was promptly discredited by the course of the war; yet it still lingers in the background and obfuscates much of our thinking about strategic bombing. It seems that a more holistic approach would be more sensible. We have to view the Allied air offensive in a broad context, as a segment of a panoply of means used to defeat the Axis. Consequently, the strategic bombing should be analyzed not in isolation but in conjunction with all other components of the overall Allied strategy.

It is beyond doubt that the Anglo-American air offensive did not rise to all the initially highly optimistic expectations of winning the war by bombardment alone. On the other hand, for nearly three years, until the Allied invasion of Italy in the summer of 1943, air attacks were the only way in which the war could be carried home to the enemy territory. This was of considerable importance to the morale of both the captive peoples of Europe and the Allied peoples. While German industry was not brought to a complete standstill, its production was ultimately reduced by the constant pounding from the air. Devastating damage was inflicted on a few vital selected targets such as the synthetic fuel factories, dams, U-boat pens, and docks, thus immobilizing such ships as the battleship *Tirpitz*. During the last stages of the war the bombing also affected the transportation infrastructure; the devastation of many communications centers in France in 1944 paved the way for Operation Overlord.

Reconsidered: A Study in Wartime Decision Making (Boston: Boston University, 1971). The bombing of Dresden was not the worst by virtue of the deaths caused. No fewer than 42,000 persons were killed in the RAF attacks on Hamburg in the summer of 1943; 25,000 deaths resulted from a single concentrated American attack on Berlin as late as February 3, 1945. The most destructive conventional bombing of any city during all of World War II occurred on the night of March 9, 1945, when almost 84,000 Japanese were killed in Tokyo by American incendiary bombs. This was considerably in excess of the death toll resulting from the atomic attack on Hiroshima on August 6, 1945.

March 7, 1945: A Soviet soldier passes a bombed German tank on the outskirts of Breslau (now Wrocław). National Archives

According to Albert Speer's postwar account, the Allied bombing had tied down a million men and 10,000 antiaircraft guns. Since the antiaircraft artillery was also used for fighting tanks, this also had far-reaching implications for the density of the antitank defenses. Speer called the American-British air offensive a substitute of the second front and stressed the effect of the offensive on German morale, because the Allied bombing brought home to the people the full impact of war with all its horrors and sufferings.[3]

The air offensive, although certainly not as successful as its original enthusiasts had anticipated, did drain the enemy's overall resources and channeled a considerable segment of them into rebuilding the bombed-out objectives: radar stations, airfields, and armament factories. As a result, the air offensive absorbed enemy resources that could have been used elsewhere. If the Allied air offensive had been better designed to dislocate supplies rather than to devastate cities, it could have produced a quicker paralysis of the enemy's defense infrastructure and fuel supplies, and hence a quicker final collapse.

To summarize the role of air power in World War II, one may say that, although aircraft did not become as dominant as their more extreme advocates had prophesied, they did revolutionize the strategy and tactics of war. Nowhere, perhaps, was this more dramatic than on the seas. Air-craft-carrier-based planes played primary roles in practically all the great naval encounters of the war, including Taranto, Matapan, Coral Sea, and Midway. Beating the German submarines in the battle of the Atlantic would also have been difficult, if not downright impossible, without airplanes of various kinds, including bombers. The U.S. Strategic Bombing Survey concluded that, despite many errors, "the Allied air power was decisive in the war in Europe." The same could be said, with far greater justification, about the Far Eastern theater of operation. Although the bombing offensive did not win the war by itself, it at least shortened it.[4]

THE BATTLE OF GERMANY

The final land assault on the Third Reich was first launched from the east on January 12, 1945. Because of the destruction of Army Group Center the previous summer, the Soviet drive on that sector resulted in the prompt capturing of Warsaw, or rather its ruins, by January 17. The German resistance to the north and south was much fiercer and more effective. Yet already by January 20 the gigantic Soviet juggernaut had reached East Prussia in the north and the foothills of the Carpathians in the south. On February 24 the Red Army, without much effort, advanced on Danzig (now Gdańsk) on the Baltic Sea. By January 26 Marshal Rokossovky besieged the city, thus virtually isolating the German forces in East Prussia. In a desperate move to delay the pressure on Brandenburg-Prussia, Hitler ordered Army Group Vistula to defend to the bitter end the very strip of land that had been his pretext for unleashing the war.

Meanwhile, to the south, by February 6 Marshal Koniev had crossed the middle Oder and laid siege to Breslau (now Wrocław). On February 14 Budapest was finally captured by the Red Army after six weeks of savage house-to-house fighting. By the end of March, Soviet troops were already in control of the main natural obstacle to their march on Berlin, the Oder. They paused for some two weeks along the river to catch their breath before the storming of the German capital where Hitler, hidden in a deep underground shelter, was desperately preparing his last stand.

On the western front the offensive was launched much later, at the beginning of March. In early 1945 the northern flank of

---

[3]See Albert Speer, *Inside the Third Reich,* New York: Macmillan and Avon, 1970, pp. 363–379.

[4]For a positive overall evaluation of the Allied bombing offensive based on U.S. and British surveys see Overy, *The Air War 1939–1945,* pp. 132–62.

the Allied front had reached the Rhine at Nijmegen, Holland, and at Strasbourg, France. In the center, the Ardennes offensive of December 1944 momentarily stopped the Allied advance. Consequently, the Allied armies reached the Rhine along its whole length only by March 1945. The German defenses were organized along the river, the most formidable water obstacle in western Europe. Besides the tactical importance, the river had a tremendous symbolic significance for the German people: It was for them "the frontier" and they were determined to hold it almost at any price. In the north Montgomery's Twenty-first Army Group faced the widest stretch of the Rhine where the defenses were especially strong; behind them was the heart of the Ruhr. To the south of the British sector the river was narrower, but fast flowing and more tricky. The crossing was preceded by a smashing barrage of some 3,000 guns.

Everywhere the defense was stiff. Bradley's Twelfth U.S. Army Group had their task made much easier by sheer accident. On March 7 an American patrol reconnoitering the left bank of the river came across an undefended and intact bridge at Remagen, which had been adandoned by the hastily retreating enemy troops. Bradley was jubilant and informed the Supreme Headquarters of the Allied Expeditionary Force, or SHAEF, about this fact, but some of its officers complained that they had to rearrange their orders because the crossing of the Rhine at Remagen had not been anticipated in their plans. Bradley was furious. He asked if SHAEF wanted him to pull his troops back and blow up the bridge. To overcome the opposition of the SHAEF staff, Bradley had to appeal to Eisenhower himself, who, equally irritated, ordered the crossing to continue at full speed. In the morning of March 23 two airborne brigades were dropped behind the enemy lines on the right bank of the river to help extend the still precarious footholds that had been gained to a depth of 6 miles or so.

Thus "the Rhine, the Rhine, the German Rhine," the last major natural obstacle before Berlin, was overcome and the Battle of Germany opened. Even Kesselring, now commander in chief of the western front, despite his mastery of delaying tactics so brilliantly demonstrated in Italy, could not cope with the overwhelming Allied superiority in men

April 29, 1945, Dachau concentration camp: Its inmates cheer at their liberation by the US Army. German Information Center, New York

and materiel. No airy talk of Goebbels or Hitler could galvanize the decimated and moribund Wehrmacht into hopeless resistance. By nightfall of April 1 the Allied forces had closed a ring around the Ruhr.

By that time many, many German units were leaderless, discouraged by the lack of air cover, and often short of rations and ammunitions; they were only too glad to surrender to the British and Americans instead of to the dreaded Russians. Town after town greeted the American and British units with white flags. Yet there were units, mostly composed of S.S. men, that fought to the bitter end.[5] Soon the German opposition began to crumble and the withdrawal often turned into a rout.

There was relatively little serious enemy resistance between the Rhine and the Elbe, but after the experience of the Battle of the Bulge, the Allied leaders became cautious. All the time, German propaganda was spreading news about a plan for the withdrawal of the remaining troops into the Bavarian Alps. Weapons and stores were to be cached there, to be used for a last-ditch fight against the invaders. In retrospect, the slogan of the Alpine Fortress appears as a fairy tale, spread to bolster German morale for a last-ditch holdout, but it was taken rather seriously by the Allies in the spring of 1945.

As the Allied troops penetrated deeper into Germany, they captured various concentration camps and discovered that even the apparently most fantastic tales about Nazi atrocities were a gross understatement. At the same time, the Red Army, approaching from the east, discovered the death mills of Majdanek and Auschwitz. The Allied soldiers were shocked by the unbelievable hells of Dachau, Buchenwald, and Bergen-Belsen. After he had seen his first extermination camp near Gotha, Eisenhower asked both London and Washington to send at once parliamentary delegations as well as a team of journalists to Germany. "I feel that the evidence should be immediately placed before the American and British publics in a fashion that would leave no room for cynical doubt."

The next Allied target was Berlin. In the last stages of the war, Churchill repeatedly urged Washington to order the U.S. troops to advance as fast as possible to meet the Russians as far to the east as possible. The western Allied armies could have rushed toward the German capital and have captured it before the Red Army arrived by using the U.S. 82nd and 101st airborne divisions reinforced by two brigades of the British parachutists. Berlin's main airfields, Tempelhof and Gatow, were to be captured by the U.S. 82nd and 101st airborne divisions; they represented a respectable force of about 20,000 men, more than the one used on the morning of D-day. These two divisions were to be transported with their equipment by about 1,000 gliders and 3,000 transport planes, escorted by 3,000 fighters. Behind them was the entire U.S. Ninth Army. When the operation was ready to be launched, its astonished commander, General William H. Simpson, or "Big Simp," was told by the SHAEF that the Allied troops were not to go beyond the Elbe.[6]

"WHO WILL TAKE BERLIN?"

On March 28, 1945, Eisenhower on his own informed Stalin that the Western armies were not going to advance on Berlin and would make their principal thrust farther to the south. Churchill was most upset by this decision. Both he and Stalin realized that where soldiers go, political influence follows. On April 2 Churchill tried again to

[5]For this subject see Bradley, *A General's Life,* pp. 405–8; Bradley noted that, in March, when Churchill came upon a captured section of the Siegfried line between Maastricht and Achen, he said to him and Alan Brooke, "Let's all go piss on the West Wall." Then he proceeded to execute his suggestion (ibid., p. 401). For the German view of the last battles of the war see Kesselring, *A Soldier's Record,* pp. 283–339.

[6]For firsthand details by the commander of the U.S. 82nd Airborne Division see James M. Gavin, *On to Berlin: Battles of an Airborne Commander, 1943–1946* (New York: Bantam, 1984).

pressure Eisenhower and dispatched a message stressing that it was "highly important that we should shake hands with the Russians as far east as possible." But Eisenhower was not to be moved: He had marshaled the support of Washington by arguing that the German capital was "nothing but a geographic location," "a prestige objective." Moreover, by that time the war in the Far East was already looming increasingly larger in American public opinion. To finish the war in Europe as quickly as possible seemed like the best alternative.

By April 15 the U.S. Ninth Army was already across the Elbe and closer to Berlin than the Russians at that moment. Churchill urged once more: "Should Berlin be in our grasp we should certainly take it."[7] All in vain, since Marshall supported Ike. Montgomery, who was a subordinate of Eisenhower, could do nothing on his own and merely pushed to secure at least Denmark and the northern German ports.

Thus by mid-April the great prize of the last campaign was abandoned by the Western Allies to the Russians. Eisenhower's decision was rationalized by his fears of high casualties. This did not square, however, with what his subordinate commanders anticipated and reported to him; by that time the German collapse was nearly complete. Eisenhower's aide, Captain Harry C. Butcher, wrote that according to his boss, "taking Berlin would be a mere show; what he wanted to do was to end the war as quickly and economically in lives as possible." Bradley admitted in his memoirs the limitations of the United States leadership in failing to recognize the basic axiom of high strategy, that war represents merely the means of achieving political ends: "As soldiers we looked naively on this British inclination to contemplate the war with political foresight and non-military objectives."[8]

The Western Allies were excessively cautious and in disagreement about their eastward drive, but Stalin had few inhibitions. He wanted to capture Berlin quickly at any price. For this purpose he amassed ten armies comprising over seventy divisions, supported by two air armies. Every detail of the great battle was carefully supervised by the Generalissimo himself. He, who had admitted to Churchill that he had exterminated 3 or 4 million people to solidify his personal power, did not hesitate to pay a high price to take Berlin. Stalin ordered Marshals Konev and Zhukov to begin their final offensives no later than dawn on April 16, 1945.

When on April 1 the marshals entered Stalin's studio, decorated with the pictures of two of Russia's most famous commanders, Alexander Suvorov and Mikhail Kutuzov (who had defeated Napoleon's Grand Army in 1812), the Soviet dictator threw a blunt question: "Who will take Berlin? We or the Allies?" "We [which meant his First Ukrainian Front] will," answered Konev. Although Zhukov waited a moment, he soon added, "We [which meant the First Belorussian Front] are at the shortest distance from Berlin. We will take Berlin." Stalin smiled and ordered both rivals to prepare their plans for the coming battle within forty-eight hours. Both army groups would be pitted as rivals against each other almost as much as against the Germans. In due time, by April 3, the two marshals reappeared with their respective plans; it was obvious that everything favored Zhukov: he had eight armies already assembled and deployed along the Oder, whereas Konev had only five more scattered along the Neisse and more in need of instant reinforcements. To put his plan of attack into action Konev needed at least two more armies. In view of this, to Zhukov went the main responsibility of capturing Berlin. Afterward he was to push for the line of the Elbe. Both Konev's First Ukrainian Front

---

[7]For Churchill's point of view see his *Triumph and Tragedy,* pp. 514–20.

[8]For Bradley's views on Berlin see *A General's Life,* pp. 420–30. Among U.S. senior commanders only Patton pressed for capturing Berlin. For conflicts among the Allied leaders concerning Berlin see David Irving, *The War Among Generals* (New York: Congdon & Weed, 1981), pp. 397–403.

and Rokossovski's Second Belorussian Front were to play an auxiliary role in the gigantic operation.

Meanwhile, the Red Army, which had brought in its baggage train a prefabricated Polish provisional government, established it in the ruins of Warsaw. Additionally, a Polish army and an armored corps, previously formed and trained in Russia, had joined Marshal Zhukov's First Belorussian Front to participate in the capturing of the German capital. Even more unceremoniously than in the case of Rumania, the Communist-dominated regime in Poland at once revealed its refusal to share real power with other political groups. The Allied Commission, established to implement Yalta's decisions on Poland, met for the first time on February 23 in Moscow and immediately set off a bitter wrangle with the Russians. In spite of the representations of Ambassador Harriman and Sir Archibald Clark Kerr, urging that three Poles should be invited from outside Poland, Molotov charged that the Yalta agreement stipulated consultation with the "Warsaw Poles" only. This caused consternation in London and Washington. Soon numerous voices began to surface in

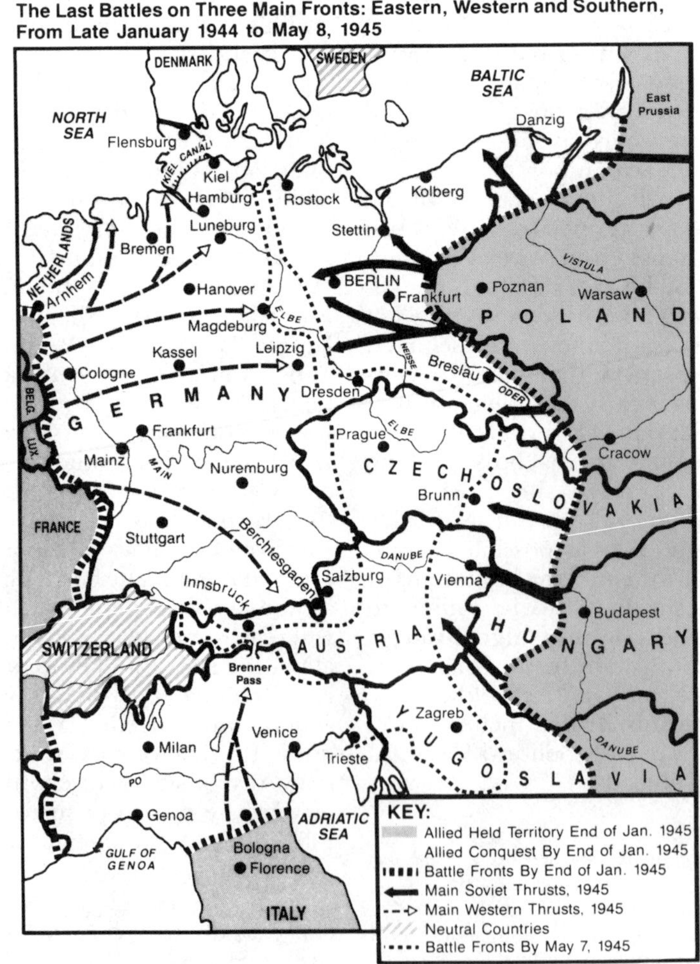

The Last Battles on Three Main Fronts: Eastern, Western and Southern, From Late January 1944 to May 8, 1945

the American mass media raising the question, How much did Roosevelt give away at Yalta, in the secret deals with Stalin? How could the President reconcile the brutal suppression of democratic voices in Rumania and Poland with the Declaration on Liberated Countries?

THE DEATH OF ROOSEVELT

While the Yalta agreements were being debated, on April 12 President Roosevelt died at Warm Springs, Georgia, of a massive cerebral hemmorhage. This caused jubilation in Berlin. When a secretary came into Goebbels's office announcing "Roosevelt is dead," the propaganda minister could not believe it. The teletype sheets were placed before him. Goebbels hugged them to his breast. "Bring our best champagne," he ordered, "and get the Führer on the phone." "My Führer!" he shouted. "I congratulate you. Roosevelt is dead. It is written in the stars that the second half of April will be the turning point for us. This is almost Friday, April thirteenth. It is the turning point!"

And indeed, Hitler greeted the President's death as the long expected "miracle" predicted by his court astrologer a long time before. In Hitler's bunker, the staff wondered aloud about the possible impact of Roosevelt's death on the war; they cited as a precedent the death of Empress Elizabeth of Russia in 1762, which had saved Frederick the Great from defeat by a coalition. Hitler was now convinced that the demise of the American president would halt the progress of the Western Allies' armies and open a prospect of a separate peace. He even hoped that an alliance with the British and the Americans against Communist Russia could be arranged.[9]

[9]The end of the war at the Führer's GHQ has been dramatically described by H. R. Trevor-Roper, *The Last Days of Hitler* (London: Macmillan, 1947) and John Toland, *The Last 100 Days* (New York: Random House, 1965).

By 1944/45, unlike Churchill and Stalin who were still in fairly good physical shape, President Roosevelt had slipped from the peak of his powers. His heart was enlarged and his body had become flaccid. His ability to concentrate was greatly impaired. His arteries were those of a much older man; they had narrowed and hardened, constricting the flow of his blood. He required at least ten to twelve hours of sleep. Death came to the President at the relatively early age of sixty-three, when the war was practically won. This was achieved largely thanks to his judicious policy of the years between 1940 to 1942 and his timely help to beleaguered Britain, as well as to Russia.

President Roosevelt was a statesman with a global vision and charismatic personality. Despite the fact that he had been stricken by polio and half paralyzed, he bravely overcame his affliction and displayed amazing activity almost up to his death. He had fought a victorious two-ocean war on opposite sides of the world, 13,000 miles apart, a unique achievement in history. His Wilsonian perception of the role of the United States in world affairs made him prepare his country, step by step, to enter the war in defiance of a powerful isolationist lobby. His efforts in this respect were carried out cautiously, but with remarkable consistency. His aid was timely and effective: Both Britain and Russia had been on the verge of defeat when the lend-lease bill provided them ships, tanks, planes, guns, and food to continue the struggle for survival. Thus the bill was a spectacular contribution to the victory of the anti-Axis coalition—one of the great acts of statesmanship. Yet the President's role as a war leader was not free from contradictions.

President Roosevelt's pragmatism, so remarkable in domestic affairs, often failed him in the international forum during the later stages of the war. His idealistic vision of world peace led him to take a rather naive view about the future of inter-Allied relations. He had literally staked his life on an honorable, equitable peace structure for the world based on cooperation of the Big

Three. For this he was willing to pay almost any price to see it realized. His misreading of Stalin was intertwined with his perception of the historical role of the United States as an arbiter between the USSR and Britain. He saw the world in terms of a steady evolution toward liberal democracy. The Axis powers represented the reactionary forces. Churchill, admirable in many ways, represented traditional imperialism and colonialism. Stalin and his Communists were moving toward the future; they were crude and occasionally brutal, yet, in his eyes, they were pioneers of the collective state of the people. The United States, with its progressive liberalism, was midway between the British and the Russians and, in spirit, actually closer to Soviet egalitarian populism than to the Tory elitist conservatism of Churchill.[10]

[10]In his war memoirs Churchill described the relationship between President Roosevelt and himself, mostly in terms of harmony, warmth, and generosity. Their recently published complete correspondence shows, however, that up until the time the United States entered the war, Churchill remained in the difficult position of being forced to beg, often in subservient terms, for America's aid. For an updated picture of the complex relationship see *Churchill & Roosevelt: The Complete Correspondence,* 3 vols.: *Alliance Emerging, Alliance Forged, Alliance Declining,* edited with commentary by Warren F. Kimball (Princeton, N.J.: Princeton University Press, 1984).

ON THE EVE OF THE FALL OF BERLIN

The last great battle of World War II in Europe, the storming of Berlin, started on April 16, 1946. The capturing of the German capital was to be a Soviet task. From the bridgeheads on the Oder, the armies of Marshal Zhukov advanced from the east. At the same time, the troops of Marshal Ivan Konev, after capturing Vienna and Dresden, swept toward the German capital from the south. Simultaneously, the Western Allies were converging toward the Elbe. Thus by mid-April the German capital was surrounded and isolated from the rest of the country, with the remnant of the Wehrmacht squared into an increasingly shrinking perimeter.

As the war was approaching its end, Hitler, encapsuled in his underground bunker, was trapped like a cornered rat. His health was deteriorating rapidly. He was often seized by violent outbreaks of maniacal rages. His head was wobbling, his hands were trembling, and his left arm was hanging slackly. His profuse sweating, the strange twitching of his face, and bouts of sultry brooding struck people who had direct dealings with him. A close aide described his decline as bordering on senility. Most of his

Hitler's youngest soldiers: German teenagers sent to the Eastern front. German Information Center, New York

fits of fury were triggered by what he regarded as the failure of his subordinates to carry out his insane orders. He was convinced that they were cowards who refused to commit themselves to all-out sacrifices in defense of their fatherland.

Hitler was determined to defend Berlin to the bitter end. He wanted to raise half a million men commanded by the Nazi's political commissars and dispatch them at once to the front to wage "the sacred war of the people." The desperate search for dwindling reserves brought about Hitler's acceptance even of General Vlasov, whom he had hitherto called a "hired Bolshevik butcher." Forgetting his racial preconceptions, he now permitted Himmler to draw Latvian, Estonian, Ukrainian and Belorussian units into the Waffen S.S. All these desperate efforts were of no avail. By the spring of 1945 the German troops were rapidly losing their cohesion and discipline. On March 1, 1945, Hitler ordered discussion of "scorched earth" tactics: the wrecking of the remaining factories, transport, and communication facilities. Full of self-pity and bitterness, he lived in a fool's paradise. To escape reality, he liked to watch the documentary films of his condemned enemies being lifted onto meat hooks.

Meanwhile, two mighty Soviet army groups were inexorably approaching the German capital: Zhukov's from Kuestrin and Konev's from Dresden. Like two hungry greyhounds unleashed by their master, they were racing to get the last big prize. The final encirclement of Berlin was finished by April 25. On the same day, Soviet and United States troops linked up on the river Elbe and exchanged formal salutes. An official United States–Soviet linkup was celebrated at 4:40 P.M. on April 25, 1945, at Torgau. There the GIs, some of them from California, met and drank euphoric toasts with a group of Red Army men, some of them from Siberia.

On the day of the encounter at Torgau the United Nations representatives convened for the first time in San Francisco to lay down the foundations of the United Nations Organizations.[11] From April 25 until June 26, shortly before the first nuclear device was exploded in secret in the Nevada desert, the world's leaders argued about the shape and structure of the organization to succeed the defunct League of Nations. They also debated the "fundamental rights" to which they professed to dedicate themselves henceforth. These rights were to include "social progress and better standard of life," as well as "the equal rights of men and women." Unlike President Roosevelt, Churchill was skeptical about the United Nations. In San Francisco, on May 11, 1945, he said bluntly to Anthony Eden, his foreign secretary: "The Russians may remain with hundreds of divisions in possession of Europe from Lübeck to Trieste, and to the Greek frontier on the Adriatic. All these things are far more vital than the amendments to a world constitution which may never come into being. . . ."

HITLER'S DEATH

When Hitler's hopes about the split in the enemy camp failed to materialize, he relapsed into a mood of total despair. On April 28 he dictated his last will. He was bent on remaining in Berlin and "would choose voluntary death" when his chancellery could no longer be held. For his misfortunes he blamed mainly "the British ruling clique," "a tool in international Jewry." He intended that after his death, the Third Reich should be destroyed because the German people were not worthy of surviving him. Yet Hitler predicted a glorious rebirth of the National Socialist movement and reestablishment of a powerful, united Germany. He condemned his closest comrades, Goering and Himmler, for leaving him, when they had recently sought a settlement with the Allies, and he appointed Admiral Doenitz as his successor.

[11]Poland, the first country to fight Nazi Germany, was not represented at San Francisco because the Soviet Union refused to accept representatives of the Polish government in London to the meeting.

Because of his utter ruthlessness, Hitler felt that Doenitz could carry out the Führer's will to the end.

The last sentence of Hitler's testament and his final message to the German people reflected his innermost, quintessential belief: "Above all I pledge the leadership of the nation and its followers to the scrupulous observation of the racial laws and to an implacable opposition against the universal poisoner of all peoples, international Jewry."[12] Martin Bormann and a few other Nazi bosses were left behind to send the final telegrams and copies of his last will outside the bunker.

On April 29 Hitler married his long-time girlfriend, Eva Braun. After the ceremony Hitler dictated his second testament, which stated that he and his bride were determined to die to avoid the shame of being captured by the enemies. They wished their bodies to be burned in the place where they had worked for the last year. Thus the ceremony resembled more a suicide pact than a wedding. Hitler ordered his favorite Alsatian dog to be poisoned; poison was also to be distributed to his secretaries. Then, early in the morning of April 30, he shook hands with the remaining members of his entourage and retired with Eva Braun. Eva took poison, and Hitler shot himself through the mouth with his pistol.

The Führer's aides carried both bodies to the nearby garden, doused them with gasoline, and burned their remains. Hitler's gnomelike propaganda minister, Joseph Goebbels, poisoned his wife and five children and then took poison himself. Both Hitler and Goebbels wanted to show that they were determined to die fighting as Aryan man's leaders in their "life or death struggle against the racial underworld," the "Jewish Bolshevism."

After the suicides of both Hitler and Goebbels, Admiral Doenitz reigned over the ruins of the Third Reich for one week. His primary efforts were to evacuate as many Germans as possible from the path of the Red Army to the areas that would be occupied by Western armies and seek a separate peace with the West. In the first task he was only partially successful; in the second he failed utterly. In the name of "Allied unity," both Washington and London stuck to the principle of "unconditional surrender to all partners of the coalition" simultaneously.

HITLER IN RETROSPECT

Hitler was a complex historical figure, and his achievements are hard to assess, even from the perspective of more than five decades. The controversies and emotions his personality still evokes are too intense to pronounce a dispassionate judgment on him. Despite numerous studies on the subject, no one has yet been able to explain adequately how a largely self-educated corporal, who in World War I had not so much as led a platoon, could assume the role of a bold and innovative military leader, create one of the mightiest armed forces in history, and challenge half the world and almost defeat it. Despite some effort to ridicule him and turn him into a lunatic, he was obviously an enduring character, and a man of no mean intelligence and impressive will power. He was endowed with a demoniacal energy and a brilliant although perverted mind. Despite his rather vulgar exterior, he did have a magnetic and even charismatic gift, which made the majority of the Germans accept his leadership to the very end of the losing struggle. During the period between 1933 and 1939, he displayed his remarkable diplomatic talents, outwitting most professional men in the field.

His military gifts were beyond doubt and commanded admiration even among many of his enemies. Besides being endowed with a restless and inquisitive mind, he had a phenomenal memory. Hitler paid considerable attention to minute material details and of-

[12]For several of his pronouncements of fundamental ideological character, including the document dictated on April 28, 1945, see François Genoud, ed., *The Testament of Adolf Hitler: The Hitler-Bormann Documents, February–April 1945*, (London: Cassell, 1961).

ten revealed an amazing grasp of the technological factors of weaponry, as well as of logistics and tactical problems. Although the idea of an independent armored force originated with Guderian and the brilliant strategic plan of the French campaign was Manstein's work, without Hitler neither Guderian nor Manstein would have prevailed against the more tradition-bound generals. Field Marshals von Manstein and von Kluge, who both looked at him as an upstart and a dilettante, had to admit that he often had an uncanny grasp of "operational opportunities" and even flashes of military "genius." Even faced with death sentences at the Nuremberg trial, Jodl and Kesselring could not bring themselves to condemn Hitler. Kluge, in the farewell letter written before his suicide, paid tribute to Hitler's "genius."[13]

Hitler represented the dominant human factor of the war on the German side. He had prepared the war, unleashed it, conducted it, and made a decisive contribution to losing it. No leader of men since Napoleon managed to determine his country's strategy, tactics, and logistics to such an extent. Hitler's mythical belief in his own infallibility, or his "intuition," made him prolong the conflict well beyond any reasonable hope of winning it. Although he professed to be a discipline of Clausewitz, he forgot his master's basic principle that wars are waged to achieve political goals. While precipitating a global war, he was deficient in global strategic thinking and aimlessly prolonged the conflict beyond any reasonable hope for victory. He was a classical berserker fighting for the sake of fighting. His morbid megalomania made him his own worst enemy, as well as the enemy of his people, whom he came to despise as "unworthy" of him. Actually it was Hitler who betrayed the German people. The seductive malevolence of this modern Pied Piper, who had bewitched millions of followers and kept them under his strange spell until the very eve of the catastrophe, made him as an English historian pointed out "the greatest demagogue in history."[14]

Cardinal Richelieu used to say that a statesman should have in his veins as much mercury as lead. In Hitler's case this balance was obviously grossly upset: His visceral reaction more than his brains increasingly dominated his decisions toward the end of his career. His grasp of international politics was unmatched since Bismarck. Yet he totally lacked the Iron Chancellor's sense of moderation. His dream of dominating Europe, and finally the world, in the name of the alleged German racial superiority, represented an insane vision for which Germany had no sufficient resources.

Had Hitler's aims been less reprehensible and his methods less criminal, his brilliant political gifts could have made him one of the great statesmen of Germany, on a par with Frederick II and Bismarck. Hitler's popularity defies rational explanation: Even while leading his country to ruin he was still idolized by his people. During the Nuremberg trial, General Jodl said that Hitler was "a great man of demonic, perverted, infernal greatness." This satanic greatness exploded into acts of incredible criminality. They made him one of the great villains of history, comparable to Attila the Hun, Genghis Khan, and his more cautious and successful rival, Stalin.

THE ITALIAN CAMPAIGN

Meanwhile, the Italian campaign proceeded at its slow pace. After the fall of Rome in June 1944 the Allied contingents kept on

[13]For an attempt at an assessment of the Führer's talents and his historic roles see Percy Ernst Schramm, *Hitler: The Man and the Military Leader* (Chicago: Quadrangle Books, 1971), especially Appendix II: "Memorandum Dictated in 1946 by General Alfred Jodl on Hitler's Military Leadership," pp. 192ff.; and Sebastian Haffner, *The Meaning of Hitler* (New York: Macmillan, 1979).

[14]Alan Bullock, *Hitler: A Study in Tyranny,* 2nd ed. (N.Y.: Harper and Row, 1964), p. 68. For an evaluation of Hitler's personality and achievement see also Joachim C. Fest, *Hitler* (San Diego: Harcourt Brace Jovanovich, 1974), pp. 75–76; and Eberhard Jaekel, *Hitler in History* (Hanover, N.H.: University Press of New England, 1984, for Brandeis University Press).

pursuing the skillfully retreating Tenth and Fourteenth German armies, which continued to apply their delaying tactics. Florence was seized, however, before its treasures could be destroyed. Yet north of the city the Allies hit new defenses in the form of the powerful Gothic line, which sheltered the last German redoubt in Lombardy. The assault on the Gothic line in the summer of 1944 saw some of the heaviest fighting of the war. The U.S. Fifth and the British Eighth armies, weakened by the shifting of some units to France, could barely cope with the Germans, reinforced by the troops meanwhile withdrawn from Greece and the Balkans. The storming of the Gothic line so exhausted the American and British contingents that all their efforts to reach Bologna before the winter rains failed. Consequently, they had to hibernate south of Ravenna and La Spezia to gather strength for the spring offensive. Bologna was captured by Polish troops by April 17–21, 1945, after bitter fighting.

Henceforth the Allied progress through southern Lombardy was relatively smooth. Mussolini's neo-Fascist republic had collapsed like a house of cards. By the spring of 1945 Il Duce was a shadow of his former self—bitter, ill, and depressed. While the German forces retreated toward the Alps, he tried to escape by hiding in the back of a German lorry, disguised in a Wehrmacht uniform. His young mistress, Clara Petacci, joined him voluntarily to share his fate. Mussolini's tragic end was precipitated by an accident. Near Milan a group of Italian guerrillas, who had intercepted and searched the German convoy, recognized both Mussolini and his companion. They were both arrested and taken to a nearby farm house where they were kept under custody. Meanwhile a group of Communist partisans burst into their bedroom, dragged them out, and stood them against the wall. Clara Petacci screamed and tried to shield her lover. Both of them were riddled through with bullets. Their bodies were taken in a van to nearby Milan. On the following day the mutilated corpses of Il Duce and his mistress were hung upside down from the girders of a partly finished garage in Piazzale Loreto. The church authorities arranged for removal of the bodies and their burial in the pauper's section of a Milan cemetery on May 1, 1945.

Mussolini's tragic end preceded Hitler's suicide by only forty-eight hours. The Italian dictator was one of the most baffling characters of the first half of the twentieth century. As with Hitler, violence and deceit initially served him well. Lurching forward from one ostensible triumph to another, his head was also turned, and he came to believe in his own propaganda of Il Duce's greatness and even infallibility. This was reflected in the slogans so often painted on the walls: "Mussolini is always right!" Yet the Fascist empire was no more than the glittering façade of a rickety edifice that the Italian people had neither the resources nor the will to sustain. From the very entry of Italy into the war, an unparalleled series of defeats shattered the façade and revealed the groundlessness of Mussolini's claims.

Constantly on the stage, performing a part, he was far more concerned about impressing people than about achieving anything of substance. The conceited expression so familiar from his official photographs reveals his inner personality, hidden behind the mask of a superhuman hero. His inner weakness Mussolini tried to cover with bombastic gestures and by applying violence. At heart he was a timid dilettante, a shallow journalist, and a cheap demagogue, craving popularity more than anything else. In his conduct of the war he was a national disaster. Behind the ever-changing masks he wore, he was actually more of an actor than a statesman. While Hitler was a "devilish genius," as Jodl called him at the Nuremberg trial, as well as a moral monster, Mussolini was simply a morbid megalomaniac and a mediocre actor always trying to play the part of an imagined hero. His wife, Donna Rachele, rightly called him simply "a miserable creature."

After the capture of Bologna on April 21, General Heinrich von Vietinghoff threw his

The German population of Eastern Germany flees in fear of the approaching Red Army. German Information Center, New York

last reserves trying to stem the Allied advance to the Po. Under relentless pressure from the Americans, the German troops pulled back to the left bank of the river, abandoning most of their heavy equipment. Continuing their drive toward the Alps, the Fifth and Eighth armies joined forces with the American and French troops advancing along the Riviera. Meanwhile Vietinghoff had already signed the unconditional surrender of his forces in Italy. The surrender became effective on May 2.[15]

The forces of northern Italy comprised the battered remnants of twenty-two German divisions and six Italian Fascist ones, half a million men altogether. The territory opened by this surrender to Allied arms included all northern Italy to the Isonzo River, the Austrian provinces of the Vorarlberg, Salzburg, and the Tirol, and portions of Carinthia and Syria. Thus, the whole southern flank of the German position in the Alps was now taken over by the Western Allies. This had important military consequences for the entire region. The quick German surrender allowed Allied troops to be the first to occupy Trieste, the key harbor of the Adriatic. If the Germans, still fighting, had fallen back in a tight defensive perimeter west of Venice, then Communist forces—either Soviet troops, coming across Hungary or Tito's Partisans, approaching from Yugoslavia—would have been in Trieste and possibly west of there before the Western Allies arrived on the spot.

GERMANY SURRENDERS

The capturing of devastated Berlin by the Soviet troops was followed by an orgy of rape, looting, and killing. The Red Army men would not be satisfied with a military triumph; they wanted revenge for the innumerable acts of cruelty that the Wehrmacht had committed on Soviet soil. Actually the reckoning had started as soon as the troops crossed the old Soviet frontiers of 1939, the Ribbentrop-Molotov line. Officially spurred on by the exhortations of the chief Soviet propagandist, the popular writer, Ilya Ehrenburg, the Red Army soldiers indulged in unbridled pillaging, raping, and burning. The slogan "Kill the Germans" was repeated over and over, apparently with the full ap-

[15]For the background of the capitulation of the German forces in Italy see Allen Dulles, *The Secret Surrender* (New York, London: Harper & Row, 1956). For the German point of view see Kesselring, *A Soldier's Record*, pp. 264–82.

May 2, 1945: Soviet tanks push toward the center of Berlin. Soviet Embassy, Washington, D.C.

proval of Stalin. This line of Soviet propaganda changed only on the eve of the battle of Berlin, marking a new approach to the German problem. On April 14, 1945, in an unprecedented editorial published by the Soviet military newspaper *Red Star,* Ehrenburg was officially reprimanded: "Comrade Ehrenburg is exaggerating. . . . We are not fighting against the German people, only against the Hitlers of the world."

This reproof came too late to affect the behavior of the Red Army soldiers in the conquered territories. Some Soviet commanders attempted to restrain their troops from looting, raping, and killing but were hardly successful. Some Russian soldiers were severely punished for such violations, but this was to no avail: Intoxicated by their triumph, the Red Army now wanted revenge and instant satisfaction of their long repressed savage instincts.[16]

Meanwhile, German resistance was collapsing everywhere. The gradual, step-by-step surrender of various sectors of the front started on May 2. The capitulation in northern Italy was followed by similar steps in Denmark and Norway on May 4. The general capitulation on all fronts came only on May 7. On that day, early in the morning at Rheims, in northeastern France, General Jodl put his signature to the unconditional surrender document affecting all German forces wherever they found themselves. The surrender was made jointly to the representatives of the United States, Great Britain, the USSR, and France. The scene of the capitulation was a brick school house at Rheims, which for a few months had been Eisenhower's Supreme Headquarters. At one side of a simple table sat three German plenipotentiaries: Admiral Hans von Friedenburg, commander in chief of the German navy; General Alfred Johl, chief of the German General Staff; and his aide, General Wilhelm Oxenius. Opposite them were the Allied representatives: British General Sir Francis Morgan, Eisenhower's Deputy Chief of Staff; General François Sevez, representing France; Admiral Sir H. M. Burrough, commander of the Allied Naval Expeditionary Force; General Walter Bedell Smith, Eisenhower's Chief of Staff; General Carl A. Spaatz, commander of the U.S. Strategic Air Force; and Generals Ivan Chermaiev and Ivan Suslaparov, who represented the Soviet

[16]For the Soviet point of view of the concluding struggles see S. M. Shtememko, *The Last Six Months: Russia's Final Battles with Hitler's Armies in World War II,* trans. Guy Daniels (New York: Doubleday, 1975). For a British point of view see John Strawson, *The Battle for Berlin* (London: B. T. Batsford, 1974).

Field Marshal Wilhelm Keitel signs the act of Germany's unconditional surrender in Berlin, on May 8, 1945. German Information Center, New York

Union. Supreme Commander General Eisenhower and his deputy, Air Chief Marshal Sir Arthur Tedder, remained in a nearby office.

The four instruments of surrender, one each for the United States, Great Britain, France, and the Soviet Union, were signed within a few minutes. Then the German emissaries were led down a hall to Eisenhower's office. In an incisive tone he asked Jodl if the German representatives thoroughly understood the provisions of the unconditional surrender. When Jodl answered "Ja" [yes], Eisenhower declared: "You will, officially and personally, be responsible if the terms of the surrender are violated, incuding its provision for German commanders to appear in Berlin at the moment set by the Russian High Command to accomplish formal surrender to that government. That is all." Jodl, whose face was like a death mask, saluted, turned around, and, with his companions, left the room.[17] On May 8 the unconditional surrender was ratified in Karlshorst near Berlin. World War II in Europe was supposed to last only a few months, according to Hitler, but it dragged on for over five years.

The Nazi Reich that was to last for a thousand years actually lasted not much more than twelve years and four months. The enraged Red Army soldiers had razed the remaining ruins of Hitler's chancellery to the ground. By the end of July 1945, on that spot there was no more than a grassy mound infested by rats and rabbits. A few days after the end of hostilities the once proud German capital was reminiscent of the ruins of Pompei.

THE END OF THE WAR IN EUROPE

The end of the war in Europe was greeted with orgies of joy and jubilation. Hysterical celebrations erupted all over the world, but especially throughout the Allied countries. Millions of relieved, overjoyed, and often intoxicated people flocked to the streets shouting "Hurrah! Victory is ours! It's over! It is all over!" Enthusiastic strangers screamed, hugged, and kissed each other. Impromptu parades preceded well-orchestrated official victory celebrations. General Eisenhower issued the Victory Order of the Day:

> Let us have no part in the profitless quarrels in which other men will inevitably engage as to what country, what service, won the European war. Every man, every woman, of every nation here represented has served according to his or her ability, and the efforts of each have contributed to the outcome. This we shall remember—and in doing so we shall be revering each honored grave, and be sending comfort to the loved ones of comrades who could not live to see this day.

Triumphant victory parades were held in all Allied capitals. The most spectacular

[17]Eisenhower, *Crusade in Europe,* pp. 425–26; see also Anne Armstrong, *Unconditional Surrender* (New Brunswick, N.J.: Rutgers University Press, 1961).

parade, however, was held at Red Square in Moscow. It was led by Marshal Zhukov, the most successful of all Soviet commanders and perhaps of the entire war, the victor of the battles of Moscow, Stalingrad, Kursk, and Berlin. The climax of the parade was reached when over 200 captured German banners were thrown at the feet of Stalin standing in his uniform of the Soviet generalissimo, in front of Lenin's tomb. From now on Stalin was to be honored in his country not only as "the great, progressive statesman of mankind" but also as "a military genius" and "the most brilliant of all military leaders in history."[18]

[18]The growth of the myth of Stalin's infallibility as a military leader has been discussed in Matthew P. Gallagher, *The Soviet History of World War II* (New York: Praeger, 1963).

19

The Potsdam Conference and the New Status Quo

THE POTSDAM CONFERENCE

The European war lasted for five years, eight months, and seven days. The end of the hostilities in Europe was followed by the third and last meeting of the Big Three. The most appropriate choice for such a gathering would be Berlin. No suitably large premises could be found, however, in the once proud but now devastated German capital full of stinking corpses and half-starved, embittered people. Consequently, Potsdam, an ancient garrison town in the Soviet sector, a historic monument of Prussian militarism, a beloved spot of Hitler's idol Frederick II, was chosen as the most suitable spot for the final summit meeting.

The Potsdam conference lasted from July 17 to August 2, 1945. It took place in the Cecilienhoff, a palace built by the last German crown prince for his wife. Stalin still hoped to persuade the United States to continue the lend-lease aid to his war-ravaged country and finance its reconstruction with Western credits. Always a meticulous planner, he tried to arrange every detail conducive to preserving the partnership that had contributed so much to his weathering the storm now passing. After inspecting the main hall in which the deliberations of the Big Three were to take place, he noticed the painting on the ceiling with a sailing ship surmounted by a dark cloud. Sensing a bad omen, he ordered the ceiling redecorated. He instructed a shining star, a symbol common to both the Soviet Union and the United States, to be painted over the dark cloud.[1]

[1]For the Potsdam conference see Herbert Feis, *Between War and Peace: The Potsdam Conference* (Princeton, N.J.: Princeton University Press, 1960); see also his *Churchill, Roosevelt and Stalin: The War They Waged and*

At Potsdam President Roosevelt's place was taken by his successor, Harry Truman, who had served only eighty-two days as vice-president and had had hardly time enough to get acquainted with the affairs of state. He had been kept completely in the dark as far as foreign affairs were concerned by President Roosevelt. Winston Churchill was to remain at the conference only until July 28, at which time his Conservative party suffered defeat in the British parliamentary election. A decisive victory of the Labour party brought a new prime minister to Potsdam as Britain's chief delegate. The humiliated Churchill had to leave for home. His place was taken by the victorious Labour party leader, Clement R. Attlee. Attlee was a short, slight, and schoolmasterly man of considerable domestic political skills, but without much first-hand experience in international affairs. At his side was Ernest Bevin as foreign secretary; he had been minister of labor and national service in Churchill's wartime coalition cabinet and author of a postwar demobilization plan that was to follow the end of hostilities. Thus, Stalin remained the only veteran of the two previous summit meetings, now facing two novices in foreign matters.

Churchill's departure was a great loss to the West. Although by that time he was already an exhausted man, his vast expertise and exceptional international prestige were a unique advantage for the West, especially Britain. The authority he had acquired as a war leader could hardly be overestimated. He had incarnated the struggle against Hitler perhaps more than anybody else. During the appeasement era he had been a Cassandra crying in the wilderness. From the very beginning of the war to its last phases, he had been Hitler's principal and most consistent enemy for nearly six years. During the fateful summer of 1940 Churchill had been the main protagonist of the fight to the end against Hitler, and the main obstacle to a negotiated peace that would have spelled Nazi victory. During the most crucial phase of the struggle, from the summer of 1940 to the end of 1941, Britain, led by Churchill, had defied Hitler's might alone. This could not be denied even by his antagonists.

the Peace They Sought (Princeton, N.J.: Princeton University Press, 1957) and Charles L. Mee, Jr., *Meeting at Potsdam* (New York: M. Evans, 1975).

Berlin in May 1945: A landscape of endless ruins.
German Information Center, New York

As a strategist, Winston Churchill was not without some aberrations and even obsessions. Although competent in naval matters, in the field of land warfare his judgment was less dependable. Unlike President Roosevelt, Churchill had few illusions about the course and outcome of the war. In 1953 he called the last volume of his memoirs *Triumph and Tragedy*. The war was a triumph because the purpose of the struggle had been accomplished: Hitler and the Third Reich were destroyed. But it was also a tragedy, because of the loss of one-third of Europe to a Communist power that stood fiercely opposed to most Western values and had swarmed over the adjacent countries "like locusts." To Churchill, Hitler was a greater danger than Stalin, and the German domination of all of Europe would have presented a far greater danger to Britain than the Soviet hegemony of the eastern part of the Continent only. At least the western segment of Germany was saved from the Soviets, to serve as a buffer to the exhausted Britons. Half of Europe was better than none.

Churchill was staunchly pro-American. Consequently, he was shocked by President Truman's desire to meet Stalin first. Since the beginning of the war he had called for the closest possible cooperation between America and Great Britain, and now was straining all his ingenuity to extend "the special relationship" between the two English-speaking countries. As long as the hostilities in Europe were going on, the cooperation with Soviet Russia was a vital necessity. It was Churchill who coined the term *Grand Alliance*. But he always realized that his slogan was fully applicable to the American-British partnership only. When applied to relations between Stalin and his Western partners, the term was largely meaningless, because the military cooperation was not based on a similarity of values and long-term objectives.

Despite contrary propaganda, the British, the Americans, and the Soviets were at best uneasy co-belligerents. The cooperation among Washington, London, and Moscow had been only military and not political. Soviet historians are actually more realistic, and in their writing on the subject use a more appropriate term: the anti-Nazi coalition. In 1941 Stalin realized that to survive he had to cooperate. As the Soviet ambassador in London pointed out: "In the jungle the strangest animals got together if they felt that their joint interests made this advisable." The Western powers and Stalin had only one imperative: to get rid of Hitler and his regime. Once this goal had been achieved, differences began to crop up at every step. Great Britain and the United States had publicly subscribed to the vaguely worded Wilsonian principles of the Atlantic Charter, which called for national self-determination, free trade, and democracy. The Soviet Union endorsed the charter only reluctantly and with menacing reservations.

One must bear in mind that, even after the West had welcomed the Soviets into the Allied camp, Stalin could not put aside his suspicion of his new partners. He feared that the old rivalry of the capitalistic world toward the Soviet Union would not be exhausted. He feared that capitalist-Communist antagonism would resume after Germany's defeat. The paranoia that gripped Stalin over almost every act of the Western Allies was constant and profound. Stalin repeatedly accused Churchill of watching Germany and the Soviet Union cripple each other, while they husbanded their resources and waited for the moment when their intervention would make the United States and Britain the arbiters of the world.

Stormy Deliberations

President Roosevelt's successor at Potsdam, Harry Truman, had a tough task. Before he became President, Truman had no experience in foreign affairs. His predecessor had kept his deputy in ignorance about many vital strategic and foreign policy matters; he was, however, aware of the Manhattan Project (the development of the atomic bomb), but not of all the details. Truman's newly appointed secretary of state, James F. Byrnes, was mainly a domes-

Stalin, Truman, and Churchill at Potsdam.
National Archives

tic politican turned international statesman by force of circumstances. He rose rapidly from local court reporter to district attorney, United States congressman, senator, Supreme Court justice, Roosevelt's economic stabilizer, director of war mobilization, and unofficial "assistant president for the homefront." At home he was regarded as a formidable political fixer, "a politician's politician." President Roosevelt took him to the Yalta conference, which was Byrnes' first and most important formative experience in international affairs and which shaped his new public image as an elder statesman. That image influenced Truman's estimate of Byrnes' allegedly unique knowledge and qualifications as the new secretary of state.[2]

On the night Truman became President, he was told that a project was under way to create "a new explosive of almost unbelievable destructive power." That was all. Before Truman left for Europe to attend the Potsdam conference, on July 16, 1945, at Alamogordo, New Mexico, the sky blazed with the first atomic explosion. A new era in the history of humanity had begun with the most powerful country on earth suffering from a succession crisis and its leaders undergoing training on the job.

Initially, President Truman was determined to follow in the footsteps of his predecessor and, therefore, disregard Churchill's pleas for resuming the British-American partnership to face the Soviets. In his *Memoirs* he admitted that at Potsdam "on several occasions when Churchill was discussing something at length, Stalin would lean on his elbow, pull on his mustache, and say, 'Why don't you agree? The Americans agree, and we agree. You will agree eventually, so why don't you do it now?' Then the argument would stop."[3]

The deliberations of the summit at Potsdam were much more stormy than those of Teheran and Yalta. The Potsdam meeting and its aftermath revealed the brittleness of the wartime alliance caused by the surfacing mutual distrust resulting from different values and goals. With the integrating pressures of wartime requirements gone, even the façade of Allied unity began to disintegrate. The old truth that military alliances are no lasting romances but merely disposable marriages of convenience was confirmed once more. After a great deal of bickering, Ger-

[2]Byrnes' experiences as secretary of state are described in his *Speaking Frankly,* pp. 67ff.

[3]Harry S. Truman, *Memoirs* (Garden City, N.Y.: Doubleday, 1953), vol. 1, p. 363.

many was split along the Elbe valley, the ancient boundary of the Carolingian Empire, more than a thousand years ago! Upper Saxony and all of Thuringia were to be occupied by the Soviet troops, and the area to the west was to be shared by the United States, Britain, and later on, France. Berlin was to be jointly occupied by the four powers. The Western garrisons in the former capital of Germany, separated by 110 miles of Soviet-controlled territory, were given guarantees of free communication by land and air with their respective occupation zones in West Germany. The economic policy to be applied to all zones of occupation was to be determined collectively.

One of the most hotly disputed issues of the Potsdam conference was the problem of territorial compensations to Poland for the loss of its eastern provinces to the USSR and the unprecedented devastation of human and material resources under the German occupation. After having made a gesture of consulting with the representative of the new provisional government in Warsaw, the Big Three decided that lands east of the Oder and western Neisse rivers were to be put "under the administration of the Polish State . . . pending final delimitation" at the future peace conference. During the last months of the war many German inhabitants had fled westward in fear of the Red Army's atrocities. The remaining 2.5 million Germans were now to be transferred to the Soviet and Western occupation zones. For this purpose the Allies put at the disposal of the Communist regime in Poland enough transport facilities to carry out this operation as quickly as possible. Meanwhile, the Czechs had expelled practically all the Germans, numbering some 3 million people, from the Sudetenland. Since, at the same time, numerous, although less forcible, deportations of Germans had taken place in Rumania, Yugoslavia, and Hungary, the ethnic map of eastern Europe had undergone a further radical change: To the extermination of over 6 million Jews by Hitler was now added the expulsion of some 10 million Germans.

By sponsoring the transfer of the Germans, as well as by encouraging their Polish vassals to push their boundaries as far as the Oder and Neisse rivers, the Russians achieved three interlocked objectives. First, they reduced the territorial base of the defeated, but potentially still dangerous, enemy; second, they denied as much land and as many resources as possible to the western powers; third, their control over the heart of the former Reich was now to be reinforced by a broad belt of buffer

Nuremberg, 1946: Trial of the main Nazi war criminals. German Information Center, New York

states that depended on Moscow politically as well as militarily. The main political instrument of control was the respective Communist parties. The Soviet hegemony was bolstered by stationing a powerful force of over twenty divisions, deployed between the Elbe and the Oder; supporting these garrisons were the armies of the vassal states. All the satellite states—Poland, Czechoslovakia, Hungary, Rumania, Bulgaria, Yugoslavia, and Albania—signed alliance treaties with the USSR as well as with each other, thus creating an intricate interlocking security net. The rise of the Soviet eastern European empire and its militant posture scared the United States and made it look for ways of coping with this new and dangerous conglomerate of power.

The Surrender of Japan

Before the Big Three finished with the German problem, they had to deal with another partner of the Axis triangle. In the summer of 1945 Japan was still fighting a bloody, bitter delaying action both on the Asian mainland and in the Pacific Ocean. At Potsdam, Stalin reaffirmed his Yalta pledge to strike against Japan three months after the end of hostilities in Europe. President Truman hesitated on whether to tell Stalin about the atomic bomb, but Byrnes remained opposed. But the President seemed determined to at least drop a hint to Stalin, in return for the Soviet leader's candor about the Japanese peace overtures. He made his approach to Stalin unofficially on the evening of July 24 after the adjournment of that day's plenary session; but even then, Stalin was not told that the bomb was about to be dropped on Japan. Instead, Truman said only that the United States had created a "new weapon" of unusual destructive power. In fact, through a cohort of his spies, Stalin already knew more about the bomb that Truman had imagined.

Two days later, on July 26, the Big Three issued a declaration threatening Japan with annihilation unless Tokyo surrendered unconditionally and immediately. On July 27 the Tokyo government rejected the Potsdam declaration and reaffirmed its resolution to continue the war to the bitter end. As a consequence of this, President Truman ordered the first atom bomb to be dropped on the naval and military bases of Hiroshima on August 6. This resulted in 135,000 casualties (66,000 killed and 69,000 wounded) and the utter destruction of some three-fifths of the city. When the Japanese still continued to fight, another bomb was dropped on another city. Nagasaki, on August 9. The devastating results of the first military application of nuclear weapons had shattered the Japanese morale. On August 10 Radio Tokyo announced that Japan would be willing to surrender, provided the future status of the Emperor was assured.

Meanwhile on August 9 the USSR had launched its long-awaited land offensive, involving seventy-six divisions with 5,500 tanks, 3,900 planes and over 1 million men. Within ten days the Soviet force had smashed the Japanese Kwantung army in Manchuria. Pursuing the retreating enemy, the Red Army entered northern China and Korea. On August 14 Tokyo finally accepted the Potsdam declaration and asked for peace. On September 2, 1945, General Douglas MacArthur, Supreme Commander of the Allied Forces in the Far East, accompanied by Soviet and British representatives, accepted Japan's capitulation on the deck of the battleship *Missouri,* anchored in Tokyo Bay. World War II, which had kept most of the people of the globe at loggerheads from 1939 to 1945, was over almost exactly six years after its beginning on September 1, 1939.

At the time of the armistice the Soviet troops pursuing the Japanese in Korea reached, roughly speaking, the thirty-eighth parallel. The line was designated as the demarcation between the American and Russian occupation zones. Although Korea, like Germany, was split between its Communist-dominated and American-controlled parts along the thirty-eighth parallel, another prize of World War II, Japan, avoided such a division, because of the stubborn opposition of Washington. Despite its short and largely

Moscow, June 24, 1945, The Victory parade on the Red Square: Banners of the Hitler Army captured in battles are lowered at Stalin's feet. Soviet Embassy, Washington, D.C.

unnecessary contribution to the Far Eastern war, the USSR obtained practically everything it had been promised at Yalta and Potsdam. Actually, the Soviet Union recovered everything imperial Russia had lost to Japan in 1905, including Southern Sakhalin, the Chinese Eastern and Manchurian railroads, Dairen, Port Arthur, and the ancient Japanese Kuril Islands. Yet, as in the case of another Axis partner, Italy, no Soviet soldiers were admitted on Japanese soil. Despite Soviet protests, Japan remained a United States preserve. Thus, Japan's fate, next to that of Germany, became another source of friction between the two main victors of World War II and one of the contributing causes of what became known as the "Cold War."

THE TRIAL AT NUREMBERG

In the course of World War II, the Nazis had violated practically every canon of human decency and committed innumerable atrocities of unprecedented magnitude. In accordance with the stipulations of the Yalta and Potsdam agreements, their leaders were to be tried by an International Military Tribunal for "the crimes against humanity." The Tribunal's legal foundations were established at a conference of jurists from four victorious powers, the United States, Britain, the Soviet Union, and France. Their representatives gathered in London on June 26, 1945, and on August 8 signed an agreement to which twenty-three nations subsequently subscribed.[4]

The Tribunal consisted of eight representatives of the United States, Britain, France, and the USSR. The indictment lodged against the original twenty-four defendants contained four counts: (1) crimes against peace—i.e., the planning, initiating, and waging of wars of aggression in violation of international treaties and agreements; (2) crimes against humanity—i.e., exterminations, deportations, and genocide; (3) war crimes—i.e., violations of the laws of the war; and (4) "a common plan or conspiracy to commit" the criminal acts listed in the first three counts.

The phrasing of the clause on the wars of aggression had caused serious differences among the victorious powers. The chief American prosecutor at Nuremberg, an Associate Justice of the U.S. Supreme Court, Robert L. Jackson, argued for the indictment of the perpetrators of any war of aggression as war criminals. He further promoted the thesis intended to carry out what was already established law: that the Kellogg-Briand Pact had, in fact, outlawed war before Germany, a signatory, unleashed the aggression and the Tribunal merely sought to enforce its provisions. The Soviets, who had themselves been declared aggressors because of their unprovoked attack on Finland in 1939, opposed such a broad concept. In reply, the Soviet delegate, General I. T. Nikitchenko, produced a narrower formula that was eventually accepted by the four powers. The formula declared the crime to be "Aggression or domination over other nations carried out by the European Axis in violation of international law and treaties."

The trial opened on November 29, 1945, at the Nuremberg Palace of Justice. The proceedings lasted for over nine months, until August 31, 1946, thus symbolically ending on the eve of the seventh anniversary of Hitler's attack on Poland. The trial took place at the city that had been designated as the "capital of the National Socialist Movement," where during the "party days" every September the blaring bands and the Führer's hoarse voice mixed with the shouts of jubilee masses to proclaim the glories of "the thousand year Reich."

It was extremely difficult for the four victorious powers, with their different conceptions of justice and their resurging rivalries, to agree on how to try the Nazi leaders, who for six years had been the scourge of Europe. It was hardly surprising that the Allies were determined to prevent a similar menace from arising in the future. The Americans and the British wanted a trial from the first. At Yalta, Stalin wanted the Nazi leaders shot without trial. Not all legal minds, even in the West, agreed that a formal trial was appropriate. The proposal for an international tribunal to try the Nazi leaders raised among lawyers everywhere, and especially in Britain, some of the most fundamental legal questions. What bothered the Nuremburg judges most was the application of *ex post facto* norms, that is, laws that did not exist at the time the war crimes were committed.

The Tribunal rejected the contention that only a state, and not individuals, could be

[4]For a full documentation: International Military Tribunal, Trial of the Major War Criminals before the International Military Tribunal, 14 November 1945–1 October 1946, 42 vols. (Blue Series). Nuremberg, 1946–1949, *Trials of War Criminals before the Nuremberg Military Under Control Council Law No. 10,* October 1946–April 1949, Vols. I–XV (Green Series). Washington, D.C.: Government Printing Office, 1949–1954. For descriptions and analysis: Ann Tusa and John Tusa, *The Nuremberg Trial* (New York: Antheneum, 1984). For a German point of view: Werner Master, *Nuremberg, A Nation on Trial* (New York: Charles Scribner's Sons, 1977).

found guilty, for "crimes against humanity." The Tribunal reasserted its original concept that crimes against basic principles of international law are committed by men and that only by punishing such individuals can the provisions of international law be enforced. Moreover, the Tribunal turned down the argument that because the trial was *ex post facto,* it could not be held. As the chief American prosecutor, Robert L. Jackson, pointed out, the Nazi leaders were to be tried for acts that have been regarded as punishable since the time of Cain. Numerous Allied warnings had given Nazi officials ample notice that they would be held responsible for their crimes, and that the Allies would "pursue them to the uttermost ends of the earth." The Tribunal pronounced that gross violations of international law and "crimes against humanity" had been regarded as punishable during World War I.

While the punishability of the crimes against humanity was not contested, bickerings of the judges over procedural matters and sentences were frequent. For instance, while the British and American members of the Tribunal wanted the Germans to be tried for having massacred 4,000 Polish officers at the Katyń forest, the Soviet judges insisted that the charge be dropped. The British and Americans, on the other hand, rejected the Soviet charge that the annexation of Austria constituted an act of aggression, because there was no visible resistance to the German troops marching into Austria in March 1938.

The Evil Henchmen

While the criminal-in-chief, Hitler, and his two major accomplices, Goebbels and Himmler, escaped justice by committing suicide, twenty-four leading Nazis, including Goering, did not. Before the trial, Goering, who in prison had lost 70 pounds and, deprived of narcotics, regained some of his youthful vigor, laid down the line to be followed by all of the accused: not a single word against the Führer. But as the trial unfolded, one defendant after another abandoned this rule and kept shifting most of the blame onto Hitler's orders and the S.S. as the main executioners of his criminal commands. These were the two main alibis for most of the defendants. The Tribunal rejected these excuses as invalid and insisted that every human being was individually responsible for his or her acts.

On October 1, 1946, the verdict on twenty-two of the original twenty-four defendants was handed down. (Meanwhile, Robert Ley committed suicide while in prison, and Gustav Krupp von Bohlen's illness prevented his being tried.) Three of the defendants were acquitted: twelve (including Martin Bormann, who was tried in absentia) were sentenced to death by hanging. Three (including Rudolf Hess) were sentenced to life imprisonment; and four (including Albert Speer) were to be imprisoned for terms ranging from ten to twenty years. Thus, four defendants (Schirach, Neurath, Funk, and Speer) escaped the death penalty. Goering cheated the hangman: Four hours before the executions began, he swallowed a capsule of cyanide. In the end, twelve defendants were sentenced to death and ten were hanged early on the morning of October 16, 1946. Their ashes, as well as those of Goering, were scattered in a place kept secret to prevent the Nazis sympathizers from erecting shrines or making pilgrimages to that spot.

"A victor's justice," Goering had sneered after learning the verdict, "Jackson's lynching law." Imperfect as it was, the verdict was far superior to Nazi justice: The defendants were free to speak, they were provided with competent legal counsels and could call witnesses who, in many cases, testified on their behalf. Thus, despite its numerous shortcomings, the Nuremberg trial was a remarkable achievement. The trial revealed to the world the grim, phantasmagoric inside story of Nazi Germany, as demonstrated by captured documents, most of them first presented at the trial, as well as numerous witnesses. Thus the trial imprinted on mankind the premeditated, mass horrors that had been inflicted on millions of innocent human beings by the Nazi leaders. The verdict made a pioneering attempt to establish new norms of justice and international law and thus created an important precedent. The principles pronounced at Nuremberg declared the primacy of individual conscience and repudiated the totalitarian axiom that orders of superiors may absolve criminal acts. The Nuremberg verdict reasserted the notion that people can be wrong and guilty when they act with the herd.

From a perspective of four decades one has to conclude that, under the circumstances prevailing after the most cruel of all wars, in an emotionally charged atmosphere, the Nuremberg Tribunal, on the whole, pronounced a fair judgment.

20

The War in Retrospect

A BEASTLY MADNESS

Leonardo da Vinci called war "a beastly madness." This is more applicable to the second world conflict than to any other. World War II was indeed the most cruel and devastating conflict in history. In terms of lives lost, geographical extent, and cities reduced to ashes, the struggle defies rational comprehension. Over 27 million combatants were killed, 17 million wounded, and nearly 20 million captured or missing. Civilian populations were more affected by this war than by any other in the past: How many millions of people not directly involved in the hostilities lost their lives is still controversial. On a per capita basis, Poland was the main victim of the war: It lost 22 percent of its 1939 population. The USSR followed with 17 percent, Germany with 16 percent, and Yugoslavia with 11 percent. The losses of France amounted to 1.5 percent; of Britain, 0.8 percent, and of the United States, 0.14 percent. Material and cultural losses, including destruction of art treasures, are beyond calculation.[1]

For all the major belligerent powers, the war was essentially a war of materiel and manpower. Only those nations that had large human reservoirs, as well as a superior industrial potential, could effectively compete in this war of attrition. Technology was almost as important as the fighting men.

---

[1]For a German estimate of the human and material losses of the war see *Bilanz Des Zweitan Weltkrieges Erkenntinisse und Verpflichtungen Für Die Auskunft* (Gerhard Stalling Verlag, Oldenburg (OLDB)/Hamburg, 1953). The main stumbling block in computing the civilian losses of the war are the unreliable and occasionally controversial figures reported in various Soviet statistical data, especially concerning civilian casualties.

The war brought about remarkable changes in the political geography of the globe. For instance, it was the expansion of its war industries, as much as its military contributions, that raised Canada to the status of a middle power on the Allied side. In Russia, the transfer of a major segment of its industrial machine beyond the Urals was a significant step toward the continuing shift of the economic center of gravity of the USSR toward the east.

In the second world conflict warfare had come to be really total because it permeated thoroughly the life of all belligerents. As a result of aerial attacks, civilians were often as affected by the hostilities as were the combatants. During World War II the struggle was among entire peoples—men, women, and even children. The dividing line between the home front and the fighting front was largely obliterated.

Another new factor was the appearance of mass resistance movements in which ordinary citizens actively participated as secret agents, messengers, or partisans carrying out acts of sabotage or conducting guerrilla warfare. Even when civilians were not active as members of an underground movement, they were, in one way or another, affected by bombardment, rationing of food, clothing, and various genocidal practices.

To this aspect one should add the fate of refugees, POWs, and displaced persons. Here, although a great deal of humanitarian effort was lavished on many victims of the war, especially the survivors of the concentration camps, numerous violations of human rights were also committed. For instance, the American and British governments repatriated, often forcibly, about 2 million people to the USSR. This was done under the agreement made at Yalta, which guaranteed the return of displaced Allied nationals on a reciprocal basis. Even later, when Allied leaders realized that repatriation would violate basic human rights, as well as international law, they continued to honor the agreement, largely because the United States wanted to ensure that the USSR repatriated the 25,000 American prisoners whom the Red Army had overrun.

Stalin viewed all prisoners as traitors. He had about 300,000 former POWs executed and about 2.5 million sent to forced labor camps. Only about 395,000 of more than 8 million Soviet citizens succeeded in remaining in the West.

Only on December 8, 1945, did the United States end this policy, after American commanders, troops, and political leaders had learned a lesson from the vigorous resistance to repatriation and from a number of suicides. The British continued forcible repatriations until June 1946.

WHY GERMANY LOST THE WAR

The reasons for the Allied victory and the defeat of the Axis are numerous and complex. Perhaps the most fundamental factor was the fact that Hitler, despite his remarkable grasp of many tactical and operational opportunities on land, was basically deficient in global strategic thinking. This was especially evident in maritime matters. Brought up in an essentially continental country, Austria, Hitler was a land rat. From the start of his rearmament program he favored the army and treated the Luftwaffe as a supplement to the land forces. Hitler always admitted his low-keyed interest in naval operations. To his naval adjutant he would say, "On land I am a lion, but with water I don't know where to begin." The only spots at the water's edge Hitler ever visited during the war were Dunkirk, on June 26, 1940, and Kiel, just before sending the *Bismarck* on its fatal raid in May 1941. His water shyness was a fatal handicap to his strategy. He assumed that sea power would not be of crucial importance in a short war to be decided in a few months, mostly on land. When he confronted the sea, first the narrow English Channel and then the vastness of the Atlantic that thwarted his boundless ambitions, he was confused and blundered almost invariably. According to Speer,

The Brandenburg Gate, a symbol of past German military glory, became a frontier post between the Soviet- and West-controlled Berlin, until November 9, 1989. German Information Center, New York.

Hitler had no deeper grasp of aerial warfare either.[2]

Hitler's concept of world mastery was rather provincial. He thought he could conquer the globe by conquering the land around him, capturing one by one the nations that stood in his way. His mistakes were similar to those of Napoleon: Both reasoned in terms of a "continental system." Hitler's ill-conceived plans to invade Britain and his attack on Russia in 1941 form a striking parallel to those of Napoleon. Both tried to bring Russia within their system; both relied on unorthodox naval strategies, which in Hitler's case assumed the form of submarine warfare, and in Napoleon's case was limited to destroying British commerce by privateers.

Many of the decisive Allied victories were essentially the result of their naval superiority and the superior sea mentality of their two principal leaders, Churchill and Roosevelt. Ultimately, from across the Atlantic came the huge stream of weapons and the armada that decisively helped the Grand Alliance to defeat the Axis. Hitler, who boasted about being a lover of history, ignored the fact that the course of all previous wars demonstrated that the sea powers conquered the land powers. World War II confirmed this axiom.

It appears that Hitler's most competent advisers were those whom he most ignored: his naval experts, starting with Admirals

[2]Speer, *Inside the Third Reich,* p. 369.

Raeder and Doenitz. Both of them had hoped there would be no large, open conflict before 1943 to 1945. By that time they planned to have ready a fleet comprising 250 to 300 U-boats, 30 battleships, and 4 aircraft carriers. When the Führer precipitated the war in 1939, Raeder was compelled to jettison his long-range program of a "balanced fleet" and hastily concentrate on the immediate tasks, mainly on building submarines. Had Hitler listened to Raeder's and Doenitz's advice and evolved a rational and consistent naval strategy, he might have capitalized on the British weaknesses and won the Battle of the Atlantic and hence the war by 1941, before the entry of the United States into the conflict.

One may also argue that once Hitler had decided to enter the contest for the Mediterranean, he should have followed Raeder's and Rommel's counsels and gone all out to win control of the entire region immediately after his Balkan campaign. Hitler's decision not to follow through upon his initial successes was caused by his resolve to remove the Soviet menace from his back before eventually dealing with Britain. Here again his ideological phobia blinded him to basic tenets of strategy.

In retrospect, one sees that Hitler's hatred of communism—as well as his personal idiosyncrasy—his fear of naval wars—upset his strategic priorities. If Britain was Germany's primary enemy, then the "peripheral strategy" should have been pushed to its logical conclusion, with Egypt, the Suez Canal, and the oil-bearing fields of the Middle East as main objectives and the Russian plans should have been shelved. If Stalin had refrained from stabbing Hitler in the back when he was fighting the Franco-British forces, would he ever have dared to challenge Hitler, who was at the peak of his power?

One of the most fundamental factors behind the defeat of the Third Reich was that the German war potential was not equal to supporting a global war. For that matter neither was Britain's, but America's material aid and Soviet Russia's ability to absorb staggering losses and then launch a formidable counteroffensive made all the difference. The most significant American contribution to the Allied war effort was the enormous material assistance that was extended against the Axis powers. Here again naval matters played a decisive role. Between 1941 and 1945, American shipyards built over 5,000 ships to maintain the sea communications.

In addition to its prodigious naval construction, America's industries provided the Allies large quantities of food, fuel, and other supplies: millions of rifles, thousands of guns, tanks, planes, and other equipment were produced for the fighting forces of the anti-Axis alliance. American industrial power, in the Second World War even more than in the First, made Allied victory possible. At the close of the war the GNP of the United States was half of the world's total. When the United States entered the war, Hitler, already locked in a life-and-death struggle in Russia, found himself in a no-win situation.

FURTHER REASONS FOR GERMANY'S DEFEAT

To the American material aid and direct military intervention much more decisive than during World War I, one must add the Soviet contribution to the triumph over the Third Reich. The contribution came late, was enforced, and limited mainly to land warfare, but there it was decisive. In the land warfare, some 80 percent of the casualties suffered by the Germans were inflicted by the Soviet forces. While on the eastern front the Wehrmacht lost some 7 million killed, wounded, POWs, and missing, similar figures for all other fronts were under 1.9 million. It was the Red Army that "tore the Wehrmacht's guts," as Churchill put it with his characteristic bluntness. Hitler and most German generals, brought up on the traditions of Clausewitz and Moltke, believed in the strategy of annihilation. They ignored the strategy of attrition, which was one of the secrets of Stalin's success. Hitler forgot that Soviet human reserves and natural resources were virtually inexhaustible. Soviet manpower alone was three times larger than that of Germany, and Soviet material assets were infinitely larger than those of the Third Reich and its vassals.

Having Italy as an ally was of little use to Hitler throughout the war. Actually, each partner conducted a separate war with diverse and often contradictory objectives. Italy was a burden to Germany most of the time. While signing the alliance with Hitler, Mussolini made a cardinal mistake: He committed his country, with its exposed coastline and vulnerable bases and without a single aircraft carrier, to a war against Europe's strongest naval power. Equally neglectful of history, Hitler, formalizing the Axis partnership, should have remembered the World War I dictum of Marshal Foch that he would rather have the Italians as enemies than as allies.

The Axis partners never developed anything even faintly resembling the Combined Chiefs of Staff. Even between the Western powers and the Soviets there was more cooperation than between Italy and Germany; the occasional meetings between Hitler and Mussolini were no substitute for regular staff contacts, which did not exist.[3] In the Combined Chiefs of staff, the United States and Britain had a unique coordinating mechanism that, despite occasional frictions and inevitable personal rivalries, did function satisfactorily and assured an overall unity of Allied strategy.

Another reason for the Axis defeat was the technological inferiority of each and every partner, especially Italy. It is noteworthy that Germany, which had started the war with a technological advantage in many fields of science and military technology, lost the race. Hitler and most of his military leaders took for granted that the scientific knowledge of the "master race" would continue to outpace that of any rival nation. How could the American "racial mongrels" outperform the tall, blond, and blue-eyed Aryan supermen, endowed by nature with superior brains? Hitler's fanatic conviction that Slavs were an inferior race excluded any possibility of Russians outsmarting the Germans. How could a bunch of "stupid Slavs" produce the best tank of the war, the T-34? How could Polish mathematicians master the secrets of the finest flower of the German mind, the Enigma coding machine? The atomic bomb was largely the work of refugees from Axis-controlled Europe. Here again Hitler paid the price of his racialism. Without Albert Einstein, Niels Bohr, Enrico Fermi, Edward Teller, and Stanisław Ulam, there would be no atom bomb.

Hitler failed also as a totalitarian leader, which he boasted to be. For all his outwardly absolute power, he proved unable to control effectively those personal and interservice rivalries raging around him. In those intrigues, political clout with the Führer was usually as important as old ties of friendship. One of the reasons Goering was able to make his point of view prevail throughout most of the war was his closeness to Hitler, who considered him an "old fighter" of the early days of the Nazi movement. It was Goering who managed to assert his slogan, "Everything that flies is mine"; thus he nipped in the bud the development of naval aviation. This, in turn, handicapped the *Kriegsmarine* disastrously, especially the U-boats. It was Goering who concluded that even with a small force of fighters he could repel any air attacks on the German industries and cities by day, and that by night the Allied bombers would fail to hit their targets. It was Goering, an ace fighter pilot of World War I, who neglected the development of a heavy bomber force.

Another cause of the German defeat was Hitler's gambling on a short lightning war. While unleashing the war, he staked its

[3]For a discussion of some crucial problems of the coalition warfare as seen from the German point of view see Burkhart Mueller-Hillebrand, *Germany and Its Allies in World War II: A Record of Axis Collaboration Problems* (Frederick, Md.: Historical Division, Headquarters United States Army, European Foreign Military Studies Branch, University Publications of America, 1980), especially pp. 79–90.

outcome on a short war, or *Blitzkrieg*, and forbade research on any weapon that could not be produced within six months. This delayed the development of the rockets, jet planes, and nuclear weapons. Both Hitler and Goering were strangely indifferent to the technological progress in the West, starting with radar and its improved version, the cavity megatron (which enabled British bombers to find their targets at night), and ending with the rapid progress of nucler research in America and Britain, which largely escaped the attention of the Abwehr. Until 1939/40, the Germans had a considerable lead in this respect over the Allies but lost it after that.

Hitler's passionate interest in modern weaponry was guided more by his capricious moods and beliefs in miraculous panacea weapons than by strict military expertise, which he held in ever-deeper contempt. Most of his experts were too terrorized to speak up. The Luftwaffe engineers, for instance, had created the world's first jet fighter, which was 125 miles per hour faster than any other aircraft in the world. The plane could have been operational within a year. Yet nobody took upon himself the responsibility to challenge Hitler's decision that only those weapons that could be available at the front line in no more than six months should be produced.

Another weakness of the Rome-Berlin Axis was its deficient intelligence services. Good intelligence is not a guarantee of winning a war, but faulty intelligence is a shortcut to disaster. The Germans never realized that one of their main alleged strong points, the coding system, had been destroyed by the Allied mastery of the Enigma machine. Convinced that the war would be short, that Enigma constituted an absolute secret for all times, they did not attach enough importance to a thorough training of their secret agents. Their profound belief in an inherent German intellectual superiority made the Nazis underestimate all other opponents, with the exception of the British. With the initial numerous failures of their intelligence service at the beginning of the war, however, even this respectful attitude was largely undermined, which, after the spring of 1940, made the Nazis look condescendingly even on the British Intelligence Service.

Yet, despite its huge size and its elaborate technical apparatus, the Abwehr was a pedantic, plodding, and unimaginative organization whose dirty tricks were numerous but whose stratagems were often clumsy and naive. The schizophrenia of the two chiefs of the Abwehr, Canaris and his deputy Oster, also played a crucial role in the malfunctioning of the German information-gathering machine. Both Canaris and Oster were torn between their sense of duty as German patriots, and their revulsion against the barbaric Nazi ways. Germany's spying and counterspying efforts were also dissipated by the internecine struggles between various intelligence-gathering bodies, mainly between the Abwehr and Himmler's secret service. This further paralyzed the functioning of German espionage agencies.

The superiority of Allied intelligence was striking in many respects. Almost five decades after the end of the war it is increasingly clear that the ability to read most of the enemy radio messages, thanks to the Allied mastery of the Enigma secrets, was crucial to the outcome of the struggle. The properly analyzed, intercepted Axis radio messages, the cracked codes, and squeezed-out secret information on troops and ship movements—all this helped the Allied leaders to anticipate and foil the enemy plans and win the war.

ARMIES AND STRATEGY

The strongest spot of the Germany military machine was its frontline men—officers, noncommissioned officers, and soldiers. As many recent studies have demonstrated, in comparison with its opponents, throughout most of the war the Wehrmacht had, by and large, a superior morale and unit cohesion. This resulted from a psychological bond forged within small teams: a fighting squad,

Two legless German veterans exchange their war reminiscences. German Information Center, New York

an aircraft crew, an infantry company, or an artillery battery; they were usually recruited on a territorial basis, drilled together for an extended period of time, and indoctrinated with a fanatical, Nazi spirit. This was particularly true of the younger soldiers shaped entirely by the system. In the stress and chaos of actual combat this cohesion, based upon trust and often on personal friendship, allowed German field commanders to use their soldiers in a more daring, not infrequently highly experimental, way. This, in turn, allowed officers and NCOs to rely on their soldiers more boldly, even in unprecedented situations, and spring surprises on the enemy. This allowed the Wehrmacht to carry out four strategic retreats of impressive length in good order, without panic or significant desertion until 1944/45. The retreats from el-Alamein to Tunisia, from the gates of Leningrad, Stalingrad, and Moscow to Berlin, from the beaches of Normandy beyond the Rhine, and from Sicily to the Alps—all are remarkable feats with hardly any precedent in the annals of warfare. One has only to remember the fate of Napoleon's disastrous retreat from Spain and from Russia.[4]

Of the two main Western armies, the British revealed higher cohesion and esprit de corps. A British military historian, David Fraser, attributed the cohesion of the British army to a longer tradition and its essentially regimental organization, which nourished strong bonds of loyalty and comradeship that a larger, more impersonal organization, such as a division, might not be able to instill. Indirectly he admits some of the shortcomings of such a system; among the most significant were the tendencies to perpetuate an excessive number of separate organizations and to overemphasize tradition, which bred conservatism.[5] The U.S. Army was considerably less bound by tradition, although not entirely free from it. Neither was the Wehrmacht. Yet the best fighting units of the Wehrmacht, the S.S. divisions, had little of a unit tradition behind them.

All the skill and discipline of the Wehrmacht, however, was no match for the toughness and ferocity of the Red Army's massive strength, backed by the nearly unlimited manpower and natural resources of the USSR. Here the seemingly irresistible power hit the immovable obstacle. In the conduct of World War II, the most important land front was in eastern, not western, Europe. The

---

[4]For an evaluation of the Wehrmacht's performance see Albert Seaton, *The German Army, 1933–45* (London: Weidenfeld and Nicolson, 1982), especially pp. 238–49. A Western historian concludes his book, *The German Army in World War II,* by saying: "The German Army was a *superb fighting organization.* In point of morale, elan, unit cohesion, and resilience, it probably had *no* equal among twentieth-century armies" (Martin van Creveld, *Fighting Power, German and US Army Performance, 1939–1945, Contributions in Military History,* No. 32 [Westport, Conn.: Greenwood Press, 1982], especially pp. 123 ff.).

[5]David Fraser, *And We Shall Shock Them, The British Army in the Second World War* (North Pomfret, Vt.: Hodder and Stoughton/David & Charles, 1985), especially pp. 108–9.

Soviet contribution to winning the war was overwhelming. The Soviet fighters' resilience was more than the Wehrmacht could cope with. The Red Army also amazed the world by retreating from the recently acquired Baltic lands, Poland, and Rumania to the suburbs of Moscow, while still retaining its ability to strike back. The Red Army confirmed the opinion of Frederick II of Prussia that it was not enough to kill a Russian soldier once; it was also necessary to push him to fall down. Except for the initial stages of the war, which saw numerous mass surrenders, an average Red Army man, even if initially badly commanded and indifferently equipped, fought to the bitter end, and his scorn of death surpassed even the most fanatical S.S. soldiers. Often the Soviet soldiers had no choice, confronted by the merciless enemy in front of them and the NKVD detachments that would not hesitate to mow down not only the deserters but even the retreating units or hesitant commanders. Many Soviet women tried to emulate their men and fought like wild cats as guerrillas or even fighter pilots. *Osoaviakhim,* a nationwide paramilitary and civil-defense organization of 36 million members, was nearly 30 percent women.

Unlike the Western leaders, especially Churchill, neither Hitler nor Stalin spared their soldiers. One of the striking features of the German casualties was the high losses among the officers of general rank and admirals: 352 were killed in action or missing and presumed dead in combat, and another 49 met accidental deaths. Natural deaths claimed 310; 101 committed suicide. After the war another 57 received death sentences from Allied war-crime courts, and 25 from German courts.[6] The percentage of Soviet officers killed in action is a controversial problem in view of the contradictory statements of Soviet historians and the notorious unreliability of their statistical data. We know that Stalin did not spare his soldiers. Neither were his commanders sparing of their men. General Eisenhower was shocked when Marshal Zhukov told him that the Soviet command valued machines over men. Zhukov admitted that the Russians placed infantry ahead of tanks to blast paths through mine fields despite heavy casualties because manpower was more available than mechanized weapons. Hitler, who condemned Paulus' Sixth Army to death at Stalingrad from the safety of his HQ, was to show that he had no regard for his own troops either. Here the two dictators were much alike. Stalin's cruelty was more than a match for Hitler's, except that it was less visceral, more calculated, and, therefore, more effective.

By far the greatest difference between the two rivals, however, was Stalin's caution in committing his country to realistic strategic objectives. Hitler, who in *Mein Kampf* had criticized William II for fighting a two-

A symbol of the Soviet hegemonial power in Eastern Europe: Marshal Konstantin Rokossovsky in the uniform of Commander-in-Chief of Poland's Armed forces. National Archives

[6]In World War I only 63 German generals had been killed in action or died on active duty, and 103 died from other causes (Seaton, *The German Army,* p. 250).

front war, ended by waging war on at least three: in Russia, in Africa, and in western Europe. In contrast, Stalin always made sure that the Red Army would fight on only one front. Even facing a half-defeated Polish army on September 17, 1939, he stabbed his victim in the back only after having concluded an armistice with the Japanese on September 15. He attacked the nearly collapsing Japan only after having annihilated the Wehrmacht and after Tokyo's peace feelers made it sure that its will to resist had been broken.

Unlike Hitler, who started the war with four masterly conducted campaigns (Polish, Scandinavian, French, and Balkan-Mediterranean), Stalin's war leadership opened with a near catastrophe from which he was rescued only by a combination of luck and his opponents' blunders. Yet after having muddled through two black summers—those of 1941 and 1942—Stalin rose to the rank of an astute strategist. This was admitted by Churchill, who was amazed at how Stalin instantly grasped the implications of the North African landing in 1942. Moreover, Stalin could be flexible. There were several cases of Stalin's military advisers persuading him to alter the orders; There are few such recorded cases as far as Hitler was concerned.[7]

Clausewitz defined strategy as the art of winning battles in order to win the war. Stalin grasped this axiom far better than Hitler. By the end of the conflict Stalin, always an astute negotiator, emerged also as a high-caliber strategist. Unlike Hitler, Stalin never boasted of having mastered Clausewitz's teaching, yet he was a better pupil of the great strategist than his German opponent or his Western counterparts. The Soviet dictator always regarded the war not as a goal but merely as an instrument for reaching his political objectives. Churchill's strategic understanding was superior to that of Roosevelt, but the British leader found himself in an increasingly inferior position because of his country's rapidly shrinking material resources. If power is the ability to get intended effects, then Stalin was closer to achieving his aims than other war leaders.

NEW METHODS OF WARFARE

More, perhaps than any previous war, the second global conflict brought about a massive technological revolution. The most important military and naval development in World War II was the rise of air power as a major factor on land and in naval warfare. The war demonstrated that an effective fighter umbrella was a necessity for surface warships. Thus it was conclusively proved that sea power without air power was no power at all. The Americans grasped this point much better than the British. The evolution of tactics and logistics was speeded up away from many traditional concepts, although the process was often too slow, painful, and costly. For instance, the division between services was blurred and the technique of combined operations was considerably developed. The distinction between land, sea, and air operations was greatly reduced. Light artillery and armored troops appeared directly onto the battlefield, brought not only by ships but also by transport planes, helicopters, and gliders. Guerrilla warfare, infiltration, and sabotage were also made possible on a large scale because of expanding airborne transport and radio communication.

As a concomitant to these novel options, several new types of specialized fighting units were evolved, for instance, parachutists, commandos, and rangers. Initially they were overlooked, especially by the more traditional commanders of the routine-bound armed forces, such as the British. As a striking example of this neglect one can quote the attitude of one of the most progressive and imaginative officers of the Royal Navy, Lord Mountbatten, the pioneer and architect of the combined operations; a

[7]Severyn Bialer, ed., *Stalin and His Generals* (New York: Pegasus, 1969), especially pp. 459–61, describing a dramatic confrontation between Marshal Rokossovsky and Stalin.

pamphlet issued by him as a sort of field regulations for the new branch of the armed forces devoted only one paragraph of four and a half lines to airborne troops, but there were fifteen lines on various methods of fighting seasickness. And this took place after the successes of the German paratroops in 1940 and 1941! During the opening stages of the war, those advocating unorthodox ways of warfare and their newly created units were treated as unwanted bastard children: neglected, starved of supplies, overlooked at the time of promotion. Only their performance at such critical times as the invasion of Sicily or D-day vindicated their value, at least partially, and assured their growing prestige.

These highly specialized units, as a rule composed mostly of volunteers, were required to undergo especially tough training before being thrown into the battle. Their highly flexible role in modern warfare and the pressing need for improvisation tended to endow them with a high degree of independence from their commanders. These special detachments were usually distinguished from conventional troops by special uniforms and by the end of the war came to be surrounded by a romantic aura.

The technical complexities of modern warfare led to a basic shift in the composition of the armed forces. The logistics of modern weapons systems had led the military profession not only to assimilate a growing variety of noncombatant skills but also to involve increasing numbers of civilians into the wartime military machines. By the close of World War II only three out of ten soldiers had to serve at the front line. The last stages of the war were already dominated by highly trained specialists, many of them civilian technicians and high-caliber academic scientists. It was war as much with slide rules, microscopes, and test tubes as with guns, tanks, planes, ships, and rockets. The appearance of nuclear weapons, with all their complexities, has made modern warfare increasingly a "wizards' war."

THE POSTWAR WORLD

World War II, more even than its predecessor, was a great historic divide. One of the most significant consequences of the war was the meteoric rise of the Soviet Union and the United States of America as superpowers. The predominance of the United States was based upon an unprecedented ability of American industry to expand and supply not only its own armed forces but also the needs of its weaker allies. By the end of the war the United States had 8 million men under arms and provided them with the most lavish and sophisticated equipment the world had ever seen. Between 1940 and 1945 the country's real output—that is, its total production—grew by 63 percent, which means an annual rate of growth of over 10 percent. This vast expansion of production allowed the United States to devote up to 42 percent of its output to war production by 1944, the year of the peak of war effort. At the same time, the civilian standard of living rose by 11 percent, while consumer prices rose by only 10 percent, feats unmatched by any other country fighting a major war on two distant fronts. With most of western and central Europe in ruins and the westernmost industrialized provinces of the USSR devastated, the United States was not merely number one but number only.

By 1945 the United States was predominant in all fields: on the land, in the air, and on the seas. Nowhere, perhaps, is the rise of the United States as a global power better reflected than in the field of naval power. The United States naval ascendancy was partly possible because of the naval leaders' flexibility: They adapted more quickly than their partners to the strategy and tactics in war at sea that air power dictated. By the end of the war, despite heavy losses suffered over nearly five years of fighting, the United States of America had six more battleships, 21 more aircraft carriers, 70 more escort carriers, and 127 more submarines than in December 1941. By 1945 the Royal Navy

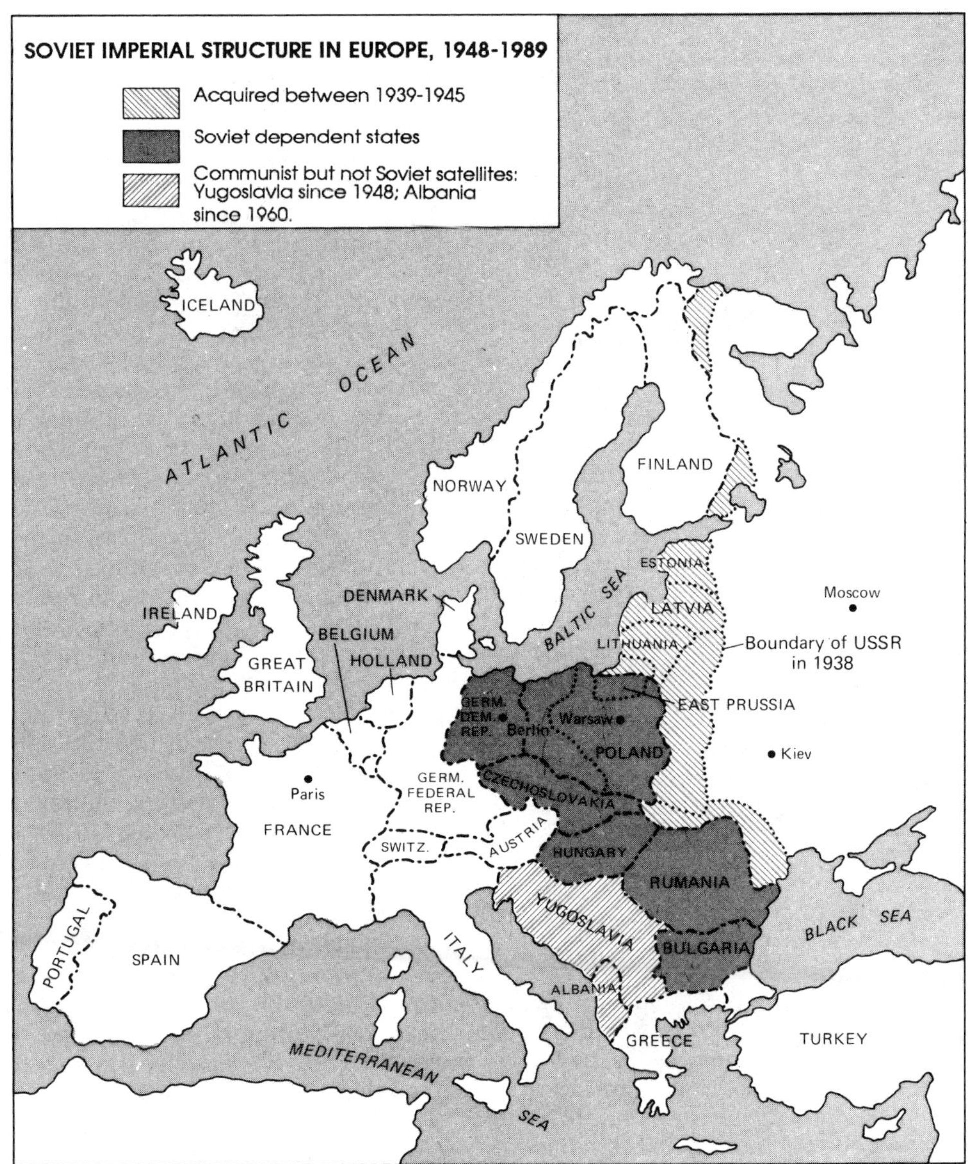

was no longer the queen of the seas, and the entire British battle fleet was no larger than the single U.S. Task Force Seven in the Pacific. By the last stages of the war, the U.S. Navy was larger than the combined fleets of the rest of the world.

The outcome of the war also revolutionized the geopolitical situation not only in Europe but in the entire world. Although Stalin failed to control the whole of Germany, his gains were most spectacular. First of all, the USSR annexed a broad belt of territories along its western borders. With the exception of Finland and central Poland, the USSR had directly recovered most of the land that the Tsarist Empire had lost at the end of World War I. In some instances, however, Stalin extended his state frontiers to include portions of east-central Europe that the tsars never had possessed, for instance northeastern East Prussia, Galicia or Transcarpathian Ukraine. In addition to that, Stalin extended his control over a vast belt of territory to the west of USSR: Poland, Czechoslovakia, Hungary, Rumania, Yugoslavia, Albania, and Bulgaria. Thus he created a vast semicolonial empire numbering well over 100 million people. While soon after the war the colonial empires of other powers, Britain, France, Belgium, Holland, and Portugal began to disintegrate, the Soviet imperial structure expanded.

There was no peace treaty at the end of World War II. Such a treaty was impossible because of the growing divergence of interests among the Big Three Powers, especially between the USSR and the United States. In Europe, Germany was the great prize of the war. Who should control the German territory and resources, and thus continental Europe, began to overshadow most other issues. Theoretically, control of the German territories was entrusted to four powers: Soviet Russia, the United States, Great Britain, and France. But already at Potsdam it was obvious that the Soviet Union and the United States were the only real victors of the war that commanded enough human and material potential to compete for leadership of the mid-twentieth-century world. This bipolarity of military resources, coupled with sharp ideological antagonism, has been the main contributing factor behind the frequent diplomatic clashes and military confrontations that are usually known as the "cold war."

The most important heritage of the war has been the development of new technologies, especially of nuclear power and of space communication. The wartime research on rockets has led humanity toward development of space satellites and space stations. Besides all the technological implications of these developments, they have revolutionized our self-image as inhabitants of a global village. This, in turn, has fostered a more cosmic perception of the role of the human species. Our globe now appears to us a fragile, sky-borne planetary sphere, the surface of which has been rather arbitrarily divided into portions the quarrel over which has threatened mankind with extinction.

During the cold war that lasted over forty years the two nuclear superpowers went at each other in every way short of direct attack. At least three times during this period humankind was brought to the verge of catastrophe. The first time arrived in 1948 as a result of Stalin's decision to deny to the Western power access to Berlin, a right guaranteed by the Potsdam agreement of 1945. For the second time, war seemed imminent when the East German Communist government, backed by Moscow, erected in 1961 a wall to prevent the communication between the citizens of the two German states—the eastern German Democratic Republic, or DDR, a member of the Warsaw Pact, and the Western-oriented Federal Republic of Germany, a member of the North Atlantic Treaty Organization (NATO). For the third time nuclear annihilation was threatened when the Soviet leader, Nikita S. Khrushchev, placed intercontinental ballistic missiles (ICBMs) in Cuba in 1962. The vision of an atomic Armageddon, however, had only a limited impact on the two main rivals, and the cold war was only intermittently interrupted by brief periods of relaxation of international tensions, or détente.

Meanwhile, as a result of the cold war, the world has witnessed a remarkable reversal of alliances: The former chief enemies of the Western democracies, Germany and Japan, became first their obedient clients and then their challenging partners. Immediately after the war, the United States, which had savaged Germany and Japan, lavished an enormous amount of aid on both of them and helped to turn both countries into economic giants. By 1980, Japan and West Germany became serious competitors of the United States in world markets. At the same time, the reconstructed West European countries have formed an increasingly integrated Economic Community of some 320 million people, a potential superpower in its own right. Thus, gradually, the bipolar world that had emerged as a result of World War II has been transformed into a multipolar world.

After much effort and cost, the two nuclear superpowers, the USSR and the United States, burdened by the staggering cost of the arms race, have attempted a fundamental reassessment of their relations. In December 1987 they concluded an agreement eliminating intermediate nuclear weapons in Europe. This created a new political climate that has had far-reaching ramifications throughout the world, especially in eastern and western Europe, where the antinuclear sentiments had grown to a considerable degree.

At the same time the gradual economic stagnation of the Soviet Union and its East European vassals combined with the ferment that had started in Poland and Hungary in the 1980s, and gradually spread to the rest of the region, including Czechoslovakia, Bulgaria and Rumania. When the revolt reached East Germany, the discontent assumed the proportion of a tidal wave and threatened Soviet control over the entire hegemony that Stalin erected in eastern and central Europe after the war. On November 9, 1989, the Berlin Wall, constructed in August 1961 to protect the Communist-controlled East Germany from the West, was breached. In December, following the example of Poland and Hungary, the DDR abolished the Communist monopoly of power.

These dramatic events pushed both superpowers, the United States and the Soviet Union, toward reexamination of the role of the two military alliances, the North Atlantic Treaty Organization and the Warsaw Pact. With Moscow's reluctant acceptance of many of the sweeping democratic changes in eastern and central Europe, and with East–West tensions easing, the role, but not the existence, of these two military coalitions has been subject to gradual reconsideration.

Thus, at the close of the twentieth century the *status quo* created by World War II in Europe has been undergoing remarkable changes. The Soviet empire revealed its feet of clay. The divisions that had emerged from the war have blurred, thus reducing somewhat the fissures that have marked the postwar partition of the Continent into rigid spheres of influence. The piercing of the Berlin Wall was, perhaps, the most dramatic tangible symbol of the gradual dismantling of what Winston Churchill called "the Iron Curtain." These changes revived the problem of German reunification, as well as the altering of the satellite status of the remaining countries of the Soviet hegemonic sphere, including the Baltic republics of Lithuania, Latvia, and Estonia. This, in turn, has put into question the long-range division of the key country of the European continent, Germany, and its further integration with western Europe. Although the Soviet leader, Mikhail S. Gorbachev, tried to veto any idea of a reunited Germany, the specter of a united Fourth German Reich of nearly 80 million people has begun to haunt many European leaders, including those of France, Britain, Poland, and Czechoslovakia.

Meanwhile, the end of Western colonialism throughout the world resulted in the redrawing of the political map of the globe and almost quadrupled the membership of the United Nations. While the old League of Nations was dominated by the European powers, especially France and Great Britain, the United Nations was overwhelmingly crowded by the largely nonwhite Third World (or "developing") nations. Thus, American and European leaders have not been comfortable dealing with this new emotionally laden factor as well as the pressure of the environmental problems that by the 1980s began to overshadow all political and military controversies. Not the least of these new global issues has been the population explosion. When World War II erupted, the population of the earth was about 2.25 billion people. By 1989 the global population far exceeded 5 billion, and it is still growing rapidly, mostly in the former colonial or developing countries.

Yet these nations have been least capable of coping with the resulting environmental near-catastrophes, like pollution, deforestation, over-farming and overgrazing, all of them threatening the already thinly stretched food and water supplies.

Consequently, after more than forty-five years since the end of World War II, its main participants, pressed by urgent common global preoccupations, are being pushed away from the arms race toward arms control and from menacing confrontation toward reluctant cooperation. Such a reorientation is badly needed to cope with the overwhelming common problems that are threatening the very survival of the human race.

Selected Bibliography

ARCHIVES

French Army Archives, Vincennes.

General Sikorski Historical Institute, London.

Hoover Institution on War, Revolution and Peace, Stanford, California.

Polish Underground Movement 1939–1945, Study Trust, London

Public Record Office, London. U.S. National Archives, Washington, D.C.

PUBLISHED DOCUMENTS, MEMOIRS, MONOGRAPHS

ABSHAGEN, KARL HEINZ. *Canaris.* London: Hutchinson, 1956.

AMBROSE, STEPHEN E. *The Supreme Commander: The War Years of General Dwight D. Eisenhower.* New York: Doubleday, 1970.

ANDERS, W. *An Army in Exile: The Story of the Second Polish Corps.* London: Macmillan, 1949.

ARENDT, HANNAH. *Eichmann in Jerusalem: A Report on the Banality of Evil.* New York: The Viking Press, 1963.

ARMSTRONG, JOHN A., ED. *Soviet Partisans in World War II.* Madison: University of Wisconsin Press, 1964.

AUSÜBEL, NATHAN, ET AL., EDS. *A Treasury of Jewish Folklore: Stories, Traditions, Legends, Humor, Wisdom and Folk Songs of the Jewish People.* New York: Crown Publishers, 1948, 24th Printing, October 1965.

BAIRD, JAY W. *The Mythical World of Nazi War Propaganda, 1939–1945.* Minneapolis: University of Minnesota Press, 1974.

BEEKER, CAIUS. *Hitler's Naval War.* New York: Doubleday, 1974.

———. *The Luftwaffe War Diaries.* Garden City, N.Y.: Doubleday, 1968.

BEHRENS, C. B. A. *Merchant Shipping and the Demands of War.* London: H.M.S.O. and Longmans, Green, 1955.

Bell, P. M. H. *A Certain Eventuality: Britain and the Fall of France.* Liverpool: Saxon House, 1973.

Bertrand, Gustave. *Enigma.* Paris: Plon, 1973.

Bethell, Nicholas. *The War Hitler Won: The Fall of Poland.* New York: Holt, Rinehart & Winston, 1972.

Bialer, Severyn, ed. *Stalin and His Generals.* New York: Pegasus, 1969.

Black, Edwin. *The Transfer Agreement: The Untold Story of the Secret Agreement between the Third Reich and Jewish of Palestine.* New York: Macmillan. London: Collier Macmillan Publishers, 1984.

Blau, G. *The German Campaign in the Balkans (Spring 1941).* Washington, D.C.: Department of the Army, 1953.

Bór-Komorowski, Tadeusz. *The Secret Army.* London: Macmillan, 1953.

Borsody, Stephen. *The Tragedy of Central Europe: The Nazi and Soviet Conquest of Central Europe.* New York: Collier, 1962. [Originally published as *The Triumph of Tyranny.* New York: Macmillan, 1960.]

Bradley, Omar N. *A General's Life.* New York: Simon & Schuster, 1983.

Bragadin, Marc Antonio. *The Italian Navy in World War II.* New York: The New York Times Company, 1980.

Breuer, William B. *Storming Hitler's Rhine, The Allied Assault: February-March 1945.* New York: St. Martin's Press, 1985.

Broszat, Martin. *Nationalsozialistische Polenpolitik, 1939–1945.* Stuttgart: Deutsche Verlags-Anstalt, 1961.

Brown, Anthony Cave. *The Bodyguard of Lies.* New York: Harper & Row, 1975.

Bullock, Alan. *Hitler: A Study in Tyranny* (rev. ed.). New York: Harper & Row, 1962.

Butler, James Ramsay Montague, ed. *Grand Strategy* (Vol. II). London: H.M.S.O., 1957.

Byrnes, James F. *Speaking Frankly.* New York: Harper, 1947.

Calvocoressi, Peter and Guy Wint. *Total War: Causes and Courses of the Second World War.* London: Penguin Books, 1972.

Campbell, John, ed. *The Experience of World War II.* New York: Oxford University Press, 1989.

Carls-Maire, Alice-Catherine. *La Ville Libre de Dantzig. en crise ouverte, 24.10.1938–1.9.1939. crise locale et crise européenne.* Warsaw: PAN, 1982.

Cecil, Robert. *Hitler's Decision to Invade Russia, 1941.* London: Davis-Poynter, 1975.

Central Intelligence Agency. *The Rote Kappelle: The CIA's History of Soviet Intelligence and Espionage Networks in Western Europe, 1936–1945.* Frederick, M.: University Publications of America, 1979.

Chuikov, Vasili I. *The End of the Third Reich.* London: Macgibbon & Kee, 1967.

———. *The Battle of Stalingrad.* New York: Holt, Rinehart & Winston, 1964.

Churchill, Winston S. *The Second World War.* (6 vols.) London: Cassell, 1948–1968. Boston: Houghton Mifflin, 1948–1968.
Vol. I: *The Gathering Storm.*
Vol. II: *Their Finest Hour.*
Vol. III: *The Grand Alliance.*
Vol. IV: *The Hinge of Fate.*
Vol. V: *Closing the Ring.*
Vol. VI: *Triumph and Tragedy.*

———. *The War Speeches of Winston Churchill.* Charles Eade, ed. (3 vols.) London: Cassell, 1952. Boston: Houghton Mifflin, 1953.

Ciano, Count Galeazzo. *Ciano's Hidden Diary, 1937–1938.* New York: E. P. Dutton, 1953.

Ciechanowski, Jan. *The Warsaw Rising of 1944.* London: Cambridge University Press, 1974.

Cienciala, Anna M. *Poland and the Western Powers, 1938–1939: A Study in the Interdependence of Eastern and Western Europe.* London: Routledge & Kegan Paul, 1968.

Clark, Alan. *Barbarossa: The Russian-German Strategy against Russia, 1939–1941.* London and New York: Oxford, Clarendon Press, 1973.

Clark, Mark W. *Calculated Risk.* New York: Harper, 1950.

Clemens, Diane Shaver. *Yalta.* New York: Oxford University Press, 1970.

Collier, Basil. *The Defence of the United Kingdom.* London: H.M.S.O., 1957.

Colville, John. *The Fringes of Power. Downing Street Diaries, 1939–1955.* London: Hodder and Stoughton, 1985.

Connell, John. *Wavell Scholar and Soldier.* New York: Harcourt, Brace & World, 1964.

Conquest, Robert. *The Nation Killers: Soviet Deportation of Nationalities.* New York: Macmillan, 1970.

Copp, DeWitt S. *Forged in Fire: Strategy and Decisions in the Air War over Europe 1940–45.* Garden City, N.Y.: Doubleday, 1982.

COULONDRE, ROBERT. *De Stalin à Hitler. Souvenirs de deux ambassades 1936–39*. Paris: Hachette, 1950.

CRAVEN, W. F, AND J. L. CATE. *The Army Air Forces in World War II. Plans and Early Operations* (Vol. I). *Men and Planes* (Vol. VI). Chicago: University of Chicago Press, 1948.

———. *The Army Air Force in WWII: Europe—Torch to Pointblank.* Chicago: University of Chicago Press, 1949.

CRUICKSHANK, CHARLES. *Greece 1940–1941*. London: Davis-Pointer, 1976.

CUNNINGHAM, ADMIRAL OF THE FLEET VISCOUNT. *A Sailor's Odyssey*. London: Hutchinson, 1951.

DALLIN, ALEXANDER. *German Rule in Russia 1941–1945*. London: The Macmillan Company, Ltd., 1957.

DAVIDSON, EUGENE. *The Trial of the Germans: An Account of the Twenty-two Defendants before the International Military Tribunal at Nuremberg.* New York: The Macmillan Company, 1966.

DAWIDOWICZ, LUCY S. *The Holocaust and the Historian.* Cambridge, Mass., and London: Harvard University Press, 1981.

DE GAULLE, CHARLES. *War Memoirs* (3 vols.) *The Call to Honour, 1940–1942* (Vol. I). New York: The Viking Press, 1955. *Unity, 1942–1944* (Vol. II). New York: Simon & Schuster, 1959.

DEAKIN, F. W. *The Brutal Friendship: Mussolini, Hitler, and the Fall of Italian Fascism.* New York: Harper & Row, 1962.

———. *The Embattled Mountain.* New York and London: Oxford University Press, 1971.

DEANE, JOHN R. *The Strange Alliance: The Story of Our Efforts at Wartime Cooperation with Russia.* New York: The Viking Press, 1947.

DE BELOT, RAYMOND. *The Struggle for the Mediterranean 1939–1945.* Princeton, N.J.: Princeton University Press, 1951.

DEDIJER, VLADIMIR. *Tito.* New York: Simon & Schuster, 1953.

DEMPSTER, D., AND D. WOOD. *The Narrow Margin: The Battle of Britain and The Rise of Airpower.* London: H.M.S.O., 1961.

DERRY, T. K. *The Campaign in Norway.* London: H.M.S.O., 1952.

DJILAS, MILOVAN. *Conservations with Stalin.* New York: Harcourt, Brace & World, Inc., 1962.

———. *Wartime.* New York and London: Harcourt Brace Jovanovich, 1977.

DOUGLAS, ROY, ED. *1939: A Retrospect Forty Years After. Proceedings of a Conference held at the University of Surrey 27 October 1979.* London: Macmillan, Archon Books, 1983.

DULLES, ALLEN. *Germany's Underground.* New York: Macmillan, 1947.

EDEN, ANTHONY. *The Reckoning.* London: Cassel & Co., Ltd., 1965.

EISENHOWER, DWIGHT D. *Crusade in Europe.* Garden City, N.Y.: Doubleday, 1948.

EISENHOWER, JOHN, S. D. *The Bitter Woods: The Dramatic Story, Told at All Echelons, from Supreme Command to Squad Leader, of the Crisis that Shook the Western Coalition: Hitler's Surprise at the Ardennes Offensive.* New York: Putnam's, 1969.

ELLIS, L. F. *Victory in the West. The Battle of Normandy* (Vol. I): London: H.M.S.O., 1962.

———. *The War in France and Flanders (1939–1940).* London: H.M.S.O., 1953.

ELLWOOD, DAVID. *Italy 1943–1945.* Bath: Leicester University Press, 1985.

ERICKSON, JOHN. *The Road to Stalingrad.* London: Weidenfeld and Nicolson, 1975. New York: Harper & Row, 1975.

———. *The Road to Berlin.* Boulder, Colo.: Westview Press, 1983.

———. *The Soviet High Command.* New York: St. Martin's Press, 1962.

FARAGO, LADISLAS. *The Game of the Foxes: The Untold Story of German Espionage in the United States and Great Britain during World War II.* New York: David McKay Company, 1971.

FEIS, HERBERT. *Between War and Peace: The Potsdam Conference.* Princeton, N.J.: Princeton University Press, 1960.

———. *Churchill, Roosevelt, Stalin: The War They Waged and the Peace They Sought.* Princeton, N.J.: Princeton University Press, 1957.

FISCHER, GEORGE. *Soviet Opposition to Stalin.* Cambridge, Mass.: Harvard University Press, 1952.

FLEMING, PETER. *Operation Sea Lion.* New York: Simon & Schuster, 1949.

FOOT, M. R. D. *SOE in France: An Account of the Work of the British Special Operations Executive in France 1940–1944.* London: H.M.S.O., 1966.

———. *Resistance: European Resistance to Nazism 1940–1945.* London: H.M.S.O., 1976.

———. *SOE: An Outline History of the Special Operations Executive, 1940–46.* London: British Broadcasting Corporation, 1984.

FRASER, DAVID. *And We Shall Shock Them: The*

British Army in the Second World War. London, Sydney, Aukland, & Toronto: Hodder and Stoughton, 1983.

FUSSEL, PAUL. *Wartime Understanding and Behavior in the Second World War.* Oxford: Oxford University Press, 1989.

GADDIS, JOHN LEWIS. *The United States and the Origins of the Cold War, 1941–1947.* New York: Columbia University Press, 1972.

GAMELIN, MAURICE. *Servir* (Vol. III). (3 vols.) Paris: Plon, 1947.

GARLINSKI, JÓZEF. *The Enigma War.* New York: Charles Scribner's Sons, 1979.

———. *Fighting Auschwitz: The Resistance Movement in the Concentration Camp.* London: Julian Friedmann Publisher, 1975.

———. *Hitler's Last Weapons.* London: Friedmann, 1978.

———. *Poland in the Second World War.* London: Macmillan, 1985.

———. *Poland, SOE and the Allies.* London: George Allen and Unwin, 1969.

———. *The Swiss Corridor Espionage Networks in Switzerland During World War II.* London, Melbourne, Toronto: J. M. Dent & Sons, 1981.

GATES, ELEANOR M. *End of the Affair, The Collapse of the Anglo-French Alliance, 1939–1940.* Berkeley: University of California Press, 1981.

GAVIN, JAMES M. *On to Berlin: Battles of an Airborne Commander 1943–1946.* New York: The Viking Press, 1978.

GEHLEN, REINHARD. *The Service.* New York: World Publishing, 1972.

GILBERT, MARTIN. *The Second World War. A Complete History.* New York: Henry Holt, 1989.

GIBSON, HUGH, ED. *The Ciano Diaries 1939–1943. The Complete, Unabridged Diaries of Count Galeazzo Ciano Italian Minister for Foreign Affairs, 1936–1943.* Garden City, N.Y.: Doubleday, 1946.

GIRAUD, HENRI-CHRISTIAN. *De Gaulle et les communistes. Le pacte secret De Gaulle–Staline.* Paris: Albin Michel, 1988.

GISEVEUS, BERNARD. *To the Bitter End.* New York: Houghton Mifflin Co., 1947.

GOERLITZ, WALTER, ED. *Paulus and Stalingrad: A Life of Field-Marshal Friedrich Paulus.* With notes, correspondence, and documents from his papers. New York: The Citadel Press, 1963.

GREAT BRITAIN. FOREIGN OFFICE. *Documents on British Foreign Policy, 1919–1939* (Vols. XVI–XXII) (22 Vols). London: H.M.S.O., 1977–1985.

GROSS, JAN TOMASZ. *Polish Society under German Occupation: The General Government, 1939–1944.* Princeton, N.J.: Princeton University Press, 1979.

GUDERIAN, HEINZ. *Panzer Leader.* New York: E. P. Dutton, 1952.

HAESTRUP, JORGEN. *European Resistance Movements, 1939–1945: A Complete History.* Westport, Conn., and London: Meckler Publishing, 1981.

HANCOCK, W. K., AND M. M. GOWING. *British War Economy.* London: H.M.S.O., 1949.

HANES, STEPHEN, AND RALPH WHITE, EDS. *Resistance in Europe 1939–1945.* London: Pelican Books, 1976.

HARRIS, SIR ARTHUR. *Bomber Offensive.* London: Collins, 1947.

HART, B. H. LIDDELL. *The German Generals Talk.* New York: William Morrow, 1948.

———. *History of the Second World War* (2 Vols.). New York: Capricorn Books, G. P. Putnam's Sons, 1970.

———. *The Other Side of the Hill.* London: Cassell, 1948.

———. *Strategy.* 2nd rev. ed. New York and Washington: Frederick A. Praeger, 1967.

HEHN, PAUL N. *The German Struggle Against Yugoslav Guerrillas in World War II: German Counter-Insurgency in Yugoslavia 1941–1943.* Boulder, Colo.: East European Quarterly, distributed by Columbia University Press, New York, 1979.

HILBERG, RAUL. *The Destruction of the European Jews* (3 Vols.). (rev. and definitive ed.). New York: Holmes & Meier, 1985.

HILGER, GUSTAV, AND ALFRED G. MEYER. *The Incompatible Allies.* New York: Macmillan, 1953.

HINSLEY, F. H. *British Intelligence in the Second World War* (Vol. I). London: H.M.S.O., 1979.

HITLER, ADOLF. *Mein Kampf.* London: Hurst and Blackett, 1938.

HOFER, WALTHER. *War Premeditated, 1939.* London: Thames and Hudson, 1955.

INFIELD, GLENN B. *The Poltava Affair. A Russian Warning: An American Tragedy.* New York: Macmillan, 1973.

INTERNATIONAL MILITARY TRIBUNAL. TRIAL OF

THE MAJOR WAR CRIMINALS BEFORE THE INTERNATIONAL MILITARY TRIBUNAL, 14 NOVEMBER 1945—1 OCTOBER 1946. 42 VOLS. (BLUE SERIES). NUREMBERG, 1946–1949. *Trials of War Criminals before the Nuremberg Military Under Control Council Law No. 10,* October 1946–April 1949. Vols. I–XV (Green Series). Washington, D.C.: Government Printing Office, 1949–1954.

IRVING, DAVID. *Hitler's War.* London, Sydney, Auckland, Toronto: Hodder and Stoughton, 1977.

———. *The War between the Generals.* New York: Congdon & Lattes, 1981.

JACKSON, W. F. G. *The North African Campaign, 1940–43.* London and Sydney: B. T. Batsford, 1975.

JAEKEL, EBERHARD. *Hitler in History.* Hanover, N.H.: University Press of New England, 1984.

JAKOBSON, MAX. *The Diplomacy of the Winter War: An Account of the Russo–Finnish War, 1939–1940.* Cambridge, Mass.: Harvard University Press, 1961.

JONES, R. V. *The Wizard War.* New York: Coward, McCann & Geoghegan, 1978.

KAHN, DAVID. *The Codebreakers.* New York: Macmillan, 1967.

———. *Hitler's Spies.* London: Hodder and Stoughton, 1978.

KEE, ROBERT. *Munich. The Eleventh Hour.* London: Hamilton, 1988.

KEEGAN, JOHN. *Six Armies in Normandy from D-Day to the Liberation of Paris, June 6th–August 25th, 1944.* New York: Viking Press, 1982.

KEEGAN, JOHN. *The Second World War.* London: Hutchinson, 1989.

KEITEL, WILHELM. *The Memoirs of Field Marshal Keitel.* Walter Goerlitz, ed. New York: Stein & Day, 1965.

KENNEDY, ROBERT M. *The German Campaign in Poland.* Washington, D.C.: U.S. Department of the Army, 1956.

KESSELRING, ALBERT. *Kesselring: A Soldier's Record.* Westport, Conn.: Greenwood Press, 1953.

KEYSERLINGH, ROBERT H. *Austria in World War II. An Anglo-American Dilemma.* Kingston and Montreal: McGill-Queen University Press, 1988.

KIMBALL, WARREN F., ED. *Churchill & Roosevelt: The Complete Correspondence* (3 Vols.). Princeton, N.J.: Princeton University Press, 1985.
Vol. I: *Alliance Emerging*
Vol. II: *Alliance Forged*
Vol. III: *Alliance Declining*

KIMCHE, JON. *The Unfought Battle.* London: Weidenfeld and Nicolson, 1968.

KLIBANSKY, RAYMOND, ED. *Benito Mussolini: Memoirs 1942–1943 with Documents Relating to the Period.* New York: Howard Fertig. 1975.

KNOX, MACGREGOR. *Mussolini Unleashed 1939–1941. Politics and Strategy in Fascist Italy's Last War.* Cambridge, London, and New York: Cambridge University Press, 1982.

KORBOŃSKI, STEFAN. *Fighting Warsaw: The Story of the Polish Underground State 1939–1945.* London: George Allen and Unwin, 1956. New York: Minerva Press, 1956.

KOZACZUK, WLADYSLAW. *Enigma: How the German Machine Cipher Was Broken, and How It Was Read by the Allies in World War II.* Frederick, Md.: University Publications of America, 1983.

LAMB, RICHARD. *Montgomery in Europe 1943–1945: Success or Failure?* London: Buchan & Enright, Publishers, 1983.

LANE, ARTHUR BLISS. *I Saw Poland Betrayed.* New York: The Bobbs-Merrill Company, 1948.

LAQUEUR, WALTER. *The Terrible Secret: Suppression of the Truth about Hitler's "Final Solution."* Boston: Little, Brown, 1980. London: Weidenfeld and Nicholson, 1980.

LE GOYET, PIERRE. *Le Mystère Gamelin.* Paris: Press de la Cité, 1975.

LEWIS, RONALD. *Ultra Goes to War: The Secret Story.* London: Hutchinson, 1978.

LINKLATER, ERIC. *The Campaign in Italy.* London: H.M.S.O., 1951.

LUKACS, JOHN. *The Last European War: September 1939-December 1941.* New York: Anchor Press/ Doubleday, 1976.

LUKAS, RICHARD C. *The Forgotten Holocaust: The Poles under German Occupation, 1939–1944.* Lawrence, Kansas: Kansas University Press, 1986.

MACKSEY, KENETH. *The Partisans of Europe in World War II.* London: Jart-Davis, 1975.

MACLEAN, FITZROY. *Eastern Approaches.* London: Jonathan Cape, 1950.

MANNERHEIM, CARL GUSTAV. *The Memoirs of Marshal Mannerheim.* London: Cassell, 1953.

MARTEL, GORDON, E., ED. *The Origins of the Second World War. The A. J. P. Taylor Debate after Twenty-*

five Years. Boston, London, Sydney: Allen and Unwin, 1986.

MARTIN, BERND. *Friedensinitiativen and Machtpolitik im Zweiten Weltkreig 1939–1941.* Dusseldorf: Droste Verlag, 1974.

MARTIN, DAVID. *Ally Betrayed, The Uncensored Story of Tito and Mihailovich.* Englewood Cliffs, N.J.: Prentice-Hall, 1946.

MASTER, WERNER. *Nuremberg, A Nation on Trial.* Richard Barry, trans. New York: Charles Scribner's Sons, 1977.

MASTNY, VOJTECH. *Russia's Road to the Cold War: Diplomacy, Warfare and the Politics of Communism, 1941–1945.* New York: Columbia University Press, 1979.

———. *The Czechs Under Nazi Rule: The Failure of National Resistance, 1939–1942.* New York: Columbia University Press, 1971.

MATLOFF, MAURICE, AND EDWIN M. SNELL. *The War Department: Strategic Planning for Coalition Warfare, 1941–1942.* Washington, D.C.: Office of the Chief of Military History, Department of the Army, 1953.

MAYER, ARNO J. *Why Did the Heavens Not Darken? The "Final Solution" in History.* New York: Pantheon Books, 1988.

MEDLICOTT, W. N. *The Economic Blockade* (Vol. I). London: H.M.S.O., 1952.

MICHEL, HENRI. *La Drôle de guerre.* Paris, 1971.

———. *Et Varsovie fut Detruite.* Paris: Editions Albin Michel, 1984.

MIKOŁAJCZYK, STANISŁAW. *The Pattern of Soviet Domination.* London: Sampson Low, Marston, 1948.

MONTAGU, EWEN. *Beyond Top Secret.* New York: Coward, McCann, 1978.

MONTGOMERY, FIELD-MARSHAL VISCOUNT. *El Alamein to the River Sangro.* London: Hutchinson, 1948.

———. *Memoirs of Field-Marshal Montgomery.* London: Collins, 1958.

———. *Normandy to the Baltic.* London: Hutchinson, 1958.

MORISON, SAMUEL ELIOT. *The Two-Ocean War 1939–1945.* New York: Little, Brown & Oxford University Press, 1963.

MOULTON, J. L. *A Study of Warfare in Three Dimensions: The Norwegian Campaign in 1940.* Athens: The Ohio University Press, 1967.

MUNCH-PETERSEN, THOMAS. *The Strategy of Phoney War. Britain, Sweden and the Iron Ore Question 1939–1940.* Stockholm: Militarhistoriska-Forlaget, 1981.

NAMIER, L. B. *Diplomatic Prelude 1938–1939.* London: Macmillan, 1948.

NEKRICH ALEXANDER M. *June 22, 1941: Soviet Historians and the German Invasion.* Columbia: University of South Carolina Press, 1968.

NEWMAN, SIMON. *March 1939, The British Guarantee to Poland: A Study in the Continuity of British Foreign Policy.* Oxford: Clarendon Press, 1976.

NÖÉL, LEON. *L'Aggression Allemande contre la Pologne.* Paris: Flammarion, 1946.

NOWAK, JAN. *Courier from Warsaw.* Detroit: Wayne State University Press, 1982.

O'BRIEN, TERENCE H. *Civil Defence.* London: H.M.S.O., 1955.

OVERY, R. J. *The Air War 1939–1945.* New York: Stein & Day, 1980.

PAVLOV, DMITRI V. *Leningrad, Nineteen Hundred Forty One: The Blocade,* trans. John C. Adams. Chicago: University of Chicago Press, 1965.

PENKOWER, MONTY NOAM. *The Jews Were Expendable: Free World Diplomacy and the Holocaust.* Urbana: University of Illinois Press, 1983.

PERSICO, JOSEPH E. *Piercing the Reich: The Penetration of Nazi Germany by American Secret Agents during World War II.* New York: The Viking Press, 1979.

PETROW, RICHARD. *The Bitter Years: The Invasion and Occupation of Denmark and Norway April 1940–May 1945.* London, Sydney, Auckland, Toronto: Hodder and Stoughton, 1974.

PLAYFAIR, I. S. O. AND OTHERS. *The Mediterranean and the Middle East.* London: H.M.S.O., 1960 (Vol. III) and *The Destruction of the Axis Forces in Africa* (Vol. IV). London: H.M.S.O., 1966.

POGUE, FORREST C. *George C. Marshall* (Vol. 2). *Ordeal and Hope 1939–1942.* New York: Viking Press, 1966.

———. *George C. Marshall* (Vol. 3). *Organizer of Victory 1943–1945.* New York: Viking Press, 1973.

———. *The Supreme Command.* Washington, D.C.: Office of the Chief of Military History, Department of the Army, 1946.

POLAND. POLISH GOVERNMENT-IN-EXILE. *Official Documents Concerning Polish-German and Polish-Soviet Relations 1933–1939.* London and Melbourne: Hutchinson & Co. Ltd., 1940.

PRAŻMOWSKA, ANITA. *Britain, Poland and the East-*

ern Front. 1939. Cambridge: Cambridge University Press, 1987.

RACZYŃSKI, EDWARD. *In Allied London.* London: Weidenfeld and Nicolson. 1962.

RAEDER, ERICH. *My Life.* New York: Arno Press, 1980.

REMPEL, GERHARD. *Hitler's Children: The Hitler's Youth and the S.S.* Chapel Hill: University of North Carolina Press, 1989.

RICH, NORMAN. *Hitler's War Aims, Vol. II: The Establishment of the New Order.* New York: W. W. Norton & Co., Inc., 1974.

RIDGWAY, MATTHEW B. *Soldier: the Memoirs of Matthew B. Ridgway.* New York: Harper & Bros., 1956.

ROKOSSOVSKY, K. *A Soldier's Duty.* Moscow: Progress Publishers, 1972.

ROMMEL, FIELD-MARSHAL ERWIN. *The Rommel Papers.* B. H. Liddell Hart, ed. London: Collins, 1953 and New York: Harcourt, Brace, 1953.

ROSKILL, STEPHAN W. *The War at Sea 1939–1945.* London: H.M.S.O., 1954–1961.

ROŻEK, EDWARD J. *Allied Wartime Diplomacy: A Pattern in Poland.* New York: Wiley, 1958.

RUBIN, BARRY. *Istambul Intrigues.* New York: McGraw-Hill, 1989.

RYAN, CORNELIUS. *The Longest Day.* New York: Fawcett, 1960.

SEATON, ALBERT. *The German Army, 1933–45.* London: Weidenfeld and Nicolson, 1982.

SHIRER, WILLIAM L. *The Rise and Fall of the Third Reich. A History of Nazi Germany.* New York: Simon & Schuster, 1960.

SIKORSKI HISTORICAL INSTITUTE. *Documents on Polish-Soviet Relations, 1939–1945.* London: Heinemann, Vol. I, 1961, and Vol. II, 1967.

SNYDER, LOUIS L. *The War: A Concise History, 1939–1945.* New York: Simon & Schuster, 1960.

SONTAG, RAYMOND J. *A Broken World, 1919–1939.* New York: Harper & Row, 1971.

———. *Nazi-Soviet Relations, 1939–1940: Documents from the Archives of the German Foreign Office.* Washington, D.C.: Department of State, 1948.

SPEER, ALBERT. *Infiltration.* New York: Macmillan, 1981.

———. *Inside the Third Reich.* New York: Macmillan, and Avon, 1970.

STAFFORD, DAVID. *Britain and European Resistance, 1940–1945, A Survey of the Special Operations Executive, with Documents.* London: Macmillan, 1980.

STALIN, J. *Correspondence between the Chairman of the Council of Ministers of the USSR and the Presidents of the USA and the Prime Ministers of Great Britain during the Great Patriotic War of 1941–1945* (2 Vols.). Moscow: Foreign Language Publishing House, 1957.

STETTINIUS, EDWARD R. *Roosevelt and the Russians: The Yalta Conference.* Garden City, N.Y.: Doubleday, 1949.

STEVENSON, WILLIAM, *A Man Called Intrepid.* New York: Harcourt Brace Jovanovich, 1976.

STONE, NORMAN. *Hitler.* London: Hodder and Stoughton, 1988.

SWEETY, JOHN JOSEPH TIMOTHY. *Iron Arm. The Mechanization of Mussolini's Army, 1920–1940.* Westport, Conn., and London: Greenwood Press, 1980.

TERRAIN, JOHN. *A Time for Courage: The Royal Air Force in the European War, 1939–1945.* New York: Macmillan, 1985.

TERRY, SARAH MEIKLEJOHN. *Poland's Place in Europe. General Sikorski and the Origin of the Oder-Neisse Line, 1939–1943.* Princeton, N.J.: Princeton University Press, 1983.

TOMASEVICH, JOZO. *The Chetniks.* Stanford, Calif.: Stanford University Press, 1975.

TREVOR-ROPER, H. R., ED. *Blitzkrieg to Defeat—Hitler's Directives 1939–1945.* New York: Holt, Rinehart & Winston, 1964.

———. *Hitler's Table Talk, 1941–44, His Private Conversations* (2d ed.). London: Weidenfeld and Nicolson, 1973.

TRITLINGER, GERALD. *The House Built on Sand. The Conflicts of German Policy in Russia 1939–1945. Westport, Conn.: Greenwood Press, 1960.*

TUSA, ANN, AND JOHN TUSA. *The Nuremberg Trial,* New York: Atheneum, 1984.

ULAM, ADAM B. *Expansion and Coexistence: The History of Soviet Foreign Policy, 1917–1967.* New York: Praeger, 1968.

U.S. AIR FORCES. USAF HISTORICAL DIVISION. *The Army Air Forces in World War II.* Wesley Frank Craven and James Lea Cate (Eds.). (7 Vols.). Chicago: University of Chicago Press, 1948–66.

U.S. DEPARTMENT OF STATE. *Foreign Relations of the United States. Diplomatic Papers: The Confer-*

ences at Cairo and Teheran 1943. Washington, D.C.: Government Printing Office, 1961.

U.S. DEPARTMENT OF STATE. *Foreign Relations of the United States. The Conference of Berlin (Potsdam) 1945* (Vol. I). Washington, D.C.: Government Printing Office, 1960.

U.S. DEPARTMENT OF STATE. *Foreign Relations of the United States. The Conference at Malta and Yalta 1945*. Washington, D.C.: Government Printing Office, 1960.

U.S. DEPARTMENT OF STATE. *Foreign Relations of the United States. The Conference at Quebec 1944*. Washington, D.C.: Government Printing Office, 1972.

VAN CREVALD, MARTIN. *Fighting Power, German and U.S. Army Performance, 1939–1945, Contributions in Military History*, Number 32. Westport, Conn.: Greenwood Press, 1982.

———. *Hitler's Strategy, 1940–41: The Balkan Cue*. Cambridge: Cambridge University Press, 1973.

VON LAND, IOCHEN, AND CLAUS SIBYLL, EDS. *Eichmann Interrogated, Transcripts from the Archives of the Israeli Police*. New York: Farrar, Straus & Giroux, 1983.

VON MANSTEIN, ERICH. *Lost Victories*. Chicago: H. Regner & Co., 1958.

WANDYCZ, PIOTR S. *The Twilight of French Eastern Alliances, 1926–36. French-Czechoslovak-Polish Relations from Locarno to the Demilitarization of the Rhineland*. Princeton, N.J.: Princeton University Press, 1988.

WARLIMONT, WALTER. *Inside Hitler's Headquarters*. London: Weidenfeld and Nicolson, 1964.

WEBSTER, SIR CHARLES, AND NOBLE FRANKLAND. *The Strategic Air Offensive against Germany, 1939–1945. Preparation* (Vol. I). *Endeavour* (Vol. II). *Victory* (Vol. III). London: H.M.S.O., 1961.

WEIGLEY, RUSSELL F. *Eisenhower's Lieutenants. The Campaign of France and Germany, 1944–1945*. Bloomington: Indiana University Press, 1981.

WEINBERG, GERHARD L. *The Foreign Policy of Hitler's Germany: Starting World War II, 1937–1939*. Chicago: University of Chicago Press, 1980.

———. *Germany and the Soviet Union, 1939–1941*. Leiden: Brill, 1954.

WILMOT, CHESTER. *The Struggle for Europe*. London: Collins, 1952.

WINTERBOTHAM, F. W. *The Ultra Secret*. New York: Dell, 1974.

WRIGHT, GORDON. *The Ordeal of Total War, 1939–1945*. New York: Harper & Row, 1968.

WYTWYCKY, BOHDAN. *The Other Holocaust: Many Circles of Hell*. Washington, D.C.: Novak Report Publishers, 1980.

YAREMEYEV, LEONID. *USSR in World War II*. Moscow: Novosti Press, 1985.

YOUNG, PETER, *Atlas of the Second World War*. New York: Putnam's, 1979.

———. *World war II, 1939–45. A Short History*. New York: Thomas Y. Crowell, 1966.

ZALOGA, STEVEN, AND VICTOR MADEJ. *The Polish Campaign, 1939*. New York: Hippocrene Books, 1985.

ZAWODNY, J. K. *Death in the Forest: The Story of the Katyn Forest Massacre*. Notre Dame: University of Notre Dame Press, 1962.

———. *Nothing but Honour: The Story of the Warsaw Uprising, 1944*. Stanford, Calif.: Stanford University Press, 1978.

ZHUKOV, GEORGI K. *Marshal Zhukov's Greatest Battles*. New York: Harper & Row, Publishers, 1969.

———. *The Memoirs of Marshal Zhukov*. New York: Delacorte Press, 1971.

ZIMKE, E. F. *The German Northern Theatre of Operations 1940–1945*. Washington, D.C.: Department of the Army, 1959.

Index

Aaland Islands (Finland), *83m*, 84, 103
Abbeville pocket, 101, 102, 104
Abwehr (German intelligence service), 93, 283, 284, 286, 357
  assassination attempt on Hitler (1944), 305
  reasons for failures, 357
Addis Ababa (Ethiopia), 142
Admiral Hipper (cruiser), 78
Admiral Scheer (battleship), 193
Adriatic Sea, 54, 216
Afghanistan, 3
Africa, 4, 54, 56, 164 (*see also* East Africa; North Africa)
Afrika Korps, 163, 164, 165, 197, 202
Aircraft carriers, 143, 194
Air Mastery (Douhet), 21
Air power, aircraft, 6, 10, 17, 18
  air cover for naval forces, 91, 298, 318, 361
  Allied bombing of Germany, 216, 243–46, 322*n*, 326, 327–28
  Allied bombing of Italy, 235–36
  Allied versus German strength in 1939–40, 71–72, 95, 96, 118–24, 127–30
  and the Battle of Poland, 62, 68, 71
  coming of age with Battle of Britain, 127
  day versus night bombing, 243–44
  German buildup in 1930s, 30–31
  German delays in development, 129–30, 356
  in the German invasion of the USSR, 173–74, 181, 183
  German theories of, 18
  Germany increases production in, 245–46
  Germany introduces jet fighter, 304, 317 (*see also* Luftwaffe; Polish Air Force; Regia Aeronautica; Royal Air Force; United States Air Force; individual battles)
  Italian theories and innovations in, 21–22, 145, 327
  Italian weaknesses in 1940, 145–46
  in the Spanish Civil War, 36
Aisne River (France), 104, 107
Alamogordo (New Mexico) testing ground, 346
Albania, 37, 155, *155m*, 188, 277, 343, 364
  Greek troops occupy (1940), 151, 158
  Italian invasion (1939), 51, 54, 149, 150, 233
Albert I of Belgium, 97
Albert Canal, 95, 97, *98m*, 99
Alexander, General Sir Harold, 200, 210, 211, 213, 214, 217, 234
Alexander I of Yugoslavia, 152
Alexandria (Egypt), 136, 157, 198, 199, 200
Algeria, *5m*, 22, 117, 189, 204, 212
Algiers, 205, 207, *208m*, 210, 280
Allied Air Force, 85, 96
Allied Expeditionary Force, 82
Allies:
  air offensive on Germany (1940–42), 243–46
  Britain becomes junior partner, 190
  British-French alliance, 103, 108
  casualties of western campaign, 112
  combined operations, 131, 189, 190–91, 234, 249, 356–57, 361
  defeat in N. Africa (1941), 165–66
  Dunkirk evacuation, 105–7
  financial and economic situation, 77
  and the German attack on the Low Countries, 97, 100–101, 104–5
  and the German invasion of Denmark, Norway, 86, 88, 89–91, 101
  German surrender to (1945), 339–

Allies (*cont.*)
41 (*see also* Casablanca Conference; Potsdam Conference; Teheran Conference; Yalta Conference)
invasion of France, Low Countries (1944), 294–304, 305–7, 311–20, 325
invasion of Sicily, Italy (1943–44), 230, 234, *236m*, 274, 304
landing in N. Africa (1942–43), 189–90, 205–10, 212–17, 277, 361
naval superiority, 77–78, 115, 354–56
negotiations with Axis allies, 211, 232
order of battle on western front, 95–97
peripheral versus direct strategy, 188–89
response to Nazi genocides, 265
and the Russo-Finnish War, 81–86, 92
Soviet request for aid from, 176, 178–79
unconditional surrender doctrine, 211, 239, 251, 277, 289, 336
U.S. joins, Grand Alliance forms (1941), 183–84, 189, 345
Alpine divisions, in Germany, 89, 90
Alsace-Lorraine, 3, 8, 9, 10, *12m*, 57
Allies capture, 311
returned to Germany, 109, 253
Altmark (prison ship), 86
Aluminum industry, 92
Ambrosio, General Vittorio, 237
Amery, Leopold, 69
Amiens (France), 108, 311
Amphibious warfare, 131, 190, 196
at Normandy, 291, 297, 298
Andalsnes (Norway), *87m*, 89
Anders, General Władysław, 242
Anderson, General Kenneth A., 205, 211
Anglo-German naval agreement (1935), 32, 77
Anglo-Polish Mutual Assistance Pact (1939), 52–54, 57, 69, 72–73
Ann-Azur spy network, 285
Anti-Comintern pact (1936), 37–38, 50, 59, 66, 168, 256, 258
Antitank guns, 17
Antonescu, General Ion, 148, 151, 258, 259, 310
Antwerp, *98m*, 292, 311, 312
Anzio, 236, 240–42
Aosta, Amadeo of Savoy, Duke of, 142
Arabs, 162, 167–68
Archangel (USSR), 177
Arctic region, 85, 183, 191
Ardennnes region, 76, 94, 95, 97
German offensive (1940), 99–100
German offensive (1944), 317–19, 321, 329
Arendt, Hannah, 261, 263
Ark Royal (aircraft carrier), 117, 194, 198
Armenians, Turkish massacre of, 270
Army Group B (Germany), 297, 300
Army Group Center (Axis); in the Western offensive (1941), 95, 99; in N. Africa, 164, 215; invades USSR (1941), *171m*, 172, 174, 176; retreat (1944), 309, 328
Army Group North (Germany), *171m*, 172, 175
Army Group South (Germany), *171m*, 172, 174, 186
Arnhem, Battle of (1944), 292, 313, 314–16
Arnum, General Juergen von, 209, 212, 213, 215
Arras (Belgium), *98m*, 104, 311
Arrow Cross, 21, 259, 311
Artificial harbors, 294, 297
ASDIC (antisubmarine detection device), 32
Athens, *152m*, 159
Atlantic, Battle of the,. 86, 134, 186, 190–96, *192m*, 356
Allies defeat U-boat menace (1943), 216, 217
British raids on German ships (1942), 194–96
German U-boats menace Allied shipping, 92, 119, 178, 189, 190–94
South Atlantic battles, 78
Atlantic Charter, 177, 323, 345
Atlantic Conference (1941), 177–79
Atlantic Wall, 190, 246, 254
Atom bomb:
dropped on Japan, 327, 348
German development of, 265, 283, 357
U.S. development of, 345, 346, 357
Attila the Hun, 337
Attlee, Clement R., 344
Auchinleck, General Claude, 197, 199
Auschwitz concentration camp, 262–63, *266p*, 266, 268, 330
Australia, 116
troops in Europe, 135, 157, 160
troops in Far East, 190
troops in North Africa, 201
Austria, 9, 10, 154, 354
Allied advances in south (1945), 339
Anschluss with Germany, 39, 41–44, 77, 112, 351
Hitler's plans for, 32, 38, 39
as Italian client, 22, 35, 37
Austro-Hungarian Empire, 3, 5, 4–5, 7, 8, 10–11
Avranches, Battle of (1944), 300, 304
Axis, Operation (1943), 230–39
Axis powers, 15, 333
and Allied intervention in Scandinavia, 85–86
and the Allied invasion of N. Africa (1942), 205, 207, 208–9, 211–17
and the Allies' unconditional surrender doctrine, 211, 239, 251
attacks Yugoslavia and Greece (1940), 154–62
British strategy against, 177
coalition begins to crumble (1943), 232, 233
Communist resistance movements in, 274–78
conquests to 1940, allies, 112
declares war on U.S. (1941), 185
declares war on USSR (1941), 170
and the defense of Sicily (1943), 236–37
as economic coalition, 252
formed (1936), 37, 38
Mediterranean and Balkan victories, 134, 135, 162, 198–99
Middle East strategy, 162, 167–68, 198–99
reasons for defeat, 351–53 (*see also* Hilter; Mussolini)
and the Soviet offensive (1942), 219, 221, 225–26, 231
Spain urged to join, 137
spheres of influence, 54, 148–49
strains between Germany and Italy, 198
treaty (1939), 55–56
Yalta provisions on (1945), 323–24
Yugoslavia urged to join, 151, 152

Babi Yar massacre, 269
Bachka (Hungary), 156
Badoglio, Pietro, 239–40, 291, 292
Baku (USSR), 172, 218
Baldwin, Stanley, 34
Balearic Islands, 5, 36
Balkans, 22, 86, 338
Axis war aims in, 110, 135, 149–50, 151, 153–54, 162, 186
British invasion plans thwarted by USSR, 247, 249
in Churchill's war strategy, 188, 190, 234, 277
Communist resistance movements, 275–78 (*see also* individual countries)
German economic offensive in, 43–44, 56, 77
guerrilla and partisan fighting in, 186, 242, 248–49, 273, 275–78
Hapbsburg expansion in, 3, 4
Italian challenges to France and Britian in, 37, 51, 54
post-WWI nations, 8, 11
pre-WWI nationalism, 2
Soviet drive toward, 309, 310–11
Baltic states:
German minorities in, 3, 9, 10
German offensive in (1941), 173, 174, 182
German territorial advances in, 51, 57–58
Nazi occupation, 259
and Roosevelt's demands at Teheran (1943), 248
Soviet advances in (1944), 308–9
Soviet alliances (1939), 72–73
Soviet occupation and annexation (1940), 147, 248
Soviet partisan fighting in, 279

as Soviet sphere of influence, 58, 59, 79–80
Soviet-sponsored deportations in, 270
units drafted into S.S., 335
Banat region, 11, 156
Bank of France, 254
Barbarossa, Operation, 149, 154, 186
Bardia (Egypt), 138, 165
Battle of, 140
Barinam (battleship), 193
Bastogne (Belgium), 318–19, 320
Battle-axe, Operation, 199, 200
Batumi (USSR), 218
Bavarian Alps, 330
Beauvoir, Simone de, 293
Beaverbrook, W.M. Aitken, Lord, 132
Beck, Jozet, 34, *46n*, 50, 54
Beck, General Ludwig, 287–88, 305
Belgium, 8, 16, 76, 79
Allied drive, German counteroffensive (1944), 311, 317–19
declares neutrality, 34–35, 96–97
German offensives in, 93–100, 104, 105, 112
Nazi occupation, 254, 255, 257, 282, 283
surrender (1940), 104, 105
Walloon-Fleming conflict, 257
and WWI, 5, 9, 16, 96–97
Belgorod (USSR), 229, *230m*
Belgrade (Yugoslavia), 153–56, 310
Belorussia, 65, 66, 172, 182, 279
Battle of (1944), 309
Nazi occupation, 259, 260, 267, 268
Belzen camp, 264, 269
Benes, Eduard, 45, 46–47, 48
Benghazi (Libya), 140–41, 165
Berchtesgaden (Germany), 42, 297
Bergen (Norway), 89, 92
Beria, Lavrenty, 174
Berlin, 227, 343
Allied air raids on, 125–26, 149, 243, 246, 328
Allied and Soviet advances toward (1944–45), 320, 330–32
postwar occupation zones, 347
Soviet siege and capture (1945), 334–35, 341
Bessarabia, *12m*, 58, 86, 147
Bevin, Ernest, 132, 344
Bir Hakeim, Battle of (1942), 189
Bismarck, Otto von, 2, 3, 337
Bismarck (battleship), 78, 193, 194
sinking of (1941), 196, 354
Bizerte (Tunisia), 208, 209, 212
Black Forest (Germany), 69
Black Orchestra (*Schwarze Kapelle*), 289
Black Sea, 148, 183
Soviet interest in straits, 148, 154
Soviet naval forces in, 219–20
Black Shirts (Italy), 20
Blaskowitz, General Johannes, 65
Bletchley Park (England), 123
Blitzkrieg ("lightning war"), 18, 55, 61, 63, 90, 194
principles of, 63
Blomberg, General Werner von, 27, 31, 32, 38, 39
Bluecher (cruiser), 78, 89
"Blue Study" (air operations manual), 128
Blummentritt, General Guenther, 111, 299
Bock, General Fedor von, 62, 95, 172, 175
Bodyguard scheme (1943–44), 295–96
Bohemia-Moravia, 10, 44
German protectorate, 50–51, 56, 62, 235, 274
Bohr, Niels, 351
Böll, Heinrich, 293
Bologna, Allied capture of, 338
Bolsheviks, 7, 8, 20, 26, 79, 262
Bombing of Dresden Reconsidered, The (Smith), 326n
Bonnet, Georges, 57, 69, 70
Bordeaux, 102, 108, 119, 311
Boris III of Bulgaria, 155, 258
Bormann, Martin, *290p*, 335, 336
Bosnia, 11
Boulogne, 126, 128, 297, 311
Bradley, General Omar, *214p*, 214, 319
criticizes U.S. strategy in Germany, 331
in Normandy, 302, 305–6
strategy in the Rhine, 312, 329
Brauchitsch, General Walther von, 54, 109, 182, 218
Braun, Eva, 336
Braun, Wernher von, 245
Bremen, 86
Brenner Pass, 42, 110
Brereton, General Lewis Hyde, 313
Breslau, siege of (1945), 328
Brest (France), *102m*, 117, 119, 194, 195, 243
Brest-Litovsk, Treaty of (1918), 7, 9, 13, 169
Briand, Aristide, 16
Britain, Battle of (1940–41), *122m*, 124–33, 137, 138–39, 143, 273
British Broadcasting Corp. (BBC), 281, 286
British Commonwealth of Nations, 116, 132, 139
troops from, 132, 135, 166 (*see also* Australia; India; New Zealand)
British Empire, 1, 2, 38, 44*n*, 114, 132, 139, 362
bases leased to U.S., 120
in Hitler's strategy, 105, 114, 115
British Expeditionary Force (B.E.F.), 77, 94, 95, 98, 101, 118
in the Battle of Greece and Crete, 157, 158–60, 164
caught in Abbeville, 101, 104, 164
evacuated from Dunkirk, 104–7
faces Rommel in N. Africa, 165–66
British Somaliland, 142
"British Strategy in Certain Eventuality" (cabinet report), 103
Brno (Brünn), *45m*, 274
Brockdorf-Ahelfeld (German general), 288
Brooke, Sir Alan, 13, 188, 213, 330n
Browning, General Frederick, 314, 315
Brussels, *98m*, 104, 311
B-17 bomber ("Flying Fortress"), 244, 283, 326
Buchenwald camp, 263, 269, 350
Budapest, 297, 311, 320, 332
Budenny, Marshall Semyon, 172, 173, 186
Bug River (Poland), 65, 67, 72, 172, 283
Bukovina, 11, *12m*, 147–48
Bulgaria, 5, *12m*, 37, 112, 148–49, 292, 320, 344, 357
and the Axis attack on Yugoslavia and partition, 155, 156, 256
becomes Axis power, 152
defection from Axis, 274
and the German invasion of Greece, 155, 156, 158, 160
as Nazi vassal state, 258
Stalin-Churchill agreement on, 320
surrender to USSR, 310
Bulge, Battle of the (1944), 318–19
Buna (synthetic rubber), 77
Burgenland, 11
Burrough, Admiral Sir H.M., 340
Butcher, Captain Harry C., 331
Butler, R.A., 115
Byrnes, James F., 323*n*, 324, 345–46, 348

Caen, Battle of (1944), 302–3
Cairo, 136, 137, 186, *208m*, 209
British defense (1932), 199
Calais (France), 308 (*see also* Pas de Calais)
Campbeltown (destroyer), 196
Camus, Albert, 290–93
Canada, 116, 354
and the Dieppe raid, 146
forces in France, 106, 305, 306, 311
forces in North Africa, 206
secures bases in North Atlantic, 92
Canaris, Admiral Wilhelm, 93, 288, 289, 305, 358
Capitalism, 1–2, 13, 74, 345
Caribbean, U.S. bases in, 120
Carol II of Rumania, 148
Carpathian Mountains, 62, 328
Carpatho-Ukraine, 51
Casablanca, Allied landing at (1942), 205, 207, 208m
Casablanca Conference (1943), 210–12, 231
strategy for bombing Germany, 245
Case White, 54
Catholic Center party (Germany), 26
Caucasus region:
German offensive in, 172, 174, 175, 176, 197, 218, 220, 221, *223m*, 225, 226
Nazi occupation, 182, 259
oil fields, 85, 172, 175, 186, 197

Caucasus region (*cont.*)
resistance movement, 183
and Stalin's deportations, 270
Cavalry units, *68n,* 170, 180, 226
Celt, Tadeusz, 256*n*
Central Intelligence Agency, 281
Central Powers (WWI), *4m,* 5, 7, 8, 11, 12, 13
Chamberlain, Houston S., 24
Chamberlain, Neville, 41, 44–48, 51–52, 77, 115, 157, 288
appeal to Mussolini, 51
appeasement at Munich, 46–48
conference with Hitler on Sudetenland, 45
and the invasion of Poland, 52, 53, 69, 72
resignation, 101–2
view of Hitler and Nazi regime, 44–45
Charlemagne Division, 257
Cherbourg, 301, 302, 303*n*
Chermaiev, General Ivan, 340
Chetniks, 249, 275
Chiang Kai-shek, 249, 322
China, 249
Japanese expansion in 1930s, 37–38
territories ceded to USSR, 323, 348–49
Chiukov, General Vasily I., 223
Choltitz, General Dietrich von, 308
Christian X of Denmark, 256
Christian Democratic party (Italy), 241
Churchill, Sir Winston, 46, 86, 120, 132, 166, 167, 176, 227, 242, 301, 319, 355
aid to Stalin, 168, 169, 178–79
and the Allied advance on Berlin, 330–31
archives, *53n, 70n*
assessment as military strategist, 355, 356–61
Atlantic meeting with Roosevelt (1941), 177–78
becomes prime minister, 101–3
"blood, sweat, and tears" speech (1940), 112–13
at Casablanca with Roosevelt (1943), 210–11
deal with Stalin on zones of influence (1944), 320, 321–22
defeated in 1945 election, 344–45
directs aid to Greece, 141, 157, 277–78
and Dunkirk, 104–5, 106, 107
"fight" speech, decision to continue war, 115–16, 344
on Japan's attack on Royal Navy, 185
Mediterranean strategy (1940–42), 135–36, 197–98, 199
meeting with Roosevelt at Malta, 321
orders air raid on Berlin, 125, 126
perspective on USSR and Stalin, 103, 116, 345, 355
perspective on WWII and Grand Alliance, 345
at Potsdam, 344–45
proposes seizure of Swedish iron mines, 84, 103
proposes union with France, 108, 117
relationship with Roosevelt, 333, 334*n*
on the UN, 335
at the Siegfried Line, 330
"soft underbelly" strategy for Italy and Balkans, 188–90, 234, 277
at Teheran, 248–50, 295
tribute to RAF, 130
Triumph and Tragedy, 345
on victories in battles of Britain and North Africa, 143
on victory at el-Alamein, 217
"V" symbol, 281
in Washington with Roosevelt (1941), 187–89
at Yalta, 320–24
and Yugoslavia, 151, 152, 277, 278*n*
Ciano, Counte Galeazzo, 35, 37, 54, 56, 110, 139, 142, 148, 156
Citadel, Operation (1943), 228, 234
Clark, General Mark, W., 206, 211, 240–42
Clausewitz, Carl von, 327, 356, 361
Clemenceau, Georges, 8, 9
Codreanu, Coreliu, 254
Cold war, 364
Cologne (Germany), 17
Colonial empires, 365 (*see also* British Empire; French Empire; German colonies)
Comintern, 13, 33, 36, 38, 231, 275, 291
Commandos, 99, 131, 190, 196, 361–62
Commonwealth Air Training School, 116
Communist movement, 23
anti-Nazi resistance opposition movements, 182, 226, 285, 291
Balkan resistance movements, 274–78
becomes supranational, 13
controlled by USSR, 231
coup d'état in Germany (1919), 15, 22, 32
in Finland, 79
in France, 33, 101, 280
growth in Germany in 1930s, 26–27, 28
in Italy, 19–20, 291, 292
Nazi crusade against, 22–23, 26, 32, 170, 182, 261
in Poland, 231, 278
in the Spanish Civil War, 35, 36
Communist party of the USSR, 7, 13, 57
Compiegne (France), 109
Concentration camps, 255, 263–66
Allied troops liberate (1945), 329, 330, 354
escapees, 292
established (1933), 28, 29
gas chambers, 265
Gleiwitz attack (1939), 59–60
scientific experiments, sexual abuse, 267
in the USSR, 72, 73, 177
"Condor" air force squadron, 36
Conservative party (England), 52, 101–2, 344
Convoy system in the Atlantic, 191, 193
Cooper, Alfred Duff, 46
Coral Sea, Battle of the (1942), 328
Corap, General André, 101
Cordon Sanitaire, 15
Corinth Canal (Greece), 159
Corradini, Philipo, 21
Corsica, 19, 22, 233, 236
Cossack (destroyer), 86
Courageous (aircraft carrier), 78
Coventry (England), 246
Cracow (Poland), 63, *67m,* 72, 253, 255
Creolite, 92
Crete, 149, 150, 159
Battle of (1940), *159m,* 160–62, 186, 194
Creveld, Martin van, 359
Crimea, *171m,* 172, 218–20, 320
Crimean War, 188, 321
Croatia, 11, *12m,* 151, 155, 275
autonomy movement, 151
Kingdom and Fascist government, 156, 258
"Crooked Legs" radio device, 123–24, 125
Crusade in Europe (Eisenhower), 251
Crusader, Operation (1941), 198
Cryptology, 31 (*see also* Enigma; Intelligence)
Cunningham, Admiral Sir Andrew, 142–43, 151, 157–58, 211
Curzon Line, 248, 322
Cuxhave (Germany), 191
Cvetkovic (premier of Yugoslavia), 154, 258
Cyrenaica, 134, *136m,* 140, 141, 165, 196
Czechoslovakia, 8, *12m,* 15, 38, 42, 324, 348, 364
alliance with France, 15, 34, 35, 46, 48, 111
alliance with USSR, 48
established, 10, 11
German frontier negotiations (1925), 16–17
German invasion and occupation, 50–51, 54, 56, 77, 112, 251, 253–54
Germans expelled from, 347
Hitler's plans to invade, 38, 39, 44–45, 46–48
Polish and Hungarian demands, 45–46
resistance movement in, 274
ties with USSR (1941), 230
Czechs, 44, 201

Dachau concentration camp, 28, 29, 261p, 263, 329p, 330
Daimler Company, 16
Dairen (Dalny) (China), 323, 348
DAK (*Deutsches Afrika Korps*) (*see* Afrika Korps)
Dakar, 118, *208m*
expedition, 206
Daladier, Edouard, 46, 82, 101
Dalmatia, 4, 11, 19, 22, 156
Danube River, region, 5, 22, 37, 42, 44, 48, 57, 86
German-Soviet tensions over, 147–48
Soviet advances in (1945), 320
Danzig (Gdansk), *12m*, 63
Germany demands for, 49–50, 56
German takeover, 72
Soviet capture of, 328
Versailles provisions on, 8, 9, 10
Darlan, Admiral Jean François, 116, 117, 207, 208
D-day landing (June 6, 1944), 298, 300–301, 362
Debrecen (Hungary), 311
"Declaration of Liberated Europe" (1945), 323–24, 332
Degrelle, Leon, 257
Dempsey, General Sir Miles C., 305
Denmark, 9, 244, 295
German invasion (1940), 86, 87, 88, 91
liberation of, 331, 340
Nazi occupation, 256, 268
"Desert rats," 140, 204
Desert warfare, 137–38, 163, 215
Destroyers, 119–20
Destruction of Dresden, The (Irving), 326
Deutschland (Lützow) (battleship), 78, 89, 193
Dieppe (France), 311
British-Canadian raid (1942), 196, 244
Dietl, General Edward, 90
Dietrich, General Joseph "Sepp," 294
Djilas, Milovan, 277*n*
Dnieper River, 170, *171m*, 175, 309
Dodecanese Islands, *5m*, 160, 162
Doenitz, Admiral Karl, 49, 78, 86, 115, 193, 216, 335, 336
promotes U-boat force, 49, 129, 196, 356
Dollman, Ben. Friedrich, 302
Donovan, Colonel William J., 153, 281–82, 287
Don River, region, 86, 220, 223, 224
Dorsetshire (cruiser), 195
Douhet, Giulio, 21–22, 129, 327
Dowding, Marshal Sir Hugh, 124, 131
Dresden, Allied bombing of, 325–27
Dual alliance (1894), 4, 5
Dulles, Allen Welsh, 287
Dunkirk, 103
evacuation from (1940), 104–7, 120, 129, 131, 189, 200, 284, 350
Dutch East Indies, 177
Dutch Nazi party, 356–57

Eagle, Operation (1940), 124
Eaker, General Ira, 244
East Africa, 6, 134, 137, 141–42
Eastern Europe:
alliances with France, 14–15, 16–17, 34–35, 51–54
British commitments in, 51–52, 57
expulsion of Germans from, 347 (*see also* Holocaust; individual countries)
German-Soviet conflicts of interest in, 147–49
in Hitler's *Lebensraum* strategy, 25, 26, 38–39, 53, 59, 255
Nazi colonial governments, 257–61
Nazi exploitation, forced labor, 250, 251–52
post-WWI territorial settlements, 8, 9, 10–11
Red Army advances in, 231, 247, 248, 308–10
resistance movements, 278–79, 292
Soviet-British division of zones of influence in (1944), 317, 318–19, 346–47
Soviet occupation 348, 363, 364, 365
Soviet occupation (1939), 73–74
Soviet political strategy in 1943, 230–31
Soviet sphere of influence established, 57–59
Yalta provisions on, 323–24
Eastern Troops, 259–60
East Prussia, 9–10, *12m*, 50, 62, 64, 163, 248, 322, 328
Eben Emael fort (Belgium), 99
Economic warfare, 77, 132
Eden, Anthony, 42, *105p*, 247, 335
Egypt, 3, 22, 167, 217
bogus Allied armies in, 295
British defense of, 191, 197, 198, 199–204
demands for British evacuation, 136
Italian defeat in, 139–40
strategic importance of, 134, 135, 143, 159, 160, 161, 356
Ehrenburg, Ilya, 220, 340
Eichmann, Adolf, 260, 261
Eighth Army (Great Britain), 166, 195, 209, 211, 212, 215, 227, 241
as cosmopolitan force, 201
defeated by Rommel (1942), 197, 198, 199
in Italy (1944–45), 337–39 (*see also* Western Desert Force)
regrouped under Montgomery, 199–202
victory at el-Alamein (1942), 202–4
Eindhoven (Netherlands), *313m*, 314, 316
Einstein, Albert, 357
Eisenhower, General Dwight D., 188, 296n, 241, 360, 298n
and the Ardennes counteroffensive, 314–16
Crusade in Europe, 251
and the land assault in Germany (1945), 329, 330, 331
and the landing in North Africa (1942), 189, 205–8
lower Rhine attack plan (1944), 312–14
made supreme commander in North Africa, 211, 214
and the Normandy invasion, strategy in France (1944), 298–99, 304–5, 306
and the surrender of Germany, 339–41
Victory Order of the Day, 341
on the Warsaw uprising (1944), 310
El Agheila (Libya), Battle of, 165
el-Alamein (Egypt), 139, 165
Battle of (1942), 198, 199, 203*n*, 202–4
Battle of (1943), *208m*, 209, 217, 226–27, 359
Elbe River, 330, 331, 334, 335, 348, *382m*
as boundary in postwar Germany, 347
Elbrus, Mount (USSR), 220
Elizabeth Petrovna, Empress of Russia, 333
Enghien, Duc d', 99–100
English Channel, 102, 104, 105, 187, 188, 195, 354
Germany closes to shipping, 119
the Normandy invasion, 295, 298–300
as protection to Britain, 116
Enigma ciphering machine, 31, 78, 95*n*, 111, 206, 298
British break codes, 123, 124, 158, 193, 195
copied by Poles, 75, 357
Kriegsmarine cipher, 193
and the Taranto attack (1940), 143
Entente Cordiale, 3, 4, 5, 19
Eritrea, 134, 141–42
Essen (Germany), 245
Estonia, *12m*, 34, 57, 58, 74, 80, 253, 279, 331
annexed to USSR, 147
Soviet mutual assistance pact (1939)
Eternal Friendship, Treaty of (1940), 152, 154
Ethiopia, 32, 134
British victory in, 142
Italian invasion, 35, 37, 46, 145, 282
Ethnic groups;
collaborators in Nazi-occupied USSR, 260–61
League of Nations Covenant rights, 11
in Nazi concentration camps, 265
Nazi racist doctrines and, 24–25
pre-WWI nationalism, 2
Eugenics, 24–25
Eupen (Belgium), 9, 253, 311, 318*n*
Exeter (cruiser), 78

Faeroe Islands, 92
Falaise, Battle of, 303, 306–7

Falange movement (Spain), 21, 36, 137
Falkenhorst, General Nikolaus von, 86, 91, 283
Famille-Interallie spy network, 286
Far East:
  Allied strategy for, 187–89, 328
  British interests in, 38, 39, 135, 197
  Hilter's strategy for, 37–38, 39
  Potsdam provisions on, 348–49 (*see also* individual countries; Southeast Asia)
  Yalta provisions on, 321, 323
Fascism, 25, 37, 145, 234, 237, 272
  doctrines, 20–21, 23
  in Eastern Europe, 258–59
  resistance movements, 291–93
  spread of, 21
  in Yugoslavia, 156, 258
Faury, General L.A.J., 70*n*–71*n*
Fellgiebel, General Erich, 288
Fermi, Enrico, 357
Finland, 8, 30, 57, 74, 151, 357–63
  attacks USSR, 170, 172
  German troops in, 148
  history, 79
  peace overtures to Allies, 211, 232
  Soviet territorial claims, 79–80
  surrender to USSR (1944), 308
  war with USSR (1939), 80–85, 92, 102–3, 350
Fischer, Franz, 5*n*
Fiume (Rijecka), 11, *12m*, 156
Flandin, Pierre, 34
Florence, Allied seizure of (1944), 338
Flying Fortress bomber (B-17), 244, 283, 323
Foch, Marshall Ferdinand, 6, 9, 104, 108, 257, 357
Foggia airfields (Italy), Allied capture of, 236*n*, 343
Fourteen Points program, 8, 9, 11, 19, 211
France, 1, 7, 114
  alliance with USSR (1935), 33–34, 48
  Allied invasion (1944), 280–81, 292, 294–308
  and the Allied invasion of North Africa (1942), 205–8
  Allies plan invasion of, 210–11, 242, 246–47, 248, 294–96
  Allied thrusts in north, 311
  and the *Anschluss* of Austria, 41, 42, 44
  assessment of failure, 111, 272
  builds Maginot Line, 17
  declares war on Germany, 66, 68, 69, 76
  defense policy, 37
  Eastern European alliances, 14–15, 16–17, 34–35, 47, 48, 52
  fall of, and armistice, 107, 108–10, 116, 138
  German bases in north, 118–21, 294–97
  German drive in, 90, 93–101, 103–5
  German frontier settlements, 16–17
  Germans takeover unoccupied zone, 208
  Hitler's plans to attack, 79, 86
  in Hitler's strategies, 25, 26, 38–39
  and the invasion of Poland, 61, 62, 67, 68–72, 111
  Italian grievances against, 19
  liberation of Paris, 307–8
  morale of troops and air force, 100–1, 103, 104, 111
  navy crippled by Britain, 116–18, 205
  Nazi "occupation costs," 254
  North African colonies, 22
  and the occupation of Germany, 347, 364
  pledge to support Poland, Rumania, Greece, 52–54, 57, 111
  Popular Front government, 33, 35, 42
  population losses, 353 (*see also* Allies)
  pre-WWI alliances, 3, 4, 5
  relations with Czechoslovakia and the Munich Conference, 46–49, 111
  resistance movement, 113, 167, 208, 210, 275, 279–81, 292, 307–8
  response to Dunkirk, 105, 106, 107
  response to German rearmament, 31–32
  response to Spanish Civil War, 36
  Reynaud reconstructs cabinet (1940), 104
  secret negotiations with Mussolini, 56
  spy networks in, 284–86
  territories under Belgian administration, 255
  and the Versailles agreements, 8, 9, 14, 15
  Vichy government, 108, 109, 112, 116, 118, 137, 206–8, 210, 254, 257, 279
  war in south with Italy, 108, 110
  and WWI, 5–6
  Yalta agreements on, 319
Francis Ferdinand of Austria, assasination of, 4, 5
Franco, General Francisco, 35, 36, 137, 257
François-Poncet (French ambassador to Germany), 46
Franco-Italian armistice (1940), 110
Franco-Polish Alliance (1921), 14, 15, 16, 17, 34, 35, 52, 69
Franco-Polish military convention (1939), 52, 57, 69
Franco-Prussian War (1870–71), 2, 3, 8
Franco-Russian Alliance (1894), 3, 5
Frank, Dr. Hans, 72, 253*n*, 255
Frankfurt (Germany), 69
Fraser, David, 333
Frederick the Great of Prussia, 330
Frederick II of Prussia, 50, 337, 343, 360
Free French movement, 113, 167, 279, 282
  enter France (1944), 307
  intelligence network, 280–81
  in the Middle East, 167, 280
  in North Africa, 198, 201
  occupy St. Pierre and Miquelon Is., 210
French air force, 111
French Empire, 44*n*, 185, 280
  de Gaulle preserves integrity of, 210
  in North Africa, *4m*, 22, 137
French Expeditionary Force, 242
French navy, 107, 109, 207, 208
  destruction of, 116–18
French Revolution, 1
Freyberg, Major-General Bernard C., 160–61, 242
Friedenburg, Admiral Hans von, 340
Fritsch (German officer), 38, 40
Fromm, General Friedrich, 290
F2 spy network, 284–85
Fuller, General J.F.C., 18
Funk, 351

Galicia, *4m*, 10, 148, 255
Galivare (Sweden), 82
Galland, Adolf, 127
Gamelin, General Maurice, 52, 70, 71, 95*n*, 103–4
  ignores intelligence reports, 97, 100
  military theories, 99–101
Gaulle, Charles de, 285, 319
  and the Allied invasion of N. Africa (1942), 206, 207–8, 210
  emergence as statesman, 210
  in England (1940–43), 112, 156, 206, 279–80, 284
  enters France, heads provisional government (1944), 307–8
  on Gamelin, 100
  moves HQ to Algiers (1943), 277
  Roosevelt's dislike for, 206, 210, 307
  speech on Free French movement (1940), 113
Gavin, General James, 315, 318
Gelsenkirchen (Germany), 310
Geneva (Switzerland), 11
Genghis Khan, 59, 337
Gensoul, Admiral Marcel, 117
German colonies, 2–3, 5, 7, 9, 10, 68, 105, 163, 250
Germans;
  in the Baltic states, 3, 9, 10
  in Hungary, 257
  intelligence gathering abroad, 31
  postwar expulsions in Eastern Europe, 347
  in Sudetenland, 10, 44, 45, 347
  in the Volga region, 270
  in western Poland after WWI, 9–10, 63
German-Soviet nonaggression pact (*see* Hilter-Stalin pact)

German Worker's party, 22–23 (*see also* Nazi party)
Germany, 1
air raids on Britain (1940–41), *122m,* 124–33
alliance with Japan, 37–38
Allied air raids on (1941–45), 125–26, 149, 243–46, 283
Allied bombing raids (1944–45), 325–27
Allied naval blockade of, 78–79
Allied and Soviet land assault (1945), 328–30
Allied subversion, sabotage, espionage in, 281–86
annexations in Eastern Europe, 72
Anschluss with Austria, 39, 41–43, *43m,* 77, 112
attacks USSR (1941), 167, 169–77, *171m,* 179–83, 186
Balkan trade offensive, 42, 43–44
bases in Northern France, 118–21, 294, 295
and the Battle of the Atlantic, 119, 178, 189, 190–96
capture of Berlin, 350–53, 334–35, 339, 340
casualties, population losses, 353, 356
collapse of central front in Eastern Europe (1944), 308–9
Communist coup (1919), 15, 22, 32
conquest of Yugoslavia and Greece, 156–62, 186
counteroffensive in Ardennes, 314, 317–20
crash rearmament program, forced labor policies, 227, 245, 253
defends Sicily and Italy (1943–44), 189, 237–43, 274
defense of Normandy, 300–303
economic recovery, 28–89, 43–44
economic situation in 1939, 77
forms Axis with Italy, 37
French-British declaration of war on, 66, 68, 69–72, 115, 116
Great Depression and growth of Communist power, 26–27, 28, 29
Greater Reich territories, 254–56, 266–67
invades Czechoslovakia (1939), 50–51, 56
invades Denmark and Norway, 86–92, *87m*
invades Poland, 60–72, *67m,* 74–75, 92
last battles, surrender in Italy, 337–39
military command in Western Europe, 295, 296, 299–300
military preparedness, 49, 70–71, 121, 123, 128–30
new offensive in USSR (1942–43), 218–31
New Order economic policy, 252–56, 266
nonaggression pact with USSR, 56–60 (*see also* Hitler-Stalin pact)
North African campaigns (1941–42), 163–66, 197–204, 205–6, 208–9, 211–17
offensive in Western Europe, 79, 87, 90, 93–101, 103–13
opposition movement in, 287–91, 293–325
plans to invade Britain, 116, 118, 119, 120–24
postwar occupation zones, 346–64
postwar treaty settlements, reparations, 8–10, *12m,* 14, 15, 22, 25, 26, 254
rapprochement with USSR, 15–16, 30
reasons for defeat, 354–61
response to Spanish Civil War, 36, 137
rise of Nazism in, 22–23
rise of Second Reich, 2–4, 25
secret rearmament, 15–16, 18, 30–31, 34, 38–39, 49
superiority of army, 358–59, 360
surrender (1945), 339–41
wartime economy, 110, 114, 133, 253
Weimar Republic, 10, 14, 15, 22–23, 26–28, 30, 31
and WWI 4–7
Yalta provisions on (1945), 321–22
Gestapo (secret police), 28, 29, 39, 40, 153, 263, 265, 289
Gibralter, 22, 118, 135, 136, 175, 284
Allied command post at, 206
offered to Franco by Hitler, 137
Giraud, General Henri, 101, 205, 206–7, 208, 210
Gleichschaltung concept, 24
Gleiwitz attack, 59–60
Gliders, 91, 98, 160, 161
Gneisenau (battleship), 78, 193, 195, 242
Goebbels, Dr. Joseph, 28, 51, 68, 86, 110, 163, 211, 330
and the Allied unconditional surrender policy, 211, 300
on the death of Roosevelt, 333
on German victories in USSR, 175
myth about Stalingrad, 226
New Order campaign, 252
propaganda against Poland, 50
suicide, 336, 357
Goering, Hermann, 39, 109, 209*n,* 335
assessment of, 357
economic exploitation policies, 253, 254
exclusive command of 3rd Air Fleet, 247, 301
and the extermination of Jews, 262, 263
as the head of air force, 29, 31, 38, 105–6, 357
and the invasion of Britain, 121, *120p,* 123–24, 127, 131, 138
police terrorism under, 27, 28
promises supplies to Stalingrad, 225
Radio Annie rumors about, 325
trial and suicide, 351
Gold reserves, 13, 77, 144, 253
Gold standard, 1
Gort, J.S.S. Prendergast, Viscount and General, 104, 105
Gothic Line, *235m,* 242, 338
Govorov, General Leonid, 225
Graf Spee (battleship), 78, 86
Grandi, Count Dino, 41, 237
Grass, Günter, 293
Graziani, Marshal Rudolfo, 138–41, 142, 156, 157, 164
Great Britain, 7, 272
aid to Greece, 150–51, 154, 156–58
aircraft production, 123, 130, 132
air and naval defenses, 118–21, 123, 130
alliance with Poland, 52–54, 57, 69, 72–73
and the *Anschluss* of Austria, 41, 42, 44
army retrained, combined operations begun, 131
assessment of army, 359, 361 (*see also* Allies)
Battle of Britain Day, 126
change of Conservative gov't (1940), 101–2
cripples French navy, 116–18, 205
decides to continue to war, 115–16
declares war on Germany (1939), 66, 68, 69, 76, 115, 116
defeats Italy in East Africa (1940), 142
defense policy, 37
and Dunkirk, 104–7
German air raids on (1940–41), *122m,* 124–33
and the German invasion of Poland, 61, 62, 67, 68–72
German naval blockade (1940), 119
German rocket attacks, 304
and Hitler's alliance plans, 25, 26, 38
in Hitler's grand strategy, 38–39
Hitler's invasion plans, 116, 118, 119, 120–24, 129
Hitler's view of, 105, 114–115
home front mobilized, war economy, 131–33
intelligence work, guerrilla tactics, 281, 282
interests in Far East, 38, 39, 135, 197
as junior partner in Alliance, 190
Labour party victory (1945), 339–40
Mediterranean naval power, 21–22
and Munich, 44–49
Near and Middle Eastern commands, 135–36, 143, 162, 166–67, 199
North African campaign (1940–42), 138–41, 145, 156, 157, 165–66, 196–204, 212, 213, 215, 217
and the occupation of Germans, 347–48, 364
peripheral war strategy, 188

Great Britain (*cont.*)
pledges support to Rumania and Greece, 51–52, 57
population losses, 353
postwar demobilization, 17, 18
prepares for Normandy landing, 235, 294
prewar alliances, 3, 4, 5
and the pre-WWI balance of power, 1, 2–3
and resistance movements in Europe, 273, 277–78, 281, 282
response to German rearmament and naval agreement (1935), 31–32, 34
repsonse to Italian aggression in Africa, 35
response to Spanish Civil War, 36
and the Russo-Finnish War, 82, 84
secret negotiations with Mussolini, 56
strategic position in Mediterranean, 134–36
strategy against Axis, 177
tensions with Germany, 2–3
U.S. Lend-Lease aid to, 144, 179
and the Versailles settlements, 9, 14, 15, 16
and WWI 5–6
and Yugoslavia, 151, 152–55
Great Depression, 26, 29, 43, 80
Great Russians, 261
Greece, 22, 37, 43, 110, 112, 135, 188, 324
Allies' bogus plan to invade, 295
Axis attack and occupation, 151, 154, *155m*, 156–62, 186, 233, 234, 235, 237
Axis plans to invade, 139, 141, 149–50
collaborationist gov't, 258
Franco-British pledge of support, 51, 52, 53, 57
Germans evacuate (1944), 310, 338
Italy defeated in (1940), 150–51, 156
occupies Albania, 150–51, 158
partisan fighting, 243
resistance movement in, 273, 275, 277–78, 292
Stalin-Churchill agreement on (1944), 320
Greenland, 92, 306
Greenwood, Arthur, 132
Greer (destroyer), 178
Grozny oil fields (USSR), 221
Guderian, General Heinz, 70–71, 99, 100, 101, 104, 108, 218, 337
advance stopped by Hitler (1940), 105–6
and the Battle of Moscow (1941), 175, 182
theories of warfare, 18
Guerrilla warfare (*see* Resistance movements)
Gulag Archipelago, 72, 73
Gustav Line (Italy), *236m*, 241–42
Gypsies, 261, 268, 270

Haakon VII of Norway, 88–89, 90
Habsburg Empire, 2, 3, 4, 7, 22, 23, 148
Hácha, Dr. Emil, 50, 255
Hagana organization, 199
Hague, The (Netherlands), 97, 98
Halder, General Franz, 194, 218, 286
Halifax, E.F. Lindley, Lord, 38, 42, 70, 115, 281
Hamburg, (Germany), 86
Allied raid (1943), 245, 304, 327*n*
Hamburg Tropical Disease Institute, 163
Hangoe Peninsula (Finland), 79, *83m*, 84, 102
Harriman, Averell, 177, 332
Harris, Marshall Sir Arthur, 71, 244
Hase, Colonel Paul von, 288
Hawker Hurricane fighter plane, 53, 123, 124, 127
Hayes, Carlton J.H., 217*n*
Heavy water plants, 91, 283
Hendave (France), Hitler-Franco meeting at (1940), 137
Henderson, Sir Nevile, 38, 115
Hercegovina, 11
Hercules, Operation (1942), 198–99
Hess, Rudolf, 109, 351
Heydrich, Reinhard, 262, 263, 274
Himmler, Heinrich, 252, 253, 260, 335, 358
and the extermination of the Jews, 264, 266, 267
foils Roehm plot, made head of S.S., 29–30
gains power after army purge, 305, 335
Hindenburg, Marshall Paul von, 26, 27, 28
Hiroshima, 327, 348
Hitler, Adolf, 13, 16, 49, 167, 208, 246, 287, 344, 345, 347, 357
and the *Anschluss* of Austria, 41–44
assassination attempts (1943–44), 289–90, 305
cancels strategic bomber force, 129–30
challenged on three fronts (1941), 186
becomes chancellor, dictator (1933), 26–28, 32
conflicts with Stalin over Eastern Europe, 147–49
conspiracies against, 46, 71, 93, 387–91, 305
and crumbling of Axis coalition, 232, 238
death (1945), 335–36, 338
on the death of Roosevelt, 333
and the defense of Italy, downfall of Mussolini (1943), 238
deficiencies in naval strategy, 129, 219, 354
demands on Czechoslovakia, 44–45
demands on Poland, 49–50
drive for victory in USSR, 199, 200, 218–19, 221–28, 231, 233, 286
early years, rise to power, 23–26
economic policy, 28–29
Far Eastern strategy, 37–38, 39
foreign responses to, 31–33
and the genocide of the Jews, 261–65, 265, 267
grand strategy (1937), 38–39, 41
halts attack at Dunkirk (1940), 105–6, 107, 129
invades Czechoslovakia, seizes Memel (1939), 50–51, 56
and the invasion of Denmark, Norway, 86, 89, 91, 92
last days, 328, 330, 333, 334
Lebensraum policy, 25, 26, 31, 38–39, 53, 254–56, 268, 270
meeting with Mussolini (1940), 110
Mein Kampf, 24, 25, 360
military policy, 29–31, 34–35, 39, 41
as military strategist, 218, 289, 336–37, 354–55, 356, 360
and the mobilization of women, 133
at Munich, 47–48
Nacht and Nebel decree (1941), 282
nonaggression pact with USSR, 56, 57–58, 59
occupation policies in Eastern Europe, 259–61
offensive in Western Europe, 79, 92, 93–97, 101
overtures to Britain, 115, 129
peace offensive (1939), 68
"peripheral war" strategy for Mediterranean, Balkans, 135, 149–50, 151, 153–54, 159, 162, 163, 164, 186, 356
plans to invade Britain, 121, 125–26, 127, 129, 355
plans to invade USSR, 127, 135, 149, 151, 162, 168, 335
and the Polish campaign, 65, 68, 72
purge of army, diplomatic corps (1938), 39–40, 287
racist philosophy, 24–25, 26, 38, 336, 337, 357
response to Anglo-Polish alliance, 53–54
response to Japanese-Soviet neutrality pact, attack on U.S., 168
response to Mussolini's policies, 35, 37, 54-56
response to Spanish Civil War, 36
and Rommel's North African campaign, (1941–42), 164, 165, 186, 198–99, 201, 203, 215–16
and the Russo-Finnish War, 81, 84
secret weapons development, 304, 357
strategy in Ardennes, 317, 318, 319
strategy on eastern front (1945), 320
strategy in France (1944), 294–95, 299–305, 306, 308, 311, 337
strategy in Soviet offensive (1941–42), 170, 172, 175–76, 180–83, 186

and the surrender of France, 108–10, 111
treatment of Soviet POWs and minorities, 182
urges France to join Axis, 137
view of the United States, 185
view of Britain and British, 25, 105, 114–15
war plans, pact with Italy, 54–56
in WWI, 23, 105, 336
Hitler-Stalin pact (1939), 57–59, 85, 102, 109–10, 280, 291
Japan's response to, 66, 168
and Polish mobilization, 61
revised version, 67
secret protocol, territorial clauses, 58, 65, 67, 73
and Soviet relaxation of frontier forces, 168–69
Stalin's attempts to justify, 173
Stalin's violations of (1940), 147–48
trade agreement, 58, 169
USSR renounces (1941), 179
and the Yalta provisions on Poland, 323
Hitler Youth, 164
Holocaust, 261–71
Allied response to Jewish resistance, 265–67
functional versus revisionists theories of, 267
against Gentile groups, 267–71
Soviet-sponsored, 270
Home Army (Germany), 288
Home Army (Poland), 273, *274p*, 278, 283, 310
Home Fleet (Great Britain), 106, 116, 118, 119, 195
Home Guard (Great Britain), 118
Hong Kong, 38, *184m*, 185
Hood (cruiser), 117, 194
Hopkins, Harry, 324
Höpner (German general), 99, 218
Homosexuals, Nazi persecution of, 261
Hore-Belisha, Isaac Leslie, 52
Horrock (British general), 313–14, 316
Horthy, Admiral Miklós, 154, 258, 259, 311
Hossbach, Colonel Friedrich, 38
Hossback Memorandum, 38–39
Hube, General Hans, 237
Hull, Cordell, 210, 249
Human rights violations, 354
Hungary, 8, 21, 42, 48, 56, 80, 112, 324, 339, 347, 348
collaborationist gov't, Fascist movement in, 258
defections from Axis, 211, 232, 277
demands on Czechoslovakia, 45, 46, 51
Fascist revolt, pro-Soviet gov't established (1944), 310–11
and the invasion of Poland, 62, 259
as Italian client, 22, 37
joins offensive in USSR, 170, 225
post-WWI frontier settlements, 10, 11
Soviet advances in (1945), 320
Stalin-Churchill agreement on, 320
Transylvania ceded to, 148
treaty with Yugoslavia, 152, 154
Yugoslavian lands ceded to, 156
Huntziger, General Charles, 101, 109
Husky, Operation (1943), 336

Iachino, Admiral Angelo, 142, 157
Iceland, 92
I G Farben Industries, 15
Ilmen, Lake (USSR), 175
India, 39, 116, 199
troops in Europe, 134, 157, 197, 200
Indochina, 36, 177, 185
Industrial revolution, 1
Intelligence:
activities of German minorities in Poland, 63
and Allied campaigns in North Africa, 202, 206 (see also Abwehr; Enigma; Ultra)
and the Allied offensive in Low Countries, 314, 316, 317
Allied spy networks, 284–88; in the USSR, 285–86
Axis deficiencies in, 128, 238, 358
and the British attack at Matapan, 157, 158
British break German naval cipher, 191, 193
British counterintelligence, 126
British and U.S. offices, 281-83
Free French network, 280
German counterespionage, 286
in German offensives in USSR, 175, 182
and the German western offensive, 93, 95, 97
"Major Martin" ruse (1943), 234–35
in neutral countries, 286–87
and the Normandy landing, 296, 298, 299
Inter-Allied Control Commission, 321
International Economic Conference (1922), 15
International Red Cross, 231
Ionian Islands (Greece), 159
Iran, 134, 135, 199
Anglo-Soviet control, 167–68 (*see also* Persia)
Iraq, 134, 167, 196, 199
Ireland, 39, 273, 286
Iron Guard (Rumania), 21, 259
Ironside, Sir William, 52–53, 72, 100*n*, 118, 129
Irving, David, 326
Istria, 10, *12m*, 19, 154
Italian East African, 134, 141–42
Italo-German treaty (1939), 55–56, 85
Italy, 2, 15, 16, 78, 80, 127, 187, 349
air power, aircraft, 21, 145
Allied invasion (1943–44), 210, 211, 233–42, 236, 277, 309
and the *Anschluss* of Austria, 44
and the anti-Comintern pact, 38
assessed as Axis partner, 357–58
and the Battle of Stalingrad, 225, 227, 231, 233
campaign in Ethiopia, 32, 35, 46, 145
defeats in Africa and Mediterranean (1940–41), 138–43, 144–46, 149–51, 156, 157–58, 159, 162, 163
dependence on Germany, 156, 189, 162, 233, 252
downfall of Mussolini (1943), 237–38
economic and military weaknesses, 145–46, 233
enters WWII, 134, 135, 137–38
and the fall of Tunisia, 215, 217, 233
grievances against France, 19
Hitler's policy toward, 25, 26, 41, 42
invades Albania, 51, 54, 149, 158, 233
invades France (1940), 108, 110, 118
invades Yugoslavia, 154, 156, 159, 233
joins Axis, 37, 39, 54, 252
last battles (1944–45), 337–39
naval strength, 55, 78, 134–35, 145–46
naval victory in Mediterranean, 148
negotiations with Allies, 236, 239, 291–92
opposition movement, 291–92, 338
postwar anarchy, rise of Fascism in, 19–22, 32, 35
response to German rearmament, 31–32
response to Spanish Civil War, 36, 37, 46, 137, 145
and Rommel's North African campaign (1941), 164, 165, 196, 197, 200, 202, 203
and the Russo-Finnish War, 85–86
sphere of influence in Mediterranean, 21–22, 26, 36, 38, 39, 54, 135, 150, 250
and the Triple Alliance, 4, 5, 19
unification, 2, 19
and the Versailles territorial settlements, 10, 11, *12m*, 19, 22, 37
and WWI, 5, 8, 110

Jachimova Dolina uranium mines, 51
Jackson, Justice Robert L., 351, 347
Jane's Fighting Ships, 129
Japan, 3, 5, 32, 78, 211
in Allied war strategies, 189, 211
as Axis power, 37–38, 135, 148, 197
drive in SE Asia, 66, 148, 176, 177, 183, *184m*, 185

Japan (*cont.*)
enters WWII, 183, 185, 198
neutrality pact with USSR (1941), 168, 176
response to Hitler-Stalin pact, 66, 168
surrender (1945), 348
U.S. occupation, 348, 349
USSR declares war on (1945), 247, 249, 323, 348
war with USSR in Manchuria, Mongolia, 58, 59, 65–66, 92, 168, 176, 361
Yalta agreements on, 321, 323
Jebb, Sir Gladwin, 321
Jekiel, Tadeusz, 284
Jet aircraft, 304–5, 317, 358
Jews:
anti-Semitism in Vichy France, 257
and the Holocaust, 261–67, 269, 270, 347
Nazi collaborators, ghetto militiamen, 264
Nazi concepts of, 22, 23, 24–25, 26, 262, 336, 337
in Nazi-occupied territories, 257, 259
Nazi persecutions of, 28, 42, 256, 259, 261, 292
in nuclear research, 265
in Palestine, 167, 261
in Poland, 72, 149, 262, 263
population losses, 265
refugees, 112, 287, 292
resistance movements, 266–67 (*see also* Concentration camps, Holocaust)
Jodl, General Alfred, 70, 244, 337, 338, 340–41
Joffre, Marshall J.-J.-C., 257
Jones, Richard V., 244
Judeo-Christian values, 25
Juin, General Alphonse, 242

Kalamata, Battle of (1940), 159
Karelian Isthmus, 79, 84
Karelian Soviet Republic, 80
Karlsruhe (cruiser), 91
Karski, Jan, 265
Kassel (Germany), 245
Kasserine Pass, Battle of (1943), 212–13
Katyn forest massacre (1940), 231, 270, 278, 351
Kaunas (Lithuanian minister), 73
Keitel, General Wilhelm, 40, 71, 109, 304, 341*n*
Kellogg-Briand Pact, 350
Kerr, Sir Archibald Clark, 332
Kesselring, General Albert, 95, 198, 238, 240–42, *238p*
career, 239
Keynes, John Maynard, 28
Khamsun (Saharan wind), 138
Kharkov (USSR), *171m*, 176, 218, 230
Kiel (Germany), 86, 244, 354
Kiev (USSR), *171m*, 174, 183, 186
King, Admiral Ernest J., 189, 211
Kingdom of Serbs, Croats, and Slovenes, 8, 11, *12m*, 19 (*see also* Yugoslavia)
King George V (battleship), 194
Kleist, Colonel-General Ewald von, 107
Kluge, Marshall Hans Gunther von, 304, 305, 337
Koch, Ilse, 269
Koenig, General Marie-Pierre, 199
Konev, Marshall Ivan S., 331, 334, 335, 338
Königsberg (East Prussia), *4m*, 49, 91, 247, 322, 294
Königsberg (cruiser), 91
Kord, Erich, 46
Korea, postwar occupation zones in, 348
Kovno uprising, 266
Krebs, Colonel Hans, 169
Kriegsmarine, 30, 49, 77, 90–91, 121, 305, 357
cipher, 193
Krupp company, 15
Krupp von Bohlen, Gustav, 351
Kuomintang, 38
Kuril Islands, *184m*, 323, 349
Kursk (USSR), 218, 219
Battle of (1943), 217, 228–30, *230m*, 231, 232, 286
Kurtrzeba, General Tadeusz, 64
Kutno-Bzura, Battle of (1939), 64, *67m*, 71
Kutuzov, General Mikhail, 225, 331
Kuusinen, Otto, 80

Ladoga, Lake (USSR), *171m*, 174, 181
Lancaster bomber, 243, 326
Lane, Arthur Bliss, 310
Langsdorff, Captain Hans, 78
Laon (France), 311
Lacquer, Walter, 265*n*
Lattre de Tasigny, General Jean de, 307, *312p*
Latvia, *12m*, 34, 57, 58, 73, 74, 80, 173, 253, 279, 335
annexed to USSR (1940), 147
Laval, Pierre, 35, 118, 251
League of German Officers, 226
League of Nations, 9, 11, 13, 14, 31, 35, 45, 82, 247, 249
Covenant, 11, 17, 33, 48
mandates, 9, 22, 30
USSR expelled from, 80
USSR joins, 32–33
Leahy, Admiral William D., 248
Lebanon, 22, 167, 280
Lebensraum policy, 25, 26, 31, 38–39, 53, 255, 268
Leclerc, General Jacques Philippe, 308
Leeb, Marshall Ritter von, 95, 172
Leese, General Sir Oliver, 241, 242
Le Havre, (France), 102, 107, 119, 311
Lend-Lease aid:
to Britain, 120, 144, 179, 183, 228, 333
to the USSR, 225, 228, 343
Lenin (V.I. Ulyanov), 13, 79
Leningrad, 74, 79, 84, *171m*, 172, 175, 183, 219, 308, 359
German siege (1941), 174, 183, 227, 228, 231
Leopold III of Belgium, 105, 257
Lerski, Jerzy, 265
Levi, Carlo, 243
Ley, Robert, 351
"Liberty" ships, 215
Libya, 134, 140, 141, 157, 164, 205, (*see also* Cyrenaica; Tripolitania)
Liddell Hart, Sir Basil, 18, 53
Lidice (Czechoslovakia), 274
Liege (Belgium), 97
Lille (France), 102, 106, 311
Lipski, Jozef, 49–50
List, Marshall Siegmund, 159, 220, 221
Lithuania, 9, *12m*, 34, 57, 74, 79, 173, 253, 266, 279, 365
annexed to USSR, 147
cedes Memel to Germany, 51, 56
Wilno agreement with USSR, 73
Little Entente, 42, 47–48
Litvinov, Maxim, 33, 48, 57
Ljubljana (Yugoslavia), *155m*, 156, 307
Lloyd, Lord Selwyn, 281
Lloyd George, David, 9
Lorcarno, Treaty of (1925), 16–17, 34, 35
Łódź (Poland), 63, 72
London, 1, 245
European gov'ts in exile in, 156, 179 (*see also* Gaulle, de; Poland; Yugoslavia)
first German air raid (1940), 125, 126
German rocket attacks, 304
Longfellow, Henry Wadsworth, 143
Lord, R.H., 9, 50
Lorient (France), 119
Lorraine, 76 (*see also* Alsace-Lorraine)
Louis XIV of France, 15, 143
Low Countries, 86 (*see also* Belgium; Luxembourg; Netherlands)
Loyalists (Spain), 36
Lublin (Poland), *67m*, 72, 255, 262
Lucas, General John, 242
"Lucy" (*see* Roessler, Rudolf)
Ludwigshafen (Germany), 325
Lufthansa airlines, 30
Luftwaffe (German air force), 30, 31, 49, 62, 63, 89, 99, 155, 193, 244, 305, 314, 326, 354
and the Allied invasion of France (1944), 295, 297–98, 301, 303, 304
attacks on Poland, 62–63
in the Battle of Britain, 120, 121, 123, 124–27, 139
in the Battle of Norway, 89, 90, 91
drained by Allied bombing, 246
in the Mediterranean, 158, 159, 161, 197
in North Africa, 164, 166

in the Soviet offensive (1941–42), 174, 181, 183
at Stalingrad (1942–43), 222, 224–26
strength in 1939, 62*n*, 71
in the western offensive (1940), 96, 105, 106, 112
Lutheran Church, 290
Lützow (*Deutschland*) (battleship), 78, 88, 91, 193
Luxembourg, 76, 94, 95*n*, 97, 99, 100, 255, 325

MacArthur, General Douglas, 189, 211, 348
McAuliffe, General Anthony C., 315
Macedonia, *4m*, 154, 156, 159, 258
Machiavelli, Niccolò, 21
Machine guns, 6
Maclean, Fitzroy, 278*n*
Madagascar, 262
Maginot Line, 17, 76, 94, 99, *102m*
in the French battle plan, 95, 100
Germans outflank, 101, 107
Maisky, Ivan, 176, 179
"Major Martin" ruse (1943), 234–35
Malava, *184m*, 185
Malenkov, Gregory M., 174
Malmedy (Belgium), 9, 255, *318m*
massacre of U.S. POWs, 319
Malta 5*m*, 22, 136, 143, 195, 216
Allied attacks on Axis shipping, 199–200
Axis fails to capture (1942), 194, 198–99, 201
Roosevelt-Churchill meeting (1945), 321
Manchukuo, 32
Manchuria, 348
Roosevelt offers compensation to Stalin on, 249
Soviet-Japanese war, 58, 59, 65–66, 92, 176–77, 225
Mandate system, 9, 22
Manhattan Project, 345, 346
Mannerheim, Baron Carl von, 79, 84
Mannerheim Line (Finland), 79, 80, 81, 85, 308
Mannheim (Germany), Allied bombing of, 243
Manstein, General Erich von, 94–95, 97, 219–20, 223, 224, 228, 230, 337
Maoris, 135
Mao Tse-tung, 38, 323
Maquis, 280
Mareth Line (Tunisia), 209, 212, 215
Market-Garden, Operation (1944), 314–16
Marne, Battle of the (1914), 6, 111
Marseilles, 102, 110, 307
Marshall, General George C., 188, 248, 331
Martell, Giffort, 18
Martin, Bernd, 70*n*
Martin, Major William, 234–35
Marxism, 1–2, 24, 173 (*see also* Communist movement)
Mata Hari, 100
Matapan, Battle of (1940), *155m*, 157–58, 159, 328
Matilda (tank), 138, 140, *144p*
Matsuoka, Yōsuke, 168, 169
May, Karl, 296
Mediterranean Sea, region, 116
Allied and Axis attacks on shipping, 193–94, 197, 199–200
Allied intelligence activities in, 284, 285
Allied naval reduction in, 78
Axis defeats, Allied strategy in (1943), 232, 234, 247
Axis strategy for, 134–36, 144–46, 149–50, 153–54, 156, 162, 163, 164, 186
British destroy French fleet, 116–18
British-French condominium over, 21–22
British strategic position in, 134, 135–36
Italian naval threat ended (1940), 142–43, 145, 156, 157–58, 159
as Italian sphere of influence, 21–22, 26, 36, 38, 39, 54, 135
Italian threats to British shipping, 118, 119
opened to Allied shipping (1943), 217
Spain's role in, 137
Mein Kampf (Hitler), 24, 25, 360
Memel (Klaipeda), 9, 10, 51, 56
Merchant marine, 107, 119
Germans conceal troops on, 88, 91
German U-boat attacks, 119, 178, 191, 193, 216
Merkalov, A.T., 49, 57
Mersa Matruh, Battle of (1942), 194
Mers El Kebir naval base (Algeria), 117–18
Messerschmidt fighter planes, 96, 109, 110, 123, 127, 130, 262 (jet), 304, 317
Messina, British landing at (1943), 237
Metaxis, Ioannis, 150, 151, 277
Metaxis Line, 158
Meuse (Maas) River (Belgium-Netherlands), 95, 97, 99, 100, 313, 314
Michael of Rumania, 148, 310
Middle East, 116
Allies outmaneuver Axis in (1941), 167–68
Anglo-Russian concessions in (1907), 3
in Axis strategy, 162, 167, 198–99
British command in, 135–36, 143, 162, 166–67, 199
German-Austrian expansion in, 3, 5
oil fields, 134, 137, 162, 167, 168, 199, 356
as Soviet sphere of influence, 148
WWI campaigns, 5
Midway, Battle of (1942), *184m*, 189, 228, 328
MI-5 (British counterintelligence), 126
Mihajlović, General Draža, 247, 274–76, *274p*
Milamt (Nazi intelligence office), 289
Milan, 20, 338
Military technology, 361–62
Axis inferiority in, 357
civilian involvement in, 362
German advances in 1930s, 31, 42–43
postwar improvement 17–18
in the Russo-Finnish War, 80, 84–85
Spanish Civil War as testing ground for, 36, 37
specialized forces, 361–62
in WWI, 6, 10 (*see also* Air power; Enigma; Radar; Submarines; Tanks; Warfare)
Milorg, 283
Milosz, Czeslaw, 293
Mincemeat, Operation (1943), 234–35
Minsk (USSR), *171m*, 172, 174
Miquelon I, 210
Missouri (*battleship*), 348
Mitchell, General William ("Billy"), 21, 91*n*, 127, 313, 327
Mitteleuropa scheme, 4
Model, General Walter, 304, 314, 315
Mogadishu (Italian Somaliland), 142
Moldavian S.S.R., 147
Molotov, Viacheslav, 57, 58, 65, 68, 73, 152, 169, 174, 247, 322, 332
meeting with Hitler (1940), 148–49
at Yalta, 317, 320
"Molotov cocktails," 81, 84
Molotov-Ribbentrop Pact (*see* Hitler-Stalin Pact)
Moltke, H.K.B. von, 356
Monastir Gap (Yugoslavia), 155, 158
Mongolia, 58, 59 (*see also* Outer Mongolia)
Montagu, Lieutenant-Commander Ewen, 234
Monte Cassino, Battle of (1944), 236, 242, *243p*
Montenegro, *4m*, 156, 258, 277*n*
Montgomery, Sir Bernard Law, Viscount, *200p*, 211, 213, 215
command in North Africa (1942), 199–201
in France (1944), 241, 303, 305–7
in Germany (1945), 229
in Low Countries, 312–14, 315, 316, 317
in Sicily and Italy (1943), 236–37 239, 240, 241
Moravia, 10, 11, 44, 50–51, 56, 62
Morgan, Sir Francis, 340
Morganthau Plan, 298, 300n
Morocco, 3, 5*m*, 22, 137, 189, 204, 205, 211
Moscow, *171m*
Battle of (1941), 92, 179–83, 186, 218, 225, 353
German plans to encircle (1942), 219, 228

Moscow (*cont.*)
German push forward, 170, 172, 174–76
victory ceremony (1945), 342
Moscow Conference (1945), 332
Moslems, 136
in Soviet troops, 260, 261
Mountbatten, Admiral Louis, 190, 195, 234, 361
Mulberries (artificial harbors), 294
Munich, 69, 227
Hitler's *putsch*, 24
Munich Conference (1938), 46–49, 54, 102, 287
Murmansk (USSR), 287
Murphy, Robert, 207, 208
Mussert, Anton, 256–57
Mussolini, Benito, 13–14, *20p*, 24, 39, 114, 142, 209, 227, 256, 258
aids Germany in Battle of Britain, 138–39
aid to Rommel in North Africa (1942), 198
and the *Anschluss* of Austria, 41, 42, 44
appeals to Hitler on Czechoslovakia, 46, 47
arrest (1943), 238, 288
asks Hitler to switch battlefront to Western Europe (1943), 227, 233
death (1945), 338
defeated in Greece, Africa (1940), 149–51, 156, 162
Ethiopian offensive, 32, 35, 37, 46
invades Albania (1939), 51, 54
march on Rome (1922), 20, 24
meeting with Hitler, war strategy (1940), 110
at Munich (1940), 47, 54
opposes German rearmament, 32
"parallel war" in Mediterranean, 135, 136, 139, 141, 144–46, 149, 156, 164, 357
rise to power, 20–21
and the Russo-Finnish War, 85–86
secret negotiations with France and Britain, 56
and the Spanish Civil War, 36, 37, 46
supports Nazi New Order, 252
visits Berlin (1937), 37
war plans, pact with Hitler, 54–56
Mussolini, Donna Rachele (wife), 338
Mustang fighter plane (P-51), 245

***Nacht und Nebel*, Operation (1941), 282**
Nagasaki, 348
Namier, G.L.B., 34*n*, 46*n*
Namsos (Norway), 89
Naples, 234
Napoleon Bonaparte, 14, 61, 126, 143, 188, 337
continental system, 355
invasion of Russia (1812), 181, 219, 331, 355, 359
Napoleon III of France, 19
Narew River (Poland), 65, 67
Narvik (Norway), 82
Battle of (1940), *87m*, 88–90, 91
Nasser, Gamal Abdel, 136
National Committee for Free Germany, 226
Nationalism, 2, 24–25, 30, 31, 73–74
National Service Act (Great Britain) (1941), 132
National Socialism, 22–23 (*see also* Nazi party)
Navies, naval power:
Allied versus German strength, 77–79, 114, 118–20, 121, 129, 191, 193
Anglo-German agreement (1935), 32, 37
Black Sea fleets, 218, 219
blockade in Russo-Finnish War, 82–84
British supremacy, 1, 2, 21–22
and the defeat of Germany, 354
German buildup in 1920s–30s, 16, 30–31
Italian strength, 55, 78, 134–35
Japanese, 66, 78, 183, 185
sailing with air cover, aircraft carriers, 89–91, 297, 328, 361
Versailles restriction on Germany, 10 (*see also* Atlantic, Battle of; Kriegsmarine; Mediterranean; *Regia Marina;* Royal Navy; Submarines; United States Navy)
Nazi party, 23–33, 37, 177, 335
anti-Semitism, anticommunism of, 22–23, 26, 32, 263
attacks Weimar Republic, 22–23
colonial gov'ts in Eastern Europe, 257–61
Colonial Office, 163
growth in 1920s–30s, 26–27
New Order in occupied Europe, 252–61, 267, 272
policy toward resistance movements, 282
racial theories, 24–25, 26, 38, 252, 261, 267–71, 302
seizes power (1933), 27–28
Socialist trends in, 28–29
terrorism in Austria, 41–42 (*see also* Concentration camps; Nuremburg Tribunal)
Near East, 4, 6, 43, 85, 150, 160, 252
British command in, 135–36, 143
League of Nation mandates, 22
Nedić, General Milan, 156, 258
Nelson (battleship), 78
Netherlands, 16, 30, 79, 93, 94, 364
Allied offensive in (1944), 312–16
German invasion of (1940), 95–99, 112, 252
Nazi occupation, 254, 256–57, 268, 284
resistance movement, spy networks in, 286, 242, 314, 316
Neurath, Baron Konstantin von, 27, 38, 39, 351
Neutral countries, *55m*, 108, 112, 119, 286–87 (*see also* Belgium; Greece, Luxembourg; Spain; Sweden; Switzerland; Turkey; United States; Yugoslavia)
Newfoundland, 120
New Guinea, 197
New Order, 251–59, 264, 271, 272
New Zealand, 116
troops in Europe, 135, 157, 160, 242
troops in North Africa, 201
Nibeiwa, Battle of (1940), 140
Nice (France), 19, 102, 110
Nicholas II of Russia, 321
Niemoeller, Martin, 290
Nietzsche, Friedrich, 21, 24
Nijmegen (Netherlands), 315, 316, 328, 329
Nikitchenko, General I.T., 350
NKVD troops, 168, 247, 273, 323, 360
Noel, Léon, 109
Nordic races, 24, 252, 269
Norfolk (cruiser), 194
Normandy, Allied invasion of (1944), 242, 243, 280, 289, 294–308, 353
Allied amphibious preparations, 300
Allied conquest of peninsula, 302–4, 305–7
battle of the beaches, 300–301
confusion in German command, 299–300
German preparations, 296–97
help from French resistance, 292, 298, 308
landing site chosen, 295–96
planned at Washington Conference (1941), 187–90
technical and logistical problems, 297–99
trial raids (1942), 190, 195–96, 294
North Africa, 108, 281
Allied landings and victory (1942), 204, 205–9, 211–16, 217, 227, 277, 361
Allied war strategy for, 189–90
Axis war aims in, 135, 196, 198–99
bogus Allied armies in, 295
British defeat Italians in (1940–41), 138–41, 144–46, 156, 157
environment, 137–38
French colonies, *5m*, 22, 137
German campaigns (1941), 163–66, 186
German push toward Egypt, British counteroffensive (1942), 196–204
North Sea naval battles, 78
Norway, 51, 78, 291, 295, 340
and the blockade of Swedish shipping, 82, 84, 85, 86
German invasion (1940), 86–92, *87m*, 101, 111, 120, 121, 188
resistance movement, 284
Novgorod (USSR), 308
Battle of (1941), *171m*, 175
Novi Sad (Yugoslavia), *155m*, 156
Nowak, Jan, 265*n*

Nuclear research;
emigration of scientists and, 265, 358
in Germany, 51, 91, 358
Norwegian sabotage and, 283
in the United States, 335, 345, 346, 358
Nuclear weapons, (*see also* Atom bomb) 362, 364
Nuremberg (Germany), 227, 325, 349
Nuremberg Laws, 28
Nuremberg Tribunal (1945–46), 70, 254, 270, 337, 338, 347*p*, 349–52

Oberlaender, Theodor, 253
O'Connor, General Richard, 139–41, 165
Oder River 5*m*, 317, 322, 347, 348
Odessa (USSR), *171m*, 175
Office of Strategic Services (OSS), 281–82, 287
Oil production, reserves, 77, 85
in Balkans, 51, 148, 149, 156
and the German offensive in the USSR, 197, 220, 221
and the invasion of Normandy, 294, 298, 301
in the Middle East, 134, 137, 162, 167, 168, 356
OKW (*Oberkommando der Wehrmacht*), 40, 86, 169–70, 172, 238 (*see also* Wehrmacht)
Olbricht, General Friedrich von, 288
Olympus, Mount (Greece), 158
Omaha Beach (Normandy), 300, 301
Oosterbeck (Netherlands), 315, 316
Operation:
Anvil (1944), 307
Axis (1943), 338–39
Barbarossa (1940–41), 149, 153–54, 186
Battle-axe (1942), 198, 199
Citadel (1943), 228, 234
Crusader (1941), 198
Eagle (1940), 142
Hercules (1942), 199
Husky (1943), 236
Market-Garden (1944), 313–16
Mincemeat (1943), 235
Night and Fog (*Nacht und Nebel*) (1941), 282
Overlord (1943–44), 248, 297–99, 338
Punishment (1940), 155–56
Sealion (1940), 121, 127, 129
Torch (1942), 189, 204–8
Operations Between Mechanized Forces (Fuller), 18
Oran (Algeria), 117, *136m*, 205
Allied landing (1942), 205, 207, *208m*
Oranienberg (Germany), 28
Orel (USSR), 228, 229, *230m*
Origins of Totalitarianism, The (Arendt), 261
Orzet (submarine), 73
Oshima, General Hiroshi, 66, 317
Oslo (Norway), 88, 89, 283
Osoaviakhum (paramilitary organization), 360
Ostend (Belgium), 311
Oster, General Hans, 93, 97, 288, 289, 305, 358
Ostland commissariat, 259
Ottoman Empire, 3, 5*m*, 7
Outer Mongolia, 66, 323 (*see also* Mongolia)
Overlord, Operation (1943–44), 248, 297–99, 338
Oxenius, General William, 310
Oxford Union Society, 32

Pacific theater, 189, 190, 211, 227
Potsdam agreements on, 348–49
Yalta agreements on, 321
Pacifist movement, 17–18, 20, 23
Pahlavi, Reza, 167
Palatinate, 70 (*see also* Rhineland)
Palestine, 167, 199, 261
Panfilov division (Red Army), 181
Pan-German movement, 3
Pantelleria (Italy), 235–36
Panther tank, 227, 229
Panzer divisions, 42–43, 61, 63, 99, 164, 186, 230, 231
in the Battle of Arnhem (1944), 314–15
in North Africa, 196, 197, 199, 200
Papagos, General Alexandros, 151
Papen, Franz von, 26–27
Paratroopers, 88, 91, 240, 361–62
German corps attacks Greece (1940), 158, 160–62, 186
at lower Rhine, 312–14
at Normandy (1944), 298
in resistance movements, 278, 283
Pareto, Vilfredo, 21
Paris, 94, 95, 103
Germans occupy (1940), 108
liberation of (1944), 300, 302, 307–8
Paris Peace Conference, 8–9, 19 (*see also* Versailles, Treaty of)
Partisan movement:
in the Baltic region, 276
in the USSR, 183, 221, 278–79
in Yugoslavia, 243, 248–49, 274 275–77, 310 (*see also* Resistance movements)
Pas de Calais, 295–96, 300, 301, 302
Patch, General Alexander, 307, 311
Patton, General George S., Jr., 213, *214p*
at Ardennes, 318, 319
and the Bodyguard scheme, 295
at Normandy (1944), 306–8, 311
personality, 214
on the Polish army, 242*n*
at the Rhine, 311
in Sicily (1943), 236–37
Paul of Yugoslavia, 151–52, 153
Paulus, General Friedrich, 221–24, 226, 360
Pavelic, Ante, 156, 258
Pavese, Cesare, 293
Pax Britannica, 1
Pearl Harbor, 183, *184m*, 187, 191
Peenemuende (Germany), 245, 283
Persia, 3, 162, 217 (*see also* Iran)
Persian Gulf, 148
Petacci, Clara, 338
Pétain, Marshall Philippe, 104, 108, 112, 114, 116, 117, 137, 167, 207, 208, 257, 258
Peter of Yugoslavia, 151, 154, 156, 275, 276
Petsamo (Finland), 79, 80, *83m*, 84
Philippine Islands, 120, 185
"Phony war" (1939–40), 76–77, 78, 79
Pieck, Wilhelm, 226
Ploesti oil fields (Rumania), 51, 148, 156
PLUTO (Pipe Lines under the Ocean), 295, 297
Poison gas, 6, 10, 15
Poland, 2, 5, 14, 15, 24, 48, 90, 348 360, 361
alliance with France, 14–17, 34, 35, 52, 69
alliance with Great Britain (1939), 52–54, 57, 69, 72–73
concentration camps in, 263–65
demands on Czechoslovakia, 45–46
eastern frontier negotiated (1943), 248, 322
German annexations (1939), 72, 255
German demands on (1938), 49–50
German exploitation, forced labor, 253, 255
German fifth-column activities in, 63
German frontier negotiations (1925), 16–17
Germany invades (1939), 60–72, *67m*, 74–75, 93, 151
gov't in London, 74, 179, 230, 231 265, 273, 278, 284, 322, 335*n*
in Hitler's strategy, 39, 54, 56, 57, 59–60
and the Hitler-Stalin pact (1939), 57, 58, 65, 66
Jewish population, 72, 255, 262, 263
military convention with France (1939), 52, 57, 69, 111
military strength, 62, 69
Nazi General Gov't, 255, 260, 268–69, 273
and neutrality of USSR, 54
nonaggression pact with Germany (1934), 49
population losses, 353
Red Army advances to German border in (1944–45), 309–10, 320,332
rejects cooperation with USSR, 34
resistance movement, 265, 266, 273, *274p*, 278, 283, *292p*, 309, 323
Soviet executions, deportations, 231, 255, 270, 273
Soviet nonaggression pact (1932), 65

Poland (*cont.*)
Soviet Provisional Gov't, 309, 316, 332
territorial compensations, transfer of Germans (1945), 347
ties with USSR (1941–43), 179, 230, 278
and the UN, 335*n*
USSR invades and occupies east, 65, 66–67, 69, 73–74, 102, 360
Versailles settlements and, 8, 9–10, *12m*
Yalta agreements on, 322–23
Poles, 2
in Allied spy networks, 284
in the Battle of Monte Cassino (1944), 242, *243p*
and the Battle of Norway, 90, 91
and the capture of Berlin (1945), 332
copy Enigma machine, 75, 357
in Germany after WWI, 9–10
Nazi genocide against, 267–68
at Normandy, 305, 306
in North Africa, 201
paratroopers' attack on Rhine (1944), 313, *313m,* 314, 315–16
POW army in Russia, 179, 230, 332
in the RAF, 130–31
in Silesia, 45
Soviets arrest resistance leaders, 323
Soviet massacre of officers (1940), 230, 270, 278
Polish air force, 62, 130–31
Polish-Americans, 248
Polish Committee of National Liberation, 278, 310
Polish Corridor, 9, *12m,* 49–50, 322, 328
Polish Workers' party, 278
Pomerania, 9, 10, 49, 62, 72, 163, 269
Popular Front:
in France, 33, 35, 42
in Spain, 35, 36
Portal, Sir Charles, *103p*
Port Arthur (Manchuria), 323, 349
Portsmouth (England), 120, 295
Portugal, 112, 137, 189, 286, 364
Potemkin, Vladimir, 54
Potsdam Conference (1945), 246, 343–49, 364
Poznan Army, 64
Poznania, 9, 10, 72
Prague (Czechoslovakia), 50–51, 54, 56, 69, 260, 274, 331
Prince of Wales (battleship), 92, 185, 195
Prinz Eugen (cruiser), 193, 194, 195
Pripet Marshes (USSR), 169, *171m*
Production Council (Great Britain), 132
Prussia, 2, 9, 10, 27
Psychological warfare, 325
Public Record Office (London), 53*n*, 70*n*
Punishment, Operation (1940), 155–56

Quattara depression (Egypt), 139, 165, 199
Quebec Conference (1943), 321
Queen Elizabeth (battleship), 198
Quisling, Major Vidkun, 86–87, 88, 90, 256, 256*n*

Radar, 119, 121, 157
antisub microradar, 215
British versus German strength, 123, 128, 130, 358
cavity megatron, 358
Radio Annie, 325
Radio communications, 96, 128, 361
"Cooked Legs" device, 123–24, 125
Raeder, Admiral Erich, 38, 78, 109, 121, 198
"balanced fleet" program, 49, 129, 196, 356
commerce raiding, 193, 195
and the invasion of Britain, 121, 129
plans seizure of bases in Norway, 36
Rajk, Laszlo, 36
Rapallo, Treaty of (1922), 15, 16, 33
Rashid Ali, 167
Rastenburg (Germany), 227, 289
Ravensbrueck camp, 263, 269, 274
Red Army, 13, 15, 34, 48, 147, 285, 356
advances toward central Europe (1943–44), 230, 231, 246, 248, 249, 294, 308, 310–11, 320, 323
Allied strategy to save (1941), 187, 188
assessment of, 356, 359–60
defense against Germans (1941–42), 172, 174–75, 180–82, 186, 218, 220, 245
dual command, 84, 220–21
in the Finnish war, 80, 84, 92
invades Eastern Poland, 65, 66–67, 69
linkup with U.S. troops at Torgau, 335
occupies territories in Far East, 348
rape and killing of Germans, 339–40
reforms and innovations (1940), 84–85, 91*n*
right of passage in Eastern Europe, 48, 57
Siberian divisions, 177, 180, 221
Stalin's reprisals on, 220
threatens Baltic states, 73
Red Devils, 315, 316
Red Orchestra (*Rote Kapelle*), 182, 285–86, 289
Refugees:
human rights violations, 354
Jews as, 112, 287, 292
and nuclear research, 265, 358
White Russians in Yugoslavia, 152
Reggio (Italy), British landing at, 239
Regia Aeronautica, 55, 155
Regia Marina, 142–43, 146
Reichenau (German general), 99
Reichstag fire (1933), 27, 28
Reichswehr, 31, 163
Reinhardt (German general), 101
Rejewski, Marian, 75*n*
Remagen (Germany), bridge at, 328
Repulse (cruiser), 92, 185
Resistance movements, 272–93, 354
in Czechoslovakia, 274, 310
in France, 113, 167, 208, 275, 279–81, 292, 307–8
in Germany, 287–91, 277–78, 325
in Greece, 188, 273, 275
intellectual leaders, 290
intelligence work, sabotage, 279–80, 314, 361
in Italy, 291–92, 335
Jewish groups, 266–67
in the Netherlands, 286, 292, 314, 316
Paris uprising (1944), 307–8
in Poland, 265, 273, 278, *292p*, 309, 323
shelter to minorities, agents, POWs, 292
uprisings in Eastern Europe (1944), 309, 310
in the USSR, 182–83, 221, 278–79
in Yugoslavia, 188, 273, 274–78
Resolution (battleship), 117
Reykjavik, 92
Reynaud, Paul, 102, 103, 104, 108, 112
Rheims (France), *98m*, 311, 337–38
German surrender at (1945), 340–41
Rhineland, 8, 9, 71
Allied attack on (1944), 300, 311–16, 325
French occupation, 9, 16–17
French offensive (1939), 70, 111
German annexation of, 255
German counteroffensive, 317–19, 359
Hitler remilitarizes, 34–35, 41, 46*n*
Rhine-Metal company, 15
Rhine River, 76, 121, 314
Allies reach (1945), symbolic significance of, 329–30
Germans occupy delta, 98
Rhodesia, 116
Ribbentrop, Joachim von, 39, 54, 56, 109, 110, 152, 168
in England (1936), 115
and the Hitler-Stalin pact (1939), 57–58, 59, 65, 66
meeting with Molotov (1940), 148–49
presents demands to Poland (1938), 49–50
Richelieu, Cardinal, 337
Richter, Hans, 293
Richthofen, Baron Manfred von, 21
Riga, Treaty of (1921), 65
Robin Moor (freighter), 178
Rockets (*see* V-1, V-2 rockets)
Rodney (Battleship), 194
Roehim, Ernst, 29
Rokossovsky, General K., 225, 309, 328, *360p*, 361*n*

Roman Catholic clergy, Nazi persecution of, 269
Roman Empire, 20, 21
Rome, 241
  Allies capture (1944), 241–43
  Mussolini marches on (1922), 20, 24
Rome-Berlin Axis, 15, 37, 39 (*see also* Axis)
Rommell, General Erwin, 63–64, 356
  defeated at el-Alamein (1942), 202–4
  in France (1943), 296–97
  injured (1944), 304
  and the invasion of France (1940), 100, 101, 107, 164
  in Italy (1943), 288, 296
  life, 163–64
  in North Africa (1941–42), 164–66, 196–201, 209, 212–14, 215
  promoted to Field Marshall (1942), 199
  response to Allied invasion (1944), 299–300, 303
  suicide (1944), 305
Roosevelt, President Franklin D., 46, 108, 168, 235, 265*n*
  aid to British in North Africa, 200
  aid to Stalin, 178–79
  Atlantic meeting with Churchill (1941), 177–78
  at Casablanca with Churchill (1943), 210–11
  conference with Churchill at Washingon (1941), 187–89, 235
  congratulates Churchill on victories (1941), 143
  death and assessment of, 333–34, 355, 361
  dislike of de Gaulle, 206, 210, 307
  and Lend-Lease aid to Britain, 120, 144, 333
  meets Churchill at Malta (1945), 321
  pressures Yugoslavia, 152–53
  at Teheran (1943), 247–50
  view of Stalin and Churchill, *248p*, 334, 334*n*
  at Yalta (1945), 320–24, 333
Roessler, Rudolf ("Lucy"), 182, 228, 285–86
Rostov-on-Don, 218, 220, 221, *223m*
Rotterdam (Netherlands), 98, 99, 246
Rouen (France), 311
Royal Air Force (RAF), 69, 94, 96, 101, 103, 105, 106, 112, 115, 116, 118, 119, 121, 166, 286, 319
  and the Battle of Britain, 124–25, 126, 127, 130–31
  Fighter and Bomber commands, 123–24
  in the Mediterranean, North Africa, 157, 161, 202
  raids on German ships in Atlantic (1942), 196
saturation bombing of Germany, 243, 244, 245, 326*n*
  strengths in 1940, 123–24
  strike plans delayed (1939), 71–72
  training, ethnic minorities in, 130–31
Royal Marines, 92
Royal Navy, 1, 17, 46, 77, 89, 91, 92, 115, 121, 167
  and the Battle of the Atlantic, 191, 195–96
  and the Battle of Crete (1940), 161, 195
  destroyer shortage, 119–20
  at Dunkirk, 106, 107
  and the invasion of Italy, 239
  in the Mediterranean, 134–35, 136, 142–43, 193–94, 197, 198
  at Oran, 117–18
  postwar strength, 362–63
Royal Oak (battleship), 78
Rozycki, Jerzy, 75*n*
Ruhr Valley, 2, *12m*, 16, 25, 34, 70, 71, 94, 96
  Allied drive toward (1944–45), 312, 313, 329, 330
Rumania, 2, 8, 11, *12m*, 14, 15, 21, 34, 42, 44, 48, 77, 86, 112, 154, 251, 258, 277, 324, 347, 348, 364
  defection from Axis, 277
  dictatorship and German military buildup in, 148, 149, 151, 259
  Franco-British pledge of support, 51, 52, 53, 57
  and the German invasion of the USSR (1941–43), 170, *171m*, 219, 221, 223, 225, 254
  northern provinces ceded to USSR and Germany, 147, 148
  oil fields, 51, 148, 156, 259
  Soviet occupation (1944), 310, 332
  Stalin-Churchill agreement on (1944), 317
Rundstedt, Marshall Gerd von, 62, 94, 95, *100p*, 107, 111, 218
  commands forces in west (1943–44), 296–304, 319
  invasion of USSR (1941), 172, 181
  offensive in Low Countries (1940), 99–101
Russia (*see also* USSR), 1, 2
  Napoleon's invasion of (1812), 181, 219, 331, 355, 359
  pre-WWI alliances of, 3, 4, 5,
  as protector of Slavs, 3, 5
  in WWI, 5, 6, 7, 13, 74, 364
Russian Liberation Army, 260–61
Russian (Bolshevik) Revolution, 7–8, 13, 19, 79, 183, 225
Russians:
  minority collaboration with Nazis, 259
  Nazi genocidal policies, 268
  in Nazi racial theories, 253, 262
  Soviet genocidal policies, 270
  White Russian refugees, 152
Russo-Finnish War (1939–40), 80–85, *83m*, 92, 102–3, 345
Russo-Japanese War (1904–05), 3, 5, 320, 349
Rydz-Smigy, Marshal Edward, 63–64, 65

S.A. (*Sturmabteilung*), 28, 29, 30, 164 (*see also* S.S.)
Saar Basin, 9, *12m*, 30, 70, 71, 76, 319
Sadat, Anwar, 136
Saint Cyr military academy, 6
Saint Nazaire (France), 119, 191, 311
  raid (1942), 195, 196
Saint Pierre I (France), 210
Saint Quentin (France), *98m*, 101
Sakhalin I, 320, 349
Salazar, Antonio, 257
Salerno, U.S. landing at, 236, 239, 340
Salonika (Greece), 152, *155m*, 158, 159
Salzburg (Austria), 56
San Francisco, UN meeting at (1945), 335
Sangro River, Battle of the (1943), 241, 243
San River (Poland), 65, 67
Sarajevo, 4, 5
Sardinia, 233, 234, *235m*, 236
Sartre, Jean-Paul, 293
Sauckel, Fritz, 254
Saudi Arabia, 167
Savannah (cruiser), 239
Savoy, 19, 156
Scandinavia, 81–86, 92, 112 (*see also* individual countries)
Scapa Flow (Scotland), 78, 90, *122m*
Schacht, Dr. Hjalmar, 28–29, 39, 43
Scharnhorst (battleship), 78, 191, 195, 243
Schirach, 351
Schleswig-Holstein, 9, *12m*, 163
Schleswig-Holstein (battleship), 63
Schlieffen plan, 95, 111
Schroeder, Kurt von, 27
Schulenberg, Count von, 65
Schuschnigg, Dr. Kurt von, 41–42
Schweinfurt (Germany), 244
Scientific revolution, 1
Sealion, Operation (1940), 121, 127, 128
Second Balkan War (1913), 159
Second Polish Army Corps, 242
Sedan (France), 76, 94, 95, 97, *98m*, 99, 100, 101, 164, 311
Seine River (France), 102, 107, 108
Senger and Etterlin, General Frido von, 242
Serbia, 4–5, 8, 151, 153, 273, 275, 277
  German puppet state, 156, 258
Serbs, 2, 258
Sevastopol (USSR), *171m*, 172, 175, 219, 220
Sevez, General François, 340
Seydlitz (German general), 226
Seyss-Inquart, Dr. Arhur, 42, 257
SHAEF (Supreme Headquarters of the Allied Expeditionary Force), 329, 330

Sherman tank, 212, *320p*
Siberia, 270
Siberian army, 177, 180, 221
Sicily, *4m*, 208
  Allied landing in (1943), 229, 234–39, *236m*, 359, 362
Siegfried Line, 49, 70, 71, 76, 79, 309, 317, 318, 325
  Churchill at (1945), 326*n*–27*n*
Sikorski, General Władysław, 74, 179, 270
Silesia, 2, 10, 45, 59–60, 62, 323 (*see also* Upper Silesia)
Silone, Ignazio, 293
Simović, General Dušan, 153, 154, 155, 258
Simpson, General William H., 330
Singapore, 38, 168, *184m*, 185, 197
Sino-Japanese War, 148
Škoda armament works, 47
Skoplye (Yugoslavia), 155
Slavs, 26, 220, 259, 261, 357
  nationalistic movements, 2
  Nazi extermination policies, 67–69
  in Nazi racial theories, 26, 262
  Russia as protector of, 3, 5
  Russian crusade against Germans, 220
Slessor, Commander Sir John, 72
Śliwinski, Leon, 284, *284p*, 285
Slovakia, 11, 45, 50, 54, 112, 170, 232
  as German annex, 255–56
  German garrisons established, 50, 54, 56, 62
  resistance uprising (1944), 310
Slovenia, 11, 155, 156, 255
Slovyanye (Panslavic magazine), 220
Smersh (Russian anti-espionage organization), 220
Smith, Melden, 326–27*n*
Smith, General Walter Bedell, 340
Smolensk (USSR), *171m*, 172, 173, 174
  Battle of (1941), 175
Socialist movements, Social Democratic parties:
  and the Communist movement, 2, 7
  in France, 33
  in Germany, 15, 22, 23, 27, 28, 29, 30, 289
  in Spain, 35
Somalia, 134, 142
Somerville, Admiral Sir James, 117
Somme River (France), 101, 104, 107, 108, 311
Sorel, Georges, 21
Sorge, Richard, 177, 182
Sosabowski, General Stanisław, 315, 319
South Africa, 116, 135, 200
Southampton (England), 295
Southeast Asia, 66, 148, 176, 177, 183, *184m*, 185
Southeast Asian Co-Prosperity sphere, 66
South Slavs, 2, 4, 5*n*
South Tirol, 2, 4, 10, 11, *12m*, 19, 22, 25, 37
Soviet Union (*see* Russia; USSR)
Spaatz, General Carl A., 340
Space technology, 364
Spain, 21, 77, 112, 189, 233, 235, 257, 273, 359
  and the balance of power in the Mediterranean, 137
  neutrality, 217
  urged to join Axis, 137
Spanish Civil War, 35–37, 46, 80, 137, 145, 282
Special Operations Executive (SOE) (Great Britain), 153, 280, 281, 286
  special training, 282
Speer, Albert, 227, 246, 253, 267*n*, 297, 328, 351, 354
Speidel (German general), 299
Sperrle, General Albert, 95
Spitfire (British fighter plane), 123, 124, *125p*, 127
Spoleto, Duke of, 258
S.S. (Storm Troopers), 28, 252, 263, 266, 269, 289, 305, 330, 351, 359
  divisions increased (1942), 227*n* (*see also* Gestapo; Waffen S.S.)
  formed (1934), 29–30
Stalin, Joseph, 13, 14, 109, 152, 162, 182, 210, 211, 218, 255, 260, 276, 278, 316, 337, 364
  alliances with France and Britain, 33, 36
  and anticommunist Yugoslavia, 152, 153
  asks Allies for help, 176, 178–79
  and the capture of Berlin, 330, 331
  conflicts with Hitler over territories in Eastern Europe (1940), 147–49
  deal with Churchill on zones of influence in Eastern Europe (1944), 320, 321
  dissolves Comintern (1943), 231
  and the Finnish War, 80, 81, 92
  and the German invasion of Poland, 65, 66, 71
  ignorance of naval strategy, 219
  ignores warning of German attack, fears Hitler, 168, 169, 173
  becomes Marshall and generalissimo (1943), 225
  military strategy assessed, 356, 360–61
  nonaggression pact with Hitler (1939), 56–69 (*see also* Hitler-Stalin pact)
  versus noncommunist resistance in Eastern Europe (1944), 309, 310, 323
  paranoid view of western allies, 345
  at Potsdam, 343, 346–48
  becomes premier of USSR, 169
  purges (1935–38), 48, 57, 174, 177, 331
  represses Poles, Russian minorities, 270
  response to Munich, accommodations with Hitler, 48–49
  response to Spanish Civil War, 36, 37
  Roosevelt's view of, 247, 334
  social engineering in Eastern Europe, 72, 73–74
  speech on German invasion (1941), 173
  strategy at Stalingrad, 225
  and the surrender of Germany, 242, 340
  at Teheran (1943), 246–50
  treatment of Soviet POWs, 354
  at Yalta (1945), 320–24, 333
Stalingrad, 218, 219
  Battle of (1942–43), 215, 217, *222p*, 221–27, *223m*, 253, 359, 360
State Defense Council (USSR), 173
Stauffenberg, Colonel Claus von, 288, 289
Stavanger (Norway), 88, 89
Stephenson, Sir William S., 126*n*
Stettinius, Edward, *322p*
Stimson, Henry L., 321
Stockholm, Treaty of, *83m*, 84–85
Storm Troopers (*see* S.S.)
Strasbourg (France), 3, 329
Strategic bomber forces, 129–30, 244, 327–28, 357
Stresa Conference (1935), 32, 35
Stresemann, Gustav, 16–17
Student, General Karl, 160
Stuka dive bombers, 63, *64p*, 129
Stülpnagel, General Karl H. von, 288
Stumme, General Georg, 203
Stuttgart (Germany), 31, 69
Submarines, 6, 10, 16, 30, 138
  antisub devices, 32, 215
  and the Battle of Norway, 86, 89, 91
  German buildup and strength in, 16, 20, 32, 49, 78–79, 114, 121*n*, 129, 191, 195, 357
  German menace ended (1943), 216, 217, 243, 245, 248
  Germans prey on Allied shipping, 119, 178, 189, 190–96, 216
  German wolf packs, 191, 193, 195
  in the Mediterranean, *193p*, 193–94, 199–200
  Schnörkel tubes, 194
Sudan, 135, 142
Sudetenland, 10, 44–45, 46, 47, 347
Suez Canal, 21, 35, 134, 135, *136m*, 160, 161, 186, 209, 216
  British defense of (1941–42), 197
  strategic importance of, 136, 138, 139, 143, 162, 356
Suffolk (Cruiser), 194
Surits, Jacob, 48–49
  Suslaparov, General Ivan, 340
  Suvorov, General Alexander, 225, 331
Sweden, 12, 30, 31, 77, 79, 80, 115
  and the German invasion of Denmark, Norway, 87
  neutrality, grants to German troops, 112, 286

and the Russo-Finnish War, 82–84, 85, 92
supplies iron ore to Germany, 77, 80, 82, 89, 91, 103
Switzerland, 12
neutrality, 286–87
and political refugees, 112, 287
spy networks in, 285–86, 287
Sydney (cruiser), 143
Syndicalists (Italy), 19
Synthetic fuel, 77, 175, 244, 297, 301
Syria, 22, 167, 280
Szálasi, Ferenc, 259

Tanks, 145
Allies versus German strength in western offensive (1940), 96
in the Ardennes campaign, 100
German improvements in, 42–43
Germany develops the Panther and Tiger (1943), 227, 229
in North African campaigns, 138, 140, 163, 164, 165, 166, 196–97, 199, *201p*, 212, 215
tested in the Spanish Civil War, 36–37
in the Soviet defense against Germany (1941), 174, 175, 221–22
in WWI, 6, 10, 17–18
Taranto (Italy) naval base, *136m*, 136, 217, 240, 328
British attack (1940), 143, 150, 157, 159, 325
Tartars, 260, 270
Tartu, Treaty of (1920), 79
Taylor, General Maxwell, 314
Tebessa (Tunisia), *212m*, 212, 213
Technology, 1, 362 (*see also* Military technology)
Tedder, Sir Arthur, 341
Teheran Conference (1943), 246–50, 274, 291, 318, 321
Teleki, Pál, 155
Teller, Edward, 354
Terboven, G.J., 90
Terijoki (Finland), 80
Terkel, Studs, 251*n*
Teutonic race, 2, 220
Thala (Tunisia), 212, 213
Thiele, Fritz, 288
Third Communist International, 13
Thoma, General Wilhelm von, 164
Thomas, Georg, 288
Thrace, 159
Tibet, 3
Tiger (Mark VI) tank, 227, *231p*
Timoshenko, Marshall Semyon, 172, 218
Tirol (*see* South Tirol)
Tirpitz (destroyer), 78, 194, 195, 327
Tiso, Father Josef, 50, 255, 256
Tito, Marshall (Josip Broz), 36*n*, 248–49, 275–77, 276, 278*n*, 339
establishes Communist gov't (1944), 310
Tobruk (Libya):
British capture (1941), 140, 165, 196, 197
British recapture (1942), 204
Germans capture (1942), *197p*, 198, 199
Todt, Dr. Fritz, 227
Togliatti, Palmiro, 36*n*, 291
Tokyo, firebombing of (1945), 326*n*
Tolbukhin, General Fyodor, 223, 310
Torch, Operation (1942), 189, 204–8
Torgau (Germany), 335
Totalitarianism, 7, 21, 56, 261, 352, 327
Toulon (France), 102, 110, 117, 118, 208, *208m*, 307
Tours (France), 102, 108
Toward a Professional Army (de Gaulle), 17–18
Trade:
Allied naval blockades, 78–79, 82
effects of WWI on, 12, 13
German agreements with Spain, Sweden, 77
German barter agreements in Balkans, 43–44
provisions in Hitler-Stalin pact, 58, 169
before WWI, 1
Transjordan, 167
Transylvania, 2, 11, 148
Trepper, Leopold, 285
Trianon, Treaty of, 8, 11, 155
Trieste, 2, 4, 10, 11, *12m*, 19, 22, 154
Allies occupy (1945), 339
Tripartite Pact, 148–49, 152, 153, 168
Triple Alliance, 4, 5, 19
Tripoli (Libya), *136m*, 157, 164, 196, 204
Tripolitania, 134, *136m*, 140–41, 157, 164
Triumph and Tragedy (Churchill), 345
Troley de Prevaux, Jacques, *280p*, 285
Trondheim (Norway), *87m*, 88, 89, 92
Tropical diseases, 142, 163
Trotsky, Leon, 37, 57
Truman, President Harry S. 343, 344–47
Memoirs, 346
T34 tank, 174, 222, 357
Tunis, 205, *208m*, 208, 209, 211
Battle of (1943), 215
Tunisia, 4, 19, 22
Battle of (1942–43), 211–16, 217, 227, 232
Germany fortifies (1942), 208–9
Turin strikes (1942–43), 288
Turkey, 1, 5, 43, 135, 149, 151, 162, 217, 270
enters war, 274
neutrality, 157, 167, 286 (*see also* Ottoman Empire)
Turtle principle, of forced labor, 282

Udet, General Ernst, 21, 128, 129–30
Uganda (Cruiser), 239
Ukraine, 25, 65, 66, 147, 151, *171m*, 172, 267, 364
German invasion (1941), 174, 175, 182, 259
guerrilla fighting, 279
membership in UN, 324
Nazi occupation, 259, 260, 261, 268, 269
Soviet offensive (1942–44), 218, 227, 231
Soviet reprisals in, 270
Ulam, Stanisław, 357
Ulbricht, Walter, 226
Ultra intelligence network, 75, 123, 124, 143, 160, 165, 194, 195, 201, 234*n*, 299, 317
Unconditional surrender policy, of Allies, 251, 277, 289, 341
and the capitulation of Italy (1943), 239
and German propaganda, 211, 300
Union of Polish Patriots, 231, 278
United Nations, 249
declaration (1942), 190
established (1945), 335
Yalta agreements on, 321, 324
United States, 2, 7, 102, 113, 116, 148, 152, 157, 166, 168, (*see also* Allies)
enters WWII (1941), 183–85, 186
German U-boats menace east coast, 191
in Hitler's foreign policy, 26, 333
increases Atlantic shipping, 216
increases industrial production, 244, 249, 362
Japanese attack at Pearl Harbor, 168
Lend-Lease aid, 120, 144, 179, 183, 228, 333
material contribution to Allied effort, 356
military strength in 1940, 120, 362
neutrality, 108, 120, 133, 177
and the occupation of Germany, 347, 364
population losses, 353
postwar economic and military strength, 362, 363
postwar isolationism, 15, 144, 333
quality of troops, 212, 315, 316, 317, 359
Roosevelt's view of role of, 333
Spanish Civil War volunteers, 36*n*
supports Finland, 80
troops join Red Army at Torgau (1945), 335
troops land in North Africa (1942), 205–7, 212
volunteers in Britain, 191*n*
and WWI, 5, 6, 12–13
United States Air Force, 244–45, 326*n*, 320, 326–27
United States Navy, 178, 191
Pacific fleet, 183, 189
postwar strength, 363
University of Cracow, 269
University of Poznań, 75
Upper Silesia, 8, 9–10, *m12*, 72
Urquart, General Brian, 315–16
USSR, 52, 116, 157 (*see also* Red Army)
alliance with Baltic states, 72–73

USSR (*cont.*)
alliance with Czechoslovakia, 48
alliance with France (1935), 33–34, 36, 48
and the appeasement at Munich, 48–49
Axis strategy against, 37–38, 39
Churchill's perspective on, 102–3, 116, 345, 360
contribution to defeat of Germany, 356
cooperates with west, joins League of Nations, 32–33
declares war on Japan, 247, 249, 323, 348
and the French-British-Polish alliances, 52, 53, 57
German attack on (1941), 167, 169–77, *171m*, 179–83, 186
German offensive (1942–43), 218–31
German persecution of minorities, POWs, 182
hegemony in Eastern Europe, 345, 347–48, 362, *363m*, 363–64
Hitler plans to invade, 127, 135, 149, 162, 168
Hitler's coalition plans against, 25, 26
industrial bases moved east, 183, 354
intelligence networks, 285–86
invasion and occupation of eastern Poland, 65, 66–67, 68, 69, 73–74, 102, 360
Lend-Lease aid to, 225, 228, 343
Nazi administration of occupied territories, 253, 254, 255, 259–61, 278
neutrality part with Japan (1941), 168, 176
neutrality toward Poland, 54
nonaggression pact with Germany (1939), 56–60 (*see also* Hitler-Stalin pact)
and the occupation of Germany, 346–47, 364
partisan movement, guerrilla warfare, 182–83, 221, 278–79
population losses, 353
POW and ethnic collaborators, 259–61, 335, 354
rapprochement with Germany (1937–38), 48–49, 57
rapprochement and military arrangements with Germany, 15–16, 30, 31, 32–33
recovers territories in Far East, 323, 349
repressions, deportations in Eastern Europe, 270
response to Spanish Civil War, 36, 37
scorns League of Nations, 11, 13, 32
spring offensive, advance toward Berlin (1945), 320, 328, 331, 332
spring offensive in Ukraine (1942), 218
ties with Poland and Czechoslovakia, 179, 230
ties with Yugoslavia, 152, 230
treatment of repatriated civilians, POWs, 354
and the Tripartite Pact, 148–49, 168
troop buildup on German frontier, 109
war on Finland (1939), 80, 85, 92, 103–4, 350
war with Japan in Manchuria, Mongolia, 58, 59, 65–66, 92, 168, 177, 360
Utaše (Croatian movement), 258

***Valiant* (battleship), 117, 197, 239**
Van der Lubbe, Marinus, 28
Vasilevsky, General Alexander, 225
Vatutin, General Nikolay, 223
Venetian Republic, 4
Venice, 154
Verdun (France), Battle of (1916), 6, 81, 99, 104, 111
captured by Patton (1944), 311
Vermork laboratories (Norway), 91, 283
Versailles, Treaty of, 8–12, 14, 16, 45, 284
German hostility toward, 22, 25–56
German renunciation of (1935), 30, 31–33
military clauses, 10, 15, 16, 30
national self-determination principle, 10, 11–12
quarrels among victors, 13–15
and the Soviet-German rapprochement, 15–16
territorial settlements, 9–11, *12m*, 16, 19, 22, 44, 253
war reparations, 8, 10, 14, 15, 16, 25, 26, 252
Victor Emmanuel III of Italy, 20, 51, 237–38, 247, 291
Vienna, 152, 334
Hitler's conference with Rumania and Hungary (1940), 148, 152
Nazi occupation, 41, 42
Red Army captures (1945), 334
Vietinghoff, General Heinrich von, 241, 338–39
Viipuri (Vyborg) (Finland), 81, *83m*, 84
Vinci, Leonardo da, 353
Vistula River, *4m*, 9, 58, 65, 66, 309, 310
Vlasov, General Andrei, 259, 260, 335
Volga Germans, 270
Volga River, 219, 221, 225, 226
V-1, V-2 rockets, 245, 283, 302, 312, 313, 358, 364
launched against Britain, 304
V-1 and V-2 compared, 301
Voronezh (USSR), 218, 221, 225, 228
Voroshilov, Marshall Kliment, 172, 248

Waal River (Netherlands), 314, 315
Waffen S.S., 29, 252, 257, 305, 335
Wannsee conference (1942), 263, 264
Warburton-Lee, Captain B.A.W., 89–90
War crimes, 349–52
Warfare:
air cover for ships, 89–91, 297, 328, 361
"all-arms" combat tactics, 201
annihilation versus attrition strategy, 31, 356–57
basic products vital to, 44*n*
blitzkrieg doctrine, 63
cavalry, use of, 68*n*, 170, 180
Clausewitz's axiom of, 327, 358
defensive-offensive method, 165–66
desert, 137–38, 163, 215
elastic defense concepts, 228
German capability in 1939, 49, 71–72
peripheral strategy, 188–89
trial raid method, 190 (*see also* Air power; Amphibious warfare; *Blitzkrieg;* Navies; Paratroopers; Psychological warfare; Tanks)
Warsaw, 72, 240, 255, 262
Germans capture (1939), 63, 64–65, *72p*
ghetto uprising (1943), 264*n*, 266
resistance uprising (1944), 309–10
Soviets capture (1945), 320, 328, 332
Warspite (battleship), 90, 143, 157, 239
Washington Conference (1941–42), 187–90, 235
Waterloo, Battle of (1815), 113
Wavell, General Sir Archibald, 111, *139p*, 157
crushes Iraqi revolt, 167
Middle and Near Eastern command, 135–36, 139, 141, 142, 164, 165, 197
Weber, Max, 2
Wehrmacht, 31, 40, 42, 63, 86, 92, 93, 94, 131, 289
assessment of, 358–60
defense of Italy, 238
defensive strategy on eastern front, 219
end of, as coherent force, 319, 320, 334
purges and executions (1944), 305
success in western offensive, 112, 178
weakness in west, 71
Weimar Republic, 10, 14, 15, 22–23, 287
Nazi attacks on, 22–23
Nazis seize power from, 26–28
secret rearmament, 15–16, 30, 31
Weizsäcker, Ernst von, 66
Werth (Hungarian general), 155
Western Desert Force, 138–41, 143, 167, 196
defeated in North Africa (1941), 165, 166, 186 (*see also* Eighth Army)

sent to Greece, 157
Western Task Force, 205
Westphal, General Siegfried, 240
Westphalia, 2
Weygand, General Maxime, 32, 104, 105
last stand against Germans, 107, 108
response to British evacuation (1940), 105, 106
White Army, 7–8, 79, 152
Wilhelmshaven (Germany), 141, 243
William II of Germany, 2, 3, 24, 109, 360
William the Conqueror, 303
Wilno (Vilnius) (Lithuania), *67m,* 73, 266
Wilson, General Maitland, 158, 159
Wilson, President Woodrow, 8, 9, 11, 19, 211, 333, 345
Windsow, Duke of, 115
Winter War (1939–40), 80–85
Witzleben, General Erwin von, 288, *291p*
Women, mobilization of:
in Britain versus Germany, 133
in the USSR, 360
Women's Land Army (Great Britain), 133
Wood, Sir Kingsley, 69, 70
World War I, 1–18, 25, 37, 96–97, 108, 110, 111, 242, 257, 322
aircraft in, 128
benefits to U.S., 12–13
breakout of, 4–5
British strategy in, 118–19, 188
conditions preceding, 1–2
course of, costs, casualties, 5–7, 360
and the emergence of the USSR, 13, 15, 74
French alliances after, 16–17
Hitler's experience in, 23, 105, 336
Nazi theories of, 22, 23
postwar military developments, 17–18
rise of Germany and realignment, 2–4
and the Russian Revolution, 7–8
social effects of, 7
Soviet-German repprochement after, 15–16
terms of Versailles Treaty, 8–12, 13–14
and the western offensive of WWII, 93, 95
World War II:
Allied naval blockades, 78–79, 87
Axis defeats and turning points (1943), 217, 226–27
British and Frensh passivity, 68–72
casualty figures, civilian losses, 353–56, 360
ended in Europe (1945), 339–42
ended in Far East, 348–49
lack of peace treaty, 364
legacy of, 362, 364–65
as a naval war, 354
perceived as "just war," 251
"phony war" (1939–40), 76–77, 78, 79
reasons for Germany's defeat, 354–62
role of air power in, 327–28 (*see also* Allies; Axis powers; Far East; Russo-Finnish War; individual countries and battles)

Yalta Conference (1945), 249, 320–24, 346, 350
conditions on Germany, 321–22, 350
conditions on Poland, 322–23
decision on Far East, 323
"Declaration on Liberated Europe," 323–24, 332
displaced nationals agreement, 354
Yugoslavia, 8, 11, 14, 15, 19, 37, 42, 48, 51, 76, 110, 112, 295, 324, 347, 348, 364
Axis attack (1940), 154–56, 158, 186, 233
economic resources, 44, 149, 156
ethnic conflicts, 151
military coup (1940), 153–54, 258
Nazi administration, genocide against Slavs, 255, 267, 268, 269
Partisan-Chetnik fighting, 243, 248–49, 273, 274–78
partitioning of, gov't in exile, 156, 258, 275, 276, 310
population losses, 353
Red Army-Partisan linkup, Communist administration (1944), 310, 339
Stalin-Churchill agreement on, 320
sympathy with Allies, 151, 152–53, 258
ties with USSR, 152, 230
Yalta agreements on (1945), 323

Zagreb (Yugoslavia), ***m155,*** **156**
Zervas, Napoleon, 277, 278
Zhukov, General George K, 66, 85, 169, 174, 177, 182, *226p*
capture of Berlin (1945), 331, 334, 335
career, 225
commander at Stalingrad, 223, 225
defense of Kursk (1943), 228, 229
on the expendability of manpower, 360
victory ceremony in Moscow, 342
Zygalski, Henry K., 75*n*